797,885 Books
are available to read at

Forgotten Books

www.ForgottenBooks.com

Forgotten Books' App
Available for mobile, tablet & eReader

ISBN 978-1-331-87706-6
PIBN 10248398

This book is a reproduction of an important historical work. Forgotten Books uses state-of-the-art technology to digitally reconstruct the work, preserving the original format whilst repairing imperfections present in the aged copy. In rare cases, an imperfection in the original, such as a blemish or missing page, may be replicated in our edition. We do, however, repair the vast majority of imperfections successfully; any imperfections that remain are intentionally left to preserve the state of such historical works.

Forgotten Books is a registered trademark of FB &c Ltd.
Copyright © 2015 FB &c Ltd.
FB &c Ltd, Dalton House, 60 Windsor Avenue, London, SW19 2RR.
Company number 08720141. Registered in England and Wales.

For support please visit www.forgottenbooks.com

1 MONTH OF FREE READING

at
www.ForgottenBooks.com

By purchasing this book you are eligible for one month membership to ForgottenBooks.com, giving you unlimited access to our entire collection of over 700,000 titles via our web site and mobile apps.

To claim your free month visit: www.forgottenbooks.com/free248398

* Offer is valid for 45 days from date of purchase. Terms and conditions apply.

Similar Books Are Available from
www.forgottenbooks.com

An Account of the Manners and Customs of the Modern Egyptians, Vol. 1 of 2
by Edward William Lane

Cults, Customs and Superstitions of India
by John Campbell Oman

Primitive Manners and Customs
by James Anson Farrer

Etiquette for Gentlemen
Or, Short Rules and Reflections for Conduct in Society, by A Gentleman

Totem and Taboo
Resemblances Between the Psychic Lives of Savages and Neurotics, by Sigmund Freud

The Sun and the Serpent
A Contribution to the History of Serpent-Worship, by C. F. Oldham

Etiquette for Americans
by A Woman Of Fashion

An Account of the Manners and Customs of Italy
With Observations, by Giuseppe Marco Antonio Baretti

The Aztecs
Their History, Manners, and Customs, by Lucien Biart

The Bell
Its Origin, History, and Uses, by Alfred Gatty

Bible Manners and Customs
by G. M. Mackie

Chinese Life and Customs
by Paul Carus

Cumberland & Westmorland, Ancient and Modern
The People, Dialect, Superstitions and Customs, by J. Sullivan

Customs and Traditions of Palestine
Illustrating the Manners of the Ancient Hebrews, by Ermete Pierotti

Oriental Customs
by Samuel Burder

Wedding Customs
Then and Now, by Carl Holliday

Dramatic Traditions of the Dark Ages
by Joseph S. Tunison

Hindu Manners, Customs and Ceremonies
by Abbe J. A. Dubois

The Kachins
Their Customs and Traditions, by O. Hanson

Manners, Customs, and Antiquities of the Indians of North and South America
by Samuel G. Goodrich

CHURCHWARDENS' ACCOUNTS

FROM THE FOURTEENTH CENTURY TO THE CLOSE OF THE SEVENTEENTH CENTURY

BY

J. CHARLES COX, LL.D., F.S.A.

"THE OFFICE OF CHURCHWARDEN, AS GUARDIAN OF THE GOODS OF THE CHURCH, DATES FROM THE LATTER PART OF THE MIDDLE AGES."
AYLIFFE'S *Parergon*

"THE OFFICE WAS WHOLLY FREE FROM ALL CIVIL FUNCTIONS UNTIL QUITE LATE IN THE REIGN OF HENRY VIII."
BISHOP HOBHOUSE

WITH THIRTY-SIX ILLUSTRATIONS

METHUEN & CO. LTD.
36 ESSEX STREET W.C.
LONDON

First Published in 1913

TO MY OLD FRIEND AND COUSIN

THE RIGHT REVEREND

THE LORD BISHOP OF WOOLWICH

THIS RECORD OF ONE PHASE OF THE

TEMPORAL HISTORY OF THE

CHURCH OF ENGLAND

IS, BY PERMISSION, DEDICATED

AS A SLIGHT TOKEN OF

AFFECTION AND RESPECT

PREFACE

IT is more than half a century since I began to make extracts from a few early parish records or wardens' accounts in West Somersetshire. Subsequently I followed up the subject in my own county of Derbyshire. In 1877 I had the good fortune, when inspecting the valuable library of Mr. Godfrey Meynell, of Meynell Langley, to find two invaluable volumes of church accounts pertaining to All Saints, Derby, beginning in 1466. They had long lain unnoticed in an attic, but have now been restored to the proper authorities. These accounts formed the chief part of a volume which was brought out in 1881, in conjunction with my friend, Dr. W. H. St. John Hope, entitled *The Chronicles of the Collegiate Church or Free Chapel of All Saints, Derby.*

From the date of this important discovery, which led to the examining of other parish accounts of an early date, I resolved to try and produce a book which should deal generally with these records, as apart from parish registers. This idea has never been lost sight of, though interrupted by a variety of causes. It was stimulated through giving considerable assistance to my good friend, the late Bishop Hobhouse, in the production of his volume, issued for the Somerset Record Society in 1890, on certain churchwarden accounts of that county, ranging in date from 1349 to 1560.

The last words of the preface to my book on Parish Registers, issued exactly three years ago, announced the definite undertaking of this companion volume, and a kindly response was made by several to the request for further information as to the existence of other examples of old churchwarden books.

The result of all this long-continued diligence in the collection of notes and extracts has proved almost overwhelming, and the difficulty of selecting the most noteworthy extracts not a little exasperating. When the time came for submitting my carefully culled minutes and comments to the courteous publishers, the material proved to be of more than double the length requisite for a volume of this series. I felt obliged to yield to their advice to compress it into one volume. This course was at last rendered easier by the reflection that it was far more my desire to interest churchfolk at large, as well as the general reading public, in these little-known local records, and to cause them to appreciate their social and economic value, rather than to produce an exhaustive work which might, after all, have only proved tedious.

The result, however, of this drastic policy of abridgment caused, in addition to general curtailment, the wholesale omission of several matters of more or less moment. These included chapters on the position and stipends of the mediæval clergy, as shown (somewhat meagrely) in these accounts; the documentary contents of various parish chests, apart from statements of accounts; all references to special Forms of Prayer, on which subject it is hoped that a separate book will ere long be forthcoming; and the analysis of all the wardens' accounts of the sixteenth and seventeenth centuries. A more serious omission is the striking out of a long section on Poor Relief, upon which a good deal of fresh light can be thrown from the study of the general parish accounts from Elizabethan days downwards, for the wardens were joined with the overseers in the administration of relief. On this subject I should like to commend Miss Leonard's recent (1900) able volume on *The Early History of English Poor Relief.*

Another subject deliberately exempted from mention at the outset is that of Briefs, though long and valuable lists may be culled from some wardens' accounts, *e.g.* Weyhill, Hants. Those desirous of following up this subject are referred to an excellent and almost exhaustive volume, issued by Mr. W. A. Bewes in 1896, under the simple heading of *Church Briefs.*

I was glad to be able to find room for the last chapter dealing with the cognate subject of Constables' Accounts. I may perhaps be forgiven for giving a long account of an extraordinary and disgraceful church disturbance, in a country parish of Oxfordshire, of so late a date as the beginning of last century. Assuredly times are improving; such a state of things would nowadays be an utter impossibility.

The number of wardens' accounts, now extant, referred to in these pages, from the earliest date down to the close of the seventeenth century, are upwards of four hundred—four or five times longer than any printed list hitherto attempted. Its compilation has been no small trouble, but it makes no claim to be by any means perfect. I shall be grateful for any additions or corrections, if merely on a post card. The lists given in Chapters II and III are supplemented not only by Addenda at the close of the book, but also by a few extra entries under the index arranged according to counties; in this last case the wardens' accounts incidentally mentioned are not put in the lists, as their initial date, etc., had not been ascertained.

It is hoped that the printing of the lists may be some

small service in the direction of the safe custody of these local records. During the time they have been under my consideration, at least five sets of old wardens' accounts, one dating back to the days of Edward iv, have hopelessly disappeared.

The custody of local records is a difficult problem; perhaps the best solution is their deposit in the charge of the respective County Councils. Such a plan was happily effected a few years ago by the mutual consent of a large number of the City of London parishes (thirty in all); the old wardens' accounts and vestry books were deposited in the Guildhall Library. The whole of these have been examined for the purpose of this book, as well as a smaller number, from different parts of the country, which are in the keeping of the British Museum.

Among the most valuable printed transcripts, with annotations, of early parish accounts, in addition to All Saints, Derby, and the Somerset volume by Bishop Hobhouse, already mentioned, are those of (1) St. Laurence, Reading, by my late friend, the Rev. Charles Kerry, printed in 1883; (2) St. Martin, Leicester, 1884, by Mr. North; (3) St. Edmund and St. Thomas, Salisbury, 1896, by the Wilts Record Society; and (4) St. Mary-at-Hill, City, 1907, by Mr. Littlehales, for the Early English Text Society.

Of volumes beginning early in the sixteenth century, the two best are those dealing with Great St. Mary, Cambridge, by Mr. J. E. Foster, and with St. Martin's-in-the-Fields, by Mr. Kitto.

The work which promises to surpass them all in extent, thoroughness, and national interest are the volumes dealing with the accounts of St. Margaret, Westminster, by Mr. A. M. Burke, F.S.A.; it is now in active preparation.

PREFACE

By rare generosity, Mr. Burke has allowed me to consult his fifteenth-century transcripts.

Though using, with sincere acknowledgments, the labours of others who have printed much or parts of these early records, I may perhaps be pardoned for saying that I had examined and made extracts from the majority of those of importance before a line had appeared in print. Among them I may mention those of St. Laurence Reading; St. Edmund, Sarum; Cratfield, Suffolk; St. Thomas, Launceston; and several in Somerset and the City.

It remains to offer my genuine thanks for much kind help. First of all I thank my old friend, the Rev. R. M. Serjeantson, rector of St. Peter's, Northampton, for much help with regard to the counties of Northampton and Salop, and especially for reading the proofs. My thanks are also due to the Rev. Canon Heanley, rector of Weyhill, for the loan of his recently recovered accounts, and for help with regard to Hampshire; to the Rev. S. Spencer Pearce, vicar of Combe, near Woodstock, for Constables' Accounts of that parish; to the Rev. J. F. Rowley, vicar of Spelsbury, Oxon, for the loan of a transcript of wardens' accounts; to the Rev. G. M. Benton, of Saffron Walden, for putting me on the track of several early accounts; to the Rev. Canon Wordsworth for leave to reproduce facsimiles of an inventory of St. Margaret's, New Fish Street; to Mrs. Goodman for transcripts of accounts of St. Botolph, Cambridge; to Dr. Ellis, of Oxford, for the loan of transcripts of the accounts of St. Michael's of that city; to Mr. Arthur C. Coldicott for the loan of a set of transcripts of the accounts of St. Nicholas, Warwick; and to Mr. Thurstan Peter, of Redruth, for transcripts of the Green Book of St. Columb Major prior to its publication.

Lastly, I desire to express my great indebtedness to a

very old friend, the late Mr. J. E. Foster, of Cambridge, the transcriber of the voluminous accounts of Great St. Mary, and a well-known leading member of the Cambridge Antiquarian Society and of the Library Association; his sudden death last October caused much sorrowful regret outside the circle of his immediate friends. It was to his kindness that I owed the loan of the transcript of the valuable Bassingbourn accounts from the Cambridge University Library, and also of Holy Trinity, Cambridge. In this connection, too, I should like to thank the authorities of the Public Record Office, Chancery Lane, for their courtesy in allowing these transcripts, as well as other original documents, to be deposited for a time in their custody for convenience of reference.

A single general reflection may be permitted—a reflection which has been irresistibly driven home during the long period wherein these hundreds of documents have been faithfully consulted. Up to the time of the introduction of compulsory church rates, a spirit of lavish generosity towards the maintenance of divine worship and the repair of church fabrics was the usual characteristic of England's parishioners both in country and in town. With the advent of compulsion, this generosity began to ebb, until at last a deplorable depth of meanness took its place in the large majority of parishes. With the abolition of compulsion in our own days, the zeal of churchmen for all that pertains to the decency and dignity of worship was quickened and remains quickened in a marvellous degree.

J. CHARLES COX

13 LONGTON AVENUE, SYDENHAM, S.E.
February 1913

CONTENTS

CHAP.		PAGE
I.	INTRODUCTORY	1
II.	EARLY WARDENS' ACCOUNTS	15
III.	CHRONOLOGICAL LIST OF WARDENS' ACCOUNTS OF THE SIXTEENTH AND SEVENTEENTH CENTURIES	44
IV.	RECEIPTS OF ST. EDMUND, SARUM	53
V.	OUTGOINGS OF ST. EDMUND, SARUM	70
VI.	THE FABRIC OF THE CHURCH	79
VII.	THE ALTAR AND THE EUCHARIST	91
VIII.	BOOKS	106
IX.	HALLOWING AND VESTMENTS	123
X.	CHURCH PLATE—IMAGES	138
XI.	FONTS AND PULPITS	149
XII.	LIGHTS AND BURIALS	160
XIII.	ROODS AND REFORMATION CHANGES	175
XIV.	CHURCH SITTINGS	186
XV.	ORGANS—OTHER MUSIC—SINGING MEN	195
XVI.	BELLS AND RINGING	211
XVII.	CLOCKS—HOUR-GLASS—ROYAL ARMS—TEN COMMANDMENTS	228
XVIII.	GARNISHING OF CHURCHES—CHURCH'S CALENDAR	238
XIX.	CHURCH OR PARISH PLAYS—CHURCH-ALES	267
XX.	LIVE STOCK—VERMIN	292
XXI.	OLLA PODRIDA	310
XXII.	CONSTABLES' ACCOUNTS	323
	APPENDIX—CONSECRATION CROSSES	349
	ADDENDA—LIST OF WARDENS' ACCOUNTS	353
	INDEX TO WARDENS' ACCOUNTS	355
	GENERAL INDEX	361

LIST OF ILLUSTRATIONS IN THE TEXT

	PAGE
MAY-DAY DANCERS: WINDOW, BETLEY HALL, STAFFS., *TEMP.* EDWARD IV	65
TITLE-PAGE OF FIRST PRAYER BOOK IN ENGLISH . . .	113
TITLE-PAGE OF "DIRECTORY OF 1644"	115
FOXE'S "BOOK OF MARTYRS," CHAINED: ST. MARY AXE, LONDON From a Drawing by J. CHARLES WALL	120
THE FONT, EAST DEREHAM . . . . From a Drawing by J. CHARLES WALL	150
THE FONT, ST. LAURENCE, READING . . . . . From a Drawing by J. CHARLES WALL	151
FONT, WIRKSWORTH, DERBYSHIRE	154
PULPIT FORMERLY AT ST. LAURENCE, READING . . . From a Drawing by J. CHARLES WALL	157
CANDLES ON HEARSE OVER COFFIN, BODLEIAN MS., DOUCE	171
JACK O' THE CLOCK, SOUTHWOLD . . . . . . From a Drawing by J. CHARLES WALL	229
HOUR-GLASS AND STAND, BLOXWORTH, DORSET . . .	232
BLESSING OF PALMS: SARUM PROCESSIONAL . . . . From a Drawing by J. CHARLES WALL	257
THE CROWE NET SET OR BENT . . . . . . From Mascall's *Sundrie Engines and Trappes*, 1590	296
A HATCH TO TAKE POLECATS, AS ALSO OTHER VERMIN From Mascall's *Sundrie Engines and Trappes*, 1590	301
THE WHIPPE OR SPRINGE TRAPPE . . . . . From Mascall's *Sundrie Engines and Trappes*, 1590	303
THE MOULL TRAPPE . . . . From Mascall's *Sundrie Engines and Trappes*, 1590	304

	PAGE
ROBERT SCARLETT, SEXTON OF PETERBOROUGH CATHEDRAL, WITH DOG-WHIP	308
From a Drawing by J. CHARLES WALL	
WOODEN DOG TONGS, CLODOCK, HEREFORDSHIRE	308
From a Drawing by J. CHARLES WALL	
ELIZABETHAN STANDARD BUSHEL: NORTHAMPTON	325
From a Drawing by J. CHARLES WALL	
DUCKING-STOOL FOR A SCOLD	337
From an old Chap Book	
STOCKS AND WHIPPING POST: UFFORD	344
From a Drawing by J. CHARLES WALL	
ANOINTING A CONSECRATION CROSS: PONTIFICALUM ROMANUM VENITIIS, 1620	349

LIST OF PLATES

THE STEEPLE, LOUTH . . . . . . *Frontispiece*	
From a Photograph	
	FACING PAGE
WEST PROSPECT OF OLD CHURCH OF ST. MARTIN'S-IN-THE-FIELDS .	14
From an old Print	
WARDENS' BALANCE SHEET, ARLINGTON, 1463-4 . . .	26
Brit. Mus. Add. 35,192	
CHURCH EXPENSES OF WARDENS OF STRATTON, 1521 . . .	44
Brit. Mus. Add. 32,243	
CHURCH RECEIPTS OF WARDENS OF STRATTON, 1534 . . .	46
Brit. Mus. Add. 32,244	
WARDENS' ACCOUNTS, SIDBURY: INVENTORY, 1648 . . .	50
Brit. Mus. Add. 34,696	
ST. PETROCK, BODMIN	82
From a Photograph by Captain CHING, R.N.	
THE TOWER, GREAT ST. MARY, CAMBRIDGE	84
From an old Print	
INVENTORY, WARDENS' ACCOUNTS, ST. MARGARET, NEW FISH STREET	106
From *The Old Service Books of the English Church*	
FIRST PAGE OF CAXTON'S "GOLDEN LEGEND"	110
FIRST PAGE OF WARDENS' ACCOUNTS OF ALL SAINTS, DERBY, 1466.	164
SEATS ROUND THE PIERS, ST. MICHAEL'S, SUTTON BONNINGTON, NOTTS	186
ELIZABETHAN HYMN, 1578	210
From a "Forme of Prayer"	
FIRE HOOKS, RAUNDS CHURCH	320
From a Photograph by POWELL, Wellingborough	

THE CHURCHWARDENS' ACCOUNTS

CHAPTER I

INTRODUCTORY

Churchwarden at outset a purely ecclesiastical official—Civil duties added by Henry VIII, Elizabeth, etc.—Number of the wardens—All elected by the parish—Sidesmen—Fines for refusing office—Women wardens—Election feasts—Days of audit—Voluntary rating—Compulsory Church rates—Select vestry—St. Martin's-in-the-Fields

CHURCHWARDENS were first appointed as officers of the Church by the first canon of the Council of London, 1127. In that learned but often prejudiced and erroneous book, *The Parish*, by Mr. Toulmin Smith, it is strenuously and emphatically asserted that "Churchwardens never were ecclesiastical officers" (2nd ed. 1857, p. 69). The truth, however, lies with Bishop Hobhouse, who, in his able introduction to a series of early Somersetshire Churchwardens' Accounts, proves by irresistible arguments that the office of churchwarden prior to the Reformation was essentially and solely ecclesiastical. They are described in 1341, in the Rolls of Parliament, as "wardens of the goods of the church." The early Latin titles of *Custodes bonorum* or *Procuratores ecclesiæ* limited the office to the comparatively narrow bounds of providing for the multifarious needs of a system of public worship in a particular church or chapel, which included the keeping of the fabric in repair. The office was wholly free from every kind of civil function, but it included the duty of presentment to the ecclesiastical court of moral delinquencies in either clergy or laity of the parish. The office was not, however, as simple as it might at first sight appear. The fiscal machinery necessary to maintain a costly form of public worship in an efficient state, in days when no one even dreamt of compulsory Church rates, was varied and complicated, and must have required constant attention and no small share of business capacity, notwithstanding the usual generosity of parishioners of all conditions. Now and again the church had lands and houses of its own, usually in connection with obit bequests, from which a steady small income would be drawn; but far oftener there was no mainstay of this nature, and the income, as will presently be seen, was drawn from farming a stock of sheep and cattle, from selling beef and wool, or cheese and milk, or varied gifts in kind, and often to a large extent from the church-ales and various entertainments, as well as from letting out on hire the different appliances of the church house for brewing, cooking, and baking. Then, too, the fees for burial within the church and for funeral knells went to the wardens, as well as the gatherings which they had to make within the church, at the times of outdoor processions, or from house to house.

It was not until late in the reign of Henry VIII that civil functions were attached to the office of churchwarden. At that time, as is explained in a subsequent section, they were ordered to provide arms for soldiers, to relieve maimed soldiers, and to discharge other like duties. From 1549 onwards these church officials were turned into relieving officers to deal with the mass of poverty created in the main by the suppression of the monasteries and through the seizure by the Crown of chantries and obits. Although a new class of parish officials were created to deal with pauperism, the wardens remained primarily responsible. Ere long, as we shall presently see, the churchwardens under Elizabeth and James I became burdened with a hotchpot of miscellaneous duties which had no conceivable relation to religious worship. They became responsible for every possible form of local government, which had formerly been in the control of Hundred and Manor Courts. On the vestry, with the wardens at its head, devolved the powers of taxing the parish, and by degrees the old duties, purely religious, became swamped by such secular responsibilities as the maintenance of army hospitals, the nursing of maimed soldiers, the relief of wayfaring Irish and other wandering persons, the upkeep of the roads and bridges, the appointment of haywards, grassmen, and such-like parish officials, the repairs of pounds, stocks, and whipping-posts, and the destruction of vermin.

It was a farce to continue to style the head parish officials *Church*wardens, but the name continued, though their accounts show but a minimum of expenditure on anything connected with divine worship. The old equivalent names, such as Churchreeves, Churchmen, Kirkmasters, or Kirkwardens, naturally dropped out of use, and those scribes who styled them, in preparing the multifarious accounts for audit, *Œconomi* were amply justified.

Churchwardens were not infrequently assisted, as in modern days, by Sidesmen, a corruption of Synodsmen, or *Testes Synodales*. They were appointed primarily to attend synods or visitation courts, as witnesses, to support the wardens' presentments. Originally their only duty was of a disciplinary character, making due inquiry as to irregular lives, and hence sometimes termed Questmen. Afterwards it came to be considered that Sidesmen were general assistants to wardens, and the appointment of two or three more discreet persons to hold this office in every parish was enjoined by the canons of 1603.

From the careful perusal of a multiplicity of seventeenth- and eighteenth-century accounts, we fear there is some foundation for the following sarcastic lines as to the duties of Sidesmen from the parish books of Childwell, Lancashire :—

> To ken and see and say nowt,
> To eat and drink and pay nowt ;
> And when the wardens drunken roam,
> Your duty is to see them home.

The offices of Chantry and Chapel Wardens came largely into being during the fifteenth century. Some were endowed with lands or stocks of cattle, or both, and they occasionally occupied an independent position and contributed to the maintenance of festival services in which all parishioners could join. The wardens of particular gilds for the upholding of lights and other objects of devotion were elected yearly by the brothers and sisters of the gild, and usually handed over the "increase" or balance of their funds to the parish churchwardens.

The number of the churchwardens was generally two, but where there were several townships or the parish was extensive, the number was sometimes raised to four or more. Now and again the exception occurs of a single warden. But the local custom in this respect varied in a remarkable degree.

The custom at St. Edmund, Sarum, in the fifteenth century, was to choose two senior and two junior churchwardens. The juniors were responsible for the goods and ornaments of the church, and they became seniors in their second year of office. In the sixteenth century only two wardens were elected; the senior one held the purse, whilst the junior became surety for the accounting churchwarden. After 1662 four sidesmen were annually appointed to assist the wardens.

At Pilton, Somerset, up to 1530, a single warden administered the parish funds, but he had four pairs of wardens under him for special work. There was but one warden, called the High Warden, at Milton Abbot, Devon, as late as 1588, but he had a multiplicity of annually elected officials under him.

The elaborate and intricate custom at Holy Trinity, Cambridge, was for the curate to nominate, on Easter Monday, two persons, and these two to choose four other parishioners. Whereupon these six elected the two churchwardens for the coming year, and also the two wardens or keepers of each of the four lights of the Rood, the Sepulchre, Our Lady, and St. Erasmus.

Two churchwardens were annually elected by the vestry at St. Thomas, Sarum, from 1545. In 1636 Charles Robson, minister, gave his written consent to the election of one of the wardens and of the four sidesmen. After 1662 four sidesmen were regularly appointed.

The parishioners of St. Peter's, Ipswich, elected both their wardens at Easter. In 1618 and subsequent years they at the same time chose two "questmen."

The old custom of the City of London with regard to the election of churchwardens provided that the parishioners were to be summoned together annually on the Sunday before the Feast of the Exaltation of the Holy Cross (14th September) after mattins, and that they were to choose one warden to act with him that had been last chosen in the previous year. (See *Archæologia*, l. 90–2.)

The two churchwardens of St. Mary-at-Hill were chosen by the parish; each warden served for two years, the junior warden becoming senior warden in his second year.

St. George, Botolph Lane, is an instance of only one warden.

Basingstoke and Wellingborough usually elected four churchwardens and two sidesmen, whilst Sidbury, on the contrary, appointed two wardens and four sidesmen.

It should always be remembered that in the mediæval Church of England neither rector nor vicar had any distinctive share in the election of wardens. They were chosen, both of them, or whatever the number might be, by the whole body of the parishioners. The modern custom of one being appointed by the incumbent and the other by the parish had its origin in a canon of 1571, by which it was laid down that "Churchwardens, according to the custom of their parish, shall be chosen by the votes of their parishioners and minister." The canon of 1603 went a good deal further in the direction of overturning the old use. It runs: "All churchwardens and questmen in every parish shall be chosen by the joint consent of the minister and parishioners, if it may be. But if they cannot agree upon such a choice, then the minister shall choose one and the parishioners another."

In the days when the sole duties of the wardens were concerned with the fabric and services of the church, there does not appear to have been the slightest difficulty in finding parishioners ready to serve; but in the post-Reformation days, when the zeal for the beauty of God's House evaporated, and every kind of secular business was thrust upon a so-called churchwarden, it is not surprising to find that many a one resisted being appointed to such an office. This reluctance to serve was met by the imposition of a fine.

In 1557 it was decided by the parishioners of Mere, Wilts, that every duly elected warden was to continue in office "by the space of too hole yeres," and that 13s. 4d. was to be the penalty for refusing to hold office.

1561 (*Spelsbury, Oxfordshire*). Hyt be agreed by ye noble parych that whosoever refusyth to be churchwarden shall pay to ye Church use ij stryk of mawlt.

Note James Suche made to ye Churche, forsakynt to be churche man in ye yere of or Lord, 1561, ij stryk of malt, to be payd at Wytesuntyde next to ye use of ye said Churche.

An order taken the same yere for the chosynge of the Chyrche men that every yere from henceforthe to change on yerly, and he that refusythe to take the offyc to pay to the Churche use ij bosshell of malte; and to have the counte at Saynte Lukes daye upon payne of vj s. viij d.

[This penalty was enforced in 1571, when William Ryman refused to be churchwarden.]

It was agreed by the vestry of St. Mary, Cambridge, in 1568, that anyone refusing the office of churchwarden was subject to a fine of 10s. This fine was imposed in 1608 and the money spent at the "visitacion supper." In 1621 the fine was increased to 40s.; this latter fine was inflicted in 1629.

In 1570 the parish of St. Martin, Leicester, imposed a fine of 10s. on refusing to be churchwarden, and the fine was enforced in the following year, in 1581, 1582, 1584, 1585, and 1597. In 1630 there were two fines of 30s. each for refusing office. In 1682 refusals were penalised at a much higher rate, namely, two instances of 50s. and one of £4; at the same time a 40s. fine was paid by a parishioner for "not serving collector for the poor."

The fine for refusing to serve as warden in the parish of St. Thomas, Sarum, was unusually heavy; it varied from 70s. to 80s., as decided in vestry "by the more voices." In 1676 Joseph Stockwell felt unable to accept office "by reason of ye faylure of his eyes and other infirmities." Nevertheless he was fined £3 10s., the vestry at the same time resolving "yt no fine less than £5 shall be accepted from any one who hath ability to serve." In 1678 two fines of £5 each were levied. A single like fine was imposed in 1680; another fine in the same year was abated 20s. "in consideration of his giving them a Treat."

In 1712 the fine for refusing the office of churchwarden in the parish of St. Alphege, London Wall, was fixed as high as £10.

At the present day women churchwardens are of fairly common occurrence, the "lady bountiful" of a country parish being not

INTRODUCTORY

infrequently persuaded to hold that office. But in old days, when the duties were much more onerous and precise, there appears to have been always a small minority of wardens of that sex. At Kilmington, Devon, a female warden was appointed in 1560, 1569, 1570, 1574, 1578, and 1581. The oldest example I have found is at St. Patrick, Ingestre, where Alice Cooke and Alice Pyppedon were wardens in 1426-7. "My Lady Dame Isabell Newton" held office at Yatton, Somerset, in 1496, and Luce Sealy held the like office single-handed for Morebath, Devon, in 1548.

At St. Budeaux, Devon, the wise custom for some time prevailed of the two wardens being chosen one from each sex.

1626. Widow Bragiton and Wm. Rowe.
1666. Margaret Roselow and Thom. Eustis.
1667. Julian Bulley [widow] and Wm. Trevill.
1669. Mary Knighton and James Reede.
1690. Jane Knighton and Thom. Steer.
1691. Mary Beele and Jeffery Knight.
1694. Ruth Nicholls and Peter Shapland.
1699. Mrs. Stucley and Thomas Graye.

A pair of widows once officiated for a Somersetshire parish.

The Account of the Widdow Farthinge and the Widdow Shattocke Church Wardens of *Stapplegrove*, Anno Do. 1645.

Under their jurisdiction the parish paid for shrouds on six occasions, at prices varying from 5s. to 7s. 6d. Such payments do not occur elsewhere in the Staplegrove accounts.

> 1684 (*Wilne, Derbyshire*). The minister and inhabitants elected Mary Jaques to bee one of the churchwardens.[1]

Although feasts at the time of auditing the accounts were not unknown in mediæval days, as can be shown from the very early records of St. Michael, Bath, yet in those, when there was anything of the kind, it usually consisted of a modest refection or breakfast for auditors and wardens, at which the chief delicacy was frequently a calf's head. But in post-Reformation times there was often a prodigal waste of parish money on extravagant feasting and drinking, of which just a few instances follow.

---

[1] I have given several seventeenth-century instances of women holding the offices of both overseer of the poor and petty constable in my *Three Centuries of Derbyshire Annals*, i. 112-3, ii. 137-8.

8   THE CHURCHWARDENS' ACCOUNTS

The accounts of St. Martin's-in-the-Fields yield good examples of the very numerous excuses made for refreshments and drinking. In 1531 bread, ale, and cheese were consumed "in the Chirche" by the parishioners on the passing of the accounts at the modest cost of 18d.; in 1537 this charge had risen to 2s. 4d. The wardens of 1559 had a much more delicate taste; they expended at the passing of their accounts—

> For cracknells vj d., for fygges Reasons and almonds xij d., for Apples iij d., for wyne xvj d., for sewgar vij d., for bere and ale iiij d.

In 1562 the more select were entertained.

> Item to make the maisters of the parishe to Drynke at the geving up of o^r accomptes . . . . vij s.

Five years later the "maisters" drank 13s. 4d. on the like occasion, and in 1569 the drink bill rose to 20s.; but in 1575 this charge dropped to 10s. In 1579

> "A Supper for the Maisters of the parishe at the gyvinge up of o^r accompte" cost 20s.

From this date a like entry occurs for many years; in 1603 it is entered that the 20s. supper was "for the Vicar and the rest of the Vestrie."

Visitations, or the swearing-in of the wardens, were always made the excuse for dinners or drinks.

> 1577. P^d the xxiijth daie of June when we went to St. Clementes to take o^r othe with the sidemen for o^r Dynner and Articles . . . . . . xiij s. iiij d.
> 1580. Paid out for our Dynners at the Bishopps visitacon . viij s.
> 1597. At the archedeacons visitacon for o^r Dynners and the sidemen . . . . . . xvj s. viij d.
> 1599. Paid for our Dinners for ourselves and our sidesmen xxj s. iiij d.
> 1603. Paid for our dinner with Mr Scott and our sidesmen, Clearke and Sexton and others . . . . vij s. ij d.

All kinds of other casual reasons for feasting and drinking were readily found, among which the following may be taken as specimens:—

> 1540. Paied for a Cowpull of Conis (rabbits) and a quarte of sacke when the Chalis was sett at Master Writtes . xiij d

1559. Payed at pooles (St. Paul's) for to make the sidesmen drinke when we presented the artycles at pooles . . viij d.
1568. Payd to make certayne of the masters of the parishe drynke when we were with the bysshopp of london at fullam vij s.
1592. Paid ye vth of November at farmer Robsons to make the vestrie men Drincke at the Chosinge of henry Russell Churchwarden . . . . . . vj s.
1600. Paide for wyne and nuttes when wee satt at Mr Knightes about o^r presentimentes . . . . . xviij d.

The habits of the officials of St. Mary, Cambridge, are illustrated by the following extracts:—

1602. Item for a bottle of Sack which was Drunke in the Chauncell of the Auditors and others at the giveinge up of the laste Churchwardens accountes . . . 2s. 0d.
1603. For wine at the Audeit in the Chauncell . 2s. 4d.
1604. For wine and cakes at the awdett . . . 2s. 4d.
1618. Layde out at the Audyt . . . . . 6s. 10d.
1625. Payed for wine and Cakes at the Accompt of the old Churchwardens . . . . . . 6s. 8d.

In the reign of James I a custom began at St. Edmund's, Sarum, of a parish "breakfast" on the day of the election of the churchwardens and other officials. The surplus charge for this meal of £2 0s. 11d. was debited to the parish in 1610, and £1 8s. 6d. in 1613. Every one present who had been a warden paid 12d., and the rest 6d. In 1620 it was formally sanctioned that the overplus for the future was always to be placed in the parish accounts provided it did not amount to more than £4. In the following year the election feast was called by the more appropriate name of "dinner," and the overplus came to £2 16s. The overplus amounted to £3 17s. 8d. in 1622; in 1623, when it was held on Easter Tuesday, the exact limit of £4 was reached; in 1625 the limit was passed, £4 6s. 8d. being entered in the accounts; in 1631 the total overplus, including wine, was recorded as £4 19s. An intermediate ordinance of 1629, limiting the overplus to 40s., was treated with derision.

The following items occur in the accounts of St. Alphege, London Wall, for 1560:—

Pd the fyrstt Day that I was chusyd wardyn for our brekfast at the taverne . . . . . . iiij s. ij d.

For our breakefast that Day that we Dyd serch abought the
p'sshe for pyctures and images that were paynted . . iij s. iiij d.
For our brekefast that Day that we dyd asemble together for to
know whether there were any anabaptystes in the p'rish . iij s. iiij d.

The dinner at the election of wardens and other officials of St. John Baptist, Walbrook, in 1595, cost the parish £6 11s. 6d. Like dinners of nine other city parishes in Elizabethan days added an average of £4 7s. each to the rates. To arrive at a correct idea of the cost of this feasting, it must be remembered that the totals must be multiplied by about ten to accord with the present value of money.

Not only were wardens' and sidesmen's dinners charged for at a high rate at Visitations, but the parish was expected to treat the visiting ecclesiastics.

1598 (*St. Michael, Worcester*).
 Layd out at the visitacion for the churche wardens and
  sydesmens dynners . . . . . iij s. iiij d.
 For a pound of suger . . . . . . xx d.
 For wyne which was bestowed upon the bushopp . iij s. viij d.
1625 (*All Saints, Derby*). For a bottle of Clarett wyne and q^{tr} of
 sugar to Mr Archdeacon . . . . . 6s. 8d.
1627. For a quart of Sacke given to Mr Archdeacon . 1s. 2d.
1630. For wyne bestowed uppon Mr Archdeacon and for beere . 2s. 10d.

The time for holding the annual audit of the parish accounts varied greatly in pre-Reformation times, and often changed repeatedly in the same parish. Christmas, Epiphany, Candlemas, Eastertide, Ascension Day, Whitsuntide, All Hallows, and various feasts of the Blessed Virgin and of different saints are all particularised as days of audit and election of new wardens. In at least three parishes the strangely unsuitable fast of Good Friday was selected. The general custom of an Easter vestry arose out of Elizabethan poor-law legislation.

The term vestry as applied to a parish meeting was almost unknown in mediæval days; it came into general use in the second half of the sixteenth century. The parish meeting had, in addition to passing the accounts and electing wardens, to see that the liability of the parish to maintain and furnish the House of God was duly fulfilled, but the parishioners were left free as to the manner

INTRODUCTORY

in which they exercised their bounty. The list of church goods required to be found by the parish by Archbishop Winchelsea's Constitution of 1305, and which was in force up to Edward VI's reign, has been repeatedly printed (Johnson's *Canons*, ii. 319); it practically included all the service books, vestments, altar plate, and other utensils. But the minimum of requisites was almost invariably outstripped by the people's zeal.

Bishop Hobhouse, after a close study of west country pre-Reformation accounts, pointed out, in a striking fashion, the whole sale distinction between a Parish Meeting and a Manor Court as shown in their respective rolls on documents. In the civil documents of the latter, the community is divided into sharply defined classes, the lord of the soil and his tenants, the tenants into bond and free, and the villeins again subdivided according to the size of their holdings. The relative duties, too, of class to class are sharply defined and enforced by fine and penalty. At the parish meeting, on the contrary, held in the church, all were equal, the women voting for the wardens as well as the men. "The bulk of the parishioners, even the serfs, were engaged in planning the amusements whereby profits were gained for the church. They were not spectators or partakers merely, but also managers sharing in the pageant and in the costs; and thereby the bonds of social fellowship were tightened, and the barrier lines between servile and free, which seem to the student of our law books to be so impassable, were melted away by the warmth of kindly fellowship."

The liability of the parish in all things pertaining to the church has already been named, but such a thing as a civilly enforced church rate was entirely unknown. The power of Interdict, *i.e.* the excommunication of the whole community, was in the hands of the Bishop in the very rare event of neglect to keep the church with its appurtenances and churchyard in repair. But compulsion of any kind for church expenses was most rarely needed, for the goodwill of the people usually prevailed to a lavish extent. Where episcopal threats had to be used, they were generally addressed to chapelries neglecting to help the mother church. Now and again there was resort to a levy or rate *juxta valorem possessionum*, as in the case of Wembdon, near Bridgwater, in 1325, cited by Bishop Hobhouse; but this was never levied until the parishioners had first consented to a voluntary rate. The following may be cited out of the three or four cases I have noted in extant wardens accounts of pre-Reformation date:—

> 1515 (*Worfield, Salop*). Hit is agreed at these accountes that every yard lond within the parish shall pay this yere to the reparacions of the church and for making the churchyard walles . . . . iiij d.

Under Elizabeth, sectaries began to flourish and Puritanism made so much headway that zeal for God's House languished to such an extent that compulsory church-rating was adopted and enforced on a resisting minority by the civil arm of the law. This disastrous law had the effect of drying up voluntary effort in a remarkable degree. After many efforts it was at last repealed in 1868, and under a voluntary system churches have again thrived. Many a parish, however, hesitated long before adopting a compulsory rate, but by the close of the sixteenth century it was frequently in operation. It is sufficient to cite a single case.

A levy was made in 1596 for the repair of the great church of Melton Mowbray, resulting in the sum of £4 5s. 10d. from 188 ratepayers, in sums varying from 6s. 3d. to 1d.

At the same time it should be remembered that the reformed Church continued to claim the power of excommunication in cases of gross neglect, though it was usually exercised only against the wardens. The church of Repton was presented for an array of broken windows in 1595. The wardens disregarded the injunction to repair, and the result appears in two consecutive entries in their book:—

> It. geven to Thomas Beldde for bryngyng a sertyfycatte for us heying excommunycatt . . . . . . viij d.
> It. att Darby when we sartyfyed that our churche was glassed

It remains to add somewhat about Select Vestries. Fairly early in the sixteenth century, a kind of parochial council for exceptional work sprang up in a few parishes. Thus at Morebath, Devon, "The Courte of the V men" is entered under 1526-7. And in 1538 it is recorded that

> Four honest men were chosen to govern the parish in all causes concerning the wealth of our church, under orders at Visitation.

INTRODUCTORY

But in this case the small council was elected by the parishioners and recognised by the Ordinary.

From this kind of a beginning there gradually emerged a small oligarchy of Masters or Rulers of the parish, termed in most cases the Select Vestry, or in certain parts of the country the Twelve or the Twenty-Four, according to their exact number. At St. Michael, Worcester, there was a body known as the Six Men, in another case the Seven Men, and in a third parish the Thirteen. They were not, however, legal bodies unless they had established themselves by lapse of time. They were not technically a representative body, and usually filled up vacancies by co-option. As to their general corruption and incompetence, see Burns' *Ecclesiastical Law, s.v.* Vestry, and the 1834 Report of the Poor Law Commissioners.

The management of parish affairs by a Select Vestry, generally consisting of 24 members, was usual throughout the diocese of Durham. The Select Vestry of 12 for the parish of Pittington began in 1584.

It is agreed by the consent of the whole parish to electe and chuse out of the same xij men to order and define all comon causes pertaininge to the churche, as shall appertaine to the profit and commoditie of the same, without molestation or troublinge of the rest of the comon people, whose names hearafter folowethe.

Once established, this Pittington Select Vestry perpetuated itself by co-option.

The Vestry of St. Mary-at-Hill, City of London, is sometimes spoken of as "The Seniors of the Parish," at other times as "The Masters of the Parish." Possibly it only numbered 12 persons; when the annual accounts were presented in 1526, a bequest of 20s. was "put in to the chirch chist in presence of xij persones of the parish."

The Vestry of St. Mary, Reading, originated in 1603, on the motion of "Mr. Docter Powell, vichar of the parishe," to be composed of 33 of "the Chiffeste and Auncientes Parishioners," who were to "associat themselves togeather at the Churche upon everie good fridaie after Eveninge Prayer to see the Accountes finished" and to transact other parish business. It was this body that imposed the first church rate of this parish in 1607.

It is of interest, in concluding this subject, to notice the gradual evolution of a Select Vestry from the accounts of an important Westminster parish.

The churchwardens of St. Martin's-in-the-Fields from 1525 to 1546 were elected "by the consent will and agreement of the whole body of the parich." From 1546 to 1583 they are simply described as "chosen and appointed." In December 1583 the wardens for the next two years were elected "by the whole assent and consent of the masters of the parishe." From the year 1561 the wardens were accustomed to render their accounts to the "masters" of the parish. There is no definite statement as to how the government of the parish passed from the full parish meeting to the select vestry or smaller body of "masters." The process was probably gradual, and may have partly come about from the general body of the parishioners ceasing to interest themselves in church government. Before the end of Elizabeth's reign a co-opted Select Vestry became firmly established and remained in power until 1834. During the eighteenth century, five separate attempts were made to eject the oligarchy, but they all failed through lack of evidence to disprove the corporation's plea of "immemorial custom." And yet, on each occasion, the unscrupulous vestry knew perfectly well that they held abundant evidence in their own hands that their "immemorial" plea was false. At last, in the 1834 suit of Simpson *v.* Holroyd, the old Churchwarden Accounts had to be produced in Court, when "the hopelessly corrupt Vestry," as Mr. Kitto rightly terms it, was dispossessed, and the parish once more resumed their ancient rights.

THE WEST PROSPECT O THE OLD CHURCH OF ST. MART N-N-THE-FIELDS
FROM AN OLD PRINT BY J. HARRIS

CHAPTER II

EARLY WARDENS' ACCOUNTS

Fourteenth Century: St. Michael, Bath ; Hedon ; Tavistock. *Fifteenth Century* : St. Michael, Oxford—All Saints, Bristol—St. Laurence, Reading ; Hythe—St. Mary-at-Hill, City—St. Petrock, Exeter—St. Peter Cheap, City ; Tintinhull — Saffron Walden — Thame — St. Peter-in-the-East, Oxford — St. Mary, Sandwich—St. Margaret, Southwark—Yatton—St. Andrew, Holborn—Walberswick—St. Ewen, Bristol—All Hallows, London Wall—Swaffham—St. Andrew Hubbard, City—St. Michael Cornhill, City—Arlington—Yeovil—St. Margaret, Westminster—Cowfold—Yarmouth—St. Edmund, Sarum—All Saints, Derby—St. Botolph, Aldersgate—St. John, Peterborough—Ludlow—St. Mary Redcliffe, Bristol—St. Martin Ongar, City—St. John Baptist, Bristol—Blythburgh—St. Stephen, Walbrook, City—Snettisham—Croscombe—Wimborne—Ashburton—Chagford—St. Thomas, Launceston ; Sutterton ; Kirton-in-Lindsey—Wigtoft—St. Nicholas, Bristol—St. Martin, Leicester—Cratfield St. Mary-de-Castro, Leicester—All Hallows, Staining—Kingston-on-Thames Bassingbourn—Pilton

IN this chapter a brief analysis is given of the extant churchwardens' records of the fourteenth and fifteenth centuries, arranged chronologically.

The wardens' accounts of St. Michael, Bath, may justly lay claim to be the oldest, and in certain respects the most interesting, in the kingdom. They were transcribed and edited by the Rev. Prebendary Pearson in 1878 for the Somersetshire Archæological and Natural History Society, and they were also briefly treated of by Bishop Hobhouse in his work of 1890 for the Somerset Record Society. These extend, with but a few missing intervals, from 1349 to 1575, and consist of 77 rolls, 67 of which are in Latin and 10 in English. They are of great value as illustrative of the working of the Church in a city parish with a trading population.

Bishop Hobhouse aptly comments on some of the peculiar

features of its fiscal system. (*a*) The occasional allowance to the wardens of a stipend (*pro stipendio*) of 12d. (*b*) The feasting at audit time, a fairly common custom in town parishes, but in this instance entered after an undisguised fashion. (*c*) A small flock of sheep, an awkward and unusual increment for a town parish. (*d*) A continually growing endowment of land and houses, rising in value from 10s. 9d. in 1347 to £11 18s. 8d. in 1540; these properties were charged with obituary payments, denoting the primary motive of the donors. (*e*) A continuance burden of house-agency on the wardens, leading to a multiplicity of entries for repairs and management. (*f*) Partition of duties between the two wardens, one being elected as bursar (*portare bursam*). (*g*) The usual sufficiency of revenue from endowment for the handsome maintenance of the church, aided by gifts and bequests, with but rare resort to church-ales or such-like expedients.

The wardens' accounts of the church or chapel of St. James, Hedon, E. R., Yorks, for the years 1350–1, 1354–5, 1356–7, 1357–8, 1358–9, 1361–2, 1394–5, 1395–6, 1410–1, 1414–5, 1424–5, 1430–1, 1442–3, 1443–4, 1447–8, 1454–5, 1460–1, 1462–3, and 1475–6, are in the hands of the Corporation of Hedon.

The wardens' accounts of St. Augustine, Hedon, for 1370–1, 1372–3, 1373–4, 1374–5, 1397–8, 1398–9, 1408–9, 1410–1, 1429–30, 1430–1, 1431–2, 1443–4, 1445–6, 1453–4, 1454–5, 1484–5, 1490–1, 1531–2, 1536–7, as well as various rolls or portions of rolls of uncertain date, are also in the hands of the Corporation; they were carefully transcribed or largely cited by Mr. J. R. Boyle in his *History of Hedon*, published in 1895. The receipts entered in the earlier of these rolls are of great and exceptional interest. The accounts of 1370–1 show that 6s. 4d. was collected on the fair day of St. Mary Magdalen, when the shrine or chest of relics was carried round the town; and 14d. was received when the relics were exposed on Holy Cross day. On the day of the Circumcision, 10s. was collected in the church. In the church stood a special Holy Cross, before which lights were maintained by a gild; before it stood an offertory box, which was opened twice a year, namely, on the feasts of the Invention and Exaltation of the Holy Cross; in 1370, 15s. was found in the box on the first of these days and 56s. 4d. on the latter occasion. There was also a box before the image of Our Lady, and this, too, was opened on these same feasts; it was found to contain 3s. 6d. and 4s. respectively. There were collections made for church expenses every Sunday in the church, with the result this year of a total of 58s. An annual gathering was made through the town, *cum tabula*, on St. Stephen's Day, producing in 1370 the sum of 5s.

The early wardens' accounts of St. Nicholas, Hedon, in the custody of the Corporation, are for the years 1379-80, 1385-6, 1402-3, 1408-9, 1409-10, 1410-1, 1411-2, 1423-4, 1430-1, 1437-8, 1443-4, 1445-6, 1456-7, 1460-1, 1461-2, 1469-70, and 1474-5. The first of these accounts shows that the receipts were chiefly obtained from rents (29s. 11d.) and from collections on diverse Sundays and festivals (12s.). The expenditure of 1379-80 was mainly concerned with the erection of a Rood-screen and loft.

In j ligno empto pro solar Crucies	v s.
In carpentariis . . . portantibus dictum solar	xxj s. vj d.
In bemefellyng pariet' cancelle	ij s. vj d.
In bordis emptis pro dicto solar	vj s. ij d.
In lignis emptis pro dicto solar	ij s. v d.
In clavis ferreis emptis pro fabricatione dicti solar	xv d.
In iij plaunkis emptis pro scannis in dicta cancella	ij s. v d.

The repair of the Rood is named in 1384-5, whilst in 1442-3 a shaft of wood was bought for 17d. to support it. There are also expenses for the light kept burning before the Rood.

Among the oldest wardens' accounts are those of Tavistock. They are very imperfect as a series, but the first roll is of the years 1385-6; this is followed by those for 1392-3, 1399-1400, 1401-2, 1405-6, 1407-8, 1411-2, 1423-4, 1425-6, and 1426-7, and next is 1470-1, and there is then a gap until 1535-6. There are a few more of the reign of Henry VIII, one of Edward VI, one of Mary, seven of Elizabeth, and a few of the seventeenth century. Transcripts or fairly full abstracts of these accounts were printed by Mr. R. N. Worth in a small volume, *Calendar of the Parish Records of Tavistock*, published in 1887; unfortunately the oldest of these, which are in Latin, have been poorly translated. The accounts run from the Feast of the Invention of the Cross to its successor. The receipts of the year 1385-6 amounted to £6 9s. 5d.; they comprised balance in hand, 3s. 2d.; rents of a park, a tenement, and four gardens, 9s. 9d.; and pence for lights, with considerable arrears, £5 16s. 6d. The total expenses were £7 6s. 6d. The cost of buying wax and tallow, and the making of tapers and candles, together with links or torches, came to £3 4s. 10d. Another large item was for the repair of diverse windows. There was an annual payment of 3s. 4d. to the sacristan of Tavistock Monastery. The altars mentioned in this account were those of Our Lady, St. Eustachius, St. Stephen, St. John Baptist, St. Katherine, St. Blaise, St. George, St. Saviour, and the Holy Trinity.

There is a fine series of churchwarden rolls of St. Michael, Oxford, beginning in the year 1403 and continuing to the end of the fifteenth century. They have been transcribed by Dr. Ellis, and it is hoped that ere long they will appear in book form.[1] The receipts of the year 1403-4 amounted to £9 13s. 4d. Diverse receipts, including balance in money and wax from the preceding proctors and wardens, and several subscriptions to the repair of the church books, amounted to 55s. 10d.; the rents of several small houses brought in 4s. 6d.; subscriptions for the church lamp, to which there were seven subscribers of sums varying from twopence to a halfpenny, 7s. 3d.; and collections on Maundy Thursday, Easter Day, and Christmas Day, 17s. 8d. The chief items of the expenditure were in lamp oil and wax; among the smaller payments were 9d. for repairing three church books, and 2d. for carrying a banner on Ascension Day.

The churchwardens' accounts of All Saints, Bristol, begin as early as 1407, and proceed onwards with but few gaps (*Archæological Journal*, vol. lviii. p. 148). A large number of interesting extracts, together with a valuable inventory of 1396, are given in Nicholls' and Taylor's *Bristol Past and Present* (1881), vol. ii. pp. 90-107. In 1410 there is an entry of 20s. 6d. for making a cross in the churchyard.

The archives of the church of St. Laurence, Reading, are among the oldest and most interesting in the kingdom. The first churchwardens' roll is for the year 1410, and from that date onward they

---

[1] I am particularly obliged to Dr. Ellis for lending me diverse transcripts of these rolls of the fifteenth century.

are fairly complete. The most salient points from these invaluable records were set forth in 1883, after a most able fashion, by the Rev. Charles Kerry, in a volume called *A History of the Municipal Church of St. Laurence, Reading*. The roll of 1410 contains the names of 150 subscribers to the re-roofing of the nave. One of the largest subscribers (13s.) was John Keat, whose brass commemorating himself and his wife Jean is in the chancel; he died in 1415. Abundant use is made of Mr. Kerry's volume under diverse heads in the subsequent pages.

The receipts and disbursements of the churchwardens of Hythe, Kent, for the year 1412-3, are printed in vol. x. of *Archæologiæ Cantiana* (1876). The receipts, amounting to £6 7s. 2d., including a balance of 8s. 1½d., were derived from four sources: (1) Rents amounting to 17s., in sums varying from 1d. to 5s.; (2) offertories collected on 26 Sundays, the one on Easter Day 10s. 6d., the remainder varying in amount from 6d. to 1s. 6d.; (3) indulgencies, which had been granted on ten days—Christmas Day, Whitsunday, All Saints, Feast of the Dedication, Corpus Christi, St. John Baptist, and Our Lady's Feasts of the Conception, Nativity, and Assumption, and St. Leonard, the patron saint—but the collective result was only 16d.; and (4) legacies, which were 24 in number and amounted to £3 6s. 1d. The payments included £5 for a Legenda and repairs to the "clokke."

A long roll of churchwardens' accounts of the same church for 1480-1, among the Corporation records, is cited in the *Fourth Report of the Historical MSS. Commission* (1874), pp. 432-3. The expenditure is chiefly concerned with the steeple and bells, for which there is a long list of subscriptions varying from 10s. to jd. The parish clerk was paid 13s. 4d. for keeping "le chyme" and "le clok," and 10s. for keeping the organs. Thomas the Bedesman, who was paid 16s. for watching the organs, was evidently a night watchman and slept in the church; he was that year provided with a gown at a charge of 4s. " for lying in the church."

The mediæval records of St. Mary-at-Hill, near London Bridge, preserved in the Guildhall Library, are contained in two large volumes of the fifteenth and sixteenth centuries. They include the churchwardens' accounts, which begin in 1420 and are continued down to 1559. Mr. Littlehales did good service in transcribing and editing these accounts for the Early English Text Society in 1905; up to 1495 they are copied verbatim, and subsequently in abstract. From 1431 to 1476 the accounts are missing, but from 1477 they are continuous.

The churchwardens' accounts of the little parish of St. Petrock, in the centre of the city of Exeter, extend from 1425 to 1692, but with a gap from 1590 to 1640. These accounts are largely cited and annotated in vol. xiv. of the *Transactions of the Devon Association* (1882). The chief receipts in the first account are from collections at Christmas, Easter, Midsummer, and Michaelmas. Among the receipts of 1426-7 are several gifts—a brass vessel weighing 20 lb., six silver spoons, a diaper napkin, and a surplice. The earlier accounts begin and end on the Feast of All Saints. There is a very full inventory in 1483-4.

The churchwardens' accounts of St. Peter Cheap, as contained in a volume of 262 folios, extend from 1431 to 1604. The earlier portions up to 1517 are comparatively scanty, but from that date they proceed with but little interruption. There is an inventory of church goods of 1431 which is marvellously rich in the number and value of its vestments and plate. St. Peter's parish, though a small one, had a large number of wealthy residential citizens. Classified extracts are given in vol. xxiv. of the *Journal of the British Archæological Association* (1868), the most important of which appear in the following pages.

Tintinhull, Somerset, possesses valuable warden accounts from 1433 to 1569. A good selection of extracts are given in vol. iv. of *Somerset Record Society*, 175-207. Two wardens were chosen annually; the day of audit and election varied considerably. The funds accrued from (1) the bakehouse (*pistrinia*); (2) the brewhouse (*brasina*); (3) the church-house (*pandoxatorium*), after 1497, (4) some strips of land on the moor; (5) live stock, horned cattle, and bees; and (6) gifts, bequests, and special gatherings. The baking and brewing tackle were let out for private hire.

Extracts are given of the churchwardens' accounts of Saffron Walden from 1439 to 1485 in Richard Lord Braybrooke's *History of Audley End and Saffron Walden* (1836), pp. 219-27. These accounts remain at Audley End.

The churchwardens' accounts of Thame, Oxon, begin in 1442.

Transcripts of the earlier years begin in vol. viii. of the *Berks, Bucks, and Oxon Archæological Journal*; only a few pages appear in each volume; in the last volume issued (xvi.) the year 1465 had not been finished. Several of the more exceptional entries are quoted in the following pages.

The valuable early churchwarden rolls of St. Peter-in-the-East, Oxford, were rescued from destruction by the late Bishop Hobhouse, when vicar, in 1845. They were bound in a volume. The earliest is 1443, and there are eight others before 1500. They then become more regular and run through the sixteenth century, but with several gaps. The accounts of 1443–4 are printed in the *Proceedings of the Society of Antiquaries*, 2nd ser. vol. x. pp. 25–8. The receipts include rents to the value of 10s. 8d., parish gatherings at Christmas and Easter, a church-ale at Whitsuntide, and fees for burials within the church. Other rolls show that (1) the house property originated with obits; (2) that the young men and maidens at Hocktide collected on the Monday and Tuesday from the opposite sex for permission to pass, handing the receipts to the church; (3) that the wardens kept a stock of players' garments and let them out for hire; (4) and that they let out torches for funerals, especially for those of academical students.

The churchwardens' accounts of St. Mary, Sandwich, Kent, date back to 1444 and are consecutive to 1449. They are also extant from 1456 to 1464, and for the years 1495–6, 1500–2, 1504–19, 1521–3, 1526–31, 1542, 1545–8, 1558, 1568, and 1582. The next book begins in 1632 and ends with 1730. Various important extracts are set forth in Boy's *History of Sandwich* (1792), 359–66. At the head of the initial account is a memorandum to the effect that when the French robbed the town of Sandwich in 1456, they bore away, amongst other goods, a book of the church of Our Lady, "where yn was conteynyd the a countis of the sayd chyrche of a xij yere afore passid or more." However, Sir Thomas Norman had copies of those accounts, and when he was churchwarden in 1474 he gave the transcripts written in his own hand to the church. The largest item in the receipts of 1444 was—

> It of mennys almeys gevyn unto ye tabyll of alabastyr at ye hygh auter for ye hygh chauncell . . iiij li. xij s. vj d.

Certain old accounts of the extinct parish of St. Margaret, Southwark, in the custody of the Corporation of Wardens of Southwark Cathedral are of much interest. There is a set of churchwarden accounts extending from 1445 to 1455. The chief source of income was from gatherings made in the church at cer tain festival seasons. These gatherings in 1445 amounted to 5s. 8d. on St. Lucy's Day, 18s. on Christmas Day, 4s. on Candlemas Day, 30s. on Easter Day, 8s. 2d. on Whitsunday, 9s. 1d. on St. Margaret's Day, 7s. 1d. on the Assumption, and 7s. on All Hallows Day. Three burials within the church produced the usual fee of 6s. 8d. each; seven weddings came to 14d.; and the executors of Nicholas Hough paid 30s. towards "Chirche Workes." The outgoings show that customary plays were held on the Feasts of St. Margaret and St. Lucy. Among the receipts of one year occurs 3s. 9d. "in dawnsyng mony of the Maydens." There are also detached sheets of churchwardens' accounts of 1481, 1487, 1491, 1497, 1508, and from 1520 to 1539. These last accounts show a change in the gatherings in church. At Easter offerings were made at the high altar. Thus in 1534, £5 6s. 8d. was "receyved at Ester at goddys bord." Some of the earlier accounts were transcribed by Mr. J. Payne Collier, and printed in vol. xxxii. (1847) of the *British Magazine*.

The highly interesting parish accounts of Yatton, Somerset, extending from 1445 to 1567, are admirably treated by Bishop Hobhouse in *Somerset Record Society*, vol. iv. pp. 78–172. "The area of the parish was divided into three portions, the east and west (Claverham and Cleve) being committed to two 'Lightmen,' sometimes called wardens, who brought their gatherings, originally made for the support of lights in the church, to the wardens' audit; central Yatton paid its offerings to the wardens direct. After the completion of the church-house, with its appliances for entertainment, the gatherings were made at the Ales, instead of from house to house, but the Lightmen of the east and west held their Ales separately."

John Bentley, churchwarden in 1584 of St. Andrew, Holborn, left behind him a book (now kept at the church) entitled *Some Monuments of Antiquities Worthy Memory*; it contains memoranda from old long-lost churchwardens' accounts, the earliest date being 1446. Some highly interesting extracts from Bentley's book are given in *Londinium Redivivium* (vol. ii. pp. 186–9, 196–8). Throughout the reigns of Henry VII and Henry VIII the four Inns or Houses of Chancery paid yearly a mark apiece to this church; the money was received by the wardens of St. Sythe, and went to the support of a chantry priest. In the first year of Edward VI, 36s. was received for brasses taken from the tombs. In 2 Elizabeth the wardens sold the remaining memorial brasses. The three Rood images "were all burned to ashes by commandment of the commissioners" in 1 Elizabeth. In 4 Mary the obit of the Pope was solemnly kept, with great ringing of the bells. We give further notes under "Fabrics" and "Church-Ales."

Many extracts from the valuable churchwardens' accounts of Walberswick, Suffolk, extending from 1450 to 1696, are given in Thomas Gardner's *History of Dunwich* (1754). These old accounts have, alas, long since disappeared. Walberswick was for a long period an important fishing port. The early receipts of the churchwardens included a considerable toll on the herrings and sperling or sprats from the various boats. In 1451 there were 22 sperling boats registered at this port and 13 deep-sea or herring boats. There was a profit to the wardens of 13s. 4d., in 1453, from a church-ale held on 6th May, and a profit of 16s. from a church-ale on All Saints' Day in the same year. There is a full account of "utensils" in the church in 1492; many of the vestments, etc., were stored "in the Lofte over the Porch."

The old churchwardens' accounts of St. Ewen, Bristol, contained in a bound volume, begin in 1454. They include some valuable inventories, showing an exceptional wealth of books, vestments, plate, and jewels. These and the earlier accounts were admirably transcribed and annotated by Sir John Maclean in vol. xv. of the *Transactions of the Bristol and Gloucestershire Archæological Society.*

The churchwardens' accounts of All Hallows, London Wall, begin in 1455. A few interesting notes from the early years are en in *Londinium Redivivium* (vol. ii. pp. 65–6); the Rood-loft was rebuilt in 1457 at a cost of £8.

The Black Book of Swaffham contains no wardens' accounts, but it is sufficiently notable to be mentioned, as it belongs to the parish. This small book was written in 1454, in Latin, by Master John Botwright, rector of Swaffham, master of Corpus Christi College, Cambridge, and chaplain to Henry VI. It contains an inventory of church goods and their donors, a terrier of all the lands belonging to the light of St. Mary, and other lands belonging to the church, and an account of all debts to the church to be collected by the wardens.

The churchwardens' accounts of St. Andrew Hubbard begin in 1454; they are particularly valuable owing to their freedom from gaps. The first volume extends from 1454 to 1524, and the second from 1525 to 1631. They are carefully transcribed, from the beginning up to 1578, in the now rare volumes (xxxi. to xxxvi.) of the *British Magazine and Monthly Register* for the years 1847-9. The receipts came chiefly from the rent of a house at five marks a year; from "knelles pyttes" (graves in the church) and bequests; and from "quaterages and houselyng silver," the latter due on Easter Day. The following are some of the noteworthy special receipts:—

1457-8. On Seint Andrewis day in May for money gadered at the church dure	ij s. viij d.
1457-8. Of Margaret the fruterr for standynge at the churche dore	vj d.
1458-60. Of Margaret Kene for sittyng at the Churchedure .	vj d.
1466-8. Of Margarete Kene for occupyynge the bench under the chirche walle for ij yeres	iij s.
1476-8. Of Margarete Kene for hir standyng at the Chirche dore for an hole yere	ij s.
1476-8. Of Pye Stacyoner for a boke called the half bible of the old testament by us to hym sold .	xxvj s. viij d.
1489-90. Of the Frenchemen and other strangers at Ester	viij s. vj d.
1491-2. Reaseyved in the stret on oure chirche holy day	vij s. iij d.
1498-9. Receyved that we gader in the Strett. . .	ix s.

These street gatherings, continued up to the Reformation, were made on 9th of May, which was the Feast of the Translation of St. Andrew.

The churchwardens' accounts of St. Michael, Cornhill, known as the "Great Book of Accounts," extending from 1456 to 1608, were privately printed in 1870, under the editorship of Mr. W. H. Overall. There is a break of 71 years from 1475 to 1546. The vestry minutes begin in 1503. The total receipts of 1456 were £4 19s. 6½d.

derived from gatherings in the church at Christmas, Easter, St. John Baptist's Feast, and Michaelmas, and from four fees for burials within the church. The chief expenses for that year were in connection with repairing parts of the church; 50 paving tiles cost 1s. 6d. All Hallows was added to the times for church collections in 1458. The details of the collections in 1471 will serve as an example of several years of that century.

RECEYTES OF GADERINGES IN THE CHIRCHE

Fonds gadered in the Chyrche on All Hallowen day	iiij s. ob. qr.
Itm gadered on Sonday next after Crystemas day a forenon	iiij s. x d. ob.
It gadered the same day at after noon	xx d. ob.
It gadered on Newrs day be fore noon	xix d. ob.
It gadered on xijth day be fore noon	xij d.
It gadered the same day at after noon	v d. ob.
It gadered the Sonday next followyng	iij d.
It gadered on Sonday next after Ester day	iij s. ob.
It gadered on Sonday next followyng	xvj d. ob.
It receyved of Wodchyrche, for hys mayde fownde it in the chyrche	iij d.
It gadered on Michelmas day	ij s. ij d.

Among memoranda at the end of the Great Book of Accounts, various ordinances are entered as agreed upon by the rector, wardens and seventeen other parishioners assembled in the vestry on 12th May 1504. The following are the chief points: The churchwardens to present the year's accounts on the day after the Purification—the wardens of every brotherhood to render accounts within six weeks of the completion of their year of office —the old wardens of brotherhoods not to deliver their stocks to the new wardens until sureties are found—churchwardens as well as wardens of stocks to deliver their accounts to the elected parish auditors—no warden to incur any expenditure above 10s. without the assent of "a vestrie"—anyone elected a warden and refusing to serve to be fined 10s.—anything requiring to be corrected or amended to be submitted to twelve of the wisest and most discreet parishioners—no churchwarden or brotherhood warden to put any priest in service in the church without the assent of the rector and "iiij or vj of the moste ancient or worshipfullest of ye p'ish." Each breach of these ordinances was subject to a penalty.

This is followed by "Rewles" of the church, drawn up in 1538.

The clerks were to ring to service for mattins at 7, for high mass at 9, and for evensong "on work dayes at ij a clock, and on holy dayes according to the lawdable custome of the Citie." Priests and clerks "after the thryd peall end shalbe present in the quyre in theire shurples singing theire from the beginnyng of Mattens, Masse and Evynsong unto the end of them all, without a reasonable excuse in payne of forfeating as oft as they shall so doo ij d."

Add. MS. 33,192, at the British Museum, consists of seventeen folios out of a fifteenth-century churchwardens' account book of the parish of Arlington, Sussex; they extend from 1456 to 1479.

The expenses of 1456 only amounted to 11s. 2d.; they are of an ordinary character, such as making the paschal taper and torches, washing linen, and mending of the bells. Nor is there anything specially noteworthy in the remaining recorded church expenditure of this small parish. With regard, however, to the receipts, two matters are well worthy of note. The parish held a considerable stock of kine. In 1458-9 and in the following year a cow was farmed at 3s. 8d. the year, and 28 other cows were farmed at 2 lb. of wax, thus producing 56 lb. of wax for the church lights per annum. The other exceptional receipt was "hognell silver," which fluctuated considerably in amount. In 1457 the receipts from "hognel sylver" were 24s. 4d.; in 1459, 23s. 2d.; in 1460, 25s. 2d.; in 1464, 25s. 6½d.; in 1475, 35s. 5d.; in 1476, 20s. 2d.; in 1477, 37s. 1½d.; and in 1478, 33s. 7½d. Hognell is probably a variant of Hogmaney, a name signifying December, but used in some places to denote Christmastide gifts, and more especially offerings on the last day of December, the eve of the Circumcision.

There is a valuable account roll of the proctors or wardens of Yeovil for the year 1457-8. The several sources of income of the first account were (1) sale of seats, 10s. 10d.; (2) fees for tolling bell and for hire of cope, cross, and censer at funerals, 16s.; (3) rents for carts standing by churchyard on market days, 1s. 4d.; (4) gifts of individuals, £2 13s. 4d.; and (5) rents for parish weights, 9s. 1d. Total receipts, independent of money in hand, £4 10s. 7d. The expenditure, amounting to £5 1s. 1¼d., was largely concerned with the bells. This roll is given *in extenso* in Nichols' *Collectanea* (1836), iii. 134-41.

WARDENS' BALANCE-SHEET OF ARLINGTON, 1403-4

The churchwardens' accounts of St. Margaret, Westminster, were collected together and bound in their present form in 1730. They begin in 1460. A full transcript has been most courteously submitted to us by Mr. A. M. Burke down to 1510. He has in active preparation a great work on the Wardens' Accounts and the Registers. During that period the following years are missing: 1462-4, 1468-74, 1476-8, 1486-8, 1492-4, 1506-8. The extracts subsequently given of a period later than 1510 are taken from Nichols' *Illustrations of Manners* (1797); but he must have had access to another copy or transcript of accounts, as they differ in several places from those now extant. The accounts are in Latin up to 1468. They date from May to May, though the exact day of the month differs. They are peculiar in being always presented in pairs of years, and the two churchwardens remained in office for two years. The exceptional feature of these returns is that they supply a mortuary register for the period covered, as the name of the person interred is always entered whether in the spacious churchyard or within the church. The receipts came largely from the charges for funeral tapers and torches. These fees amounted in 1490-2 to £22 12s. 9d.; a child's funeral with two tapers paid 2d., and an adult from 2d. to 6d.; with four tapers, 10d.; with two torches and four tapers, 3s. 4d. A knell from the great bell was 6d. Two tapers at an obit were 4d., four 8d.; eight torches and six tapers, 13s. 4d. The fee of half a mark (6s. 8d.) was paid for burial within the church, which was usual throughout the kingdom. A charge was made for a marble stone over the grave, varying presumably according to size; the fees in three cases in 1460-2 were 3s., 8s., and 20s.

A second source of income was from the collections made in church on six days, namely, Whitsunday, St. Margaret's Day, All Saints, Christmas Day, Good Friday, and Easter Day. In the first account these collections amounted to £14 5s. 5d.

The third head is "Le Puez"; in 1460-2, twenty-seven pews or seats were allotted to as many wives, varying in price, according to position, from 4d. to 20d. By the end of the century the allotment of paid seats had greatly increased, and they were occasionally claimed by men. It seems to have been the custom to pay for a life seat, but the fee had to be renewed if the seat was changed.

28   THE CHURCHWARDENS' ACCOUNTS

A fourth head of receipts is legacies or gifts, sometimes in money, sometimes in kind. In the first account their value was 34s. 6¾d., but this included 2¾d. picked up in the church porch. Perhaps the quaintest gift is one that occurs in 1500—

> Item a fether bede w^t a bolster of the gefte of the syster of the byshop of Seynt Asse to thentent that he shall Remayne in the Westir as long as he last for the clerkes of the chireh to ley upon.

Michael Deacon, Bishop of St. Asaph, appears to have died that year at Westminster. There is an entry—

> For the knell of the bysehopp of Saynt Asse w^t the grett belle   vj d.

Various other entries show that a clerk or clerks usually occupied a vestry chamber. Thus in 1495—

> For makyng of a bedde in the vestry for the clerkys   vj d.

The special observance of St. Margaret's Day constantly occurs in these accounts. A bonfire was kindled in the churchyard, opposite the chief entrance, on St. Margaret's Eve; the general charge for the faggots was 3d. The singers from the King's chapel assisted in the services, and were rewarded with "brede ale and wyne." The Keeper of the King's palace lent cloth of Arras for hanging in the quire, and the "vesterer" of the abbey lent "clothis of sylke and of golde" which were hung above the altar; both of these officials received "rewardes." The bonfire was probably the cause of the invariable engagement of two watchmen on "Sainte Margarets night." The church and churchyard were swept and garnished before this festival of 20th July, and in 1485 we read that a penny was paid for "wasshing of the Ymage of Sainte Margarete." In 1505 four shillings was paid to the "Waitts of London for to goo a for the procession" on St. Margaret's Day.

In the parish chest of Cowfold, Sussex, is a small leather-covered paper book of twenty folios, which contains, in a somewhat defaced condition, churchwarden accounts extending from 1460 to 1485. They are a strange medley of Latin and English; all the legible portions were transcribed in vol. ii. of the *Sussex Archæological Collections* (1849). The general expenses of the church and the maintenance of certain lights were sustained by cattle which were pastured on different farms. The accounts for 1473-4 show that there were nine oxen and four cows the property of the church. Two of the cows sustained four tapers in honour of St. Katherine, whilst two other cows had been bequeathed "to fynde a tapre afore Sante Antonie et unum afore Our Lady." Interspersed among the accounts are several memoranda of a miscellaneous character, including receipts against the plague and lockjaw, and the lucky days for bloodletting in each month.

Blomfield and other early writers on Great Yarmouth give extracts from churchwarden accounts of 1460 and of immediate subsequent years, but we can only conclude that they are lost.[1]

The parish accounts of St. Edmund, Salisbury, begin in the year 1463; they are fairly complete up to the end of the seventeenth century. There are also the accounts of the stewards of the Fraternity of the Jesus Mass, in connection with this church, from 1476, until the dissolution of the gilds in 1547. They were printed by the Wilts Record Society in 1896, together with the accounts of St. Thomas, Salisbury, the whole prefaced by an able introduction.[2] These accounts are of much interest and value in connection with the changes in sources of income: the rise and growth of the poor relief system; the visits of royalty and other distinguished persons to the city; the bountiful store of valuable church goods and lights in the earlier days of free-will offerings; the meanness of such provision in the times of church rates, save in the matter of a gaudy and extravagantly dressed pulpit; the admission to Holy Communion by tokens; and, above all, the evil growth of a paid pew system, beginning with two or three seat payments in the fifteenth century down to the unblushing sale of every possible seat or pew, with the exception of a few back benches branded in big red lettering "For the Poore." The main features of these and of other details will be found in subsequent sections, but two particulars, rarely met with in old churchwarden accounts, may be here mentioned.

[1] This is almost the only instance in which my inquiries have been treated with discourtesy. Letters asking for brief information, and enclosing a post card for reply, have been addressed respectively to (1) Vicar, (2) Churchwardens, and (3) Parish Clerk, and in each case they have been ignored.

[2] These accounts form a volume of upwards of 450 closely printed pages; unhappily there is no subject index.

The oblations and devotions of diverse persons to this church were kindled by papal letters of indulgence or remission of penance granted to penitents making offerings to the fabric of the church at Michaelmas and the Annunciation. On these occasions the Hand of St. Edmund, encased in a hand-shaped silver reliquary, his ring of gold in an ivory box bound with silver, the comb, part of a shirt, and a cruet belonging to the same saint, a piece of the stole of St. Dunstan, and "a pece of ye skull of seynt Wolfrine[1] standyng in a fote of silver and parcelgilt" were exposed to the faithful making oblations. This indulgence, made in "old time," appears to have been lost sight of, but in 1473-4 5d. was spent in proclaiming it, and 6s. 8d. was obtained in offerings at the ensuing Michaelmas. In 1475-6 considerable pains were taken to make the pardon more widely known. A shilling was paid for making six bills or copies of it in English, 4d. for rewards in distributing or affixing them, and 2s. 4d. in rewards to children who attended the formal declaration. A child was hired for 6d. "to kepe the pardon" at the Annunciation, and one Robert Glasyen to fulfil the same office for 8d. at Michaelmas. This keeping of the pardon probably implies responsibility for offerings in money. There was no striking response to this expenditure. The pardon receipts were 2s. 4d. in 1476, 2s. 8d. in 1480, 4s. 4d. in 1483-4, 1s. 7d. in 1490-1, and 2s. 10d. in 1494-5. An entry of the year 1480 records the suspension of the pardon, "all manner of pardons were annulled by reason of the Indulgence of Seynt Jonys of Jerl'm." The Knights of St. John were at that time besieged at Rhodes by Mahomet II; their situation was so urgent that the Pope suspended all other indulgences in their favour, so as to secure them the more generous support of all Christendom. This papal restriction was, however, removed by 1483, when six English copies of this Sarum indulgence were again made; on this occasion they were written gratuitously by the deacon of the church. The money offerings of 1499-1500 only amounted to sixpence, but the matter is thus detailed at length on the roll:—

Oblacions for the pardon of the Popis bullis in ye same Churche this yere. Of dyverse persons for the pardon the Popis bullis in the fest of Michelmas iiij d., and in the fest of thannunciation of our lady ij d.

---

[1] St. Wolfrida, abbess of Wilton.

EARLY WARDENS' ACCOUNTS

The last entry relative to the pardon occurs in 1500-1, when the amount offered was only 7½d. Presumably, however, various of the gifts in kind to the church fabric, made from time to time and entered under another heading, were due to the papal indulgence. A favourite gift or bequest by women householders was a brass pot; one of those given at this period weighed 38 lb.

The elections of mayors, bailiff, and other town officials were frequently held in churches in the old days. The mayor of Salisbury was elected within the church of St. Edmund. In 1579 the election was moved to the church of St. Thomas because the plague was then " hot " around the former church. In one of the subsequent plague years 2d. was charged "for Frankinnsense to burne in the churche agaynst ye masters come to chose Master Mayre."

The following is a summary of the oldest of the perfect account rolls, extending from 2nd April 1461 to 15th April 1462 :—

> Balance from last account, £3 15s. 8¾d. ; collection of pence on Maundy Thursday and Easter for the church fabric, £2 0s. 3½d. ; collection of pence for the font taper, 4s. 9½d. ; bequests of money, five in number, £3 2s. ; bequests of a brass pot, *magna pond.*, a silver spoon, and a silk girdle ; fees for four burials within the church, 22s. ; Scot ale, £18 8s. 10d. Total receipts, £31 1s. 7¾d.
>
> Maundy expenses, 5s. 8d. ; new wax and making tapers, 4s. 3¾d ; obits, 5s. 1d. ; necessary expenses, repairs, etc., 19s. 9d. ; purchase of candlesticks, etc., £20 17s. 10½d. ; two silver-gilt candlesticks, weighing 160 ounces at 3s. 4d. the ounce, £20 in part payment, and 3s. 4d. for bringing them on horseback from London ; purchase of 1016 lb. of lead and carriage to storehouse, £2 0s. 7d. Total payments, £24 13s. 3¼d.

The parish books of All Saints, Derby, are quite exceptionally complete and voluminous, beginning as early as 1465 and continuing down to the present time. The two earliest books were lost or stolen when the body of the church was rebuilt in 1724. Various entries appear as to their loss, and eventually, in 1728, the town crier was paid 4d. to offer a reward for their recovery. In 1877 the present writer had the good fortune to find them in an attic at Meynell-Langley, and Mr. Godfrey Meynell restored them to their proper custody. The first of these two highly interesting and invaluable paper books has well-written entries from 1465 to 1527 in the same handwriting, and is clearly a transcript made at the latter date from original accounts which had probably been made on detached rolls. The maintenance income of this once important collegiate church was derived in the main from the rents of divers lands and tenements. The chief of the casual receipts was from burials within the church. The first of these accounts is prefaced by an elaborate inventory of all the goods and ornaments of the church, which were of a costly and most varied character. There is another comprehensive inventory of the year 1527.[1]

There are 103 rolls of churchwardens' accounts, several of two or four years, pertaining to the parish of St. Botolph, Aldersgate, in the Guildhall Library. They extend from 1406–7 to 1632–3, with gaps from 1602 to 1608 and from 1611 to 1632, are in good condition and of much value. The rolls follow a set form. The receipts always begin with certain quit-rents, followed by the rent of a tenement called the Church House, which was next door to the "Peacock" in Aldersgate; the third entry was always concerned with the rent of a garden "without Temple Bar." Other receipts were for "pitts and knells," for the hire of torches and tapers for funeral or obit purposes, and gatherings for special objects. The same marginal headings are often repeated even if there was nothing to chronicle. Thus two headings always appear in the receipts: " Money gadered for surplyces and rochetts," and " Money gadered for Vestmentes." The following are the returns under these items in 1489–90:—

Of any money gadered among the paryshioners thys yere for surplices and Rochetts they Answer not Forasmuche as no such money was gadered thys yere. Nevertheless in the furst yere of the Reyne of the forsayd Kyng Henry the Seventh hit was answered of suche gaderyngs iiij s. iiij d. ob.

Of any money by thym gadered among the paryshioners for vestmentes, forasmoche as there was no suche gaderynge thys yere. Neverthless in the second yere of the Reyne of the sayd Kyng Henry the Seventh there was gadered for vestmentes xxxv li. ix s. vj d. ob.

Amongst the "casual recipes" of the days of Henry VII and Henry VIII are curious entries, which at first sight look puzzling,

---

[1] Exact transcripts of the whole of these accounts, with facsimiles of the first three pages, appear in a quarto volume by Rev. Dr. Cox and W. H. St. John Hope, entitled *Chronicles of All Saints, Derby*, published by Bemrose & Sons in 1881.

as to moneys received " for standyng aboute the churche" on St. Bartholomew's Day. Thus, in 1507, 3s. 1d. was received on this plea from "Henry Browne Herdwerman (hardware man) and dyvers other persons." In 1509 the receipts under this head were 4s. 8d.; in 1519 they had grown to 7s. 1d., and an additional 6d. from one standing "at este ende of the churche gate." The explanation is obvious from the entry of 1534, when 9s. 11d. was obtained from persons "standing at St. Bartelomew's Fayer." Standings on church ground were let to certain dealers in small wares during the holding of the great St. Bartholomew's fair on Smithfield; the fair charter was granted by Henry II, and it was not suppressed until 1855. The receipts from this source in 1601-2 amounted to 30s.

There is a chartulary of the Gild of the Trinity and of SS. Fabian and Sebastian of this church in the British Museum (Add. MS. 37,664). It was founded in 1377, and refounded in 1446. The brethren and sisters paid a penny each to find "xiij taperes aboute ye sepulcre of Criste at Este in ye churche of seynt Botulphe w'oute Alderesgate in Loundone." Accompts of the fraternity are given from 1432 to 1456, with one or two omissions. There are various lists of the members, headed by the two masters. In 1377 they numbered 80, including many married couples; they paid annual sums chiefly of 12d., but extending in a few cases to 2s. and 4s.

The churchwarden accounts of St. John, Peterborough, begin in 1467 and continue up to 1571. The pre-Reformation entries are of exceptional interest, and they would well repay printing *in extenso*. Details as to the repairs and purchase of vestments are frequent. Various items are quoted under subsequent headings; a few of the more important, which cannot be readily classified, are here cited:—

1473. Payd for ryngyng agense my lord of Lyngkcoln at hys vysytacyon	ij d.
1474. Payd for the yere tyme of Abbot Genge . . .	vj d.

---

[1] A knell for a woman burnt at the stake. The law of England, up to 1790, provided that women guilty of high or petty treason should suffer this form of capital punishment. Petty treason included murder of a husband or an employer. The last instance was at Portsmouth in 1784.

1475. Rec of the woman y^t was byrnt for the bellys[1]	ij d.
1476. Payd to the ryngers to the worschypp of God and for the Duke of York sowle and honys commyng to Fodrynghey [1]	iiij d.
1476. Rec of the wyffys of Pet'burgh that Elyn Man and Elyn Watson gadyrd among them for the qwythyng[2] of the chyrche and to the west ward	x s.
Item payd for qwythlymyngs of the chyrche. .	xiij s. iiij d.
1500. For the dirige of the Founders	xvj d.
1512. For meyt and drynke at the fownders deryge and messe	ij s. iiij d.
1515. Payd for a lattys to the shryvyng howse[3] .	ij s.
1536. Payd for Ryngers when my Lady Katern was buryed[4] .	ij s. vj d.
Item payd for mendyng a flower for a candellstyke of ower Ladys chappell	ij d.

In 1889 the *Shropshire Archæological Society* (N.S. vol. i.) printed the churchwarden accounts of 1469 and 1471, which are in the possession of Ludlow Corporation. Between 1471 and 1540 there is a prolonged gap. The accounts *temp.* Edward IV are of value as dealing with the latter period of the erection of the great central tower.

The churchwardens' accounts of Ludlow, extending from 1540 to the end of Elizabeth's reign, were for the most part transcribed by Mr. Thomas Wright, and printed by the Camden Society in 1869. The receipts of the first year of these accounts and for all its successors were chiefly obtained by gatherings at Easter; in 1840 they amounted to 37s. 9d., and in the following year to 39s. 2d. The next highest item of the receipts was 26s. 8d. for four "leystalles"; Mr. Wright failed to understand this entry, and thought it was a kind of pew, but the word simply means a grave within the church, for which the general charge throughout the kingdom was half a mark. The receipts for 1541 include 6d. of Thomas Heytone " for the reversyonn of his fathers pew," and 8d. for a " knelynge place for Rycharde Rawlens wyf."

The parish accounts of St. Mary Redcliffe, Bristol, begin 1470. See extracts in *Bristol Past and Present* (1881), vol ii. pp. 206–10.

The churchwardens' accounts of St. Martin Ongar (Guildhall Library) do not begin until 1710, but the first volume of the vestry

---

[1] Duke Richard fell in battle at Wakefield, 1460, and was buried at Pontefract; but the body was subsequently translated to the royal collegiate church of Fotheringhay.

[2] Quickliming, *i.e.* whitewashing. [3] Confessional.

[4] The divorced Katherine of Aragon.

minute books extends from 1471 to 1615. This great volume is thus headed:—

"This boke belongith to the Church of Seynt Martyns Ongar beside Candehoyk strete in London begun the xxv day of Juyn the yere of oure Lorde god MCCCCLXXJ, that tyme beyng parson Maist' Elysaunder Broun, than beyng Wardeyns Harry Jacom drap' and John Wysall Grocer, the which had ye Rowle of all the Rentis of iij chaunterys belonging to the sayde Church yat is fortosay of Westons Rentis, Hyde, and Crowners Rentis as hyt appoints folowynge, every chantery be hymself."

The property of Westons Rents is entered as of the annual value of £13 5s., and that of Hydes £13 16s. 8d.; the next folio is missing. The particulars are given of the obits of William Hyde, and of John Mathew, alderman and mayor of London. The churchwardens' accounts for two years, 1469–71, are set forth in full. The receipts show that during this period the wardens received from three donors five barrels and a kilderkin of "godeale," valued at 20s. 4d. Later on in the book occurs the churchwardens' accounts for 1577–91, and a large number of the seventeenth century.

The churchwardens' or proctors' accounts of St. John Baptist, Bristol, begin in 1472, and are of much value in the pre-Reformation period. Various extracts appear in Nicholls' and Taylor's *Bristol Past and Present* (1881), vol. ii. pp. 154–7. Among the archives of the church is the original writ, of 1st June 1409, for the consecration of the burial-ground in St. John Street.

In the *East Anglian*, N.S. vol. ii. 180–1 (1887–8), a few extracts are given, as alleged, from old churchwarden accounts of Blythburgh, Suffolk, beginning in 1472; but it is not stated from whence they are taken. In Suckling's *Suffolk*, vol. ii. 155–7 (1848), other extracts are given, and mention is made of an old tattered churchwardens' book, bearing the date 1547. The present writer was permitted to make a careful search in 1903, but no early accounts could be found.

The churchwardens' accounts of St. Stephen, Walbrook (Guildhall Library), begin in 1474 and continue to 1487. The first volume also contains the accounts for 1507, 1510, 1518–9, 1522, 1525–7, 1529, 1531, 1534, 1536–7, 1577, 1580, and 1583. Three more volumes carry on the accounts consecutively from 1649 to 1812. The first account covers the period from 1474 to 1478. During those years voluntary gifts to the amount of £26 9s. 2d. were made by parishioners to the "Reparacon of the stepull"; and £13 2s. 10d. was raised by assessments granted to "the feneysyng of the stepull."

There is a folio volume of wardens' accounts of Snettisham, extending from 1474 to 1536, and another from 1588 to 1661. They are both in the library of Hunstanton Hall, Norfolk.

The early churchwarden accounts of Croscombe, Somerset, are in a paper book mutilated at both ends. They run from 1474-5 with a few exceptions, 1547-8, when spoliation set in with cruel vigour. From the latter date to 1559-60 the accounts occur irregularly. The audit was generally held in January when the two wardens were elected by the parishioners. The gilds who presented their offerings at the audit were generally six, namely, the Young Men or "Younglyngs," the Maidens, the Webbers (weavers), the Tuckers (fullers), the Archers (represented by Robin Hood and Little John), and the Hagglers (labourers). On one occasion (1483-4) 6s. 8d. was contributed of "the Wyfes dansyng." Each gild received a stock of one or two shillings for immediate charges, such as the maintenance of a light; this was supplemented by a gathering or profits on their special revel or feast day. After fulfilling their social and religious obligations, they brought back at the audit to the wardens the "new and old," namely, the stock with which they had been entrusted, together with the "crese" or increase which had been made during the year. Occasionally there was no profit, when it is entered that they "broughte yn noughte."

The gild offerings are entered after a quaint fashion, which we have not observed in any other warden accounts; the phraseology brings before us, after a lively fashion, the audit in the church, with the "approach" to the wardens and the chief parishioners, in due order of the representatives of each gild, with their balance or offerings, as well as of those who desired to make a special gift. Here, as an example, are entries made at the audit of 11th January 1476:—

> Comes Thomas Blowre and John Hill and presents in of Roben Hod's recones (reckonings) . . . . . xl s.

Comes John Joyce and Roger and presents in of font tapur and Kendal of encres	iij s.
Comes Walter Mayow and presents in of the gyfte of Isobel Mayow j payer vestments of white damaske and delyvered into churche	...
Comes the Weyhers Harry Mewe and Thomas Symonds and presents in xxij d., and they receive a yeu for a stoke .	xij d.
Comes William Brabuck and presents in of old and new of Synt Myghel light which remayns al in his hands	vj s. viij d.
Comes the Hogglers, and presents in of old and new iij s. x d., and they received a yeu for a stoke	ij s.
Comes Youngmen William Cogen and Nichol Edmonds and bryng in of encres of the past iij s. ix d. that remayns in their hands delyvered to them more by Heyman of his gaderyng of old	ij s. ij d.
Comes Tokers and Roger and Costrell and presents in clere ii s. ij d. and Roger and Braunch received a stok of . .	xij d.
Comes the maydens and bryng in of encres cler .	ix d.
Comes Mayster John Toker (a master fuller) and gyfes to the new legent	vj s. viij d.

The largest item of this year's receipts came from the "Crok" or "Croke," *i.e.* the great processional cross; it had its special keeper, who bore it through the parish at festal seasons, on which occasions alms were gathered.

The money of the Crok of the yere comes to	lix s. vij d.
Paid to Harper for his yers wages	v s.
Paid to Harper for kepyng of the Croke . . .	xx d.

The Croke money was usually considerably higher; it exceeded £5 at two or three of the fifteenth-century audits.

The gifts to this church were most varied and sometimes of considerable value. Occasionally a gift accompanied the fee for the burying or pit within the church. Here are a few examples:—

1476-7. Jane Fenton at her det gaf to our lady a ring gylt.
    Of the gyfte of Maud Malleny a sylver ring gilt and a token gyrdel of sylver.
1477-8. William May, an ewer, bras.
    Thomas Blower, j vyolet long gowne ingrayne, a ryng gold with a torcus (turquoise) and a kerchef of syper (Cyprus silk) to mak a wiper.

38   THE CHURCHWARDENS' ACCOUNTS

> 1481-2. Of the gefte of the Lady Schefton a ryng of gold with a ruby.
> 1483-4. Richard Down for a kow of the gyfte of his dowgter .   vj s. viij d.
> 1488-9. Of the gyfte of Syr John Comb, parson of Corscombe, a gretté maser with a stone.
> Of the gyfte of Syr John Camell ij powchys of felewote (velvet), one of rede felewote and another of blake.
> 1496-7. Of Master Richard Mawley and Alsun his wife a portoss called a leger, a grayll and precessioner, ij new couchers (large books), and ther wedyng ryng of gold to our lady.
> 1497-8. Of John Jons a neue and a lam (an ewe and a lamb).
> 1498-9. Of my lady Mayow a gold ring to our lady and a nobule (noble) for her pytt.

Wimborne Minster, Dorset, has three volumes of early wardens' accounts — (1) 1475-1580; (2) 1581-1640; and (3) 1640-96. There is a gap from 1550 to 1560. The chief receipts came from the church-ale (*taberna cerevisiæ*); the profits were £6 in 1475. The wardens let out brewing utensils from the church-house on hire. Oblations brought to the feet of St. Cuthberga, St. Laurence, and other saints realised in this year 31s. The wardens received fair tolls, in the churchyard, on the Sunday after the Feast of St. Cuthberga. Fee for burial in the church was 6s. 8d. ; for those under fourteen, 3s. 4d. No seat-letting is named until 1565; usual seat payments were 2d. and 4d. A large number of entries are cited in *History of Wimborne Minster* (1860), pp. 87-125. The "wyve of the cuntrey" and the "wyfe of the towne" were two women who made and sold cakes for the benefit of the church; they jointly gained £5 in 1510; in 1516 the former obtained £4 13s. 4d. and the latter £4 6s. 8d.

The sacristan or sexton and his deputies and other servants of the church received as wages the offerings that were made on the occasion of three parochial processions, namely, on St. Stephen's Day, Easter Monday, and Whitsun Tuesday; but the amount was occasionally increased by further sums from the wardens' common fund.

The old churchwardens' account book of Ashburton, Devon, is a quarto of paper with parchment cover, extending from 1479-80 to 1579-80, with only two omissions, namely, those of 1480-1 and

1481–2. A pamphlet of 50 pages was printed in 1870 by Mr. J. H. Butcher, giving a large number of selected extracts. The chief annual receipt came from a Whitsuntide church-ale, and secondly from the surplus of the annual collection of wax-silver. The Whitsuntide church-ales of Ashburton were the principal source of income in that parish. In 1482–3 the profits were £5 13s. 4d.; in 1558–9, £6.

There were a considerable number of separate "stores" in this parish, all of which contributed to the general fund of the churchwardens. Thus in 1511–2 the wardens of the following stores contributed as follows: The wardens of the store of the Great Torches, 13s. 4d.; of the Junior Torches, £2; of the Blessed Virgin, £7; of the Blessed Mary at the font, 10s.; of the Wyvyn (wives) Store of the Blessed Mary, £2; of the High Cross, £4; of St. George, 26s. 8d.; of SS. Katherine and Margaret, 20s.; of St. Clement, £2; of SS. James and Eligius, 20s.; and of St. Thomas of Canterbury, 2s. Each of these gilds or fraternities maintained lights before the respective images, and put aside the surplus contributions for the general church funds. The entries of this particular year represent the debts or accumulations of several years which were then paid into the common fund. The church was shortly afterwards reseated and reglazed.

The wardens' accounts of Chagford, Devon, begin in 1480. A few desultory extracts occur in the *Transactions of the Devonshire Association*.

The earliest wardens' accounts of St. Thomas, Launceston, begin in 1480. A valuable series of extracts are given in R. and B. Peter's *Histories of Launceston and Dunheved* (1885), pp. 356–83. The gilds of All Saints and of St. Mary held stocks of cattle. There are various curious entries in Elizabethan days relative to the burial of criminals executed at the Castle and the disposal of their clothes.

The churchwardens' accounts of Sutterton, Lincoln, from 1483 to 1536, are at the Bodleian (Rawl. MSS. Miscell. 951). The main receipts of 1483 were from small payments for candles burnt for the dead, varying in amount from 1d. to 10d. The "kyrk house" is often mentioned from 1484 onwards. Various extracts are given in a paper in vol. xxxix. of the *Archæological Journal* (1882).

The churchwardens' accounts of Kirton-in-Lindsey, Lincolnshire, begin in 1484 ; with them are the accounts of one of the five gilds, that of Corpus Christi, associated with the church. There is a good short paper on these parish records in the *Antiquary*, vol. xix. (1889). The other gilds were those of the Holy Sepulchre, St. John Baptist, the " May gilde," and the " Pluygh (plough) gilde."

Considerable extracts are given in Nichols' *Illustrations of Manners* (1797) from the churchwardens' accounts of Wigtoft, Lincolnshire, for 1484-6, 1487, 1499, 1500, 1505, 1507, 1509, 1512, 1519, 1520, 1523, 1524, 1525, 1532, 1533, 1535, 1543, 1544, 1549-58, and for several years of Elizabeth's reign down to 1612. The date for giving in the accounts varied considerably; the financial year of the first entry began and ended with the Feast of St. Peter in Cathedra (Feb. 22), and soon afterwards was changed to that of St. Peter ad Vincula (Aug. 1), and in 1561 it was Good Friday. The most unusual feature of the receipts is an annual rent of 14d. for a "salt panne"; Wigtoft was at that time a sea-board parish. There were gatherings both in money and corn of the parishioners, and it is of special interest to note—

Item reasvyd of gaderyng in ye kyrk of strangers . . . iij s.

The chief outgoings of the first account included charges for keeping and dressing the clock, and also 11d. for

Scouryng of iiij candelsticks afore ye hye auter, and ye candelstyk afore Seynt Peter and for saudryng of the holy water fatte.

In 1580 the "orgun pllayur" received 7s., and 7½d. for his expenses.

The parish accounts of St. Nicholas, Bristol, both of the upper and of the crypt church, are of considerable interest, particularly in pre-Reformation days. Those of the latter church begin in 1489, and are much concerned with the observance of obits. An obit was held "for all good dowers" (doers) on the eve of Holy Rood Day, when the services, attended by ten priests and two clerks, were followed by considerable feasting. The festival of the boy-bishop was celebrated at this church on 6th December (St. Nicholas' Day) with great completeness. All the services, except Mass, were conducted by the youthful bishop and his fellow quire boys. The mayor, sheriff, and the town council attended evensong to hear the boy-bishop's sermon, and to receive his blessing. Many extracts from these parish accounts are given in Nicholls' and Taylor's *Bristol Past and Present* (1881), vol. ii. pp. 160–4.

The accounts of the Upper or High Church begin in 1520.

The churchwardens' accounts of St. Martin, Leicester, were printed by the late Mr. Thomas North in 1884. The volume contains (1) a few extracts from Nichols' *Leicestershire*, between 1489 and 1513, taken from a book of accounts long since missing; (2) an exact transcript of entries from 1544 to 1566; (3) copious extracts from 1566 to 1644; (4) extracts by Nichols from 1645 to 1737; and (5) extracts from original documents from 1744 to 1844. The accounts for 1634–5 supply many particulars as to preparations for a visit from Charles I. The royal arms were repainted; two rows of seats were removed; two loads of rushes were provided for 20d.—they must have come from a distance, for their carriage cost 3s.; the mayor and brethren's seats were taken away, and a fee of 4s. was paid to the " Kings Officer for the Floare where his majestie satt." The ringers, eight in number, were paid 15s.; a new surplice was provided at a cost of 49s. 4d.; and 3d. was paid " for flowers for the Kings Cushion."

The King was again in Leicester in 1643–4; two entries refer to this visit:—

> Paid to Norman for flowers and herbs to straw the church at the Kings comeing . . . . 1s. 8d.
> Paid to Knowles for six burdens of rushes for the church at the Kings comeing . . . . 2s. 0d.

The churchwarden accounts of the small country parish of Cratfield, Suffolk, begin in 1490 and continue to 1642. The earliest accounts, down to 1502, were transcribed verbatim, with extracts and abstracts of the remainder by the Rev. W. Holland, the rector of an adjacent parish, and printed posthumously, with an introduction by Dr. Raven, in 1895. They are of considerable interest, and contain separate accounts of the parish gild from 1534 to 1540. The receipts of 1490 were entirely raised from church-ales; four of them produced 33s. 8d.; the results of a fifth ale are not set down. The expenses were only 12s. 4d., including 4s. 4d. for the sexton's or rather sacristan's wages. The receipts for 1491 amounted to 56s. 7d., and included gatherings on Plough Monday in addition to various ales.

The awkward habit was adopted in 1585 of each churchwarden keeping a separate account, a custom which prevailed down to the Commonwealth. A large portion of the later accounts pertain more strictly to the constable's office. There is a good deal of matter relative to the vexatious system of purveyance for the royal household in Elizabeth's reign, which is discussed in the last chapter.

The churchwardens' accounts of St. Mary-de-Castro, Leicester, from 1491 to 1571, are largely cited in Nichols' great history of the county (1795), vol. i. pp. 309-11. The receipts were largely augmented by church-ales; three of these ales in 1495 produced 51s. in clear profit. The wardens made special gatherings in church for particular objects on Sundays, such as for new quire stalls in 1495, and for mending the windows in 1498. Up to 1520 the churchwardens are termed "churchmasters."

In 1887 an old wardens' account book of this parish, from 1652 to 1729, was restored to the church by the will of Joshua Chawner. These accounts are fully cited in vols. vi. and vii. of the *Transactions of the Leicestershire Archæological Society*. The vestrymen of this period were known as "The Thirteen."

The churchwardens' books of All Hallows, Staining, begin, according to *Londinium Redivivium*, in 1492; interesting extracts are given (vol. ii. pp. 19-22); the church was rich in costly images and tabernacles, and exceptionally well furnished with vestments and plate.

The Kingston-on-Thames accounts extend from 1496 to 1681. See *Hist. MSS. Commission, Third Report*, pp. 331-2.

The churchwarden accounts of Bassingbourn, Cambridgeshire, begin in 1497, and are continued in the same volume down to 1538, but with several gaps. The book opens with an elaborate inventory of church goods, dated 17th April 1498. Various long quotations appear in subsequent pages. A transcript of these accounts was made by Mr. Alfred Rogers for Mr. Henry Bradshaw about 1870. This transcript is in the Cambridge University Library, Add. 2792.

EARLY WARDENS' ACCOUNTS

The earliest church accounts of Pilton, Somerset, date from 1498 to 1530, but with several omissions. After a great gap comes a second volume, beginning in 1584, and a third which begins in 1626 and ends in 1641. Up to 1530 a single warden administered the parish funds; but under him were four pairs of wardens annually elected, namely, those of Our Lady, of St. John's Gild, of the Highlight on the Rood-loft, and those of the Key, Kye, or Kine, that is, the Cows pertaining to the church. Within the parish was the chapel of North Wootton, with its own pair of wardens, but they appear to have been independent and directly responsible to the diocesan authorities. See *Somerset Record Society*, vol. iv. pp. 49–77.

CHAPTER III

CHRONOLOGICAL LIST OF WARDENS' ACCOUNTS OF THE SIXTEENTH AND SEVENTEENTH CENTURIES

AN analysis of the extant accounts of the sixteenth and seventeenth centuries, on the same lines as the earlier instances in the previous chapter, had been prepared, but exigencies of space has compelled their omission. In their place a table has been prepared, in chronological order, setting forth the initial year of each cited instance, with a reference to any work wherein extracts have been printed. Unless stated to the contrary, it is to be assumed that the account book or books are in the parish to which they belong. Where the third column is left blank, I am not aware of any matter in print. It is not to be assumed that these lists are complete, especially in the seventeenth century, but much diligence has been expended in endeavours to make them thorough.

Date.	Place.	Printed References, etc.
1500–1648	Worfield, Salop	*Trans. of Salop Arch. Soc.*, Third Series, vol. iii., etc.
1501–1521	Louth, Linc.	*Archæologia*, vol. x. (1792)
1502–1547	Stoke Courcy, Som.	*Hist. MSS. Com., Sixth Report*, 348–351
1504–1633	Great St. Mary, Cambridge	Printed by *Camb. Antiq. Soc.*
1504–1635	Holy Trinity, Cambridge	Transcript in *Camb. Antiq. Soc.* Library
1504–1557	Lambeth	*Archæologia*, vol. vii. A few extracts
1507–1525 (resumed 1547)	St. Margaret Pattens, City	*Sacristy*, vol. i. 258–262 (1871)
1507–9, 1518–28	Horley, Surr.	Brit. Mus. Add. MSS. 6173
1510–1540	Fordwich, Kent	*Hist. MSS. Com., Fifth Report*, 607–608

The a compte of William Smyth & John Harter wardens of
the Cherch of Stratton Anno H. viij xiij [1521]

And payed for the Cherch as in old tyme &c.

Expens

It p for expens at the visitacon at Launcestou ... xij d
It p to a smyth Wicke for the wyssoll ... vj d
It p to Nyc Goddou & Nyc Par̃g Wardew ... xd ob
It p for wey to make candells ... vj d
It for mendyng of the fest colores for M^s ... iij d
It for mendyng of a sept ... j d
It p̃ for the chache bagg ... j d
It for ang wasshyg of the chur̃ch clothes ... iij d
It for brekyg of of the grete candelor ... ij d
It for p̃ssheon ... iij d

Sm̃ expens ... iiij s v d ob

pendyng to the church ... vj d
John Harter yot hard[y]

CHRONOLOGICAL LIST OF WARDENS' ACCOUNTS

DATE.	PLACE.	PRINTED REFERENCES, ETC.
1511–1797	Shipdam, Norf.	Brit. Mus. Add. MSS. 23,009
1515–1539	St. Martin Outwich, City	Lond. Rediv., iv. 407–410
1515–1714	Hawkhurst, Kent	Arch. Cant., v. 55–86
1516–1546 (Gild Accts. 1371–1547)	Bardwell, Suff.	Suff. Inst. of Arch., vol. xi. (1903)
1517–19, 1565–69	Rainham, Kent	Arch. Cant., xv. 333–337
1518–1546	St. Giles, Reading	Printed by Rev. W. L. Nash, 1881
1519–1520	St. Helen, Worcester	Worc. Hist. Soc., 1896
1520	St. Nicholas, Bristol	St. Paul's Eccles. Soc., vi. 53–67
1520–1548	Huntingfield, Suff	Inv. of 1534, Proc. Soc. of Antiq., N.S., i.
1520–1545	Ecclesfield, Yorks	Registers of Ecclesfield, by Sir A. S. Gatty, 148–162
1520–1557	Morebath, Dev.	Som. Rec. Soc., iv. 208–224
1521 onwards	Bramley, Hants	Vict. Co. Hist. of Hants, iv. 144
1523–1853	Bungay, Suff.	East Anglian, vols. i., ii., and iii.
1524–1613	South Tawton, Dev.	Trans. Rec. Soc., vols. xxxviii.–xli.
1525–1699	Spelsbury, Oxon.	Typed copy by Dr. Oldfield
1525–1603	St. Martin's-in-the-Fields	Printed by Mr. J. V. Kitto in 1903
1527	St. Alphege, London Wall	Guildhall Library. Pamphlet by G. B. Hall, 1880
1527	Wing, Bucks	Archæologia, xxxvi.
1529	St. Nicholas Cole Abbey, City	Lond. Rediv., iv. 548–551
1529–1596	Boxford, Camb.	Camb. Antiq. Soc., vol. i. (1859)
1529–1709	Badsey, Worc.	Midland Antiquary, vol. i. (1852)
1530	Christ Church, Bristol	Bristol Past and Present, vol. ii. (1748)
1530–1663	Elmsett, Suff.	East Anglian, vol. i.
1531–1614	Culworth, Northants	N'hants Herald, 1902, Feb. and March
1534	Christ Church, Bristol	
1536–1558	St. Mary, Dover	Brit. Mus. Egerton MSS. 1912
1536–1602	Snowdon, Kent	Arch. Cant., ix. 224–235
1536–1565	St. Mary-on-the-Hill, Chester	
1536	Bolney, Sussex	Suss. Arch. Coll., vol. vi.
1538–1628	North Elmham, Norf.	Brit. Mus. Add. MSS. 23,008
1538	St. Andrew, Clifton	
1539–1603	St. Michael-in-Bedwardine, Warwick	Worc. Hist. Soc., 1896
1539–1640	St. Mary Woolnotte, City	Extracts by J. M. S. Brooke, 1881
1540–1560	St. Mary Magdalen, Milk Street	Kept at church of St. Laurence, Jewry
1541–1696	Mendlesham, Suff.	Hist. MSS. Com., Fifth Report, 593–594
1541–1728	Stoke Charity, Hants	C.C.C., Oxford
1543 to present day	Crondall	In five vols.
1543–1608	Steeple Ashton, Wilts	Wilts Notes and Queries, 1908–1912
1543–1699	Weyhill, Hants	Restored to parish from Queen's Coll., Oxford, 1912
1544–1628	Cheswardine, Salop	
1544–1649	Worksop, Notts	White's Worksop, 315–321

46 THE CHURCHWARDENS' ACCOUNTS

DATE.	PLACE.	PRINTED REFERENCES, ETC.
1544	St. Thomas, Bristol	
1544	St. Martin, Leicester	
1544	Ellingham, Hants	
1546–1592	St. Olave, Southwark	Kept at Bermondsey Town Hall
1546–1612	Melton Mowbray	*Trans. of Leic. Arch. Soc.*, vol. iii.
1547–1603	St. Matthew, Friday Street, City	*Brit. Arch. Journ.*, vol. xxv
1547–1731	St. Botolph, Aldgate, City	Rev. A. G. B. Atkinson, 1898
1547–1621	St. Nicholas, Warwick	Trans. in *Par. Mag.*, 1890, etc.
1548	St. Werburgh, Bristol	*Bristol Past and Present*, ii. 220–224
1549	St. John, Winchester	
1549–1693	St. Benedict, Gracechurch	*Lond. Rediv.*, i. 314–318
1550–1602	Stanford, Berks	*Antiquary*, vol. xvii.
1550–1662	St. Mary, Reading	Printed 1893, preface by Bishop Stubbs
1551–1569	Saxilby, Linc.	*Assoc. Soc. Reports*, xix. 376–389
1553	Brockdish, Norf.	Blomefield's *Norfolk* (1769), vol. v. 338
1554 to present day	Loddon, Norf.	*Norf. Arch.*, vol. ii.
1554–1600	Eltham, Kent	*Archæologia*, xxxiv. 51–64
1554–1569	Mildenhall, Suff.	*East Anglian*, vol. i.
1555–1713	Minchinhampton, Glouc.	*Archæologia*, xxxv.
1555–1763	Strood, Kent	Brit. Mus. Add. MSS. 36,937
1555	St. Pancras, Soper Lane, City	*Lond. Rediv.*, vol. ii. 167–171
1555–1689	Wilmslow, Cheshire	Earwaker's *E. Cheshire*, vol. ii. 111–117
1555–1615	All Hallows, Hoo, Kent	*Kent Records*, 22–25
1556–1853	Mere, Wilts	*Wilts Arch. Mag.*, vol. xxxv.
1556	St. Katherine, Aldgate	*Lond. Rediv.*, vol. iii. 303, 334
1557–1613	Bungay, Suffolk	
1557–1668	Chelmsford	*Cath. Ch. of See of Essex*, 1908
1557–1620	Pulham St. Mary, Norf.	*East Anglian*, vol. iv.
1557	Holy Trinity, York	*Assoc. Soc. Reports*, xxx. 641–654
1558–1620	Pulham St. Mary Magd., Norf.	Brit. Mus. Add. MSS. 23,610
1558–1747	Prestbury, Cheshire	Earwaker's *E. Cheshire*, vol. ii. 217–231
1558–1614	Chudleigh, Devon	Jones' *Hist. of Chudleigh*, 1852
1558–1675	Wootton, Hants	Kitchen's *Manor of Manydown*, 171–175
1558	SS. Philip and James, Bristol	*Bristol Past and Present*, ii. 236
1558	Barnstaple	Wainwright's *Barnstaple Records*
1558	St. Mary-le-Port, Bristol	*Bristol Past and Present*, ii. 225–229
1559–1708	Burton Latimer, N'hants	
1559–1564, 1588–1723	Seal, Surrey	*Surr. Arch. Coll.*, vol. ii.
1560–1725	Holme Pierrepoint, Notts	*Old Nottinghamshire*, Second Series, 93–104
1560–1669	St. Mary Woolchurch, City	Extracts printed by Rev. J. M. S. Brooke
1560	Portsmouth	*Portsmouth Records*
1561–1631	Thatcham, Berks	Barfield's *Thatcham*, i. 121–126; ii. 92–115

CHURCH RECEIPTS OF WARDENS OF STRATTON, 1534

CHRONOLOGICAL LIST OF WARDENS' ACCOUNTS

DATE.	PLACE.	PRINTED REFERENCES, ETC.
1561 to present day	Wigan, Lancs	
1563-1604	St. Peter, Ipswich	Brit. Mus. Add. MSS. 25,344
1565	Chiddingstone, Kent	Kent Records, 35-36
1565	St. Helen, Bishopsgate	
1565	Kingsthorpe, N'hants	Kingsthorpiana, 1883
1565	Abbey Church, Shrewsbury	
1566	St. James, Bristol	Bristol Past and Present, ii. 36-40
1566 to present day	St. Peter Chesil, Winchester	
1567-1741	St. Laurence, Southampton	Davis' Southampton, 372-375
1567	St. Martin, Salisbury	Wilts Arch. Mag., xxi. 384-388
1568-1715	St. Martin, Ludgate	St. Paul's Eccles. Soc., v. 117-128
1568	St. Botolph, Bishopsgate	Lond. Rediv., i. 226-230
1569-1599	St. Stephen, Norwich	East Anglian, N.S., viii.
1569	Bewdley, Worc.	Burton's Bewdley, xii -xxxv.
1569	St. Ethelburga	A few extracts in pamphlet by Dr. Cobb
1569	St. Peter, Mancroft, Norwich	
1570	St. James, Clerkenwell	Lond. Rediv., iii. 202-209
1570	St. Mary Aldermanbury, City	Lond. Rediv., ii. 127-128
1571-1612	St. Saviour, Southwark	
1573	St. Ives, Cornwall	Matthews' Hist. of St. Ives
1573-1899	Redenhall with Harleston, Norf.	East Anglian, vol. i.
1574-1850	St. Antholin, City	Guildhall Library
1574	St. Gregory, Norwich	
1574-1676	St. Matthew, Ipswich	East Anglian, N.S., vol. iv.
1575	St. Martin Ongar, City	
1575-1602	St. Christopher-le-Stocks, City	Privately printed by Dr. Freshfield
1575	St. Michael, Bristol	Bristol Past and Present, ii. 169-170
1576-1678	St. Margaret, New Fish Street, City	Guildhall Library
1576-1609	Little Cornand, Suff.	East Anglian, N.S., vol. i.
1577-1596	Condover, Salop	
1577-1816	Oswestry, Salop	
1578-1840	Mortlake, Surrey	Vict. Co. Hist. Surrey, vol. v. 73, etc.
1579 intermittently to 1662	Lindfield, Sussex	Suss. Arch. Coll., vol. xix.
1580-1700	St. Oswald, Durham	Surtees Soc., vol. lxxxiv.
1583-1691	Loughborough, Leic.	Fletcher's Loughborough, 1883
1583-1685	Repton, Derb.	Derb. Arch. Journ., vol. i.
1584-1748	Berkhamsted, Herts	Brit. Mus. Add. MSS. 18,773
1584-1699	Pittington, Durham	Surtees Soc., vol. lxxxiv.
1585	St. Columb Major, Cornwall	
1585	St. John Evangelist, York	Assoc. Soc. Reports, xxix. 304
1585-1623	Staplegrove, Som.	Brit. Mus. Add. MSS. 30,278
1586	St. Mary, Norwich	
1586	Wakefield Cathedral	Walker's Wakefield Church, 267-276

THE CHURCHWARDENS' ACCOUNTS

Date.	Place.	Printed References, etc.
1587-1731	Weybread, Suff	*East Anglian*, vols. i. and ii.
1588	Great Paxton, Hunts	
1588 to present day	Wootton St. Laurence, Hants	
1588	Milton Abbot, Devon	*Monthly Magazine*, vol. xxix. (1818)
1590-1800	St. George, Botolph Lane, City	Guildhall Library
1590	St. Laurence, Norwich	
1591-1785	St. John Zachary, City	Guildhall Library
1592-1642	Morton, Derb.	*Reliquary*, vol. xxv. 17-25
1593 to present day	Marlow, Bucks	
1594-1652	Lilleshall, Salop	
1594-1652	St. Clement, Ipswich	*East Anglian*, N.S., vols. iii. and iv.
1595-1865	St. John Baptist, Walbrook	Guildhall Library
1595	St. Augustine, Farringdon Within	*Lond. Rediv.*, ii. 86-91
1595-1699	Houghton-le-Spring, Durham	*Surtees Soc.*, vol. lxxxiv.
1596-1698	St. Bartholomew, Exchange, City	Privately printed by Dr. Freshfield, 1893
1596 to present day	North Waltham, Hants	
1596-1669	Cottingham, N'hants	
1597-1701	Hartland, Devon	*Hist. MSS. Com.*, *Fifth Report*, 572-575
1598-1677	Stockton, Salop	
1598-1857	St. Botolph, Billingsgate	Guildhall Library
1598-1609	Knebworth, Herts	William's Library, Gower Street
1598 to present day	Yateley, Hants	
1598	Ryton, Salop	*Notes and Queries*, Eighth Series, v. 188
1598-1714	Cowden, Kent	*Suss. Arch. Coll.*, vol. xx.
1598	Flitton, Beds	*Vict. Co. Hist. Beds.*, ii. 332
1599	Childwall, Lanc.	
1600-1645	St. Botolph, Cambridge	
1600-1709	St. Neots, Cornwall	*Arch. Journ.*, vol. xlviii.
1600	Ringwood, Hants	
1601-1662	Whitegate, Chester	*The Cheshire Sheaf*, N.S., vol. i.
1601-1657	Kenley, Salop	Much mutilated
1602-1894	Bray, Berks	
1602-1891	St. Swithin, London Wall	Guildhall Library
1602-1827	Marston-sur-Dove	*Churches of Derbyshire*, iii. 206-7
1602	Southam, Warw.	*Proc. of Warw. Field Club*, 1892
1602	Henley, Suff.	*East Anglian*, N.S., vol. iv.
1603	Toft Monks, Norf.	*East Anglian*, N.S., vol. iii.
1603-1649	Lowick, N'hants	
1604-1669	Marston Trussell, N'hants	
1604-1783	Chirbury, Salop	
1604-1755	Youlgrave, Derb.	*Churches of Derbyshire*, ii. 333-343
1605-1850	St. Benet, Paul's Wharf	Guildhall Library
1607-1619	Hampnett, Glouc.	*Glouc. Notes and Queries*, ii.
1608-1844	St. Benedict, Norwich	*East Anglian*, vol. iv.
1609-1642	Woodford Halse, N'hants	*N'hants Notes and Queries*, 1884-1885, 41

CHRONOLOGICAL LIST OF WARDENS' ACCOUNTS

Date.	Place.	Printed References, etc.
1610–1869	St. Katherine, Coleman	Guildhall Library
1610	St. Benet Fink, City	Guildhall Library
1610	Yarnlow, Oxon	Stapleton's *Three Oxon. Parishes*
1611–1645	Mellis, Suff.	*Proc. W. Suff. Arch. Inst.*, vol. i.
1612–1674 (single leaf of 1599)	Cheddar, Som.	*Hist. MSS. Com.*, Third Report, 329 330
1612–1681	Hartshorn, Derb.	*Derb. Arch. Soc. Journal*, vol. vii.
1613–1673	St. Werburgh, Derb.	*Reliquary*, vols. i. and ii.
1614–1662	St. Stephen, Ipswich	*East Anglian*, N.S., vol. i.
1614 to present day	St. Mary - le - Tower, Ipswich	
1616–1712	Wellingborough, N'hants	
1616–1756	Eastington, Glouc.	*Glouc. Notes and Queries*, iii. 246–25
1616–1861	All Hallows the Great, City	Guildhall Library
1618	All Hallows, Honey Lane, City	
1618–1723	Sidbury, Devon	Brit. Mus. Add. MSS. 34,696
1619–1873	St. Michael, Wood Street, City	Guildhall Library
1619–1874	Whitchurch, Salop	
1620–1662	Clunbury, Salop	
1620	St. Mabyn, Cornwall	*London Society*, vol. xliv.
1620–1680	Birchington, Kent	*Archæologiæ Cantiana*, vol. xii. 406–
1621–1750	St. Julian, Shrewsbury	
1622	Barnsley, Yorks	Jackson's *Hist. of Barnsley*
1624	St. George, Southwark	Kept at Southwark Town Hall
1625	St. Bartholomew the Great, City	
1625–1680	Beccles, Suff.	*East Anglian*, N.S., vol. ii.
1625–1723	Stockton, Norf.	*Norfolk Arch.*, vol. i.
1625–1801	St. Dionis, Backchurch, City	
1625–1810	Cound, Salop	
1625–1710	Lydbury North, Salop	
1627	Basingstoke, Hants	Baigent's *Hist. of Basingstoke*, 499 532
1627–1693	Uffington, Salop	*Trans. Salop Arch. Soc.*, vol. xii. 357 369
1627–1702	St. Mary, Shrewsbury	
1627	Weedon Bec, N'hants	
1628–1639 and 1653–1678	St. Giles, N'ton	Serjeantson's *Hist. of St. Giles*, 212 239
1629–1782	Barrow, Salop	
1629–1811	Donnington, Salop	
1630–1710	Great Weldon, N'hants	A few fragments
1630–1855	All Hallows the Less, City	Guildhall Library
1630–1662	St. Michael, Wood Street	Guildhall Library
1630–1680	Tong, Salop	
1631–1712	Swainswick, Som.	Peach's *Annals of Swainswick*
1633–1711	Shawbury, Salop	
1634–1674	St. Sepulchre, N'ton	*Hist. of St. Sepulchre*, 220–228
1635	St. Mary Bourne, Hants	Stevens' *Parochial Hist.*, 228–254
1635–1637	Byfield, N'hants	*N'hants Notes and Queries*, 1884 1885, pp. 25–28

Date.	Place.	Printed References, etc.
1635–1905	Collyweston, N'hants	
1635–1700	Great Houghton, N'hants	
1636–1697	Langton-Long-Blandford, Dor.	*Som. and Nor. Notes and Queries*, vol. iii.
1636–1662	St. Ann's, Aldersgate	Guildhall Library
1636	St. Clement, Eastcheap	Guildhall Library
1638–1753	Eastbourne, Sussex	*Suss. Arch. Coll.*, vol. xiv.
1638–1686	Collingtree, N'hants	
1639	St. Magnus, City	Guildhall Library
1639–1647	Ashton-under-Lyne, Lanc.	
1640–1660	Upham, Hants	
1643–1695	Mavesyn Ridware, Staff.	Shaw's *Staffordshire*, i. 197–199
1647	Middleton, Lanc.	Transcribed by Mr. Giles Shaw
1647	Prestwick, Lanc.	Boston s *Memorials of Prestwich*, 18–46
1648–1662	St. Mary Magdalen, Old Fish Street	Guildhall Library
1648–1712	Mainstone, Salop	
1649–1872	St. Martin, Ludgate Hill	Guildhall Library
1650	Ribchester, Lanc.	T. C. Smith's *Ribchester*
1650–1878	Edgmond, Salop	
1650	St Katherine Cree, City	Guildhall Library
1650	Aldwinkle St. Peter's, N'hants	
1651–1848	Wenhaston, Suff.	*Curious Parish Records*, 20–23
1651–1710	More, Salop	
1652	Elstead, Surrey	
1653	St. Peter, Bristol	*Bristol Past and Present*, ii. 132–135
1653–1672	Church Pulverbatch	
1654–1723	Dallington, N'hants	*N'hants Notes and Queries*, N.S., vol. iii.
1656–1809	Hammersmith	Faulkner's *Hist. of Hammersmith*, 216–223
1656	Bolton, Lanc.	
1656	St. Michael, Southampton	
1656–1702	Alberbury, Salop	
1658	Wirksworth, Derb.	*Churches of Derbyshire*, ii. 539, 552
1658	Kendal, Westmoreland	*Camb. and West. Arch. Trans.*, vol. ix. 269–283
1658–1673 and 1687–1713	Wroxeter, Salop	
1659–1813	Glinton, N'hants	
1659–1773	Enstone, Oxon.	Jordan's *Hist. of Enstone*, 1857
1660–1696	Bromfield, Salop	
1661–1738	Piddington, N'hants	
1662–1720	Chetwynd, Salop	
1663–1714	Stokesay, Salop	
1663	Cobham, Kent	*Kent Records*
1663–1693	Thornby, N'hants	
1663–1703	Thornhaugh, N'hants	
1663–1712	Ufford and Ashton, N'hants	
1663–1686	Kinnerley, Salop	
1664–1763	Greenwich, Kent	Hasted's *Kent*, i. 103

WARDENS' ACCOUNTS, SIDBURY: INVENTORY, 1648

CHRONOLOGICAL LIST OF WARDENS' ACCOUNTS

Date.	Place.	Printed References, etc
1664	East Budleigh, Devon	*Trans. of Devon. Assoc.*, vols. xxii xxiii.
1665	Deptford, Kent	Hasted's *Kent*, i. 34–35
1665–1703	St. Nicholas, Durham	*Surtees Soc.*, vol. lxxxiv.
1667	St. Michael - on - Wyre, Lanc.	
1667–1697	Prees, Salop	
1668	St. Leonard, Eastcheap, City	
1669	Liskeard, Cornwall	Allen's *Hist. of Liskeard*, 143–14 148–149
1669 to present day	Lymington, Hants	Bostock's *Hist. of Parish Church*, 19)
1670–1887	Bolnhurst, Beds	
1670–1705	Stapleton, Salop	
1670–1793	Broughton, N'hants	
1670–1885	Ashby St. Legers, N'hants	
1671–1710	Overstone, N'hants	
1671–1768	East Haddon, N'hants	Overseers of the Poor
1672	Forncett St. Peter, Norf.	*East Anglian*, vols. ii. and iii.
1672–1678	Clungunford, Salop	
1672	Torpenhow, Cumberland	
1673–1698	Rostherne, Cheshire	*Cheshire Sheaf*, vol. i.
1674–1839	Quatford, Salop	
1674–1798	Acton Round, N'hants	
1675–1769	Sudborough, N'hants	
1676–1728	Dunham Parva, Norf.	Brit. Mus. Add. MSS. 23,008
1676	St. Swithin - over - Kingsgate, Winchester	
1676	Waberthwaite, Cumberland	
1677–1653	Ruardon, Glouc.	*Trans. Bristol and Glouc. Arch. So.* vol. viii.
1678–1688	Lydham, Salop	
1679	Badger, Salop	
1680–1830	Berrington, Salop	
1681–1719	Diddlebury, Salop	
1682–1694	Castle Ashby, N'hants	
1683–1796	Great Harrowden, N'hants	
1683–1816	St. Martin, Chester	*Hist. Soc. of Chester and N. Wal.* vol. viii.
1684–1833	Yarwell, N'hants	
1684–1756	St. Peter the Less, Chichester	*Suss. Arch. Coll.*, vol. xliv.
1685 to present day	High Ercall, Salop	*Salop Arch. Soc.*, Second Series, vol.
1685–1728	Kensington	Faulkner's *Hist. of Kensington*, 27 286
1688–1780	Clun, Salop	
1689	Ibsley, Hants	
1690	Flixton, Lanc.	Lawson's *Flixton*, 24, 43; Longto *Flixton*, 53–71
1691	Sherfield - upon - Lodon, Hants	

THE CHURCHWARDENS' ACCOUNTS

Date.	Place.	Printed References, etc.
1692-1764	Ruyton Eleven Towns, Salop	
1692	Bedhampton, Hants	
1693-1753	Culmington, Salop	
1693 to present day	Atcham, Salop	
1693-1785	Thruxton, Hants	
1695-1864	Newport, Salop	
1696	Hawkshead, Lanc.	Cooper's *Hist. of Hawkshead*, 1899
1696-1803	Woolwich	Hasted's *Kent*, vol. i. 167
1698-1760	Silchester, Hants	
1698-1782	Pitchford, Salop	
1699	Hexham, Northumberland	
1699	Holy Rood, Southampton	
1699-1748	Lamport, N'hants	
1699-1799	Bolas Magnar, Salop	

CHAPTER IV

RECEIPTS OF ST. EDMUND, SARUM

Receipts of St. Edmund, Sarum — Receipts — Gatherings — Font Taper — Paschal money — *Dona et Legata* — Burial fees — The Holy Loaf — "Increase" from lights — Standings or stalls — Hire of vestments — The Bede Roll — Church-ales — Hocktide — Dancing — Seats or pews

THE church account rolls of St. Edmund, Sarum, from 1463 onwards are so unusually full of detail, and so aptly illustrate the varied sources of income upon which the mediæval warden depended, as well as the methods in which the income was expended, that it has been thought well to confine this and the following chapter to an exclusive consideration of the receipts and payments of this one parish. The general working of a town parish church in mediæval days will thereby be abundantly illustrated.

The various pre-Reformation methods for obtaining money to sustain the fabric and services of the church of St. Edmund, Sarum, were unusually diversified. The oblations in connection with special papal pardon days have been already named.

(1) The gatherings at the church door or in church on a few special days, at Eastertide, usually come first in these accounts. The following is a table of the days and amounts thus collected on the first twelve of the complete extant rolls:—

Years	Days	Amount
1461–2.	Maundy Thursday and Easter Day	£2 0 4
1462–3.	,, ,,	2 11 2
1468–9.	,, ,,	2 14 11½
1469–70.	,, ,,	2 8 10¼
1473–4.	Good Friday	2 7 0
1474–5.	Maundy Thursday	1 7 0
1477–8.	,,	2 3 0

THE CHURCHWARDENS' ACCOUNTS

Years	Days	Amount
1481-2.	Easter Eve and Easter Day	£2 14 8
1483-4.	,, ,,	2 13 4
1490-1.	Good Friday, Easter Eve, and Easter Day	3 0 3½
1491-2.	,, ,, ,,	2 10 7½
1495-6.	Maundy Thursday and Easter Eve	2 13 1

(2) The gatherings are usually followed by the sums received for the Font Taper. The collections *ad seru 1 fontis* were usually made on Easter Eve and Easter Day. This gathering appears annually in the accounts until Elizabeth's reign, when it became intermittent, and though the name occasionally appeared, it is practically certain that the ceremonial taper was no longer made. In 1564 the sum collected under this head was 40s.; the last entry is 1588, " for the fontaper 53s. 4d." Afterwards an approximately similar amount appears as " The Hawpence " for Easter dues, and thus continues till 1641, when it became merged in the Quarter Book. Reverting to the earlier accounts, the amount gathered was 4s. 9½d. in 1461; 50s. 1d. in 1462; 7s. 11d. in 1468; 43s. in 1469; 47s. 2d. in 1473; 44s. 8d. in 1474; 57s. 11d. in 1480; and 49s. 3½d. in 1490. The considerable variation in the collection at once shows that the exact sum could never have been spent on font tapers. Indeed, the opposite side of the accounts at once proves this, for the making of the font tapers is always included in the expenses under the head of Wax. The cost is usually associated with that of the great Paschal Taper, and the two together never exceeded a few shillings. The number of font tapers required varied in accordance with the number of baptisms; occasionally three were required during the twelve months. The following are a few specimen entries :—

1468-9. In iij[bus] Fontaperis cum pascall' Taper renovatis hoc anno in toto . . . . . . vj s. viij d.
1474-5. In factura xxxiiij lb cere nove et veteris ad pascale sereum et iij cerea fontes . . . . . xvij d.
1477-8. In cerea ad Pascal' et le fontapere cum fectura eorundem hoc anno in toto . . . . . vj s. iiij d.
1483-4. Pro factura sex librorum cere pascereis fontes de Instauro ecclesie tempore grave infirmitatis . iij d.

In this last entry the cost of the wax is not included. The probable meaning of the phrasing is that it was a plague year, and that various font tapers were made to avoid infection.

It becomes evident from these and like entries in other accounts that font taper money, originally intended for that special purpose, went either to the general fabric fund, or was ear-marked for some other definite expenditure. At St. Thomas, Sarum, this collection was made under the title " Font Taper and Deacon's Wages," which was afterwards termed " Deacon's Wages and Halfpence at Easter."

(3) The Paschal money, originally devised for providing the great Paschal Taper, was paid by all parishioners of houseling age, when they "took their rights," which meant confession, absolution, and Easter Communion. The Paschal Taper was blessed on Easter Eve, was kept lighted till Holy Thursday, and was lighted again at Whitsuntide. It was elevated on a large stock, and entries occur for painting and dressing the same, and also for mending the case in which the taper was moulded. At St. Edmund, Sarum, where the weight of the great taper is given, apart from font tapers and other candles, it usually weighed about thirty pounds; in 1491 the weight was thirty-six pounds.

"Coleys on est^r eve for holy fyre," in 1491, cost a penny; and an entry in Latin in 1495 names

"Pro una mensura Carbonis in Vigilia Pasche apud benediccionem ignis j d."

These entries refer to the Holy Fire, kindled by burning glass or flint on Easter Eve, whence all lamps and tapers, previously extinguished, were relighted by hallowed tapers.

The paschal money eventually became merged in the general gatherings at Eastertide already named.

(4) *Dona et Legata* is another frequent heading among the receipts. These gifts and bequests in kind are most varied; they include live stock such as sheep and bees, gowns, cloths, brass pots or mortars, oak coffers, silver spoons, jewels, and rings. A few instances of such entries must suffice. Such goods were usually placed in the treasury to await a convenient opportunity for sale,

whilst live stock (especially in country parishes) was more usually farmed.

1474-5. Et de xx d. rec' de pretio j debilis et veteris toge provenientis ex legac' uxoris Roberti Beller.
1481-2. Unum manutergium de Dyaper de leg' Ade uxoris.
1482-3. Et de x s. vid rec' pro una olla enea ponderante lxiij libr precij libr ij d. ex legat' Alicie nuper uxoris Roberti Drover.
1491-2. j peire of bedys of coralle with gaudys gilt, a Woman's girdelle of silver and over gylt, both of Jone Taverners gifte.
1523-4. ij schepe yt was gevyn by a man of the countre   xx d.

Money gifts were usually for a specific purpose, such as three donations of 4d. and two of 2d., in an undated roll of Henry VIII, towards "the crosse and candelstyckes." Sometimes money was left or given to the church fabric or general fund; such gifts were contributed by all classes of the community. A tailor gave 4d. in 1469, and another groat was the contribution in 1482 of the wife of a barber. Half a mark was bequeathed in 1499 by Thomas Blakker, "late mair of this Citie," whilst in the following year 4d. was the gift "cujusdam pauperis in la bedredyn rowe."

(5) Burial fees and tollings went to the general fund of the churchwardens. Up to the end of Henry VIII's reign there was a definite charge for the passing bell, picturesquely known as the "Forthfare," which was rung for those *in extremis*, as the soul was passing forth on its last journey. It served the twofold purpose of summoning the priest to the administration of the Church's last offices, and of inviting the intercession of the faithful. A shilling was the charge "pro magna compana in extremis pulsante" in 1468-9, when there were four such entries, and six in the following year. In 1474-5 there were three cases of 10d. charged for "fourthfare," but in each of these instances 6s. 8d. was also paid for interment within the church. The fee for the great bell was dropped to 8d. in 1477-8, and remained so for more than a decade, when it reverted to 12d. and soon afterwards (1494-5, etc.) advanced to 20d.

The forthfare seems to have ceased with the advent of

Edward VI, when knylls or knells rung after death took their place, at a charge of two shillings.

In the days of Queen Mary (1557–8) occur these entries:—

Mystrys short' for her husbandes knyll and for all the belles at his buryal	ix s. vj d.
Goodwyf Marshall for the fyve belles	viij d.
Sir harrys twelmonethis mynd	viij d.

The fee for burial in the church, including as a rule a gravestone, remained at 6s. 8d. up to about 1640, when it was raised to 10s. There are occasional entries of a fee for a gravestone in the Litten or churchyard, varying from 4d. to 4s.

An elaborate fee table was drawn up in 1608 as to the fees for bells at burials and their division.

VI Belles. Imprimis for all the bells x s. Whereof to the Churche vij s. iiij d. If the partye be buried in the Churche for the grave and stone xj s. Whereof to the Churche vij s. ij d. If the partye be buried in the Churchyard and Chested, the Churche must have for the grave and Chest iiij d., without a Chest ij d.

Item for the V Belles vij s. x d. Whereof Due to the Churche yf the partye be chested v s. iiij d., without a Chest v s. ij d.

For the iiij belles iiij s. ij d. Whereof Due the Churche yf the partye be Chested iij s., without a Cheste ij s. x d.

For the iij belles. Whereof Due to the Churche yf chested ij s., without x d.

For the ij belles xij d. Whereof Due to the Churche viij d.

Mem[d] when the Fyfth bell maye be Ronge wth one man, then the Churche is to have iiij d. more for every burial.

Further we agree that a straunger shall paye for the belles as abovesayde, but shall paye to the Churche for his knell only ij s. vj d. Yf he be not buried in the parishe, he shall paye for his knell only ij s. vj d.

The remainder of the bell fees not taken by the wardens was divided between the minister and clerk.

"Ornamentes" were occasionally hired from the wardens for funerals in the earlier days. Thus a hearse cloth was hired for 16d. in 1491–3; the best candlesticks in 1494–5 for 12d.; in 1510, 5d. for a black pall, 12d. for the best cross and candlesticks on two occasions, and 4d. for the second best. Fourpence was charged in 1538 for the cross and candlesticks used at the burial of the sexton of St. Thomas, and a similar charge for the same occurs in 1543-4.

No charge seems to have been made for the use of the "bere," "paleborde," or "shrowdeborde." The ordinary plan for burial was to place the shrouded body on the parish bier or open coffin and thus carry it to the church and afterwards to the graveside, whence it was lifted, uncoffined, into the earth. Fees for "Buryalles, Christenynges, and Banes" began with the reign of Elizabeth and continued to the Commonwealth. They brought in a considerable annual income, varying from £3 to £9. The burial fees produced by far the largest share. Thus in 1575-6 the burials stood at £3 14s. 3d., the christenings 5s. 10d., and the banns 4s. 6d. It seems probable that the baptismal money was a voluntary offering and not, it is to be hoped, expected from the poor "Weddinge offringes" first appear in 1611-2, when six wedded couples offered sums varying from 4s. to 18d.; it is clear that the wedding entries of this period were not compulsory fees. When entered, the name of the married couple is always set down, and in some years when the return under this head is *nil*, the registers show that there were marriages.

(6) The Holy Loaf or *panis sanctificatus* occurs occasionally in these accounts. This loaf was brought into the quire after Mass on Sunday, and, after being blessed (not consecrated) by the priest, was cut up and distributed to the congregation to be consumed in token of friendly amity. Amongst the payments on the roll of 1510-1 is the entry—

> Pro uno Coffane ad portandum imponendum panem sanctificatum . vj d.

The entry in 1534-5 of "bred on' palme sonday 1d." probably refers to the holy loaf. A collection was made at the time that it was carried round. On this same roll, among the receipts, occurs—"the Holy cake cantell ij d." Cantell or cantle is a term implying a small piece, a corner, or a slice of anything, and it came to be used in the meaning of pieces of the holy loaf. An undated roll, *te¹ p.* Henry VIII, includes amongst the receipts—

> Cantell, gatheryd for one Hole yer after viij d. a wek for the cantell . . . . xxxiiij s. viij d.

RECEIPTS OF ST. EDMUND, SARUM

The Cantell gatherings for 1560-1 produced 17s. 4d., and the like in 1563-4, 1567-8, and 1568-9. In 1570-1 £1 14s. 8d., at the old rate of 8d. per week, is entered.

> Gathered from trynitie Sundaye laste paste after viij d. the wyke for the Cantell . . . . . . xxxj s. iiij d.

is the entry for 1575-6. Entries at the like rate for the Cantell continue up to 1588, when they cease; but a like amount continues to be entered up to 1641 under the heading of "Bread and Wyne."

(7) Among the receipts occur, from time to time, such terms as "Incresis," "Encrese of lightes," or "Incrementes of lightes." These are the sums brought into the general fund by the various Gilds at their annual festival. When the stewards found that they had an "increase" or balance, after the due maintenance of their light and the fulfilment of their religious and social obligations, and also after retaining a sufficient stock in hand wherewith to start another year, they brought the surplus to the church to be hallowed, and transferred it to the churchwardens.

> 1473-4. Incresis. It y receyved of the stuards of the lighte of senct Christopher and at halowyn of Increse of this yere . . . . xj d.

The churchwardens were fortunate in 1494-5 in obtaining "increase" from the Fraternity of Jesus Mass to the amount of 57s., from the light of St. Catherine 8d., and 4s. from the light of St. Christopher.

In 1497-8, the steward of the light of St. James gave an increase of 3s. 4d., and two stewardesses of the maidens' light 6s. 4d. In the same year the wives of the parish presented the handsome sum of £9 " de incremento luminis beate Marie virginis in ecclesia predicta."

The City trades gilds of the Bakers, Ironmongers, Joiners, Parchment-makers, Shoemakers, and Weavers are among the crafts making offerings at St. Edmund's.

Lights were so distinctive a feature of England's mediæval churches that it may be well here to briefly chronicle the lights and gilds of St. Edmund's as revealed in those accounts. In the Lady Chapel to the south of the quire were two altar lights, and a lamp before the Blessed Virgin sustained by the gild of the wives.

At the high altar in the quire were two lights, and a lamp supported by a gild before the Blessed Sacrament. At Christmastide there were also "two torches of rosom," and in 1501-2 mention is made of two for the high altar on double festivals, weighing 30½ pounds. Over the Sepulchre at Eastertide, in addition to the great sepulchre taper and the Paschal taper, were a hundred candles fixed on prickets or pins of beech. The chapel of the Jesus Mass, with its special well-endowed gild, had two tapers for the altar and a torch of rosin weighing 11 pounds. This gild supported the Morrow Mass held at 6 a.m. at the Holy Cross altar, and the accounts show that there was a yearly supply of six pounds of tallow candles for the Morrow Mass in winter-time. The Weavers' gild had a chaplain who used the Morrow Mass altar. In the nave was the specially supported Rood light, in addition to the Trendall or hanging corona of lights, as well as candles on the Rood-beam. In the north aisle was a chapel of St. John Baptist with a light, and mention is also made of the lights of the Trinity, Maidens, Servants, and of St. Christopher, St. Catherine, St. James, and St. Sebastian.

Each year a special wax taper or tapers were made for carrying before the Blessed Sacrament at times of visitation. This, for example, is the entry in 1482-3:—

> Pro candelis cereis ad usum Sacramenti Altaris in tempore visitationis Infirmorum . . . . . . iij d. ob.

A lantern had been bought in 1481-2 to shelter the tapers.

> Pro una laterna emptu ad usum ecclesie ad portandum diebus et noctibus cam sacramento altaris . . . . . vij d.

There are fairly constant references to the cost of making up the wax for the greater tapers, mixing the old wax with new. The following late instance must suffice:—

> 1543-4. Makynge lxx li. of olde waxe for the roodlyght . ij s. xj d.
> xxx li. of new waxe at vj d. the li. . . . xv s.
> xxx li. of old waxe makynge for the pascall xx d. ob.
> v li. of new waxe for the same . . . . ij s. vj d.
> makynge ij li. of olde wax for the foonte taper . . j d.
> v li. of new waxe for the same . . . . ij s. vj d.

(8) The Standings or Stalls at St. Edmund's fair, both without and immediately within the walls of the litten or churchyard, brought in a small but steady income to the churchwardens. Under the "Foreyne Receites" of 1490–1 is entered—

> Rec of dyverse men chese sellers which stode at the Church Walle . xviij d.

The "Perquis' Nundine" of 1495–6 amounted to 16d., received of those who had stalls within the cemetery. In the following year the fair rents paid by stallholders within and without the cemetery amounted to 2s., and in 1900 to 22d. The entry is longer and the amount larger for 1510–1 :—

> Rec "de perquis" nundinarum Sci Edmund's pew stallis et stationibus diversis frimatutoribus et aliis Artificiariis traditis et dimissis infra interiorem partem et exteriorem muri lapidis Cimiterii ecclesie predicte tempore nundinarum predictarum . . . . iıj s. vııj d. ob.

Three undated rolls, *te 1 p.* Henry VIII, record the respective receipts of 3s., 2s. 6d., and 20d. "of the Cheesemen that stode under the Churche wall." In 1550–1 the receipts from the Cheesemen amounted to 23d., and the like amount in 1556–7. In the following year the sum fell to 16d., but it rose to 2s. in 1560–1, and to 7s. 8d. in 1561–2. The last time apparently that the cheesemongers were permitted to take up their stations at the churchyard wall was in 1576, when the receipts amounted to 2s. 10d.

If the churchyard wall was to be used for wares at fair time, the sale of cheeses was a tolerably cleanly trade, but at least on one occasion butchers' stalls were sanctioned :—

> 1474–5. It. of the Gift of the Bōchers for grounde for ther Stallys without the letton . . . . . . ij s.

(9) The Hire of Vestments was an occasional source of income. Thus in 1475–6 the wardens received 3s. 4d. from Mr. John Dagoad, of the chapel of St. Mary, for the loan of vestments out of the church store to celebrate Mass for his parents. In the same year these funeral vestments were again loaned to Mr. William Nessyngwyke for a like sum to enable him to celebrate on behalf of Andrew Brante and other of his benefactors.

(10) Gifts in kind and in money were made, from time to time,

with the object of having the donors' names, or those of their ancestors, placed upon the Bede Roll. The bede roll was always recited from the pulpit by the parish priest on Christmas Day, Michaelmas, and on every Sunday. For fulfilling this duty the priest usually received 4s. per annum.

Among "Giftys and bequests" of 1478-9 is—

It. paide to the Paryshe prest for the prayers of the bedrolle . vj s.

The following is a long entry under 1499-1500 :—

Giftes for namys to be put in the bede rolle this yere. It. rec' of the gift of Robert South Gent at the namys of hym Alys his wiffe their faders and their moders be set in the bede rolle of the seide Churche of Saynt Edmunde that the pepulle then beyng present may pray for ther Sowlys Amongist all Cristyn every Sonday when the parisshe preste rehersithe thare then in all xl s. Of the gift of Stephyn Walwyn and Kateryne his wif' a vestment for the pryst of Crymson Velvet with alle thapparelle at their namys be put in the same bede rolle for like cause.

The accounts clerk for 1500-1 duly entered the heading "Nomina in le bede rolle hoc A° registrata," but he had to add—

Null. quia nemo hoc Anno desideravit.

A bequest of Master Copper to the bede roll of 6s. 8d. is entered under 1538-9.[1]

(11) Church-ales, in pre-Reformation days, were generally among the most prolific and popular methods of obtaining income both in town and country. St. Edmund was no exception, especially between 1461 and 1497. The Scotale House stood near the church in a small street still known as Scotts Lane; there are various charges for its repair, *e.g.* It. in 1474-5 "pro domo scotali." There are no entries for malt or brewing vessels; it may therefore be assumed that the ale was bought and then sold at a profit. The Maundy ale was certainly purchased, for the names of the sellers are several times set forth.

Ales were held on three occasions, namely, the week before and the week after Whitsunday, and at the translation of St. Edmund (9th June). They were called King ales, because a man and a woman were chosen to preside (*regnare*) over them; anyone failing

[1] As to the Bede Roll, see subsequent chapter, also Abbot Gasquet's *Parish Life*, 222-5. Its place has been taken by the later form of the Bidding Prayer.

when appointed was fined 8d. In 1461 the Scotales, *diversis jocalibus regibus et reginis*, actually produced for the churchwardens the sum of £23 8s. 10d., equal to about £300 of the present day. In 1469-70 four ales produced £9 18s. 6d.

Et de xliij s. vid rec' de denar' hoc anno collect' per Willm Smythe et Aliciam uxorem Roberti South de servisia regali viz. in Septimana proxima ante festum Pentecoste. Et de xx s. rec' de denar' collect' per Johannem Payne Vever (weaver) et Johannem Noke Vever de servisia regali viz. in Septi'a Pentecoste. Et de lx s. rec' per Johannem Chapman et uxorem Radulfi Hayne de servisia regali viz. in Septi'a profine post festum Pentecoste. Et de lxxv s. rec' per Willm Harrys et ux'm Willi Pole de servisia regali viz. in Septi'a qua accidit festum translacionis Sei Edmundi.

An Ale was the chief means of raising money for any extraordinary demand. Such Ales were usually promoted and managed by two of the parishioners. The accounts for 1474-5, when gatherings were made for the great bell, show that three of these Scotales produced £9 5s. 5d.

Scotalis with Gifts to the grete Belle.
It. of the gaderyng of Robert Parche and Xtoper Flemynge   xxxiij s. ij d.
It. of Robert A Neve and Walter Dawbeny in lyke wise   .   liij s.
It. of John Holberne in lyke wise   .   .   .   .   ix s. iij d.

In 1490 the word "kyng" is erased, and the phrase is thus entered—

Also receyved of Alys Plaies that yere in the somertyme as it apperyd in oure qweyer for our remembrance made and upon this accompt examyned and shewed iij li. xj s. xj d.

These Ale plays were probably religious mysteries or miracle plays, not infrequently in naves of churches; but their performance in the quire (not the presbytery or sanctuary) was surely most exceptional. In the 1461 accounts are charges amounting to 16s. 10½d. for players' apparel and properties, such as chevrons or perukes, fustian, and tinfoil. Other properties and labour were supplied gratuitously. The charges also included 2s. for 34 dozen tickets (*signorum jocallum*), and 14d. for a pyx in which to collect and take care of the money. It would appear, from the conjunction of the accounts, that the receipts from these Corpus Christi plays went towards the payment of two silver-gilt candelabra recently purchased.

In 1469–70 the sum of 11s. 10d. was paid for the apparel of the Corpus Christi players, in addition to 4d. for a woollen shroud for " le Kingplay."

The waits, who were musicians attached to the Corporation, served for orchestra on such occasions. The waits are named in accounts for 1538–9 and 1543–4 as " bryngynge in of ye processyon," for which they received the respective payments of 8d. and 12d.

The chief part of the clerk's salary came from his annual Ale for a long period. It was not abolished until 1697, when the vestry allowed him henceforth 40s. " uppon ye accompt of not keeping an Ale." At the neighbouring church of St. Thomas the clerk's Ale was abolished, in favour of a regular money payment, in 1651.

(12) Among the receipts of St. Edmund's from 1497 until 1581 are the collections for church work at Hocktide. The Hock days were the second Monday and Tuesday after Easter. The accounts for 1497–8 name 15s. 10½d. as collected by the wives " in festo Hokkes." In 1499 the churchwardens received 5s. " of diverse wiffes and maydens to save them from byndynge in Hok Tuysday."

There is a much longer Latin entry in 1510–1 :—

Colleciones in festo lez hokkis. Et de iiij s. rec' et collectis in festo de les hokkis de donacionibus diversarum feminarum sexuum quos deder' ad commodum ecclesie predicte ad custodiend' illas a ligacione eodem tempore ut ab antiqua consuetudine in quolibet consimili festo colligi solent per Gardianos et Custodes ibidem pro tempore existentes.

In 1532–3 the " devocyon of the people on Hocke Tuysday" produced 6s. 8d., and in 1538–9, 8s. 6d. The gatherings at Hocktide on an undated Henry VIII roll produced the much larger sum for the churchwardens of 36s., and another roll of doubtful date (probably Henry VII) reaches the far higher total of 60s. A third undated Elizabethan roll, probably 1572, also yields a total gathering of 60s. A further sixteenth-century roll, as to whose date there is some doubt, is of interest as showing gatherings on both the Hock days; on the Monday there was a collection of 13s., and on the Tuesday of 4s. 5d. The double entry for 1540-1 also testifies to receipts on both days, gathered by the two sexes—

Hocketyde. Itm the sayde gatherede at Hocketyde by the chirchemen viij s. iij d. Itm thy receyved of the gatherynges whiche the Women gathered at hocktyde and at Wytsontyde xxj s. iiij d.

In 1561 the Hocktide gatherings amounted to 20s. 1d., but in 1562 and 1563 to 40s. The amount had increased to £3 in 1572, and in 1576 to £3 15s. The last entry occurs in 1581, when the sum gathered was £3 1s.

Once or twice there are payments on the other side of the accounts towards Hocktide refreshments. Of this there is an amusing instance in 1510-1. The gatherings amounted to 4s., and of this sum the churchwardens expended 3s. 4d. in a dinner to the women "in die le Hockes," leaving a net balance of 8d. for the church funds.

MAY-DAY DANCERS: WINDOW, BETLEY HALL, STAFFS
TEMP. EDWARD IV

(13) Dancing. The mediæval Church of England was ever ready, not only to maintain and regulate and bend to its own ends ancient customs such as that of Hocktide, but also to promote and take in hand other amusements in addition to the mystery plays. The accounts of St. Edmund's show that sums were not infrequently "gotten to the profitte of the churche" by dancing. Dancing at Whitsuntide was taken advantage of in the way of gatherings for the church. An undated roll, *te_mp*. Henry VII, records amongst the receipts 3s. 4d. for "Whytsontyde dawnsynge." There are frequent entries throughout Elizabeth's reign of the receipt of 3s. 4d. from this dance gathering, and in 1567 it amounted to 6s. There was a further advance in the earlier years of James' reign. The Whitsun dance produced 20s. in 1607, and 10s. in each of the four following years. At that period it seems to have died out.

A much more interesting dance recorded as bringing profit in these accounts was the Maypole dance of the children. The first definite mention of this entertainment occurs on the 1490 roll, where this entry is found among the payments:—

> To Willm Belrynger for clensinge of the Churche at ye Dawnse
> of Powles . . . . viij d.

From this it is clear that the dance took place within the church, almost certainly in the nave. This dance evidently required a special framework; the repairs for 1491-2 include the following :—

> For a pece of Tymber for a ynner grounselle of Powlis Daunce
> and bordes for other necessaries . . . . . iij s. j d.
> To Will Joynour for workmanship of the seid Powlis Daunce . x s. ij d.
> For nayles bi the hands of Stephyn Rotherforde . . iij s. x d.
> To John Lokyar for xxiiij grete nailes for the Daunce of Powles . iiij d.

An entry in 1468-9 for an ash pole and ironwork connected with it may refer to the accessories of this dance, but it is stated in the introduction to these Sarum Accounts that "the Beden or Birch pole used at these dances probably gave its name to Beden Row running on one side of the Litten." The last reference to this dance is in 1594, when the "childrens daunce" procured 20s. 1d. towards the church funds.

(14) Seats and Pews. A considerable income was eventually

gained by the churchwardens of St. Edmund from the odious system of letting seats and pews. We know of no other parish accounts wherein the scandal of mapping out the whole area of God's House in accordance with the wealth and position of the parishioners attained to such egregious proportions, or where the evil can be shown to have originated from such small and comparatively innocent beginnings.

The first entry in the printed accounts is in 1477-8 under the heading "Assertaciones Seditium," when 6d. was received for the assigning of a seat to Robert Romsey, and 12d. for two seats for John Thornton. In 1480, seat money, "Conduccio sed' il'," for four persons produced 2s. 8d.; one of them was for the mother of John Saunders, chaplain. The letting of four seats in 1482-3 yielded 5s. 4d.; 20d. each was paid for two seats. Under the head of "Conduccio sedil'" in 1483-4 is the entry "nil hoc Anno." In the following year 10s. 6d. is put to the credit of the church fund from 13 seats, chiefly assigned to women. "Hyrynge 17 Setys" yielded 5s. 4d. in 1490-1, six out of eight were for women. The "Setys assigned" of 1491-2 brought in 3s. 1d.; in 1494-5, 10s. 2d., and in 1495-6, 10s., when all but one were for women. The receipts were 10s. 4d. in 1499-1510, but dropped to 4s. in the following year; they rose again to 9s. 8d. in 1510-1. The word "Pewes" first occurs in an undated roll of a little later date, when the receipts sprang up to 23s. 6d.; these pews or sittings were chiefly appropriated to householders' wives. "The goodwiefe of the blew bore" secured one for 4d.; but in the following year "the goodwyffes doughter of the Blew bore" had to pay 20d. for her seat. In 1523-4 "the Settes in the Churche" produced 17s. 1d.; "Cecyly Maneforde and Wascottes wife for thyre ij Pewis" paid 10d. Among the entries for "Pewys" in 1532-3 are "a woman syttyng under the clock iiij d." and "ij other women syttyng by Robert viij d." An undated roll, *te 1 p.* Henry VIII, yielded the large seat income of 29s. 3d.

With the changes that began in Edward VI's reign, when the pulpit was exalted above the altar, the income from this source occasionally rose; in 1560-1, 24s. 6½d., and in 1568-9, 32s. 8d. In 1587-8 the price per seat was advanced to 12d. each; in 1589-90 the receipts realised £2 0s. 6d., and in 1602-3, 33s. 2d. During James' reign the large income from pews of 50s. occurred in 1607-8. In 1620 a record appeared, for the first time, of the seats in the different pews. There were five pews under the north wall; 20s. was paid for the front one. Eight pews were against the west end of the church. Thirteen pews are described as "againste the piller where Mr. Willyams pewe is." Three pews were "aboute the pulpitte piller," for the front one of which 30s. was paid. Six pews were "on both sids of the Quire doore." Twelve "weomens pewes were on the north side of the north Rowe." Twelve pews were on the south side of the north row; whilst eleven pews were on the north side of the south row. The total receipts for this new arrangement were £10 10s. 8d. The pew receipts of 1622-3 were £4 14s. 10d. The payments of 1623-4 included

A painter for wryttinge figures in everie seat in our Church   2s. 6d.

On 6th January 1624 it was ordered by the Vestry

That the Seates on the northe side of the Churche nexte to the northe wall shall be enlardged at the ends towards the walke, and the Seates to be narrower, to the ende that more Pewes maye be made in that space, for the benefitt of the Churche, the speciall purpose beinge that seates maye be prepared and afforded for the sonnes and daughters of the Aldermen, 24, and 48 : And for the Children of other of the better sort of the parishe, for wch the fathers and friends of them are to give to the Church suche somes of monie as shalbe taxed by the Vestrie.

It is now declared accordinge to annciently use That boathe the Seates at the ends of the two foremost Pewes in the Churche, where the maior and Aldermen sitt, are proper onelie to be preserved and kepte for the 24 onelie, It being the Ancient Use of this Cittie, that not onlye the Aldermen and ancientes of the 24 of the Parishe wherein they dwell are to sitt and be placed in those foremoste Pewes in the parish Churche where they dwell, but alsoe in everie other parishe Church of this Cittye yf they come thither. It is ordred and declared That when anye persone of this parishe be chosen and sworne of the 24, he is to yeald of the seate where he sate before to the Churche, and to take his place in one of these Pewes of the 24, accordinge to his place, And his wyfe is lykewise to give of her seate where she sate before to the Churche and to take her places in the Pewes of there wives of the 24.

1627-8. Goody Langley for a small hanging (flap) seate 6d.

16 January, 1629. All the poore of the new Almeshouse and all other the Church Poore shall sitt in the Church, according to former orders made, upon Formes sett of purpose for them. And the Churchwardens are to see who are missing, and to keepe backe that weekes pay unles they can excuse it. And that the Formes may be knowen and not sate upon by others, there shalbe these wordes painted in great Red letters upon the Formes, *For the Poore*. Nevertheless old John George and John Fudges and Susan Beckett, and such others

as have already used stooles may use their former places, if it prove not inconvenient. Item the Churchwardens are to place every person in the Pewe where he or she shall sitt in the time of morning prayer on the Sundayes, and noe person shall presume to place him or herselfe in any Seat or Pew in any other manner.

1633-4. Pew receipts £10 14s. 6d.

1637-8. Rec for yᵉ Portable Seats that are set up for the youth of the Parish in yᵉ Iles of the Church—for yᵉ long and portable seate in yᵉ North Ile 13s. Mr. M. Aylerugge for yᵉ litle portable seate in yᵉ N. Ile against his owne seate dore for his children 2s., and he hath agreed to paie 2s. per an' for this seate soe long as he lives in the Parish. Mr. T. Lawes for one of yᵉ litle seates in yᵉ S. Ile to place in Eliz., Dorothy, Margaret, and Anne his daughters 6s., etc. . . .

1641-2. Pew receipts £13 9s.

1648-9. Mr. G. Masters and Jane with 3 children, Mary, Samuell and Abigall, also a bench for servants, 20s. Mr. Ambrose Smith with Mary and 4 children, he to fix a new bench for his Servants at his own charges, 15s.

In 1651-2 an elaborate new scheme for sittings with names of parishioners was drawn up; the following are among the items:—

Nic. Billen and his wife for a bench fixt to the maiors pew, 2s.—Mrs. An Carter hanging seat for servant, 1s.—Jone wife to Perigan Dawes sliding seat before Magistrates Pew in S. row, 2s. 6d.—Ric. Blacke and Kath. hanging seat against Aldermens Pew N. row, 2s.—Mrs. Battes widow a clap seat fixt to her owne for servant, 6d.—J. Willice widow to a clap seat fixt to Mrs. Foster her seat in Midle Ile for nothing.

After the fall of the tower, the nave of the church was pulled down and the quire reconstructed in 1653, when a new scheme of appropriated and rented seats was devised.

CHAPTER V

OUTGOINGS OF ST. EDMUND, SARUM

The Payments or Outgoings of St. Edmund, Sarum—Keeping the Accounts—The Maundy—The Gang-week—Banners—Wages—Repairs to fittings—Clock Smoke Farthings—Repairs to Fabric—Fall of tower, 1653—Rebuilding scheme—Litten or Churchyard—Trees—Specimen "Solutyon" roll

(1) A NECESSARY annual charge was that of Keeping the Accounts. In 1461 and the following year the charge was 3s. 4d. Subsequently for several years the payment rose to 5s. At the end of the account roll for 1481-2 is this entry:—

Mem: that Rob Southe made this boke of accompte at his owne charge. Nothing asking for his labor which hath savyd to the Churche v s. which William Wynne was wont to have yerely for makyng of th' accompte.

In 1495 the charge for a clerk writing the accounts was 3s. 4d. and 3d. for parchment. The price paid in 1539 was 2s., and only 1s. in 1542 and the following year. The charge rose to 4s. in 1551. In the earlier part of Elizabeth's reign the charge was again a quarter of a mark or 3s. 4d.; in 1594 the charge had risen to 4s. 4d., but the clerk was to find his own parchment. This latter fee was paid till 1626, when this entry occurs:—

Parchmentt and wrytinge this accounte . . . . 4s. 8d.

In 1632 the charge was raised to 6s. 8d., and thus remained until the close of the Commonwealth.

(2) Among the earliest outgoings of these accounts are those connected with the Maundy, or Mandatum Novum, as it is set down in Latin. The accounts of the church and of the Jesus Mass were annually made up on Maundy Thursday, *in die parascenes.* In 1461 twenty-four gallons of good ale were purchased at a halfpenny a gallon, and twelve cups of ashwood for 7d. where-

with to drink it. The drinkers were presumably the auditors, the wardens, and other invited parishioners. Like entries under these two heads occur, with certain variants, for upwards of a century. In 1468 two gallons and a bottle of wine were bought, in addition to the ale, and one gallon in the following year. The ale averaged about 2s. 3d., computed according to a variety of measures. The white or ashen cups increased in price to 12d. by 1517; they numbered three dozen in 1527. The entry in 1538 is as follows:—

iiij dosen of mawndy cups ij s.—a Cowle of Ale on Mawndy thursdaye xviij d. —the hyer of ij dosen of mawndy cruses.

There are several like entries up to the close of Henry VIII's reign. The Maundy is not mentioned in the accounts during Edward VI's reign. The last entry pertaining to it that we have noticed occurs in 1562–3:—

iij dosyn maundy dyshes iiij s. vj d. Ale for the maundy ij s. iiij d.— mayngates (manchets) an Cakes vj s.

In addition to the keeping of the Maundy by drinking when the accounts were made up—always within the church, presumably in the vestry—there was another charge, constantly entered, for a *jantaculum*, sometimes translated a breakfast and sometimes a dinner, on the morning of Easter Day, of which the accountants or auditors and the wardens partook. It was no extravagant meal, for the usual cost was 6d. The customary dish was "*calvishede cum le henge*," that is calf's head, with the heart, liver, and lights.

(3) In the Gang-week or Rogationtide, with its ceremonial processions round the bounds of the parish, there was an invariable charge for boys and men carrying the banners on this occasion. The entries respecting it are usually associated with like outside processions on other great days or festivals, such as Corpus Christi, Whitsuntide, St. Mark, St. Thomas the Martyr, etc.

1461-2. Et pueris hastas et vexilla portant' diebus rogacionum ascenscionis domini foris in Septimana Penthecostis et corporis Christi . . . . . xviij d.
1480-1. Paid to divers men and children beryng Baners in processions at Seynt Marks tyde, etc. . xvij d.
1490-1. In money paid to dyvers Children and men for berynge of baners as well in the Rogacion Weke as at Whitsontyde and Corpus Xpi day . . xvj d.

1499-1500. For bred and ale for diverse persones that renge the bellys and bere the banerys ther in all the Rogacione Weke and afterwards in Holy days scil Whitsontide Trynyte Sonday and Corpus Xpi day in alle . . . . ij s. ix d.

1532-3. Baner barers in the Procession weke . viij d.
,, on the Ascension Day iij d.
,, the Thursday in the Whitson weke . iij d.
,, on Corpus Xpi day . iij d.

The banners themselves were no small initial cost, and their repair involved fairly frequent charges. Small bells were attached to their fringes. On festivals, when not in procession, they decked the church walls, and at other times were kept in the vestry. Among the particular banners of this church were those depicting St. Edmund, Our Lady, the Passion, St. George, St. Nicholas, and St. Eustace; they numbered seventeen.

1468-9. In viij banerstavis empt' per Will'm Taverner precii in toto . . . . x s.
1483-4. For hepys and stapplys to make fast the baners at churche . . . . viij d.
1491-2. To Will Joynour for ij crukhis to bere up the banerstaffes in the vestry . . . .
1501. Johi Coplande stayner pro le steynynge de magno vexillo . . . . . . vj s. viij d.
Pro j frenge de cerico pro eodem vexillo . . . v s.
Pro filo de cerico circa idem vexillum occupato . ij d.
Pro j baculo pro eodem . . . . . viij d.
Johi Shirville brawderer pro emendacione divers' vexill' xx d.
Pro filis lineis circa eadem vexilla occupatis . ij d.
Michl Smythe pro xvj Canillis (bells) de ferro ad pendende predicta vexilla per easdem canillas in toto xij d.
ij doss' de punctis de leder circa eadem vexilla occupatis ij d.
1523. Whyte lether for to mende the banars and for ij clappers to the bellis of ye banars . . . iiij d.

The banners were sold in 1552-3, but they were restored under Queen Mary. In 1556-7 the banner-bearers received 3d. for drink on each of the three Rogation days and on Holy Thursday. On Corpus Xpi day they received 4d., whilst 3d. was bestowed on those "that dyd were copes." When Elizabeth came to the throne, the banners were again sold, and no further Gang-week payments occur except to the bell-ringers.

(4) Wages or payments of the parish clerk, sexton, those in charge of clock, bells, organ, the priest for reading the bede roll, and a variety of incidental craftsmen and labourers occur in abundance in these, as in all other accounts. The more striking of these items appear under subsequent general headings. Washing of the church linen and scouring of the brass and latten utensils also come under this head.

(5) So too with regard to church fittings and ornaments, such as sepulchre, plate, font, pulpit, clock, organ, books, vestments, seats, etc., which constantly required repair or renewal. Their noteworthy points will be afterwards mentioned. It may, however, be here remarked that the first clock, mentioned in the earlier accounts, was obviously one in the interior of the church; it had a jack or figure which struck the hours. The bells perpetually needed attention, and the expenditure over them was often a serious item. Payments to the ringers on particular occasions are discussed elsewhere, and so too are payments for special forms of prayer. Certain valuable Rood and Rood-loft entries are cited later on under that specific heading, but one class of exceptional entry as to interior repairs may as well be just mentioned in this place.

In the quire stood a "grete chere," which must have been of some size, for on one occasion 13 feet of board as well as iron rings were used for its repair. Payments are also entered for chairs that stood by the altars of Our Lady and St. Nicholas.

1477-8. Et sol' pro emendacione unius Cathedre ad altare beate Marie deserviendum . . . . . vj d.
1480-1. Et solut' pro emendacione unius Sedile juxta Altare Sei Nicholai . . . . ij d.

It has been suggested, with some probability, that these chairs were used by priests when hearing confessions.

(6) Smoke farthings, more often described as Pentecostals or Whitsun farthings, in old church accounts, caused a small and interesting payment during the sixteenth century. A tax of a penny or less on each hearth was collected from Saxon times on St. Peter's day, and sent to support the English College in Rome, hence the name of Romescot or Peter's Pence. In the thirteenth

century definite sums were allotted to each diocese, and this was subdivided among the parishes. The share of Sarum diocese was £7, and the annual amount required from St. Edmund's was 5s. 0½d. This tax was for a time forbidden by Edward III. It first appears in these accounts in 1510; it was diverted from Rome by Henry VIII in 1534, but restored by Queen Mary in 1556. Though the house-to-house collection of Peter's Pence was generally made on St. Peter's Day, it became customary to carry this parochial offering in procession with cross and banners to the cathedral or chief minster church of the district in Whitsun week. The sum collected was usually less than the amount required, and hence the difference was entered on the payment side of the accounts. If the full amount was gathered there was no necessity for the Smoke farthings to be in any way named. In Elizabeth's days this due was again diverted from Rome, but continued to be claimed long afterwards by cathedrals and old minster churches. In this later period it was usual to take the whole sum from the general accounts.

 1510–1. Et pro oblacionibus a retro existent' ecclesie Cathedr'
   Sarum vocatis Smoke vorthyngis   . xvijd. ob.
 1517–8. At oure lady churche for smoke sylver .   . xxijd. ob.
 1518–9. Smoke farthynges to oure lady Churche .   . xxij d.
 1541–2. At Wytsontyde at our lady Chirche for smoke farthynges . ij s. x d.
 1556–7. Of the parishoners for Smoke Farthynges   . iijs. iijd.
 1574–5. Oʳ Ladye Church for Smok' Fardinges .   v s. ob.

(7) The gravest and most frequent charge on this and other parishes was the continuous strain of keeping the fabric in repair. In this instance the building was of considerable size. The old church was 176 feet long, with central tower and transepts, and both quire and nave had aisles and three-gabled roofs. The walls required repair or buttressing from time to time, and the interior painting or whitewashing, the parapets renewing, the windows reglazing, and more especially the roofs restoring. The "Reparatio infra ecclesiam et extra" of 1469–70 amounted to 64s. 4d. These expenses included the reroofing of the south quire aisle, which was the Lady Chapel; it was covered with stone tiling from the celebrated Wilts quarries of Chilmark, and 4000 "stone nayles"

or wooden pins for securing the stone tiles were bought for 4s. 8d. In 1473-4 there was a far heavier outlay, £26 9s. 0¼d. being spent on "Expenses necessary with the cost of the Steple." This steeple was a short spire of lead-covered timber on the summit of the tower, which was at that time reconstructed. New lead cost £18 2s. 1d., and the casting and laying of 95 cwt. of old and new lead £3 19s. 9½d. The repairs of 1483-4 amounted to £17 6s. 6½d. By far the heaviest item was lead for roofing, but the account included 49 feet of glass for the great west window at 3d. a foot, and also 14d. for mending two panes of (coloured) glass in the same. Occasionally the repairs were of far less moment—thus "Reparacyons done uppon ye Churche" in 1523-4 only amounted to 46s. 9d.

A close study of the early repair accounts of this or any other old church will always result in interesting and detailed particulars. Thus the accounts of St. Edmund's show that the upper room of the south porch was used as the sexton's chamber; it was reached by a newel stairway, at the top of which was a door on to the leads secured by a padlock or "hanginge lokke."

There but seldom appears to have been any difficulty in raising extra money by voluntary appeals for any unusual expenditure in pre-Reformation days, when enforced church rates were unknown. This was particularly the case in the event of new bells being required. Thus at St. Edmund's in 1474-5, when the great bell required rehanging, a new clapper, and a new frame, etc., £8 18s. was specially raised for the purpose. Again in 1497-8 the wives collected 15s. 10½d. for a new window, and the total of voluntary gifts amounted to £2 10s. 10½d.

In post-Reformation days, when forcible levies could be raised, the matter was far simpler. In 1619-20 the total disbursements were £73 17s. 1½d., when the chief expenses were for a new "Ringinge Lofte" under the central tower, fitted with pews. Another year of somewhat heavy expenditure was 1624-5, when the quire and its aisles were repaired, and particularly "the great windowe at the East end of the Churche."

The great catastrophe of the fall of the tower in 1653, when the western half of the fabric was reduced to ruins, produced a fairly generous response from the parishioners when their donations were solicited, but the work of making the body of the church fit for worship, and that on a reduced scale, could not be carried out save by the imposing of a heavy rate to be levied in the course of the next ten years.

In May 1651 a motion was made "to take downe the bell upon the top of the Tower" of St. Edmund, Sarum, "it being hurtfull to the Tower," but the matter was adjourned. On 6th June 1653 the sexton was ordered to ring no bells save one for a knell or a sermon. On 8th June it was reported that the tower was in jeopardy through the foundering of the foundation of the south-west pillars, and it was resolved in order to ease it of some of the weight to take down the bell on the top of the tower, together with its lead-covered frame; the sexton was to ring the treble bell at 5 o'clock a.m. in place of the one removed. On 19th June the whole parish as well as the vestry was summoned; they found that the tower was "so clift with shaking by meanes of the Ringing of the Belles," that the churchwardens were ordered to remove all the bells except the great bell for summoning the people to church and the treble for five o'clock ringing.

The tower fell with a crash on Monday, 27th June 1653, destroying much of the nave of the church. A long and magniloquent entry as to the catastrophe was made in the vestry book, from which some sentences are cited. On Sunday, 26th June, the church was crowded with a large congregation, including the mayor and principal inhabitants of the city.

"The maine pillars did bulge out and sensiblely shake; the cleftes in the walles were seen to open and shutt with Ringing the Sermon Bell yt day, neither were there any considerable Proppes under set to Support it, So yt nothing but the very hand of God did keep the Stones and Timber from falling untill the next morning yt his own people were all Secure at home, and then he so sweetly Ordered the fall of the Tower yt (albeit many woorkemen were about it yt day) neither Man Woman nor Child received any hurt thereby. When wee consider what God hath formerly permitted when the Tower of Siloa fell, and when the Church of Blake fryers in London fell upon a people mett as wee were for worship but in another Religion ... wee cannot but Breake foorth in to Praise and say Salvation and glory, and honour, and Power unto the Lord our

God. . . . Wee doe Order and Appoynt yt the twenty-six day of June yearly shall bee unto the people of Edmundes parish a day of soleme and publique Thankesgiving so long as ther shall bee one stone upon another in Edmundes Church and an Inhabitant left alive in Edmundes parish. . . ."

A systematic scheme for collecting funds for the rebuilding of the tower and body of the church was at once set on foot, service in the meanwhile being held in the chancel. The moneys collected being not sufficient, a ten years' rate was imposed in December, the parishioners' subscriptions to be therefrom deducted. The accounts of 1653-4 show that the subscriptions amounted to £702 13s. 3d. In 1655 a committee was appointed to ask for subscriptions from." Thomas parish, Martines parish, and the Close," and others, towards setting up the tower. "Free Guift Money" was subscribed in answer to this appeal to the amount of £91 1s. 4d., the largest donation being that of Earl Pembroke for £20.

The Litten or churchyard was also a source of fairly frequent payment. It was entered by a lychgate, sometimes called the style; the gate beneath it had a lock, and when locked entrance was by a whirligig or turnstile.

1462-3. Et pro ij capit' mearemii pro le lychegate et impositionem ejusdem . . . . viij d.
1477-8. Amendyng of the church Style xij d., yrepere to the same vj d., a laborer to helpe make ij d., a pece of Tymber to the Whirlegogge ij d.
1648. Ordered to wall up the place where the great gate stood that the Carts came in and out at, and only leave a door convenient to bring the Corps in.

Small sums were frequently expended on the walls, and also on clearing the churchyard of weeds and worse nuisances.

1475-6. To John Gibbes for the weding' of diverse anoysance within in the Churche yerde . . . . . iiij d.
1499-1500. To John Frye for cuttyng downe of the Netylles and Wedes in the Churchyerde . . . . ij d

In 1644, when an extra rate was being raised for the repair of the church and the south windows, it was ordered that six of the churchyard elms were to be felled and the rest lopped and sold for that purpose. Soon after this successors must have been planted, for there is an entry in the 1650-1 accounts of

> Wattring the young Trees this last somner . . . . 5s.

In December 1693 it was resolved that

Elm trees be planted in the room of those that are dead, and as many more as the C. W. shall think convenient.

Thereupon William Baker, gardener, supplied 16 English elms at 2s. 6d. each, and 3 sycamore trees at 3s. each, and promised

to keepe and make grow the above said trees together with those planted last year.

The following will serve as an example of the general payments; it is taken from an undated English roll, about the beginning of Henry VIII's reign:—

Solutyons—The sayde Accomptantes asketh Alowaunce for suche solutions as they have layde out in the yere aforesayde for the sayde Chirche as here after foloweth'—Jn primis for squarynge iij peces of Tymber ij s.—Jtem for ffellynge of an Elme and for the loppynge thereof byfore vi d.—for sawynge of vij hundreth' and dī of borde and leges vij s. vi d.—for xxviij li. of souder and the workemanshyppe xiij s. iiij d.—for an C leade spent on our lady yle and the body of the Chirche iiij s. viij d.—for redyng of the Beade rolle the hole yere iiij s.—for wasshynge of the Chirche Ornamentes ij s.—to Will Androw for kepynge the Cloke from Ester vntylle mydsomer xx d.—for makynge cleane the gutters and the wyndowes iiij d.—for makynge of lxxvi $^{li.}$ of olde waxe for the roode lyght iij s. ij d.—for xxxvi $^{li.}$ of new wax for the same lyght' xviij s.—for talow candle ij d.—for j $^{li.}$ of vysytatione lyght' vi d.—for torches agaynst Corpus Crysti daye viij s. j d.—makynge xxvi $^{li.}$ of olde waxe for the paschalle xiij d.—for v $^{li.}$ of New wax to the same ij s. vi d.—for makynge of ij $^{li.}$ and dī of olde waxe for the fonte taper jd.—for iiij $^{li.}$ and dī of newe waxe for the same ij s. iij d.—for kepyng the roode lyght' xij d.—Jtem payde at our lady Chirche for smoke ferthinges iij s. iiij d.—to the waytes for hryngynge in of the processyon xii d.—to the ryngers on mundaye twysdaye wendensdaye and thursdaye in Crosse Weke on the processyon daye and Corpus X pī daye ev'y daye iiij d. and ev'y one of those dayes in breade and drynke spent upon' the Baner berers ij d., iij s.—for iij dosen of mawndy dysshes ij s. vi d.—for the hyer of ij dos' crewses ij d.—for a Cowle of Ale xviij d.—for holy oyle j d.—to Peryn Goldesmythe for mendynge the crosse and candelstyckes iiij s.—for ij Bawdryckes ij s. iiij d.—for a Bawdrycke for the V belle xxi d.—for a Bawdrycke for the Dawbneye belle vi d.—for ij whyte lether stroppes for the orgauns iij d.—for a shepes skynne to mende the bellowes of the orgauns ij d.—for a spade for the chirche v d.—for besomes ij d.—for ij sackes of Coles vi d.—for makynge of this Accompte xij d.—to Robert Martyn for yron for the V^t belle and the workemanshype and for mendynge of a Cofer in the vestrye x d. S'ma totalis solut' iiij li. xvi s. xi d.

CHAPTER VI

THE FABRIC OF THE CHURCH

Native workmanship—Fifteenth-century examples—St. Michael, Bath; St. Laurence, Reading; St. Mary, Sandwich; St. Andrew, Holborn; Ludlow; Bodmin; Great St. Mary, Cambridge—Roofing, shingles, stone-tiles—Flints for walling—Porch and other chambers—Glazing—Whitewash—Galleries

WARDENS' accounts bear abundant testimony to the generous free-will offerings of parishioners towards the due maintenance or rebuilding of their church, in days long before the institution of compulsory church rates. The following are a few noteworthy instances from fifteenth-century returns.

It may here be remarked that throughout the hundreds of parish accounts, both printed and in manuscript, which have been consulted in the compilation of this book, not one single statement or even hint has been detected of the importation of foreign labour or of foreign material in the construction of church fabrics or their fittings, with the single exception of bringing Caen stone from across the seas.

The wardens of St. Michael, Bath, set about building a new Lady Chapel in 1425. Towards the cost a church-ale (one of the only ones in these long accounts) realised 24s. There was a payment of 4d. for horse hire for one seeking a mason; 1d. for placing in position the foundation stone; 33s. 4d. to the mason; 4s. 8d. for clearing away the old walls of the chancel and chapel; 7s. for the carriage of the stone; and 4s. for stone purchased at Claverton. Every item is entered in connection with the carpenter's work in roof and doors, in the tiling and leadwork, and in the glazing and ironwork of the windows. Two men were paid 8d. for moving the old Lady Altar, whilst a fee of 6s. 8d. was paid to the suffragan bishop for consecrating the new altar. The total cost of erecting the chapel was £17 7s. 10d.

The account roll of St. Laurence, Reading, for 1440-1 gives a list of subscribers to the *opus ecclesie* "then in progress." There were 86 subscribers and the total gathering came to £9 6s. 5½d. There were two subscribers of half a mark, and four (including the vicar) of a quarter of a mark; on the other hand nine subscribed twopence each, and one a penny. The singularly fine and well-proportioned tower, the pinnacles of which rise to. a height of 111 feet, was brought into its present form in 1458; a considerable portion of the materials of its Norman predecessor were reused. The roll for that year originally gave a long list of the donors to the "Emendation of the Campanile," but unfortunately the parchment has suffered so much from damp that only 26 names are partially legible. Considerable church repairs were begun in 1518 and continued until 1521.

1518. Gyven by dyverse persons toward the reperacon of the church gatherid every Sonday after new yers day unto Sonday after Michelmas day which amounteth to the sm of . . . . xxj li. ij s. j d.
Payd to Meller the Joynor in pte of payment of iiij li. vj s. viij d. for makyng of the p'close in the new chapell   xxvj s. viij d.
Payd to Harry Horthorne for tymber workmanshipp and for bowrdyng of men as apperith by his bills   vij li. iiij d.

The south window of the tower lost its tracery in 1567, when the great bell was lowered to be recast.

Anno 1567. For xlii foote of boorde for ye south window in the steple when the bell was taken out and in, and one hondreth and a half of nayles . . . . xj s. vj d.

The accounts of St. Mary, Sandwich, supply interesting particulars as to the stone used in 1446 in the rebuilding of the steeple.

To Robert carpenter for ye takyng down of the stepill and to cover hit agen . . . . iiij li.
For a m^{ll} of breke . . . . . . iiij s. vj d.
Spendit on the mason of Crystchirche for to have an ynsyght yn the Cane (Caen) stone for the stepill . . . . v d.
For v ton of Cane stone . . . . . . xxv s.
For iiij of bere (Beer, S. Devon) stone for the stepill   xx s.
For iiij^c fete of okyn bord and a half and ix odde fete for ye stepyll, prec de C. ij s. iiij d. Sum' . . . . xj s. x d.
For vj ton and j pip of Folston (Folkestone) rag . . . vij s.

THE FABRIC OF THE CHURCH 81

For xx yong elmys for scaffold tymbyr . . ij s. ij d.
To ye masones for ye castyng of ye stepill without with mortar . . . . . . xxvj s. viij d.
To J. C. carpenter yn party of payment of xvj li. xiij s. iiij d. for the makyng of ye spere of ye stepyll . . vij li.

Bentley's MS. book (1584) at St. Andrew, Holborn, says that the steeple of the church was begun in 1446 and the bells placed in it in 1456, but not completely finished until 1467–8. The north and south aisles were rebuilt about the same period.

And note that all this, as many things else in the church in those days, even when the church had most lands, were nevertheless builded by money given of devotion of good people, then used to be gathered by the men and women of the parish in boxes, at ales, shootings, etc., for the only purpose, through the parish weekly, during the time of these works as by their accounts, yet remaining, may and doth appear.

Certain detached Ludlow accounts of 1469–71, as well as an undated portion of the same period, deal largely with the later work of the erection of the fine central tower. The executors of John Hosier paid 6s. 8d. as the wages of the master-mason for two weeks. Bequests and gifts were made "to help forthe yᵉ quarriers"; among the donors were the Crafts or Gilds of the carpenters, cordwainers, tailors, smiths, dyers, barbers, bakers, and butchers. One Hugh Lotrier contributed 9d. towards a grindstone, and the same man received 8d. "for styling and mendyng of axes." John Hope paid 3s. "for iij dosen lyme." Among the payments of 1469–70 were 9s. 10d. "for belyng of the steple," and 39s. 8d. for the carriage of 122 "fother" of stone. The fother was 19 cwt. Hughley and Felton are named as places from which stone was fetched.

The accounts for 1577–8 abound in details as to the taking down and re-erecting of the great "pole of the weather cocke." Felling and sawing the tree selected for the new pole, covering it with lead, making the iron cross to surmount it, hauling it up, with frequent ale to the wainmen, sawyers, and every kind of labourer, etc., brought the expenses to about £7.

The church accounts of Bodmin, giving full details of the rebuilding of the greater part of the fine parish church of St. Petrock between 1469 and 1472, afford striking evidence of the wholehearted spirit and marvellous unanimity with which church restoration was undertaken in the fifteenth century.[1] There is no reason of which we are aware to consider the zeal of Bodmin in this direction as anything of an exceptional nature, save that a remarkable wave of Celtic fervour for the enlargement and beautifying of the Houses of God was at this time flowing from one end of the Duchy to the other, and that it naturally culminated in what was then its most important town. Bodmin, too, had even for those days an exceptional number of gilds, the members of which vied with each other not only in contributing from their common funds, but also in their individual gifts in money or in kind. Of these fraternities, numbering about forty, five were Trades Gilds founded to sustain certain crafts. These were the Gilds of St. Petrock, for skinners and glovers; of SS. Dunstan and Eloy, for smiths; of St. Anian, for shoemakers; of St. Martin, for millers; and of St. John Baptist, for drapers and tailors. The large number of smaller associations were brotherhoods united together under some special patron saint for the furtherance of social and religious obligations, and connected with the parish church or other subsidiary places of worship within the town. An interesting contribution was 5s. from William Mason and his fellows, the players "yn the Church Hay" or churchyard.

Every one seems to have given according to his means. Not a few who gave money gave labour in addition, and some only labour. The well-to-do gave trees off their estate, others gave stone, lime, timber, and parcels of nails. Now and again the wardens received gifts in kind, such as a cow sold for 7s. 6d., a lamb 5d., and a goose 2d. One woman, in addition to her subscription, gave her "crokke," and it realised 20d. The vicar gave his year's stipend, whilst a "hold woman" in the poorest quarter of the town contributed 3s. 2½d. A house-to-house gathering resulted in voluntary gifts from 460 inhabitants, including several servants. The principal folk lived in Fore Street; here there were four subscriptions of a mark (13s. 4d.), thirteen of half a mark, and one as low as 2d. Reyn Street was in one of the poorest quarters, and here there were several gifts of a penny. The women of the congregation had a special collection on Easter

[1] These accounts were printed in the *Camden Society Miscellany*, vol. vii. p. 875.

ST. PETROCK, BODMIN

THE FABRIC OF THE CHURCH

Eve; the "maidenys yn Forstret" contributed 6s., and the "maidenys of the borestret xvij d." A certain number of persons agreed to contribute a penny a week, and others a halfpenny whilst the work continued. The whole sum was raised within the limits of the parish, with the exception of some trifling donations from strangers passing through the town.

The total receipts from all sources during the first three years of the work amounted to £196 7s. 4d. This has to be multiplied by at least ten to give any idea of the present value of money. The expenditure would also have been far greater, probably quite double, had not so much of the material been freely granted. Thus an expenditure of 1½d. in wine seems to have sufficed to secure stone from the quarry of Tregarthyn; and many costly windows were erected and glazed by individual donors.

The parish had not much breathing-time wherein to recover from their great effort in church-building, before they realised that the old fittings were not worthy of the new fabric. In 1491 a contract was entered into for new seating and a new pulpit, to be completed by Michaelmas 1495, at a cost of £92, the parish providing the timber.

Valuable historical and architectural notes on the church of Great St. Mary, Cambridge, by Mr. Sandars were printed by the Cambridge Antiquarian Society in 1869, together with the "Annals of the Church" by Canon Venables. The church was used for the public purposes of the University as early as the thirteenth century. In 1522–3 the magnificent rood-loft or *Theatrum imaginis Crucifixi*, extending across the church from wall to wall, was erected at a cost of £92 6s. 8d. The original contract is still preserved in the parish chest; it was to be made after the models of the rood-lofts in the churches of Gazeley, Suffolk, and Triplow, Cambridgeshire. During the celebrations of the Commencements in Arts, the church was fitted up with stages like a theatre for the accommodation of the University. This custom was continued on a diminished scale until about 1740, when what remained of the ceremony was transferred to the Senate House.

The foundation-stone of the tower was laid in 1491, but funds came in very slowly, though the University diligently begged in all directions. About forty years after its commencement, namely, in 1530, it had but reached the level of the top of the west window. From that date its progress was still slower. The upper or belfry stage, which gave the tower a height of 131 feet, was at last taken in hand in 1593, and completed in 1608. The original design of a spire was never attempted.

On Easter Monday 1593 the elaborate system of electing wardens for Great St. Mary, Cambridge, resulted in the appointment of Richard Love and Richard Golsborows. At the same time it was entered that—

> The said Electors and all the other parishioners of this parish have named and appoynted Mr. Ball, Mr. Norkott, Mr. harvie, Mr. Poley, Mr. Wolfe, and Mr. Skarlett to go forwardes in the building and fynishinge of St. maries steple and to do their best indevor to procure things necessarie, And what they or any two of them shall do the whole parishe do promise to ratifie.

A subsequent entry stated that—

> The whole Sum of the money Received by one John Poley towards the bulding of greate St. maries Steple in Cambridg as yt dothe appear in anno 1593 and 1594 the Som of . . 179 li. 12s. 7d.

The several items of these contributions numbered 193. All sorts and conditions of men were among the donors. "Straungers whose names I colde not take" subscribed £11 11s. 10d. The Earls of Essex, Shrewsbury, and Rutland, the Bishop of Lincoln ("his Surname was Wickham"), aldermen of London and Bristol, and a variety of knights and squires of different counties were among the contributors; and so too were the "fellowes and scollers" of the colleges of Trinity, Christ's, King's, Emanuel, Gonville and Caius, Queen's, and Bennet's, together with aldermen, doctors, vintners, stationers, printers, tailors, joiners, shoemakers, and "Lychfielde barber of Trinite colledge."

The fullest details are supplied of the building accounts. "Fremasons" were paid at the rate of 14d. a day, "roughe masons" at 12d., and labourers at 8d. A large number of bricks were bought at 18d. the hundred. In June 1594 fifty-eight tons of "Asheler or freston from Ramsey" were purchased at 6s. 8d. the ton, including carriage to the Antelope. In August sixteen tons of stone were bought of the "quarrey man of Eversden" at 4s 8d. the ton. At the same time fourteen tons of "Ragge and ij Tonne of freston were

THE TOWER, GREAT ST. MARY, CAMBRIDGE
FROM AN OLD PRINT

purchased for 52s. 6d." Later in the year various other small quantities of stone were obtained from Eversden, and large freestone or ashlar from Thorney Abbey at 8s. the ton, as well as a large amount of rag at 4s. the ton.

Two other entries are worth citing, for they show the exceptional pains taken to secure subscribers:—

> Item paid for iij paste bords to make iij platformes of the Steple when we did gather for yt at the commensement . iij d.
> Item paid to a paynter for drawing of a plotform of St. maries Steple apon velam parchement for my Lorde archebyshopp of Caunterburie . . . . xviij d.

The earliest material used for roofing English churches was thatch; many thatched churches remain in Norfolk and Suffolk. The next most frequent use, at all events in wooded districts, was a covering of shingles, that is of thin pieces of oak forming small wooden tiles. These shingles are still in use as the covering of timber spires and wooden belfries in several parts of England; but the employment of shingles in other parts of the building has died out so rapidly with the last century that the nave of only a single old church, that of Tenterden, Sussex, remains thus roofed at the present day. Wardens' accounts simply abound with references to shingle roofing.

> 1550 (*St. Nicholas, Warwick*). Payd to the shyngler for shynglyng of the body off the churche in sertin places . . xiij d.
> To Thomas Harris for iij C. off nayles being occupyed in the same worke off shynglyng . . . . xviij d.
> 1568 (*Eltham, Kent*). Payments to Sylvester Page, the Shingler for the Reparations of the Church Steeple.
> Paid to Sylvester Page . . . . . iij li. iij s. iiij d.
> The like . . . . iij li. iij s. iiij d.
> Pd to Sylvester Page for 200 shingles . . . . vj s.
> Pd to Sylvester Page for 7 dayes work and 3 men xxxij s. viij d.

In addition to roofing with lead, baked tiles, and slates proper, thin slabs of stone, usually termed stone-tiles, were frequently used and are still employed in certain districts, as in Oxfordshire, Northamptonshire, Surrey, and Sussex. The following is an example of their use at Staplegrove, Somerset, in 1620:—

> For ix thousand ij hundred of healing stones from Huish iij li. vj s. iij d.

Flints for church walling were constantly used in East Anglia, Essex, parts of Wilts and Hants, and in other stoneless districts. For this purpose the flints were usually gathered from the surface of the soil. In the accounts of North Elmham, Norfolk, 1538–9, it is interesting to note that child labour was employed when the chapel of St. James was under repair.

>   To ye scolers for bred and drynk when they gathered stones   ij d.
> 1590 (*Exning, Suffolk*). Paid to Sparrow of Moulton the firste day of maye for gatheringe of ten lodes of flinte stones for the Church walls . . . . xxij d.

Priests' or clerks' chambers in towers, over vestries, and over porches were of fairly frequent occurrence. Especially were they provided in towns and cities for the convenience of the morrow-mass priest, who said the first mass often as early as five o'clock. The old church of St. Peter Cheap, destroyed in the Great Fire and never rebuilt, had a large vestry on the north side, abutting upon Cock Alley. This vestry was built by special benefactions in 1475, and had three upper chambers, which were apportioned to as many priests.

> 1519. Sr Wyllam Abee, Sr Thomas bostocke, Sr Rauffe Yonge, each a chamber.
> 1574. Off the Rent off the morowe masse preests chambre which is gevyn hym . . . . . vj s. viij d.
> 1533. The paryshe preest for hys chambre   vj s. viij d.
>   Syr Thomas Dybon for hys chambre . vj s. viij d.
>   Syr Wyllam the morrow masse preestys chambre   vj s. viij d.
> 1526–7 (*St. Mary-at-Hill*). For a Bedsted for the priestes chambre that kepeth the first mas . . . . . xiiij d.

Chambers over the porches—by an absolute misnomer often termed "parvis" or "parvise"—were undoubtedly constructed, as a rule, for the occupation of a priest, deacon, or sacristan, who acted as church-watcher.

> 1594–5 (*Ludlow*). For Tymbre for the Roofe of the deacons chambre over the churche porche . . . . . iij s.
> 1620. Pd to Roger Lea for setting up Thomas Hinde his bed in the Belfry, and for puttinge one barr into the olde grate . x d.

The repairing of the glazing of windows, and the supplying them with new pictures are of continual occurrence in the old

THE FABRIC OF THE CHURCH

parish accounts. Here are a few examples set out in chronological order:—

1385-6 (*Tavistock*). To repairing a glass window in the vestry . . . . . . vij s. iiij d. ob.
To making three figures in the vestry window xij d.
To six feet of new glass . . . . . vij s.
To eight feet of old glass . . . . iij s. iiij d.
To repairing three shutters (*cloturias*) to the great window in the end of the church . . . . ij d.
1447 (*St. Peter Cheap*). To the Glasyer for makynge of ij ymagies heds . . . . . . xij d.
1496 (*Walberswick, Suffolk*). By a gadering of the Wyvys in the Towne for a Glaswyndow . . . . . ix s.
1503-4 (*St. Mary-at-Hill*). To the glassyng of the gret wynddow wythe the Trenyte in the south yell . xxv s. iiij d.
1521-2 For settyng in of xxiij newe quarrelles in the wyndowe of the Trynyte whiche was blown downe with the wynde . xx d
1521 (*St. Margaret, Westminster*). To Symond Symonds for mendyng of the glass windows and the ymagery works that were broken with the grete wynds before Christmas ij li.
1539. To the glazier, in reward fro the parish, tooards the setting up of the Kinges armes and of my Lord Princes armes and of my Lord Privy Seals armes in the east window in the Trinity chapellee . . . . . x s.
1540. To Symon Symones glasier for making and setting up of divers armes in the Trinity chapell by the advice and commandement of Mr. Lancaster Herrold at armes x s.

A good deal of old glass suffered at the time of the Reformation, but the beautiful glass of the fine church of Ludlow, much of which remains to the present day, was not only spared, but from time to time repaired.

1550 (*Ludlow*). For mendynge of saynt Katherine wyndow vj s. viij d.
For mendynge of saynt Margetts wyndow . . xx d.
For ix fote of new glasse to the west wyndow vj s.
1581-2. Payd to Season for takinge downe the glasse and settinge it up agayne in the Weavers chauncell . . ij s. x d.
1592-3. For vj fete of new glasse . . . . . iij s.
For the making iiij foote of or owne glasse . . xij d.
For fourescore and thertene quarreys at j d. a quarel vij s. ix d.
For bonds for the glasse windowes and iij li. of leade . vj d.

Hardly anything was done during Elizabeth's long reign to

beautify the churches; contrariwise, for the most part they suffered severely, but occasionally blazoned arms were inserted in the windows.

> 1567-8 (*Tavistock*). For the quenes armes and my lord of Bedfords and for Setting of the same and for xxx quarrels sett at the same tyme . . . . . xv s. viij d.
> For master Fytz armes and for the Setting the armes and mendyng certyn quarrells att the same tyme . . x s. iiij d.
> 1570-1 (*St. Matthew, Friday Street*). For the new glasing of the windows in the Quire contayninge j'xli foote at 5d. ob. ye foote . . . . . iij li. iiij s. vij d. ob.
> For placeing of the armes in the quyre wyndows . iij s.
> For the quenes armes to sete in the quyar wyndow xiij s. iiij d.
> For the goldesmythes armes to seate in the same wyndow . x s.
> For the Salltars armes to seate in the same wyndow . viij s.

Instances are fairly frequent of substituting plain glass for coloured where Puritanism was in the ascendant.

It was ordered by the vestry of St. Edmund, Sarum, in 1629

> That Mr. Recorder may, if it please him, take down the windowe wherein God is painted in many places, as if he were there creating the world: so he doe in steed there of new make the same window with white glasse, for that the sayde window is somewhat decaied and broken, and is very darksome, whereby such as sitt neere to the same cannot see to reade in their bookes.

Henry Sherfield, the Puritanical Recorder, was not, however, satisfied with having the offending window removed after an orderly fashion, but publicly broke it with his staff by way of protest. For this offence he was punished by the Star Chamber—"Laud, who, though a disciplinarian, was strictly just, explaining that although sacred art might be within its province in depicting the humanity of Christ, it could not be defended in an attempt to represent the Father; yet, granting this, nothing could justify contempt."

A somewhat similar window had been mutilated about half a century earlier at St. Thomas, Sarum. The accounts of 1583-4 contain the following entry:—

> Hacker putting out the picture of the father in ye east windowe at Mr. subdeanes comandement . . . . . iiij d.

THE FABRIC OF THE CHURCH

In August 1641 the Puritans, "those poor withered souls" as Sir W. Richmond, R.A. justly styles them, in order to remove all that was fair and beautiful from the Houses of God, succeeded in inducing the Commons to insist upon "the taking away of all scandalous Pictures out of Churches." Soon afterwards one William Dowsing, an uncompromising and blatant iconoclast, was appointed parliamentary visitor of the Associated Eastern Counties. This miscreant and his agents dealt dire destruction to painted glass in many hundreds of churches. Dowsing left behind him a diary as to his evil progress, containing such entries as this pertaining to Gorleston, Suffolk :—

> We broke seven popish pictures in the chancel window, one of Christ, another of St. Andrew, another of St. James, etc. . . . A picture of St. George with divers pictures in the windows which we could not reach, neither would they help us to raise ladders, so we left a warrant with the constable to do it in 14 days.

We are content to give two instances from scores of wardens' accounts of this wave of desolation :—

1643 (*Toft Monks, Norfolk*). Laid out to Ruseles the Glaysher for taken Down of the painted Glase . . . . 1s. 6d.
1644 (*Lowick, Northants*). P for glasing the windowes when the Crucifixis and scandalus pictures was taken downe xij of July . . . . 12s.

The once prevalent notion that the whitewashing of the interior of churches was a debasing idea of post-Reformation origin can be easily refuted by record evidence from the time of the white-liming of the retroquire of Peterborough in 1190 down to numerous entries in sacrist rolls of the first half of the sixteenth century. Notwithstanding the abundance of good mural figure and design painting, there were frequently large surfaces in our parish churches which, from their uneven surface or from lack of funds, were treated, from time to time, with the whitewasher's brush.

In the 1394 accounts of St. Michael, Bath, full record is made of the whitewashing of the church both within and without (*tam infra qua ı extra*); the lime cost 12s. 4d.

1482-3 (*St. Edmund, Sarum*). Et sol' circa dealbacione pariet' capelle Sci Jobis Baptist ex una parte Chori ecclesie capiendo in toto . . . . . iiij s. iiij d.

1490 (*St. Dunstan, Canterbury*). Receyvid of the beqweth of Mother Bollyng to the whyte lymynge of the Churche vj s. viij d

Payde to Wyllyam Ingram a bargain penny for the whyte lymyng of our Churche . . . . j d.

Payde to the same Wyllyam for whyt lymyng of the Churche . . . . . . vj s. viij d.

Considerable sums were spent on galleries in the seventeenth century.

1641 (*St. Margaret, Westminster*). Worke about the new gallery (in all) . . . . . . £221 11s. 2d.

1670 (*Sidbury, Devon*). To John Shoulders for building ye gallery . . . . . . £10 9s. 3d.

CHAPTER VII

THE ALTAR AND THE EUCHARIST

Altars of St. Laurence, Reading—Diverse altar excerpts—The Pyx and cover—Communion Wines, excessive quantities—Nature of the Wines—Odious distinctions—The Holy Loaf—Wafer Bread—Cost of the Elements, St. Margaret, Westminster—Communions of the Commons—Communion Tokens—Number of Celebrations—Poor Folk and Sacrament Sundays—Processional Canopies—Houseling Cloths—Altar Rails—Altar Coverings

IT may be well to follow up the church-book entries as to altars in a single typical case.

The accounts of St. Laurence, Reading, beginning in 1410, name no fewer than twelve altars, but possibly they did not all exist at the same time. Those mentioned, in addition to the High Altar, are the altar of St. John Baptist in the north quire aisle, the altars of Jesus and Our Lady on either side of the chancel entrance, those of St. Blaise, St. Thomas, the Sepulchre, St. George, St. Nicholas, the Trinity, St. Clement, and one erected in the vestry in 1518. There are a variety of highly interesting entries relative to the High Altar.

 1503. Payed for whipcord to draw the blak cloth at sakeryng of masse . . . . j d.
 1508. Payed for a carpyntors lyne to draw the black sarsenet before the Sacrament at the Hy Auter [1] . j d.
 1510. Payed for a small lyne to hang the Kanape over the Hy auter . . . . j d.

In 1513 the "front" (probably the slab or *1 ensa*) of the High Altar was transferred to the altar in St. John's Chapel and a

[1] Mr. Kerry's note (p. 26) to this entry runs as follows: "It was a custom in the old English Church to draw a vail before the altar during the consecration of the elements, in accordance with the words: 'Eye hath not seen, nor ear heard, nor have entered into the heart of man to conceive the things which God hath prepared for them that love Him.'"

new High Altar stone erected at a cost of 14s. This involved the consecration of both.

> 1513. Payd to a Suffrygan for Halowyng of the High Awt', Seynt Johns awt', and a supaltare . . . . vj s. viij d.
> Payd to John Knyght for makyng crossis to the Hygh Awtar and other service . . . . . viij d.
> 1526. To the paynter for payntyng the transfiguracon over the hygh Awt' . . . . . . vj li. xiij s. iiij d.
> Rec' of dyvers persones towards the gyldyng and payntyng of the transfyguracon over the high aut' as by a byll it doth apere . . . . . . iiij li. xiij s. j d.
> To Robt Pasteler for making a skaffold and enlargeyng the High awt' . . . . . . iij s. iiij d.
> 1528. For enlargyng the Awt' clothes for the hygh Awt' with all man' of stuff therto belongyng . . . xxij s. ix d.

In 1548 the High Altar was bought by Mr. Bell for 6s. 8d., but when Mary came to the throne there is a 1553 entry:—

> Paid for making of the high Awt' and paving in the churche . xij s.

The irreverent Puritanism of Elizabeth's days finds due entrance in the accounts.

> 1560. For dressyng the high alter and the wall beneth and the bourdes where the altar stode . ij s. viij d.
> 1568. To Martyn Woodnett for makinge of the Frame for the comunion table . . . . . . xxij d.
> To Edmund Paynter for colloringe of ye same . iij d.
> 1569. To the joynor for makyng the comunion table and benches, with a doore . . . . . iiij s.

There was a return to the old position in the Laudian days.

> 1638. Pd to the jynor for making the new and mendinge the oulde winscotte above the comunion table . £1 1s.
> 1638. One velvet cover for the Com' Table with silke fringe of the gift of Mrs. Saunders £8
> One velvet quisheon and a booke of Comon prayer gilt for the Com' Table of the gift of James Read and Mr. Henry £3

There are many entries relative to the numerous subsidiary altars of the church, especially those of the Lady Mass and the Jesus Mass, and the one in St. John's Chapel. The 1524 inventory gives lists of the vestments and ornaments pertaining to each. All these altars were destroyed in 1547, and the slabs or *mensæ* sold for two or three shillings.

The chief altars were re-established and hallowed under Queen Mary.

M^d that in the yere of our lorde 1557 and the iij^d and iiijth yers of the reignes of our Souveraigne lord and lady Phillipp and Marye by the grace of God Kyng and Quene of England, etc., the Second Day of May beyng Sonday, Willm Fynche Suffrigan unto the Bisshoppe of Bathe and welles hath hallowed the churchyarde of the p'rishe of Saynt Laurence in Redyng. And also the same day and yere hath hallowed in the seid p'rishe fyve awters of stone, that site with the High Awter of Saynt Laurence; in the chauncell next called St. Johns Chauncell one awter called Saynte Johns Alter: in the body of the churche the myddell alter ther called Jesus Alter: in the South syde ther one Alter called our ladye Awter of the Nativitie: and in the north side ther one Awter called Saynt Thomas Awter.

The following are selected as brief examples of various altar references elsewhere :—

    1448 (*Yatton*). Vor lyme to wassche the awterys . . ij d.
    1495 (*Ibid.*). For makyng of an awter to Thomas Cotyng . vj s. viij d.
    For a stone to hale (cover) the auter . . . . ij s.
    1474-6 (*St. Margaret, Westminster*). For an auter cloth of Golde . iij li.
    To Robert Nevill for makyng of thaut' cloth and frontell . xx d.
    For frenges for ye same frontell . . . ij s. iiij d.
    1493-4 (*St. Mary-at-Hill*). For makyng of the crossys on the superaltarys . . . . iiij d.
    1554 (*Stanford, Berks*). Rec of henry Snodam gent for a tabull w^t a frame ye whiche served in ye churche for ye comunion in the wycked tyme of sysme [pen struck through last six words] . . . . v s.

The English use of placing the Reserved Sacrament in a pyx or box suspended above the high altar is fully treated of in *English Church Furniture*, 39-45. The reference to the cords for suspending the pyx are very frequent in wardens' accounts.

    1491 (*St. Edmund, Sarum*). For a corde to fastene the sacrament   iij d.
    1510-1 (*Ashburton, Devon*). For a cord to hang the pyx . . iij d.

Above the pyx was usually a small canopy with a fringe, of which a solitary example remains at Hessett, Suffolk.

1507 (*Tintinhull*). For makynge of a frenge with bottyns and
tassels to a kerchew to hang over the sakerment   ij s. viij d.
1554 (*Yatton*). For yᵉ nette clothe ower yᵉ pyxe . . xviij d.
For tassells for ye pyxk . . . . . ij d.
1555. For ye pyxe and palle cloth for ye same   xx s. viij d.

Communion Wine

The amount of wine consumed at Celebrations in post-Reformation days—even after making allowance for the large number of communicants in times when absence was, alas, penalised in various ways—is most startling. The conclusion is inevitable that there must often have been peculation in connection with such returns by the wardens and their allies.

1561 (*St. Peter Cheap*). For breade and one gallon of wyne the
25 day of October for cviii comunycants .   j s. ix d.
[In this year there were also, on 19th July, 68 communicants; at Christmas, 96; 2nd February, 56; Easter Day, 112.]
For a pynte of wyne 13 daye of Aprill for xxij comunycants
at the marriage of Gabriel newman . ij d.
1562. For Bread, and wyne for clxvij comunicants xjᵗʰ of Aprill
1562-3 (*St. Martin, Leicester*). Payd for wyne for the Communeon
at Estur iij quartes of mamse and ix quartes of claret
wyne . . . . iiij s. vj d.
1590 (*Exning, Suffolk*). Paid for bread and a gallonde of
Malmesye agaynste Easter Daye . . iiij s. iiij d.
For a quarte of wine and bread agayn marndye Thur. for
the communion . . . . . . xij d.
For iij pintes of wine and for bread agaynste ester evene   xix d. ob.
For a quarte of wyne and bread agayn the sondaye after
ester . . . . xij d.
For a pynte of wyne and for breade agaynste trinitie
sondaye . . . . vij d.
1591. Inprimis for a pint of muscadine and for breade agaynste
the sondaye before easter . . . . vij d.
Item for iij pintes of muscadine and for breade agaynste
marnde thursdaye . . . . . xx d.
Item for a pottell of malmeseye againste ester evene and
for breade . . . . ij s. ij d.
1605 (*St. Mary, Reading*). For our Easters Comunions for
Wine . . . . . . xiiij s. vjd.
For 25 quartes and a pinte of wine for the monthelie Communione . . . xxj s. iij d.

1614 (*St. Mary, Reading*). For xlij quartes of muskydine and a pinte at xjd. the quarte . xxxviij s. xj d. ob.

1617. For lvij quartes of muskidine for the monthlie Comunion . . . . . . liij s. lij d.

The amount expended on wine at Hartland, Devon, although it was a wide and fairly populous parish, was amazing. In 1614 twelve gallons and a quart of Canary wine were bought "against Easter," at 9d. a quart, amounting to £1 16s. 9d.

The most scandalous case of excess of wine, purporting to be for the Easter Communion, is that of St. Neots, Cornwall. In 1618 the charge is 34s., and in 1619 35s. 7d.; the quantity is not stated, but the usual price at that period, judging from other accounts, was 6d. a quart. But this extravagance was far surpassed after the Restoration. In 1664 ten gallons of sack for Easter Communion were purchased at £2 3s. 4d. Under 3rd May 1695 comes the following entry:—

We have examined this account, but finding that the 23 quarte of wine which was provided for the comunion at Easter to be soe exceedingly bad and that the churchwardens have charged 2s. 4d. for each quart of it, whereas the wine was not really worth 12d. a quart. However wee are contented to deduct out of the superfluous charge only 13s. 9d. for the whole.

1625 (*Beccles, Suffolk*). Paid to nathainyell Browne and Abraham Tood for xxxviij quarts of muskdine for ye Comuneon ye Sonday after Ester; xxiij quarts from Browne at xij d. ye quarte and xiiij quarts Todds at xiiijd. ye quart xl s. iiij d.
[On Easter Day 33 quarts of muskadine had been supplied.]

1679 (*Wirksworth, Derbyshire*). Paid to Edward Millond for 31 quarts of wine at 14d. a quart for 4 Comunion Days £1 16s. 2d.

1694 (*Ibid.*). Paid for 18 quarts of wine for Michaelmass and Christmas Coms . . . . . . £1 9s.

As to the wines most usually named in wardens' accounts, in addition to claret—*Malmsey*, a strong, sweet wine, first made in Greece; *Muscadel* or *Muskadine* (spelt variously), a rich, sweet-smelling wine from Spain, and corresponded in some respects to *Tent*, the usual Communion wine of the early Victorian period; *Bastard*, a sweet red wine from Spain and Corsica, usually mixed, hence the name; *Sack*, the name given to any Spanish white wine, and equivalent to sherry; *Canary*, or Canary Sack, a superior white wine from the Canary Isles and from Malaga.

A most odious distinction was made in a few churches, notably at Salisbury, whereby the well-to-do were supplied with the luscious and more expensive wine, and the ordinary folk with the lighter and cheaper claret.

1573-4 (*St. Edmund, Sarum*) Mrs Smallam wyne 22s. 9d., and bought besydes for v^e masters and Mrs. 7 pintes of muscodal . . . . 2s. 4d.

1629. It is ordered that the Churchwardens shall provide Muscadine only for the wine at the Comunions, and shall not provide any more Claret wine for that use.

Holy Loaf

Entries as to Holy Loaf are of continuous occurrence. As to the accounts of Sutterton, Lincolnshire, Mr. Peacock says:—

"This year (1512) the wardens bought 'ij holybred maundes' (baskets) for 10d. This is an additional proof, if proof on such a matter is needed, that the holy bread or eulogiæ was almost universally distributed in this country before the Reformation. . . . This holy loaf had nothing whatever to do with the eucharistic elements, but was ordinary unleavened bread, such as was commonly eaten in the parish, which was blessed by the priest after he had said Mass, cut into small pieces, and given to the people to eat. When the custom originated, it is perhaps hardly safe to affirm. It was intended as a symbol of the brotherly love which ought to exist among Christians. . . . One of the demands of the Devonshire men, when they broke out into rebellion in 1549, for the purpose of resisting the changes in faith and ritual, was that they should have 'holy bread and holy water every Sunday.' The holy bread was distributed as long as the old services continued in use. Baskets for containing it are mentioned several times among the things removed as 'monuments of superstition' from the Lincolnshire churches, 8 Elizabeth."[1]

To this clear statement on a matter so constantly misunderstood and wrongly described, it may be added that the cost of providing and baking the weekly holy loaf was imposed in some parishes on certain landholders in rotation; that in other parishes

[1] See also interesting depositions as to providing Holy Bread at St. Oswald's, Durham, in *Surtees Society Proceedings*, vol. xxi.

THE ALTAR AND THE EUCHARIST

it was always baked in the Church-house (sometimes called, as at St. Michael, Bath, the " Holybrede House "), and the cost defrayed by a definite gathering; that the name and not the reality lingered in many places right through Elizabeth's reign, and even later; and that the gathering, when continued, was used for providing bread, and in some cases wine, for the Holy Communion.

A sufficient number of excerpts are given from wardens' accounts to establish these various points:—

1511 (*St. Edmund, Sarum*). Pro uno Coffane ad portandum et imponendum panem Sanctificatum . . . . v d.

c. 1538 (*Bolney*). Thys be the Hole breds of the parysh of Bolney
John Bolney pays for Blast Wayseld and v acres of land   iij
Holybreds, ii s. iiij d. ob. for taper and treyndell.
William Lang for iij lands pays iij holybred.
John Gratwek pays for on land on holebred.
Hari Costredell pays for Wylvorn land on holy bred.
Myderd Byrtynshaw for Barnards land pays on holy bred.
John Dunstall on holy bred.
[Followed by 41 other payers of holy bred.]

1537 (*St. Alphege, London Wall*). For the holy bread baskett . iiij d.

1542-3 (*Tintinhull, Somerset*). Rec' of the increase (surplus) of the holy loffe . . . . . . iiij s. iij d.

1551 (*St. Laurence, Reading*). It was concludid and agreed that from hensforthe every inhabitant of the p'sche shall bere and pay every Sonday in the yere v d. for every tenement as of old tyme the Holy Lofe was used to be paid and be received by the p'sche clark wekely, the seid clark to have every Sonday for his paynes 1d. And iiij d. residewe to be paied and delyvered every Sonday to the churchwardens to be employed for bred and wyne for the communyon. And if any overplus therof shall be, of suche money so received to be to the use of the churche; and if any shall lacke, to be borne and paied by the seid churchwardens; provided allwey that all such persons as ar poore and not able to pay the whole, be to have Ayde of such others as shall be thoughte good, by the discrecon of the Church-warden.

1555. Rec' of money gathered for the holy lofe . ix s. iiij d.
1560 (*Melton Mowbray*). For ye holly lof v sondays in lent . xvj d.
1588. Recevid for the holye loffe for lxij days at iiij d. the daye xx s. viij d.

Entries under the head of "The holy Loafe" occur in the Mere, Wilts, accounts up to 1590, and were then continued for some years after a like fashion, but under the head of "The Comunion bread."

> 1585.—Item receyved of Robte Goodyn for the rent of the holy loafe over and above iij d. wch the Bedman yearly hath accustomably receyved to his owne use on Easter day . xij s. ix d.
>
> 1591. Item receyved of Robte Gowdden for the rent of the Comunion bread this yeare over and above iij d. gyven the bedman for collecting the same as in the yeare before . . . . . . xij s. ix d.

The Holy Loaf appears in the St. Mary, Reading, accounts from 1564 to 1618. The cessation of this entry coincides with the imposition of a penny from each communicant for the elements. It was agreed in that year that every householder should pay 2d. "for the holle Loffe every yere according to the Olde Custome."

The belief that the use of wafers at the Communion was forbidden at the Reformation is a common blunder; the exact contrary is the truth. In 1549 it was ordered that the Eucharistic Bread was to be "throughout the realm after one sort and fashion, unleavened, round as it was before, but without all manner of fruit."

In Queen Elizabeth's Inquisitions it is ordered that the sacramental bread shall be of the same fineness and fashion, though somewhat bigger in compass and thickness, as the usual bread and wafer heretofore named singing cakes, which served for the use of the private mass."

"Houseling bread" was the smaller form of wafer for the communion of the people; "singing bread" (so called from the chanting with which its manufacture used to be accompanied) was the larger or priest's wafer.

Wafer bread was used by Archbishop Parker, and its use was maintained at Westminster Abbey up to 1643.

The evidence from wardens' accounts as to the use of wafer breads throughout Elizabethan and Stuart times is overwhelming; it may also be remarked that the paten-covers of the Elizabethan chalices were obviously made for wafers. Five quotations must suffice:—

> 1549 (*St. Mary Redcliffe*). To a pair of wafer Irons . iij s. iiij d.
> 1565 (*Wimborne*). Singing bread . . . . . ij d.

1573 (*Redenhall, Norfolk*). Payde for wafer breade . viij d.
1579 (*Eltham*). Paide unto John Browne for wafers for ye Comunion . . . . vj d.
1597 (*Worksdp*). For ij hundrethes and a halfe of Comunion breades or wafers . . . . . . xv d.
[We have found " wafer irons " included in several Jacobean church inventories.]

Various difficulties arose in the Elizabethan and subsequent days as to the cost of the Elements.

1575 (*Spelsbury*). Yt ys agreed by the worshipfull and all the pryshoners there that every comunicant within the paryche shall gyve one ob. (farthing) to by bred and wyne for the blessed Comunion, not only agaynst Easter, but to serve for every monthe in ye yere for ye same purpose, as yt ys there ministered and receyved ; and that every howse holder shall answer and pay for all those that be within hys howse, and ye tythyng man within every towne and village shall gether or take up the same sume of every hose boulder, and the same so gethered or taken shall withoute delay delyver the same unto the churchwardens for that tyme beyng ; and they to provyde for bred and wyne at all tymes as ys before named. And further yt ys agrede that yf any house holder denye to paye for all ye comunicants within hys howse that then the sayde tythyngman shall strayne for the same sum, and the stresse so taken shall cari and beare awaye and make saile thereof for so much as ye summe comyth to in that howse, and ye stress to kepe tyll yt be anncered.

Meanwhile it was found that this compulsory levy of a farthing from each communicant did not suffice to supply the materials for the Celebration, and at a parish meeting in 1580 it was resolved that every communicant was to pay an annual halfpenny for this purpose, that the tithingman was to collect the sum from house to house on or before Mid-Lent Sunday, and that if any person made default they were not to " receyve the Sacrament untill they have discharged the same."

The " Paschall money at Easter" occurs in the St. Mary, Reading, accounts for 1557, and continues under the one word " Paschall" until 1598. The paschal taper continued to be made for the first two years of Elizabeth. In 1599 the entry " Communion at Easter " begins to take the place of Pascall. The sum raised under this head paid for the Elements at the Easter Communion. The surplus was divided between the vicar and the wardens' fund.

1601 (*Berkhamstead*). Mem^d it is now concluded upon and agreed by the minister, churchwardens, and the rest of the Vestrie that all single communycants shall paye for ever hereafter towardes the charge of the bread and wine at Easter for evrie of themselves 1d., and the rest of the parishioners accordinge to theire abillyties.

1625 (*Pittington, Durham*). That for the provision of bread and wine every communicant shall pay one penny to the churchwardens, and that every maister of the family shall pay for himself, wife, children, and servants.

1663 (*St. Thomas, Sarum*). Every person rated to the poor to pay for himself wife and children and apprentices that are fit to use the Sacrament a groat apiece besides a convenient allowance for bread and wine.

A special interest attaches itself to the subjoined excerpts, and their phraseology, from the accounts of the important church of St. Margaret, Westminster.

1502. For a brekefaste upon Ester day for them wch helpen the pepull to be husleth . . . . . ij s. iiij d.
1538. For matts for the parishioners to kneel upon when they reverenced their Maker . . . . iiij s. iiij d.
1548. For bread, ale, and wyne for the gentlemen and children of the Kings chapel for their paynes in helping of the divine service at the blessed communion on our Ladys day in Lent . . . . ij s. xj d.
1620. For 14 loads of gravel laid into the churchyard against the comunion of the lower house of parliament . xvij s. viij d.
1625. Rec. of the Commons House of Parliament when they took the Comunion on July 3rd xlvij li. v s. viij d.
1627. For bread and wine when the Commons (being 468 persons) received the Comunion in 1626 . . . . £5 17s.

It has usually been supposed that the objectionable custom of supplying tokens as a warrant of admission to Holy Communion was a post-Reformation device. The following entries, however, from the accounts of St. Martin's-in-the-Fields prove that it was of earlier origin, but probably of quite exceptional occurrence:—

1535. Received and gathered for the howsellyng tokens in the Churche . . . . . . xiij s. vij d.
1540. Receved and gathered on Ester daye in the church for hoslyng tokons . . . . . . x s.
1542. Receyvyd on Ester day for howseling tokyns . xxxj s.

In the next two years, receipts under this head exceeded 40s. In post-Reformation days the custom was firmly established,

THE ALTAR AND THE EUCHARIST

in the parishes of St. Thomas and St. Edmund, Sarum, of each communicant, on some day in the week preceding the Celebration, notifying his intention to the clerk and receiving a metal token. One halfpenny was paid to the churchwardens at the time of communicating, when the token was given back. These sums are sometimes entered as "halfpence for monthly communion." A steel die was used to strike these tokens, which were sometimes of brass, but more usually of lead. The following entries occur, *inter alia*, in these two Sarum accounts:—

    1572–3. Altering of the stampe and strikinge of ye tokens .   6d.
    1573–4. Alteringe yᵉ stampe and strikinge of the tokens .   6d.
    1574–5. Alteringe of the stampe and strykinge of the Tokens   6d.
    1575–6. Gravinge the stampe . . . . .   4d.
    1622–3 (*St. Edmund*). Tokens to deliver to the Comunicantes   12d.
    1641. Comunicants that pay to the relief of the poor and are able to do so, to pay 2d. each time they come, or send for tokens in order to their receiving the Lordes supper
    1651–2. Brasse Tokens and for a Box to put them in and Two steele stamps . . . . . . 18s. 2d.

The following brief extracts give other instances of this town use:—

    1559 (*St. Michael, Worcester*). For ledd and makyng of tokens at Easter. . . . . vj d.
    1583 (*St. James, Bristol*). Paid for tokans to deliver to the howselynge people at Easter. . . . . vj d.
    1628 (*Sidbury, Devon*). For twoo hundred of tokens   x d.

The most remarkable and detailed evidence of the use of Communion tokens are the returns for the years 1619, 1620, and 1621 of St. Saviour's, Southwark. The book for 1619 begins with Winchester House, ten tokens being obtained by Sir Charles Montagu, Bart.; then follows Rochester House, and afterwards all the streets and "rents" of the parish; the number of tokens issued was 1489. In 1621 they amounted to 1722, and in 1622 to 1936. Communion tokens were very largely used in Scotland in Presbyterian and in some Episcopalian churches. See Wood's *Scottish Pewter Ware*, pp. 106–21; they were first introduced in 1560.

In post-Reformation days the number of Celebrations were usually surprisingly few, but opportunities for communicating were often multiplied at Eastertide. At Holy Trinity, Cambridge, there were Celebrations on Palm Sunday, Maundy Thursday, Easter Eve, Easter Day, Easter Monday, and Low Sunday.

In 1585 at Staplegrove, Somerset, there were eight Celebrations, namely, on Palm Sunday, Maundy Thursday, Easter Eve, Easter Day, May, August, All-Hallowtide, and Christmas Day.

At Seal, Surrey, in 1588, there were only three Celebrations, namely, at Easter, All-Hallows, and Candlemas. In 1589 like provision was only made at Easter and Hallowtide, and in 1590 merely for the one great feast of Easter. The accounts of 1591 include the quantity of wine purchased. In 1592, and for several subsequent years, the Communion was administered at Candlemas, Easter, Midsummer, Hallowtide, and Bartholomewtide; but in 1609 there was a new departure, Palm Sunday being added to the list. In 1618 there were administrations on Palm Sunday, Easter Eve, and Easter Sunday, and in 1634 and 1639 on Good Friday.

There were daily Celebrations of the Holy Communion in the church of St. Oswald, Durham, in 1610, from Palm Sunday to Easter Day inclusive, when a total of 34 quarts of wine were supplied at 8d. the quart. The following year 31 quarts were supplied for a like period, and 33 quarts in 1613.

The bread and wine at the Communion cost the parish of Holy Cross, Canterbury, £1 4s. 4d. for the year 1698; it was only administered four times a year. In 1718 there were the like number of administrations; fifteen pints of tent were bought at 2s. a pint, and the bread cost 8d.

Kindly provision was now and again made, at the expense of the rates, for poor folk attending church from a distance on "Sacrament Sundays."

 1676 (*Leek, Staffs*). P^d 7 dinners on Sacrament dayes   7s.
 1766 (*Hayfield, Derbyshire*). P^d for two mens Dinners 3 Sacrament Days . . . .   3s.

Canopies over the Reserved Sacrament when carried in procession were naturally objects upon which much cost and art were expended. The two great days for such processions were the festivals of Palm Sunday and Corpus Christi. The latter was by far the most important, for on that occasion the procession traversed the main streets or roads of the town or village, instead of merely going round the churchyard.

1475-6 (*St. Edmund, Sarum*). Costs of the new portable Canape.
Paied for ij yerds di and j nayle of Satyn to the same   xxij s.
Paiede for iiij unce j quart of selken frenge to the same . v s. ij d.
In iij Ellys of Garnesey cloth to the same .   .   .   xx d.
In iij yerdes of purpul Velvet to the same   .   xlviij s.

1515-6 (*Holy Trinity, Cambridge*). The Costes and Charges of
the Canopy.
Furst vij yardis dim of Blake velvet the prise of a yard
ix s. vj d.   .   .   .   .   .   .   iij li. xj s. iij d.
For the valance iij yardis dim and halfe quartum Cremesyne
velvet   .   .   .   .   .   .   xlj s. iij d.
For the ymage of the Trinitie with xiiij Chales (chalices)
for the same   .   .   .   .   .   xxxiij s. vj d.
For xvij unces dim of fring to the same   .   xvij s.
For vj yardis of Bakeram for the lyneyng .   .   iij s.
For makyng of the Canopy .   .   .   .   . v s. iiij d.
                Summa   x li. vij s. vij d.
For mendyng and payntyng of the frame and iiij staves   ij s. vij d.
For a dosen silke poyntes   .   .   .   .   .   xv d.
For haspis and staplis for the same frame .   viij d.
For Cariage home from London of the Canopy   .   vj d.
For twys Rydyng to London, horse mete and mans mete
and horse hyre   .   .   .   .   .   vj s. viij d.
To Robert Taylore   .   .   .   .   .   .   xx d.
To Richard Rolfe   .   .   .   .   .   .   viij d.
       Summa totalis alloc'   . xiij li. xv s. ix d.

When chancel screens were the invariable rule of the Church of England, there was no need for altar rails, so far as keeping dogs and other profanities at a distance was concerned. It was probably always the custom to place kneeling benches for the infirm or aged communicants, and thereon would be placed the white linen houseling cloths, which were otherwise held by clerks at the time of the laity's communion. Only a single pre-Reformation example need be given:—

1546 (*Ashburton, Devon*). For x yards of linen for towels called
housslyng cloths   .   .   .   .   .   .   xx d.

The use of the houseling cloth has been of late years restored in several churches; it is said never to have died out at Wimborne minster. In many places it survived the Reformation, as is evident from the long towels mentioned in various Elizabethan and seventeenth-century inventories, and also by direct evidence, of which the following entries are examples:—

    1602 (*St. Botolph, Cambridge*). Two Lyninge Towells for the Chancell at Comunion tymes . . . .
    1617 (*St. Margaret, Westminster*). For twenty yards of diaper towelling for the desks . . . . j li. iij s. iiij d.

That the large majority of English churches had altar rails in Elizabethan or early seventeenth-century days has been completely established in *English Church Furniture*, pp. 17–9, and the statements need not be here repeated. The earliest wardens' accounts entry as to altar rails, hitherto noticed, occurs in 1574 at Hawkhurst, Kent.

    For makyng the partycyon of the chauncell lower and makyng the Rayles about the place of the Comunyon Table   liij s. vj d.

A 1602 inventory of St. Bartholomew Exchange names "certayne *ould*, Rayles that have stood aboute the Comunion Table." This phrase is repeated year by year up to 1611. At St. Mary, Reading, "a *newe* rayle about the Comunion table" was erected in 1635 at a cost of £6 10s., clearly showing that these rails succeeded an older set. Altar rails were provided at St. Werburgh, Bristol, in 1620.

The use of forms and other conveniences for communicants are illustrated by the subjoined excerpts:—

    1550-1 (*St. Edmund, Sarum*). The leggyng of a Forme to serve for people when the do receyd the Comunyon . j d.
    1622-3. Joyner for a Seven foote of Brackettes to mend the place to kneele uppon at the Comunion beinge made to narrow at firste . . . . 2s. 6d.
    xl yards of newe matt for the Comunicauntes to kneele uppon   5s.
    1626. That furmes be provyded for the comunicantes to knell at in the Quire . . . .
    1560 (*Ludlow*). For a planke to knele upon at the communyon tabulle . . . . iiij d.
    1566-7 (*St. Mary Woolnoth*). For a borde of tenne foote long for the bench to kneel on before the Comunyon table   ij d.
    1593-4 (*St. Martin, Leicester*). Payd to goodman Kyrke for ij mats for the formes to the Communion table . . viij d.
    1603 (*Wimborne*). For fotestoles in the quier about the Communion Table . . . .

THE ALTAR AND THE EUCHARIST

1625 (*St. Mary, Cambridge*). For 18 yardes of Matt for the parishioners to kneele on at the Comunion . . . iiij s. vj d.

1638 (*All Saints, Derby*). For mattinge and rushes in ye chancell to kneele on . . . . 5s. 3d.

The visitation by Archbishop Laud of his province in 1633 brought about the restoration of rails in several puritanical churches whence they had been ejected or never erected, and caused the position of others to be changed so as to run north and south straight across the chancel.

1635 (*All Saints, Derby*). Pd Mr. Aderly for Raile about ye Comunion table . . . . . . £2 6s. 8d.
Given Frierson for Henges and for Cariage of ye Raile to ye Church . . . . 3s. 3d.

1636 (*Cratfield, Suffolk*). For setting up the rails in the Chancell £2
For fetching of the rails from Laxfield . . . 3s. 4d.

In 1641 Parliament took upon itself to forbid altar rails; but the order was at first disregarded in the loyalist half of England.

1646-7 (*St. Thomas, Sarum*) Rec^d for ye railes about ye Comunion table . . . . 17s. 6d.

Once removed, altar rails were not readily resupplied in out-of-the-way or poorly supervised districts. In his visitations of 1703-4 of the diocese of Carlisle, Bishop Nicholson found 35 unrailed chancels.

The following illustrate the occasional care taken to provide good coverings for the Holy Table in the seventeenth century:—

1608 (*St. Margaret, Westminster*). Bought a cloth of gold and a cushion for the comunion table and a cushion for the pulpit . . . . xx li.

1624 (*Seal, Surrey*). P^d for three yeards of Cloyth for the Comunion Table and Pulpit at iij s. vj d. per yeard . . x s. vj d.
Pd for the greene frindge for them . . iij s. iij d.
P^d for makinge them . . . . . . iij d.

1628-9 (*St. Martin, Leicester*). For 4 yards the quarter and halfe quarter of broad cloth at xij s. vj d. ye yard for a carpett cloth for the Comunion table . . liiij s. x d.
For fringe and silke . . . . . xxvij s. iij d.
For making of the Comⁿ Carpett cloth . . . xij d.

CHAPTER VIII

BOOKS

MS. Service Books—Bassingbourn inventory—Binding—Printed Books—Caxton's *Golden Legend*—Reformed Service Books—The Commonwealth Directory—The Homilies—The Bible—Erasmus' Paraphrase—Foxe's *Martyrs*—Jewel's Works—Chained Books—Other Books

THE early book entries of St. Michael, Bath, are interesting. Thus in 1349, William de Wyke bequeathed 2s. towards a missal; 2d. was paid for a skin to bind it; and 46s. 2d. was the full cost of the missal. In 1370, 5s. was paid for binding books, and 13d. for sheepskins and thread. A breviary cost £1 3s. 4d. in 1371; and a processional 5s. 11d. in 1426, of which 5s. 1½d. was collected towards the purchase. A manual was bought at Bristol, in 1439, for 16s. 8d.; an additional 18d. being spent on two men riding to fetch the book.

The following entries serve as reminders of the prices of the old service books:—

1401-2 (*Tavistock*). A new missal for the church . iiij li. xiij s. iiij d.
1442 (*Thame*). For a manuel . . . . . x s. vj d.
1474-6 (*St. Margaret, Westminster*). For ij grett Bokes called Antiphoners . . . . xxij li.
1484 (*St. John, Peterborough*). Solut' Dno Johni Crowland pro scripto unius libri de servicio bte Marie . xxiij s. ij d.
1485 (*St. Dunstan, Canterbury*). Payde to the prest of Amery for owr Antifyner . . . . . liij s. iiij d.
Payd to Syr Rychard Lang for owr Massebooke . xl s.
1499 (*St. Margaret, Westminster*). To Thom Herte xx s. in parte of payment of xl s. for the makyng writtyng notyng lumynyng byndyng and for the stuffe of iij newe festis that is to sey, the visitacion of our ladi, de nomine Jhu and transfiguracion of our lorde, that is to witte in v antiphoners and a legende, iiij graelles, iiij masse bokes and iiij processionares . . . . . . xx s.

INVENTORY, WARDENS' ACCOUNTS; ST. MARGARET, NEW FISH STREET, 1472

INVENTORY, WARDENS' ACCOUNTS; ST. MARGARET, NEW FISH STREET, 1472
(CONTINUED)

The 1472 inventory of St. Edmund, Sarum, shows that the church possessed a large number of service books. There were 5 missals, 9 grayles (the mass music), a gospeler, an epistoler, 4 breviaries, 6 antiphoners (music for the canonical hours), 14 processionals, 2 legends (book of the lessons for mattins), "J newe grete legant bought by the church godes called a Temperall" (the lessons from Advent to Trinity), a collection or book of short lessons, a dirge book, a psalter, an ordinal or collection of rubrical directions, a book of the lives of the Saints (*Legenda Aurea*), and "J boke for the organes."

Another most interesting item of this list is: "Hugucon y chaynyd in our lady Chapell." This volume was also chained in the lady chapel of All Saints, Derby. It was the *Vocabularium* of Hugutio of Pisa, a book never printed, but fairly frequent in manuscript. An admirable book of reference.[1]

It is singular to note that there is no mention of a manual, the book of occasional services, in the 1472 list. Its omission must be accidental, for no church could possibly be destitute of at least one copy of this essential service book. A subsequent entry, of 1482–3, tells of the binding of a manual.

Bishop Beauchamp secured in 1456 the canonisation of Osmund the founder of the cathedral church of Old Sarum. In 1472 a special indulgence was granted by Pope Sixtus IV to all penitents visiting St. Osmund's shrine on 17th July, the day of his festival. The authorities of St. Edmund's bought parchment and caused the life of St. Osmund to be engrossed thereon in 1474, doubtless to read to the congregation and thus further the cause of the cathedral pardon. The accounts of 1474–5 name this and also supply interesting particulars relative to the binding and care of the service books.

1474–5. In pergamento empto ad inscribendam Historiam Sci Osmundi . . . . xvij d.
In scripture Sequenc' Sci Osmundi . iiij d.

In 1479 a further copy of the life of St. Osmund was made for the same church, apparently for use in the Lady Chapel.

[1] See Mr. Albert Way's Preface to the *Promptorium Parvulorum*, p. xxiii.

Item paid for viij quayres of Velum bought to write the Visitacion of our Lady and Seynt Osmand stories to the use of the Church . . . . vj s.
Item paid to Sir John Odlond for wrytyng of the same ingrosse . . . . v s.
1475-6. Paid for a boke called a Sentenciall for the use of the church. . . . . xxj d.
[The Greate Sentence, or commination of sinners, ordered to be read on 1st Sunday in 'Advent, 1st Sunday in Lent, Sunday after Whitsuntide, and Sunday after the Assumption.]
1477-8. Sol' pro uno libro vocato a legende empto ad usum ecclesie   xl s.

The full inventory of church goods of 1498 in the wardens' accounts of the country parish of Bassingbourn, Cambs, is of much interest in the book entries. It has not hitherto been printed.

Item iij messbokes one off the gifte of Ric hychen late of Bass' with Claspes of sylver over giltid. Item the ijth of the gifte of parson Goldburne sometym parson of the seid Bass' as it is expressid in the seid mess book bitwixt the prefacis and the canon that he gaff it. Item the thyrdde a lesser than any of the ij with the prefacis canon and sequences in newe quayeres wrytten. Item be yt remembrid the said Masboke of Ric hychen gyfte hasse a Rigestir pynne of sylver and over gyltid with regesteries of sylk.

Item ij Masse bokes of printe yat one of William lyon geft and ye other of Thomas Bolnest geft and agn' his moder.

Item an other masbok havyng ye colet of Saint Andre in ye hend of ye bok.

Item iij Gradualles one of the gift of Katar Bolnest somtyme the wiff of Thomas Bolnest as it showith in the begynyng of the booke of the giff'r thereof. Item the seconde of a lesser volume with viij bolsteres of latayne. Item the thirde of the gyft of parsone goldeburne bifor spokyn of as it showith in the seyd Grad' in the leefe betwixe the observances of Buryinge and the fest of seynt Andrewe.

Item a graylle with ye serves of ye vycytacion of our lady in ye begyning of ye boke.

Item a Cowcher of the gifte of one Thomas Bolnest and Katar' his wyffe as it is expressid in the said cowcher aftir the sawtyr in the next leefe befor the Derige. Item a Portays with sylver Claspis of the gift of Mr. Ric' Caudry somtym parson of Bass' as it shewithe in the seyde book for the nexte leeffe before the Comune of the Apostelles with his Armes their pyctured.

Item iij othir Bookes of the seyd parson gift as it shewithe in the sayd Portays that is to saye j antiphonare with newe quayres of the Chaptures Colettes of the hole yer with the fest of Corpus Christi and Seynt Anne next bifor ye Fest of seynt Andrewe and ther the foresaid armes pyctured. Item one legendar with the saids armes ordrid in nexte leef bifor the viij day of our lady the nativite of her. Item ij processionarys with the seid armes in thende off bothe bookes.

M^d that ther ys In quayres for the masse of Ihu for ij gradualles for the processyon as for iij processyonaryes wound up in a skyn.

Item another cowcher of the gyft of the holle pareche with the Rolle of jesse.

Item ij bookes of the gyft of Sr John Hubbertes one the bybull one other book begynnyng with manipulus curatorum.

Item a py in pryntt with a calander for ytt.

Item a nother processionar of the gift of the holle pareche having Omnes sancti befor Rex sanctorum in the mydst of the book.

Item j othir processionar of a mor volume than any of the othir ij. Item one Epistoll book with the Invitatores and venites in the fyrst parte of the book with iiij Bolsteres of latyne. Item ij manuelles a newe with an olde the newer orderid with the Genealogies of the fest of cristemasse day and the fest of the Epiphanie with the halowinge of the Fonte next bifor the vij psalmes nye the myddes of the boke. Item in the old manuall the vij psalmes yn the latter ende of the book. Item j olde Sawter with an olde antiphonar with the legend ther yn. Item j olde Ordinall.

An inventory of 1516 shows how bountifully St. Laurence, Reading, was supplied with service books. In addition to two costly books—a gospeler and epistoler—bound in silver, there were 5 antiphoners, 7 missals, 4 manuals, 6 graduals, an ordinal, a martyloge, a legend, 2 psalters, and 4 processionals, as well as the following, which had better be given in the exact phraseology :—

A portos (breviary) not Sarum.
A legend Scor' (the Golden Legend) chayned byfore the vicars stall.
ij quaires in prent of the visitacon of our lady.
A queire of the fest' of Cristmas.
A new legend prynted of the gyft of John Barefote.
A grale pryntyd of the gyft of Thomas Whyt.

Bokes of Pricksong

A great boce of vellem bourded for masses of the gifte of Willm Stannford.
Another boke bourded of paper w^t masses and antemfines.
An old boke bourded w^t antemfines.
Anoyther of vellame bordyd w^t antems and exultavits.

1466 (*Croscombe, Somerset*). Item the Wardenes have paid for stoff and writtyng of the new legent which is xlvi queyres, pres per queyer iij s. Suma   vj li. xviij s.
1500 (*St. Dunstan's, Canterbury*). To the parson of Harbaldowne for a book callyd Legenda Sanctoris   .   .   .   xx s.
1538 (*Wimborne*). For a new Legend of the Story of St. Cuthborow   .   .   .   .   .   .   vj s. viij d.

With the accession of Edward VI came a grievous destruction of the costly and often beautiful service books. Occasionally they were sold at an absurdly low price.

1550 (*North Elmham*). Rec. of Henry Holme for ye gret Antyphoners Grayles Legends Masbokes and all other kynds of boks of ye old service . . . . x s.

Under Queen Mary the Latin books, both written and printed, were again in demand. In certain cases the old concealed books came once more to light, but many parishes had to pay for new copies.

1553-4 (*St. Edmund, Sarum*). An Antyfoner and ij Grayles xxx s. iiij d.
A processhyonell . . . . . . iij s.
1554-5 (*Yatton*). For a missall . . . . . xvj s.
For a manwell . . . . . vj s. viij d.

Before leaving the old service books some other extracts may be given showing that binding and repairing was a heavy charge on the mediæval parish. The size of the volumes and their daily use made repairs inevitable.

A fourteenth-century entry in the accounts of St. Augustine, Hedon (E. R., Yorks), is of much interest as showing the use of sealskin :—

1397-8. Pro iiij sele skynnes pro cooperturis . . . . vij d.
1442 (*Thame*). For a manuel . . . xx s. vj d.
1453. For a bagg of a bukskyn to ye massboke . viij d.
1457. For makyng of a bagge for ye grete legger for ye p'sche p'st vj d.
1461. For mendyng of ye gret portiform . . . . xviij d.
1465. We payde for byndyng of ye best masboke . . . xl d.
1451 (*Yatton, Somerset*). For the byndyng of the boks v s.
1458. For byndyng of ij portoes bokys . . . iij s. iiij d.
1480. For the byndyng of the sawter . . . . xvj d.
1486. Payd to the bokebyner . . . . xxvj s. viij d.
1537. To ye buckebynddar . . . . . xxiij s. iiij d.
More to ye buckebynddar . . . . . xv s.
For ye furst buke to ye sayd buckebynddar . . . vj d.
To ye buckebynddar for another bargayne . xxvj s. ix d.
To ye buckebyndar . . . . . vj s. viij d.
1491-2 (*St. Edmund, Sarum*). For mendynge byndynge and coverynge of a grayle lyenge daily in the South syde of the queer byfore y^e parisshe preste . iij s. iiij d.

The holy & blessed doctour saynt Jerom sayth thys auctorite / do alwey somme good werke / to thende that the deuyl fynde the not ydle / And the holy doctour saynt austyn sayth in the book of the laboui of monkes / that no man stronge or myghty to laboure ought to be ydle for whiche cause whan I had parfourmed & accomplisshed dyuers werkys & hystoryes translated out of frensshe in to englysshe at the requeste of certayn lordes / ladyes and gentylmen / as thystorye of the siege of Troye / the book of the chesse / the hystorye of Jason / The hystorye of the myrrour of the world / the xv bookes of Metamorphoseos in whyche ben contyned

FIRST PAGE OF CAXTON'S "GOLDEN LEGEND"

1499-1500 (*Bassingbourn, Cambs*). Payed to a book bynder of Cambrigg repayryng and mendyng deffaurtes off v bookes, ij antiphon', j portas, ij gradual, psalter, a pystilbot, ij processionar', ij myssalles, with kevering a legendar' . . . . . . xvij s. iiij d.

1509-10 (*Holy Trinity, Cambridge*). Payed to Frier Jeffrey for the bindyng and new covering and penyng of one Antiphoner and a great legend in ij volums . xvj s. viij d.

With regard to printed books, it is interesting to find that Caxton bequeathed a copy of his *Golden Legend* to St. Margaret's, Westminster. He died about 1492; he first printed this book in 1483; it was again issued in 1487, and for a third time in 1493.

1502 (*St. Margaret, Westminster*). A prynted legende booke of the bequest of Willm Caxton.

An elaborate inventory of church goods in the wardens' accounts of Pilton, Somerset, of the year 1507, shows that printed service books were coming into general use; the church possessed "a masse booke prynted," "iiij prosessionaries prynted," "a manel boke prynted," and "a grete portuas of prynte."

1509-10 (*Bassingbourn, Cambs*). Payd for a newe antiphonar in pryntte . . . . . . viij s. j d. ob.

1520-1. Rec' att the gaderyng in the cherche to mende the legende and the printydd mass boke . . iij s. ix d.

1527 (*Wimborne*). For a prynt legend . . . . x s. iiij d.

Reformed Service Books

In June 1544 a litany in English was put forth by authority shortly before the king set forth to invade France. Litanies at that time were always sung in procession, and the words were usually called a "processioner." In the following year Cranmer was instructed to draw up a revised English litany, translated from the Latin procession. This was practically the same as the Litany now in use. It was first sung at St. Paul's on Sunday, 18th October 1545, and was printed with the Primer.

1544 (*Worksop*). For makyng iiij bowks in ynglyesh for the prossessyons . . . . vj d.

1544 (*St. Margaret, Westminster*). For vj books of the Litany in English . . . . xviij d.

1545 (*St. Mary, Cambridge*). For iiij Inglyeshe processioners . xvj d.
    To the clerke for wrytyng ij Englyeshe processioners   xvj d.
1546 (*Croscombe, Somerset*). Paid for bokes for the prossyon   xj d.

For the due understanding of the following selected references to the English service books, a few words may be helpful. An "Order of Communion," approved by Convocation, 30th November 1547, and ratified by Parliament on 20th December, was issued under a proclamation by the Crown on 8th March 1547–8. The first Prayer Book of Edward VI was issued in 1549, the second Prayer Book of Edward VI in 1552, and the first Prayer Book of Elizabeth in 1559. The Psalter was frequently translated into Anglo-Saxon and mediæval English. After the issue of the first authorised version of the Bible in 1540, English Psalters were taken from that text; it was printed in that year both in Latin and English.

1547–8 (*Melton Mowbray*). For a book off the nue service   vj s.
    For a salltre in ynglishe . . . . . xij d.
1547–8 (*St. Nicholas, Warwick*). The Communion boke   iiij s.
1548 (*Yatton*). To Syr Nicholas Poore for wrytynge ye masse
    in Englych . . . . . . viij d.
1548 (*St. Edmund, Sarum*). For viij Salters in English   xiij s. iiij d.
1549–50 (*St. Thomas, Sarum*). Payed for ij bokes of the Comunyon
    called the ordynall' thone for the preste and thother for
    the quyer . . . . viij s.
    Syr Bartram for a Saulter boke for the quyer . . ij s. iiij d.
    For a Saulter boke for Syr John Rusdean . xvj d.
    To the Curate for a Sawter boke . . xvj d.
1551 (*St. Mary, Cambridge*). For ij prymers bowt at ye fyrst
    tyme of ye inglyse servys . . . . xvj d.
    For ij bookes of ye servys for ye comunyon . viij s.
1551 (*St. Martin's-in-the-Fields*). For a comunion booke for y^e
    chyrche . . . . . . iij s. viij d.
    For a salter and a homyly book . . . iij s. iij d.
    For ij salters more . . . . . iij s. iij d.
1551–2 (*Yatton*). For a boke for the Comunion . . iij s. iij d.
1551–2 (*St. Mary, Dover*). Payed for a new boke of the servyce
    of the Churche caulid the Communyon boke agaynste
    hallowtyde and for charge in fetchinge the same boke
    at Canterbury . . . . . vj s. viij d.
1552 (*St. Mary, Devizes*). P^d for the new Books of Common
    Prayer . . . . . . iij s. viij d.

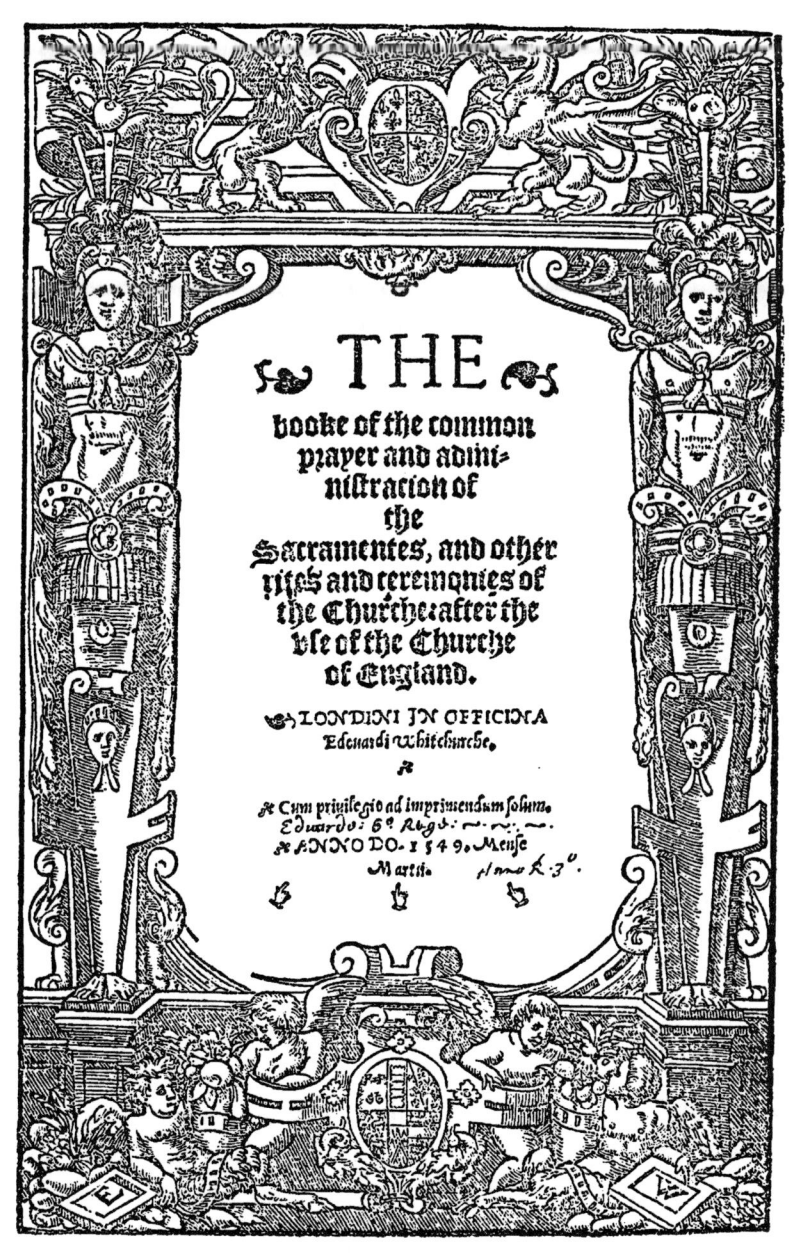

TITLE-PAGE OF FIRST PRAYER BOOK IN ENGLISH

THE CHURCHWARDENS' ACCOUNTS

1553 (*St. Mary, Cambridge*). For iij commewnyon bookes   xv s. iiij d.
    For iij saulter bookes in ynglyse to sing or say yᵉ
    salmes of yᵉ servys . . . . . vij s.
    Ye copy of ye servys in inglys sette oute by note .   iij s. iij d.
    For wryghtynge and notyng part of yt to syng on bothe
    sydes of ye quyre . . . . . . xvj d.
1555 For presheoneres and imnals . . . . vj s.
1558–9 (*Yatton, Somerset*). For a booke of the prossessyon
    (Litany) in English . . . . . ij d.
1559. For the boke of common prayer . . . . v s.
1559–60 (*St. Thomas, Sarum*). 3 bokes of the prosessyon . . 4s. 9½d.
    4 communion bookes and 3 psalters . . . 21s.
1596 (*Seal, Surrey*). For a newe booke of Common Praier
    bought at London . . . . iij s. vj d.
1596 (*St. Nicholas, Warwick*). For a Communion Booke of
    the great vollem . . . . . . vij s.
1616 (*St. Nicholas, Warwick*). For a new Booke of Common
    prayer . . . . . . vij s. vj d.
1662 (*St. Edmund, Sarum*). Paid for a Common Prayer Book,
    and binding Bishop Hall's works, belonging to the
    church . . . . 17s. 6d.
1661–2 (*St. Giles, Northampton*). Payd to the parritor for bringing
    the booke of Common Prayer . . . . 1s.
    Payd for the Common Prayer Booke . 10s. 8d.
1707 (*All Saints, Derby*). Mʳ Nisbett for a Common prayer booke   12s. 6d.
1717. For a Church Communion prayer booke . . . 15s.
1723. 1 Common Prayer and Playfords Psalms to Job Grice   7s.
    2 Common Prayer Books . . . . . £1 12s.
1770. Paid Mʳ Roome for a Prayer Book for yᵉ Clerk . 18s.
1789. Mʳ Drewry for hymns for Christmas . . . 2s. 6d.
1793. April 1. Ordered that one hundred Books containing the
    new Version of Psalms be ordered of Mʳ John Sanders
    and distributed amongst the Inhabitants of this Parish
    by the Churchwardens.

The Commonwealth provided certain service books after their own fashion. "The Directory for the Public Worship of God," put forth by the Assembly of Westminster Divines, was enforced on the nation by Parliament in 1644–5. Every parish was bound to purchase this Presbyterian formulary, and anyone found using the Book of Common Prayer, publicly or privately, was to be fined £5 for the first offence, £10 for the second, and imprisonment and loss of all goods for the third.

A DIRECTORY
FOR
The Publique Worship of *GOD*,
Throughout the Three
KINGDOMS
OF
England, Scotland, and *Ireland.*

Together with an Ordinance of Parliament for the taking away of the Book of
COMMON-PRAYER:
AND
For establishing and observing of this present DIRECTORY throughout the Kingdom of *England*, and Dominion of *Wales*.

Die Jovis, 13. *Martii*, 1644.

ORdered by the Lords and Commons assembled in Parliament, That this *Ordinance* and *Directory* bee forthwith Printed and Published:

Joh: Brown, Cleric.   *H. Elsynge, Cler.*
Parliamentorum.   *Parl.D.Com.*

march 18th LONDON:
Printed for *Evan Tyler, Alexander Fifield, Ralph Smith,* and *John Field*; And are to be sold at the Sign of the Bible in Cornhill, neer the ROYALL-EXCHANGE. 1644.

TITLE-PAGE OF "DIRECTORY" OF 1644

1645–6 (*Stroud, Kent*). For the Directory and the Covenant . . 4s. 6d.
1646 (*All Saints, Derby*). For a Directory . . 1s.
1657 (*All Saints, Derby*). For a Psalme Book to Church . . 2s. 8d.
1647 (*St. Edmund, Sarum*). For a Directory and a Psalme booke . . . . 3s. 4d.
1648–9. A booke of Ordinances for Presbyterial government . 9d.

The first book of Homilies was enjoined to be procured in every parish by Edward VI's Council in 1547; the second book was put forth by Convocation in 1563. They were to serve in lieu of sermons where there was no licensed preacher.

1541 (*St. Mary, Cambridge*). For a booke of ye homylys   xx d.
1547–8 (*Yatton, Somerset*). For the Omelys and injuncsions   ij s.
1560 (*St. Edmund, Sarum*). A booke of the homyles .   vj d.
1562–3 (*St. Nicholas, Warwick*). For the Boocks of the Homilies. v s. iiij d.
1566 (*St. Peter, Ipswich*). For the homelies booke of the Seconde tome . . . . . . iiij s. iiij d.
1570 (*St. John, Winchester*). Omelies book . . . xij d.

For the due understanding of the frequent references to Bibles in parish accounts, a few preliminary words are essential. Considerable portions of the Scriptures had been translated into Anglo-Saxon and mediæval English; but it was to Wyclif that England owed the first translation of the whole Bible. That translation was so deliberately falsified in parts, and so marred by prologues and glosses of an extreme levelling character, that the Church naturally did its best to suppress it. The same is true, though in a less degree, of both Tyndale and Coverdale's sixteenth-century translations. Sir Thomas More's *Dyalogue* ought to be read by anyone desirous of understanding the objections to Tyndale's New Testament; his well-weighed perversions are there set forth in detail.

In August 1536, Crumwell, as the King's vicar-general, issued a set of injunctions to the clergy, one of which required "every parson or propriatary of any parish church within this realm" to provide before 1st August 1537 a whole Bible in Latin and also in English, and to lay them in the quire for anyone to read. This is one of the numerous contradictory orders of that period of flux. There was then no printed authorised version; all that was available was Coverdale's rendering, avowedly made from the

"Douche (German) and Latyn in to Englishe"; it took no account of either Hebrew or Greek. This version was printed abroad in October 1535, and though dedicated to Henry VIII was not then authorised for sale in this country. Probably there was a very restricted obedience paid to the 1536 injunction. Bible purchase at that period only appears in one or two parish accounts; but it must be remembered that the clergy were directed to supply this English Version, and if they complied there would be no charge on the parish.

In August 1537, another English Bible appeared, dedicated to the King by Thomas Matthew. It gave great satisfaction to Cranmer, but was in reality no new translation; it was a compilation, with a few minor alterations, from Tyndale and Coverdale. The work was begun abroad, but finished in London, and Richard Grafton was licensed to sell it. A new set of injunctions was issued by Crumwell, ordering, *inter alia*, the setting up of this large English Bible in every church, the people to be admonished to read it. The expense was to be divided between the minister and the parishioners, hence the expression "half Bible" in several accounts, an entry which has been supposed by more than one good recent writer to mean one Testament, not the whole book !

The Great Bible of 1540, often termed Cranmer's Bible, was but a reproduction on a larger scale of that attributed to Thomas Matthew. An injunction of Edward VI, in 1547, ordered each parish to provide "one Boke of the whole Bible of largest volume in English"; this injunction was repeated in 1559. The Genevan Bible, completed by three English exiles at Geneva in 1560, went through many editions, and was for threequarters of a century the popular Bible for private use; it but seldom found its way into churches. Archbishop Parker's version, called the Bishops' Bible, was issued in 1568. Several parish accounts bear witness to the fact that the old Bible was sold when the new version was purchased, and the like took place when the Authorised Version of 1611 was issued. Two or three instances are given of the extravagantly high prices paid for church Bibles towards the close of the seventeenth, and throughout the eighteenth, century.

1535 (*St. Alphege, London Wall*). For a bybyll for ye chirch . iiij s.
1548. For a Bybyll of the large volome . . xxvj s.

THE CHURCHWARDENS' ACCOUNTS

1538–9	(*Yatton, Somerset*). Payd for a bybyll	ix s. vj d.
1548–9	(*Ibid.*). Payd for a bybull of the largyst volume	xj s.
1539	(*St. Mary, Cambridge*). For halfe the byble	ij s. vj d.
1540.	For halfe the byble	ij s.
1540.	For halfe the gret byble	ix s.
1548.	For halfe the byble	vij s.
1539	(*St. Mary Woolnoth*). For the half of the Bybill in the church whiche cost xiij s. iiij d.	vj s. viij d.
1541–2	(*Tintinhull, Somerset*). For the halfe price of the Bible this year bought	vj s. v d.
1561–2	(*Tavistock*). For a bybyll of the largis volume	xxvj s. viij d.
1568–9	(*St. John, Winchester*). Pd for a Bible	xiij s. iiij d.
	Rec for an old Bible	vj s.
1570–1	(*St. Thomas, Sarum*). For a greate Bible	2 1 6
1573–4.	Harry Hamon seting of boses on yᵉ bybyll and 2 large strapes also for the savinge of him	2 6
1578	(*St. Mary, Cambridge*). For an englyshe geneva bible	xvij s.
1597.	For a large bible for the churche	xxviij s.
1590	(*Exning, Suffolk*). Paid for the byble at London and for bringinge of yᵗ from the Stationers to my ende	xxviij s. ij d.
1612	(*Wimborne*). For the Church Bible	ij li. xvj s.
1614	(*St. Mary, Devizes*). Samˡ Clark for a new Bible of the new Translation	ij li. vj s.
1619	(*Youlgrave, Derbyshire*). A newe byble	2 4 (
1620	(*Great Wigston, Leicestershire*). Paid for the New Bible	2 0 0
	Sold the Old Bible	10 (
1662	(*Wirksworth, Derbyshire*). Pd Mr. Heape for the Church Byble	2 13 4
1673	(*Prestbury, Cheshire*). Pᵈ for a New Church Byble	5 6 0
	Pᵈ for carriage thereof from London	5 9
1696	(*St. Edmund, Sarum*). Paid for a large Bible ruled for the church	4 0 c
1731	(*Youlgrave, Derbyshire*). A new Bible for the church	5 10 0
1762	(*All Saints, Derby*). George Killar for a Large Bible	9 9 0

The injunction of Edward VI, 31st July 1547, ordered the setting up "in some convenient place within the church within one twelvemonth" of a translation, pronounced by scholars to be a very bad one, of Erasmus' Paraphrase of the New Testament.[1] This injunction was afterwards enforced by Archbishops Parker and Bancroft.

---

[1] For a list of the few churches still retaining copies of the Paraphrase, see *English Church Furniture* (1907), pp. 337–40.

1548–9 (*Yatton*). For a bucke callyd paraphrasas and Erasmus   xj s. iiij d.
1550–1 (*Croscombe, Somerset*). For the perrafrase   .   . v s. ij d.
1551 (*St. Mary, Cambridge*). For dim' y⁰ parafrases of Erasmy   v s. vj d.
1566 (*St. Peter, Ipswich*). For the Paraphrases of the Epistles and
  Gospels of Erasmus .   .   .   .   .   .   xij s.

John Foxe, when in exile, produced two editions of his *Book of Martyrs*. An English edition, purged of many gross detected errors, but still most inaccurate, appeared in 1563. "The Government commanded it to be placed in each parish church; more than any other influence, it fanned the flame of that fierce hatred of Spain and the Inquisition which was the master passion of the age. Nor was its influence transient. For generations the popular conception of popery has been derived from its melancholy and bitter pages" (*Encyc. Brit.*). It is singular to find so very few entries in Elizabethan parish accounts relative to the purchase of these volumes, but finding of chains for their preservation and binding them at later dates are of frequent occurrence.

A third work ordered in 1564 to be placed in every church was Bishop Jewel's *Apology for the Church of England*. Archbishop Bancroft renewed this order in the days of James I. About two score copies remain in our churches; they are mostly of early seventeenth-century date.

1611 (*Youlgrave, Derbyshire*). For a boke called Jewells Works . 1 6 0

Chained Books

Incidental reference has already been made to early examples of chained books in churches both in pre-Reformation and Reformation days. A long list of such books now extant, either chained or showing traces of former chaining, is given in *English Church Furniture* (1907), pp. 336–40. The following are a few details as to the purchase of chains, etc., by the parish authorities for this purpose. But first of all the highly interesting list, c. 1525, must be cited from the All Saints, Derby, accounts:—

These be the bokes in our lady Chapell tyed with chenes yᵗ were gyffen to Alhaloes Church in Derby.
In primis one Boke called summa summarum.
Item A boke called Summa Raumundi.

Item Anoyer called pupilla occuli.
Item Anoyer called the Sexte.
Item A boke called Hugucyon.
Item A boke called Vitas patrum.
Item Anoyer boke called pauls pistols (English).
Item A boke called Januensis super evangeliis dominicalibus.
Item A greete portuose.
Item Anoyer boke called legenda Aurea (probably printed).

[Mr. Henry Bradshaw, University Librarian, Cambridge, supplied a valuable series of notes on these books to the *Chronicles of All Saints*, pp. 175-7.]

FOXE'S "BOOK OF MARTYRS," CHAINED
ST. MARY AXE, LONDON

1475 (*St. Michael, Cornhill*). For lengyng of an yron cheyne and makyng to serve to the glosed sawter in our Lady chapell . . . . ij d.
1540 (*St. Mary Woolnoth*). For makyng a deske to sett on the bibill . . . . vj d.
For ij stapulls for the chayne of the said bibill . ij d.
1542 (*Wimborne*). For a desk and chain for the Bybyll . xiiij d.
For a Chayne and settyng in thereof for the fastenynge of the Dictionarie in the Scholehowse . ix d.
For Three Chaynes of Iren with plates and for the fastenynge of the Bible, Paraphras of Erasmus, and Mr. Juells booke in the Churche . . . . iij s. ij d.
1593-4 (*St. Martin, Leicester*). Also receaved 7 bookes that were chaynedd in the Church and geven by Symon Crafter.
Pd to John Langford for bayndding of seven bookes v s.

BOOKS

    Pd to christofer nedome for one chene and stapiles for the bookes . . . . xiiij d.
1616). For a chaine for the booke of Martyrs and another booke   vj d.
1632-3 (*St. Nicholas, Warwick*). Mending the Ch : booke and setting on the chainis to ye Bookes of Martirs   10d.
1636 (*St. Mary, Devizes*). Pd for the Chaynes wherewith the Bookes of Martyrs are tyed .   j s. viij d.
    Pd for a Chayne and Staple to tye the booke of the paraphrases of Erasmus . . . . viij d.

OTHER BOOKS

Libraries of books were frequently placed in church during the seventeenth and eighteenth centuries for the use of parishioners; a long list of these is given in *English Church Furniture* (1907), pp. 131-6. They very rarely, however, obtain mention in churchwardens' accounts, as they were the gift of private donors. Repton is an exception; the following interesting list of books, placed in the custody of the wardens, appears in the parish books of 1622-3 :—

Bookes sent by Mr Willm Bladone to be emploied for the use of the parrishe, and to be disposed of at the discretione of Mr Thomas Whiteheade.

Rec^d by Mr Robert Kellett, Godfry Cantrell, Roger Bishope, and Robert Orchard, Churchwardens 1622, the xxvth of December, the said bookes, videlicet :—

    First, a faire Bible well bound.
2. B^p Babingtone, his worckes.
3. Mr Elton on the Colossians.
4. Mr Perkins on the Creede.
5. Mr Dod and Cleaver on ye Commandements.
6. Bellymy his Catechesmie.
7. Mr Young his Household Govermentte.
8. The first and second partte of the new Watche.
9. The third partte of the said by Mr Brinsley.
10. The Plaine Manne's Pathewaye, & Sermon of Repentance by Mr Dentte.
11. Bradshawes P'paraĉon to ye Receavinge of ye Bodye & Bloude.
12. Hieron his Helpe to Devotione.
13 and 14. Allsoe towe bookes of Martters.

The peculiar feature of this benefaction is that none of the books were to be chained or retained definitely in the church. The gift was accompanied by certain "Condicions to be observed concerning the using and lendinge of the foresaid bookes" by the minister and churchwardens. Is not this the earliest known instance of a church lending library?

 1630 (*St. Oswald, Durham*) King David his psalmes translated by King James and commanded to be had in all churches   2   4
  [Sir William Alexander, afterwards Earl of Sterling, is supposed to have been the chief author.]

 1633 (*St. Petrock, Exeter*). For a book lately set forth for Recreatyon . . . .   vj d.
  [The Book of Sports and Pastimes issued by James I was re-issued by Charles I.]

CHAPTER IX

HALLOWING AND VESTMENTS

Setting apart for holy purposes of churches, churchyards, altars, vestments, etc.—Consecration Crosses—St. Mary-at-Hill; Yatton; Tintinhull; St. Edmund, Sarum; Sutterton; Holy Trinity, Cambridge—Reconciling St. Mary, Cambridge—Martin Bucer—Short References—Louth Steeple Vestments—Early Extracts—St. Edmund, Sarum; St. Mary-at-Hill; Bassingbourn, Cambs; St. Laurence, Reading; St. Mary, Cambridge; St. Stephen, Walbrook—In Elizabethan days—The Surplice—Gloves—Hoods—Surplices for clerks—Rochets—Gowns

THE Benediction, Blessing, or Consecrating of altars, altar plate, vestments, bells, etc., as well as the consecrating or dedicating of churches or churchyards, and their reconciliation, if polluted, naturally occupies a frequent place in pre-Reformation wardens' accounts. In these documents the ceremony is usually termed "hallowing," that is the setting apart for holy purposes.

The subject of consecration crosses at the dedication of a church, about which many blunders have been published, is fully treated in an appendix to this book; see also the able article by Rev. E. S. Dewick in the *Archæological Journal*, lxv. No. 257. The same article gives a list of the various requisites for a mediæval church consecration. The two ells of cloth, supplied by the wardens of Yatton in 1486 "for my lords apryn," were probably intended to screen his pontificals from the holy oil, etc.

The consecration of altars, superaltars, and bells was strictly reserved to bishops. The hallowing of altar plate and of various vestments was usually performed by bishops, and parishes went to the expense of having such articles taken to cathedral cities or to episcopal manor-houses to secure their due hallowing; but such matters were also in the power of parish priests, provided they had received a faculty at the hands of the bishop for the exercise of such functions.

The various phases of hallowing or solemnly blessing of fabrics and of church vestments and furniture for sacramental use are well illustrated by the following selected entries from various accounts:—

1426–7 (*St. Mary-at-Hill*). To Sir John Norfolke for halwenge of the auter clothis . . . . . . iiij d.
1489–90. For the halowing of a vestyment . . . . vj d.
1493–4. To the soffrican of London for halowyng of Sentt Stevyn ys autyr . . . . x s. iiij d.
To mastyr parson for hallowyng of the westementes xij d.
1500–1. To Maister John for hallowyng of iiij Awtrys . iiij d.
1503–4 (S. aisle rebuilt). For box at the hallowyng of the Cherche to vasche (wash) the Aultyres . . . . . j d.
For a skop and a grat laddyll . . . . . ij d. ob.
For bred ale and vyne at the hallowyng of the Cherche . vij d.
To the sufficans man for the barrellys and tubbys . iiij d.
1510–1. For hallowyng of xi Albis, v Amyses and iiij Surplises for children . . . . xij d.
1511–2. Paid the Suffregan for haloyng of a Chales, iiij Corporasses and iiij Vestimenttis . . . . iij s. vij d.
1519–20. For a reward gevyng to the Bishoppis servant at the halowyng of the vestmenttis . . . . xij d.
1520–1. To John Balahans for ij days to make clene the Steple agenst the halowyng of the bellis . . . . viij d.
1555–6. For the dynner of the suffrican yat day he halowed the altars and others yᵗ did service with hym . . . xiij s.
Payde in Claret wyne, sacke and sugar . iij s. xj d.
1453 (*Yatton, Somerset*). Pro consecratione campane, suffraganeo vj s.
1482. Paide to the Bushop ys man for halowyng of the new sute of vestements . . . . vj d.
For the blessynge of the Chalys . . . . ij d.
1486. Payed for dyverse costs for hawluyng of the Cherche erde .
Imprimis payd to the Byschepe . xxxiij s. iiij d.
It payd for ij ellys of cloth for My Lords apryn . . xviij d.
It payd for the brekefast of the Lords men . iiij d.
It payd for rydyng to Wellys ij tymes xij d.
It payd for rydyng to Bristowe . . . . xij d.
It payd for dyverse vessells ybought to the halowyng of the Cherchyerd . . . . ij s. viij d.
1499. Payd for yᵉ halowyng of yᵉ chalys . . viij d.
1503. Payd for blessyng of ye vestment . ix d.

1508. Payd to yᵉ monke for caryng of ye awter cloth to Wells for to be blessyd . . . . . . v d.
1517. Payd for blessyng ye chales that was new cast . . ij s.
1527. For halowyng of iiij awter clothys . viij d.
1536. Payd at Banwell for halowyng yᵉ sewte of vestments . viij d.
1504 (*Tintinhull, Somerset*). In expensis apud Kyngesbury pro consecratione ij corporalium. . . . . iiij d.
1508. For costs done at the halowynge of the bellys and of the High Awter . . . . vij s. x d.
1514. For blessyng of a pair of vestments . . . . ij d.

An entry in the Yatton accounts for 1476 clearly refers to the hallowing of a superaltar, or small portable altar slab:—

For the caryage (probably on horseback) of the Altar and table from Wellys . . . . ij d.

In 1526 John Holcum gave to the church of Morebath "a super-altar yblessyd," price iij s. iiij d.

1474-5 (*St. Edmund, Sarum*). In cleansyng of the Lytton (churchyard) . . . . . . xj d.
Paid to John Lumbard for his labour to the Suffragans costs and hors hure for to halowe the letton . iij s. iiij d.
1483-4. Pro attachiatione trium personarum qui polluerunt Cimiterium ac pro implitacione eorum . . xj d.
Sol' pro expensis Suffraganei tempore quo fuit apud Sarum . . . . . . xxviij s. viij d.
Et in regardo facto eidem Suffraganeo ad consecrandum dictum Cimiterium . . . . . . iiij li.
Et in regardo facto famulis suffraganei pro laboribujs suis . xvj d.
Et in regardo facto Ballivo Sarum pro auxiliorum ad recuperandem versus transgressores qui polluerunt Cimiterium . . . . . . vj s. viij d.
Et inden' sol' pro commissione acquista de Domino Episcopo Sarum . . . . x s.

In the 1474 case the pollution of the churchyard was evidently caused by some accident, and the process used was "reconciling." The offence of 1483 was evidently one of such gravity and deliberation that the Bishop decided on the costly ceremony of rededication. The receipts for 1483-4 show that the three offenders, William Sawyer, Roger Carpynter, and Thomas Carpynter, paid over to the church fund the respective sums of 38s., 31s., and 30s., so that the parish suffered but little monetary expense.

Sutterton church, Lincolnshire, was so much rebuilt in 1493 that it required consecration. The fee paid to the suffragan bishop was five marks, which probably covered all the various incidental expenses of the elaborate ceremonial. The wardens, however, included in "ye costes for halloyng of ye chyrche" the provisions for a great parish feast or dinner, for which a swan, beef, mutton, lamb, chickens, "ij pygges," butter, eggs, spice, bread, wine, and beer were liberally provided.

There are interesting entries in the 1510–1 accounts of Holy Trinity, Cambridge, as to the hallowing of that church. The fee to the suffragan was 53s. 4d. Red wine, salt, frankincense, and two ladles were provided for the ceremony at a small cost. The three last entries are well worth citing in full. Lighted tapers were affixed to the walls before the consecration crosses.

> For ij pounds wax for the Crosses . . . . xliij d.
> To the peynter for making of the Crosses about the church iij s. iij d.
> Item to a masone for settyng up of the seyntes in the Cherch . iiij d.

The dinner, in addition to two calves' heads, two breasts of veal, and a quarter of lamb, included such delicacies as "a Marebone j d." and "an henne iij d." "An hoggett of hostell ale" and "a quarte of Maumisey" were also provided.

An entry in the 1557 accounts of St. Mary, Cambridge, calls for brief explanation.

> For the new halloweinge or Reconcyleing of our chyrche for beyng Interdycted for the buryall of Mr. bucer, and the charge thereto belongeing frankensens and swate perfumes for the sacrament and herbes etc. . . . . . . viij d. ob.

Martin Bucer, the German Reformer, was originally a Dominican friar, but he abandoned his order and married a nun. Archbishop Cranmer invited him to England in 1549. He was appointed teacher of theology in the University of Cambridge, and was a *persona grata* with the young King's advisers. He died in 1551, and his burial in St. Mary's was made an occasion of much pomp. The accounts for that year indicate a crowd: "Item for nayles to mend ye seates in ye chyrche when Mr. doctor busar was buryed ij d." Five years later his body was disinterred and burnt and his tomb demolished. Queen Elizabeth in her turn ordered the reconstruction of the monument.

1561. Payd to long and barnes for pavyng of the quire and coveryng Bucers grave . . . . . . xxij d.

1452 (*Walberswick, Suffolk*). At Bilbro for halwyng of the Pyx, auter clothis, and a Towyell, an Aube, an Amyce and expenses . . . . xx d.

1471 (*St. Michael, Cornhill*). Paid to Maist^r John for hallowyng of the corpres and for halowyng of sten' awlt' clothes . xviij d.

1501 (*Worfield, Saldp*). It pro emendacione altaris beate marie et pavimenti coram altari . . . . . xv s.

It pro sanctificacions ejusdem altaris . . . . v s. x d.

It pro vestibus episcopo necessaris Rogero Rowlowe viij d.

1511 (*St. Margaret, Westminster*). Of the gift of my Lady Clinton j tabilcloth sore worn now hallowed for the high awter by the hands of Mr Curate.

1531 (*Wimborne*). Paid for haloing of the Clock Bell vj s. viij d. and for halowyng of the new pyx and chesybles with awter cloth xij d. : and to the suffrycans serwants viij d. : and for iiij ells of lyn cloth for the Suffrygan xj s. : and for ij ells of bockram and ij ells of canvis xj s. : and for frankynsense iiij d. : and for wyne and the Clerks labour iiij s. viij d.

1542-3 (*St. Laurence, Reading*). Payd to the Suffregan in money for reconsyleyng the churche . . . . xl s.

[This entry is followed by the fines received from the culprits who had defiled the church, probably by some bloody affray, Robert Watlyngton 20s., Mark Awrepp 10s., and Robert Lewsham 3s. 4d.]

1554 (*St. Margaret, Westminster*). Paid for iij capons for the bishop's dinner at the reconciliation of the church . vij s.

1556 (*St. Michael, Cornhill*). To the Suffirican for hallowinge the Aulters and to iij prestes an ell of linnon clothe w^t other things thereto belonginge . . xxvij s. iij d. ob.

1620 (*St. Margaret, Westminster*). For carrying of formes cushions and hassocks into the new churchyard at the consecration therof . . . . ij d.

1627. For twelve bundles of rushes to fitt the churchyard for consecration 1 0
For carrying and recarrying the tent and other things 1 8
Dr Pope for his fee at the consecration . . . 2 10 0
Mr. Walsall the register for his fee 3 10 0
The appariter for his pains 10 0
Spent at a dinner at the said consecration . . . 1 19 :

We cannot do better than conclude these scattered references to hallowing than by citing, from the parish books of Louth, this jubilant entry as to the triumphant crowning of that most noble broach or steeple which had been fourteen years in building, and at last attained to a height of 360 feet:—

Memorandum, the xvth Sunday after Holy Trinity of this year (1518) the weathercock was set upon the broach on Holy Rood Eve, there being William Ayleby, parish priest, with many of his brethren priests there present, hallowing the said weathercock and the stone that it stands upon, and so conveyed upon the said broach : and then the said priests singing Te Deum Laudamus with organs, and then the kirkwardens would ring all the bells, and caused all the people there being to have bread and ale, and all the loving of God, Our Lady, and all saints.

Vestments

The entries in wardens' accounts as to vestments—using the term in its wider sense and not limiting it to chasubles—are of course exceedingly numerous, and in many cases bear witness to high expenditure.

1385-6 (*Tavistock*). To five yards of linen to make a rochet	ij s. ij d. ob.
To making the said rochet	vj d.
To eight feet for a girdle	viij d.
1426-7. Eight yards of Cornub' (*Cornish*) cloth for rochets for the clerks	v s.
For making the same	xvj d.
1449 (*Thame*). To Thom Waltar for the bryng' of a payr of vestementy of the quest of ye besshope of lynkolne	xij d.
1473-4 (*St. Ewen, Bristol*). Memorandum that the new blew sewte of Vestementes of vellewett cost xxx li. Also xij d. the halowinge of the same.	
1481 (*Yatton, Somerset*). Paide att Bristowe for a sewte of vestments and a cope	xxvj li.

The vestments named in a 1472 inventory of St. Edmund, Sarum, were numerous and costly; they included a suit of white damask wrought with gold eagles, and two copes and altar cloths of the same ; a suit of blue damask and two copes, with gold eagles ; a suit of purple, with branches of gold ; a suit and two copes of cloth of gold, with white dogs ; a suit and a cope of cloth of gold, with red . . . ; a cope of blue velvet with the Passion on needlework orphreys, called St. Edmund's cope ; a cope of green, with crowns of gold ; 7 copes of white, "with puffe fethers in manner of escalloppys"; a cope of purple velvet with eagles of

HALLOWING AND VESTMENTS

gold, the gift of John Chapman, fishmonger; a suit and cope of black; and an old suit of cloth of sylver, "the ground blewe with bestys and byrds." There were also two palls of cloth of gold for the Sepulchre, and one for the canopy; 16 albs and 5 amices; various altar cloths; a store of towels and napkins; and 15 banners, 2 streamers (*getons*), and 20 staves. There was also, in the hands of the deacon, another store of vestments, which comprised 5 complete suits, a chasuble, 8 copes, 4 palls, and an altar cloth.

The following items in the accounts of 1491-2 tell of the parish purchasing two most costly copes:—

For a newe cope boughte bi Mr Briges and Mr Hampton at london . . . . . . ix li. xviij s. iiij d.
To the Carior for Carryyng of the same Cope from London to Sarum . . . . xij d.

The vestment entries in the accounts and inventories of St. Mary-at-Hill are of exceptional interest.

The inventory of 1496-7 includes

vj Copes for children of dyvers sorttes.
A Myter for a bysshop at seint Nycholas tyde, garnyshed with sylver and an'elyd and perle and Counterfetestones.
vij Rochettes for children.
vj Albys for chyldren, and vj Ameses with parelles, and iij Albys and Ameses withowte paralles.

The inventory of goods delivered up in 1553 to Edward VI's commissioners enumerates "viij Chilldrens Copes."

The following entries relate to surplices:—

1512-3. For x elles of holand cloth for a surples for Mr Doctor
x d. the ell . . . . . . viij s. iiij d.
For makyng of the same surples to woodhokes wyffe . xx d.
1523-4. For makyng of xij Surplices for men . . . vj s.
For makyng of xij Surplices for children . . . v s.
For makyng of iij Children Surplices, of the which Surplices
Mr Clayton gave the clothe of them . . . xv d.
[Forty-eight ells of linen cloth had been bought for these surplices.]
1531-2. Paid for xx elles of holland cloth at vj d. ob. the elle, for surplices, x s. x d. And for makyng of v surplices ij s. vj d. for the conducter. And for iiij surplices for the childern x elles at 6d. the elle and for makyng the same iiij surplices xvj d. Suma . xix s. viij d.

9

130 THE CHURCHWARDENS' ACCOUNTS

Badger skins were purchased in 1531-2 to make warm hoods or tippets for the two rectors, or directors, of the quire.

For ij stolys for the Rectours in the quyre and ij Greyes skynnes. iij s. ij d.

The vestment inventory of 1498, among the wardens' accounts of Bassingbourn, Cambs, is unusually full for a small country parish. It has not hitherto been printed; the main portion is now given *in extenso* :—

Item a clothe of velewet of purpur Colour for the Canopy to be born over the blyssid Sacrament with the ymage of the Crucifige broydr'd in the myddes of the seid clothe and the namys of the gifferes in the iiij Corneres.

Item iiij Sewtes of vestimentes to yche sewte bilonging a Cope and a vestment for the priste with the vestures for a dyacon and subdyacon with all their apperaunce—Fyrst sewt of the iiij of Rede velewet purpur colour with aungelles wrought or broydryd in golde, off the gift of Ric' lychen. The seconde, of the gifte of George lonkyn of Blewe velewett. The thirde of the gift of Mr Ric' Caudry beyng of Rede colour, the Cope of velewett broydryed with aungelles of gold, incloudes the vestyment thereof of Red sylke wroughte in the myddes thereof with colores and flowres of delic' in golde the grownde thereof in the seid myddes beyng of blewe velewett. The iiijth sewte, beyng of the g^r pt of parson goldebourne bifor spokyn of, of the salutacion of our blyssid lady in silke.

Item iiij othir synglar vestymentes, iij of them for sondays and other duble festes, the firste of the iij of wyghte silk strayled with grene sylke, the seconde of Rede sylk wroughte with lyons and swannes yn golde, the third of velewet wroughte in Chekir with a red cross and broydryd with Crownys of golde. The iiijth of blacke silke with a Rede Cross with the armes of parson Caudry the giffer therof in Red velewet and wyghte servyng for Masse of Requiem.

Item v othir vestymentes iiij of theym for Feriall dayes, the first of the iiij of Gren sylk with a blak cross broydryed in the crosse with braunchis of golde, the ij of Rede sylk with a Crosse of grene, the iij^d lynon with a Crosse of Rede, the iiijth of wyght fustion for lentan, ij of these v vestymentes wantyng albes and amysses as the Red and a wyteth.

Item ij Copes for a priste, the one of Rede silk with a Crosse broydryd in Golde, the othir of Grene sylke medled with blew with lebardes yn Golde broydryd. Item ij small Copes for Chylder of Rede sylke. Item one wyghte Chesible of sylk with the phanon lacking and stole and albe with the amysse. Item ij amysses of Red sylke broydrid with Egles of gold.

There were also 6 corporas cases, 6 "stenyd surplysses," 21 rochets for men, and 11 rochets for children.

The high altar had 5 altar cloths, 3 frontals, 2 hangings, and 2 pair of curtains; the lady altar 6 altar cloths, 2 frontals, and

3 hangings. Side altars had 2 new frontals; St. John's altar, 6 altar cloths, 1 frontal, and 2 hangings.

Linen: 5 long towels, 29, 19, 8, 5, and 3 yards respectively in length, and 8 small towels.

There were also 3 herse cloths, 3 lectern cloths, 6 banners with banner poles, 3 Lent cloths, 8 sheets of linen, 4 old cloths lying in the rood-loft, and other linen cloths for covering the tabernacles of the Trinity and Our Lady in the chapel.

According to the inventory of 1517, St. Laurence, Reading, was singularly rich in apparel. There were 26 copes, most of which were evidently fine examples. Here are two of the descriptions:—

> A Cope of crymson velvett w^t orphrays imbrowdred and angels flowres imbrowdred of the gifte of Mr Thomas Justice vicar.
> A Cope of White Damask tissue w^t orfrey of Bawdekyn and rosis of gold of the gifte of Raphe White of Okyngham.

There were 25 suits of vestments; also 25 altar cloths. Of the latter two or three of the more detailed descriptions are given:—

> An Awter Cloth of panes of cloth of gold and velvett imbrowdred w^t Arch angells and flowres.
> ij Awt' Clothes of tissue red and grene w^t a cover of the halpase (high pace) of the same and ij Curteyns.
> An Awter Cloth of black velvett and bawdekyn paned with an Image of Saynt Laurence.
> An awter cloth of black velvett and bawdekyn w^t an Image of Saynt Edward and for the nether pte of the same an Awter cloth of Sarsenett orenge color and blew paned w^t curtyns of the same.
> ij Awter clothes of blew saten a brydges imbrowdred w^t flowres w^t an Image of Saynt Clement for o^r Lady Awt', and ij Curteyns of blew taffeta.
> ij awt' cloths w^t red cross^s for lent w^t Curteyns to the same.

There were fifteen cushions or pillows, chiefly used for missal rests on the altars; but "iiij pillows of russett ray for weddyngs" would doubtless be used as kneelers for bride and bridegroom.

Also nine corporas cases; one of them, according to the 1503 inventory, was a royal gift.

> Also another corpas case the one syde of cloth of gold and the other syde of blak velvett w^t l'res of gold R. and S. of the gyft of quene Elizabeth by the procuryng of Mr Richard Smyth yoman of the quenys robys w^t iiij knoppis of sylver w^t a corpas cloth to the same.

Five palls are named in the inventory, followed by an entry which is difficult to explain :—

A Cloth of gotis to ley in the weddyng cheyre.

Eight banners and three streamers are enumerated; five of the former bore the arms of England, and one the images of the Trinity and Our Lady. The following items are specially noteworthy :—

A sepulcre Cloth of right Crymson Satten imbrowdered w Imagerye w^t a frontaill of panys conteyning in length iiij yards w^t ij clothes of lawude for the sepulcre.
A canape of tissue for the Sacrament and a lawude w^t iiij botons wrought w^t gold and tassells of gold for the pix.
A Canapye of Crymson velvett imbrowdred w^t gold flowres and the Holy lombe in the mydle.
A cloth of ray Silk to bere the crysmatory at Est^r.
A purse of crymysin cloth of gold pyrled for the vets.

The slight puzzle as to this last entry is cleared up by the variant of the 1523 inventory, where the purse is described as "pyrleyd for visytacons."

Twenty "Awter Clothes of Lynen"; the size of each is set forth. The first one is of the great length of five yards, and several are fully four yards—this would allow for the cloth hanging down at the ends; the breadth varies from a yard to a yard and a half. There were also seven towels of diaper; the great length of several of them, eleven to nine yards, denotes their use, as in the Bassingbourn inventory, for houseling cloths before communicants.

The 1503 inventory of St. Laurence, Reading, has a remarkable list of stained, *i.e.* painted, cloths :—

ij staynyd clothis w ryddeles to the same and a coveryng for the halpace (high pace) over the hy awlt' stayned w^t red damaske warke and an ymage of Seynt Laurence in the mydd^e.
A cloth staynd w^t the byrthe of o^r Lord for the fonte and a noy' cloth for the same of lynnyn w^t panys white and blew.
An aut clothe staynyd w^t an ymage of o^r lady of Pyte and ij angels, and a nother w^t the sepulcre, and ij angells for the hy awlt' in lent.
An ault' cloth of ray silke for the nether parte of the hy awter w^t a frontell of styrrs of gold.
A nother awt' clothe staynyd w^t an ymage of o^r lady onely.
A nother aut' clothe staynyd w^t o^r lady, Seynt Gregory Pyte, and Seynt Anne.

A nother awt' cloth of the salutacon and of the byrthe of o^r lorde.

A coverlynt of blak and grene w^t M and rosys white and red of the gyft of Alyce Adene.

An awt' cloth stayned of thassumpcion of o^r lady, seynt Anne, and seynt Margaret.

The accounts of St. Mary, Cambridge, for 1525 supply interesting details relative to the making of a festival cope within the parish.

> For v yardes and iij quarters for the cowpe and the halfe quarter of whytte dammaske at v s. viij d. ye yarde and for 1 unce of golde at iij s. viij d. ye unce . . . . . xxxvj s. xi d.
> For vij yardes of grene bukeram at vj d. ye yarde . iij s. vj d.
> For ij elles of Canvas at iiij d. ob. per ell . . . . ix d.
> For v unces of Sylke and iij skenes of blacke Sylke vj d. at xij the unce . . . . v s. vj d.
> For whytte threyde . . . . ij d.
> Paid unto the Brothers for viij wekes and iij days workyn of the Cowppe . . . . xxiij s. iij d.
> For iij unces and a quarteryn of Fenys (Venice) gold at iij s. viij d. ye unce . . . . . . xj s. xj d.
> For iij unces of fyssemen (vestment) rebyn at xij d. ye unce . iij s.

The vestments and other church goods of St. Stephen Walbrook were exceptionally rich and varied. In 1550 the parishioners were shrewd enough to make merchandise of the "Vestementys and other Implementes of the churche" in their own interests, rather than suffer spoliation at the hands of the Crown. Their sale realised (without any plate) the great sum of £132 11s. 10d.; the names of all purchasers are entered in the accounts.

The subjoined entries bear witness to the fact that chasubles, copes, albs, rochets, etc., remained (apparently in use) in many churches far into the reign of Elizabeth. They corroborate in a remarkable manner the common-sense view of the "Vestment Controversy," namely, that vestments were understood to be sanctioned by the Ornaments Rubric, but that their use *gradually* died out, owing to the frequent ascendency of a Puritan spirit and the great cost necessary for their maintenance.

1561-2 (*Tavistock*). One payre of Sarples.
    A payre of Reade Sylke vestement.

> A pere of whette Damaske vestement for Decon and Subdecon.
> A sute of vestemente of yelow Sylke Decon and Subdecon.
> One whytte Coppe of Sattyn bourgis.
> 1565 (*Strood*). A cope a vest an alb, 2 stoles, and a yellow and blue silke alt clo', a torch and a crysmatury.
> 1568. Pyx, pair of censers, baner stuff.
> 1571. Sold at St. Dunstun time "the crosse and other gere" 6s.
> 1573. A cope.

An Elizabethan inventory, of 1560-1, of All Saints, Derby, shows that the church retained a cope and suit of vestments of black velvet, as well as "a fyne Vestment that Mr Reyd gave." An inventory of 1563-4 names, in addition, "A Coope of blew Chamlet." The last year in which copes are mentioned in the yearly inventories is 1567-8, but albs are enumerated year by year up to 1576-7.

An inventory of St. Michael, Worcester, of 18th January 1561, included an old vestment, two albs with apparels, and six stoles.

> 1562 (*St. Margaret, Westminster*). One vestment of blew cloath of tissue with the tunicles for deacon and subdeacon.
> One cope of crymson cloth of tyssue.
> ij coorse copes of blew tissue.
> One cope of purple cloth of tissue.
> One other cope of crymson velvet with skall of shells of silver.
> One cope of crymson velvet with flowrs of gold.

In 1565 Christ Church, Bristol, retained four costly copes and five chasubles. The list of "implements" belonging to the church of St. Werburgh in the same city, for the year 1567, specifies a cope of blue velvet.

> 1584-5 (*Ludlow*). Receaved for an olde Blewe Coape being worne oute and full of holes . . . . . ij s.
> For other old Coapes . . . . . v s.

"A cope and a Vestemente and three stooles" in the church of St. Ewen, Bristol, appear in an inventory of 1596. Two years later they were sold for 50s. "by consent."

A costly cope remained in the church of St. Christopher-le-Stocks, London, up to 1618, when it was sold for 50s.

The once generally used post-Reformation vestment, the surplice, eventually rose to a considerable price.

1547 (*St. Nicholas, Warwick*). vj elles of lynen Clothe for a
surplese . . . . iiij s.
1566 (*St. Peter, Ipswich*). For a newe Surplis . xj s.
1572-3 (*St. Thomas, Sarum*). Making of 2 surplises yt were made
of iiij of the albs wche be in ye vestry v s. vj d.
1584 (*St. John, Winchester*). Ten ells for a surplece of Holland xx s.
Making of the same . . . . . . xvj d.
1590 (*Seal, Surrey*). For sixe elles of holland to make the
surplusse at xx d. the ell . . . . . x s.
For cutting of the surplusse . . . . . ij d.
For twopenyworthe of white threede . . . ij d.
For making of the surplusse. . . . . xij d.
1603-4 (*St. Botolph, Cambridge*). For a new surplusse xxv s. v d.
1632-3 (*St. Martin, Leicester*). P^d for viij elles and iij quarters of
Holland for a surplesse at 4s. 7d. . . . ii li. ij d.
P^d for making of yt . . . . . v s.
1638. For 8 ells of Holland to make a surplice . £1 8 0
Item for making the same 5 0
1695. For 12 yards of fine Holland £3, for making of a surplice 7s. 6d.

Entries for gloves are of occasional occurrence.

1524-5 (*St. Mary-at-Hill*). For Glovys at Estur for the churchwarden and the clerk . . . . . vj d.
Item more for that was paid at Estur for ij peyre of gloves
for the churchwardens the Summe of vj d., which shall
not be for no presedent hereafter.
1545 (*St. Michael, Worcester*). For a peare of gloves for the
clerkes ease . . . . . . ij d.
1561-2 (*Tavistock*). For a payre of glovys for Mr Vicar . xv d.
1584 (*St. Christópher-le-Stocks*). For a payer of Gloves geven
unto the Bushopp of St. Androues in the name of the
whole parish by Mr Parson . . . . iiij s.

The 58th canon of 1603 provides that "such ministers as are graduated shall wear upon their surplices such Hoods, as by the orders of the Universities are agreable to their degrees." The same canon orders that the surplice was to be provided "at the charge of the parish." Some ministers were ingenious enough to persuade their parishes that the canon intended the hood to be provided after a like fashion; but it is quite obvious that this was never intended.

1612 (*St. Mary, Reading*). For Mr Wolfes hood contayninge one
yeard and a quarter of Read Clothe at xiiij s. a yarde and
for one Elle of Rydee Taffetie with the Silke and makinge 34s.

1626. For a Scarlet hood for Mr Doctor Denison . . . 1 7 10
1634 (*All Saints, Derby*). To Dr Williamate for his Hood   1 10 0
1637. For a Hood for Mr Crawftur 15 4
1663 (*Redenhall, Norfolk*). For a master of Arte his hood for the Minister . . . . 1 6 c
1670 (*St. Martin, Leicester*). Ordered that the churchwardens provide a hood for Mr William Barton, at the charge of the parish, and so to be kept for the use of the parish.
1680 (*Edenbridge*). Will Stephens for silke to new Lyne ye Hood. 5s. 8d.

In several town parishes, surplices were provided in the sixteenth and seventeenth centuries for clerks and sextons; it should be remembered that "sexton" is a corruption of "sacristan."

1551 (*St. Michael, Worcester*). The clerks sorples (Inventory).
1568. For mendyng the clerks surplls . . . . ij d.
1563 (*St. Martin's-in-the-Fields*). Makyng the preste Surplese and mendyng the clarke ij surplesses . . . . ij s.
1565. For washinge of the Clarkes Surples . . . . vj d.
1567. For washinge the vicars clarkes and sextons surplyses for or lady day quarter . . . . . . xij d.
1574 (*Ludlow*). For lynen clothe to make ij surpleses for Higges sounes and for makinge the same . v s.
1628 (*St. Margaret, Westminster*). For thirteen ells of Holland to make surplisses for the two clerks and sextons, at 3s. 4d. the ell . . . . 3 16 c

The accounts of the Durham parishes of St. Oswald and St. Nicholas, and of Pittington and Houghton, co. Durham, show that the use of the surplice by the parish clerk in the sixteenth and seventeenth centuries prevailed in all four instances; it appears in the accounts of St. Nicholas as late as 1679.

The rochet, or sleeveless surplice, continued in occasional use long after Reformation days.

1571-2 (*St. Petrock, Exeter*). For x yardes of morles (Morlaix) clothe for a surplece . . . . . xv s.
For iij yardes of dowlus, to make a rochet for the clerk .
1591 (*Stâplegrove, Somerset*). Two surplices and one Racheit used a(t) comunion.
1602 (*St. Botolph, Cambridge*). An old Rouchett without Sleves.
1626 (*Sidbury, Devon*). A Surplisse and rochett.
[Like entries up to 1648.]

The following are instances of parish-provided gowns:—

1595–6 (*St. Thomas, Sarum*). Mr Lascombe the preiste for his Gowne . . . . 10s.

1662 (*St. Thomas, Sarum*). M Hussey to provide a convenient handsome gown, at a cost not exceeding £3, to lie in the Vestry for the use of any strange minister coming here to preach at lecture.

1681 (*St. Martin, Leicester*). Paid for cloth for the clerk's gown £1 4 6
For trimming and making it 4 8

CHAPTER X

CHURCH PLATE—IMAGES

Chronological entries of exceptional plate—Tavistock, 1385, to St. Martin, Ludgate, 1611—Inventories of St. Laurence, Reading—Inventory, 1498, of Bassingbourne—Lectern

Images — St. Laurence, Reading—Patron Saint — Tabernacles — Chronological extracts—Saffron Walden, 1464, to images of the Marian revival—Boxes for offerings — Cult of St. George — Articles of personal jewellery — Image decking

ALTAR Plate—consisting of the Chalice, Paten, Cruets, Pyxes, and Ciboria, and at a later date the Monstrance—is necessarily of frequent occurrence in the parish accounts, as well as Censers and Incense Vessels, the Pax, the Chrismatory, the altar or processional Cross, and Candlesticks. To these may be added Croziers or Pastoral Staffs, Mitres, and the occasional jewelled binding of the Missal or Textus. All these are dealt with, explained, and illustrated in *English Church Furniture* of this series of books (pp. 28–59).

A few extracts may be given to illustrate the value and elaborate character of Church Plate both in town and country.

A Tavistock inventory of 1385–6 enters a cup and cover of silver, with two silver-gilt angels holding a glass receptacle (*vitreu¹ clausu¹*) wherein the Body of our Lord is borne.

1464. (*Yatton, Somerset*). Pro emptura nove calicis . v li. vj s. viij d.
    Isa wyts to ryde to Woke (Bp. Bekynton's manorhouse) to
        blesse the chals . . . . . iij d.
    For a case for the chals . . . . . viij d.

In 1488–9 the churchwardens of *St. Botolph, Aldersgate*, "Answer of cxiiij s. ij d. by theym recevyd for an olde crosse of sylver and gylt solde by the assent and agrement of the parishioners, pond" xxxij unc.

1470–1 (*Tavistock*). One beryl set in silver and with a chain of
    silver, to hang to the pyx with the Body of Christ on
    the principal feasts.

CHURCH PLATE—IMAGES 139

1538-9. For mendyng of a lock to the Coffur that kepithe the
Syngying bredd in . . . . . j d.
1478-9 (*St. Ewen, Bristol*). Rec. of the bequest of Gilliam Sampson a
Sylver Cup covered, weying xxv unces and iij quarters, price the
unce iij s. Suma iij li. xvij s. iij d. The which cup is altered and
changed into a Chalice to the use and behof of the church.

The inventory of St. Edmund. Sarum, for 1472, shows a considerable wealth of plate. There were 15 chalices with their patens of silver gilt, five of them enamelled; 6 silver-gilt crosses with staffs; 4 candlesticks, a pair of censers and ships, a bason, 4 cruets, a pix, a cup, a monstrance, a pax, 2 chrismatories, and a small bell, all of silver, and either gilt or parcel-gilt.

1480-2 (*St. Margaret, Westminster*). For peyntyng of the nether
parte of the Crosse staffe . . . . . xx d.
For gyltyng and burnysshyng of the upper parte . iiij s.
For the new crosse weying $^{xx}_{vj}$ unc p'ce every unc v s.
Sma . . . . . . xxxij li. x s.
1482-4. For a pair of basons of silver . . . xxiiij iij d.
1480-2 (*St. Andrew Hubbard*). For ij Candelstikes of Selver to
the high aulter weying xl unces and a quarter price the
unce workmanship and weight iiij s. Suma viij li. xij d.
Of the which some certyn well disposed men of the
parissh gave of their gode willes toward the charge of
the seid candelstikke, as it appeareth hereafter xviij s.
iiij d. And so was paid of the chirche mony outt of the
box . . . . vij li. ij s. viij d.

The first entry of the 1483-4 inventory of St. Petrock, Exeter, is

"A box of gold with a berell to bare the Sacrament in ponderyng xviij di unc."

This pyx was then valued at £24. The silver-gilt plate, including six chalices, weighed 281¼ ounces, and was valued at £40 4s. 2d.

In 1509 a payment was made of £5 4s. to the wardens of St. Botolph, Aldersgate, by

John Marlow parish clerk, price of chalis by hys neclygence lost.

It appears from the accounts of North Elmham that there was an unusually early sale of church plate, etc., in 1542; these sales were probably to some extent the result of heavy fabric charges during that year; but the tone of the parish must have been towards reform, to have admitted of making merchandise of church plate of the character.

> Rec. of Symond Newton of Norwyche for certen plate after iiij s. ye unce . . . . xxiij s.
> Rec. of ye same Symond for ye Sylver yt was upon the Crosse y^t the relyques wher yn' . . . . xix s. ij d.
> Rec. of Mr Nycholle for ye sylver shews wych wer upon ye brown rodes fete . . . . x s.
> 1544 (*Mendlesham, Suff.*). x day of January, Wyltur Seynard and Thomas, etc., have soulde unto Gylbart ye gouldsmyth of Ipyswch j payre of sensers, j payre of chalys of dubyll gylte, j pyxe, a schepe and a spone, after iij s. vj d. the ounce, the wyche same mountythe unto xvj li. ij s. vj d., by ye consente of Wylliam Singulton gentyll and Willyam Dunckyn ye elder. And a croslyt of plate and gylt w^t stones and ij payre of challysys of paarsyl gylt.
> 1543. Item sould the iij daye of February a crosse of gylt for xij li.

In 1611, Henry Swedall, churchwarden, gave to the church of St. Martin, Ludgate, a second cup of silver, double gilt, weighing 36 ounces, owing to the number of communicants which had necessitated the borrowing of another cup whenever there was a celebration.

The earliest book of church accounts of St. Laurence, Reading, contains three inventories, dated respectively 1503, 1517, and 1524. The one of 1517 is unusually full, and sets forth the magnificent appointments of this church in detail. It is given *in extenso* in Mr. Kerry's annals. The total weight of the church plate, mostly of silver-gilt and parcel-gilt, amounted in that year to 583 ounces, but by 1523 it had been increased to at least 700 ounces. All kinds of altar vessels and ornaments were included; the two following items merit special mention:—

> It. ij bokes a gospellor lxix unc' and a pistellor lxv unc' the one side cov^rd w^t silver p'cell gilt w^t Images uppon the same and the other side w^t boces of silver weyng yn all cxxxiii unc' of the gifte of Mr Richard Smyth yemen of the robes w^t our sovrayne lord the kyng.
> It. a gredyson of silver and gilt w^t a bone of Saynt Laurence therein weyng iij q'rt of an unc' of the gifte of Thomas Lynde senyer.

In 1538, when Henry VIII's spoliation schemes first began to develop, the churchwardens sold plate to the value of £20 11s. 11d., and again in 1544 to the value of £26 13s. 4½d. So soon as

CHURCH PLATE—IMAGES

Edward VI came to the throne, the Reading authorities realised that the policy of sacrilege was about to be carried to its extreme limit, and they are not to be blamed for doing what they could to dispose of much of their plate for the advantage of the parish, rather than suffer it to be absorbed by the insatiable greed of the Crown. Plate, therefore, was sold in 1547-8 to the value of £47 18s. It only just escaped the clutch of the royal commissioner. In the same year's accounts are the three following entries:—

Paid to Mr Bell, Mayor, of that was made of a chalice for pavyng in the strets. . . . . . . iiij s. iiij d.
Paid and delyvered to Mr Bell, Mayor, by M. Nicholas uppon the ij Chalices by him sold towards the pavyng of the Strets by the assent of the p'sche. . . . . . v li.
Paid for makyng of Inventories for the Church goods to the Comyssioners at ij tymes . . . . . iij. s. iiij d.

It is some satisfaction to feel that the forethought of the wardens saved upwards of one hundred pounds' worth of plate from passing to the Crown.

The following is the first part of the elaborate 1498 inventory of church goods of Bassingbourn, Cambridge, not hitherto printed:—

In primis iiij Crossis ij of Copir and over gilted, with ayther of theyme a fote of the same, and one of the same Crosses having a staffe of coper and over giltid with ij knottes of the sam metalles. Item to the saide Crosses ayther of theym having a Clothe of sylke the best of Rede sylk the secunde of yalowe sylk with the ymage of trinite pyctured in ayther of theym. Item the othir ij Crossis beyng of laten the one of theis ij havyng a staffe with a cloth pyctured with the ymage of seynt John the baptiste nyghe worne.

Item a baner Clothe of Rede sylk of Elnor lyon maid gift with the ymage of the trynitie ther uppon.

Item a pyxe of laten with a crucifixe of silver for the hyghe altar.

Item to the same pixe iij Clothis one of Rede silke the othirs of wyghte lawne and ayther of the thre clothes having iij tacelles.

Item a crysmatorye of pewter ij Cruetes of Coper and over gilted.

Item iij Crewettes and a wyne Botell of pewter. Item a pott for water of pewter.

Item ij holywater stoppis of laten. Item j Basyn and ij laverys of lateyn. Item j styppe of lateyn. Item one othir clothe for the seid pixe of lawn with the frenges of gren sylk and reed and iiij tasilles of Reed sylke with the blyssid full name of ihesu broydryd in iiij places of the seid clothes.

Item ij kercheff of lawn to leye uppon the crucifixe.

Item iij smalle frontylles of lawne to the ymages of Seynt Kataryn. Item ij frontynelles to the ymage of ye salutac' of our ladye.

Item j Chalys of the gift of Robert bolnest of sylver with his name and his wyff uppon the fote of ytt.

Item j chalis bylonging to the trinite gild of the giftes of sur hughe Wyche and dame Alic his wyff and that other of Kateryne Bantlowe.

Item ij Chalis mor one of the geft of Ric Gelyngate and the other of Mrs Jone lynn.

The following post-Reformation entries of city church accounts may perhaps find a place under "Church Plate":—

1564 (*St. Michael, Cornhill*). For makinge cleane the greate deske of Latten called the Fawcon. . . . . ij s.
1566. For skowringe the Egill at Ester . . . . ij s.
1581 (*St. Christdpher-le-Stocks*). Rec. for the Egle of Lattin or brasse . . . . xlj s. vj d.
1555 (*St. Peter Chedp*). For a deske called a fawton with feete of lyons all latten . . . . . iij li. vij s. vij d
[A subsequent entry shows that this was an "Egele of Bras."]

The accounts of St. Laurence, Reading, afford a good instance of the number and richness of the Images in the more important town churches. In addition to the invariable Rood with SS. Mary and John, there were statues or images of Our Lady (2), St. Laurence (3), St. John Baptist, St. Michael, St. Mary Magdalene, St. Clement, St. George, St. Vincent, St. Katherine, and St. Leonard. There were also several smaller ones standing in niches on the piers of the nave and aisles. There were two external images of the patron saint, the one on the right hand of the west entrance of the tower, the other, of late date, at the east end.

1520. Paid for boards for makyng of the fentice over the Image of Saynt Lawrence and for setting upp the same Image without the church at that end of the quere iiij s. ij d.

But the chief figure of St. Laurence was in the proper place for the patron saint's image, namely, immediately to the north of the high altar against the east wall. The chief images of a church were usually of an earlier date and of a better style than those of the fifteenth century, and hence are rarely named in extant accounts save by way of embellishment. The following entry helps us to realise the magnificence and beauty of church adornments; and it may here be remarked that the "tabernacles" of church accounts, whether expressed in English or Latin, usually signify the

CHURCH PLATE—IMAGES 143

canopied recesses, of either stone or wood, wherein images stood, and not "shrines," which is a frequent but erroneous explanation.

> 1519. Paid to John Paynter in Ernest of xiiij li. xiij s. iij d. for gilding of the ij Tab'nacles in the quere with all necessaries thereto . . . . . . xx s.

The cost of this work, according to our present money standard, and including the wages of a good craftsman and his assistant, would be about £140. Another entry about this date mentions a fee of 6s. 8d. paid to the "Kyngs paynter" for seeing or passing judgment on the work of embellishing a tabernacle.

The second tabernacle in the quire, which was gilded after so costly a fashion, would doubtless be one to Our Lady immediately to the south of the altar. There was another image of the Blessed Virgin by the Lady altar at the east end of the nave on the south side of the chancel arch. A cloth and a kerchief were given to this altar by Juliania Roche in 1436; a new bench (for kneeling purposes) was placed before this image of St. Mary in 1441, at the cost of 8d.; and an entry of 1506 names 6d. for mending "one of the grate candlestikks before O^r Lady." The wardens of the Lady Mass, sung at this altar, were charged with an annual payment of 33s. 4d. towards the sexton's or sacristan's wages.

There must have been an image of St. John Baptist in the important north chapel of the quire usually termed "St. John's Channcell," by the side of his altar; the great candlesticks before that altar, supplied in 1503, weighed 103 lb., and cost 51s. 6d.

> 1523. To an Alabast' man for makeying clene the table at Saynt Johns Autr' and other ymages . . xvj d.

An image of St. Michael was supplied at a late date; the cost is not set forth in the accounts — it was probably the donation of some modest benefactor, but there are entries of certain particulars.

> 1519. Paid for canvas for coveryng of Saynt Michell iij d.
> Paid for cariage of the Image from Maynard of London . iiij d.

The following entry tells of an image of St. Vincent:—

> 1524. To John Paynters wyff for gyldynge of pte of Saynt Vyncent Tabernacle . . . . . . iij s. iiij d.

St. Clement's altar, with his image, stood in the north aisle.

1516. Paid for mendyng of the beame for Saynt Clement's light . viij d.
1520. Payd for mendyng of the cloth before Saynt Clement . iiij d.

Mr. Kerry gives good reasons for believing that this altar, as well as the great mounted figure of St. George, stood on a continuation of the rood-loft at the entrance to St. John's chapel, and over the altar of St. Thomas. The following interesting items occur in 1534, under the heading "Charge of Saynt George"; they show that St. George was given a realistic horse.

For iiij Caffes skynes and ij horse skynnes.	iiij s. vj d.
For makinge the loft (dais) that Saynt George standeth upon	. vj d.
For ij planks for the same loft	. viij d.
For iiij peeces of clowt lether	. ij s. ij d.
For makeyng the yron that the hors resteth upon .	vj d.
To John Paynter for his labor	. xlv s.
For roses bells gyrdle swerd and dager .	iij s. iiij d.
For settyng on the bells and roses	. iij d.
For nayles necessarie therto	. x d. ob.

The image of St. Mary Magdalene was one of those which were dressed or specially garbed, usually only on festivals. The cloth-of-gold coat was probably a royal mantle with falling sleeves; one phase of her legend represented her as of royal extraction and of the castle of Magdala. The following entry is made in the full inventory of 1517, under the head of Vestments:—

Id. a Cotte for Marmawdlyn of clothe of gold.

The lights of St. Catherine were in the chapel of St. John; they are first mentioned in 1433, and again in 1436. Where there were lights, there would certainly be an image.

The following brief excerpts from a variety of parish accounts, arranged chronologically, will help to give an idea of the expenditure and skill bestowed upon these representations of the saints both in town and country:—

1464 (*Saffron Walden*). Solut' Johi Dawys pro uno grosso arbore
ad faciend imag' be' Marie . . . . . iiij s.
[The carving and painting of this image and its tabernacle cost £9 12s. 11d.]

CHURCH PLATE—IMAGES

1467 (*Yatton, Somerset*). To the peynter to peynt oure Lady . iiij li.
For peyntyng the Crystofer . . ij li. iij s. v d.
1474-5 (*St. Nicholas, Hedon*). Pro pictacione tabernaculi Sancti
Nicholai . . . . . . ij s. iiij d.
1479 (*St. Botolph, Aldersgate*). For amendyng of the tabernacle of
Seynt Botulph . . . . . . x s.
To a kerver for half a day for settyng up of the Image of
Seynt Botolph . . . . . . iiij d.
1493 (*Eastfield, Suffolk*). To Thomas Bottre for peyngtyng of ye
image of our lady . . . . . ij li. xiij s. iiij d.
To ye seyd Thomas for ye peyngtyng of tabernacell of Seynt
Edmund . . . . viij s.
1494. To Thomas Bottre for y^t tabernacell peyntyng of our lady vij li.
1498. To Thomas Bottre for ye peyntyng of the image of Saynt
Edmunde i y^t tabernacle . . viij li. vj s. viij d.
1497-1500 (*St. Andrew Hubbard*). For the settyng in off the ymage
of Our lady in her tabernakyll to a Joyner . v d.
1498 (*Bassingbourn, Cambs*). John turpyn senior bequethed to
the peynting off the Tabernacle off seynte James x s.
1502. Robert Knott off lyttllyngton off George Kenton byquest to
the peynting off the Rodeloft . . . vj s. viij d.
John Turpyn the yonger byquethid and gaff to a Booke for
bass' Chyrche by his executor to be boughte viij marks
1507. In Ernest to a Kerver for the ymage off seynt Marg' i d.
Delivered to the Kerver for the ymage off seynt Margar' . x s.
Payd to the peyntur of Barkwey for iiij panes and the ymages
off seynt Margar and saynt Kateryn with their tabernacles
peynting . . . . . . iiij li. vj s. viij d.
1515. John Dykan of bass'dy off Ric' sely byquest to the peynting
of seynte Christoffer and off seynt Nicholas xx d.
To the peynting off the ymage of seynt Margar' and seynt
Kateryn and the tabernacle . . . . iij s. iiij d.
1518 (*Wimborne*). John Rekeman hath paid x pounds for the gilt-
inge of oure lady with the images about her in oure lady
chapel: for which x pounds he is discharged for ever, and
no man shall put him nor charge him to be Churchman
(*i.e.* Churchwarden).

"Pixes" or boxes stood at the feet of images of St. Cuthberge, St. James, St. Laurence, Our Lady, and "King Harry" (Henry VI) and the Rood, in Wimborne Minster, to receive offerings.

There was a remarkable development in many parts of England, at the beginning of the sixteenth century, in the devotion shown to the patron saint, St. George.

146   THE CHURCHWARDENS' ACCOUNTS

A chapel was added to the north side of the chancel of Croscombe, Somerset, to provide for the cult of the newly established gild of St. George. A "Gorgemaker" was employed to make a great trophy, at considerable outlay, of England's patron saint on horseback in his encounter with the dragon.

1506-7. John Carter, Gorgemaker, Vremassyn (Free mason) of
    Exeter recyved of the parish of Croscombe the sum of .   iiij li.
    Item payd the fryst of January to the same man .   .   iiij li.
1508-9. The wardens hath y payd owtte of the box of the church money xxx s. unto John Carter, the Gorge maker at the settyng uppe of the Gorge.
1511-2. Item the cost of the Gorge, the holle sum of all the coste . . . . . xxvij li. xj s. viij d.

The accounts of 1515-6 and subsequent years show that this gild of St. George maintained a light before the image, presented an annual sum to the wardens of their profits, and had a box in the chapel for offerings. In 1522-3 there was an ale of St. George, the "crysse" of which amounted to 13s. 7d.

1506-7 (*Holy Trinity, Cambridge*). Money R' by Harry Cryswell
    and Roland Smythe toward the setting uppe off seynt
    Gorge in the Church . . . . .
    R' Gaddert off the kynges Grasse and hys lordes at Seynt
    Jorge day anno xv^{c}iijth . . . . xxxv s. iij d.
    R' off the Gyld money off seynt Gorge the same year and
    tyme . . . . . . xxviij s. xj d. ob.
    R' and gaddert off the Chanons when the Chapter was at
    Barnewell . . . . x s. j d.
    R' off Mr Mowrons and hys wyfe for the bequest off
    Mastrys Cope in parte off pament off a mont sum . xxv s.
    R' off Mr Wood for Mastrys bolton .   vj s. viij d.
    R' off the parrych that was Gaddert by Wylliam Wortwall
    and Jamus Goldsmyth . . . . . xxvj s.
                    Summa . vj li. xij s. ob.
1547 (*Ludlow*). Rec. for the lofte that saynte George stode one   vj s.
    For the image of saynt George that stode in the chapelle . xviij d.
    For a volte . . . that the image stode on .   iij s. iiij d.
    For a image of Jesus that stood Beawpie chapelle .   x d.
    For a tabernacle that saynt Margett stode in   vj d.
    For a image of Jhesus that stode in Beawpie chapelle   x d.
    For a tabernacle that saynt Margett stode in   vj d.
    For the dragan that the image of saynt George stode upon   vij d.

CHURCH PLATE—IMAGES

<table>
<tr><td colspan="2">For the tabernacle of the image of saynt Kateryne</td><td>vj d.</td></tr>
<tr><td colspan="2">For the case that stode in Trynitie chancelle</td><td>ij s. ij d.</td></tr>
<tr><td colspan="2">For the tabernacle that saynte Anne stode in</td><td>vııj d.</td></tr>
<tr><td>1531</td><td>(St. Margaret, Westminster). To the payntour for payntyng and gyldyng of the lx storys of saynt Margaretts tabernacle.</td><td>iij li. vj s. viij d.</td></tr>
<tr><td></td><td>For gyldyng of xij small images for the small tabernacle</td><td>ij li. viij s.</td></tr>
<tr><td>1533</td><td>Payd to Willm Hulle, carvar, for makyng the gorge and the dragonne</td><td>vııj s. vııj d.</td></tr>
<tr><td colspan="2">For nayles and yarn warke to ye gorges</td><td>xvj d. ob.</td></tr>
</table>

Under Queen Mary, not only were the Roods re-supplied, but also images of the patron saints.

<table>
<tr><td>1556 (St. Michael, Cornhill). To Peter the Joyner for Saint Mihell</td><td>iii li.</td></tr>
<tr><td>For a stone that Saint Mihell standes on</td><td>iiij s.</td></tr>
<tr><td>Labor to sett it upe</td><td>v s.</td></tr>
<tr><td>1556 (Smarden, Kent). For the ymage of Saint Michell
[The patron saint.]</td><td>xx s.</td></tr>
<tr><td>1557 (St. Peter Cheap). To lewes the copper smyth in gutter lane for the Image of Saynte Peter</td><td>li s.</td></tr>
</table>

The parish accounts frequently afford evidence of the multiplicity of gifts and bequests of articles of jewellery, especially of wedding rings, assigned to the church. Occasionally such gifts were sold by the wardens and the proceeds added to the general church fund; but much more frequently they were used to deck favourite images. Special jewellery or costly vestures were sometimes reserved to brighten particular festivals.

Among the bequests at St. Margaret, Westminster, in 1499 were included:—

A paire of Coral beds banded wᵗ silver and giltt wᵗ a litill Rynge wᵗ a knop of perle gyven to the worship of God and our ladi and Seynte Margarett to be hanged uppon the ymage of Seynte Margaret every day or else every halyday as they will.

On the apron of the image of St. Cuthberga, Wimborne, in 1530, there actually hung 130 rings, 3 silver spoons, and 4 " great Buckylls of sylver and gilt."

The inventory of the chapel of St. Mary of the Bridge, Derby, in 1488, among the wardens' accounts of All Saints, appears the most remarkable example I know of the decking and adorning of images:—

Our Lady of the Bryge

In p'mis on' Cote of crymyson Velvett ende'ted w^t gold that my lady Gray gaffe / & opon hytt ys lxvj penyes ii gilte penies on' gylte ob (farthing) ij penese of ij d. on' grotte An' Ee' (?) of silver ij shells of sylver / on' herte of silver / A mowne (moon) of silver on' broche of Copeer & gylte / ij shafts of silv'r on' cristall ston inclosed In silver.

Also on' Cote of blewe velvett y^t my lady chamburlayn gaffe Ther' opon ys A crown of sylver & gylte that John boroes gaff Itm a grett broche of silv' & gylte w^t A stonne In hytt Also on casse of Redde satten w^t buttons of silv' & gilt Itm lx pens iiij Gylte pens / on' peny of ij^d / on crosse of sylv' Itm a casse of velvett / on' broche / & on' peny of hytt And a crystall stonne.

Itm on' Garment y^t my lady longforth gaff of blewe velvett and Rede And on' y^t ys A crucifix of silv' & gylt w^t A Ryng of Golde that Maistres bonyton gaff Itm on' tablet of golde y^t Maistres Stanlay gaffe Also A Ryng of silv' & gilte Anoy^r of Cop^r / vi ster D & iiij D & vj halfepens / iiij grotes iiij pens of ij^d vi flewers of silver & gilte Itm x Curall bedes w^t ij silver Gawdyse.

Itm on Cote to o^r lorde of Crymyson velvett furred w^t menyver y^t my lady longforth gaff Opon hyt y^s A shylde of sylv' w^t v bende pens Itm xi pens And v gylte pens / A peny of ij^d Itm on' payr of beds of silver / gaudred wt chorall y oxle wyff gaff Itm on' ston closed in silv' w^t on cros of silver / on' brōch of silver / ij oy broches of silv' & gilte w^t on' colar of blak perle w^t xvij belles of silver And gylte.

Itm on' payr of bedes of Corall gauded havyg gaudeses of silv' & gilte w^t iiij Ryngs & ij c^{u}cfix^s of silv' & gylte w^t a c'stall ston sett ī silv' And a ston of curall that Richerd Baker wyfe gaffe.

Itm Anay^r payr of bedes of Corall w^t gaudeses of silv' and gylte w^t on' golde Ryng & ij Rings of silv' and gilte w^t ij crucifix' of sylv' & gylte that Richerd Sale wyfe gaffe.

Itm on payr of bedes of Corall gaudede w^t sylv' y^t Richerd Colyar wyffe gaffe.

Itm on' payr of bedes of blak Jette.

Itm on' payr of bedes of Corall w^t p'ciose stones w^t xxv gaudres of silv' w a tufte sett w^t perles y^t Rog' Justice wyf gaffe.

Itm on' gylte gyrdel y^t maistress entwysel gaffe.

Itm on' p'pull gyrdel yEdmunde dey wyfe gaffe.

Itm on' blewe gyrdell sylv' herneste w^t vij studds on hytt y^t John hyll wyffe gaffe.

CHAPTER XI

FONTS AND PULPITS

East Dereham font—Cowfold—St. Laurence, Reading—Font-cover, Yatton Chrismatory clothes—Font locks—St. Mary, Cambridge—Brass locks—Font cloths—Fonts forbidden under the Commonwealth—Fonts of St. Giles, Northampton and Wirksworth—Pulpits universal—Entries from Arlington, 1458, to St. Mabyn, 1654—Puritan love for costly pulpit hangings and cushions—The Bede Roll from the pulpit

ENTRIES relative to fonts are naturally often found in wardens' accounts. Full details are fortunately preserved in the accounts of East Dereham, Norfolk, for 1466, of the cost of the material (brought over the seas from Caen) and the workmanship of one of the finest of the East Anglian fonts. See *Archæologia*, x. 196. The font cost about £150 of our money.

Imprimis, payd to the mason quan he toke the said funte in arneft	iiij d.
Item, payd for makyng of an oblegaceon in the which he was bound for the seyd work	iiij d.
Item, payd for lying of the frestone, that was for the seyd funte atte Lynne	xxij d.
Item, payd for carryng of the seyd stone	ij s. viij d.
Item, payd for carrying iiij lods of the seyd fre stone fro Lynne to Est Derham per i lod carying ij s. vj d. summa	x s.
Item, payd to Thomas Platfote for carrying of iij lodes of frestone the seyd space takyng for a lode, iij s. summa	ix s.
Item, payd for di chalder of lyme xx d. and cc tyle bourt at Norwich xvj d. summa	iij s.
Item, payd to Robert Crane, for carrying of the seyd lyme and tyle	xx d.
Item, payd to Ric Wefthave, for ironwork to the seyd funte	xi d.
Item, in expens upon help quan the funte was in the reeping	ii d.
Item, payd to the mason for workmanship of the seyd funte	xli s.
Item, to his reward	xx s.
Item, payd to Will. Plomer for ledyng of the new funte	ij s. v d.
Item, payd to Will. Pylche for makyng of the stole to the funte and keverying of the same	xx d.
Item, payd for making of a quetance betwixt our mason and us	ij d.

The following particulars relate to font-making on a much meaner scale:—

1471-2 (*Cowfold, Sussex*). Solvere to the masyn for makyng of
    the fonte . . . . v s.
    For cariage of stone . . . . . viij d.
    For lym iiij d. and for fechyng ij d.
    Helpyng of mortar and other stuf . . . . ij d.

Some of the font entries in the accounts of St. Laurence,

THE FONT, EAST DEREHAM

Reading, are noteworthy. Master Cheney was employed at Cardinal Wolsey's new works at Hampton Court when an honorarium secured his services as a font-maker at Reading. Cheney's font, though much scraped, still stands in the church; it is a fairly handsome one of a usual and diagonal design; a few remains of the original colouring could still be traced on both bowl and shaft when we saw it in the "eighties" of last century. It was in this font that Archbishop Laud was baptized.

FONTS AND PULPITS

1520. For a Hose cloth gyven to the overseer of my lord Cardynalls werks to license Chayney the mason to cum fro them . . . . . iiij s. iiij d.
For chargis in Ridyng for Chaney the mason . iij s. iiij d.
1521-2. Rec' for led of the old font sold . . vij s.
Payd for boarding of the olde seatts where the olde font stode . . . . xviij d.
1572-5. To Chenye the mason for makeyng the fonte . xxxj s. viij d.
To the plumar for makeyng the font and mendyng of the stepall . . . . ix s. x d.

A single example must serve to illustrate entries as to font covers:—

1449 (*Yatton, Somerset*). Johanni Crosse carpentario pro coopertione baptysterii . xvj s.
Proglutino et clavi eidem baptysterio vj d.
For a lyne to the font ij d.
For the poley of gren to the fonte . . xviij d.

Various entries in wardens' accounts and church inventories show the costly nature—usually silver-gilt and often jewelled—of the chrismatory, or box containing the hallowed oils and chrism. This box was always locked, and usually kept in an almonry or locker in the chancel. It was treated with much reverence, and when carried from the chancel to the font for baptismal use

THE FONT, ST. LAURENCE READING

was always wrapped up in a special cloth reserved for that purpose. At St. Ewen, Bristol, the chrismatory cloth was of "rede silke"; at St. Mary, Worcester, of "turkey silke"; and at St. Laurence, Reading, of "ray silke."

1504 (*St. Mary, Cambridge*). (Inventory.) An olde Clothe of silke to lie in the Crysmatorye to the Fownte.
1527 (*Wimborne*). To the somner for bryngyng home of the holy oyle from Sarum at Easter . . . . xi d.
For a Towell of sylke to lay on the holy oyle Boxe . ij s. vj d.
1538. For a purse to carry the holy oyle box . xij d.

Three or four of these silk-embroidered chrismatory cloths fell into private hands at the time of the Reformation, and are mistakenly used for carrying infants to the fonts, a use for which they are obviously unsuited.

Locks for font covers are fairly common entries in the earlier accounts.

    1519 (*St. Mary, Cambridge*). For a lokke for the fonte . . ijˢd.
    1540. For a keye and mendyng of the loke of the fonte . . ij d.

The few following extracts will serve to illustrate the treatment of certain fonts in post-Reformation days, though archidiaconal records show how frequently they were neglected. The custom of painting the stonework of fonts continued.

    1571-2 (*St. Martin, Leicester*). For iiij li. of leayde to set fast yᵉ hooke over the font . . . . . iij d.
    To a plumar for settinge fast of yᵉ same . . . iiij d.
    Payde unto Christovar Nede for woorkmanshipe abowt yᵉ fonte . . . . vj d.
    Receyved of Mʳ Byshope for the beever that did hynge over the font . . . . . . xviij d.
    1622-3 (*St. Edmund, Sarum*). For mending the Cover of the Faunte and the Painter for newe dressinge of the Faunte . . . . 11s.
    1631-2 (*Stockton, Norfolk*). For coullering for the fonte . 1s.
    For the Cover of the funte . . . . . 13s. 4d.
    For the painting of the funte . . . . 4s.
    1633 (*St. Mary, Cambridge*). To George Tompson for the makeinge the funt £2
    For bread and beare spent on him and his servants 3s.
    For a barrell of Lintseed oyle to painte the fonte the porch and church dores . . . . . 14s. 6d.
    To David Blisse for payntinge the fonte etc. £1
    For makeinge the rayles about the fonte £2 7s. 9d.
    1634 (*Hawkhurst, Kent*). For the font cover . . . 10s.
    For a cord to draw it up . . . . . 8d.
    1639 (*St. Martin, Leicester*). To John Milkesop for a brasse cock for the font . . . . . . 4s.

A brass tap of seventeenth-century date may still be seen driven into the side of the mediæval font of Talland, Cornwall. There used to be one of these uncanonical abominations in the font of

Castleton, Derbyshire, and we believe there is another still in the ancient font of Mellor in the same county.

It was customary, preparatory to baptism, after the locked cover had been raised or removed to cover the font with a fair linen cloth. Out of more than a score of collected references to font cloths from wardens' accounts and inventories, it must suffice to cite two.

> 1455 (*St. Ewen, Bristol*). A white cloth for the font.
> 1556 (*St. Nicholas, Warwick*). Payd for Iron and workemanshype to hange the clothe on over the Font . iiij d.

A special use of the font cloth is named in a rubric of the Sarum Manual. In the midst of the office of *Benedictio Fontis*—an elaborate ceremony used on the eves of Easter and Pentecost, the seasons when in old days it was customary to baptize—after the taper had been immersed in the water, the priest is directed to pause, and if there were none to be baptized, the oil and chrism were not to be added, but the font was to be covered with a fair linen cloth (*linteamine mundo*), and thus reserved until the end of Easter or Pentecost.

When the Puritans came into power in the Commonwealth days, the use of the old fonts was forbidden; baptism was to be administered out of a mere bason, for which a stand or bracket near the minister's seat was sometimes provided. The bason was usually a mean thing of pewter; accounts show in a score or more of cases that it was provided, as at Aldwincle St. Peter, Northants, at a cost of 6d. The following are among the more noteworthy entries relative to font destruction and their subsequent restoration. The destruction began in many parishes immediately on the issue of the Presbyterian Directory of 1644-5.

> 1644-5 (*Strood, Kent*). For pavenyng the place wheare the Fonte stood . . . . 2s. 6d.
> 1645 (*St. Martin, Leicester*). For a bason to be used at baptism 5s.
> For a standard to bear the same . . . . 15s.
> For laying the same in marble colour . 5s.
> 1661. Agreed that the font of stone formerly belonging to the church shall be set up in the ancient place, and that the other now standing near the desk be taken down.
> Pd Widow Smith for the font stone, being the price her husband paid for it . . . . . 7s.

1647, April 7 (*St. Edmund, Sarum*). By virtue of an order from yᵉ Comittee presented to yᵉ Vestry Concerning the taking downe of ye Fontes in all the Parish Churches in this Cittie and Close of Sarum. It is ordered that Mʳ Nicholas Beach doe take downe yᵉ Font wherein baptisme was formerly administered and ye place where it stood made plaine with pavement stone and yt a frame for a font be forthwith sett up in a Convenient place neere yᵉ Ministers seat for ye administration of ye Sacrament. Mʳ Beach to set up in the place where the old Font did stand Portable seates of wainscott for the benefit of the Church.

1647–8 (*St. Thomas, Sarum*). Takeing downe the fonte and laying the stones ... 8s. 0d.

1660. Forthwith sett up the Font in the place where it formerly stood and allso to place the seat for the midwife adjoyninge to it as here to fore.

1650 (*Hawkhurst, Kent*). Rec. for the lead of the old font and for old brasse . 13s. 1d.

1656 (*St. Peter, Ipswich*). One bason for baptizing and a frame.

FONT, WIRKSWORTH, DERBYSHIRE

The old font of St. Giles, Northampton, was removed in 1658, and the lead with which it was lined sold for 16s. The churchwardens' accounts for 1661–2 contain the following items:—

Laide out for yᵉ font worke	3s. 4d.
Paide for taking downe the Presbiterian font . . .	1s.

The first of these entries refers to the repairs of the ejected font. The font now in use is a handsome one of fifteenth-century

FONTS AND PULPITS

design, much restored, but parts undoubtedly original. By a "Presbiterian font," a bason on an iron stand is probably signified.

The most elaborate font and font cover of any English church of Restoration date is that of Wirksworth, Derbyshire. The following items appear in the wardens' accounts of 1662:—

P^d ye Joyner for ye Cover of ye funt	£1 15s.
P^d John Ashmore And ye Carrier and Ashmore's man for settinge ye funt and other worke	£4 7s.
P^d Wm Greene for painting ye funt, etc.	11 0
And for Ale at the hanginge up of ye funt cover .	6d.

The whole question of fonts, and of the fonts of different counties, is treated of at length in *English Church Furniture*, pp. 160–235. See also Mr. Francis Bond's *Fonts and Font Covers* (1908) and Mr. Wall's *Porches and Fonts* (1912). The hallowing of the font is treated of under Holy Week.

Pulpits

The common notion that mediæval pulpits were exceptional in English churches is completely disproved by a study of parish accounts. Almost all those of pre-Reformation date contain entries relative to the repair of the pulpit, usually of a trivial character and not worth citing. Preaching was a continuous feature of the old Catholic days; it received a severe rebuff during the changes of the sixteenth century, when the authorities dared not permit the open expression of the views of the clergy. There was far less preaching in Elizabethan days than at any other period in the history of the Church of England. Matters somewhat improved towards the close of the century; but a full clergy list of 1602 for the diocese of Lichfield shows that out of 433 clergy less than a tenth, namely 42, were licensed to preach.

Here are a few of the more important pulpit entries from the earlier accounts and from those of the seventeenth century:—

1458 (*Arlington, Sussex*). Et ij s. iiij d. ob. p' faciend' de la pulpitte.	
1478–80 (*St. Margaret, Westminster*). For a pulpite in the Chirche Yerde agenst the preching of Doctour Penkey	ij s. viij d.
1447–8 (*Yatton*). For the makyng of the pulpyt	iij s. iiij d.

1503-4 (*St. Mary-at-Hill*). To John bull for hys labyr for mak-
kyng the pulppet . . . . . ix s. viij d.
To hys man for xiij dayys wark to the sam xiiij s. iiij d.
For Nayllys to the sam pulppet . . . . ij d.
[Other items for fixing it 2s. 7½d.]

1517-8. Resc' of Mr Doctor for the olde pulpet that stode in the
chirch . . . . v s.

1553 (*St. Margaret, Westminster*). For the pulpet where the
Curate and the Clarke did reed the chapter at service
tim . . . . xiij s. iiij d.

1578-9 (*St. Thomas, Sarum*). Mychell Joynes for a cover over the
powlpete 10 10

1583-4 (*St. Matthew, Friday Street*). To the joiner for makinge
the pulpitt . . . . . . iij li. xv s.
To the carpenter for a planck and for makinge the way
to the pulpitt . . . . . viij s. iij d.
To the Smyth for Iron Work about the pulpitt vj s.

1584-5. For a candelstyck for the pullpytt . . . . viij s.

1603-4 (*St. Botolph, Cambridge*). For Lininge the pulpitt with
greene Bayees, flockes and workmanship . iiij s. x d.

1609-10 (*Hartland, Devon*). Paid for a new pulpite . xxxiij s. iij d.

1634 (*St. Mabyn, Cornwall*). To making a new Pulpit ix li. v s.
To ye Painter for painting ye Pulpet . . . . v s.

The accounts of St. Laurence, Reading, show that a new pulpit was purchased in 1639.

It. by a tax of the parishioners towardes the new pulpett and church
reperations . . . . . . 13 li. 19s. 3d.
It. pd goodman hine for mooving the pulpit and setting him lower 4s. 3d.

But in 1741 this pulpit was sold to the churchwardens of Aldworth, Berks, for four guineas; and it can still be seen in that church. The accompanying drawing taken from Mr. Kerry's book shows that this pulpit is of a distinctly good Renaissance design.

The Puritan element which objected so strongly to bright colours in vestments, altar cloths, and even in painted glass, and desired to reduce the Houses of God to a dreary greyness, apparently found it impossible to reduce everything to neutral tints, and gave way in the case of pulpit hangings and cushions. It was the easier to do this as the pulpit exalted preaching, the most human part of the service. Bishop Stubbs, when writing about seventeenth-century pulpits, says: "The cushion of which seems to have been an object of special devotion."

FONTS AND PULPITS

1593 (*St. Martin's-in-the-Fields*). P^d for the olde Churchwarden beinge presented before Mr Doctor Stanhope for not having a pulpett cloth . . . . . x s.
1594. P^d for iij yardes and iij q^ths of blacke velvett for a cloth for ye pulpett and for frindge and Buckeram . . . iiij li.
For ye flowres theron ymbrodered . . . . xxiiij s.
1603-4 (*St. Martin, Leicester*). Payd to Coldwest for Worke abowte the pulpitt . . . . vj s.
Item for paintinge of it . . . . . v s.
1605-6. For halfe a yarde and a reale of grene carsie for a cushione for the pulpitt . . . . . . iij s.

PULPIT FORMERLY AT ST. LAURENCE, READING

For j read skyne and white skyne for the same . xviij d.
For vij and a halfe of fethers fringe and Crewell for the same . . . . . . iiij s. iiij d.
1620 (*St. Mary, Reading*). For Silke for the pulpit cussen and for canvis . . . . . . vij s. viij d.
For halfe yard of greene broddcloth for the cussen . vj s. vj d.
For making the cussen and triming of the pulpit . . iij s.
1621 (*Youlgrave, Derbyshire*). Three quarters of yellow serg for the pulpit quishen 0 2 6
Two brazile skinnes 0 2 4
Seven yeards of fringe and fyfteen skeynes of silke for the sayde quishen 0 3 11

158 THE CHURCHWARDENS' ACCOUNTS

For making the s^d quishen	0	2 5
Fyve li. of flocke to stuff the s^d quishen	0 2	0

1622 (*Basingstoke*). Received a pulpit cloth of green velvet which is the gift of Julian Hatfield, gentlewoman, and she desireth that it might serve and be hung upon the pulpit every festival day and Sabbath day and every Lecture day. [If used at a burial or christening, 12d. to be given to the wardens for the poor.]

1678-9 (*St. Martin, Leicester*). For a new cover for the pullpit and the coveringe it . . . . . xxj s. vj d.
For a pullpitt cloth of velvet and a cushion of the same . . . . . . xvj li. xviij s. viij d.
For two yardes of grene cotton at xvj d. the yard for a case for the velvet cushion . . . . ij s. viij d.
[These heavy charges for the beautifying the pulpit were disallowed at the vestry meeting, the minute being signed by 18 parishioners.]

1634-5 (*St. Oswald, Durham*). For 5 yeardes of Padua Serge togither with Silke for making the pulpitt cloth and cushion 3 2 1
For making the pulpitt cloth and cushion .
For workinge the fringe for the pulpitt cloth and cushion and for fethers and a ledd 11 0

1635-6 (*St. Edmund, Sarum*). Stuffe and fringe for ye Pulpit Cusheon 1 3 0

1646-7. Eleven yardes and a quarter of velvett at 15d. the yard for the Pulpitt cloth and Pulpitt Cusheon . . . 3 8 9
Eleven ounces of fringe ingraine and 3 quarters at 2s. 6d. per ounce 1 9 1
Foure Tassells for the Cusheon 8 0
Embroydering the figures on ye Cloth . . . 12 0
Buckrum and silke and making up the Pulpitt Cloth and Cusheon 1 4 0
More to B. Beckham for woorke don, as by his bill 2 10 0

1652. The pulpit Cloth bee forborne to bee layd because the Color is offensive to the sight of some of the parish. . . . The laying of the Pulpit cloth to be left to the discrecion of the C.W.

1666. (*Wirksworth, Derbyshire*). Payd to Mr Anthony Bunting for the Pullpitt Cushion 5 15 0

1669 (*Leek, Staffs*). Pulpit-cloath and fringe . . . 3 0 0
Thos. Hulme for making itt 0 2 0

In connection with the pulpit, mention ought to be made of the Bede-roll, to which reference has already been entered in the accounts of St. Edmund, Sarum.

FONTS AND PULPITS

The bede-roll, afterwards termed the bidding prayer, *i.e.* bidding the prayers of the congregation for the souls of benefactors, was read from the pulpit, usually by the parish priest, but occasionally by clerk or sexton. A small payment from the parish accounts was usually made to the " bedeman " for this service.

1477-9 (*St. Mary-at Hill*). To the parish preste to Remember in the pulpite the sowle of Richard Eliot which gave to the Churche workis vj s. viij d. . . . . ij d.

1489-90. To Mr John Redy (parish priest) for rehersing of the bederoll . . . . viij d.

1490-1. To Mr John Redye for the Rehersing of the names of Founderes of the chauntryes in the bederoll for a hole yer at Michelmus . . . . . . xvj d.

1498-9. For makyng of a tabyll for the beyd Roll . . . ij d.

1520-1. To Mr Alen for the Bede Rowle of the Church . . ij s.

1477-8 (*Tintinhull*). For the bedrowyll to the prest at iiij tymes . xij d.

CHAPTER XII

LIGHTS AND BURIALS

Ceremonial lights—Early use—Wax—Tallow for illumination—Torches—Serges—Paschal candle—Font taper—Special lights at St. Mary-at-Hill; St. Botolph, Aldersgate; All Saints, Derby; Spelsbury, Oxon—Trendle or Roundle—Square tapers—Judas candles—Snuffers—Short extracts—Under Queen Mary—Under Elizabeth—Ludlow—Under James I

Burials in churches—" Lairstall "—Crowded churches and churchyards—Charnell House—Hearse—Bier fees for passing corpses—Burial without coffins—Funeral knells—Loan of funeral gear—Historical entries

THE employment of ceremonial lights during the celebration of the Eucharist and other religious offices is one of the best authenticated and earliest uses of the Christian Church. The custom prevailed in a stronger degree in England than in any other part of Christendom, owing probably to the greater gloom of our climate. On the general use of lights see Rock's *Hierurgia*, pp. 391–411; and on their use in English churches, Dr. Cox's " The Lights of a Mediæval Church " in *Curious Church Gleanings* (1896) and *English Church Furniture* (1907), pp. 320–30; also Staley's *Studies in Ceremonial* (1901), pp. 169–94.

The candles used at Mass were always to be of pure wax, save that in Masses for the dead they might be *de communi cera*, *i.e.* of yellow wax. The use of lights at funerals goes back to the fourth century. Torches—*torchæ*, originally of twisted wax " *intorticia* "—were used at Lincoln Cathedral *ad corporis Christi levacionem*, and occasionally at other ceremonial functions; but latterly the term was generally used for a coarse form of taper, largely mixed with resin, and employed in escorting the corpse to the church, and from the church to the grave. Most ·churches kept a stock of these torches, and they were loaned for funeral purposes. The large tapers burning by the corpse in the church, and lighted again at the "month's mind," or at definite obit services, were of wax, and a usual name for them was Serges (Fr *cierge*) Tallow candles were quite admissible in church, provided they were only used for illuminating purposes, as at early Christmas services, or at mattins.

The great Paschal candle, or column of wax of exceptional size, stood in a massive candlestick on the gospel side of the high altar. It was lighted with much ceremonial from the newly blessed fire on Easter morn, and remained in the Sanctuary until Ascension Day.

The Font taper—quite distinct from the small candle placed in the hand of the infant or person at baptism according to the Sarum rite—was a large candle used at the solemn ceremony of the blessing of the font on the eves of Easter and Whitsunday, and apparently lighted at all times of baptism.

The providing of ceremonial lights of various kinds was the most costly of all church charges in mediæval England. Up to the time of the Reformation, they were provided most readily by all classes of the community, not only in towns but in the smallest country parishes.

The copy of the will of John Causton, 1353, "englished" in 1486, among the parish records of St. Mary-at-Hill, is of much interest as to special lighting of the old church in the middle of the fourteenth century. He provided that two tapers were to be kept

brennyng upon the Iren Beame afore the image of our lady atte high awter on Sondayes and halidays, and ij tapers brennyng before the Aungelles Salutacion of the ymage of our lady in the body of the said Church every evenyng at the tyme of syngyng of Salve Regina from the begynnyng to the endyng.

A fifth taper was to burn at the south altar between the figures of St. Thomas and St. Nicholas.

John Warton, by will of 1407, provided for

ij torches of waxe to burne every Sunday and other holy daies at the high awltr in the masse tyme at the levacion of the blessed Sacrament and after as is the use.

Richard Gosselyn, by will of 1428, provided for a five-pound taper to burn beside the altar of St. Katharine on Sundays and feast days. John Bedham, by will of 1472, instructed the wardens to fynde and sustayn for evermore a lampe with oyle in the quire and high Chauncell to burne alwey as well on Dayes as on nyghts before the blessed Sacrament.

Gatherings for the "bemelyght"—that is, for the light or lights on the rood-beam—are continuous throughout the accounts of St. Mary-at-Hill.

    1477–9. For the beme light, Receyved in the said ij years . . xlij s.
    1490–2. For the Beamelighte . . . . xvj s. xj d.
    1496–7. Receved for the biemlight this yere besydes them that wold not paye er the light neare sett upe and them that be owyng . . . . . . xviij s. iiij d.

In the sixteenth century the beam-light money dropped considerably, and is usually entered jointly with the paschal money.

    1530–1. Rec' for pascal money and Beame light this yere . xj s. vijd. ob.
    1537–8. Rec' for the pascall money and the beame light gaddred this yere . . . . xj s. ij d.

As to candlesticks, the following are the more important entries:—

    1431 (Inventory.) vj candelstykkis of laton more or lasse and a kandelstyk of laton with foure nosis.
    1490–1. For the Scouryng of ye laten desk standardes candilstickes and laten bolles anent oure lady day Ester and Christmas . . . . iiij s.
    1496–7 (Inventory.) ij standardes of laton.
    On the high auter ij gret candylstykes and iij small.
    On Sent Stephyns Awter ij Candylstykes.
    iij small Candylstykis of laton for Tapors.
    iiij Candylstkes of laton with braunches for Talough candell.
    1509–10. For ij hand canstickes . . . . . j d.
    1531–2. For ij hangyng candylstykis for the quyre v d.

In 1525–6 six sconces were provided for the quire, and in the same year occurs a most rare entry of "ij lamp stands for the chirche ij d."

The parish of St. Botolph, Aldersgate, spent £4 0s. 3¼d. in 1466–7

LIGHTS AND BURIALS

on "wax for the beme light and other lightes in the churche"; as well as 18s. 6d. for 18½ gallons of oil.

Fyrste paide for lj lb. and di of new wax bought for the beme lighte agayn Alhalowen day	xxij s. j d.
It. for makyng of xxvj tapers for the said beme light .	v s. v d. ob.
It. for ij grett tapyrs weying vj lb. to sette up at buryinges .	iij s.
It. for ij grett tapyrs of iiij lb. to sette up byfor the Rode while the beme lights was in makyng	ij s.
It. for lvj lb. of new wax bought for the beme light agyne Esterday	xxviij s. vj d.
It. for makyng of xxxj tapers for the said beme light .	v s. v d. ob.

From later accounts it appears that there were occasional gatherings for special lights in this church for St. Katherine and St. Christopher, St. George, St. Margaret, and the Salve light. Mention is also made of lights before Our Lady of Pity in the Trinity chapel, and before SS. Fabian and Sebastian. The receipts of 1468–9 name 5s. from the "Wardyns of the Brotherhed of Seynt Fabyan and Seynt Sebastian."

The following is a transcript from the accounts of the sepulchre or funeral serges and craft serges maintained in the collegiate church of All Saints, Derby, in 1483. It was by no means unusual for the great wax candles which burnt by the side of bodies in the church to be afterwards removed to burn before some particular altar or image, where they were renewed by special bequest or by sorrowing relatives.

Sepulcur Serges

Inp ms on Sepulc^r serge In the holdyng of John hardyng that now kepeth uppe Richerde Strynger delyv'de to hym by the church Reves that tyme beyng.

Itm Anoy^r in the holdyng of Williā Cowp' yt aft^r was delyv'de to conay bargear by the churchwardyns y^t nowe holdes up Edmu'de Rawlynson.

Itm Anoy^r in the holdyng of John Hoghton delyv'de aft' to John Newton by the church reves nowe in the kepyng of Rawfe Coke.

Itm Anoy^r in the holdyng of Roberte Weste de lynde aft^r to thomus bradshae by ye churchreves And aft^r his dethe to Richerde Hatfelde or els wolde Elise stokks that wedded Thomus Bradshae wyfe have had ye Away aft^r hyr decesse to Sancte Werbur church, whe' he dwelled att thabbey barnes. [A list of 23 other sepulchre serges follows.]

Serges Holden up by Crafts

& oy'wyse as foloeth.

Inp'mis Sancte Catne lyght ys upholden by gederyng of the candyllyght' and conteneth xx serges.

Itm Sayncte Nicholas lyght ys upholden by the parische clerke, by his gederyng of sancte Nicholas nyghte & conteneth xij serges.

Itm whosoe ev' ys scolemayster by gederyng amonge hys scolers upholdrs before Sancte Nicholas iiij wax serges.

Item vj wax serges befor' sancte loy that be upholden by the farrers.

Item v serges before Sancte Clemente upholden by the Bakars.

Item v serges before o^r lady upholden by the Shoemakers.

Item v serges before the Roode Williā Walkar one John drap.

Anoy^r Thos. ffarynto' the thrydde, Thoms payn the forthe, Thomas Bradshae the ffyfte.

Itm v serges before the mary of pety holden up by Rawfe Mayre wyfe.

Itm in o^r lady Chapell before o^r lady ys ffonde iij serges, Williā Walkar one, Thomas Knolles anoy^r Richerde baker ye thrydde.

Itm in the same chapelle ys on' before sancte John baptiste holden up by Williā Walkar.

Itm v serges before sancte cristofer Att the fyndyng of Mastres Willugby, John farynton, John peneston wyffe, William bancrofte, and Edmunde busby.

Itm iij serges y^t Ant^r Gēy^r fonde on' before o^r lady Anoy^r before sancte Cat'ne the third before the trinite Alter.

Itm ij serges befor' sancte Edmu'de holde' up by the gederyng of the Clerke on sancte edmu'de nyghte And goyng with sancte Edmunde w^t in the parishe As ye doe of sancte Nicholas nyght.

The wardens' accounts of Holy Trinity, Cambridge, of Wing, Berks, and of St. Thomas, Sarum, have many light entries of exceptional interest, but the extracts are suppressed on the score of space. Room has been found, however, for these notes from the unprinted accounts of a comparatively small country parish of Oxfordshire.

These were the lights of Spelsbury church, in 1531, together with the amount collected for their sustenance, and the day appointed for the respective gatherings:—(1) The Trinity light, Candlemas Day, 22s. 8d.; (2) Our Lady's light, the Annunciation, 4s.; (3) The "Hersse" light, any day before Allhallowtide, 16s. 10d.; (4) St. Nicholas light, 16s. 2d.; (5) St. George's light, St. Matthias Day, 22s. 10d.; (6) St. Clement's light, St. Clement's Eve, 5s. 7d.; (7) St. Katherine's light, St. Thomas of Canterbury, 8s. 4d. and 3½ strike of barley; (8) St. Erasmus' light, St. Stephen's Day, 4s. 8d., a sheep worth 20d. and two bushels of barley; (9) St. Christopher's light, New Year's Eve, 4s. 4d. and two bushels of barley; (10) St. Anthony's light, Shrove Monday, 14s.; (11) St. Michael's light, St. Michael's Day, 2s. and 4 bushels

Liber compotus princi-
capelle Regie collegia-
tor in Derbeia.

Memorandum that fyrst day of ... Lord m cccc lxvj
indentur George Styholme to be clerke for of sayd
collegiate Chapelle of all Saints then beyng
churche wardens Henry Cartewright and John
Ashbey and the sayde John and Henry delyverd
to the sayde George to have the naments And
gods of the sayd collegiate chapell or churche
in all charges to the belongyng duryng all the
tyme of hys Clerkshyppe As folowth ...

Bokes

Inprimis ij myssals or massboks / ij gospellar
... antiphoners / ij manuelles / ij processionals
and collectar / ij grelles / ij ordinales / ... other
the ... of smalle valure /

FIRST PAGE OF WARDENS' ACCOUNTS, ALL SAINTS, DERBY, 1466

of barley; (12) St. Andrew's light. There are somewhat varying details as to these lights from 1525 to 1530, but the accounts for 1531 are the fullest in this respect. There were two wardens (custodes) for each light, who were responsible for the gatherings and had to make a yearly account. There were also two more wardens or keepers of the bells, who gathered this year 3s. 5d. and 1½ strike of barley, and other wardens who provided the torches for funerals and obits. In some years there was also a gathering made for the light of the Pieta, or Virgin with the Dead Christ, as distinct from the image of the Virgin in the Lady Chapel. It therefore follows that there were about thirty male parishioners responsible for diverse church collections in addition to the general churchwardens.

Nor would it be right to omit the following single extract from the valuable and unprinted accounts of Bassingbourn, Cambridgeshire:—

> 1514-15 (Torches). Payd for xliiij li. of Rawe waxe bought att Sterbyryche (Stourbridge) Fayer with the caryage for the Rod lyghts at Mydsomer and Michaelmass quarters and for Waxe to iiij Torches thys Madsummer   xix s. iiij d.
> Item payd for xl li. Rosen and viiij li. wyke to those iiij torches . . . . . . ij s. viij d.
> Item payd for gold foyle and Colours off those iiij torchis   viij d.
> Item payd for fyr wood and meyt and drynk to those iiij torchis making . . . . . . x d.
> Item payd to the werkeman Robert Blane chaunndelor for his labur in makyng . . . . . xvj d.

Trendal or Trendle was the name for the ring, circle, or hoop wherein candles were fixed; it was suspended in front of the Rood. It corresponded with the Roundel, which was the more usual term in the Midlands and East Anglia.

> 1439 (*Tintinhull, Somerset*). Pro una corda empta ad le trendel .   iij d.
> 1440   ,,   Pro vj libris uno quartero caree emptis pro le pascal taper, et le trendell . . . iij s. ix d.
> 1440 (*Yatton, Somerset*). For makyng of the trendyl . x s. iiij d.
>   For colours to the trendyl . . . . . xx d.
>   For peyntyng of the trendyl . . . . . xij d.
> 1508 (*Pilton, Somerset*). For waxe and makyng of the trendell   ij s. iij d.
> 1510   ,,   ,,   For a rope for the trendell   ix d.

The great majority of tapers were round, but occasionally they were cast or moulded in a square form.

1474-6 (*St. Margaret, Westminster*). Item in Square lyghtes in ye Rodeloft weying $_{iiij}^{xx}$ xvj lb.

1480. For new wexe in tapers square and Rownde and making of broken waxe and a pascall . . iiij li. ij s. vj d. ob.
For iiij newe torchis weyng xxix lb. p'ce the lb. v d. xxxvij s. j d.
For ij torchis and a torchet weyng xlvij lb. p'ce the lb. v. d. . . . . . . xix s. vij d.

1515 (*St. Ewen, Bristol*). For xij new Judas for the square tapers . . . . vj d.

The "Judas," about which much would-be learning has been wasted, was a wooden painted stock to imitate a candle. Those for the pascal candle were often of great size, others were smaller, of the nature of a "saveall." A most appropriate name; Judas was apparently an apostle, but he was in truth a sham, and gave forth no light.

1451 (*Tintinhull, Somerset*). Ad faciendum de novo xl Judaces ligneas ad portandum luminaria stantia coram alta cruce   x d.

1553 (*St. Peter Cheap*). For Judas Candell weying ij li. for pascall taper . . . . ij s.

1524 (*St. Margaret, Westminster*). For xij Judaiis to stand with the tapers . . . . ij s.

Snuffers are occasionally mentioned in the accounts.

1517-8 (*St. Mary-at-Hill*). For Snoffers of plate for to put owte the tapours . . . . . . v d.

1574 (*St. Edmund, Sarum*). The makynge of the Snoffer to serve candelles in the churche . . . . iiij d.

The following are a brief selection of short "light" extracts arranged chronologically:—

1476-8 (*St. Andrew Hubbard*). For Ironwerk for the droppyng of the Tapirs before our lady of pitie . . . ix d.

1485 (*St. Dunstan, Canterbury*). For strykyng of the pascall and the font taper . . . . . . ij s. iij d.

1501 (*St. Margaret, Westminster*). Payde to Richard Chaun deller for iij li. v q'trn of newe waxe in small tapers for the tenables (tenebræ) lyghts and a curse candell for the halowyng of the fire on Ester Even . . . xxiij d.

1505 (*St. Margaret, Westminster*). For a dossen of Candyll to
    set aboute the Churche uppon Cristenmasday in the
    Mornyng . . . . xii d.
    For Candyll for burning in the lanteryn on Wynter
    mornings in the body of the Churche . x d.
1536 (*St. Mary, Cambridge*). Resceyved of the wyffes that
    Gadir for our ladylyght . . xxxvij s. iiij d.
1537 . . . . Payed for xxxv li wex for the
    sepulcre and the Roode lyghtes price of a li. vij d. ob.
    Summa . . . . . . xxj s. x d. ob.
    Payed for the making of the said wex . . . v s.
    Payed for a Dyner at the making of the said wex . ij s. iij d. ob.
    Payed to John Capper for settyng up the hyrse and
    kepyng of the Sepulcre lyght . . . . ij s.
1537-8 (*St. Mary, Dover*). Paid for strekyng[1] of the pascall, the
    processioners, the Angelle tapers, the Judas Candeles,
    the font taper, and for mete and drynke . ij s.
    Paid to them that take paynes with settyng up of the
    pascall in mete and drynke . . . . iiij d.
1508 (*Heybridge, Essex*). Memorandum that in the 21st yere
    of Kynge Henrye VIII the bachellers of the paryshe of
    Heybryge have delyvarede the ix tapers belongynge to
    the sepulker, at the feste of Ester, each taper con-
    taynynge v pownde of waxe.
    Also in the said yere the maydens of the said parishe
    have delyvered on to the ix tapers belongynge to the
    seid sepulkre, at the feste of Ester, every taper
    contaynynge v. pownde of waxe.
1544 (*Smarden, Kent*). First layd out for liij li. of waxe for the
    crosse lyght . . . . . xxvj s. vj d.
    It. for iij li. of waxe candyll strekyng . . . xxj d.
    It. for ij li. of waxe for depyng of torches . xij d.
    It. to Holnesse for strekyng of the crosse lygth and the
    paschall and for strekyng of ij li. of small candles iij s. iiij d.
    It. to Holnesse for strekyng of the torches . xviij d.
    It. payd for a li. of talow candell . . . ij d.

During Queen Mary's reign the ceremonial use of lights at
once revived.

1554 (*Stanford, Berks*). For ye pascall Tryndell christening taper
    and font Taper agaynst Est^r . . . . vj s. ij d.

---

[1] Streking or striking as applied to tapers has been erroneously explained to mean painting them in streaks or stripes ! It is, however, simply an old term for casting or moulding the wax in taper form.

1556. For wax candull that wer burned the wensday thursday and fryday before est' at ye Tenebree . . vj d.
1555 (*Yatton*). For ix poundes of wax and a quarter against Ester . . . . ix s. iij d.
1556 (*St. Nicholas, Warwick*). Payd to Thomas Payne for a li. off talow candelle one crystemas day in the mornyng . ij d.

The following entry tells of King Philip's visit to St. Paul's:—

1555-6 (*St. Matthew, Friday Street*). For candells for to lyght ye Chirche in the mornyng when ye Kynge came to powlls . . . . j d.

Throughout Elizabeth's reign mattins were said in cathedral and many town churches at 5 a.m. in the summer and at 6 a.m. in the winter; and the practice continued during most of the seventeenth century. Hence charges for candles are frequent in post-Reformation accounts, of which Ludlow affords striking examples.

1571-2. 2 lynkes and 2 li. of great candels to lyght in the churche at the entry of the Queenes Ma'ties at service tyme and sermon . . . . 20 d.
1572. For a lynke to servise at the Comunion on Christmas daie . . . . viij d.
1574-5. For ij li. of candles on Christmas daie in the mornyng vj d.
To the deacon the 19 of decembre a pound of candles iij d.
ij li. of greate candles for the table and the organ . vj d.
More to the deacon ij. li of candles . . . . vj d.
ij platys of Candles . . . . . . v d.
a pounde of sise candles . . . . . xij d.
ij lynks . . . . xviij d.
To the deacon a pound of Candles the weke after Xmas iij d.
the 16 of february ij li. of Candles . . . . vij d.
half a li. of Sise Candles the same tyme . . vj d.
To the deacon the 27 of Septembre a pounde of candles . iij d. ob.
To him the 8 of October . . . . . iij d. ob.
more a li. of candles to the deacon . . . . xj d. ob.
The 10 of november a pounde of candle . . . iij d. ob.
The 16 of november   „   „   . . . iij d. ob.
[Further candle entries of this year amount to 3s. 5½d.]
1611 (*St. Mary, Reading*). For vj pounde of Candles for Morninge Prayer . . . . . . ij s.
For eight Plate Candlesticks and for nayles to fasten them . . . . ij s. j d.
For iij poundes of Candles more used for Morning Prayer j s.
1612. For xv pounde of Candels for Morninge Prayer . . v s.

LIGHTS AND BURIALS

Burials in Churches.—"Pit money," as it was often termed, or payment for burial within the church, was such an easy way of adding to church funds that it was doubtlessly often encouraged by the wardens. This odious custom, originating with reverence towards the bodies of the faithful departed, was carried to such an excess that many a church became literally a pest house for the living, and was among the primary causes of the constant outbreaks of the plague in the sixteenth and seventeenth centuries. Not a few churches were packed with dead bodies gradually decomposing in shallow graves from end to end and from side to side, and they were constantly being disturbed by new arrivals. Take the case of St. Neots, Cornwall. The number of intramural interments from 1606 to 1708 was 548. The internal area of the church is 85 ft. by 52 ft., but from this must be deducted about 100 square feet for the footing of the six pillars on each side of the nave. It thus follows that the whole area of the church must have been stocked with corpses considerably more than twice over within a century. And the process was considerably increased within many town churches.

In sixteenth-century parish accounts of co. Durham the obsolete word "lairstall," for which the wardens received payment, is of frequent occurrence. It meant a grave within a church, the stone laid over such a grave being called a "lairstone." The term corresponds with the "leystalle" or "laystalle" of the Ludlow accounts. The usual fee for burial within the church was 6s. 8d. throughout England.

The old churchyards of England, especially in towns, became almost as crowded with interments as the churches. Hence we find continuous references to the bone-holes or charnel houses that were required for the disposal of the bones disturbed by fresh interments; they usually took the form of vaults beneath the fabric. The following examples are selected from several score of a like character·—

    1510-1 (*Holy Trinity, Cambridge*). For making clene of the
        Charnell house . . . . . . ij d.
    1616 (*St. Margaret, Westminster*). To several men for foure
        daies worke apiece in digging a large pit of twelve foot
        deepe, thirty foot long, and about ten foot broad to bury
        the bones in the churchyard, at xviij d. a day apiece . ij li. ij s.

1653-4 (*St. Mary, Warwick*). P^d to Andrew Kington for a scuttle
for the gravemaker to gather up bones .   1s.
P^d to John Glendall and his boyes for piling up the bones
in the bonehouse . . . . . .   1s.

The word *hearse* or *herse* is nowadays exclusively used for a funeral car; but its original English meaning was a frame for holding candles. When a corpse was brought into the church this wooden framework was placed over the body. Over it was placed the pall or hearse-cover, whilst at the angles and sometimes on the ridge were iron sockets for candles. Occasionally these wooden hearses were reproduced in iron or other metal and made prominent parts of the tombs of persons of distinction buried within the church, tapers being lighted at the obit and anniversary of death. A few of these survive, notably at Tanfield and Bedall, Yorks, and at Spratton, Northants. Over Richard Earl of Warwick's effigy, in the Beauchamp Chapel, Warwick, is a *hearse* in brass, to bear the pall, thus styled in the contract for the tomb, 1439.[1]

The accounts and inventories of St. Mary, Cambridge, amply illustrate the use of the word *hearse*.

1511. A covering of Tappestry work for the herse.
A Grene Coverlyght for the said herse.
1551. One herse clothe of black velvet.
1568. For making of ye hearse cover . . . . xx d.
For Bords for the hearse . . . . . xvj d.
Two Iron Pinns and a Iron plate for the herse   vj d.
For Inch bord to make a cover to the herse .   xx d.
For a Borde at the side of yt . . . . . iij d.
1570. For mendyng ye bear and hearse . . . . xij d.
1600. A pall Cloth for the hearse.
1625. Payd to Neale Peerc for a newe hearse makinge   xl s.
Paid to the Smith for ironwork for the same .   x s.

The bier for carrying the body to the church was sometimes called a *fertor*, or *fertur*, from Lat. *ferere*, to carry.

1514-5 (*Holy Trinity, Cambridge*). Resceyved of the gyfte of
Elizabeth Williferd wydow towardes the bying of a
Fertur . . . . vj s. viij d.

---

[1] On the evolution of the word *hearse*, see a learned chapter by Mr. Peacock in Andrew's *Church Gleanings* (1895).

CANDLES ON HEARSE OVER COFFIN, BODLEIAN MS., DOUCE

> Resceyved of money geven by the M^r and Brethern of seint
> George's Guylde towardes the hying of the said Fertor   v s.
> Resc' of the gyfte of the Dukke of Bukkyngham towardes
> the bying of the said Fertor   .   iij s. iiij d.

Now and again the term *hearse* was used as equivalent to bier three centuries ago, of which certain particulars as to the burial of prisoners at St. Nicholas, Warwick, afford an example.

> 1608. Bell for Mr Phippes a prisoner   .   .   .   xij d.
> [The usual charge for the passing bell was 4d.]
> „ Also rec. for the hearse to bring Mr Phippes from the
> Jubett (gibbet) .   .   .   .   xij d.
> „ Also rec. of Richard Hendes, for the same reason, to bring
> a prisoner from the Jubett .   .   .   .   .   viij d.

When dealing with *Parish Registers* (pp. 126–7) attention was drawn to an illegal but customary claim made by church officials in the case of a corpse being carried through the parish. Burial was offered, and if refused the usual burial fees claimed. This custom is met with in various wardens' accounts.

> 1623 (*Basingstoke*). Received for the passage of the corpse of a
> knight   .   .   .   .   6s. 8d.
> 1627. Received for the passage of the corpse of the Bishop of Bath
> and Wells .   .   .   .   6s. 8d.
> 1631. Received for the passing of Lord of Pembroke's corpse
> through the toun   .   .   .   .   .   .   6s. 8d.

On the subject of uncoffined burials see Dr. Cox's *Parish Registers*, 119–21. Up to the end of the eighteenth century, in the large majority of burials, the corpse was simply in its shroud. It was the custom for each parish to provide one or more shells or coffins to rest on the bier; the body was lifted out of the coffin at the edge of the grave. The Yorkshire churches of Easingwold and Howden still retain these parish coffins.

> 1501 (*St. Margaret, Westminster*). For a new bere and a coffyn
> for chyldren .   .   .   .   .   .   vj s. viij d.
> For meynding of the olde beres [three in number, each with
> its own coffin]   .   .   .   .   .   .   iij d. ob.
> 1545 (*St. Martin's-in-the-Fields*). To John myller for styropes and
> nayles for the coffyn .   .   .   .   .   .   viij d.
> For the making of the Coffyns   .   .   .   vj s. viij d.

1538. For makynge a Coffyn for the beere . . . ij s. iij d.
1554 (*St. Michael, Cornhill*). For mendynge of the coffin that carrys the corsses to the churche . . . . xij d.
1567-9 (*St. Michael, Friday Street*). For ij coffyns bought to cary corses to the church . . . . . v s. viij d.
1569 (*St. Alphege, London Wall*). For a newe coffin for the use of the P'sch . . . . v s.
For making of a penthouse in the church yarde for the keeping drye of the said coffen . . . vj s. viij d.

An inventory of the church goods of Hartshorn, Derbyshire, for the year 1612 makes mention of "a beare with a coffin." But the parish was soon afterwards presented with a new one.

Memord that Mr. James Roylle of Shorthaselles gave to the churche a newe beere beinge made att his owne coste and charges, box woode and workmanshipp this presente yeare 1626.

Reference has already been made to funeral knells, but a few extracts pertaining thereto had better be set forth in this place.

Burials were paid for at St. Martin, Leicester, according to the number of bells rung. The ordinary use was three bells, for which there was a charge of 8d. Three cases of five bells, in 1544, incurred a fee of 5s. 4d. These fees are confirmed by various subsequent entries, and also the payment of 20d. for four bells. The charge for five bells "and lyenge in ye church" was 12s. The bells for obits were on a like scale.

1636 (*St. Thomas, Sarum*). Sexton not to ring any knell on the death of any person above the space of one Houre.

In 1653 it was agreed at St. Edmund, Sarum, that the ringers were to be paid 6s. on the death of any parishioner who had the bells; the sexton 3s. for ringing a single bell and making a grave in church, chancel, or chapel; and for such as are buried in the churchyard with a coffin 18d., and without a coffin 8d.

The last clause was repeated in 1673.

In several parishes a small but steady income was made by the letting out on hire of the great funeral candlesticks and suchlike ornaments of the church. (See pp. 26, 57–8.)

1504-5 (*Holy Trinity, Cambridge*). Off Adam Sampyll wyff at the beryyng off hyr husband for the ij standers . iiij d.
Off Mistres Potecare for to borow our copys and westment at hyr husbondes monyth day . iiij d.

THE CHURCHWARDENS' ACCOUNTS

Off Mastres Merns for mastres cope for her derege for ij stander and ij small tapers . . . . viij d.
Off Wylliam berbur goldsmythe for hys wydyr derege and for the borowyng off the ornamentes off the churche with the standers . . . . . iij s. iiij d.

On the occasion of a funeral mass for royalty, or other distinguished persons, it was customary in the larger churches to place the parish hearse, with lighted tapers, in position as though the corpse was really present.

1547 (*St. Nicholas, Warwick*). At the Kyngs Highness dirige a masse. For fyve Tapers x d.—a masse ij d.—for mendynge of the bere and hearse ij d.—for the colourynge of two wodden canstykys blacke ij d.—for bred and ale for the ringers then iiij d. ob.—for ryngynge vj d.—for two papers of the Kynges Armes to sett on the Kyngs herse iij d.

The two following entries from St. Margaret, Westminster, tell of the terrible death-rate of the prisoners of the battle of Worcester, and of the crowds at the Great Protector's funeral.

1651. To Thomas Wright for 67 load of soyle laid on the graves in Tothill fields, wherein 1200 Scotch prisoners taken at the fight at Worcester were buried, and for other pains taken with his teeme of horse about mending the Sanctury highway when general Ireton was buried . 1 10 (

1658. Rec. for 240 foot of ground in the old church yard lett to build scaffolds at the Lord Protectors funerall, at the rate of 1s. the foot . . . . . . 12 (

CHAPTER XIII

ROODS AND REFORMATION CHANGES

Roods and Rood-screens—Yatton ; St. Mary-at-Hill ; Thame—Short extracts
The four periods of Reformation changes—St. Martin, Leicester ; St. Mary,
Cambridge ; St. Mary, Devizes

ROODS and rood-lofts and the screens which carried them formed the most striking feature of our old parish churches, both small and great. Their elaboration and ritual character were essentially English. The story of these rood-screens is told at length, together with county lists of surviving examples, in *English Church Furniture* (pp. 72–144). See also Mr. Francis Bond's *Screens and Galleries* (1908), and especially Mr. Aymer Vallance's admirable articles on the screens of Kent, Derbyshire, Surrey, Middlesex, Lancashire, Yorkshire, and Nottinghamshire, in the *County Memorial* series of Messrs. G. Allen & Co.

The wardens' accounts throughout the kingdom simply teem with entries relative to roods and rood-screens; the difficulty of making a sufficiently brief selection out of hundreds of transcripts has been considerable.

The wardens of Yatton, in 1446–7, rode forth to Easton-in-Gordano to see a model rood-loft with an "alle" or alwie, *i.e.* gallery, and to inquire the cost before proceeding with one for their own church. They also rode to Selwood Forest to procure timber, and selected a special oak for felling. In 1447–8 a considerable supply of timber was felled and brought to the church. Crosse the carpenter was paid £5 19s. 8d. in the following year for making the rood-loft; and in 1450 £2 6s. 8d. for the same, as well as 13s. 4d. *pro solario*. Crosse worked steadily on at the fixing and carving of the rood-screen and loft; at different dates in 1451 he was paid £2 13s. 7d. "for the Aler," in addition to such small entries as 11d.

"for glewe to the Aler," or 20d. "to Crosse ys chylde in reward." The carpenter's work was not completed until 1454, and this was followed by the painting.

Johanni Crosse pro solario	xxvj s. viij d.
For divers colers to the Aler.	vj s. vj d.
Costage for settyng uppe of the Aler the fyrste daye	ij s. vij d.
For colers late boffte at Bristow	. ij s. j d.
For the paynter ys hyre a wyke	. xx d.
For the same payenter ys bedde	. ij d.
For feschyng of a stone from Chelsey to grynde colers therewith .	j d.
For a quarte of peyntyng oyll	. v d.
For dyvers colers boffte	. xxij d.
For golde to paynte the angell	. vj s.
For colers	xiij s. vj d.

This same year Crosse proceeded to work at the "syler" or ceiling of the rood-screen, receiving £2 6s. 8d. for the same. He was presented with a pair of gloves, price 10d., as a complimentary fee when the ceiling was finished; on another occasion 2½d. was spent on "ale gevyn to Crosse to make him wel wellede" (well-willed)! Special timber was bought for this delicate work, both at Southampton and Bristol, at a cost, including carriage, of £1 0s. 10d. In 1455 there were many disbursements of large sums for varnish, painter's oil and colours "for the loffte," together with painter's and carpenter's work. Also

For expenses at Crosse ys ale yn settyng uppe of the posts of the rodelofte	iij d.
For the chandeler yn the rodelofte, to Jenken Smyth of Comysbury	xiij s. iiij d.
For ernest peny to the ymage maker . . .	. j d.
To settyng up of the ymages	. iiij d.
For the ymages to the rodelofte yn number lxix	. iij li. x s. iiij d.

Finally, in 1458, 33s. was spent in foreign (*walsche*) timber "for to cely (ceil) the Rodlofte," and £3 for painting the same.

A rood-loft was set up or considerably reconstructed at St. Mary-at-Hill in 1426-8; to this work 21 persons subscribed £29 4s. 2d. A contract was entered into with William Serle, carpenter, but the items of expenditure are confused, because an "under clerkes chambre" attached to the church was being built at the same time.

ROODS AND REFORMATION CHANGES

In 1496-7 the old rood-loft was reconstructed at a cost of about £7. A "master workeman" received 21d. for three days' labour, whilst several "karvers" were paid at the rate of 8d. a day; ordinary labourers' wages were 5d. a day.

To Sir John Plumer for makyng of the fygyrres .	xx d.
To the karvare for makyng of iij dyadems and of one of the Evangelystes, and for mendyng the Roode, the Crosse, the Mary and John, the Crown of thorn with all othyr fawles .	x s.
To Undirwood for payntyng and gyldynge of the Roode, the Crosse, Mary and John the iiij Evangelistes and iij dyadems, with the ij nobilles that I owe to hym in moneye .	v li.

Further interesting details as to the "costes made for settyng up of the Roode" appear in the accounts for 1497-8, including the following:—

	For cartage of borde from Suthwarke for the skaffold .	iiij d.
	For xv foot of bord for the pilars of the marye and John and for the mastes of the Crosse	ij s. ix d.
	To Bakar mason for a days labor settyng up of the Steyebare	viij d.
	To Undirwood the peynter for a Reward mor than his covnant	vj s. viij d.
	To Richard Garrett Smythe for xxiiij li. new Iryns to strengthen the steybare of the Roode that goeth from wall to wall at j d. ob. the li.	iij s.
	For iiij Stayes of new Iryns weyng xx li. . . .	lj s. vj d.
	For the long bolt of Iryn comyng down from the Roofe and for stapilles and spekynges to fasten it to the Roode weyng xliiij li.	v s. vj d.
	For ij hookes for the lentyn cloth byfore the Roode .	ij d.
1499-1500.	For iij elles lynyn clothe for to mende the cloth afore the Roode	lj s. vj d.
	To Harry Mershe for peyntyng of the same clothe .	iiij s.
1501-2.	For makyng of a lectorne in the Roodloftes .	xij d.
1520-1.	For mendyng of ye Judassis in the Roodeloftes .	viiij d.
1547-8.	For cariage of tymbre for scaffoldes for the Rode loft when yt was paynted	xiiij d.
	For paynting of the Rode lofte with sculptures	iiij li.

In 1555-6 the Rood was restored.

	For the Roode Mary and John . .	vij li.
	For xxvj bolles of laton for the Roode lofte	xxxiij s. viij d.
1556-7.	For iiij wooden pynnes for the tapers in the Roodeloftes .	xij d.

1559. For takyng downe of rood ye Mary and the John   xvj d.
For bringying downe of ye Imagis to romeland and other things to be burnt. . . . . . xij d.

The following is an early example of popular gifts and bequests to the rood and rood-light in the parish of Thame in 1444:—

Of Jone carp'y'ter for a testemente to the rodelyte . . . iiij d.
Of Marchory hoggs for a testemente to the rodelyte   vj d.
Of Verdur of schyllydon for hys modyr to the rode ij boschel malte . . . . viij d.
Of John powly to the rode a boschel of malte . . . . iij d. ob.
Of hew grene for hareyn hodde to the rode . . . . ij d.
It. also we rescyved atte Kyrstimasse to the rode lyte . . xiiij s.
Of thomas schapman for hysse modir to the rode . iiij d.
Of John sage for hys wyffe to the rode . . . . iiij d.
Of mykole stone to the rode . . . . . . iiij d.
Of halyson mowlschofe for her hosbonde to the rodelyte . . ij d.
Of wyllyam hogge for hys wyffe to the rodelyte a boschell barly iij d.
Of pyrrse mapuldram to the rode a boschell barly . . . iij d.
Of tomas bosse for hys Wyffe to the rode . . . . vj d.
Of harry torch for hys Wyffe to the rode lyte . . . iiij d.

The rest of the selected items are arranged chronologically.

1454–6 (*St. Andrew Hubbard*). For new Rode lofte clothe   iiij s. vj d.
For steynyng of the same clothe . . . . xxiiij s.
1511–2. For makyng of the pewys in the Rode lofte   vj s. viij d.
1455 (*St. Margaret, Southwark*). For peyntyng of the Rode lofte . . . xx d.
For makyng of the mortasis for the baners in the Rode lofte . . . . xx d.
1475 (*St. Michael, Cornhill*). For makyng of the yron warke in the Rodelofte the whiche stondyth by the orgones and holdythe ye Rodeloft together . xxj s.
To the carpenter for workmanshyppe in the Rodeloft to make stondyng for the seyd organes . . v s. vij d.
1556. To Peter the Joyner for makinge the Roode Mary and John . . . . . . viij li. x s.
1478–80 (*St. Margaret, Westminster*). For a dore in the Rode lofte to save and keep the people from the organyns . xij d.
For makyng a newe staire into the Rodelofte and the stuffe . . . . xxx s.
For brede ale and wyne in to the Rode lofte on Saynte Margarits day . . . . . . xx s.
To a carpenter for makyng the crucyfix and the Beme he standith upon . . . . . . xl s.

ROODS AND REFORMATION CHANGES

  For karvyng of Mary and John and the making newe xxxiij s. iiij d.
  For gilding of the same Mary and John and the crosse
  and iiij evaungelystes . . . . vj li. vj s. viiij d.
  For gytyng down of a beme in the body of the chirche afore
   the crucifix and settyng up a newe one Archewyse and
   borde to sealyng thereof and other stuffe . xxvj s. viij d.
1491. For iij li. wyre to hold up the tapers of the roode light . xij d.
1495–6. Johanni Coleyn pro pictura Crucis cum Maria et Johanne
   et pro deauracione Imageium cum stellis deauratis in toto   xvj li.
  Johi Sendall prolex Crampayne' ponendis al fixand'
   Crucem nov operis cum Maria et Johanne in toto . . ij s.
1511. For money gathered for the roode lighte on crystmas daye ix s. iiij d.
1503–4. (*Bassingbourn, Cambs*). For sewing togeder the sheetes
   and wasshing bifor the Rod loft . . . . iij d.
  To the smyth for ij stapilles of yron and wyre for that clothe vj d. ob.
  For whyppe Cord to the sam Cloth . . . . j d.
  For Rynges for the clothe before the Rode loft . iiij d.
1507. Item giffen in Ernest to a peyntur for iij panes and ij ymages
   with their Tabernacles in the Rodloft . . iiij d.
1515. Payed for a lyne for the basyn bifor the crucyfixe . iiij d.
1508 (*Pilton, Somerset*). Payed to David Jonys the paynter of
   the Rode loftie . . . . . xxvj s. viij d.
  To John Foreste smythe for yron worke for ye Rode lofte . ij s. v d.
  To David Jonys peynter . . iij li. vj s. viij d.
  To the peynters . . . . . iij li. viij s. j d.
  For xij ellys of lenyn clothe for the Rode lofte   vij s. vij d.
  For lynes and rynges for the sayed clothe . . vij d.
1525 (*St. Dunstan, Canterbury*). For the ledding of the newe
   wyndow agen the Rode . . . . . v s.
  To the plumber hymself for the seid wyndow   v s.
1528 (*St. Mary, Cambridge*). For the guyldyng of the Trinite in
   the Rode lofte . . . . . . lx s.
1533 (*St. Peter Cheap*). To the goodman gante for paynting of the
   Judas or stook of the Roode lyght . iiij s. iiij d.
1535. To Mounslowe for a newe Rode with Mary and John . vij li
  For ix ells of canvas for to hange before the Rode   iiij s. vj d.
1533 (*St. John Baptist, Bristol*). Paid unto old Solbe for peynting
   of oure rode lofte and mending the images . iij li.
  Unto the said Solbe for peynting of the nether roode and
   lofte more with the ij small images and the xij apostles
   with the angels . . . . . ij li. xiij s. iiij d.
1536 (*St. Alphege, London Wall*). For payntyng of the Rode
   Marye and John . . . . . . x s.
1555. For ye Roode and the hymmages of Mary and John w^t the
   Crosse . . . . . . v li. vj s. viij d.

1538-9 (*Ashburton, Devon*). For painting the south part of the
Roodloft with the separation of the ij aisles   xvj li. xiij s. iiij d.
1545-6. For the settyng up of Mary and John .   . . . xvj d.
1547-8. For taking down the Rood and other images   iij s. iiij d.
1549-50. For the takyng down the Image and the Tabernacles and
burnyng the same .   . . . . iij s. iiij d.
1554-5. For mending of the rode loft .   . . . . vj d.
For strykyng oute of the scription opon the rode loft   vj d.
For staples for the banners to stand yn   . iiij d.
1555-60. To Martyn the kerver for makyng of the Rode   . xl s.
For the full payment of the crosse   . xiij s. iiij d.
To George Wyndegate for his paynes in settynge up the Rode   ij d.
1559-60. For taking down the rode .   . . . . viij d.
1563-4. For pullyng downe of the Roode loufte   . ij s. viij d.
1547 (*St. Margaret, Westminster*). For xxxv ells of clothe for the
fronte of the rode lofte whereon the Commandments be
written .   . . . . . xxiij s. iiij d.
1555-6 (*St. Mary, Dover*). Boughte and paied for a Roode at
Canterbury to be set up yn the Churche accordinge to
the Kynge and Quenes procedinges and the Auncient
use .   . . . . xxvij s iiij d.
Paied for the payntinge and guyldinge of the saied Roode . x s. x d.
Paied for bringinge the saied Rode from Canterbury   . xxij d.
Paied for nailes occupied yn setting up the Roode .   . ij d.
Paied yn expenses at Canterbury and for ij horse hires
when I made bargain for the Roode   . v s. iiij d.
1559-61 (*Mere, Wilts*). For takynge downe of the Rode in the
Churche .   . . . vj d.
For wasshyng oute of the Rode and the trynyte   . viij d.
For lyme for the same .   . . . . . vij d.
For the defacynge of the Images of the xij Apostles which
were paynted in the Face of the Rode lofte   xij d.
1562-3. For the takyng downe of the Rode loft by the commandement of the Byshop .   . . . . . x d.
For lyme to amende the same place ageyn .   xvj d.
For the amendynge of the same ynewe   . iij s. iiij. d.
For lathes to amende the Rode lofte .   . . . xvj d.
1603-4 (*St. Botolph, Cambridge*). For all the timber and for deales
used about the p'ticion twixt the church and chancell
and for sawing the same for deales .   . . xlj s.
1639 (*Hartland, Devon*). 2nd Nov. It is agreed on that John
Gibbins shall before Christmas next erect and new build
upon the rood lofte in our church, on both sides of the
organs there, so many seates as the same will conveniently
containe ; and the said John is to have the benefit of the

first sitting of the same for the term of their lives that shall be therein respectively placed, and for their only use that shall be so placed; and that the said John shall not nominate or place anyone in any of the said seates without the approbation and consent of the 24 governors of the parish church of Hartland or the most part of them, and each one that shall sit in any of the said seates is to pay yearly towards the reparation of the said Parish church one penny.

Scores of the wardens' accounts testify to the four marvellously rapid changes in the ritual and doctrine of the National Church in less than a quarter of a century, from the time when Henry VIII flung off papal allegiance in 1534 down to the accession of Elizabeth in 1558. There is nothing so astounding in history, ancient or modern, as the four startling transformation scenes that took place within the whole of England's churches during those few short years. The chief sadness of it all was that England as a whole (with many notable exceptions) was content to follow blindly four successive sovereigns in their completely diverse notions as to the nature of public worship to be offered to the Most High. To form any true idea of the bewildering rapidity of these transitions, it is necessary to recollect that the religious revolutions brought about successively by Henry VIII, Edward VI, Mary, and Elizabeth took place in a shorter period of time than that which has elapsed since Victoria's first jubilee!

We now proceed to draw examples from three sets of parish records as to the outward signs of these upheavals, which may fairly be taken as typical of the external changes in worship in all the churches of the land.

It is but seldom that church plate was sold before the advent of Edward VI to the throne. But the accounts of 1545–6 of St. Martin, Leicester, show that plate to the value of £24 5s. was sold by the wardens "to Mr. Tallance then maire of Coventre." The sales from this church in 1547 included seven cloths hanging before the Rood, 3s. 8d.; eight tabernacles, 17s.; old iron, 6s. 2½d.; brass vessels and ornaments to the value of £5 11s. 6d.; wax, 32s. 9d.; and the chamber (case) of the organ and some pipes, 24s. 6d; also "the hors yᵗ the Georg Roode on," 12d., and the "forth and the vente that the George stood on," 3s. 10d., making a total of £13 2s. 2½d. In the following year, vestments and hangings and other "old gere" were sold to the value of £8 5s. 3d. Three men were paid 18d. for taking down the rood-loft. A crown of wood and two crowns of wood covered with silver realised £3 6s. 8d. in 1552. The accounts presented in 1553 included the sale of several superior copes and vestments, two copes and a vestment being of blue velvet, which produced £20 3s. 4d.

The accounts presented in 1554 record the sale of "an olde black vestment and a tunycle" for 10s.; but on the 6th of July the boy-king died and was succeeded by Queen Mary, when the other side of the scale went up. The selfsame accounts show that the wardens were apparently quite willing to purchase two copes and a vestment of blue velvet, quite possibly the very ones that they had so recently sold. The altars were remade, a rood provided, pyx, candlesticks, corporas cases, banners, further copes and vestments, a canopy for the altar, St. George and his banners, etc., were purchased. An organ was replaced and repaired by Sir William Burrows, one of the priests of the church. Sir William had evidently bided his time with patience and had rescued some of the books of the ancient services which they were expected to destroy. Consequently the wardens were able to purchase from him, at the modest expense of 16s. 6d., a missal, a psalter, processional, a manual, and a coucher. In 1556 the rood-loft was repaired and re-erected, and it was supplied with "ix taper dysshes." In 1557 "a thyng to loke the Sacrament in" (a pyx) was purchased for 16d., whilst the making and gilding of the "Roode Mary and John" cost 16s. 8d.

After various payments for the Lenten veil and hanging it up before Lent 1558, comes an entry "for ale to the Ryngers when the quenes grace was proclamyd, viij d." Mary died on 17th of November, and soon after the accession of her sister Elizabeth the making desolate of the church was again renewed. In 1559 four men were given drink to the value of 3d. when taking down the altar, and new service books were bought at a cost of 14s. 1d. In 1561-2 vestments, banner clothes, and a rood cloth were again sold. The following entries relate to the destruction of the rood and rood-loft:—

> Pd to John Wyntershall and is man for ij dayes worke to graunseyll ye setes and to make up ye holles where ye bame was in ye Rode louft . . . . xx d.
> Pd to boddeley for taking up ye border in ye Roode lorft . . iiij d.

Meanwhile the organ was suffered to remain, and 6s. 8d. was paid for a dinner "that wast bestode upon ye Clarkes y^t kept ye quyre at crissenmas." Puritanism, however, soon came to a head, and in 1562–3 "the organ chamber" was pulled down at a cost of 2s. In the same year iij s. iiij d. was paid to a "clevar carvar" for making a frame to the Communion Table. In 1566–7 the sum of 4d. was expended in "puttyng out the Imageyse out of the pulpyte," and in 1570–1 further mutilations were carried out which are thus described:—

> Payd unto yreland for cuttynge downe the ymages hedes in ye churche . . . . xx d.
> Payd unto hyme for cuttynge downe a bord over the font . . xiiij d.
> Payd unto hyme more for takynge down the angels wynge and removynge of his fether . . . . . . xij d.

The accounts of St. Mary, Cambridge, for 1548 name the sale of an unusually large cross.

> For a crosse of sylver parsell gylt sold to Henry Ryngsted by the account of the paryshenors the xij day of October anno domini 1547, weynge iiij score and xij unces at iiij s. x d. ye unce. xxij li. iiij s. viij d.

Also two silver censers with their ships, weighing over five score ounces, were sold for £23 11s. 4d.; whilst "sartyn old ymplymentes of ye churche," such as painted cloths, latten candlesticks and wooden images, brought in a further sum of 22s.

In 1550, certain parcels of old church stuff, chiefly vestments and hangings, were sold for about 80s. In 1551, the sale of the two great candlesticks of latten and other small candlesticks realised £3 6s. 10d. Two candlesticks of silver, 5 chalices, 2 paxes, and a crysmatory, all of silver, and a great variety of vestments and hangings remained in the hands of the churchwardens.

In the first half of 1553, the churchwardens expended 22s. 5d.

in new English Communion books and psalters, sold some remnants of "churche stuffe," and paid for bread and wine for the Communion; but in July the boy-king died, Queen Mary succeeded, and the same wardens set to work to supply the church again with cheap reproductions of the very details they had been selling. Candlesticks were bought for 8s., a vestment, albe, cope, and three books for 28s., a fayer messe boke and a legent for 14s., a manual for 5s., and a crysmatory for 2s. 6d., etc.; whilst two altar cloths of blue velvet were bought back for 50s. from Doctor Blythe, who had been churchwarden in the worst spoliation year under Edward VI. The Rood was restored; the painting of it in 1555 cost 6s. 8d. The inventory of 1556 attained to fairly decent proportions, though infinitely inferior to the richness of the church prior to its pillaging; it included "xiij lattyn candylstyckes to ye Roode Loft." The tapers burning before the Sacrament for the whole year cost 10s. 5d., and the "synging bredes" for the year cost 12d.

In 1558, as the parish was recovering from the shock of the strenuous action of Edward VI's rulers, a pair of chalices, double gilt, were bought in London for £6 0s. 10d.; but in November of that year Mary died, and with Elizabeth came a renewed but more gradual "purifying" of the church. In 1560, "takyn downe the alteres" cost 2s. 8d., taking down the tabernacle 10d., and "ye communyon table" 6s. The 1562 accounts record the receipt of 4s. "for a piece of tymber y^t ye Rood stoode on"; and a penny was paid for "a booke y^t was sent to us for ye pullying down of ye Rood lofte." Incense continued, however, to be used; its purchase appears in the accounts for the years 1559, 1566, 1568, 1571, 1572, 1573, and 1575. Queen Elizabeth does not appear to have been popular at Cambridge; in the 1566 accounts there is an entry of 2s. 2d. which was given to "ye Quens Almoners servaunte for not ringinge at ye Quens comminge."

Sales of church goods and ornaments continued throughout 1568, when it was stated that the total result of such sales amounted to £30 10s. 2d. The sales included candlesticks and lamp of the rood-loft, the Lenten veil, and a further selection of vestments and hangings. "One William a Singing man" gave 6s. for "the Image of our ladie which was taken of the blewe velvet alter cloth be the comaundement of the archdeacon." In the same year William Prime was paid 4d. for "washing owte Images oute of the glass windowes." In the following year 3d. was paid for pulling down the rood-loft, whilst the sale of its fragments realised about 20s.

The following items indicative of the rapid changes of church policy and ritual in the midst of the sixteenth century occur in the accounts of St. Mary, Devizes :—

1550. 4 Edw. VI. Pd for their labor at the plucking down of the Alters, and for meat and drinke	xiiij d.
Pd for their labor at the taking downe of the side Altar	xij d.
1553. 1 Mary. Pd to Bartlett for setting up the great Altar	viij d.
Pd to James Benett the mason for his work about the Altar	vj d.
1554. 2 Mary. Pd for holye oyle	iiij d.
To Wm. Jefferies for ij tapers of a pound and a half and more	xviij d.
For the new making of the same tapers against Easter	xj d.
There is to be accounted for of old ix days work for George Tylar and his man, at vij d. the day, for putting and making up of the organ loft	v s. iij d.
1555. 3 Mary. Pd for defacing the Scriptures on the walls	ij s. iiij d.
Pd for making of the altar and for defacing the x commandments and putting . . . in the Rodloft	vj s.
Pd for making Mary and Joseph (? John)	v s. iiij d.
1557. 5 Mary. Pd for makyn of ij alters	iij s. viij d.
Pd for stones for the same alters	ij s. viij d.
For tymber to make the pyctor that standeth by the Rode named Mary and John	ij s.
For mendyng of a crewet	j d.
For mendyng of ij Albes	ij d.
For frankinscens	j d.
1561. 4 Elizabeth. For taking down of the Roodloft	vj s.

CHAPTER XIV

CHURCH SITTINGS

Stone bench-tables—Pre-Reformation examples of sale of seats—St. Laurence, Reading; St. Ewen, Bristol; Ludlow—Short extracts—Quire desks Pew doors and locks—Numbered pews—Poppy-heads—Separation of sexes Seats for the wealthy—A seat on the pulpit stairs—Corporation seats Shriving pews—Churching pews

PROBABLY the early general rule for a congregation in England, as in other churches of Christendom, was to stand when not kneeling. Stone bench-tables against the walls or round the piers, many of which still remain of considerable antiquity (*English Church Furniture*, 261-2), would suffice for the aged and infirm. The custom of providing wooden seats for the congregation seems to have originated with patrons and founders of chantries and chapels causing seats to be fixed within their parcloses or screens, and thence gradually spreading to the body of the church. There is no proof, however, of any general pewing of churches until the fifteenth century is reached. Mr. W. J. Hardy's paper of 1890, "Remarks on the History of Seat-Reservation in Churches" (*Archæologia*, vol. liii. pp. 94-106), has completely vindicated the Reformers from the often repeated charge of inventing appropriated seats and pews, though reservation and sale naturally grew with startling rapidity as soon as the listening to sermons came to be considered by many as almost the chief object of church attendance.

The grievous evil of seat-rents, through which the Church of England has for centuries so bitterly suffered, by making the Houses of God the very centres of class distinctions engendered by wealth, was begun from comparatively innocent motives in early days as shown in the previous discussion as to seats at St.

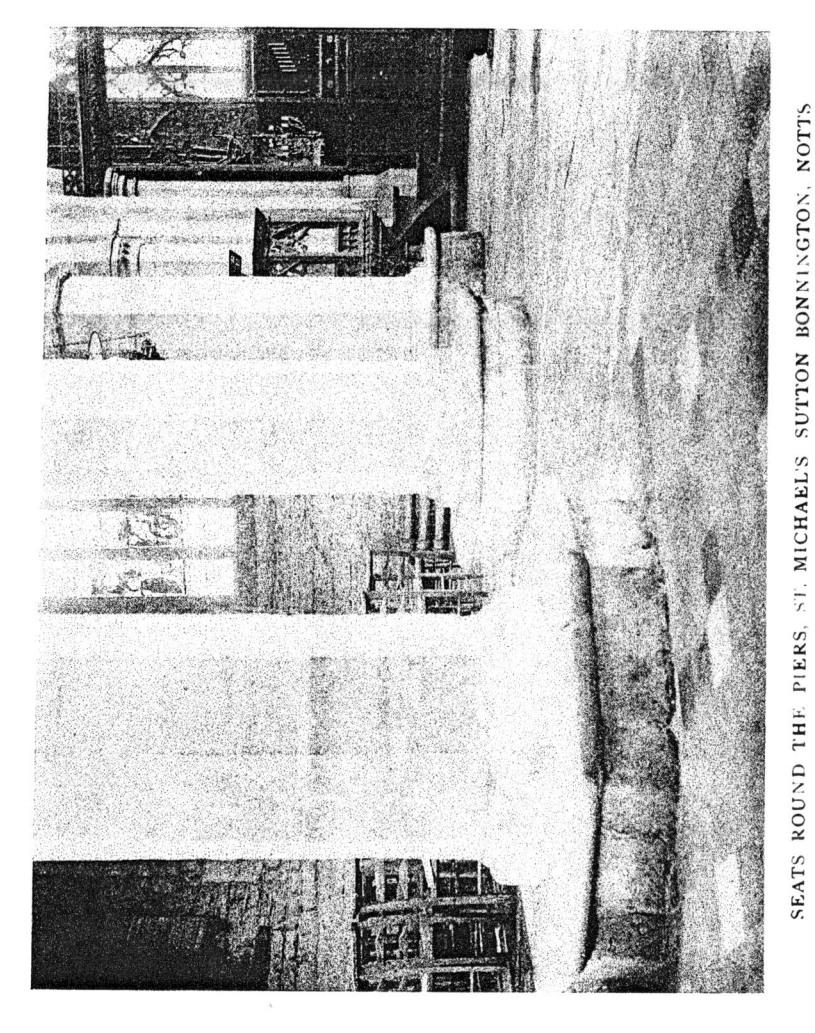

SEATS ROUND THE PIERS, ST. MICHAEL'S SUTTON BONNINGTON, NOTTS

Edmund, Sarum. The evidence supplied by the accounts of St. Laurence, Reading shows, in common with several others, that the idea originated in the fifteenth century with the supplying of women only, and those probably of an aged or delicate nature, with an allotted seat. Here is the first entry of the kind, in the wardens' rolls of this church, which begin in 1420:—

   1441-2. Et de iiij d. de dono ux^ris John Tamer j^r j setell.

A groat was also paid by three other wives, and 6d. in a single case. By 1498—for the evil soon began to grow—the seat-rents amounted to 6s. 6d., which was the sum paid for sittings exclusively pertaining to wives of the congregation. In 1515-6 it was agreed that all women taking seats were to pay 6d. each,

> except in the mydle range and the north range beneath the font, the which shall pay but iiij d. and that every woman to take her place every day as they cumyth to churche excepte such as have ben mayors wyfs.

There is a somewhat remarkable and pathetic entry in 1520-1:—

   Item of my lord for his moder sete . . . . . iiij d.

By "my lord" is signified the lord abbot of the great abbey of Reading. At this time that high spiritual office was held by Hugh Faringdon, a man of good family, who had just been promoted to the abbacy. It is of interest to note that he placed his mother among those who occupied the cheaper front seats. It will be remembered that Abbot Faringdon was judicially murdered by Crumwell before the abbey gateway in 1539, the sentence being fixed before the trial began.

In 1522 a number of new seats were provided at a cost of £8 12s. 2d.

> 1527. Rec' of Mr Barton for a seate for his madens   viij d.
> Rec' of Mr Hyde for his mades seat . . iiij d.
> 1529. Rec' of Willm, barb^r to my lord abbot, for his wyffes seat   vj d.
> 1545. It is ordered and enacted that all women of the parrishe whose husbands now be or heretofore have been bretherne of the Mass of Ihc shall from hensforth sitt and have the highest seats or pewes next unto the mayors wifs seate towards the pulpitt.

The Reformation gave a great impetus to the seat-letting

movement. An ordinance of 1573, from the St. Laurence records, is well worth quoting *in extenso* :—

In consideracion that the collecions or gatheringes heretofore accostomably used for and towards the mayntenance of the Church as well on the feast of All Saintes, the Feast of the Byrthe of our Lord god, as on Hocke Monday, Hocke Teuesday, Maye Daye, and at the feast of Penticost comonly called Whitsontyde, togyther with the Chauntry Landes are lefte of, and cleane taken from the Churche to the great Impoverishment thereof, the wch heretofore dyd muche healpe the same. It is theretofore of necessytye by and with the assent, consent and aggreament of the p'isheners then and there beinge present for and towardes the mayntenaunce of the contynuall chardges of the Churche by these presentes for evermore Ordayned concluded upon and fully aggreed as hereafter followith, That is, that every woman that heretofore bathe byn sett by any of the Churchwardens, or that of themselves do or have used to sitt on the Sondayes or holydayes in any of the seates beneathe the pulpett and above the southe syde church doore, or in any of the seates in the mydel Raynge of seats above the saide churche doore Shall yerely pay iiij d. a pece for the church profytt and towardes the contynuall chardgs therof at two Feasts in the yere, That is to say at the feast of the Byrthe of o^r Lord god, and at the feast of pentycost by even porcions. And that all women that be or have byn sett by or without the Churchwardens in any of the seates on the south side rainge above the pulpett Shall yerely paye vj d. apece at the foresaid feasts by even porcions. The same to be gathered by the Churchwardens or their assignes for the tyme beinge at theire perell.

Matters continued to advance in this evil direction, and by the year 1607 the parish was ripe for parcelling out the whole area of God's House into ranges of pews or seats in accordance with the position or wealth of the occupants of both sexes, the whole of the names being duly entered. In " St. John's Chancell " were placed 8 men at 4d. each. In " the North Ile " were placed 28 men at 4d. each in the five front pews, 76 men at 3d. each in the next thirteen pews, and 3 " goodwives " in the back seat. In " the Middle Ile " 4 men were allotted seats in the front pew at 1s. each, 10 men at 8d. each in the next two pews, 6 men in the fourth pew at 6d. each, 5 women in the fifth pew at 4d. each, 37 women in the next six pews at 3d. each, 18 men at 2d. each in the three next pews, whilst in the last four pews 12 women were allowed to sit at a penny apiece. In " the South Ile " the two front seats were allotted to Sir Francis and Lady Knollis; 63 women were seated at 4d. each, and 21 women in the back pews at 2d. apiece.

1637. Item p^d Wm Meerbancke for rearing the seate higher for the Burgesses wives. 9 0

The accounts of St. Ewen, Bristol, afford early (1454–5) proof of the sale of seats, the two first of this short list being the wardens or proctors.

Receytes for the saal of segys.
In primis, of Richard Batyn, Goldsmythe, the procurator forseid,
   for his sege & his Wyf . . . . . . xij d.
Item, Robert Core procurator forseid for his Wyf is Sege . vj d.
Item, of Lawrence Wolf for his sege and his Wyf is xij d.
Item, of John Wolf for his sege and his Wyf is . xij d.
Item, of Jamys Swetmane for his sege . . . vj d.
                            Summa . . iiij s.

The Ludlow accounts afford another sad instance of the monstrous growth of the appropriated pew-rent system. The accounts begin fairly well. In 1541 the receipts record:—

Res' of Walter Torites wyf for Annes Davis knelynge place . xij d.
Res' of Rycharde Rawlens wyf for Elsabeth Gwyns knelynge place . . . . viij d.

In 1542, 8s. 4d. was spent over the making and repairing of "the comyn pewis"; but there are also entries of three private pews, paying collectively 13s. 4d. With the advent of Edward VI, the pew system got into full swing. In 1550 fifteen parishioners bought "pew places" of the wardens at prices varying from 13s. 4d. to 1s. The "pew place" signified a specified area within the church whereon the purchaser usually built his pew, which became his property, and he could sell it or bequeath it, or otherwise his heir inherited it. It became, however, the Ludlow custom (as in modified forms in other town churches) for a form of surrender to be made to the parish at the death of the owner, when a further fee was exacted. In 1571–2 the wardens granted eight pews, for which they received the aggregate sum of 24s. 8d. Here are two of these entries:—

Of William Allsope, for hallfe a pewe with William Browne,
   late beinge his mothers, in the north yle afore the pulpite x d. ob.
Of Richard Brasir, for hallfe a pewe on the north syde the
   churche, with John Clee, surrendered into the parishes bandes
   by master Wayliefe Brasier late his wyffes . . . xij d.

THE CHURCHWARDENS' ACCOUNTS

In the accounts of St. Michael, Bath, there are two fifteenth-century entries as to the payment for church seats, and others are cited in chronological order.

 1441. P^d pro una sede de Thom. Bradwey.
 1494. R^d pro sede una in ecclesia de Eleanor Tyler.
 1449 (*Thame*). For makyng of the setys yn ye norye quarter of
  the chyrch at seynt jemys tyde . . xiij s. iiij d.
  For makyng of the setys at Seynt hew ys tyde . xiij s. iiij d.
  Item to Wyllyam karpentyre at hocketyde . . xiijs. iiij d.
  For bed and borde and x days tym and ys schilde . xvij d.
  Item yn bred and hale to men to helpe hym to drive the
   setys to the wall . . . . . . ij d.
  Item to on of ys neyborys for the karyg of the tymbyr from
   schylton bedyes man . . . . . . xvij d.
 1495 (*St. Mary, Leicester*). Memorandum on St. Vincent day the
  churchmasters began to gadyr for the desks in the great
  quire, and received xxj d.; Sexagesima Sunday received
  xj d.; and so they continued to gadyr every Sunday.
  For free stone for the desks . . viij s. iiij d.
  For carrying the same . . . . . . ij d.
  For sawing timbir for the desks and other matters about the
   desks which this year were made in the great quire iiij s. vij d.
  For making the images before the desks . vj s. viij d.
 1515 (*St. Margaret Pattens*). A Kaye for masster Waddell's pew
  dowre . . . . ij d.

In the 1546 accounts of St. Michael, Worcester, there is an entry of 22d. "for makyng of dores to seats in the churche"; but from the amount paid it can only refer to a few seats. As a rule the sexes were separated, as is clearly shown by entries of 1596 and 1597. Here as elsewhere the evil of paying for seats—the price from 4d. to 1s. depending on position—steadily grew from small beginnings. From 1595 to 1602 there were 116 allotted seats for which payments were made.

 1570 (*St. Matthew, Friday Street*). On 5 of Januarye hyt was
  agreed that the xvj woomens pewes shoulde be nombred
  as hyt ys nowe sett uppon.
 1548-9. For ix Benches to knylle upon in the pewes . xij s.
  For ix matts to lay in pewes . . iij s.
 1569-70. For payntinge numbers uppon pewes . . . vj d.
 1572-3. For v dossen of pynes to hange capes on . xix d.
 1572 (*St. Martin's-in-the-Fields*). Payde for the Carvinge of xxvij
  poppee heeds for the leftt side of the church . . xxxvj s.

CHURCH SITTINGS

    Payde for the Carvinge of xxv for the Right of the
Churche . . . . . . xlj s. viij d.

1574 (*Stroud, Kent*). For makinge of the Seates for the preste
and the clerke to sitt with their faces towardes the people   v s.

At Pittington, Durham, the vestry in 1584 allotted the seats or "rooms," by name, to every male householder, "as well gentlemen as also husbandmen and cote men," at a charge of "iiij d. a roume att everye first entrye."

The two following excerpts are cited as examples of parish expenditure on the seating of the wealthy :—

  1563-4 (*St. Martin, Leicester*). P^d to Thomas Oliver for a day worke
aboute my lordes seate (Earl of Huntingdon)   x d.
P^d to Them w^h holpe us about mi lordes seate   j d.
P^d for mattes for my lordes chappel .   iiij s. iiij d.
P^d for a skin of red lether and halfe a thousand red neles
for mi lordes seate . . . . . . xvj d.
P^d to Richard Perker for v yerdes of broade grene, and
iij quarters of narrow grene for my lordes seate . vj s. ij d.

  1577 (*St. Stephen, Walbrook*). For Alderman Bondes pewe, viz.—xxxj yeardes greene saie at xvj d. le yeard xlj s. iiij d. : for xvj dosen of lace at viij d. the dos. x s. viij d. Three workmenn ij dais a pece xij s. : ij Mattes xx d. : Candels one pound iij d. : for Coles viij d. Bredd beare and butter xij d. To a painter vj d. Nailes v^m v s. And to a Carpenter iiij d. In all the charges of this pew iij li. xiij s. v d.

  1602 (*St. Botolph, Cambridge*). 3 formes for youth to sitt one, 2 longe one short.

  1608 (*St. Oswald, Durham*). That no younge man, journaman nor prentice, beinge parishioners, shall presume in the Quire to sytt or above the crosse alleye upon payne of ij d. for everye default and tyme except he can reade and helpe to saye service and have a convenient place assignede hime by the Churchwardyns to sytt in.

That no younge women or maide servantes shall presume to sytt in any wives stalls above the crosse allye upon payne of ij d. everye default, except gentlewomens waytinge maides or others having convenient places assigned them by the churchwardens as to do.

That no man younge or olde shall in tyme of Divine Service sytt upon the sides or edges of womens stales upon payne of ij d.

  1609 (*St. Mary, Reading*). It is agreed that whosoever hereafter shalbe Removid by the Churche Wardens from their Seates to anie others, And her or thaie beinge so Removid will not tarrie and Abyde in the seid Seat but Will or Doe come backe again, shall paie for everie time so Doinge to the Churche Wardens xij d. for the mayntenance of the Churche, And if it be a Woman wch bathe a husband That shall so Offende, Then her husband to paie xij d. for her, And if it be a widowe then shee to paie xij d. for her selfe.

A list of "them which have seates" was set up in the church of Horley, Surrey, in 1604. The foremost and the two next seats were each allotted to four persons, and the fourth seat to five persons. Half of these seats were assigned to special lands, probably those that brought in the heaviest rates, and the rest to certain names or "to whome he shall assigne it." The system of seating at the expense of individual proprietors was further extended in 1634, when an entry was made, after a long list of seat holders, to the effect that

These setes were winescoted and planked and repared and paide for by them above writen.

1610 (*Spelsbury*). M^d that the churchwardens and the parishe have permitted Thomas Collinge, the younger, of Deane, and John Sansome of Spelsbury to set up a newe seate adjoyninge to the font, for their wives, under this condition that they shall avoide the seate as often as the fonte is used. If they refuse so to doe, then they shall claime noe title any longer to the seate, but must leave it to be disposed of by the minister, churchwardens, and the paryshe, And they paie to the Churche for the place to sett it up viij d.

1616–7 (*St. Peter, Ipswich*). Delivered unto ye Churchwardens 2 newe long formes of 3 inch plank for ye midle ally for ye poore to sitt on.

1621 (*St. Mary, Cambridge*). A locke for ye Ministers pew doore j s. iiij d.

1625. For two formes for the poor to sitt on . . . iiij s.

1630–1. Cularyng the Ministers seate and mending my Lord Bishopes pewe . . . . . . 6 (

1641–2 (*St. Edmund, Sarum*). P^d to Joseph Bradley for peggs for the 48 mens batts 1 8

1642–3. Given to Mr White, the Countess of Devon gent, for setting up the Kings throne in our Church . . . 5 0

1664. Paid for railing the seats in the middle aisle 14 0

1669. For work about the catechising seat for boys 2 8

1679. For removing the schoolmaster's seat . . . 4 0

1681. For 45 yards of rails and banisters for the Aldermen and 48 men's seats, at 17d. the yard 3 3 9

1697. Agreed that the Churchwardens shall take off the two locks of the seat formerly called Mr Inge's seat, lately set on by order of Mr Inge and by order of Mr G. Bent late churchwarden, and if any controversy shall arise, the parish shall bear them harmless.

1658 (*Wimborne*). Sold to Francis Frost the cooper one roome
on the pulpit stayers for himself to sit on .   1   6

The following are two or three examples of the provision of seats in town churches for corporation officials:—

1490-1 (*St. Martin, Leicester*). M^r mayor's pew made.
1572 (*St. Peter Cheap*). For payntinge over my ladye mayres pewe .   .   .   .   x s.
For a pece of sages for my lorde mayres and my ladyes pewes   xl s.
For lattyn naylls and blacke nayles for my lord mayres pewe and my ladies .   .   .   .   .   .   vij d.
For lace for them Twos pewes .   .   .   .   iiij s.
To a plasterer for whiting over my ladye mayres pewe .   xx d.
To the joyner for the silke for my lorde mayres pewe   iij li. x s. iij d.
For xij li. of flax to make ij settills for my lorde mayres and my ladye mayres pewe at iij d. ob. .   .   .   .   iij s.
1593-4. For latches and catches for the outer Dores where the Eyght and forty sytts .   .   .   .   .   xvj d.
1628-9 (*St. Thomas, Sarum*). Setting a bord against an Eight and Fortye seate.
Any seat or pew that hath bene used by anye of the xxiiij or by their wieves not to be let to any other person but by the consent of a Vestrye according to the Anncyent custom.
1665-6 (*St. Mary, Leicester*). For a new Bench in the 48 mens wives seats making it a little wider 1 11
For matting the 48 wives seat   2   3

There is abundant proof that confessions in the mediæval Church of England were for the most part made by the chancel screen or within the chancel; but two or three instances in city wardens' accounts refer to shriving pews or confessionals.

1493-4 (*St. Mary-at-Hill*). For a matte for the shrevyng pewe .   iij d.
1499-1500 (*St. Andrew Hubbard*). For gere for the Shryvyng pewe .   j d. ob.
1511 (*St. Margaret Pattens*). A clothe for Lent to hang before the Screvyng pewe .   .   .   .
1515. Dressing ye yrons of the shrevyng pew .   .   j d.
1548 (*St. Michael, Cornhill*). To the joyner for takynge down the shryvyng pew and making another pew in the same place   iij s.
1589-90 (*All Saints, Bristol*). Payd for mendinge of a pewe called the shrivinge pewe .   .   .   .   .   1s.

A sixteenth-century custom in some churches, continued long after the Reformation, was to have a certain seat or pew set apart for women who came to be "churched," who were usually accompanied by the midwife. There was, of course, no need for such a pew under the Commonwealth, when churching was abolished.

1538–9 (*St. Mary, Dover*). Paid for the pullynge downe of the chyldewyffes pue of saynt Martyns Churche and for the bryngyng of hit home . . . . . iij d.
1617 (*St. Margaret, Westminster*). Midwives Pew £2 5 0
1634 (*Cundall, Yorks*). A Childwife Pew . . . . 26s. 8d.
1646–7 (*St. Thomas, Sarum*). For the Midwives old Pew for Ric Bristow . . . . 20 c
1683 (*Edenbridge*). P^d to Thomas Wells for a Matt and a Trott for ye Churching Seate . . . . . . 6s. 8d.

CHAPTER XV

ORGANS—OTHER MUSIC—SINGING MEN

Origin of organs—"Pairs of organs"—Partial suppression under Elizabeth—Extinction under Commonwealth—Organ notes of St. Laurence, Reading, Wimborne Minster, St. Mary-at-Hill, and shorter notes—Organ opening at Ashborne—Other instruments of music—Shawm—At Church-ales Church bands—The bassoon—Singing men and boys, at St. Mary-at-Hill and St. Edmund's, Sarum—Short extracts—"Hymns" in honour of Elizabeth

ORGANS

CHURCH organs were introduced into England at least as early as the dawn of the eighth century. Aldhelm, *ob.* 709, states that native workmen ornamented the front pipes of their organs with gilding. From that date onwards, the evidence of organs in the large minsters or abbeys accumulates. By degrees it came about that the ordinary parish church became possessed of these aids to vocal music, until at last their adoption was practically universal. So far as the investigation of pre-Reformation churchwarden accounts is concerned, not one single case has been found wherein the mention of these instruments is omitted. They are always described as organs in the plural, and usually as "a pair of organs." This latter term, often erroneously explained, is simply an equivalent to the word "set," and means an instrument of more pipes than one. A "pair of beads" used to be an equally common expression, not meaning two but a set; nearly a score of like examples of the use of the word "pair" in the sixteenth and seventeenth centuries could be given; we still speak or write of a pair of steps or stairs when a flight of several steps is intended. The parish accounts very rarely mention the small "regals" or other portative organs which could be carried and played at the same time. As to the construction, use, and gradual development of organs, with their bellows and other accessories, reference should be made to Hopkins and Rimbault's *The Organ*, 3rd ed. (1877), and more especially to Galpin's *English Instruments of Music* (1910). English church organs of the time of which we are treating usually stood on the rood-loft, or occasionally on a special loft of their own. A smaller pair of organs, in the larger churches, often stood in the quire or in the Lady Chapel. There are also various references to the comparatively small positive organs, which, though played from a stand, could be moved about as required from one part of the building to another or even transferred for a time to another church. The frequent entries in the old accounts as to ropes for the organs refer mainly to their use in working the bellows.

Objections to the use of organs were strongly urged by the more puritanical of the reformers in the sixteenth century.

On 13th February 1562 among articles put down for discussion by the Geneva element in the Lower House of Convocation was one to the effect "That the use of Organs be removed." There were 117 votes recorded, and organs were only saved by a majority of one! In 1561 Bishops Grindal and Horne wrote to their Continental supporters that they disapproved of the use of organs. It is no wonder, then, that various parishes got rid of their organs about the middle of Elizabeth's fickle reign, anticipating that they would shortly be seized by the Crown or by Church officials. This is the explanation of an entry subsequently cited from the accounts of St. Peter Cheap. The attack on organs was renewed some ten years later, and certain parishes, like St. Laurence, Reading, avowedly sold their instruments lest they should be "forfeited into the hands of the organ-takers."

In 1644, ordinances of the Lords and Commons of 9th May enjoined that "all organs and the frames and cases in which they stand, in all churches and chappels shall be taken away and utterly defaced, and none other hereafter set up in their places." Nevertheless some escaped, but chiefly in cathedral or collegiate churches.

Organ references are so very numerous in wardens' accounts, coming next in many of them to bells, that it is difficult to select the more telling or interesting notes. Of a few churches, a fair

ORGANS—OTHER MUSIC—SINGING MEN

number of items are given; such are those of St. Laurence, Reading; St. Mary-at-Hill; Wimborne; St. Peter Cheap; and St. Mary, Cambridge; in a large number of other cases, arranged so far as may be chronologically, only an odd item or two are cited.

The fickleness of payment to the organ player is strikingly illustrated throughout these extracts. In the earlier days much was done gratuitously in this direction by those attached to the church in minor orders, or by chaplain priests.

The organ entries in the St. Laurence, Reading, accounts have various interesting points. The old organs were removed from the rood-loft in 1506.

1505. For whitleder to the belys of the organs	iij d.
1506. For setting up the rode Mary and John, for removing of th' organs and for making ye sete for the player of the same organs	xx d.
1510. Payd to Barkeleye uppon a bargen of a peyre of organnes at the instaunce of the p'rishe at ij times	iiij li.
1512. Rec' for bryk and mort' left at the makyng of the vowt (vault) for the belys of the organs	xxj d.
Paied to Robt Barkle organ maker	xiij s. iiij d.
To Mr White for waynscott to the new organs	xxxj s.
To Robt Turner for such stuff as he delyvered to the same organs	xv s. x d.
For carrying of the leder fo the belys of the same organs	ij s. ij d.
For vj waynscotts at London	xiiij s.
To Ric' Turner and John Kent for the organ made at one tyme	xxxj s. vj d.
To Ric' Turner and John Kent for the organ made at another tyme	j s.
For led to ley upon the belis of the organ	vj s. viij d.

The bellows for this large instrument were evidently in a vault beneath the floor-level. In addition to the above items, masons and labourers were paid 12s. 1d. for making the vault during the same year. The old instrument was retained, for 7d. was paid in mending "the belis of the old organs and for a li. of glew" in 1512.

1513. To Hew Smyth for iron worke in the new organ loft	x d.
For ij lokks to the organs, one for the stopps and the other the keys	xj d.
To Robt Berkle organ maker for a reward	v s. iiij d.

> For rydyng to Wyndsor to set Mr. Wod to see the new organs   x d.
> To the same M^r for his costs at hys comyng   vij s. x d.
> For mendying and grownde pynnyng of the posts under the organs . . . . ij d.

All was not right with the new instrument, hence the visit of the organist of St. George's, Windsor. In 1514-5 legal proceedings were taken against Barkley, the organ builder, and in 1519 the pipes weighing 291 lbs. were sold to Segemond, another organ maker, for 40s.

> 1520. Paid to Segemond for transposing of the grete organs   vj li. xx d.
> 1521. Paid to Segemond by thadvyse of the p'yde tranposyng and new castyng ye for fronte of the organs and settynge yn ye new stope . . . . . . xiij s. iiij d.

Segemond's organ also proved a failure, law proceedings were taken against him in 1522-3, and it cost 4s. in repairs in 1524. In 1524-5 another new organ was purchased, but from the cost it was evidently but a small instrument for the quire. It was bought ready made, for 15d. was paid in carrying it "from the water to the churche."

> 1529. For mendyng the case of the lytell organs in the chauncell and the bellows of the same at ij times . ij s. vj d.
> 1531. For mendyng the stopps of the grete organs   ij d.
> 1533. Rec' of the Freres in Oxford for the great organs . x li.

Subsequent entries show that the great organ was sold to the friars for £12 10s., but the remaining 50s. never reached Reading owing to the destruction of all friaries.

The next organ fell a victim to Puritanism within the Church.

> 1578. In^d on St. Andrews Day, 1578, it was agreed that the organs in St. Johns chauncell, for that they shoude not be forfeited into the hands of the organ takers shoulde be taken downe and solde; and the tymber of them be applied to sett up two seats higher for Mr. Main and his brethrene above the seate yt now they sett in.
> Pd for taking downe ye organies . . xj d.
> Solde to Rocke 37 li. of leade which was organ metall   viij s. vj d.
> Item xxiiij li. of leade . . . . . . iij s.

Organ entries in the accounts of Wimborne Minster are exceptionally interesting. Richard Gilbert and John Harris, of Christchurch, received 11s. 2d. for mending the organs in the Lady

Chapel in 1495, and Thomas Green, in the same year, 11d. for "glyw and lether" for the organs in the rood-loft. Gilbert received 2s. 8d. as keeper of the organ. In 1526 the organ player received 3s. 4d., and 2s. 4d. was charged for a manual or keyboard. In 1526 "lether to amend the organs" cost 3s. 4d., whilst 4s. 4d. was paid to "the Pryst for mending of them." John Vaucks received 12s. for mending the great organ in 1531, and at the same time £2 0s. 7d. was expended on new (small) organs; there were numerous other small payments this year incidental to the organs, including a reward to the bedeman as blower. Vaucks received 9s. 3d. in 1534 for further organ repairs, and 41s. 5d. for the like in 1535. "John Clifford organ pleyar" received the large sum of £4 for a year's wages in 1539. The sum of 21s. 3d. was paid in 1590 for "8½ ells of holland to make a surplisse for the orgenyst." "Taking down the orgaynes," in 1609, cost 16s. 6d., but in the following year they were again set in their place. "The Great Organ" was tuned and repaired in 1620, but it seems to have been destroyed in the Commonwealth struggle; in 1643 the wardens received 6d. "for sum of the organ pipes." But the organ loft, *i.e.* the rood-loft, still remained, for in 1650 the wardens sold "3 roames in a seat in the organloft" for 20s. In 1663 a rate was levied for repairing the church and buying a new organ; it produced the sum of £253 13s. Of this sum £188 15s. 6d. was expended on "a payre of organs erect and set up by Robert Hayward of the City of Bath organ master." Messrs. Tompkins & Silver, of Sarum, obtained £5 for coming over "to prove the organ where it was sufficient according to our Covenants." Setting up a canopy over the organ in 1666 cost £5 4s. 3d. In 1668 a gift of £5 towards the organ by Sir J. Rogers was disposed of by putting his armes on the three biggest pipes, and by beautifying the king's arms on the top of the organ in gold.

There were two organs at the church of St. Mary-at-Hill, the smaller one in the quire and the larger one probably on the rood-loft. The inventory of 1496 names "ij peyre of old organs," whilst the inventory of 1553 mentions "ij paire of Organs ye one gretter yen ye other." The accounts for the latter year enter 5s. 6d. "for mending the great organs and mendynge the bellowes and for mendynge the lytell organs." In 1477 one Walter Pleasance was paid 6d. "for playing at the organs" on St. Barnabas day.

1519-20.	For Bryngyng of the Orgons from Seint Andrewys to our chirche agent Seint Barnabas Eve . . .	ij d.
	For the beryng home of the Orgon to Seint Andrewys .	iij d.
1521-2.	To the Orgonmaker for the Orgons in money besidse that was gaderid and for bryngyng home of the same orgons	x s. viij d.
	To the Orgonmaker as aperith by Indenture for the oversight of the orgons for certen yeris, yerely to now	xij d.
1523-4.	To John Northfolke for a Rewarde for kepyng the Quere and the Orgons all the xij days in Cristemas .	vj s. viij d.
	Paid for brede and Drynk spent uppon the Orgonmaker and other of the parisshe in the tyme of the Amendyng of the Orgons	xj d.
1524-5.	To the Orgonmaker for mendyng the Orgons accordyng to the Mynde of Mr Northfolke and at his devyse .	ij s.
	To the iij Almesmen, to every of them ij d. for theyre weke when they do blaw the orgons when ther weke comyth	viij s. viij d.

Father Howe, the organ maker, mentioned in the St. Peter Cheap accounts as tuning the organs of that church for a shilling yearly fee from 1547 to 1560, did the like service at St. Helen, Bishopsgate, for a two shillings annual fee. On April 23rd, 1561, "Thomas How, organ maker, was brought up before the Lord Mayor on a charge of not having received the Communion since the Queen's accession" (*Dom. State Papers*, Eliz. xvi. 60); he was doubtless a priest of the unreformed faith, and his arrest brought his organ tuning services to an end.

1433	(*St. Peter Cheap*). For ye Organs mendyng .	vj s. viij d.
1522.	To the organ maker for the new organys . .	vij li.
1524.	For iiij porters for Removynge of the organs into the Roode lofte	xij d.
	For mendyng of the lyttyl organs . .	xij d.
1525.	For the bryngng downe of the organs oute of the Rode lofte	viij d.
1526.	For one of the yrons of the stoppys of the organs . .	xij d.
	For the Forme and the deske at the organs .	ij s. iiij d.
1555.	To Howe organ maker for his fee for kepynge the organs .	ij s.
	To Howe the organ maker for makynge sprynges to the doble regalls and for tonges of the ij regalls which is called the prynceypalls in the base regalls . . .	iij s.

ORGANS—OTHER MUSIC—SINGING MEN

1556. To Howe for ij new pypes for the organs and brasse to the regalls	ij s.
1566-7. Rec' more for the orgaynes sold by consent of the whole parishe	iiij li.
1513 (*St. Mary, Cambridge*). Payed to a blak Fryer in Estir holidaies for to pley atte Orgaynes	xvj d.
1526. For a skynne ledir to amend the organs .	ix d.
1527. For a new handell makyng for the orgayne to keylle	ij d.
P^d for a quartt off Suett wyne to the orgyn makyr for ys re-labor	iiij d.
1537. Payed for ij lokkes and iij Jemens (hinges) for the Organnys	xiiij d.
Payd for a staffe for the Belowes of the said Organnys .	iiij d.
1543. Item of Thomas Canam for xliiij li. of tynne comyng of the old orgayne pypes	xj s.
1557. Payd to Dyall for playeng of our orgaynes from the xijth of May to the iiijth of June	ij s. viij d.
1559. For a booke called a grayle for the organys	iij s. iiij d.
For byndyng of the booke for the orgayns .	viij d.
1564. To betts ye synggeman for mendyng ye orgaynes and makyng new pypes	xij s.
[In an inventory of 1583 the organs are entered as "broken."]	
[The inventory for 1601 names "An Organ Case with some pypes."]	
1613. Received of Mr Fawle Thompson for the Oargen case .	xx d.
1455 (*St. Margaret, Southwark*). For a peyre of newe Organes	v li. vj s. viij d
For a pleyer to pley upon the same Organes hyred in Chepe	xiij s. iiij d.
To Mychell for pleying upon the organes .	xij s.
1457. To John Fychelle Organ pleyer	xl s.

The accounts of St. Petrock, Exeter, show that a rood-loft was erected in 1458-9. In 1472-3 a seat was made at a cost of 7s. for use when playing on the organs in the rood-loft; about this date the clerk of the church received 6s. 8d. a year for playing the organs. In 1519 new organs were purchased for £10 and "the olde pair sold."

1510 (*St. Stephen, Walbrook*). For makyng of the lofte for the organs and translatyng of the rode loft Payd to the carpent' for lxvj ft of stron borde tember	x s. viij d.
[Twelve other items, including the "Bynch of ye organs," came to 44s. 11d.]	
1497 (*Cratfield, Suffolk*). Payd for horgans	ij s. viij d.

1499. For Bord ye iiij days of a man for guldyng (gilding) of y^e
ordell (organ) . . . . . . viij d.
1576. For takynge downe the organ case . . . . iiij s.
1511-2 (*Bassingbourne, Cambs*). Payed for mending or Reparaton'
don on the organes, as his wages xl d., his bord iiij dayes
viij d., iij skynes xxj d., ij calf skynnes and j shepis skyn.
For glewe and nayles, colys, ale v d. ob. The hole
summa . . . . . . vj s. ij d. ob.
1513 (*Shipdham, Norfolk*). Payd to the clarke for ye mendyng
ye orgwanys, and he shall take charge of ye pypys and y^e
bellows ye space of ij yerys at hys owne charge . v s.
Payd to the new clarke for ye fryst quarter x s.
1514-5 (*Holy Trinity, Cambridge*). For the amendyng of th organs xj s.
For a weighte of leade for the belowes of the said organs . xij d.
1520-1. Resceyvyd of money and other of the parochyanours by
them graunted towardes the makyng of a newe peyer of
organs as apperith by a bill owen and examyned upon
this accompte . . . . . v li. vij s. x d.
Rec' for the olde Organ pypis . . . . viij s.
Rec' of the gyft of the master and brethern of seint
Katryn giylde towardes the sam newe organs . . xij s.
Suma . vj li. vij s. x d. ob.
9 Hen. VIII. (*St. Andrew, Holborn*). The little organs were made
and bought at the charges of the parish and devotion of
good people and cost £6. The loft cost 40s.
2 Edward VI. My Lord of Lincoln gave a pair of organs.
1 Mary. The parish gave young White £5 for the great organs
which his father gave to the church.
1519 (*St. Helen, Worcester*). For the taking downe of the old
organs and the lofte of them and for mending of the
Rode loft . . . . . . iiij s. iiij d.
1526 (*All Saints, Bristol*). A new paire of organs was bowt yt
cost x li. ye cariage xiij s. iiij d.
1528 (*St. Alphege, London Wall*). To an organ pleyar for
Wytsonday and Corpscristi day . . . viij d.
1532 (*St. Mary Woolnoth*). To Gregorie the clerk for playing
at the organse one hole yere . . . xiij s. iiij d.
1540 (*Ludlow*). To the organ bloere for his yeares wages ij s. viij d.
1543. For a corde to oure Ladye organs . . . . j d.
1547. For the olde case of the organs . . . xij d.
1551. For mendynge ij peyre of organs . . xij d.
1556. For a corde to the organs in the lofte . . . j d.
1558. For makynge a barrelle to the organs . . . xij d.
1583. For turninge and putting up of xiiij pillars before the
organs . . . . vj s.

ORGANS—OTHER MUSIC—SINGING MEN

For tymber to mak iiij of them	xvj d.
For payntinge the said pillors and the defaced places in the chaunsell	iij s. iiij d.

The accounts of St. Andrew Hubbard for various years show casual disbursements for organists on special occasions or for certain periods; *e.g.* the following sums in 1495:—

To a Organ player	iij s. iiij d.
For an Organ player	iij s. iiij d.
For an Orgyn player for a day	ij d.
For an orgyn player at witson tyde	xiij d.

Subsequently this parish reverted for a time to the employment of a regular organist.

1506-7. Paid to John Smyth organ plaier for A quarter ending at our Lady Day in lent . . . . . v s.

The organist of St. Martin's-in-the-Fields was paid, in 1528, by quarterly gatherings in the church, which amounted to 12s. 10d. In 1526, Mr. Watts received 16s. 5d. "for his Child to pley at Organs by all that yeres." "Nicholas our Clarke" received 13s. 4d. for playing on the organs in 1533. For many years the organ maker received 12d. a year "as his fee in lokyng to the Organs and mendyng of them." At a later period in Elizabeth's reign he received 6d. a quarter for discharging the same duties. Two organs were purchased in 1544-5 by subscription at a cost of £6 13s. 4d. There were 45 donors in sums varying from 40s. to 2d.

1549 (*Smarsden, Kent*). For the olde orgaine pippes sold — x s. vij d.
1500 (*St. Mary, Devizes*). for mending the Organs — viij d.
1529 ,, ,, pd for mendyng of the Orgheyn bellows — j d.
1533 ,, pd for the Organs — xiiij s.
1562 ,, Recv^d for xxxx pound of the organ pypes at vj d. the pound — xx s.
1562 ,, ,, Recv^d of the bellows of the organist — ij s.
1554 (*St. Michael, Cornhill*). For mendinge of the greate Orgaynes and the small paire being broken in the takinge downe — xxiij s.
1556-7 (*Mere, Wilts*). To Jerande for blowynge of the byllows of the Organs for the hole yere nowe endyd — viij s.

1558 (*SS. Philip and James, Bristol*). Payd for a coat and a pair of hosen for the organ player — vij s. iiij d.
Payd for the making of his coat, doublet and hosen — iij s.
1561-2 (*Tavistock*). Unto Ellis Drake for the blowynge of the organs . . . . xvj d.
1639 (*Sidbury, Devon*). For mending the Organs — £5 0 0
For wax and candle used about the Organs — 0 0 4
For men and horses to help hand the Organes . — 0 1 8
1645 (*St. Margaret, Westminster*). Rec. for the organ pipes . 4 0 0

These desultory organ notes can scarcely be better concluded than by the following remarkable notes as to the opening of an organ at Ashborne, Derbyshire.

10 May, 1710. Henry Valentine of Leicester first brought hither the great Organ, and some days after began to work at it towards fitting it up.

"The great Organ being sett up and almost compleated on Sunday the 6th of this month (August, 1710) Thomas Cook of Trusley Esq. and his servant and Mr. Richard Bassano came in the afternoon, and after evening prayers and sermon ended they first plaid a grave Sonata as Voluntary, then Mr. Bassano before the Church full of people sang the 121 Psalm—'I will lift up mine eyes'—as an Anthem.

"September, 1710. The great Organ in the Church being now compleated and put in tune, and ye iron standard Rods and curtains of the Organ loft being sett up it was opened and dedicated in the manner following. On Sunday (16th) the Vicar preached from Psalm 92—1, 2, 3 (here follows an abstract of the sermon, and an account of the part taken by the organ in the services). But in the afternoon Mr. Matthew Haines, one of the singing men of the Quire at Lichfield, gave a fine long anthem just after the Italian manner. The anthem has much variety of musick in it, and is contrived with intermixture of frequent Symphonies or Riturnalles, which Riturnalles were touched and plaid upon two Violins by two gentlemen who stood behind the curtain in the Organ loft. This performance was very fine as well as grave and solemn.

"But the grand performance was on the following Wednesday, when there were many voices and instruments (of which a full list is given) and an audience of five thousand people. Mr Rathbone of Nottingham played the Organ, and Mr. Henry Valentine, who made the Organ, stood by him with a trumpet. At night in the great parlour of the Blackmore's Head they made a fine consert both of Instrumental and Vocal Musick, and so concluded the musick of the day."

OTHER INSTRUMENTS OF MUSIC

The close study of hundreds of early churchwardens' accounts has only resulted in the discovery of a single entry of a musical

ORGANS—OTHER MUSIC—SINGING MEN

instrument for church use other than organs until the seventeenth century was far advanced. In the Wimborne accounts of 1531, the somewhat puzzling entry occurs of "an iron bar for the shalms, viij d." The shalm was a form of pipe or trumpet, somewhat resembling the later clarionet. In various accounts mention is made of trimming banners with little bells, sometimes of silver; their tinkling sound, on great procession days, would be heard within the church, as well as in the open air. Small chiming bells were used as an occasional accompaniment to organs, and possibly some of the chimes named in the accounts served partly for such a purpose and not merely as adjuncts to the clocks in the interior of the churches.

In connection with the church-ales, the payment of special instrumentalists is occasionally named, such as a harper at Reading in 1504, pipers at St. Ives, Cornwall, and a drummer at Seal, Surrey, the last two in Elizabethan days. Minstrels are frequently mentioned in connection with ales and plays, and now and again, as at Barnstaple, it is expressly stated that they played in church. Then again, town waits, or professional musicians, were now and again hired to take part in church holyday processions.

In the eighteenth and early part of the nineteenth centuries, church bands were common adjuncts to church music, especially in country villages. The most usual instruments were the bassoon, violin, base viol or violoncello, flute, clarinet, and hautbois.

It must suffice to cite a few instances of eighteenth-century church music from certain Derbyshire parish accounts. At Youlgrave these two entries occur:—

    1742. For hairing the bowe of the viole . . . . 8d.
    1751. Gave Ben Jones to buy Reeds for ye Basoon . 3 0

From a loose sheet of paper in the church chest, it appears that the parish acquired a "Base Voile" in 1785, and it was decided at a vestry meeting that it should be appropriated solely to the use of the church, "and not be handled about to Wakes or any other places of profaneness and Diversion," excepting the club feasts of Youlgrave, Elton, and Winster.

1772 (*Hayfield*). Spent with Singers when new Bazoon came	£0	2	6
1772. Charges when the Bassoune came	. 0		6
1779. For repairing the Bassoon	. 0		6
1783. For reeds for the Bassoon	. 0		0
1793. Paid John Line for a Hautboy.	. 1		0
1789 (*Hartshorne*). Paid for one Haughtboy for the Church	. 0	1	0
1790. Paid for a Haughtboy and Reeds	. 0	1	0
1818 (*Marston-on-Dove*). Pd to repairing the Bassoon	1		0

At Church Broughton the old church bassoon is still preserved in the parish chest, though not played within the memory of man.

The present writer well remembers the village band in front of the west gallery of Luccombe Church, of which his father was for some years rector. When old Robert Ketnor, the clerk, called upon us to "sing to the honour and glory of God," the whole congregation turned round to face west. The Luccombe church band expired in 1859; in the neighbouring village of Selworthy the church orchestra remained in the gallery until after the death of "Old Sir Thomas Acland" in 1871. In fact, throughout West Somerset, there were far more village church bands than organs down to 1850 or somewhat later. The Rev. F. W. Galpin, however, in his delightful *Old English Instruments of Music* (1910), brings down the survival of a Dorsetshire church band to a much later date; it did not expire at Winterbourne Abbas till about 1895.

SINGING MEN AND BOYS

References in town accounts to singers in the quire, both men and boys, are fairly frequent. A variety of extracts are given from the wardens' books of St. Mary-at-Hill and St. Edmund, Sarum. These are followed by a series of shorter entries from numerous other churches, especially those of the City of London. It is hardly necessary to state—but there is some ignorance on the matter—that the reformed Prayer Books of Edward VI and Elizabeth abound in rubrics as to "singing," not only at mattins and evensong, but at the Holy Eucharist. Marbeck's *Booke of Common Praise noted* was issued in 1550. The 49th of Queen Elizabeth's Inquisitions, of 1559, was most explicit as to the continuance of "syngynge or musycke in the churche."

ORGANS—OTHER MUSIC—SINGING MEN

Special reference is made in a later chapter to the singers on Palm Sunday.

There are frequent entries in the St. Mary-at-Hill accounts as to singing men and boys in the quire.

The descriptive word "conduct" occurs fairly often; it means a hired man, and usually is applied to a singing man, whether lay or cleric; the term is still in use at Eton College for a chaplain. Occasionally the singer was a priest, as is implied by the prefix "Sir."

1477–9.	To Sir John Henley for syngyng (St. Barnabas day)	viij d.
	To iiij Childre of Saynt Magnus for syngynge	iiij d.
1484–5.	To syngers on St. Barnabas evynyn wyne at Easter and at many other festes of the yer to syngers within the quere	v s.
1493–4.	To a chylde that songe a trebyll to helpe the quere in crystmas halydayis	xij d.
1498–9.	To William Raynesford, conduct, which weas hired from shroftyde to lammas	xxij s.
	To Symond Vaireson for helpyng of the quiere all the halydays of Crystmas	iij s. iiij d.
1502–3.	To Wylliam Wylde for a reward in helpyng of the quere at Ester and Whytsontyde	iij s. iiij d.
1527–8.	To a singingman of Sent Anthis for keping of our ladymas in thabscence of gose and the clerk when they were takin to Ipswich	iij s. iiij d.
1529–30.	For Brede and Drynk att the hyring off Sir Symond the Bass that cam from Saint Antony's	iiij d.
1531–2.	To Richard the Bass for ix daies wages that he served before Michelmas	iij s. iiij d.
1534.	iij syngyng men at easter for helpyng the quyer	v s.
1535.	ij singing men to singe in the ester hollydayes and upon loo sondaye	vj s.
	To seven conductes to sing ev'songe upon our Ladis even	xx d.
1539–40.	To a trebyll for synging in the quier	iij s. iiij d.
1551–2.	To William Dawe, our base, for his wholle yeares wages	vj li.
1556–7.	To Sir John Parkyur, a base, for to helpe the quere when Hobbes was dead and to have viij d. day everie holy daye and sundayes	xv s. viij d.
	To John Hobbes, condocke, for one quarters wages endynge at thannunciacion of our Ladye and borrowed xvj s. viij d. of the nexte quarter and dyed	lvj s. viij d.
1556–8.	To Tamor, the basse, for one quarter from mykellmase to chrystmas	ij li.

To a pryste that dyd synge a basse for vij wyckes at ij s. viij d. the wycke	xviij s. viij d.
To a syngynge man on palme sonday .	xij d.
To a syngynge man in the ester holy days	v s.
To a syngynge man at Whyttsontyde .	iij s. iiij d.

The accounts of the Fraternity of Jesus Mass within the church of St. Edmund, Sarum, contain various references to singing men and choristers on special occasions, from which the following selections are taken:—

1476-7. In clericis cantantibus Salve qualibet die Veneris quadragesima	xviij d.
1505-6. Propend et Servicia pro potacionibus Cantorum qui cantant Salve qualibet die Veneris in XL^{ms} .	ij s.
1507-9. Pro potacionibus presbiterum et Clericorum cantantum Salve	ij s. ix d.
1532-3. For brede and ale for prestes and Clarkes syngyng at Salve in Lent	v s. viij d.
1538-9. Drynkynges in lente after Salve on the Frydayes	iij s. iiij d.
1539-40. Bread and ale spent on the Frydayes in lent after Salve upon the syngynge men and quyristers	iiij s. vj d.

At the dedication of the eastern part of the new cathedral of Sarum in 1223, Bishop Poore instituted the daily Mass of the Blessed Virgin known as *Salve*.[1]

This special Salve Mass was revived during Lent in the time of Queen Mary, as shown by the following entries in the general accounts of the church of St. Edmund:—

1556-7. The fyrst Fryday in the lent to make the syngynge men drynke	xij d.
The secon Fryday in lent to make the syngynge men drynke after Salve	iij d.
Thyrde Fryday in lent to make the syngynge men drynke after Salve	xxiij d.
Fourth Fryday in lent to make the syngynge men drynke after Salve	xx d.
The Fyveth Fryday in lent to make the syngynge men drynke after Salve	xvij d.
1557-8. ij pounde of Fygges[2] for them that dyd helpe to syng at Salve the fyrst fryday in the lent . . .	vj d.

---

[1] "Salve sancta parens." See *Missale Sarum*, p. 779, and Wordsworth's *Notes on Mediæval Services* (1898), pp. 273-4.

[2] Smyrna figs are still known in parts of Wiltshire as "Lent figs."

ORGANS—OTHER MUSIC—SINGING MEN

  vij li. of fygges . . . . . xvij d. ob.
  iij li. for the Syngyn men that sang at Salvy the frydeyes
   in the lent . . . . . . vj d. ob.
  In all for brede and drynke for the Syngyn men that dyd
   Synge at Salvy . . . . . v. s iiij d.
  Edmond the syngynge man . . . iij s. ij d.
1560-1. John Saunderis for to helpe synge in the quyer . . iiij s.
1572-3. John Sanders for to helpe synge in the quyre . v s. iiij d.
1574. A strange Singinge man of Steple Ashtone yt dyd
  labour for S'vice . . . . . . iij s.
  John Mill for the travel to Steple Ashtone to cause the
   sayde Singinge man to come to the Master of the
   parisshe abowte service . . . . . vj d.
1472 (*St. Michael, Cornhill*). To Clydrowe for singing in the
  Chirch by all Cristemas halydaies . vj s. viij d.
1473. To my Ladye Bokyngham clerkes for their syngyng . viij d.
1484-6 (*St. Margaret, Westminster*). For brede ale and wyne
  on Corpus Xtiday for syngers of the Kyngs Chappell . xij d. ob.
1496-7 (*St. Andrew Hubbard*). For wyne for Singers on our
  Chircheholyday . . . . . . viij d.
1528-9. To the conducke for senggyng in the holydays . xvj d.
1531-2. Apone sent Andrewes day to the Syngyne men . xij d.
  To the porter for syngen yn ye queer v s. iiij d.
1518 (*St. Stephen, Walbrook*). To the syngers on o^r church
  holyday . . . . xx d.
  To the syngers on the Invencyon off Synt stevyn xx d.
1531-2 (*Ashburton, Devon*). Given to a boy John Bartlett for
  singing in the church this year for a reward . iij s. iiij d.
1541 (*St. Mary Woolnoth*). To iiij Preists and ij clarks of this
  church for kepyng of our Lady masse by note in the
  time of the vacation of a Conduct . xij s.
  To our Conduct for lyke service doon by him and his
   children for iij quarters of a yere . . . vj s.
1561-2. To the children of Paules for helping . vj d.
1543 (*St. Nicholas, Cole Abbey*). Paid to Mr Reynolds and his
  company for their pains in the Lent season for
  anthems . . . . ij s.
1526 (*St. Stephen, Walbrook*). Payde at the ale house over
  the syngers on Seynt Stephyn Evyn . vj d.
  Payde in Rewarde to the syngers that day vj s. viij d.
  Spent on them at the ale house after the last evynsong . vij d. ob.
1549-50 (*St. Matthew, Friday Street*). Paid to Mr Russell for a
  synging man at Ester to sett the quire in order . iiij s.
1560-1. To v syngyng men on Sant Mathewes daye for sarvyng
  in ye Churche and for boroyng of song bouckes . iiij s.

1557 (*Ludlow*). For a lynke of iij li. and iij quarters to lyght at after evensonge to synge carolles at the same tyme . xij d.
1564 (*Ludlow*). For a booke for one of the singeinge boyes . vj d.
1576–7. For songes singed upon the Q. Maties birthedaie . . viij d.
To a sumner for bringing the same songes . . iiij d.

It was not until 1576 that it was decided, on obvious political grounds, to have an elaborate " Fourme of Prayer with Thankes givinge to be used of all the Queenes Majesties loving subjectes every yeere, the 17 of November, being the day of her Highnes entrie to her Kingdom." At the end of this ultra-loyal special form of prayer is a doggerel effort in rhyme, of fourteen long stanzas divided into two parts. These are evidently the " songes " of the Ludlow entry. The writer blundered in considering the form was for Elizabeth's birthday ; 17th November was the day of her accession. On the opposite page the first three stanzas are reproduced from an original copy.

1584 (*St. James', Bristol*). Paid to the singing men of the College at Christmas . . . . . x s.
1585. Payd unto the waytes at Christmas for a carroll . . ij s. vj d.
1601–2 (*St. Botolph, Aldersgate*). Money received amongst the parishioners towards the payment of the stipendes and wages of the Clarke Sexton and others healpinge to singe and serve in the Quyer . . xiij li.

Occasionally a chorister was recompensed in kind.

1582–3 (*St. Thomas, Sarum*). 5¾ yards to make Distine the boye wch singeth in the quire a coat and a pair of breches . 7 8

A thankesgiuing, to be
sung as the 81. Psalme.

BE light and glad, in God reioyce,
which is our strength and stay:
Be ioyfull and lift vp your voyce,
for this most happie daye.
Sing, sing, O sing vnto the Lorde,
with melodie most sweete:
Let heart and tongue in one accorde,
as it is iust and meete.

2 Sing lawde vnto the Lorde aboue,
serue him with glad intent:
O clappe your handes in signe of loue,
for this which he hath sent.
Sing prayse, sing prayse with Harpe and Lute,
with ioy let vs be seene:
Before our God let none be mute,
but lawde him for our Queene.

3 Sound out the trumpe courageously,
blowe as on solemne dayes:
Both high and lowe come fill the skye,
with sweete resounding prayse.
For why? When we were bound in thrall,
and eke in griefe did stand,
The Lord did set vs free from all,
by this his seruants hand.

4 Our selues therefore we wholly binde,
a Sacrifice to bee,
In token of our thankefull minde
(O God most deare) to thee.
To thee we crye, and also giue
most high thankes, lawde and prayse,
For thy good giftes which we receiue,
both nowe and all our dayes.

ELIZABETHAN HYMN: FROM "A FORME OF PRAYER," 15

CHAPTER XVI

BELLS AND RINGING

Bell repairs—Explanation of terms—The passing bell—Bell ringing against Thunderstorms—Festival ringing—Early Mattins—Ringing for Royalty—Fines for neglect—Elizabethan ringings—Stuart ringings at Salisbury—Historical Ringing selections—Episcopal ringing—Curious ringings

THERE is no one subject which occupies near so much space in wardens' accounts as that concerned with the casting, purchasing, and continuous repairs of bells, and the supplying them with bell ropes. Nevertheless the story of the actual bells is almost entirely excluded from these pages to make space for other material; and this can be done with hardly any regret, because the majority of English counties are already in possession of good monographs on church bells, wherein liberal extracts constantly appear from churchwardens' books of various periods. There are, too, several valuable books on church bells in general, the best and most comprehensive of which is *The Bells of England* (1906), by the late Dr. Raven.

A brief paragraph or two may, however, be spared, for the help of those who are not campanologists, and who may be puzzled by unusual terms of frequent occurrence in old parish books relative to bells and their repairs.

Baldrick—spelt in an almost infinite variety of ways, such as "baudrik," "bawdrick," "balltrix," etc.—was a leather thong, by which the clapper was suspended from a staple in the crown of the bell; it naturally required frequent renewal. It has since been superseded by a wooden block.

Cotter is a small wedge of iron put through a rod to prevent a nut coming off; the term is still in use.

Brasses are the sockets in which the *gudgeons* or axles of the bells work.

Quartering a bell is turning a bell round, after it has hung many years, so that the clapper may strike on a fresh place.

Brief references to the blessing of bells will be found under the section on hallowing.

The passing or soul-bell has been discussed under the receipts of the wardens of St. Edmund, Sarum, where it was known by the picturesque name of the forthfare bell. This mediæval and beautiful custom, said to be peculiar to England, fell for the most part into disuse with the Reformation, when the knell at the time of burial took its place. These knells produced a good income for the wardens of populous parishes, *e.g.* St. Martin's-in-the-Fields and St. Margaret, Westminster. Occasionally, as at present, the knell was tolled immediately after the death, and still retained the incorrect name of the passing bell. Kindly provision was made by some parishes for knell-ringing without a fee when the friends or relatives of the deceased were poor.

Thus at St. Mary, Warwick, the regular charge for ringing the passing bell at death was 2s. 6d. for the great bell, 1s. for the seventh bell, and 6d. for the fifth bell. It was, however, provided, in 1686,

"that every person that dyeth, having not money to pay for the ringing of the 5th bell, may have liberty to send any person to ring that bell without paying for the same. And if the party dec'd hath none to ring the bell for him, nor money to pay for the same, the clarke shall ring the said bell without receiving any pay for ringing the said bell."

There was an old superstition that bells had the power of dispersing tempests. Here are four early instances from parish accounts:—

    1450 (*St. Mary-at-Hill, City*). Dat' hominibus pulsantibus in nocte Sci Petri pro tornitura . .. . viij d.
    1457-8 (*Yeovil*). In potacione dat' pulsatoribus dum tonatruat   j d.
    1464 (*St. Mary, Sandwich*). For bred and drynke for ryngers in the great thunderyng . . . . . iij d. ob.
    1519 (*Spalding*). Pd for ryngyng when the Tempest was . iij d.

This custom was preached against vehemently by the Reformers, although Lord Bacon thought there was a certain scientific

BELLS AND RINGING

basis in justification of the practice. The idea did not readily die out. We have found an Elizabethan entry of its continuance in a Norfolk parish, and one of the seventeenth century in Kent; but most unfortunately both these excerpts, culled many years ago, have been mislaid.

The early ringing of bells for Mass and the services of the Hours was usually done by clerks of the church; it was consequently gratuitous and is not named in wardens' accounts; but it was different at the times of popular festivals.

1483-4 (*St. Edmund, Sarum*). For the beringe of the banners and
    for ryngyng in Rogacyon weke . . . . iiij d.
    Payd on holly thersday and on oure thankyng Day and on
    Corpus cryts day for ye baners beringe and for Rynkers vj d.
    [Several similar later entries.]
1517-8. Payde for ale for the Rvngers the gang weke and ye wytson
    wyke . . . . ij s.
1518-9. Rynggers at Seynt Martynes . . . . . iiij d.
    Rynggers on the dawnsynge day . . . . ij d.
    Ryngyn on Corpus Xtiday . . . . . ij d.
    The Rynggars for Rynggynge off generalle prossessyone . iiij d.
1506 (*St. Laurence, Reading*). Payed for bred and ale to the
    ryngers in the rogacion weke . . . . ij d.
1508. For ij galons of ale for the Ryngers on Dedycacion . iij d.
    To the ryngers on Holy Thursday of coustom to ryng at
    p'cession . . . . iij d.
    For ryngyng on Corp' Xtiday at p'cession . iij d.
1523-4 (*St. Mary-at Hill, City*). To the Ryngers on our lady day
    for Ryngyng . . . . viij d.
1525-6. For Ryngyng of None Curfew and day pele, and Courfew
    and other pelis on our lady day the Assumpcion . xij d.

A dish of calves' head is mentioned in several accounts as a customary reward to ringers and others on Corpus Christi day.

1524 (*St. Dunstan's. Canterbury*). For calves heddes for the
    ryngers for ij yeres . . . . . . xiiij d.
1525. For a calves hede flagges and thredde at Corpus Christi
    day for ryngaris . . . . . . vij d.

A shortened form of mattins at five or six o'clock was customary in various town churches in the days of Edward VI and throughout Elizabethan times. This was the case at St. Edmund, Sarum.

1553-4. Ringinge to mornynge prayer . vj s. viij d.
Rynginge of none for sayntes yeves and saturdays for one whole yere xviij d. a quarter . . . . vj s.
1560-1. Ryngyng to the mornyng prayer . vj s. viij d.

Ringing for none or nones, *i.e.* 3 p.m. evensong on saints' eves and on Saturdays, continued at the same church throughout Elizabeth's reign.

1568-9. Ryngynge none on Satterdays and sayntes yeves . v s.
1592-3. Ringing at noon (sic) on Satterdays for ye whole year 6s.

The ringings on special festivals are often entered separately.

1581-2. For whitsonday, against cristmas, on Candlemas day, at ester day . . . . 21s.
1587-8. Ascension day 4d., Christmas day 6d., Ester day 6d. 1s. 4d.
1591-2. Ascension daye, Witsondaye, Christmas day, and Easter daye . . . . 2s.
1603-4. Quarter Ringinge . . . . . . 6s.
For the Ringers at iiij severall feasts of the yeare that is to saye the feaste of the Ascension, of pentecoste, of our Lord God (Christmas), and Easter . . . . 2s.
1625-6. Ringing on Feastifull dayes in the morning . 8s.
1622-3 (*St. Martin, Leicester*). For ringeinge to praiers every Sabboth and Holie daie . . . . . iij s.

Six honest able men were appointed ringers at this latter church, in 1664, at 4s. each per annum, "for ringing and chiming on Sundays, holydays, and other days, as the churchwardens shall appoint, for giving convenient notice to the parishioners for preparation to come to church."

The earliest entry in parish accounts of ringing on the advent of royalty, of which we have any knowledge, was on the occasion of Queen Margaret visiting Saffron Walden in 1444.

For ryngyng wanne y[e] quene was her . iiij d.

On a second visit in 1455 the entry is in Latin—

Pulsantibus quando dna Regina vent[t] in istam villam iiij d.

Henry VI about this period visited Bristol in two successive years, as recorded in the accounts of All Saints in that city:—

1448. To ryngnys aganst ye Kynge. . . . viij d.
1449, ii March. For ryngyng ageynst ye Kyng . iiij d.

BELLS AND RINGING

It was customary for the church bells of each parish through which the king or queen passed to be rung on both entry and exit. The royal almoner claimed the right to levy a fine on the neglect of this loyal custom, and he, or others of the king's servants, went so far as to seal up the church doors until the fine was paid. This happened when Henry VI visited the abbey of Saffron Walden in 1445. The wardens had to pay a fine which is thus entered:—

> Sol' servis dne Regie p defect' p pulsacionis qn' vent' ad Abbathiam . . . . ij s.
> 1510 (*Wimborne*). To the kyng hys servant for defawte of ryngyng at the Quenes departyng . . . .

Catherine of Aragon's visit to Reading in 1528 caused the wardens of St. Laurence to be fined.

> To the quens servants, for that the bells were not rung at her comyng in to the towne . . . . . . viij d.

On the visit of Henry VIII to Dover in 1538–9, the bells of St. Mary's were duly rung; but a fine of 5s. was enforced for neglect on his departure.

> For the ryngyng in of the Kinge to the ryngers . . viij d.
> For the sealyng up of the Church dores at the Kynges departyng owt of the town . . . . v s.

The accounts of St. Margaret's, Westminster, for 1548 show that that parish got off with a lighter fine in the case of the boy-king Edward VI:—

> Paid to the King's amner when he would have sealed up the church door at the departure of the King majesty the 2^d day of July because the bells were not rung . . . ij s. iiij d.

Queen Elizabeth was characteristically determined to uphold enforced ringing as the accompaniment of her constant movements. This became a somewhat serious tax upon Westminster and London parishes. There are at least four recorded cases of the sealing of church doors and the exacting of penalties through neglecting to be prepared for her movements. Were all the extant Elizabethan ringings in wardens' accounts to be set down in these pages they would about fill the volume. Of course there were ringings throughout the land on her birthday and her day of accession. The wardens' accounts of St. Martin's-in-the-Fields fairly bristle with Elizabethan peals. Here are three entries of the Michaelmas quarter of 1566, which must serve as an example :—

> For ringinge at the quenes remove from grenewich to St. James the 29 of June . . . . viij d.
> For ringinge at ye quenes remove from St. James to hir progress theight of Julye . . . . viij d.
> For ringing the 27 day of September at ye quenes remove from Rychmonde to Whithall . . . . . . viij d.

Visits to Salisbury, especially to Wilton, the residence of the Earls of Pembroke, were frequently undertaken by the Stuart kings. The wardens of St. Edmund, Sarum, had to be watchful to escape fines. The following are examples of a large number of like entries :—

> 1613-4. Ringers the 3rd of August for the Kenge and Queenes comminge to Sarum . . . . . 12 (
> At the Kenges goinge awaye (5th August) . (
> At the Queenes goinge awaie. . . . . (
> 1625-6. Ringing for the Kinge Sept 12 . . . . 1 (
> Ringing when the Quene rod to Wilton . (
> More when the queene come into the Close 1 (
> Ringing when the Kinge went away . . . (
> When the Queene went away . . . . o

Analogous to the royal compulsion as to the use of church bells was the action of the Palatine Bishops of Durham in insisting, *subpœna*, on visitation ringing.

> 1630 (*St. Oswald, Durham*). At the Bishopps going in his visitacion not being formerly fined for not ringing . 2 9

The Cavalier General Lord Goring insisted on similar belfry recognition during the Civil War.

> 1644-5 (*St. Edmund, Sarum*). The martiall gen'all of the Lord Gorings Army for not ringing the Bells wch he demannded for his fee 1q 0

A very limited selection is now given of the ringings recorded in parish books to commemorate historical events under different reigns. The following from St. Mary-at-Hill, City, refers to the betrothal at Paul's Cross of Margaret, the eldest daughter of Henry VII, to James IV of Scotland, "in rejoycement whereof Te Deum was sung, and other signes of publike joy declared":—

1502-3. For ryngyng of our bellys when the kyng came from Waynardes castell to powelles (St. Paul's) . . iij d.

Henry VIII

1508-9 (*St. Mary-at-Hill*). To sevyn men that rang the bellis when the Kynges grace whent to Westmyster to be crownpyd . . . . j s. ij d.

1509 (*St. Laurence, Reading*). For x Rynggers at the parting of the Kyng and for drynke and to the sexton . . ij s. ob.

1513. For a galon of ale for the Ryngers at the getting of Turwyn . . . . ij d.

For a galon of ale for the Ryngers at the deth of the Kyng of Scots [Flodden Field] . . . . ij d.

1513 (*St. Andrew, Holborn*). Election of Leo X. Bently, referring to the old accounts, writing in 1586, says: "The bells were accustomed to be rung always at the election of the Pope in this parish as in 5 Hen. VIII is in all lands over."

1524-5 (*St. Mary-at-Hill*). For Ryngyng of the belles at the Triumphe for the takyng of the French Kyng [Battle of Pavia] . . . . iij d.

1533 (*St. Laurence, Reading*). For ryngyng at the birth of the princes (Elizabeth) . . . . . iiij d.

1536 (*St. Alphege, London Wall*). To v Ryngars for Deryge and Masse of queene Jane . . . ij s. viij d.

1539 (*St. Andrew Hubbard*). Payd for Rynggen for the empourers wyffe (Isabella, wife of Charles V) . vj d.

1546 (*St. Mary Woolnoth*). For ryngying at the French kings funrall . . . . xx d.

1546-7 (*Ashburton, Devon*). For ringing after the death of King Henry viij[th] for whose soul may God be propitiated . xvj d.

For ryngyng the peales at y[e] Kynges buryal . . ij s. vj d.

(*St. Martin's-in-the-Fields*). Payed to the Ryngers and holders of Torches when our late Souveraygne lorde King Henry theyght went to buriall . ij s.

Edward VI

1547 (*St. Michael, Worcester*). To iij men for rynginge at the procession for the victorye in Skotlande [Battle of Pinkie] iij d.

(*Christ Church, Bristol*). For rynging of the bellis at the generall processyon for the Kyng when peace was taken at Bollen [Boulogne] . . . . . iiij d.
1552-3 (*St. Edmund, Sarum*). Ryngers at ye cumynge of ye Kinges grace . . . . . . xiiij d.

Mary

1553 (*St. Margaret, Westminster*). For bread and drink on Ash Wednesday to the ringers at the victory and overthrow of Wyat and his adherents . . . . viij d.
1554 (*St. Michael, Cornhill*). Paide the vijth daye of February when Captayne Wyat (Sir Thomas Wyatt) was taken, for ringinge the belles and singeinge Tedu (Te Deum), to the clerkes and sexton for all beadesmen . . ij s.
1555. To vj Ringgars when the Kinge and the Quene cam thorrow the Cittie . . . . . . ij s.
Paide to Ringgers (30 April) when worde was brought that the Quene was brought to bed . . . . ij s.
1553-4 (*St. Laurence, Reading*). Pd to Ringers at the Kyng and Quenys cumyng and goyng . . . . xx d.
1555 (*St. John Baptist, Bristol*). Paid the sexton to ring for our holy father the pope . . . . . ij s.
1556. Paid for ringing the bells for the visitation of our holy father the pope [Cardinal Pole's visitation] . iiij s.
1556 (*Strood, Kent*). Paid to ye Ryngers when my lord Cardenall came to Rochester in Lente . . . vj d.
1556-7 (*St. Mary-at-Hill*). To fyve ryng that ronge the same daye that the Kynge and Quenes hignes came through London, by commaundement of the bishop to rynge . . . . xx d.
1558-9 (*Ashburton, Devon*). For ryngyng of Quenes majestys knyll . . . . viij d.
(*St. Martin's-in-the-Fields*). For ryngynge at the buryall of Queene . . . . vij d.

Elizabeth

1558 (*St. Nicholas, Warwick*). Item for brede and aylle to the ryngeris at the generalle prosessyon for quyne elsabethe . viij d.
1568 (*St. Laurence, Reading*). To the Ryngers at the Queens comynge in . . . . . . xvj d.
1569 (*St. Michael, Worcester*). Ryngyng at the daye of the Quenes entry . . . . . . viij d.
1570 (*St. Margaret, Westminster*). For ringing when the Queen's Majesty went to the Burse . . . . iiij d.

BELLS AND RINGING

["Burse" given the name of "Royal Exchange" on the occasion of Queen's visit 23 Jan. 1570.]

When the Queen went to Sir Thomas Greshame and came back again . . . . . . viij d.

1571. For joy of the great victory that the Christians have gotten of the Turks . . . . . . ij s. vj d.

(*St. Martin's-in-the-Fields*). Payd for brede and drink for the Ringinge at the overthroe of ye turk [Battle of Lepanto] . . . . vij d.

1585–6 (*St. Thomas, Sarum*). Geven to the Ringers the Kinge of Portingalles beinge heare . . . . 6d.

1586–7 Ringinge the Quenesma^{ties} escape from the treason conspired [The Babington Conspiracy] . 6d.

Ringers when newes came of the Queene of scottes beheddinge . . . . . . 6d.

Lest it should be imagined that the ringing for the Queen of Scots' beheading was of the nature of a dirge, the following coarse entry made by the parish clerk of St. Botolph, Aldgate, may be cited. The execution was on 8th February 1586–7.

Mem^d that we did ringe at oure parish churche the ix day of Febrarie in ano 1586 and was for joye that the Queene of Skotts that ennemy to oure most noble Queens Matie and ower contrie was beheaded for the wch the Lorde God be praysed and I wold to God that all her confederates weare knowne and cut of by the lyke means.

There is something peculiarly repellent in the ringing of joy peals over an execution, but it was commonly done throughout England as well as in every belfry of the City of London.

1586 (*Minehead, Somerset*). Ringers for joy when newes reached us of beheadinge of quene of scottes . . xij d.

1586 (*Stanford, Berks*). Ringers 10 Februarie for the execucon of ye Quene of Scotts on scaffolde . j s. iiij d.

1585–6 (*St. Christopher-le-Stocks*). For ringing when Babington with the other traytors were ap'hended and were taken and also when the quene of scotts was p'claimed conspirator to ye quene and our realme . iij s. iij d.

For ringing on the daye of execution of ye Skotts queene ij s.

1588 (*St. Martin's-in-the-Fields*). P^d for ringinge at her ma^{ties} goinge and comynge to and from ye Campe at Tilbury in Essex . . . . ij s.

1588–9 (*St. Thomas, Sarum*). On the twesdie and followinge for the great Victorie against the spanyardes by the mightie hand of God 8 0

THE CHURCHWARDENS' ACCOUNTS

Ringers breakfast at that tyme	2 10

1590 (*St. Martin's-in-the-Fields*). Paid ye xvth day of marche for ij Dayes ringinge for the victorie the kinge of Navar then obtyned (Battle of Ivry, 14 March) and for a prayer Booke . . . . . iiij s. iiij d.

1592-3 (*St. Edmund, Sarum*). For ringing the Triumphing daye (Armada) . . . . 4s.

1595 (*St. Alphege, London Wall*). Spent on the Ringers at the returne of or ships from callis . . . . ij s. ij d.

1595-6 (*St. Martin's-in-the-Fields*). Paid for Ringing the viijth of Auguste being upon Comaundment from the Counsell for the good success that the Erle of Essex and the reste of his followers had at Cales voyadge . . iij d.

1601-2 (*St. Edmund, Sarum*). Ringers for ringinge for ye Triumphe in Ireland (defeat of O'Neil at Kinsale) 12d.

JAMES I

1603-4 (*St. Edmund, Sarum*). On the Kinges byrthdaye being the xxix of June . . . . . . 4s.

On the v of August being the Kinges holiedaye in the which it pleased almightie God to deliver him from his enemies in Scotland [alleged Gowrie Conspiracy] . 6s.

For his Coronation being St. James his day 6s. 8d.

When O^r Kinges Majestie came in his progresse for iiij dayes followinge and parte of nightes from ye xxvj of August unto the xxx . . . . . 34s.

On the xxth of October when the Queens majestie came to the Close of Sarum and the xxj of the same moneth when the Kings ma^{tie} and the younge Prince roade through Sarum to Wilton . . . . . . 14s.

When the Kinge and Queene came to o^r Ladie church to the sermon upon all saintes Daye, and at other times when his ma^{tie} Roade through the Cittie towardes the Parke to hunt . . . . . . 7s.

When the Kinge removed from Wilton . . . 5s.

Beinge the xxiv of march in which day he was proclaimed Kinge of this Lande . . . . . 6s. 8d.

When the Lord of Pembrooke passed through ye Cittie . 12d.

1605 (*St. Margaret, Westminster*). When the parliament house should have been blown up [chosen out of a number of like entries for its quaint language] . xxx s.

1606. Augt. 4th. When the King of Denmark came to the Abbey ij s. vj d.

1610. When the citizens met the Prince, when he was created Prince of Wales, and when the fireworks were made . vij s. ij d.

BELLS AND RINGING

1614. When the King of Denmark came to Londen . . . ij s.
1623. When the Kings Majesty feasted the Spanish ambassydor in July . . . . ij s. vj d.
1617-8 (*St. Edmund, Sarum*). For the birthe of the Prince Palgraves child . . . . . . 3s. 4d.
1623-4. Ringeing when newes came of the princes saffe returne from Spain . . . . 2s.
Ringing when newes came that the matche was broken off between the Prince and the Infanta of Spain . 2s.
[Many like entries up and down the country.]
1623-4 (*St. Mary, Cambridge*). Payed to John Hall money that he sayethe he spent uppon the ringers the vjth, vijth, and viijth dayes of October when the prince returned from Spayne . iij s.

CHARLES I

1625-6. For Boniferes and Ringers at the Quenes Coming . vj s. vj d.
1628. For a Bonfyre and ringinge, by Mr Vice Chancellor and M^r ma'iors appoyntment for joy of the Queens conceiption iij s. iiij d.
1633-4. For the Ringers whenn the duke of York was borne by Command of the vicechanclor and bonfiars . 5s.
1624-5 (*St. Edmund, Sarum*). Ringinge when Kinge Charles was proclaymed Kinge of England, Scotland, France, and Ireland . . . . 8s.
1624-5 (*St. Martin, Leicester*). Pd to 5 Ringers for Ringinge at the first and second time proclaiminge the Kinge . v s.
1630-1. For Ringing of the Bells when newse was brought the Queene was brought to bed . . . . ij s. vj d.
1633-4. Given the Ringers for ringing at the birth of the young Duke . . . . xviij d.
1628 (*St. Margaret, Westminster*). When his Majesty granted the petition of right . . . . . . 5s.
1630. On the conclusion of the peace with the King of Spain . 2s. 6d.
1640. On that day which the Triennial Parliament was agreed upon in the House of Parliament . . . . 5s.
1641. When there was a Thanksgiving for our unity with the Scots . . . . 5s.

PARLIAMENT STRUGGLE

1641 (*St. Mary, Reading*). Ringing the Kings returne from Scotland (25 Nov.) . . . . . .
1642 (*St. Benedict, Gracechurch*). To ringers when the bishops were voted downe by parliament 2 6
1642-3 (*St. Mary, Reading*). For ringing for the King at his reterne from Branford (Brentford, after battle of Edgehill) 1 6

1644-5. For ringing when the King came to Coley (Royalist army came from Newbury to Reading on 16 May 1644; king's headquarters at Coley House) . . . 5 6

The town of Leicester was in the thick of the conflict.

1646 (*St. Martin, Leicester*). Paid the 7th of May to the ringers when New-worke was surrendered up unto Parliament . 2 6
Paid to the ringers when the Lords and Commons, and Judges were at Leicester . . . . . 4 (
Paid to the ringers Jan. 22, 1646, when the Lords and Commons came to Leicester, by appointment of the Committee . . . . 6 (
Paid to the ringers when his Excellency came to Leicester 2 6
Paid to the ringers when the King came to Leicester 3 0

The Leicester ringings during the fateful year 1648 included peals for a victory over the Scots, for good tidings from Wales, on the day of thanksgiving for regaining of Leicester, and for a victory over the enemy at Willoughby. The bells continued to celebrate the 18th of June, the day of regaining the town, until the close of the Commonwealth.

In 1652 the ringers were paid 2s. 6d. on 25th August in honour of General Cromwell's passing by, and 3s. 4d. on the news of beating the Scots.

Salisbury was another town well in the line of conflict.

1646-7. (*St. Edmund, Sarum*). Ringing when Sir Thomas Farefax came through the towne with his great gunnes . 5 6
Ringers upon the Publeque day of thanksgiving (Nov. 22) for the delivering the Castles and Fortes into the bandes of the Parliament . . . . 8 (
1648 (*St. Thomas, Sarum*). 7th day of Sept. for a great victory over the Scotts 8 0
1650-1. Ringing for the Scots overthrow per order Mr Maior . 5 6
1651-2. Ringing for the Victory at Worcester against the Scòttes by Mr Mayors orders . . . . . 12s.
1653-4. Ringers April 3d for victory over the Hollanders . 10s.
1655-6. Ringing thanksgiving day the 26 of June . . . 12s.

The title of Lord Protector was conferred on Cromwell, 16th December 1653.

1653-4 (*St. Mary, Reading*). For ringing for the Lord Protector 6s.

BELLS AND RINGING

It is not a little remarkable that some degree of respect was paid to the King by way of ringing the bells on his birthday in most of the towns of the kingdom throughout the strife, and even on his last birthday, 19th November 1648.

1645 (*St. Margaret, Westminster*). On 5th February being a day of publick thanksgiving for Dartmouth, Hereford, and the West . . . . . . 5 ⸱

1648. Paid to the ringers for ringing on the King's Majestys birthday (19 Nov.) . . . . . 5 ⸱

1651. On 4th September upon intelligence of the overthrow of the Scottish armey at Worcester . . . 6 ⸱

On 24th October, being a day of thanksgiving for the victorie over the Scots at Worcester . . . 7 ⸱

1653. On that day when the Lord Protector was installed 3 ⸱

1653 (*St. Christopher-le-Stocks*). For ringing ye Bells when ye Lord Protector dyn at Egromes Hall . . . 2 6

1657-8 (*St. Mary, Reading*). For ringing the day the Lord Protector proclaimed . . . . . . 5 ⸱

[On refusing kingship, Cromwell was formally installed Lord Protector with much pomp on 26 June 1657.]

1658-9. For ringing att ye proclaiming the Lord Protector 5 ⸱

[Richard Cromwell accepted as Protector 27 January 1659.]

CHARLES II

1660 (*St. Michael, Worcester*). On the day that the King landed and on the day that his Majesty came to Whitehall . 11 0

1660 (*St. Mary, Reading*). For ringing proclaiming day and for 5th of November . . . . . 14 ⸱

1660-2. For ringing on Coronation Day . . . . 15 ⸱

1680 (*St. Alphege, London Wall*). Ringing the Bells when his Matie was at Supper at Fishmongers Hall 5

1660-1 (*St. Thomas, Sarum*). Ringing on the day the Kinge was proclaimed . . . . . . 18s.

Ringinge of Bells of Mr T. Cutlers desire at the Kings Landinge . . . . 5s.

1669. Ringing for the Tuskie Prince by order of the Vestery . 2s. 6d.

[Cosmo, Grand Duke of Tuscany.]

1673-4. Ringing when Peace was proclaimed . . . 1 0 ⸱

1677-8. Ringing for the Prince of Orange . . . 18 ⸱

1682-3. Ringing at the Duke of Yorkes deliverance 15 ⸱

Ringing June 1 for the restauracon of the King to his health . . . . 18 ⸱

1683-4. June 28 for the recovery of the King . 18 ⸱

James II and William III

1685–6 (*St. Thomas, Sarum*). Ringing for his Majesties most gracious speech to the Parl^t 12 0
    May 25th 1 2 0
    For joy of Arguiles (Duke of Argyle) being taken . 10 6
    For Monmouth and Grayes being taken . 10 0
    When Monmouth was taken 1 2 0
    For the deliverance of his Majestie from his enemies, on a Thanksgiving day 1 2 0

1688–9. Ringing for ye Prince of Wales ye 1 of July 1 0
    „ for ye Bishops 1 0
    „ when the King came to town . 1 0
    „ when the Prince of Orange came to town 0
    when the King was proclaimed . 0
    „ to King William and Queen Maries Coronation . 1 0

1685 (*St. Peter, Bristol*). To the ringers when Sir John Churchill (Duke of Marlborough) was made Master of the Rowles, order of Mr Mayor 6 0

1688. To the ringers on the Bishops being admitted to Bale . 5s.
    To the Ringers when the Bishops was discharged out of ye Tower . . . . 5s.

1689. Augt. 5th (*St. Giles, Northampton*). To the ringers at the joyfull news of the death of Dundee (Killiecrankie) . 3s.

1688 (*Edenbridge*). For ye Dyatt given to ye Ringers when ye Bishopps were Acquitted . . . . . 4s.
    To ye Ringers when ye Prince of Orange came to London . . . . 4s.

1694. P^d John Eeles for Ringing ye Bells when Queen Mary dyed . . . . 3s.

1691 (*Kensington*). Paid the ringers when the news came of Limerick's being taken, and 'twas false 1 6
    Paid that night when the true news came for faggots for a bonfire at Little Chelsea and for drink 15 0

1689 (*St. Martin, Leicester*). Paid November the last for ringing for the Princess Ann 5 6

1695. Paid for tolling at the Queen's interment . . . 2 0

1696. Paid for ringing on the King's birthday, and the King coming through Leicester the same day . . 5 0

Historical Ringing of Eighteenth and Nineteenth Centuries

Two or three paragraphs must suffice to make a brief record, after a superficial fashion, as to the parish-book entries of bell-ringing of the eighteenth century and of the early part of the nineteenth century. The capture of the fleet at Vigo in 1702 was observed in all town and in many country belfries. The Duke of Marlborough's vigorous campaigns must have been specially gratifying to the general body of ringers for several years.

The ringers of the parish church of Kensington had a busy and profitable time of it during those wars, for on each of these patriotic occasions they received a mark, *i.e.* 13s. 4d., from the parish. In 1709 they were paid for the taking of Tournay, for the taking of the citadel of Tournay, for the taking of Mons, for the Thanksgiving day of 22nd November, and for "forcing the French lines." In the following year they received a mark on the occasions of the taking of Douay, Bethune, and Aire, and also for the two Spanish victories of Almanara and Saragossa. They also had a good time through the frequent passage of royalty to and from Hampton Court, and on the various royal birthdays. On 2nd November 1714 a mark was given by the parish to the ringers "on the King's coronation," and another mark "for the pious memory of Queen Anne." The accession of the Hanoverians proved a godsend to the ringers of the east coast, for the Georges were constantly crossing and recrossing to Hanover by way of Harwich.

The ringers of Holy Cross, Canterbury, obtained four 5s. payments in 1728 for royal peals; namely, for ringing on George II's accession and coronation, for the Queen's birthday, and for "ye prince of whale Birthday."

In the second half of the century came stirring events, such as the capture of Quebec, the taking of Pondicherry and the Havanah, and the victories of Admiral Rodney and Lord Duncan. A good list of the chief bell-ringings of this century will be found in the *Chronicles of All Saints, Derby* (1881).

Nelson's and Wellington's achievements are chronicled in several hundreds of extant wardens' accounts; here are two or three brief notes from those of St. Mary, Warwick :—

 1802-3. "Sept. 3^d gave the ringers for ringing for Lord Nelson,
  at Warwick, by order of the Mayor" . . £1
 1805-6. "Nov. 7th gave the ringers for Nelson's victory £1 1s.;
  Nov. 23^d gave the ringers for tolling and buffing the
  bells one hour for Lord Nelson's burial, 10s."

226   THE CHURCHWARDENS' ACCOUNTS

1815-16. "Paid to the ringers for news of the battle of Waterloo, £2 2s.; ditto for taking of Bonaparte, £1 11s. 6d."

EPISCOPAL RINGING.

It was a mediæval custom for the church bells to be rung when the bishop passed through the parish when on visitation or otherwise. A single extract must suffice.

1509-10 (*Bassingbourn, Cambs*). In expenses on Ryngers at the coming by of the bisshope of Ely . . . . j d.

The following are a few of the sixteenth-century ringings for bishops among the parish records of St. Edmund, Sarum:—

1501-2. Diversis personis pro laboribus suis inpulsand' campan' ibm erga invencionem Episcopi Sarum ad Civitatem predictam in visitatione . . . . . vj d.
[Primary Visitation of Bishop Audley.]
1557-8. Ryngers that Range my lord bysshoppes beyll   xvj d.
[John Salcot, ob. 6 Oct.]
1560-1. Ryngers when my lorde byshop cam in .   xiv d.
[John Jewel consecrated 22 Jan. 1560.]
1571-2. Allowed to the ryngers at the buryal of Bisshop Juel   iiij d.
[Ob. 23 Sept. 1571.]
1592-3. Ringers for Ringing in of the Bushope . . .   2s.
[Bishop Coldwell, consecrated 26 Dec. 1591.]
1641-2. Ringers when yᵉ Bishop was installed . . .   8s.
[Bishop Brian Duppay translated to Sarum 1641]

The accounts of All Saints, Derby, bear witness to the loyalty of the bells to the episcopate when visiting the county town. Some of these seventeenth-century extracts must serve as examples of many others.

1620. Paid to the ringers for ringing at my Lᵈ Bushops coming to visit 5 8
1630. For ringing twise for the Bishop 4 4
1663. To the ringers when Bishop was in towne . 13 4
To ringers when Bishop came from Chesterfield   5 0
1666. Pᵈ for ringing for yᵉ Bishopp 12 6
1669. Ringing at the Bishopp's Visitation 10 0

Episcopal visits in 1673, 1679, and 1685 brought equally liberal payment to the ringers. The exact orthography of the last of such entries for this century is worth preserving.

1693-4. For wringing at yᵉ bishops coming . . . .

Curious Ringings

1733 (*All Saints, Derby*). April 19. The dealers in tobacco caused all the bells, in each of the churches at Derby, to be rung on the arrival of the news of the duty on that article being taken of.

1736. March 18. Upon receiving the news, on Monday last, that the dissenters had miscarried in their endeavours to get the Corporation and Test Acts repealed, orders were given for ringing all the bells in each of the parish churches, which was continued most of the afternoon.

1626 (*St. Martin, Leicester*). P^d to the Ringers for Ringinge 3 dayes when the Earls came to the Chusinge of the knights for the shire . . . . . ij s. vj d.

1639–40 (*St. Thomas, Sarum*). Ringinge two dayes at the chusinge the Knightes of the shire . . . . . 10s.

1646–7 (*St. Edmund, Sarum*). Ringing the Race day that ye Erll of Pembrook his horse woon the cuppe . 5 0

1687 (*St. Peter, Bristol*). To the Ringers a duck hunting day . 3s. 6d.

1689 June 21st.. To ye Ringers for duck hunting . 3s.

CHAPTER XVII

CLOCKS—HOUR-GLASS—ROYAL ARMS—TEN COMMANDMENTS

Clocks in England in seventeenth century—Dials not till fourteenth century Tower clocks without dials—Clock usually inside churches—St. Laurence, Reading—Short extracts—Chimes—Sundials—Hour-glasses—Short extracts—Royal arms in churches—Henry VIII—Elizabeth—The Stuarts—Commonwealth—Charles II—Lymington—Ten Commandments

CLOCKS

MECHANICAL clocks were known in England in the twelfth century, or perhaps a little earlier, but dials were not introduced till the fourteenth century. In 1344, the dean and chapter of St. Paul's entered into a contract with Walter the Orgoner of Southwark to supply and fix a dial, from which it has been inferred that the previous clock had no dial. The earlier clocks simply struck the hours and usually the quarters. Well on into the seventeenth century village church clocks had often no dials. The clock in the church tower of Luccombe, Somerset, dated 1672, struck the hours on one bell and the half-hours on another bell. As a youth the writer often examined it. It had no face or dial. The majority of the clocks, even in large town churches, such as St. Edmund, Sarum, in the fifteenth and sixteenth centuries, had no outside faces, and were in clock-houses within the church. This can often be proved from a careful examination of wardens' accounts. The clock bell or bells were frequently struck by figures called jacks. There are striking jacks still at work at Rye, Sussex, St. Mary Steps, Exeter, and at several cathedral churches. In a few cases old jacks have been recently restored. There are interesting old disused jacks at Southwold and Blythborough, Suffolk, and at Minehead, Somerset.

It is a common but bad mistake to imagine that church clocks were a great rarity. Even a scholar like Dean Burgon, when writing of the church of St. Helen's, Bishopsgate, in early days, stated that it had a clock, "that rare luxury." The fact is there was hardly a clockless church to be found in either town or country in the fifteenth century. The present writer has not as yet examined the extant records of fifteenth or early sixteenth centuries date, of any single parish, without finding evidence of clock repairs among the older entries. The following is a very small selection of such entries. In the first case a number of entries are cited, but in the other instances we have to be content with briefer extracts. The clock is mentioned at St. Petrock, Exeter, in 1435-6.

The story of the successive clocks of St. Laurence, Reading, is revealed in the accounts. In common with the majority of mediæval church clocks, it was inside the fabric in sight of the congregation without any external dial, struck by a jack, and lighted for late services.

JACK O' THE CLOCK, SOUTHWOLD

1433. In resol' John' Tylere p' custodia orologii et illuminacioe' lumen' . . . . vij s.
In stipendis factoris orologii . . . . . ij s.
1495. Payed for the settyng of jak, with the hanging of his bell and mendyng his hond . . . . . . iiij d.
Payed for makyng part of the cloke howse with ij pec' of tymber set into the walls with a mason . viij d.
For wyer to the same cloke . . . . . xj d. ob.
For settyng of a pece of tymber at the clok ham' with nayles . . . . iij d. ob.
For led to make the payce (weight) of the clok . v s. vj d.
For cartyng the payce . . . . . . iiij d.
1510. Rec[d] of Willm Velde for a seate for hymself under the clock hows . . . . iiij d.

The successor of the old clock obviously stood in the tower and had an outer dial.

 1520. To the clockmaker for a new clok in pte of payment of v^{li} xl s.
 1521. To the clockemaker in pte payment of vj li. x s. for the new cloke and the dyall . . . . . . iij li.
 1522. For glayssyng the stepell wyndow over the dyal with pt of the old glass and pt newe . . . . vij s. vj d.
 1586. Paid to H. Osmund for mending ye clocke broken with the fall of ye gret bell clapp . . . . . ij s. vj d.

In the following year the dial was repaired and gilt, etc., at a cost of £3 13s. 8d. Timber and boards for a new clock-house cost 10s. 1d. in 1596.

William Young, locksmith, of Oxford, covenanted in 1673 with the churchwardens for the sum of 20s. in hand, and for a further sum of £29, to supply and set up "a firme, good, substantiall, and tuneable sett of Chymes to two Tunes"—the tunes of the cxlviii. and cxiii. Psalms, or any other two tunes best approved by the wardens—"to strike upon all the eight bells in the tower of equall and good notes." He further covenanted to make "a good and substantial Quarterne clock to strike on the aforesaid eight bells in an orderly manner," and also to put the clock then standing in the tower in thorough repair. All this work was satisfactorily accomplished in 1680.

 1436 (*Tintinhull, Somerset*). Pro oleo pro clocke . . . j d.
 1439. In emendatione oriscopii ville . . . . . v d.
 1448. Pro j corda empta ad le payse oriscopii . . xxj d.
 1449. Cuidam fabro de Kyngsbury locato ad emendandum unum karrillum oriscopii ferreum portantem le sayllor [1] . iiij d.
 1443 (*Thame*). For kepyng of ye kloke to harry sexton for iij yer . . . . x s.
 1473 (*St. John, Peterborough*). Payd to Syr Wyllm Wellys for keping of the chyrch clocke chyme at Morrowmesse for half a yere . . . . . . iij s. iv d.
 1537 (*Yatton, Somerset*). To William Sensam in ernes for makyng a clock and chyme . . . . . j d.
 1539. To William Sensam for ye clocke . . . . xx s.
   To ye clocke howse makyng in ye church   iij li. xiij s. iiij d.
 1540. For takyng down of ye (old) clocke howse . xij d.
   In part for ye clocke . . . . . xxxiij s. iiij d.

---

[1] Perhaps a jack in the form of a sailor.

CLOCKS—HOUR-GLASS—ROYAL ARMS, ETC. 231

And to ye seid clockemaker	xx s.
For bryngyng home ye clocke . . .	ij s. vij d.
For bryngyng home ye frame of ye clocke . . .	vj d.

1544-5 (*St. Martin, Leicester*). Paid to Rodis for a rope for the clock — iiij d.
Paid to Syr William borough for mending the Cloke and chyme . . . . — ij d.

1546-7. For a gret rope for the plome of the Cloke . . . xiiij d.
For mendynge of the harrells that the chyme goyth with to the smyth at the west bridge . . . . xij d.

1597-8. For 3 yardes great Wyer to make a Soon Dyall with which Master Belgrave made to set the Clock by at the end of the New Ospitall . . . . xij d.

1664. Agreed that Francis Molloy for making a tuneable pair of chimes shall have £12, 4s. od.; and for keeping them yearly 20s. with the materials of the old chimes now in the vestry.

1687. Agreed that a new clock shall be made at the charge of the parish. Received for the old clock 20s. of Mr. Wilkin.

1563 (*Ludlow*). For mendyng the chymes and the barrelle and jake of the clocke house . . . . . viij d.

The 1611-2 accounts of St. Mary, Reading, show that there were special collections for a new clock. The subscriptions of 104 parishioners amounted to £27 4s. 10d. A further subscription raised the amount to £39 10s. 2d. The total outlay on the clock and dial was £40 0s. 9d. The clockmaker was Robert Duglas; he was paid 5s. a year for keeping it in order.

1633 (*St. Giles, Northampton*). Paid Sheffield for the clock	5	0	0
For mending the clock			6
1642 (*Yarnton, Oxon*). Paid for the Clock besides the old Clock .	5	18	0
To Francis Mull for seven daies work about the clock and clockhouse		6	0
1651. A pond of wire for the clock		1	4
The smith and his boy for coming over to mend it .		3	8
For mending him again when the Rogue pulled him in pieces		1	0
For carrying the wheels on my back to Oxford three times to mend			
1670 (*Wirksworth, Derbyshire*). Payed to Francis Mattison for makinge of a New Clocke	7	0	0

References to Sundials are but rarely found in the earlier wardens' accounts. The following may be cited in addition to the one already named at St. Martin, Leicester:—

1615 (*St. Mary, Reading*). For a Brasse for the Sunn Dyall .	xij d.
For Payntinge the Dyall and gravinge over the Porche .	ij s. vj d.

1663-4 (*St. Thomas, Sarum*). A new Sundial to be made in the place where the old one was or else in some more convenient place according to the discression of the Churchwardens.

1672-3. Two Sundialls on the south and west side of the Tower . 3 10 0

The religious controversies of the sixteenth century brought longer sermons into use, and hour-glasses became the pulpit accompaniment of theologians of different schools. The preacher in Holbein's "Dance of Death" has an hour-glass beside him in his pulpit. The frontispiece of the "Bishops' Bible," of 1569, represents Archbishop Parker with an hour-glass on his right hand. Their use by clergy of the unreformed faith is illustrated in a tract called "Fatal Vespers," relative to an incident that occurred at a meeting of Papists in Blackfriars in 1623:—
"About three o'clock the expected preacher came in . . . attended by a man that brought after him his book and hour glass." See *English Church Furniture*, 2nd ed., pp. 156–9, where nearly 100 instances of hour-glass stands (and occasionally the actual glasses) are given as still remaining in parish churches. There must have been vehement preachers at St. Peter Cheap. A shilling was paid for an hour-glass, a stiff price, in 1563, and in the following year another was purchased for a like sum. In 1584 are the entries:—

HOUR-GLASS AND STAND
BLOXWORTH, DORSET

Payde for the hower glasse the xxijth of October . .	xij d.
Payde the same daie to the Turner for the foote for hower glasse to stand uppon	xij d.
1572 (*Barnstaple*). Paid to John Blackman for an hour glass for the Preacher	4d.
1577-8 (*St. Martin, Leicester*). Payd for an houre glase . .	iiij d.
1598 (*Ludlow*). For makinge of the frame for the hower glasse .	xx d.
For oyling and coloringe yt	ij d.
1612 (*St. Edmund, Sarum*). Makeinge the foote to holde the hower glasse standing on the Pulpitt . . .	12d.
An Hower glasse and the Cadge to sett him on	14d.

CLOCKS—HOUR-GLASS—ROYAL ARMS, ETC.

1622-3. Frame for the Oure glasse standinge uppon the Byble deske . . . . 3s. 2d.
1648-9. An Houre glasse . . . . . . 8d.
1611 (*Berkhampstead*). Payed for an hour glasse . x d.
Payed for the Irone that the houre glasse standeth in . xviij d.
1629 (*St. Mary, Devizes*). Pd to John Bennett, Cutler, for a branch to carry the hour glass in the church . ij s. vj d.
1673-4 (*St. Edmund, Sarum*). Frame for the Ower glasse standinge upon the Byble deske . . . . 3s. 2d.
1672 (*Prestbury, Cheshire*). Pd. for the Houre Glasse, Houre Glasse Case, and the guildinge and the setting upp the same . . . . 1 / 0

From the frequency of hour-glass entries in parish accounts during the seventeenth century it may fairly be assumed that they were owned by at least the majority of churches. An hour-glass at Seal cost 8d. in 1639; one at Bletchingley (where the stand is preserved) 7d. in 1643; one at Chippenham 7d. in 1657; whilst at Church Pulverbatch the hour-glass of 1653 cost 12d., and another in 1683, 9d.

Royal Arms

As to the occurrence of Royal Arms in churches, much has been said in *English Church Furniture* (pp. 351-6), but we were not able then to adduce, as is now done, a definite instance of Henry VIII's arms. The following extracts from wardens' accounts do not infringe on what is set forth in that volume.

1541-2 (*Yatton, Somerset*). To a gylter of Brystow for gyltyng ye kyngs armys . . . . . xiii s. vii d.
1565 (*Strood, Kent*). For payntyng and wrytynge ye Armes and Rood lofte . . . . . xiij s. iiij d.
For makyng ye table for ye quenes ma^{ties} armes and nayles to it . . . . xiiij d.
1572-3 (*St. Thomas, Sarum*). Making of the waull hyer w'che is in the uper end of ye quire for makinge of the quenes armes and ye Comaundementes . . . . 5 (
1573-4. Adam Marbell peynting and gilting of ye queenes armes and making ye x Comaundementes and other skripture at the uper ende of ye quire 2 13 4
1593-4 (*St. Martin, Leicester*). Payd to george Longlaye the paynter in payment for washing and payntynge and gyldinge the queenes armes in our church bye sevrall portyons . iiiij li. xj s. viij d.

THE CHURCHWARDENS' ACCOUNTS

> 1599 (*St. Mary Woodchurch*) Unto Benge the Smith for 6 irons for the Quenes Arms 4 0
> Unto Daniel the painter for painting Jehovah over the Quenes Arms 2 6
> 1605-6 (*St. Edmund, Sarum*). Payed for the Kinges Armes . £7
> 1613-4 (*St. Thomas, Sarum*). For the Kinges Armes frame . 1 9 0
> 1612 (*Hartshorne, Derby*). Itm. march 23 p^d ffor inlarging ye Kings Armes wth Helmett Crest & mantell & paintinge lords praier and ye beleivfe 5 4
> 1623. Ite. p^d goodman Johnson for makinge a frame for the paintinge of the kinges armes for wood, workmanshippe, and nailes . . . . . . vij s vj d.

Most churches during the Commonwealth seem to have been content with destroying or defacing the King's Arms; but in a few cases the States Arms (a plain cross) were put up. The wardens of St. Thomas, Sarum, spent 4s. 6d., in 1650, in "washing out" the Royal Arms. At Hartshorne, Derbyshire, the "washing out" only cost 5d.; whilst at St. Martin's, Leicester, the "washing down" of the King's Arms cost 6s.

> 1651 (*St. Mary Woodchurch*). Paid my Lord Maiors officer and clark for a warrant he brought for the putting out of the church the late Kings Armes . . . .
> 1651 (*St. Margaret, Westminster*). To John Gomersall for paintinge and guilding of the States armes in several places of the church and vestry 50 0
> 1652 (*Uffington, Salop*). To John Dickens for drawing of ye Armes of ye Comonwealth . . . . . 10s.

At the Restoration the process was reversed. In country churches they were sometimes content at the outset to clear off the States Arms from the surface of the old Royal Arms, and to spend a small sum on restoring the latter. Thus at Uffington, Salop, 12d. was spent in "blotting out ye states armes," and 21s. 2d. in restoring those of royalty; and at Wootton Courtney, Somerset, 2s. 6d. was laid out in "cleaninge off the States arms," and 4s. in "paintinge againe the Kings arms." Even in a town church like St. Thomas, Sarum, the wardens in 1660-1 only spent 3s. 4d. in "washinge ye Kinges Armes and makinge them cleane"; whilst at Strood, Kent, 12s. was laid out for "the new beutiffieing of the King's Armes."

Many parishes, however, showed their loyalty by a large

expenditure on the new arms of Charles II. St. Columb Major, Cornwall, paid the highest of any accounts I have seen, namely, £18; St. Mary, Reading, spent ten guineas; the City church of St. Mary Woodchurch paid ten pounds, and St. Mary, Warwick, paid the like with the addition of 12d. for a pint of sack for the limner. The exact entries from four parishes are given out of over fifty that have been copied.

 1660 (*All Saints, Derby*). Gave Ralph Richardson and other workmen at severall tymes to drinke at setting up ye Kings armes 2 1
 To Ralph Richardson for drawing ye Kings armes   10 0 1
 To William Carew for 2 frames for ye Kings armes   14 4
 More for 3 ell of Canvis to draw ye armes in .   14 0
 1660–1 (*Beccles, Suffolk*). Paid to Mr Parrish of Yarmouth in part of the Kinges Armes the sume of 4 10 0
 Item more for the Cherubim over the Kings Armes . 1 0 0
 1662 (*Redenhall, Norfolk*). P^d for the King's Arms at London, for a box and bringing downe 4 7 0
 For the frame for the Kings Armes 9 0
 1676 (*Lymington, Hants*). Gave the men to drink to help to set up the Kings Armes . . . . .
 1716 (*Lymington, Hants*). To workmen in beere about helping downe the King's Armes 1 0
 To John Cleves for painting the King's Armes . 1 10 0

These last-named Arms, well painted on panel, still hang in Lymington church. They are those of 1676; in 1716 the date was altered, the churchwardens' names at the bottom of the frame changed, and the white horse of Hanover introduced on an escutcheon of pretence.

The Ten Commandments

On the general subject of affixing the Ten Commandments to the church or chancel walls see *English Church Furniture*, pp.356–7. The following is a much abbreviated collection of references from wardens' accounts arranged in chronological order:—

 1547 (*St. Michael, Worcester*). For the pane of the Pater Noster the Articles of our Faith with the Ten Commandments of God . . . . ij d.

236   THE CHURCHWARDENS' ACCOUNTS

1548 (*St. Mary, Dover*). Payed to John Pullyn for payntynge of
the x Comaundementes in the Rode lofte . iij s.

1558 (*Stanford, Berks*). For a paper of the tenne Commandements
and a calender boke to say servis by in ye churche . xvj d.

1559 (*St. Martin's-in-the-Fields*). For the payntenge of the ten
Comaundementes . . . . . . v s.

Queen Elizabeth's letter to the Commissioners for causes ecclesiastical, of 22nd January 1560-1, orders that "the tables of the commandments be comlye set or hung up in the east end of the chauncell, to be read not only for edification, but also to give some comlye ornament and demonstration that the same is a place of religion and prayer."

1560 (*St. Mary Woolnoth*). To the Bysshoppe of London
somner for a table of commandementes and a booke with
calendar howe the chapters shal be read in the Church

1560-1. For moyses tables to set at the high altar . . . 18d.

1561 (*Ludlow*). 26 Marche paid for the table of commaundementes and the new kalender . . xviij d.

3 April for settinge of the commaundementes in a
forme, etc. . . . . . . iij s.

1561-2 (*St. Martin, Leicester*). P^d for a tabyell of ye Commandementes and a Kallynder . . . . xvj s.

For ye paint to ye ten commandementes . xiij d. ob.

To Wyllam Bargard for wrytyng ye ten commandementes ij s.

1563-4 (*St. Petrock, Exeter*). For a hundred of nails for the
painter to nail up the cloth for the Ten Commandementes . . . . ij d.

1565 (*Wimborne*). For the x Commandments in Collers
(colours) . . . . xx d.

1576 (*St. Mary, Devizes*). To the painters for writing the
x commandments on the church wall . xv s.

1597 (*Exning, Suffolk*). Paid to Thomas Orders for making of
a table of bord for the tenn Commaundementes, and
one other table for the degres prohibited in marryadge ij s. iij d.

Paid to Owldfyld the Smithe for makinge of certain Irone
worke to hang the sayde table of the tenn commaundementes in the church . . . . . vj d.

1606 (*Minchinhampton, Gloucester*). For a ringe to hange the
table of the commandements . . . iiij d.

1607 (*Pittington, Durham*). Payed in the court when William
Hall was cyted about Christmas and enjoyned to provide
a table of the x commandmentes . . . ij s

1634 (*St. Mary, Cambridge*). For James Priest for paynting ye Comandements the Creed and Lords prayer.   1
　To him more for wryting 2 tables upon ye wall paynting the woodwork 17 6
1657 (*All Saints, Derby*). Pd old Hawley for setting upp 10 Comandments, Beliefs, Lords Prayers, and Death and Tyme　.　.　.　.　.　.　. 1 15 10

CHAPTER XVIII

GARNISHING OF CHURCHES—CHURCH'S CALENDAR

Flowers in processions—Birch, Box, Willow—Garlands of roses worn by clergy—St. Mary-at-Hill; St. Andrew Hubbard; St. Peter Cheap; St. Martin's-in-the-Fields; Morebath — Short extracts — Under Queen Mary — Post-Reformation garnishing — Rushes — Christmas decorations — Prohibited by Commonwealth — Star at Epiphany — Plough Monday — Lent, white the liturgical colour—The Lent veil—Rood veil—Image veils—Lent crosses and banners—Licences for flesh—Penance in white sheet—Palm Sunday—St. Peter Cheap; St. Mary-at-Hill—Short extracts—The Palms—Tenebrae—Washing the altars—Discipline with the rod—Creeping to the Cross—Easter Sepulchre—Holy Fire—Hocktide—Rogation days—Whitsuntide—Corpus Christi

THE decking of churches with flowers and greenery, usually termed "garnishing," at the chief festivals was a usual custom throughout mediæval England. The wardens' accounts or parish books of cities and towns bear abundant testimony to the prevalence of these customs; contrariwise, such entries are very rarely found in country accounts, and that for the very natural reason that flowers and garniture were readily and most gladly offered without any charge, as is the case at the present day. The special uses at Christmastide and on Palm Sunday are discussed separately; but the various entries immediately cited bear testimony to decorations at Easter, Ascensiontide, Whitsuntide, and the vigil of St. John Baptist, or Midsummer Day, and also on the patronal festivals of the respective churches. Birch was the customary garnishment of Midsummer Day, as it still is in many parts of the Continent. The decking of the churches with yew at Eastertide, as the special emblem of immortality, was widely prevalent particularly in country

GARNISHING OF CHURCHES

districts; indeed, this significant custom prevailed very widely up to the midst of the nineteenth century throughout Herefordshire and in parts of Worcestershire and West Somerset. Box and willow (the English "palm") were widely used on Palm Sunday, as will be presently noted. The flowers often distinctively named are red roses, usually woven into garlands for use on Corpus Christi Day and other great festivals. By way of contrast, there were other garlands of white sweet-woodruff, and sometimes the two were mingled. Garlands were hung on the processional crosses, and flowers bedecked the great processional tapers. On the return of the processions it was customary to hang the garlands in suitable places within the quire or on the screen. Other flowers that are specifically named in wardens' accounts are lilies, St. John's wort, and gillyflowers. The nature of the herbs that were strewn is very seldom mentioned, save rosemary and fennel.

It has more than once been stated, with some show of authority, that rose garlands borne in procession by clergy or clerks were carried in the hands. But this is a blunder. For instance, old Stow (1598) in his *Survey* tells us that at the procession at St. Paul's, on the feast of the Apostle, the dean and chapter, "apparelled in coats and vestments, with garlands of roses on their heads, issued out at the west door." It is the same chronicler who states that "on the vigil of St. John Baptist and on SS. Peter and Paul the Apostles, every man's door in London was shadowed with green birch, long fennel, St. John's wort, orpin, white lilies, and such like, garnished upon with beautiful flowers."

The entries in the accounts of St. Mary-at-Hill as to decking the church with flowers and greenery are full of interest.

1477–9.	Payd for birche at Midsomer	viij d.
	For Garlondis one Corpus Christi day	x d.
	For Rose garlondis and wodrofe garlondis on Saynt Barnebes day (11 June)	xj d.
1487–8.	For ij dossen and a halffe Roose garlondes on seynte Barnabas daye	viij d. ob.
1490–1.	For Birch at Midsomer	iiij d.
	For Roose garlandes and off Wodroffe for Corpus Christi day and Seynte barnabe daye	ix d. ob.
1519–20.	For iij dossen Garlondis on Corpus Christi day for the procession	xv d.

	For ij dossen of Grene Garlondis for that procession	ij d.
	For ij Garlondis for Mr Doctor and the parish prest	iij d.
	For iij Garlondis for the iij Crossis.	viij d.
1522-3.	On Seint Barnabis day for v dossen of Roose garlondis for the crosses and for the queer.	ij s. iiij d.
1539-40.	For garllandes on the Ascencion daye	xj d.
	For garlondes on corpus crysti daye	ij s.
	For byrche at Mydsomer	vj d.
1485-6	(*St. Andrew Hubbard*). For bircche and lylies at mydsomer.	ij d.
1487-8.	For fenell and erbis.	j d. ob.
1488-9.	For bircche and fenell at mydsomer	iiij d.
1491.	Paid at Corpus Cristi tyde for garnysshyng of xij torches at iij d. the pece	iij s.
	Pd for Rose garlandes	xiij d.
	Paid at mydsomer for byrche and flowers for the chyrche and the dore	vj d.
1492-3.	Paid on corpus Cristi day for garlandys of Rossys and woodroffe for the quyre	xiij d.
1495-6.	For Bows (boughs) and flowrys at witsontyde	v d. ob.
1498-9.	Paid at mydsomer for fynell for the chirche dore.	v d.
1499-1502.	For byrcche and flowers at mydsomer	vj d.
1505.	Mydsomer. For birche and flowres for Dressing the Church door	viij d.
1501-3.	Apone the Assencione day for Swytt Erbes and for garlandes.	x d.
1524	(*St. Margaret Pattens*). For birch for the chirch agenst midsom	ij d.
	For garlondis on Corps Xti day for the quere	vj d.
	For ij doss garlondes on seint Mgretts day	xiij d.
	[Gillyflowers were named for St. Margaret's Day in an earlier account.]	

Here are a few of the decorative entries from St. Peter Cheap:—

1534.	For garlands on White Sonday, corp' Xti Daye, Holy Thursday, and Saynt Peters Day	ij s. vj d.
1555.	For garlandes and strawing herbes for assension daye	vj d.
1598.	For yerbes on Easter daye	1 6

On Corpus Christi Day, at St. Martin's-in-the-Fields, garlands of red roses were carried in procession. For these garlands 8d. was paid in 1543, and 7d. and 6d. in other years, when doubtless the roses were blooming more freely. The processional torches were

GARNISHING OF CHURCHES

also garnished with flowers. In 1555, 10d. was paid upon Corpus Christi Day "For Flowers and herbs." Garlands were also provided for Holy Thursday; in 1546 and 1547 they cost 6d., and in 1555 10d. Birch was used at Midsummer.

> 1525. Payd for byrche at Midsom' . . . . . ij d.
> [Like entries occur until the accession of Elizabeth.]
> 1528 (*Morebath, Devon*). Johan Hyllyer gave a canstycke of lattyn to stonde afore Sent Sydwell, prisse. vj d.
> Upon the wyche canstycke sche doth mayntayn a taper before Sent Sydwell trymmyd with flowrs to borne there every hye and prinscypall fests: this she doth entende to mayntayne whyll sche lyvyth, gracia divina.

Garlands were used in processions at St. Botolph, Aldersgate, on St. Botolph's Day (17th June), as well as on Corpus Christi Day.

> 1474-6 (*St. Margaret, Westminster*). On Corpus Cristy day for garlands for iiij torches . . . . . j d.
> 1484-6. For garlonds of Reed Rosis on Corpus Xti day . v d.
> 1489. To moder Kateryn for Rosis for garlands on Saynt Margarets day . . . . . . ij d.
> 1490. For bowis (boughs) on Seynt Margarets day . j d.

The floral decorations in the sixteenth century of St. Matthew, Friday Street, corresponded closely with those of St. Peter Cheap on the opposite side of Cheapside. Palms (willow blooms) were obtained for Palm Sunday; holly, ivy, and rosemary for Christmas; birch for Midsummer; and garlands of roses for Ascension Day and Corpus Christi.

> 1528 (*St. Alphege, London Wall*). For Garlons on holy thursday x d.
> [Several like entries.]

There was considerable revival of garnishing during the short reign of Queen Mary.

> 1555 (*St. Benedict Gracechurch*). 12 garlands on St. Benedicts day 1s. and strewing herbs 4d.
> 1556 (*St. Michael, Cornhill*). For Garlandes on Corpes Cristye daie for them that caried the canapye and otheres . xvj d.
> 1557. For Garlandes on Ascencyone daie . . . . vij d.
> 1557-8 (*St. Edmund, Sarum*). Makyng of xxx garlons at Whytesontyde for the prestes . . . . . xvj d.

Here follow a few seventeenth-century extracts from parish books as to the garnishing of churches. It is not a little interesting to note that the Puritans of the Commonwealth, though endeavouring, with but small success, to suppress Christmastide garnishing, were ready enough to strew herbs on their own days of either victory or humiliation.

> 1615 (*St. Petrock, Exeter*). For bays and flowers in the church . 2 0
> 1634. For flowers and herbs for the church . . . .
> 1645. For roasmay and bay to put about the church at Christide and Easter . . . .
> [Of frequent subsequent occurrence.]
> 1624 (*St. Mary, Reading*). For Decking of the Church with Rosemarie and bayes, holly and ivey at Christmas, Easter, and Witsontide 6 0
> [A like entry the next year with the addition "and greene bowes."]
> 1644 (*St. Laurence, Reading*). P⁴ for Ewe for the church against Easter, and for sticking itt upp 1 8
> 1647. Strewing aubes (herbs) and flowers to strowe the sitis in the Church win the Ginerall was in the towne . 10d.
> 1650 (*St. Margaret, Westminster*). For herbs that were strewed in the windows of the church and about the same att two severall daies of humiliation 3 10
> For herbs that were strewed in the church upon a day of thanksgiving 2 6
> 1651. For hearbs strewed in the church on the 24ᵗʰ day of May being a day of humiliation 3 0
> For hearhes and lawrell strewed in the church on October 24ᵗʰ [Thanksgiving for victory at Worcester] 8 0

As to post-Restoration garnishing, two or three excerpts from a single parish book may suffice as an example :—

> 1662 (*St. Peter, Bristol*). Given to yᵉ Saxton for herbes to dress ye church against Eastir 1 0
> 1663. Gave the Saxton for Holly and bay against All Saints day. 6
> 1664. To Goodope clark to buy Earbs and flowers to dress the church against whitson tide 6
> 1678. Rosemary and bayes for the Church, All saints day . 1 0

"Birkes," or branches of birch, cost 1s. 8d. for setting up in the church of St. Nicholas, Durham, in 1670, at Whitsuntide. There is a like entry in 1672.

GARNISHING OF CHURCHES

1673. For seting the birches and strowing the reshes and dresing the church 2 6
1674. For 11 burthen of rushes 4 0
For 11 burthen of birkes 3 8
1676. For birkes and rushes, being 4 of birch and 6 of rushes . 4 6
For the church and pewes clensing and the birkes putting up and the rushes stroweing therein . . . 2 6

RUSHES

At a time when our churches were for the most part unpaved, the habit of strewing Rushes on the floor at certain seasons must have been welcome both for cleanliness and warmth. In town and country it became a general use to spread rushes at particular festivals or in honour of distinguished visitors, and in the seventeenth century on "Sacrament Sundays" in the chancel.

Throughout the first quarter of last century the custom was general in the north of Derbyshire and Cheshire of having the floor litter of rushes renewed every summer. The rushes were carted to the church, bedecked with garlands and flowers, and spread throughout the church and pews on some Sunday in July and August.

1732 (*Prestbury, Cheshire*). Spent on nine several Townships at the Rushbearings, when they brought rushes and flowers . 1 7 8
1766 (*Hayfield, Derbyshire*). Upon the account of the Rush Cart. 5 0
[Like entries as to rush cart nearly every year down to 1794, when the accounts end.]

This custom of rush-bearing tarried, to the writer's knowledge, in several village churches of Westmoreland and Cumberland, in the "fifties" and early "sixties" of last century. It is still maintained at Grasmere, but merely as a show for the visitors and for no purpose of utility or honour. See full account, *Churches of Derbyshire*, ii. 202-4; Dyer's *Churchlore Gleanings*, 328-32; and Vaux's *Church Folklore*, 264-5.

The following are some of the earlier rush entries:—

1385-6 (*Tavistock*). To rushes gathered against the feast of St. John Baptist . . . . . . iiij d.
[An annual entry.]
1392-3. Rushes bought for strewing the rood loft . . . j d.
1493-4 (*St. Mary-at-Hill, London*). For ij burdens of Russhys for the newe pewys . . . . . iij d.

Rushes were in constant use at St. Margaret, Westminster, on their chief festivals.

> 1501. Paid to John Wrigar for ij dos' burden of Russhes agenst Whytsonday iijs. Itm paide to hym for ij dos' burden of Russhes agenst the feste of All Halowen iij s. Item paide to hym for ij dos' burden of Russhes agenst St. Margeretes Day iij s. Item paide to hym for ij dos' burden of Russhes ageynst Cristmasse iij s. Item paide to hym for ij dos' and di burden of Russhes ageynst Ester day iij s. ix d. Sum totales xv s. ix d.

Rushes were freely used in the City church of St. Andrew Hubbard; the following entries occur for the year 1522-3:—

> For Rushes . . . . . . iiij d.
> The ix day of May for rushes, garlondes, etc. vj d. ob.
> For a borden of russhes on whitson evyn . . ij d.
> For garlondes and russhes on corpus christi day vj d.
> For iiij burdens of Russhes agenst the dedycacon day kept the iij^d day of October . . . . . v d.
> For Russhes agenst alhalow day . . . . iiij d. ob.
> For Russhes on Saint Andrews evyn . . . iij d.
> For Rushes . . . . ij d.
>
> 1535-6 (*St. Mary-on-the-Hill, Chester*). Russhis Agaynst Est' ix d.
> Russhis Agaynst Penticost . . . . iij d.
>
> 1559-60 (*St. Botolph, Aldersgate*). For carriage of Russhes at Christemas . . . . iiij d.
>
> 1571 (*St. Martin's-in-the-Fields*). For Rishes and strawing herbes when the bishoppe came in visitacion to ye churche . . . . xij d.
>
> 1572 (*Ludlow*). For two burden of roshes to straw master baylyes seate . . . . viij d.
>
> 1580 (*St. Ives, Cornwall*). Payde for x horses to carye morash Russches frome connerton gevyn unto the parysche churche of seynt yves yerlye by Sr John Arundell of lanhorne knyght and hys awncetors tyme out of mynde and ther labours that gatheryde the same Russches v s. viij d.
>
> 1602 (*St. Laurence, Reading*). For flowers and Rushes for the Churche when the Queene was in towne . . . xx d.
>
> 1620 (*All Saints, Derby*). For rushes for my Lord Bishops seate 4d.
> 1626. For two burthens of Rushes . . . . 4d.
> 1627. For Rushes for two Communions . . . 8d.
> For Rushes at other Communions . . . 1s. 2d.
> 1631. For 3 burthen of Rushes at Easter . . . 6d.
> 1636. A burne of rushes . . . . . 4d.

For rushes for the chancell	3d.
For 2 burn of rushes	6d.
1663 (*Kendal*). Payd for Bent (long coarse grass) to strawe in the High quire against Sir Joseph Cradock (Archdeacon of Richmond) come	2d.
1665 Payd for 8 burden of Rushes to straw in the High quire	1 0

Straw occasionally took the place of rushes in the winter, as at Mailsham, Sussex. At Scarcliffe, Derbyshire, the abbey of Darley provided 12d. a year *pro stramento ecelie Skarcli in hyeme*.

1605 (*Pittington, Durham*). For two thrave of strawe for the stalls (seats) in the church . . . . . . vj d.

Christmastide

The earliest wardens' accounts testify to the decking of English churches with holly and ivy at Christmastide, and occasionally, at a later date, with rosemary and bayes. By bayes or bays, laurel or bay-laurel would be implied. It was one of the few old English customs which received no check at the time of the Reformation. The Puritan Parliament attempted to suppress Christmas, and hence the adorning of churches at that season. But, as will be seen, they were disobeyed in the very church at their gates, St. Margaret's, Westminster. A few scattered references as to this custom are cited; they are chiefly gleaned from town accounts; doubtless the custom was just as closely followed in the country, but in the villages there would be no necessity to purchase evergreens, and hence they do not appear in the wardens' books.

1465 (*Thame*). We gave to Chyldryn to gadr yvy   ob. (a halfpenny)
1457-8 (*St. Ewen, Bristol*). For condels and bowes ageyne Cristesmas . . . . iiij d.
1468-9. For talowe candels and holmyn bowes agaynes Cristmas . v d. ob.
1474-5. For tallow candell holme and Ivye agens Cristmesse . iiij d.

The wardens of St. Martin, Leicester, paid a halfpenny for holly and ivy at Christmas in 1493; a penny in 1494; twopence in 1495; and so on for many years.

At Christmas the church of St. Mary-at-Hill was always decked with holly and ivy; up to 1539 holly is entered under its older name of "holm" or "holme."

1427-8. For holme and yve anenst Cristmas . j d.
1556-7. For holy and Ivye agaynst Cristmas to garnishe the
   Churche . . . . . . ij s. viij d.
1422-4 (*St. Margaret, Westminster*). For holme (holly) and yve   iij d.
   1503. For holy and Ive agenst the fest of Crystenmas . iiij d.
   For candyll for the holy Busche . . . .
   1524 (*St. Margaret Pattens*). For holly and Ivy agenyst
   cresmas . . . . . ij d. ob.

The wardens of St. Martin's-in-the-Fields spent 2d. on holly and ivy for Christmas in 1525; ere long the annual expense under this head rose to 4d., in 1564 to 12d., in 1565 to 16d.; at which last figure it remained right through Elizabeth's reign; in the later years "rosemary and bayes" are usually included.

1529 (*St. Helen, Worcester*). Holly and eyvy agenst Crestomas   ij d.
1534 (*St. Peter Cheap*). For holly and Ivey at Xmas   iiij d.
1572. For hollye Rosemarye and bayes on Christemas daye . xij d.
1599. Rosemary and bayes at Christide . . . 3 4
1535-6 (*St. Mary-on-the-Hill, Chester*). For the Holyn   v d.
1536-7. For holyns to make the bolyn of . . . . v d.
   1539 (*St. Mary Woolnoth*). For Holy and Ive against
   Chrystmas . . . . . . iiij d.
1566-7. To Goodman Plommer the xxiiij[th] day of December for to
   buy holly for the churche and for packthryd to tuy up
   the same . . . . ix d.
   1547 (*St. Michael, Worcester*). For flowers (Christmas) for the
   Tapers of the Roode lyght . . . . ij d.
   1540 (*Ludlow*). For yve and holye at Chrystemas . ij d.
   1543. For candles, evy, and holle at Christmas . . . iij d.
   1555. For cordes to hange evy and candelles upon at Christmas   vj d.
   1564. For cordes to hange up evy at Christmas about the
   churche . . . . viij d.
1557-8 (*St. Edmund, Sarum*). Holly at crystmas   j d.
1579-80. For holle . . . . j d.
   1580 (*St. Mary-le-Port, Bristol*). Payed for hollye bayes and
   rosemary at Christmas . . . . . vj d.
   1668. Payd for rosemary and bay and an almanack for the
   church . . . .
   1693. To money gave Gammer Morgan, Crism, for bay and
   lorrell to dress ye churche 2 0
   1619. (*St. Mary, Cambridge*). For flowers and herbes in the
   Church on Christmas and Easter daies . iij s. vj d.
   1624-5. For Triming the Church against Christmas . . ij s. vj d.

1637 (*St. Mary Woolchurch*). For Rosemary and bayes at Christmas . . . . . .

1644 (*St. Laurence, Reading*). P^d for Holly and Ivy, Rosemary and Bayes at Christmass 1 10

1644 (*St. Michael, Bristol*). Paid for holly ivy and other herbage to White . . . . . ij s. vj d.

1647 (*St. Margaret, Westminster*). For rosemarie and baies that was stuck about the Church at Christmas . 1 6

Paid in fees unto Mr Freind and Mr Denham, twoe of the messengers unto the serjeant att armes, attending the Common House of Parliamant, when their accomptants were committed for permitting ministers to preach upon Christmas day and for adorning the church . . . . 3 (

1660-1 (*St. Thomas, Sarum*). Rosemary and Bayes 1 0

1661-2. Holly and bayes at Christmas 1 0

1676-7. Boughs and Rosemary to deck the church 2 6

1670. Dec. 17 (*St. James, Bristol*). Rosemary and bay to dress the church . . . . . . 1s. 6d.

Epiphany

In certain churches the feast of the Epiphany was observed by the display of the Star which drew the wise men to Bethlehem.

In the wardens' accounts of Yarmouth, between 1462 and 1512, there are several entries as to making a new Star, leading the Star, and "a new balk line to the star and ryving the same star," etc. With regard to these Mr. Bolingbroke writes (*Norfolk Archæology*, vol. xii):—

"These items relate to the mechanical contrivances employed in the production of the ceremony known as the 'Feast of the Star,' as performed upon the festival of Epiphany. The magi entered the church by the west door, and proceeded up the nave, until, on approaching the chancel, they perceived a star hanging before the great crucifix on the rood-loft, whereupon they exclaimed, 'Behold the star of the east.' The star, moving back by means of lines and pulleys, led them to the high altar, where, drawing a curtain aside, a living child would be discovered, representing the infant Saviour. At the same time the magi dressed as three Kings made their offerings ... and a boy, representing an angel, said, 'All things which the prophets said are fulfilled,' and then the festival concluded with chanting."

THE CHURCHWARDENS' ACCOUNTS

The following entries from the accounts of St. Mary, Cambridge, refer to annual Epiphany pageants of a like kind :—

1540–1.	For the bolyn	v d.
	For naylis and tymber to make the mone under the bolyn	iiij d.
	For Condullis under the holyn	v s.
	For makyng a skaffolde to take downe the mone	ij d.
1541–2.	Candles to the bolyn	iij s. iiij d.
1545–6.	For candels to ye sterr and to yᵉ hollyn	. iij s. v d.
1555–6.	For iiij li. candles for the bolyn	. xviij d.
	For holend to the stare and mone	. vj d.
1557–8.	For makyng of a stare	. xx d.
	For the pentyng and gyldyng of the same stere	xx d.
	For wyer to the stere	. ij d. ob.
	For a rope to the stere	. ix d.
	For the bolyn	vj d.
	For a man to get the rope into the polley	ij d.
	For candylls for the stare and the holyn	iij s.

Plough Monday

An occasional form of church receipts is met with in early accounts as accruing from gatherings made on Plough Monday, of which one example may be quoted :—

1529 (*Boxford, Cambs*). Resceyved off the gaderyng on Plow mundy clerely . . . . iij s. viij d.

Such receipts are notable in the village accounts of Cratfield, Suffolk, beginning in 1491. The collections are entered annually up to 1499; they varied in amount from 9s. 10d. to 4s. Plough Monday, the Monday after the Epiphany, was the season when the labour of the plough and other rustic toil began. The young men were in the habit of dressing up fantastically and yoking themselves to a plough. They went about from house to house soliciting money, or gifts in kind, and if it was refused the ground before the door was ploughed up. In the old days the Church made this an occasion of blessing the tilling of the ground. The plough used for this purpose was kept in the church, and it was solemnly censed before the procession started. In many churches there was a Plough Light kept burning by the husbandmen, and chiefly from the Plough Monday collections. In 1547 the wardens of Cratfield bought a plough for this purpose for 8d.; but in 1548 all Plough Mondays, Wakes, etc., were abolished. It was found impossible, however, to stamp out this well-rooted custom, and here and there church gatherings continued in connection with it in post-Reformation days. Thus at Wigtoft, Lincolnshire, the churchwardens in 1575 received 20s.. "of ye plougadrin." As a rule the later collections were solely used for feasting the plough-boys and their friends. The custom survived in certain districts within memory, and possibly still lingers in remote parts.[1]

LENT

Mr. St. John Hope has abundantly established the fact, in his valuable paper on "The English Liturgical Colours" (*St. Paul's Eccl. Soc. Trans.* ii.), that the usual old English colour for Lent was white; there is no necessity to cite from the various inventories among parish accounts to confirm this fact. It is, however, of some interest to note that returned chrisom cloths were sometimes used in the fashionings of Lent hangings.

1448 (*Thame*). Aparell made of crysomes for lent.
    ij aut' clothes of crysomes for Lent time.

The Lent veil hung in parish churches a little distance in front of the high altar, and not, as is so often asserted, at the chancel arch; it has been discussed in *English Church Furniture* of this series, p. 83. On Wednesday in Holy Week, in the reading of the Passion, at the words "And the Veil of the Temple was rent in twain," it was dropped and not put up again until the next year.

The great Cross of the rood-loft had its own special Lent cloth suspended in front of it; it was dramatically withdrawn, by an arrangement of pulleys, rings, and cords, on Palm Sunday.

White cloths or veils were also used throughout Lent for covering up the various images and pictures of the church; they remained thus covered until mattins on Easter morning.

The following are a few selections from wardens' accounts; others have been printed by Mr. Feasey.

---

[1] I am old enough to remember the custom, at Parwich, Derbyshire, in the "forties" of last century, when, as a small boy, I saw a surly farmer's strip of front garden roughly ploughed over.

THE LENTEN VEIL

1431 (*St. Peter Cheap*). j veil steyned w^t j crosse of red for lent in the quer.

1436 (*Tintinhull, Somerset*). Pro una lente clothe . xiiij s. ij d.

1447. Pro una corde empta pro le lente clothe suspendendo . j d.

1448. (*Thame*). A white veyle for the Church in lent tyme and another whyte veyle to be hangyng in the chancell before the hy aut^r in lenten tyme.

1454 (*Yatton, Somerset*). For a lyne to the leynte clothe ij d.

1501. To John Haryce for mendyng of ye Lent clothe . iiij d.

1509. For xiiij yerds of lynyn to make ye Lent clothe iiij s. viiij d.

For steynyng of ye seyd Lent clothe . . . vj s. viij d.

1507 (*Pilton, Somerset*). For lynes for lent clothe . . . vj d.

1521. For hangyn uppe of ye Lent clothe . . . . iiij d.

1510-1 (*Ashburton, Devon*). For xx yards of straunge (cord) for hanging the Lent cloth . . . . . iiij d.

For xxxiij rings for the said Lent cloth . iij d.

1526 (*Morebath, Somerset*). John Holann gave to this churche a Lent clothe ypaynted, a red clothe ypaynted, and a sepulture clothe ypaynted, price of all . . . x s.

1527-8 (*St. Mary-at-Hill*). For a grett iron to hang the veill of the chauncell against lent . . . . . xij d.

For mending of the same veill and for curten ringes xij d.

1537 (*St. Mary, Cambridge*). Paied for a lyne for the veile atte heigh aulter . . . . iiij d.

1504. A vayle for Lenton of white clothe.

1556. A vale for lent with a Rope and ij stapelles.

1568. Rec. for the vaile used in lent of linnen clothe vj s.

1540 (*Ludlow*). For rynges and crule and the sowynge on of them on the clothe on the mydys of the heygh chancelle iij d.

1557 (*St. Martin, Leicester*). For steynnyng the veyle . . vij s.

1558. For soying of the veale . . . . . vj d.

For a Cord for the veale . . . . . v d.

For ij yrdes about the same veale . . . . iij d.

THE ROOD VEIL

1508 (*Yatton*). Payd for ix yardes of bukeram for ye Rood clothe iij s.

1555. For iij yards of Green cloth for ye Rode . . . ij s.

1524 (*St. Laurence, Reading*). For a lyne to pull upp the clothe before the rode . . . . vj d.

1538 (*St. Mary, Cambridge*). For making a poly to draw up the vale before the rode . . . . . vj d.

1548-9 (*Holy Trinity, Cambridge*). A clothe to hange before the Roode in Lent.

GARNISHING OF CHURCHES

1549 (*St. Dunstan-in-the-East*). A greate cloth that dyd hange before the Roode in the Lente.

Image Veils

1495-6 (*St. Edmund, Sarum*). Pro anulis pro lente clothe Coram Sce Niche Epi iiij d., et pro factura eiusdem iiij d.

1507-8 (*Bassingbourne, Cambs*). Paid for a barr of yron or rodde with ij stapilles and x Ryngges to hangg uppon a Clothe bifor the ymages of Seynt Mary and seynt Kateryn . iiij d.
For mending of Clothes to Kever the sayntes in Lenton . ij d.

1521 (*St. Laurence, Reading*). Paid for canvas for coveringe of Saynt Michell . . . . . . iij d.

1527 (*Wimborne*). Paid to the ij Clerks for hanging up of the Lent Cloths upon Ashe Wednesday . . . ij d.

1529-30 (*Stoke Courcy, Somerset*). To the two clerks for coveringe the images in Lent . . . . . . ij d.

A special plain cross, without the crucifix, was reserved for processional use in Lent. The Sarum use directed it to be painted red, but the London use was to paint it green.

1486 (*St. Margaret Pattens*). A crosse and a crosse staffe to serve for lentten, paynted green withoute ymages wt iij white silver nailes

1531 (*St. Peter Cheap*). Paid for paytynge the greene cross for lent . . . . ij d.

1555 (*St. Michael, Cornhill*). Paide for a Crosse and a staffe for Lente of wood . . . . . . xij d.

Special banners were also used during Lent.

1541 (*St. Margaret Pattens*). Two Banar Clothes of the paschion steyned for lent.

1554 (*St. Ewen, Bristol*). Two banars of the Passion for lent.

The money paid for licences to eat flesh in Lent and from butchers for licences to kill, in accordance with the statutory proclamations of Edward VI and Elizabeth, went to the poor. Hence examples are usually found under overseers' accounts when they were kept separate from those of the wardens'. The following are examples culled from the poor accounts of St. Margaret, Westminster.

1571. Of John Dod for his lisense for kylling of flesh in lent vj s. viij d.
Of Mr. Harye dudle for his lisense for etynge of flesh vj s. viij d.

1618. Of the right worll Mr. Doctor Townson, Deane, license by him made to eat fleshe in the Lent season videlicet.
Of the Right honourable Lord Pagett for a license   xxvj s. viij d.

Twenty-six like receipts are entered for this year as granted by the Dean, including the Bishop of Lichfield, Sir Christopher Perkins, Sir Randolph Crewe, Lord Knevitt, and Lady Fortescue, all residents in the parish. The fees were £2 6s. 8d. for the nobility, 13s. 4d. for knights and ladies, and 6s. 8d. for commoners. Applications for these dispensations had to be accompanied by certificates from physicians.

The following are four other sample references to Lenten abstinence from city wardens' accounts:—

1596 (*St. Alphege, London Wall*). June 23d. Mr. French and Mr. Dager for March followinge for to look for meat in Cookes shopes and taverns . . . .
1605 (*St. Benet, Paul's Wharf*). Received of Mr. Frankwoode for a license to eate fleshe in Lent . . . . 6s. 8d.
1621-2 (*St. Anthonie*). Receyved of Mr. Bridges for his flesh license   6s. 8d. [Two similar licences that year.]
1609-10 (*St. Mary Woolnoth*). Licence to eat flesh . 6s. 8d.

Licences of this description are also frequently entered in parish registers. See Cox's *Parish Registers of England*, 222-5.

At Henley-on-Thames, in 1596, the wardens presented Robert Chamberlain "for roasting a pigg in his house on 24 March (Lent)," Henry Wauker "for seethinge ij pec of bacon," and Thomas Widmore for "rosting a shoulder of veal."

PENANCE

Penance is so closely associated with Lent, that it may be well in this place to cite a few examples of its public performance in post-Reformation days, as mentioned in wardens' accounts; much under this head, as recorded in registers, is set forth in *Parish Registers of England*, 217-20. The churchwardens of the Peculiars of Canterbury were ordered early in the seventeenth century

to provide a convenient large sheet and a white wand, to be had and kept within your church and vestry, to be used at such time as offenders are censured for their grievous and notorious crimes.

The offences for which public penance was enjoined were for the most part incontinence and slander.

The *Ecclesiologist* (vol. xxiii. 199) cites the following from the parish books of All Saints, Huntingdon :—

1621. Johannes Tomlinson, Rector. Oliverus Cromwell, filius Roberti, reprehensus coram totam ecclesiam pro factis.

1626. Hoc anno Oliverus Cromwell fecit penitentiam coram totam ecclesiam.

A few eighteenth-century entries are cited as examples.

1701-2 (*Woodbury, Devon*). Pd. for the charges of a woman doeing penance . . . . 9d.
1702-3. Pd. the charge for a woman doing penance . 7d.

At Wakefield, in this century, it was customary to hire sheets for penance, of which the entries are frequent.

1732. Oct. 8. Pd. for the loan of 7 sheetes for penances 1s. 9d.
1714 (*Otterton, Devon*). Paid to procure sheet and wand for Peter Longworth standing penance . . . . 1s.
1735. Paid for washing the Parish sheet for Club's wife to stand penance in . . . . 2d.
1764. 20 June. It is agreed at a parish meeting by us the parishioners who were then present, that the Churchwardens shall take out an Order of Penance against Pascho Potter who was presented at the last visitation of a Bad child, and that the expenses of it be allowed and reinfurced then either out of the poor or Church Rate.
1764 (*Little Glenham, Suffolk*). Pd. the Parish when the Widow Chrisp did penance . . . . . . 5s.
For ye use of a sheet and washing it . . . . 6d.

As to nineteenth-century public penance records, the latest in 1882, see Vaux's *Church Folklore* (1899), 173-8, and Dyer's *Churchlore Gleanings* (1891), 53-60.

Palm Sunday

On Palm Sunday, the usual procession before Mass went outside the church and round the churchyard bearing palms which had been previously blessed. The Holy Sacrament was carried beneath a canopy. On returning to the church by the south entrance, a station was made at the porch, where a scaffold was usually erected, when the boys sang the *Gloria*

Laus. From the porch roof or from the tower, it was customary to throw down flowers and cakes among the people.

A chief feature of the Palm Sunday Mass was the chanting of the long Gospel of the day, usually termed the "Singing of the Passion," during which the Lenten veil before the rood was drawn aside. It was sung from the rood-loft. A tenor voice (*vox media*) rendered the evangelistic narrative in recitative; but a treble or trebles (*vox alta*) sang any sayings of the Jews or the disciples, whilst a bass (*vox bassa*) sang the words uttered by the Saviour. After the Gospel, a prophetic lesson was sung by one or more Prophets, who were usually quire boys, garbed and bearded to look the parts—"an acolyte in the guise of a prophet," as the *Sarum Processionale* has it.

The various points are all illustrated in the following extracts from churchwardens' accounts. By far the best and fullest description of the Old Palm Sunday rites will be found in Feasey's *Ancient English Holy Week Ceremonial* (1897), pp. 53-83.

1447	(*St. Peter Cheap*). Payd on Palme Sunday for brede and wyne to the Reders of ye passion	iij d.
1519.	For hyering of the heres (wigs) for the p'fetys uppon Palme sondeye	xij d.
1521.	Spent uppon palme sonday for cut flowers box and palme	vij d.
	For nayls for ye frame over ye churche dore	j d.
	For lathe and nayls for the skafolde	ij d.
	For the hyer of ye heyr for the profytts	xij d.
1522.	For hyre of heyrs for ye profytts upon palme sundy	xij d.
1523.	For brede wyn and alle for them that rede the passyon	vj d.
1525.	Palme sondaye. For lathes naeylles and hooks for the pageante and for settyng up the same	x d.
1529.	For bowes flowrys caakes and for pynnys for lathys and for makyng of the Framys on palme sondeye	ij s.
1534.	For the settyng up of the stages for the prophetts on Palme Sonday	iiij d.
1556.	For palme flowers and cakes for palme Sondaye	xij d.
1557.	For palme and Ewe on palme Sondaye	xij d. ob.
1565.	To the sexton on palme sonday for hearbes	ij d.
1451	(*St. Mary-at-Hill*). Pd to Loreman for playing the p'het on Palme Sonday	iiij d.
1493.	For setting up the frame over the porch on Palm Sunday Eve	vj d.
1518-9.	Paid a pece for the frame that standeth on the lede for palme sonday	viij d.

GARNISHING OF CHURCHES

1519–20.	For the skaffold over the porche agenst palme sonday and for a carpenters labour to mend the same .	vij d.
1534–5.	For the frame over the north dore of the chirche that is for the profettes on palme sonday, for workmanship .	iij d.
1530–1.	For papur for the profettes on palme sonday in ther bondes	j d.
	For clothes for one Towre on palme sonday .	xij d.
	For heres (wigs) Berdis and garmenttes on palme sonday .	xij d.
	[There are several other entries for hire of raiment for the prophets in subsequent years.]	
1480–2	(*St. Andrew Hubbard*). For a frame and workmanshippe over the chirch dore for palme sundaye .	vij d.
1492–3.	For a laddyr for the chirche porche on palme sonday	x d.
1520.	For the hire of an angell	viij d.
1535.	For a Preest and a chylde that playd a messenger .	viij d.
1509–10.	For palme flours and kakes	vij d.
1491	(*St. Margaret, Westminster*). For brede and wyne for them that Redd the passyon on palme sonday	viij d. ob.
1505	(*St. Laurence, Reading*). To the clerk for syngyng of the passion on Palme Sonday in ale	j d.
1509.	For a quart of bastard for ye syngers of the Passhyon on Palm Sonday	iiij d.
1524.	For drynk in the roode loft uppon Palme Sonday .	j d.
1541.	For a quarte of Malmesey for the clerks upon Palme Sonday	iiij d.
1549.	For a quarte of wyne on Palme Sonday at Redyng the Passion	iiij d.
1518	(*St. Stephen, Walbrook*). Paid on Palm sonday for brede and ale and for wyne	xv d. ob.
1519.	For hyere of a berde for a proffyt on Palme Sondaye	ij d.
	For bred ale and wyne and dressyng of the proffyttes the same daye	xx d.
1525.	For bred ale and wyne for the syngers and profetts on palme sondaye	xiiij d. ob.
	For the hyre of the hayres for the profette on palme sondaye	vj d.
1524	(*St. Margaret Pattens*). For palme flowers and cake against palme Sunday	iiij d.
1539	(*St. Mary Woolnoth*). For brede ale and wyne geven to the preists and clarkes at reding of the Passion on Palme Sunday	vij d.
	For Palme flowers and cakes on Palme Sunday .	v d.
1545.	For setting up the railes for profhetes . . .	ij d.
1556.	For palme ewe and boxe and cakes for the chirche .	6d.
1540	(*St. Alphege, London Wall*). Payde to the Chyldern that playyd the p'fytes on Palme Sonday . . .	ij d.

1555 (*Ludlow*). Charges for "pyns and poynts to dress the canopie to bear over the sacrament on Palme Sondaye" "pyns and poynts upon Palme Sondaye to tye up the coverelette in the churche over the offrynge place."

1557 (*St. John Baptist, Bristol*). Pd to the parson for syngyng the Passion on Palme Sunday . . . . vj d.

1548-9 (*St. Ewen, Bristol*). For Readynge the Passion . j d.

1562 (*St. Michael, Cornhill*). Paide to a clerke on Palme Sonday for syngyng . . . . iiij d.

The following entries relate to the dramatic withdrawal of the rood-veil on Palm Sunday, to which reference has already been made under Lent.

1540 (*Ludlow*). For ij cordes to draw up the clothe afore the roode on Palme Sondayese . . . . . ij d.

1555. For hangynge the clothe before the rood in seat and iij cordes for the same . . . . iiij d.

1556. For cordes and packethrede for the rood clothe agaynst Palme sonday . . . . . viiij d. ob.

1558 (*St. Mary-on-the-Hill, Chester*). For a corde to ye Roode clothe for pame Sondays . . . . . ij d.

As to the actual *Palms* which were blessed, carried in procession, and distributed in the mediæval Church of England on Palm Sunday, controversy has arisen from time to time. There can, however, be no doubt that the recent revival of the use of the true Eastern palm on this occasion is in full accord with the old English precedent.[1] Without multiplying arguments, it is sufficient to reproduce the woodcut from the printed *Sarum Processionale* of 1502. The *rami pro clericis* are clearly true palms, whilst the *frondes et cetera pro laicis* are the catkin-bearing willow branches. The former, owing to its cost and difficulty of transit, would be but rarely used even by the clergy, save in cathedral or great conventual churches; whilst the latter is doubtless the "palm" of scores of early wardens' accounts. The flowering willow is still known in English villages throughout the land as "palm;" it is gathered by the children under that name and placed in the churches or houses. Another common English substitute for palm was the evergreen box, and a third was the yew. The use of the yew as a palm was

[1] The old English word *Palmer*, a pilgrim, had its origin in the custom of returning with palms as a testimony of the journey to the Holy Land.

exceptional, for as the emblem of immortality, the true and general English use of the churchyard yew was for garnishing the church on Easter Day.

The purchases of palm (flowering willow), box, and flowers and occasionally yew are continuous throughout the St. Mary-at-Hill accounts.

BLESSING OF PALMS: SARUM PROCESSIONAL

1490–1. For palmes and flowres for palme sondey . vij d.
1492–3. For palme boxe and flowrys on palmson eve . . . viij d.
1539–40. For pallme box and yue . . . . . xiiij d.

For Palm Sunday the garnishing entries of St. Martin's-in-the-Fields are constant until Elizabeth's accession. In 1525 the entry simply runs:—

For palme Agaynst palme sonday . . . . iij d. ob.

and there are several like entries.

1533. For palme yoeu and boox agaynste palme sonday iiij d.

This threefold form of Palm Sunday decoration occurs under many years; the variant spellings of yew are quaint, *e.g.* "ew," "ewe," "you," and "ewghe." In 1542 and 1546 "flowers" are also named. "Palme and boxflowers" are named in the St. Martin, Outwich, accounts of 1510; "palme and yew" at St. Andrew Cheap in 1511, and palme and box in 1527; and "palmes and flowers" at St. Botolph, Aldersgate, in 1519. It is in vain, as has been already said, to look for such entries, save very rarely, in country accounts, for abundance of greenery could readily be obtained without purchase.

Tenebrae and Good Friday

The ancient office of *Tenebrae* was sung on the evenings of Wednesday, Thursday, and Friday in Holy Week. At this night office, originally said at midnight, a triangular candlestick or hearse, of latten or iron, was placed on the south of the altar. The tenebrae candles of yellow wax, usually twenty-four in number, typifying the twelve prophets and apostles, were extinguished, one by one, at the beginning of each antiphon and responsary whilst the office was being sung. A single white taper representing our Lord was left burning.

> 1525-6 (*St. Andrew Hubbard*). Payd for j lb dim of tenebrae Candylls . . . . x d.
> 1535 (*St. Michael, Cornhill*). Payd for the Paskcull with the crosse candell, and ij lbs of Tenebre candles weiyinge all vij lbs at xj d. a pounde . . . . . . vj s. v d.

After evensong the altars were stripped and the *mensæ* or altar slabs washed.

On Good Friday the altar slabs were rubbed with fragrant herbs, or carefully dusted. The following entries may relate to this ceremonial :—

> 1503 (*St. Mary-at-Hill*). For box at the hallowing of the chirche to washe the aultyr . . . . j d.
> 1493 (*Walberswick*). For a Bessume of Pekoks Fethers . iiij d.

Disciplining with the rod was a Good Friday public penance,

GARNISHING OF CHURCHES

when the priest smote the hands of those who desired it with a bundle of small rods.

1510 (*St. Mary-at-Hill*). For disseplynyng roddis . ij d.

The Adoration of the Cross, usually known as "Creeping to the Cross," was an invariable Good Friday usage in the Church of England from Anglo-Saxon days onwards. At this adoration offerings were made in money or in kind.

1514 (*St. Ewen, Bristol*). Yn Offryng money to the Crose.
1541 (*St. Margaret, Westminster*). Received on Good Friday, for crepinge to the Cross the same yere . v d.

The Easter Sepulchre

Nothing need be stated here as to the nature of the Easter Sepulchre and the various rites connected with it, for the subject has been so often explained; it is fully discussed in *English Church Furniture*, 74–78; it may, however, be as well just to cite some pertinent entries from a few parish accounts.

1426-7 (*St. Mary-at-Hill*). For the sepulcre for divers naylis and wyres and glu . . . . . . ix d. ob.
To Thomas Joynour for makyng of the sepulcre . iiij s.
1492-3. For takyng downe of the sepulture . . . ij d.
1517-8. For a wayneskot for the Sepulcre . . . x d.
For a newe boorde and nayles for the sepulcre . . iiij d.
1529-30. For iij Tapurs for the Sepulcre more than were gadred of the parish . . . . . . xiij d.
1468-9 (*St. Edmund, Sarum*). Et in uno Nomine conducto pro laboro suo circa Sepulctrum, videlicet Petro Joynor in toto . . . . xx d.
Et in candelis emptis et expentered' circa opus sepulchri j d.
Et Johi Smythe pro xvj lib' ferri occuput' circa sepulchrum . . . . ij s. vj d.
Et eidem Johi Smythe pro labore suo in operatione proprii ecclesie circa sepulchrum occupat' . . xij d.
Et Johi Russhe Turner pro factura xlvij pynis de Beche et Asshe ad standum supra sepulcur' pro cerce ibidem ardente . . . . xviij d.
1475-6. Et sol' pro ferramento de novo ocupto pro firmacione et factura de la Sepultur' ibidem . . xiij s. iiij d.
1476-7. To William Karver for the makyng of a newe Sepultur' . vj s. iiij d.
For the beryng of the same to the Church . iiij d.

1477-8. Et sol' pro ferramento de novo empto pro firmacione et factura de la Sepultur' . . xiij s. iiij d.
1557-8. Watchyng of the Sepulker . . . . . vj d.
Setting upp of the Sepulker. . . . . ij d.
Pynnes to pyn the Sepulker . . . . j d.
1507-8 (*Holy Trinity, Cambridge*). To a warkeman for makyng of a Cofer to the Sepulcur . . . vj s. viij d.
Item paied to Richard Rolfe for two waynskottes to the same Cofer . . . . . . iij d.
Item paied to George Foyster for nailes and claspys to the same Cofer . . . . . . iij d.
To the clerk for kepyng of the sepulcr lyght . ij s.
1514-15. The sepulkyr lyght weyd when yt was taken down nyne skorre and xviij pound the vij yere of Kyng Henre viijth.
1500 (*St. Mary, Devizes*). To iiij men for keeping of the Sepulchre ij nights . . . . . xiij d.
For the making of the Sepulchre and taking down ij d.
1557. For the Sextane watching at the Sepulcre . . . iiij d.
1527. For watchyng of the sepulcre and for pynnys and naylls and other necessaryes to hange up the clothe and for wat'g upon good fryedaye and on Ester Evyn xiij d.
Payd a Reward to Ambros Barkars s'vant for mendyng of the clothe that henge abowte the sepulcre by consent was droppyd with candyll . . . ij s. iiij d.
1533. To the carpenter for mendyng of the sepulcre . xx d.
For watchynge the sepulcre at easter and for brede and drynke for them that watched . . . . ij s.
For ij sakks of coles for the wachmen to make fyer w^t all on Easter Eve . . . . . . xviij d.
1536 (*St. Mary, Cambridge*). Payed for a peece of Tymber for the sepulcer . . . . . . x d.
Payed for sawyng of the same Tymber . . . ij d.
Payed to the joyner for workyng of the Tymber in the sepulcer . . . . xiiij d.
Payed to Thomas Grene for payntyng the sepulcer . xij d.
1537. „ for mendyng of the wice (device) of the Resurrexcion . . . . iiij d.
1539. To John Capper for watching the sepulcre and hys meate ij s x d.
For pynnes spent abought the sepulcre . ob.
1542. Payd for xiiij li. wax putt to the sepulcre light vij s.
For settng up the sepulcre and watchyng the same ij s.
1544. For makyng of the vyce (device) of the sepulcre . xiij d.

The hallowing of the New Fire, though generally carried out on Holy or Easter Saturday Eve, was occasionally accomplished

GARNISHING OF CHURCHES

in England on Maundy Thursday. All lights were extinguished throughout the church, and they were again rekindled from renewed flames solemnly lighted by a burning glass or by flint and steel.

1540-1 (*St. Mary, Dover*). Payd for a bushell of charcoles at Easter evyn . . . . . . iiij d.
1555-6. Paied for woode for the hallowed fire ester evyn for lacke of cole . . . . ij d.

The devout parishioners usually rekindled their cold hearths by a brand from the Holy Fire.

HOCKTIDE [1]

Hocktide, with its quaint customs, judging from old parish accounts, used to be observed in all parts of England. Antiquaries have differed much as to its origin, but the most generally accepted opinion is that it commemorated the massacre of the Danes on St. Brice's Day, 1002. Collections were then made and the proceeds handed over to the churchwardens. The Hocktide festivities were held on Monday and Tuesday of the week following Easter week. On the Monday the men, and on the Tuesday the women, intersected the public roads with ropes, impounding, respectively, after a merry fashion, the opposite sex, and only releasing the captives on their paying a fine to the church. The women usually met with more success than the men. A few selections are made from scores of examples. There has been much learned as well as fanciful discussion as to the meaning of the term *Hock*. The Oxford Dictionary decides that none of the conjectures as to its origin are correct, but fails to supply a solution. The word in its earliest form was *Hoke*, a dissyllable. As to the survival of a portion of this eccentric custom up to a recent date, see the Bishop of Oxford's preface (p. ix.) to the Churchwardens' Accounts of St. Mary's, Reading.

In the Hocktide gatherings at St. Mary-at-Hill the women were as usual more successful on the Monday than the men on the Tuesday. In 1496 the men gathered 6s. 8d. and the women 20s. 1d.; in 1497 the men 5s. 8d. and the women 14s. 8d. In the latter year the wardens gave a dinner to the wives that gathered, consisting of "iij Rybbes of bief ale and bred," at a cost of 16d.

[1] See also pp. 21, 64-5.

The like proportion of receipts continued for many years. By 1526 it appears that the men's action fell into abeyance, only the wives are entered.

  Rec of the Gadryng of the wyffes on hok Monday .   xx s.

The following are a few extracts, taken from scores of others, arranged in chronological order:—

 1457 (*Thame*). We ressevyd of hockmoney of ye womanys gaderyng . . . . . . vj s. viij d.
 1497 (*Bassingbourn, Cambs*). Payed toward a Torche besides xl d. off hokyng money the whiche was Rec' off the wiff of Robt Bolne of that he and his company gadered the last hocke tuesday.
 1498 (*St. Laurence, Reading*). Rec' of Hok money gaderyd of women . . . . xx s.
 Rec' of Hok money gaderyd of men . iiij s.
  [In 1500 the women gathered 17s. 6d. and the men 5s ; in 1546, women 31s. 3d. and the men 8s. 4d.]
 1498 (*St. Margaret, Westminster*). Rec. of Maistres Bough Maistres Burgeys and Maistres Morland for hotckyng mony . . . . . . xxx s. iiij d.
 Rec. of Maister Bough Maister Morland and Maister Rabley for hokkyng money . xvj s. vij d. ob.
 1508–9 (*Holy Trinity, Cambridge*). R' that was gaddert in hokeyng money . . . . . ij s. viij d.
 1516–7 (*Lambeth*). For oke money of the men . v s.
 For ooke money of the wyffs . . . vj s. iiij d.
 1518–9. Of William Elyot and John Chamberlayne for hoke money gyderd in the pareys . iij s. ix d.
 Of the gaderynge of the churchwardyns wyffes on Hoke Monday . . . . . . viij s. iij d.

The Hocktide gathering of St. Martin's-in-the-Fields on Monday and Tuesday, 1525, amounted to 13s. 2d.; in 1526, 15s. 4d.; in 1527, 13s. 1d.; and in 1528, 13s. 4d. The women's gatherings on Hock Monday 1531–2 were used towards new altar hangings.

 1555 (*St. Mary, Reading*). Rec. for Hoc money and Whytsontyde money . . . . . . vj li. ixs. x d.
 1556. Pd. for the wymens sopper at hoctyde . iij s. iiij d.
 1557. Rec. of the mens gathering wymens gathering and Maydens gathering at Hoctyde and uppon Mayday . . xxxix s.
 1559. Rec. of the mens gatheringe . . . . vij s. iij d.
 Rec. of the womens gatheringe . . . xxvij s. v d.

GARNISHING OF CHURCHES

[In 1560 the men gathered 5s. and the women 23s.; in 1561, the men 4s., the women 12s. The last entry of hocktyde money is under 1568-9, when the total was 15s.]

ROGATION TIDE

Parochial Perambulations or processions were customary from an early date on the three days before Holy Thursday or Ascension Day, when litanies were sung for the prevention of pestilence or plague, and for a blessing on the fields or crops. Hence these days were usually termed Rogation Days. The parish books abound in references of this nature.

The Yeovil accounts of 1457-8 show that 2½ ells of linen cloth were bought for 15d., to make two banners to be carried round the fields; 1d. was spent on dyeing the same; 6d. in making the banners; and 2½d. for seven wooden rods to carry them in procession.

1484 (*Saffron Walden*). To the gawing forth of viij baners on ye Monday in going wyk		viij d.
1503-7 (*Bassingbourne, Cambs*). For the Banyeres bering about the Feldes in theis iij yeres		xxiij d.
1540-1 (*St. Mary, Dover*). Paid to them that bare the banners upon the Assencyon and Corpus Xtiday		vij d.
1557-8 (*St. Thomas, Sarum*). To the baner bearers and to the ryngers upon Saynt Thursday		vj d.
For iiij belles to hange at the endes of the baners		viij d.
To the Baner Bearers to the ryngers and for drynke the Monday, Tuesday and Wednesday and Thursday in the Rogation weke		xxij d.
1605 (*St. Margaret, Westminster*). For bread, drink, cheese, cream and other necessaries when the Worshipfull and others of the parish went the perambulation to Kensington		xv li.
1610 (*Yarnton, Oxon*). Paid for bread and beere at the tyme of goinge in Procession		16d.
1612. P^d forty for the processioning 22d. For bread and beare at the Procession 2s.		
1620. Cakes and bread for the Perambulation		2s. 5d.
1639 (*St. Peter, Ipswich*). For a dinner at the bell at the Perambulation		17s.
For bread and beere for the boyes		8s.
1638-9 (*St. Martin, Leicester*). For bread and beere at the Perambulacon		3 6
For poynts and ribbons given to children the same time		3 0

THE CHURCHWARDENS' ACCOUNTS

	Gave to Mr Lins a quart of wine when we went on perambulacon	1 4
1641–2.	P^d for expenses at our perambulacon and points given away	4 9
1666.	P^d for bread and drink upon the people and parson when we went upon perambulation . . .	6s.
	To the young people in points	2s. 6d.
1688.	Paid for ale, bread, and tobacco on Holy Thursday	19s.
	For points 18d., marking the bounds 1s.	

The Perambulation entries in the accounts of All Saints, Derby, are very frequent during the seventeenth and eighteenth centuries. Fifty selected entries are given in the *Chronicles of All Saints*; seven or eight must suffice for quotation in these pages.

1623.	For dynners, ringing, and preparing ye way for perambulation	3 8
1632.	For makeinge ye gappes at perambulation .	8
1668.	Two quarts of Clarit at perambulation . . .	1 6
1672.	Given to 2 maids wch Attended us in O^r perambulation at Little Chester	2
1690.	For Buns and Ayle att Darly Hill	6
1756.	For meat for the Prossessioning Dinner . . .	8
	For meat for the Singers and Ringers . . .	4
1782.	For 16 doz. Buns for ye prossessioning . . .	16 8
1663	(*Sidbury, Devon*). For the dinner and dressing for them that did ride to vew the bounds of the parish at the perambulacon	22 9
1664.	For the perambulation in Beefe and Mutton .	9 0
	For to Legs of Veale 2s 8d., for bread 1s. 8d.	4 4
	For baken, flower, fruits, saferon and clovis .	3 1
	For beare 3s. 6d., for dressing the dinner 2s. .	5 6
1673	(*Hawkhurst, Kent*). For ribbon and plumes for ye boyes y^t went ye bounds	5 6
	For vittles and beere when we went ye bounds	1 0
1684.	May 8 (*Deptford*). Pd Mr Douse for a processioning dinner £4. 7. 0.; p^d Mr Cox at the halfway house for meat, bread, beer, and cakes at the processioning £2. 16. 0.; pd the widow Spett for cakes £1; p^d Rob Phipps for bread and beer at ye Black Jack and Shovel 4s. 6d.; p^d for 2 bottles of Canary which we had in Peckham Lane, 4s.; pd to make ye boys drink when we came home 1s.; pd more ye same day with ye gentlemen of ye parish at Mr Douse's after dinner, 8s. 6d.	

The sum of £9 7s. 8½d. was spent in the City parish of St. Alphege, London Wall, on an Ascension Day dinner in 1707, after the beating of the bounds. Other expenses included 4s. 5d. for ale in the vestry, 8s. for ale for the boys and girls, 7s. 6d. for 300 wands for the boys, 14s. 1½d. for ribbons, 28s. for " four grosse of Taggs and 8 Dozen of Laces," and, by way of bathos, 3s. "for a Leg of Mutton for the poor."

> 1546 (*St. Margaret, Westminster*). Pd on Ascension even for bread, ale, beer and wyne for the prebendaries and quyer of the mynster after mass was done . j s. ij d.
> 1555. For spiced bread on the Ascension even and on the Ascension Day . . . . . . j s.

Whitsuntide

To impress the lessons of Pentecost or Whitsuntide a pageant was frequently arranged, especially in the larger churches, to signify the descent of the Holy Ghost in the form of a dove. Here are three out of many references in old parish books.

> 1500 (*Walberswick, Suffolk*). John Alpeyngham left money to provide for "the Holy Ghost goyng upp and down with a cheyne."
> 1510 (*Louth*). Robert Boston for the Holy Ghost appearing in the kirk roof . . . . . . ij s.
> 1540–2 (*St. Mary-on-the-Hill, Chester*). Paide for wyre to sett up the holy goste . . . . . . j d.

Corpus Christi

The festival of Corpus Christi, on the Thursday after Trinity Sunday, used to be greatly honoured by processions throughout mediæval England. It was usual to have a feast at the conclusion of the outdoor procession.

At St. Ewen, Bristol, the Corpus Christi breakfast or dinner for clergy and choir, after the great procession, continued to grow in substance and expense throughout the fifteenth and early years of the sixteenth century. In 1479 six gallons of ale, and three rounds of beef, in addition to other pieces of beef and mutton, were consumed. In 1489 the meat included "a double Rybbe of beef, the purtenance of a lambe, powdered (salted) beeff, a chekyn, and a Gose." Eventually on 19th February 1535,

"It is agreyd by the consent of the whole paryshoners That the procktors for the tyme byeng shal be alowed for the brekefast upon Corpus Cristi day 2s. for the parson priestes and the clerkes and for no more.

1530 (*St. John Baptist, Bristol*). Payd to iij priests upon Corpus
Xtiday	xij d.
Payd to the sexton upon that day	iiij d.
Payd for ij quarts of wyne	iiij d.
Payd to ij chyldn that bare the candlesticks . . .	ij d.

CHAPTER XIX

CHURCH OR PARISH PLAYS—CHURCH-ALES

Plays in churches—Plays at Harling; St. Margaret, Southwark; St. Michael, Bath; Ashburton; St. Laurence, Reading; Bassingbourne; Braintree; Heybridge; Bungay—Short extracts—The Boy-bishop—Churchyard of St. Katherine Cree—Summer games at St. Ives; St. Columb Major, Wootton, Hants—Robin Hood plays—Mayday and Whitsuntide games—Church-ales—Church House, Yatton, Cratfield, Bassingbourn, Seal, and Mere

Church or Parish Plays

THIS is a vast subject. If all that could be found relative to plays in wardens' accounts were duly set forth and briefly annotated, it would occupy far more space than the whole of this book. By far the best book to study on this question is Chambers' *Mediæval Stage* (1903), two vols., especially appendix, vol. ii. 329–406. There is a good article by Mr. L. G. Bolingbroke on "Pre-Elizabethan Plays and Players in Norfolk" in *Norfolk Archæology* (1892), vol. xi. At Braintree, Chelmsford, Halstead, Heybridge, Leicester, and Salisbury there is direct evidence of play-acting within the church; at Bungay and St. Katherine Cree (London) in the churchyard; at Harling at the church gate; at Bassingbourn in a croft near the church; and at Louth, Reading, etc., in the market-place. They were invariably acted to bring profit to the general church fund. The long accounts relative to the Bassingbourn play of 1511 are set forth at length, as they have not hitherto been printed; twenty-seven adjacent villages contributed to make this play a success. Remarkable evidence is here given, much for the first time, of the survival of these church plays right through Elizabeth's reign. Mr. Chambers, usually so accurate, is quite mistaken in stating that the last of these parish plays occurred at Hascombe, in

Surrey, in 1549. The latest I have found is at Wootton, Hants, in the year 1680.

The earliest is in the accounts of St. Augustine, Hedon, for the year 1339-40, when 7s. was received from players in the church on the feast of the Epiphany. Certain liturgical plays were, of course, always enacted within the church, such as that of the Epiphany, and the more striking drama of Palm Sunday.

In the year 1500 the church of St. Dunstan, Canterbury, possessed upwards of fifty books, about a dozen of which were religious plays—such as, according to the inventory, "A queer off Corpus Xti and Saint Anne," and "ij queers off the story of Saint Anne"—they formed part of what is known as the cycle of Corpus Christi Plays.

The following references to church plays up and down the country are arranged in chronological sequence:—

1452 (*Harling, Norfolk*). Pd for the original of an Interlude played at the Church gate	. . . .	...
1457. Pd for bread and ale when Lopham Game came to this town		xij d.
For bread and ale to Garblesham Game	. . .	vj d.
1463. In expenses when Keningale Game came	.	vj d.
1467. Bred and ale to ye Kenyngale Players	. . .	vj d.

The plays performed within the church of St. Margaret, Southwark, on the feasts of St. Margaret and St. Lucy are several times named after a brief fashion in the accounts of the reign of Henry VI.

1453-4. Peid for a pley upon seynt lucy day, and for a pley upon seynt Margrete day	. .	xiij s. iiij d.
1454. For the grete procession upon seynt Margrete day	.	xx s.
1458. Upon seynt lucy day to the Clerkes for a pley	.	vj s. viij d.
1460. To the Pleyers upon seynt Margrete day (a frequent entry)		vij s.
1460. To the Mynstrell for the procession	. . .	xvj d.
1460. For hyryng of the Germentes	. . .	xiiij d.
1466. To Hary for his Chyldren upon Seynt Lucy day	. .	xij d.
1481-2 (*St. Michael, Bath*). Pro potacione le players in recordacione ludorum diversis vicibus	. .	iiij d.
Pro ij busels frumenti ad idem ludum	. . .	ij s.
Waltero Comyar pro liquo ad faciendum scrinium dicto tempore	. . . . . .	viij d.
Johi Slugg pro pane et floribus ad idem	.	. v s. vj d.
Pro ij dosyns servicie ad idem ludum		iij s. iiij d.

CHURCH OR PARISH PLAYS—CHURCH-ALES 269

        Robto Chapman pro caseo ix d, et Johe Guntschere pro caseo iiij d.
        Ricdo Tanner pro pelles ad idem ludum . . . xx d.
1490–1 (*Ashburton, Devon*). For the profit of ale called the
        playerin ale . . . . . . xxxiij s. iiij d.
1491–2. From Widelambe for players clothinge . xij d.
1519–20. For keeping the players clothes . . . ij s. viij d.
1528–9. For painting cloth for the players and making their tunics
        and for making staves for them and crests upon their
        heads on the festival of Corpus Xti   ix s. ix d.
1533–4. Recomded and alowed to the pleirs of Crystmas game that
        pleyd in the churche . . . . . ij s.
1534–5. To the stenar for payntyng of the playyng clothes and gold
        skynnys bought to the same . iiij s. iiij d.
        To the pleyers of Exeter playyng a Chrissmas game   ij s.
1536–7. For playing gammys . . . . . . iiij s.
        For ij schepe skynnes for playing cloths . vj d.
        For a hed of here (hair) and other thynges for the players . ij s.
1537–8. For a pair of silk garments for Herod on Corpus Xtiday . xij d.
1542–3. For ij devils heads and other necessary things for the
        players . . . . ij s. j d.
1555–6. For a payr of glovys for hym that played God Almighty
        at Corpus Xti daye . . . . . ij d.
        For wyne for hym that played Saynt Resinent . vj d.
1556–7. For payntyng the players clothes at Totnes . xx d.
1558–9. For a payr of glovys to hym that played Christ on Corpus
        Xti daye . . . . ij d.
1562–3. To the bearwards of Lord Robert Dudley . iij s. iiij d.

The entries as to plays are frequent in the accounts of St. Laurence, Reading; they were for the most part acted on the open space, near the church, termed the Forbury

        1498. Rec. of the gaderyng of a stage play . xvij s.
        1507. Rec. of the Sonday afore Bartylmastyde for the pley in the
        Forbery . . . . . . xxiij s. viij d.
        To the labourers in the Forbury for setting up the polls for
        the schafhold . . . . . . ix d.
        To the Bereman for ber for the pley in the Forbury x d.
        For bred and ale and bere yt longyd to the pley . ij s. vj d.
        For j ell quart' of croscloth to make j payr of hosyn and j ell
        of a doublett . . . . x d.
        For course canvass to make xiij capps wt the makyng and wt
        the hers (ears) thereto longyng . . . ij s. iiij d.
        For ij ells di of croscloth for to make Eve a cote . x d.
        For dyed flax (for wigs) iij li. . . . . . v d.

> For makyng of a dublett of lethur and j payr of hosyn of
> lethur agaynst Corp' Xti day . . . . viij d.

The valuable Reading accounts also bear witness to the performing of a Resurrection play. The entry of 1507, wherein there is mention of 3d. paid "for rosyn to the resurrecyon play," has been ingeniously interpreted by Mr. Kerry to resin used for the burst of light at the moment of the Resurrection.

> 1534. Payd to Mr. Laborne for reformyng the Resurrecion Play viij s. iiij d.
> 1535. Payd to Sr Laborne for a boke of the resurrecion play for
> a qu'r of paper and for byndyng thereof . ix s. ix d.
>
> 1510-2 (*Bassingbourn, Cambs*). Rec' atte the play had on seynte Margar' day anno domini M^l v^c and xj^{mo} had in brassingburn off the holy martir seynt georg, att that tyme Chirchewardeyns John Ayworthe and John good the elder in bass' in the westend by theym rec' than as apth followith :
>
> First rec' off the Townshyppe off Royston suma . . xij s.
> Item rec' off the townshyppe off Therfeld suma . vj s. viij d.
> ,, ,, Melburne v s. iiij d., off Lyttellyngton v s. ij d. ob.
> suma . . . . . . x s. vj d. ob.
> ,, Whaddon iij s. iiij d. ob., off Stepulmorden iij s. j d.
> suma . . . . . . viij s. v d. ob.
> ,, ,, Berly iiij s j d., off Asshiwell iiij s. suma viij s. j d.
> ,, ,, Alyngton iij s. iiij d., off Orwell iij s. suma . vj s. iiij d.
> ,, ,, Wendey ij s. ix d., off Wyndpole ij s. vij d. suma v s. iiij d.
> ,, ,, Meldreth ij s. iiij d., off Arryngton ij s. iiij d. suma iiij s. viij d.
> ,, ,, Shepreth ij s. iiij d., off Kelsey ij s. v d. suma . iiij s. ix d.
> ,, ,, Wyllyngham xvij d., off Fulmar xxv d., suma . iij s. vj d.
> ,, ,, Gyldymorden xvj d., off Tadlowe xij d. suma . ij s. iiij d.
> ,, ,, Crawdyn xvj d., off Hattely x d. suma . ij s. ij d.
> ,, ,, Wrasthyngworthe ix d., off Hasselyngfeld ix d. suma . xviij d.
> ,, ,, Bankwey viij d., off Foxtoun iiij d. suma xij d.
> ,, ,, Kneseworthe with vj of hekys suma . . ij s. vj d.
> ,, ,, the townshipps off bass' on the Mondaye and on
> the Tewysday next after the playe, together with
> other commeres on the Mondaye xiiij s. v d.
> upon the Wednesdaye next after the playye with a
> potte of ale at Kneseworthe all wch deduct suma . xix d.
> Item rec' for food ale and small ale sold out suma . x d. ob.
> ,, ,, off Thomas taylor in bass', bocher, in money of his gyft . xx d.
> ,, ,, William Pynk off his gyft in mony . . . x d.
> ,, ,, John Dubur iiij d., off Thomas Marchall servant of Mr.
> Mulvey iiij d. suma . . . . . viij d.
> ,, ,, Robert Freeman iiij d., off John Good at Cross iij d. . vij d.
> ,, ,, Frank leon and Robert Serle ayther of them ij d. . iiij d.

CHURCH OR PARISH PLAYS—CHURCH-ALES

Item rec' off William lamkyn ij d., off John Comes ij d., and John Dykon. Item of Will' Taylor suma . . viij d.
,, ,, Robert blandes geft of buntford suma . . xij d.
,, ,, John good karpentur and whelewhryght off his geft in workemanshippe off falchons, and tourmentours, axes, parts of the stuffys of his own and for a Rymbyll of a whele suma together . . . xvj d.
,, ,, John Hobard priste towardes theyse costes in all out of his labour for beryng the playe booke, with iij d. for a boss' of malte suma . . . . xxj d.
Mem^d the gefftes in Brewing of the maltes
First ux' Egidii asshewell j quarter . . . . . x d.
Item ux' Thomas Taylor bocher a j quarter malte brewing . x d.
,, ux' John Good the Elder gaff the brewing of iiij boss' v d.
,, ux' Roberti Serle ,, ,, ,, v d.
,, ux' Waltur Taylor ,, ,, ,, v d.
,, ux' John Thomas gaffe the brewing a quarter . v d.
,, ux' Georg Noorthe ,, ,, . . . v d.
,, ux' Thomas bolnest . . . v d.
,, Maryon loskyn wydow ,, . . . v d.
,, ux' Roberti bolnest ,, ,, . . . ij d.
,, ux' John Good at Cross ,, ,, . . . ij d.
,, rec' off Morgan gyft of Gylden mordon a shepe pc . xxij d.
,, ,, John Gosselyn geft in bass' a shepe pric' xx d.
,, ,, fur ale lefte summa mor than afor rec' . xj d. ob.
Item rec' in maltes first of Mr. Antony Malare . j quarter
Item off John lyon Corss . . . . . ij quarter
,, ,, Robt holnest . . . . . . j quarter
,, ,, Thomas bolnest and his wiff and Robert Laurence . v boss'
,, ,, Thomas Asshewell . . . . . iiij boss'
,, ,, Georg noorthe . . . . . . ,,
,, ,, Will Thomas of Wyndpole . . . .
,, John Ayworthe . . . . . .
,, ,, John Thomas of bass' . . . . .
,, ,, Booz' hasyldeyn . . . . . ,,
,, ,, Will frodde parysh clerk . . . . ,,
,, ,, John game of kness' . . . . . iij boss'
,, ,, Will Edsyn . . . . . . ij boss'
,, ,, John Catell . . . . . . ,,
,, good senior in westend . . . . iiij boss'
,, ,, Will Asshewell . . . . . j boss'
,, ,, Robt Taddelowe . . . . . ,,
,, ,, W. Soyleyard . . . . .
,, ,, Robert Crane . . . . .
,, ,, John Pynk . . . . . .

Item off	Maryon loskyn		j boss'
,, ,,	Rie gibbs		,,
,, ,,	John Cran		
,, ,,	John Gibson		,,
,, ,,	Robert Skampion		,,
,, ,,	Robert lane and J. grouger		ij boss'
,, ,,	Harr' lavenok		j boss'
,, ,,	John Stephenson		iij pakes
,, ,,	Will good and Everard		,,
,, ,,	Agnes Katell		j pak

Summa in maltes xj quarter iij boss' iij pekes.

M^d in wheetes rec' of Mr. Malary iij boss', item of Gyles Asshe iiij boss'.

Item of Will Soyland of W. Watters, of Th' gyfte in Kness' of John Hobard prist ayther of them a boss'. Suma . xij boss'

Expenses and Charges off the sayde playe as followith:

First paid to the garnement man for garnementes and proprytes and play books	xv s. ij d.
Item payd to mynystrelles and iij waytes of Cambrigg for the Wednesdaye sondaye and monday ij of theym the first day and iij the other dayes	v s. vj d.
,, in expenses on the playeres when that the playe was shewed in bred and ale and for other vytalles att ryston on those players	iij s. ij d.
,, in expenses on the playday for the bodyes off vj shape one of theym of Morgan of Morden	ix s. ij d.
,, for iij Calfis and halfe a lambe pric' . . .	viij s. ij d.
,, a shepe giffen off John Gosselyn pric'	xxij d.
,, payd to Thomas taylor and Gyles Asshewell for ij quarter of whete	viij s.
,, ,, to John goode off the westend for j lode of wood	ij s. viij d.
,, ,, for v days bord off one pyke propyrter making for himselfe and hys servaunte one daye and for his horss pastur vj days Summa	xvj d.
,, ,, Thomas polgrave Coke ix d., and to Frank Asselar iiij d.	xiij d.
,, ,, turneres off spittes and for salte ij d. togeder	ix d.
,, ,, Anne Ayworthe for iij Chekynes to the gentylmen .	iiij d.
,, ,, Yssabell Asshewell for Fysshe and bred .	iiij d.
,, ,, for nayles to lamkyn Smyth paid j d. and for a Jorrny to Westwell	ij d.
,, ,, John bocher for peynting of iij Fawchones and iiij tormentoures axes	xvj d.
,, ,, Gyles asshewell for Easement of his Crofft to play in	xij d.
,, ,, John hobarde brotherid priste for the play book beryng	ij s. viij d.

M brewinges of maltes and ayworthe for di quartr paid	v d.
Item to Kateryn taylor for di quarter malte brewing paid .	v d.
„ Jone bolnest ux' Robert for j quarter brewing	x d
„ Jone taylor ux' Thomas taylor „ „	x d.
„ Maryon loskyn wydow for di quarter „	v d.
„ helyn good for j quarter malte brewing . . .	x d.
„ yssabell Asshwell „ „ . . .	x d.
„ Jone Scerle for di quarter „ . . .	v d.
„ Agnes good „ „ . . .	v d.
„ Margarett Thomas for j quarter „ . . .	x d.
„ Alic Noorthe ux' Georg for di quarter brewing	v d.
„ Jone bolnest ux' Thamas „ „	v d.
„ Kateryn lyon for a quarter and to Elyn pynke for di a quarter	xv d.
„ payd for halfe a shepe mor on the tewysdaye after the playe	x d.
„ „ for spyces to that sayd besynes and play	xlj d.
„ „ for bred bought off Jone bolnest uxor upon Rob' .	iij d.
„ „ for fetchyng the dragon in expenses biside the car'	viij d.
„ „ for gryndyng off x quarter malte and dim'	ix d.
„ „ for bred and vitalles and also setting uppe the stages	v d.
„ „ to Will gronger one of the asselares on the play day	ij d.
„ „ for pastes uppon the tewsdaye as for the flower	iiij d.

M^d the bakyng off the wheetes viz. iij quarter and dim ny uppon gyffen except the gorgond thei had.

uxor Thome Taylor dim a quarter, Item uxor Gyles j quarter Item uxor John Pynk dim quarter, Item uxor John good sen' dim quarter. Item uxor John lyon Corss dim quarter, Item uxor Thomas boln' and the wyff off georg noorth betwyx theym dim a quarter.

M^d all thynges allowed and accowyntyd the suma totalis off the Reman' xxxij s. j ob.

M^d the sumes off mony gaderid towardes an ymage off george primo die marcii anno domini M^l v^c and xj First delyveryd at this datte by John ayworthe to Thomas taylor than electe Chirche ward' the sayd xxxiij s. ob.

Item at this daye in the handes off gyles asshewell xj s.

Item at this daye in the bandes off Kateryn lyon uxor John xxviij s. iij d. ob.

Summa iij li. viij s. iij d. ob.

M^d dettes besyde owing graunted to seynt Georg.

Fyrst John ayworthe d' vith vj boss'.

M^d graunted for the mony occuping his tyme.

Item Summa xiiij boss' maltes.

Item thomas soyland in boss' d' in Rye ij boss'.

Item the same thomas soyland and John Gosselyn for Thomas Rooyn of Kneseworthe j bos' malte.
Item Ryc' buckenell off his promyss d' . . . iiij d.
Item Ric' Wightnys d' off his promyss . . . . ij d.
Summa in hi' xv boss'
Item in Rye ij boss'
Item in mony vj d.

The wardens' accounts of Braintree, Essex, mention, in 1523, a play of St. Swithin, acted in the church on a Wednesday, net profits to the church, £3 13s. 7½d.; in 1525, play of St. Andrew, acted in the church on a Sunday, profits £3 17s. 8d.; and, in 1534, play of Placidas *alias* St. Eustace, profits £8 2s. 8½d. In 1567 the wardens received £5 of the play money; in 1570, £9 7s. 7d., and also 1s. 3d. for letting players' garments; and in 1571, for a play book 20d., and 8s. 7d. for play gere. Finally, in 1574, the players' apparel was sold for 50s. See Karl Pearson's *Chances of Death* (1897), ii. 413–4.

On the Sunday before Whitsunday, 1532, a play was acted at Weybridge, Essex, which made a considerable stir in the countryside. Unfortunately the accounts, which are imperfect, do not give the name of the play or pageant. It was well supported by many of the adjacent townships.

Thys ys the sume of moneys of all the Townes the wryde was browgte in att the day of ower playe :—

	£	s.	d.		£	s.	d.
Maldon . . .	1	3	4	Tottam and Gold Angere		8	6
Bylygh . . .		8	1	Terlynge .		12	2
Cockshall			11	Tolfonte Magna .		4	2
Braested Magna.		6	0	Wycham .		5	4
Inford .		1	1	Woddam Ferys .		1	0
Braested Parva .		4	3	Felstede . . .		6	8
Purly .		4	2	Keldon . . .		1	1½
Woddam Mortymers		2	1½	Ferynge . . .		1	0
Tolesbury			7	Hatfield . . .		6	8
Woddam Walters		2	4	Tolfonte Daffys		3	6
Langforde		3	5	Moche Tottam		10	0
Owlde . . .		1	5		5	17	11

Gatherings were made to supply abundant provision for feasting the visitors and players in wheat for baking, and in malt for brewing; whilst the meat included " a quartere of ij beffes,

CHURCH OR PARISH PLAYS—CHURCH-ALES

7 cawys (calves), 6 shepe and 8 lambys." Gatherings in ready money amounted to £1 15s. 7½d. The total receipts in cash on the day of the play were £7 10s. 2½d., and they also "resayved of the parson the next daye" 13s. 1d.

The following are among the payments:—

For 4 dosen potts	2 2
To the pagentt players	13
For baryng of the boke	
To 5 payr of gloves	
To the minstrell	1
To Colben for his tabor	
To Hoowe that playd the folle	1
To the cookes	1
To she that turned the spitt	
To the basteter	

Two items that relate to the gilding of the tabernacle and for "a locke for the porche door" show that the performance of this play was within the church. When the accounts were made up there "remayneth clere above all charge £7 10s., the wych restyth in the churchwardeyns handys."

1558 (*Holy Trinity, Bungay, Suffolk*). Pd to William Ellys for
the interlude and game book . . . . iiij d.
Pd for writing the parte . . . . . ij s.
1561. For making the scaffold for the interlude in the churchyarde,
meat and wages . . . . . . v s.
Pd at Norwiche for expense when my lord of Surrey, his
apparel, was borrowed for the interlude . xx d.
Pd for staynyg certayn clothes for the interlude . xij d.
Given to Kelsage the vyll (fool) for his pastyme before the
plaie and after the play both daies . . . . ij s.
To Holbrook for his visors (masks) . . . . iiij d.
For carrying home the apparell agayne to Norwich xij d.
For dying heares (wigs) for ye interlude players . ij d.

Similar items appear in the accounts of 1567 at 13s. 6d., the performance in the latter year taking place in the castle yard. In 1577 the warden acknowledges the receipt from his predecessor of

All the game players gownes and coats that were made of certayne peces of olld copes.

The last item relative to the plays occurs, in 1591, when 5s. was received for the "players cootes."

The following are a few desultory extracts and notes in chronological sequence.

In 1451 a play called "Christmasse play" resulted in a profit of 6s. 8d. to the church account of Tintinhull.

The old church accounts of Yarmouth show that the wardens drew a considerable income from plays; plays on Corpus Christi day are mentioned in 1473 and 1486; at Bartholomewtide in 1484; and on Christmas Day in 1493:—

>1474 (*St. John, Peterborough*). Rec of men of depyng (Deeping) for
>hyryng of iiij garments . . . . . xvj d.
>1479. To the players that playd in the church at crystemesse . xx d.

Vestments for the Boy-bishop and his companions often occur

>1487-8 (*St. Andrew Hubbard*). For makying of seint Nicolas
>cope . . . . ij s. ij d.
>1488-9. For iij yardes bokeram for a childes cope . . xv d.
>1469-70 (*Holy Trinity, Cambridge*). For the makyng of seint
>Nicholas Coops and for dim elle bokeram xv d. ob.
>For canvas for seynte Nicholas Coope bought of annye
>Matterhead by thodore of the Clerks . vj d.
>For a Rochet makyng by thordore of the Clerkes vj d.
>1492 (*St. Martin, Leicester*). Paid to the players on New years
>day at even in the church . . . . . vj d.

There are various references to plays in the Sutterton accounts, Lincolnshire. In 1519, "For ye pluars rewarde of Quoublods (Whaplode) ix d." There are charges for candles for the players in 1521 and 1522. In 1524 the wardens received from sundry people 9s. 6d. "for increments for the play playd on the day of the assumption of our lady." In the following year players from Swineshead received 3s. 4d., and those of Donington 12d.; and in 1526, Sutterton was visited by two other bands of players from Frampton and Kirton.

>1525 (*St. Martin's-in-the-Fields*). Payed for the Pagantes played
>on palme sunday . . . . . . xvj d.
>1538. Resceyved of the pleyers that played in the church ij s.
>1555. Paide to the players uppon Ester Daye in the morenenge . xvj d.
>1535 (*Boxford, Cambs*). M^d here after follows all the sumes of
>money receyved by a play made in ye yere of o^r lord god

mccccxxxv by William Cox and John Scott Chirche Wardyns in that yere.
> [This entry is followed by 19 items from different individuals and townships amounting to £17 12s. 6d., as "profets on the play," which were assigned towards the rebuilding of the steeple.]

1539 (*St. Mary Woolnoth*). On Alhalowen day for v herps for
virgyns to play . . . . . . ij s.
For garlandes for the same virgyns . . . . ij d.
For lampes for the same virgyns . . . . iiij d.
1548-9 (*Barnstaple*). Paied to the players that played at Church ij s. viij d.
1552-3 Paid to minstrells for playing and singing in the church iij s. iiij d.
1554. Paid to the King's Juggler on St. Peters day . . v s.
1560. Paid to my Lord Bishop's players who played in the church. . . . .
1561-2 (*Tavistock*). Payed unto the players vj s. viij d.
Payed unto the quenes majestyse is players . xiij s. iiij d.
1561 (*St. Martin, Leicester*). Receved for serten stuff lent to the players of fosson . . . . . vj d.

In the wardens' accounts of Chelmsford for 1562 occurs the following interesting list of properties stored in the church ready for the acting of miracle plays:—

Garments

Fyrst iiij gownes of red velvet.
It^m a longe gowne of blew velvet.
It^m a short gowne of blew velvet.
It^m ij gownes of red satten.
It^m a gowne of borders.
It^m a gowne of clothe of tyssew.
It^m a jyrkyn of blew velvet wth sleeves.
It^m a jirkyn of borders without sleeves.
Itm. viij jyrkyns without sleeves.
Itm. ij vyces coats and ij skalpes, ij daggers.
It^m v prophets cappes.
It^m vj capes of furre and one of velvet.
It^m iij jyrkyns, iiij sloppes for devils.
It^m iiij shepehokes, iiij whyppes.
It^m a red gowne of sage.
It^m xxiij Bredes [beards] and xxj hares [wigs].
It^m a fornet of blew velvet with borders.
It^m a mantell of red bawdekyn wth sleves.
It^m iij jerkes of red bawdekyn with sleves,

This list is followed by entries as to the payment of 20s. to the minstrels on two occasions, in addition to 10s. for a trumpeter, 3s. 4d. for a flute-player, and 5s. for a man "playeing on ye Drome." There were also further charges for their meat and drink. The plays were evidently committed to writing, for in 1562 one Christopher received 2s. for writing out seven parts. The cost of ironwork for making "the hell" was 4s. Amongst various other entries of this year, one Lawrence received 4d. "for watchinge in the Churche when the Temple was a drying." This evidently refers to the drying of the paint on a part of the scenery. It is quite clear from various entries that the play was performed in the nave of the church on Sunday and on the following Monday. Watchers remained in the church on Sunday night to guard the scaffold. Mention is made of a third play during this year. Our Lord was evidently one of the characters, for John Wright received 16d. "for makynge a cotte of lether for Christe." Another man received 7s. for "payntenge the Jeiants and the pajeaunte and writtinge the plaiers names."

From various entries of the years 1563–76 it appears that the churchwardens of Chelmsford received a considerable addition to their income from letting out the players' garments for the use of other parishes. Thus in 1563 they received from the men of Colchester "for the here of our garments" 53s. 4d. on two different occasions; from Billericay, 26s. 8d. and 20s.; from Walden, in Hertfordshire, for the hire of three gowns, 10s.; from Stratford, £3 6s. 8d.; from Little Baddow, 26s. 8d., and from the children of Baddow, 6s. 8d. In subsequent years substantial payments were received for the same reason from Boreham, Langham, Witham, Colchester, Brentwood, Writtle, and Hatfield. In 1570 the Earl of Sussex's players paid 26s. 8d. for the hire of the players' garments of Chelmsford. Occasionally the Chelmsford players performed outside their own parish, particularly at Braintree and Maldon, and possibly the larger sums mentioned above included the hire and expenses of some of the actors as well as their properties.

We believe that the performance of miracle plays within a church was an exceptional custom in Elizabethan days, and it is singular to find it so prevalent at Chelmsford and in this part of Essex. The last performance in Chelmsford church occurred in

1576, and from an entry of that year it would appear that there was probably some little disturbance. Eightpence was paid to one Drane "for mendinge of x broken holes in the church windowes which was done at the late playe." Various other players' extracts from these accounts appear in Karl Pearson's *Chances of Death* (1897), ii. 415–23.

In Bentley's MS Book (1564), citing from old wardens' accounts of St. Andrew, Holborn, occurs this passage:—

19, 21 & 22 Henry VII. The wardens and parishioners were accustomed yearly to make plays in convenient places, and great shooting matches among the parishioners; as also to keep ales or drinkings, with barrels of ale given by some well-disposed parishioners to the church, and all to the intent that the overplus and gain thereof might be received and converted to the use of the church works, as appeared at large in many accounts.

1565 (*St. Katherine Cree*). Receyved of Hugh Grieves for lycens geven to certen players to playe their enterludes in the churche-yarde, from the feast of Easter, 1565, untyll the feaste of Seynt Michaell Tharchengell next evenynge, every holye daye, to the use of the parysche . . . . . . xxvij s. viij d.

Receyved of Rychard Dyckenson for lycens geven to hym to make scaffoldes in the churche-yard; and the paryshe to have the thyrde penny; bearying no charge for that he doth receyve of the persons that dothe stand upon the scaffolde for 3 holy daies in the Easter weeke, 1565 : to the use of ye paryshe . vj s. viij d.

Receyved more of Richard Dyckenson, for Lent Sunday 1565, and for Maye Daye followinge, and the Sunday after, beinge the syxt of Maye, for the thyrde peny for those persons that stoode upon the scaffolde within the churche-yarde, to the use of the paryshe, the some of xj s. viij d.

Receyved of Richard Dykenson, for vj Sonday and iij holy dayes, reckonnynge the 13th day of Maye, 1565, and endynge the 18 daye of June and iij holy dayes, Ascension daye and ij holy dayes in Whytson weeke; of the wyche 3 of these dayes, the players did not paye for the thyrde peny of the Persons that stode upon ye scaffolde in ye churche-yard to the use of the paryshe 5s.

An entry in the wardens' accounts of Bewdley in 1572 records the payment of 6s. 8d. to "the quenes plaiers in the Churche."

A King and Queen of the Summer Games were chosen annually at St. Ives, Cornwall. It was the King's duty to hand over his receipts for the relief of the poor; this amounted in 1575 to 14s. 6d. Plays were acted apart from the games; they were repeated for several days, and appear to have been popular in the district. The following are the receipt entries in 1575:—

Received the firste daye of the playe	. . . .	xij s.
Received the seconde daye wch amounteth to	.	j li. xij s. ij d.
,, third ,, ,,	.	iiij li. x s. xij d.
,, fourth ,,		j li. xix s. ij d.
,, 5. ,,		. iij li. ij s.
,, sixt ,,		. iij li. j d.
More received for drincke money	. . . .	. j s. ij d.
More received of William Trimrith in the churche veard whiche amounteth to	. . . . .	j li. xv s. ij d.
Received for drinck money after the playe	. . . .	ij d.
Pd to the pypers for ther wages (town).		

In Dyde's *History of Tewkesbury* (1803) it is stated that the churchwardens' accounts for 1578 have an entry—"Payd for the players geers, six sheepskins for Christs Garments." Also in an inventory of 1585 occur "eight heads of hair for the apostles, and ten beards, and a face or vizer for the devil."

Among the church goods of St. Columb Major were certain stage properties as well as costumes for Morris dancers. The list of parish goods for 1585 includes " v coates for dancers, a Fryer's Coate, 24 dansing belles, a Streamer of Red Moccado and locram, six yards of white wollen clothe." In 1585 the coats for dancers were reduced to three. From an entry of 1595, when 2s. was paid " for hedding three Moryse pykes," it would appear that the parish armour was lent to the stage when not required for more serious use. Sometimes the stage wardrobe of St. Columb was lent to other parishes; thus in 1588 the wardens received 18d. " for the lone of the Robbyn hoodes clothes," and in 1595 there is an entry to the effect that " Thomas Brabin hathe brought in the dancyng Coate."

The church books of Great Marlow, Bucks, beginning in 1592-3, are cited in Nichols' *Illustrations of Manners* (1797); they show the retention of play-acting in the church towards the close

CHURCH OR PARISH PLAYS—CHURCH-ALES

of Elizabeth's reign, and of the keeping of players' properties in the days of James I.

>   1595. Received of players for playinge in the church lofte .   2 4
>   Payde to one for the carrying of the morrys coate to Maydenhed . . . .   4d.
>   1608. Among goods belonging to the church, fyve payr of garters of bells, fyve coats, fower fethers.
>   1612. Received of the churchwardens of Bysham, loane of our Morris coats and bells 2 6

The accounts of a church-ale at Wootton, Hants, in 1610 show that the proceedings included a play—

>   Receipts for the Kingale [as followeth for the Sunday after Midsumer Day, Juni xxix, 1600.
>   Rec. at the first table . . . . . . xv s.
>   „ seconde table . . . . . ij s. viij d.
>   „ „ thirde „ . . . . . . xj s. ij d.
>   „ „ fowerth „ . . . . . . x s. iij d.
>   „ „ fifte „ . . . . . viij s. iiij d.
>   „ „ sixth „ . . . . . xj s.
>   „ the same day at the tronke . . . . . ij s. x d.
>   „ for pewtre the same day . . . . x s. vij d.
>   „ out of the Churchowse for drink thear . . xij d.
>   „ for the felles . . . . . . xvj d.
>   „ more out of the Churchowse . . . . viij d.
>   Summe . iij li. xiij s. ix d.

The receipts on the following Sunday, 6th of July, amounted to £4 2s. The payments for this King-ale, extending over two Sundays, included 23s. 10d. "To the minstrills for minstrelsie" and 2s. "to Whitburn for his play." The meat purchased were three calves, five lambs, three sheep, and a couple of chickens. Fish, eggs, butter, fruit, and spice were also purchased, as well as malt and hops for brewing the ale.

Robin Hood and Maid Marian were frequent characters in May and summer games, and often took the part of "king" and "queen" of the revels. They were usually accompanied by Little John, Friar Tuck, and "the whole joyous fellowship of Sherwood Forest." Expenses with regard to their equipment appear with considerable frequency in wardens' accounts, whilst the collections or gatherings made by Robin and his merry men often appear on the other side of the balance-sheet. On the question of this celebrated outlaw, see Child's *Ballads*; also Chambers' *Mediæval Stage*, vol. i. 171–81.

The Robin Hood gatherings were for many years by far the most popular of the six parish gilds or fraternities of Croscombe, Somerset. Thus in 1480–1 the "Roben Hode money" amounted to 40s. 4d. In 1483–4 "Ric Willes was Roben Hode and presents in for yere past xxiij s."; the next highest offering at that audit was 9s. 6d. from the maidens. At the audit of 1486–7 "Robyn Hode" presented to the wardens £3 6s. 8½d.; the maidens came next with 20s. 4d. In 1490–1 Robin offered 50s. and the next highest was 25s. In 1500–1 there was a considerable drop— "Camyth in Robyn Hode and Lytyll John and presentyd in xv s."; but the next highest that year was 4s. 4d. from the young men. The audit of 1505–6 shows that 53s. 4d. was "presented in of the spoil of Roburt Hode and hys company," whilst the maidens came second with 17s. 5d. In 1510–1 Robin's contribution was £3 6s. 8d. and the next highest only 16s. 10d. The last appearance of Robin in the Croscombe accounts was at the audit of 1526–7, when he and his company of archers presented the wardens with the handsome contribution of £4 0s. 4d.

The Robin Hood references in the accounts of St. Laurence, Reading, are numerous.

1499. Rec of the gaderyng of Robyn Hod	xix s.
1502. Rec of the May play callyd Robyn Hod on the payne day .	vj s.
For ij^c (200) Coverays (badges or ribbon) .	viij d.
For makyng up of the maydens banner cloth .	viij d.
1504. Rec of the gaderyng of Robin Hod x busshells malt (for brewing church ale)	v s.
Rec of the gaderyng of same Robyn Hod j busshell of whete	xij d.
Rec' of the gaderyng of the seid Robyn Hod in money .	xlix s.
Payed to an harper on the church holyday . .	iiij d.
Payed for bred and ale to Robyn Hod and hys company the 5 day	iiij d.
Payed for a cote to Robyn Hod . .	v s. iiij d.
Payed to a Taberer on Philips Day and Jacob for his wagis mete and drink and bed	viij d.
For fellyng and bryngyng home of the kow set in the m'cat place for settyng up of the same mete and drynk . .	viij d.

CHURCH OR PARISH PLAYS—CHURCH-ALES

1505. For Robin Hods cote and he's house.   vj s. vij d.
     Rec of the maydens gadering at whitsontyde at the tre at
       the church dore, clerely . . . . *. ij s. xj d.
     For wyne to Robyn Hod of Handley and his company . vj s.
     To the taberer . . . . vj s.
1506. For a supper to Robyn Hod and his company when he
       came from Fynchamsted . . . . . xviij d.
1508. Rec' of the gadering of Robyn Hod pley   xvij s. x d.
1510. Rec' on Seynt Phylypp and Jacob day for ij stondyngs at
       the church porch . . . . . . vj d.
1529. For Fyve ells of Canves for a cote for made Maryon   xvij d. ob.
     To the carpyntre for ij dayes to make a ladder of the May
       poole and for hys mete and drynk . . . . xiiij d.
1557. For the yeough tree . . . . . iiij d.
     For fetchinge the summar pole . . . . ij d.
     For a breakfast for the yonge men . . . . xvj d.
     For a quartre of veale and quartre of lambe   iij s. iiij d.
1504. (*Kingston-upon-Thames*). Paid for ye mensterell apon may
       day, iiij d. ; for their drink, j d.
     Painting the banner of Robin Hood, iij d. ; a gown for the
       lady, viij d. ; bells, xij d.
1509. Rec'd for the gaderyng of ye Kynge at Whitsontyde, 19s.
       and at hoctyde, 17s.
     while the gathering at the Kyngham [1] and the Robyn Hode
       produced 4 marks, 20d.
     Paid for mete and drynke for ye mor^s (morris) daunsers,
       ij d., and on Corpus Christi day, iiij d.
     Sylver paper for the mor^s daunce . . . . viij d.
     Paid to Robert Neyll for goyng to Wyndesor for Master
       Doctors horse, ageynes the Kyngham day   iiij d.
     to a loborer for beryng home of ye gere after ye Kyngham
       was done . . . . j d.
     For vj peyre of shone [shoes] for ye mor^s daunsers   iiij s.
     Thomas tothe for half Robyn hod^s cote   vij s. vj d.
     bote hire going up to Waltar Kyngham . . . x d.
     for Kendall for Robyn hod^s cote . . . xv d.
     Rec^d at ye Kyngham . . . . . . iiij s.
     Robyn hod^s gaderyng . . . . . iiij marks
     Paid out of ye churche box at Walton Kyngham   iij s. vj d.
     Paid out of ye churche box at Sonbury Kyngham . xxij d.
1510. Paid for Robyn Hods cote and for littell Johnys cote and
       for ye frer^s [friar's] cote . . . . xxx s. vj d.

---

[1] Kingham is probably a corruption of "King Game."

1514. Rec^d for Robyn hods gaderyng		xij s.
Robyn hod gaderyng at Croyden		ix s. iiij d.
1538-40 (*St. Andrew Hubbard*). Resceyved of mestres maryan		xiij s. iiij d.
Resceyved in the Churche of the players		xij d.
1566 (*Abingdon*). For setting up Robin Hoodes bowere		18d.

Mayday and Whitsuntide were usually the occasions of festivities under the control of the wardens, the profits or gatherings being handed to the church funds. Morris, Maypole, hobbyhorse, and other kinds of dancing, with much minstrelsy and music, were common forms of amusement at both these festivals. At Reading it was customary to act the King Play at one or other of these seasons; it represented the adoration of the Magi, traditionally true kings; their heads were eventually enshrined at Cologne, hence described as Kyngs of Colen. The chief part of the drama took place within the church, the Star of the Epiphany being displayed from the rood-loft, as at St. Margaret's, Westminster.

This play must not be confused with Mayday or Whitsuntide frolics, which were sometimes called "King's Revels," the name being taken from the king and queen, or lord and lady, chosen to superintend the Ale and its accompanying sports.

King's revels brought income to the wardens of Croscombe on three occasions, namely, in 1476, 1498, and 1504. A king's revel was held on a large scale at Yatton in 1534.

1499 (*St. Laurence, Reading*). For horse mete to the horssys for the Kyngs of Colen on May Day		vj d.
To mynstrells the same day		xij d.
1503. Rec' of the Kyng play		xj s.
1508. For carrying of a bough for the King play at Whitsontyde		iiij d.
To the taberer at Whyssontyde		iiij s. viij d.
1515. For a Kylthenkyn of bere agenst Wytsontyde		xvj d.
For a dosen of good ale and iij galons of penyale		xx d.
For carriage of the tree at Witsontyde		vj d.
1517. Of the yong men for the gatheryng at the Kyng play		xxiij s.
For the tree of the Kyng play late stondyng in the m'catt place		xij d.
1519. To Thomas Taberer for the Kyng pley at Whisontide		x s.
1539. Forwarding the sepulc' and for Colen		x d.
1541. Rec of the Kyng game this yere		iij li. viij s.
1557. The churchwardens gatheringe at ye Kingale in the Whytsontyde at the church ale suppars		xlviij s.

CHURCH OR PARISH PLAYS—CHURCH-ALES 285

1483 (*St. Margaret, Westminster*). For the Corde to the Sterre
in the rode lofte . . . iiij d.
For amending and dressing of the Sterre . . . ij s. vj d.
1484. For hanging up of the sterre in the rode lofte vj d.
1563 (*Wing, Bucks*). Receaved of the May ale . . . lj s. vj d.
1564. Item, Resavyd of the Maye ale . . iij li. ix s. vij d.
Memorandum that this yere at Whytsontyde was chosen for the Lorde John Taylor of Ascot, and Catheryn Chapman of Crofton. Note—an ordre mentioned in the end of this boke for the Lord and Lady at Wytsontyde made this yere, 1565.
[The order here referred to is as follows, viz.:—]
Memorandum that S. Wylliam Dormer knyght, ffraunc^s darrell and John a more gentlemen, with the consent of the churche wardens th^r beyng, and the rest of the parryshe have agreed and taken an order that all suche yonge men as shall hereafter by order of the hole parryshe be chosen for to be lorde at Whyts-ontyde for the behafe of the churche, and refuse so to be, shall forfeyt and pay for the use of the churche iij s. iiij d. to be levyed vppon the sayde yonge men and theyr fathers and maysters wherere the just default can be founde, and every mayde refusyng to be lady for the sayd purpose to forfet vnto the sayde vse xx d. to be levyed in lyke order as is before expressed. And yt is provydyd that all suche howses out of the whiche the sayde lordes or ladyes, or one of them, are chosen to stand fre from that purpose and charge for the space of vj yere then next ensuynge. This order was taken, agreed upon, and in this boke noted the xth day of June, in the yere of our lorde god MCCCCCLXV.
1565. Item thys yere above wrytten was harrye kene chosen lorde and refused, and so payde to the Churche . iij s. iiij d.
Robarte Rychardeson the servaunte of Thomas Lygo was then chosen lorde and Kateryn Godfrey lady.
Item receaved of the Maye ale all thynges thereto belonging dis-charged . . . . . iij li. xiiij s. viij d.

The following are some desultory excerpts relative to these two seasons:—

1464-5 (*Tavistock*). To Mayers child for dawnsyng with the hobye hors . . . . ij d.
1499 (*St. Margaret, Westminster*). Rec. of Symand Smyttes wyffe and Lymken barbers wyffe of money by them gadered wyth Vyrgens upon May day . . vj s. vij d. ob.

1518. Given by the children of the May game	xiij d.
1513 (*St. Laurence, Reading*). Payed for a hope (quart pot) for the joyaunt and for ale to the Moreys dawncers on the dedicacon day.	iij d.
Payed to the Mynstrells for iiij days	xxij d.
1529. For bells for the Morece dauncers	iij s. vj d.
For iij batts for the Morece dauncers	vj d.
For iij yerds of bockerham for the morece daunsers	xij d.
1530. For a grosse of bells for the morece dauncers	iij s.
1541. For lyverge and payntyng the mores cotes	xj d.

Payments made to minstrels constantly occur in the later Yatton accounts, usually at Whitsuntide.

1528. To a mynstrelle for pleyng at Saynt James Day	xij d.
1530. To a mynstrell at Wytsonday.	ij s. viij d.
1537. To ye Mynstrells	x s. j d.
1540. For ij mynstrells	vj s. ix d.
1555. Unto Menstrells at Wyttsondaye	v s.
1538–9 (*St. Edmund, Sarum*). The gatherynge of the wyffes dawnce	xiij s. iiij d.
1574. The gatherynge of the wyffes at Whytsontyde for Daunsynge	iij s. iiij d.
1541 (*Culworth*). Payntyng of the hoby horse clothes	iij s.
1557 (*St. Mary, Reading*). Payed to the minstrelles and the hobby horse uppon May day	iij s.
1558 (*St. Martin, Leicester*). Rec^d for the mawrys daunce of the chyldren	iij s.
1594–5 (*St. Thomas, Sarum*). Childrens Daunce	20s. 1d.
1613 (*Lowick, Northants*). Payd to Robert Brandin for makeinge the Maypole	iiij s.

CHURCH-ALES

In discussing Church-ales, it should be remembered that the mediæval Church of England prohibited labour on festal days, and required the people of all classes to attend the church services as a religious obligation. Hence it came about that the Church busied itself to find entertainment and amusement for the assembled people, and thus the Holy Day became identified in the Holiday. Every kind of popular amusement contributed towards the general or particular church funds. "The Church-ale," says Bishop Hobhouse, "was, by the end of the fifteenth century, the most universal churchwardens' resort for eliciting the bounty of the parish." It was a parish feast, a main feature of which was doubtless ale-drinking. The ale and food were usually given and sold for the benefit of the general church fund, or for some particular object, such as the building of the steeple, the providing a bell, or the erection of a rood-loft. Occasionally the ale was held within the church itself even at a comparatively late date. Thus in the St. Laurence, Reading, accounts—

> 1506. To Macrell for makyng clene of the Church agaynst the day
> of drynking in the seid Church . . iiij d.
> For flesh spyce and bakyng of pasteys agaynst the said
> drynkyng . . . . . . ij s. ix d. ob.
> For ale at the same drynkyng . . . . xviij d.
> For mete and drynke to the Taberer . . ix d.

For the most part, however, the ale was held in the church house, a building close to the church, erected or bought for the purpose of becoming the focus of the social life of the parish. Bishop Hobhouse is probably right in thinking that its origin was the providing a place for the baking of the holy loaf, and possibly, too, of the altar wafers. Afterwards brewing gear was added for providing what was sometimes called the "holy ale" of Christian fellowship. The wardens sometimes added to the church income by letting the oven and the brewing vessels for the use of private persons. Eventually the church house was usually of sufficient size for the entertainment of large numbers of general parishioners or members of particular gilds, or of anyone wishing to help in a certain church object. With the leave of the wardens, one or more parishioners proclaimed an ale (termed in churchwardens' Latin a *taberna* or tavern), and the inhabitants were generally ready to flock to it and bring their contributions in kind. At the church house were held Bride-ales, to celebrate the wedding of those too poor to provide their own wedding feast; Clerk-ales, to find the stipend of the parish clerk; or Bid-ales, to help some poor man in trouble. As they grew in size, parishioners were sometimes enabled to extend the hospitality of the church houses to neighbouring parishes at the times of their dedication or other special festivals, as can be shown from extant accounts of Somersetshire, Cornwall, Derbyshire, and Norfolk. These parish houses were usually well supplied with utensils.

This be perselles that longyth to the Cherche howse (Yatton) the yere A.D. mcccclxxxxij delyveryd to the Wardens that yere.

Imprmis a chettyll	
It. ij grett crocks	It. ij kyve vates
,, ij lyttl crocks	,, ij trowys (troughs)
,, iiij pannys	,, ix stands
,, a botum for a panne	,, barellys
,, a brandyre	,, xxj trendyllys (trendles)
v tun vats	,, vj borde clothis

Entries as to the purchase of wooden bowls and cups and platters or trenchers are frequent in wardens' accounts up and down the country. Even the young folk were anxious to keep their church house well equipped.

> 1583 (*Stanford, Berks*). There was brought to the churche this yeere fowre newe platters and too newe potyngers the w[ch] were of the colection and provision of the young youthes of this Toune such as were betwyxt x years of age and xiij haveing one bushell of the churche whayte towards theyre charges.

The revelry and excess that occasionally attended these church-ales probably helped to their gradual extinction; but that their influence was often towards innocent social enjoyment and levelling of too rigid class distinctions cannot possibly be doubted. Stubbes, in his *Anatomie of Abuses* (1583), attacks these ales with his usual puritanical virulence. Against this abuse should be set the absolutely opposite judgment of Carew as to Cornish ales, and of Aubrey as to those of Wilts in the next century. Moreover, the Bishop of Bath and Wells (William Piers) wrote warmly and with some eloquence in favour of these ales, then rapidly being suppressed, in 1633, to Archbishop Laud.[1]

The early accounts of Yatton, Somerset, show the constant dependence of the wardens on this means of raising funds.

> 1446. Received of the Wardenys of the ale making at Whytteson day . . . . iiij li. xx d.

---

[1] All these authorities and others are cited in full in *Hieronima Anglicana*, iii. 129-137. It ill becomes Churchmen of the twentieth century, with their bazaars, fêtes, refreshments, whist-drives, and every variety of dramatical and musical entertainments, to speak slightingly of the church-ales of our forefathers; and certainly the old ales were never disgraced by imitations of palmistry and fortune-telling, which are contrary to the laws of God and man.

CHURCH OR PARISH PLAYS—CHURCH-ALES

1447. Received of the Wardenys of making of Ale at Wyttsundey to the cherche	iiij li.
1448. For a taverne that ys made of ye Church Ale	v marcs xj d.
1451. Pro taberna servicie in festo Pentecoste	iij li.
1464. For vij tavernys made at the Churche house	ix s. iiij d.
1509. Receyvd of Saynt Jamys Ale	iij mark iiij s.
1527. For ij dosyn and a halfe drynkyng bowls and a dosyn and a halfe of mate dysses and iiij dosyn trenchers and a ladyle	xvj s.
1546. For our taverne Ale at Whytsondey	iiij li. xiiij s. iiij d.
1547. Our taverne Ale at Wysontyde	v li. xx d.

In the sixteenth century it became customary at Yatton to hold three parish ales annually,—namely, at Whitsuntide, at Midsummer Day, and at Hocktide in the second week after Easter week. In 1524-5 the three ales realised £23, and in 1547-8 the great sum of £24 2s.

The receipts from ales of the Somersetshire parish of Tintinhull were on a much smaller scale. The ale of 1443 only realised 2s. The accounts of 1447-8 show an ale profit on St. Margaret's Day of 12s. 1d., and on the feast of SS. Philip and James of 13s. 4d. These two ales were subsequently of annual occurrence.

Three "drynkys made by the chyrchrevys" of Shipdham, Norfolk, in 1551, produced a profit of 38s. 4d.

The country parish of Cratfield, Suffolk, was exceptionally dependent on church-ales for funds for the general sustentation of the church. In 1490 a *Potatio ecclesiastica* (the only time we have met with this Latinised form) was held on Passion Sunday, at Whitsuntide and on All Saints Day, and there were two others of private origin. In 1493 "churche-ales" were held on Passion Sunday, Whitsunday, in harvest, and on All Souls Day, and a fifth for Thomas Kebyll. These five also produced profits of £2 13s. 11d. for the church expenses; and the whole receipts for that year were only £3 16s. 9d. The receipts for 1494 were £3 15s. 7d., and the whole of that sum, save 7s. 1d., came from six ales. Other days on which parish ales were held about this period were the Dedication day, first Sunday in Lent, second Sunday in Lent, Midlent Sunday, and Candlemas.

There are frequent entries as to ales in the Bassingbourne, Cambs, accounts. In 1497-8 ten ales were held, which realised

£14 7s. 3½d., towards the cost and carriage of a new treble bell from London.

Rec' att the Fryste may ale and all charges borne	xviij s. ij d.
Rec' att an Ale next after the seid may ale	vij s. xj d. ob.
Rec' att one other Ale in the Feste off the transfiguracion off our lorde ihesu criste	x s. ij d. ob.
Rec' att an ale the next sondaye after the Assumpcion off our blyssid ladye	vj s. ij d.
Rec' att an Ale the next Sondey after Mich'daye	vij s. viij d.
Rec' att an ale that day xiiij[th] next after	v s. ij d.
Rec' atte one othir ale on the next Sunday aftyr the Feste of seynt Kataryn the virgin and martyr	vj s. viij d.
Rec' att an ale on Rogacion sondaye	vj s. x d.
Rec' att the laste maye ale with the towne and beynes obitt, as with bred and ale	xxvj s. viij d.
Rec' att an ale on Mydlenton sonday	vj s. xj d. ob.
In losse off evyll money taken at the may ale	viij s.

Transcripts had been made of church-ale entries from Stoke Courcy and Croscombe, Somerset; St. Nicholas, Warwick; Wimborne, Dorset; Great Marlow, Bucks; All Saints, Derby, etc. etc., but lack of space forbids their insertion. Room must, however, be found for details of the festivities in two other parishes.

A Whitsuntide church-ale at Seal, Surrey, in 1592, is set forth with much circumstance in the wardens' book.

Charges laide out concerning our Churchayle

In. primis for iij Bushells of wheatte	xiij s.
It. for ix Barrells of Beere	xl s.
It. for veele and lame	xxij s. ix d.
It. for a loade of woode and the carriadg	v s. vj d.
It. for spice and frutte	vij s. j d.
It. for Butter, Creame, and mylke	iiij s.
It. fer clettes and nailes to the smythe	xiiij d.
It. for Gune powder	iiij s.
It. for more wheatte	viij s. ij d.
It. paide to the musitions for v days play	xx s.
It. to the drumer	ij s.
It. for more Butter and Creame	ij s. iij d.
It. for more spice and frutte	iij s. ij d.
It. to Goodman Shrubbs wyfe for helpinge att the tyme	xij d.
It. for meatt and Beere for the musitions and other helpers	viij s. iij d.

CHURCH OR PARISH PLAYS—CHURCH-ALES

The accounts of the church-ale of 1611, which lasted for four days, are still more elaborate in detail. The meat on that occasion included three calves, a fat sheep, and eleven lambs.

> P^d the Vice, otherwise the Footle . . . . . v s.
> Pd for silke points and laces . . . . . . xij s.

The church-ale was the great source of income at Mere, Wilts. In 1557 the profits were £12 0s. 6d.; in 1567, £6 16s. 9½d.; in 1574, £7 0s. 11d.; and in 1578, £7 6s. 10d. In 1579 the ale was superseded by a definite collection for the church and for the payment of the clerks' wages; it amounted that year to £16 18s. 4d.

> 1566. For Tynnen spoones and trenchers and potts bought to thuse of the Church . . . . . . vij s.
> 1567. John Watts the soone of Thomas Watts is appointed to be Cuckowe King this next yeare according to the old order, because hee was Prince the last yeare. And Thomas Barnerd thunger is elected Prince for this next yeare. And because John Watts hath ben long sick hit is agreed that if hee be not able to serve at the tyme of the Church ale, that then John Cowend shall serve and be King in his place for this yeare. [Like appointments up to 1578.]

In 1588, however, the "collection" gave way to the old church-ale, the profits from which amounted to £14 2s. 6d. In 1593 "there was not Church ale made nor other collecion for the repayre of the Church." The ale was resumed in 1594, when a profit was made of £9. The ale profits of 1605 amounted to £15 6s., and in 1607 to the great sum of £23 6s. 8d. The last ale entry occurs in 1613, after which a definite rating system was adopted.

CHAPTER XX

LIVE STOCK—VERMIN

Gifts of Live Stock: Sheep, Cattle, Pigs, Bees—Bassingbourn, Cambs Short extracts—Common Bulls—Bees, Wax, and Honey—Crow Nets—"Noyfull Fowles and Vermyn"—Sparrow heads—St. Neots, Cornwall—Sidbury, Devon —Eastington, Gloucestershire—Short extracts—Birds in Churches—Rats in Churches—The Dog-whipper—Dog-tongs—A Dog Wicket

Live Stock

THE gifts of live stock to the Church were frequent. Occasionally such gifts or bequests were speedily sold and the cash received entered in the accounts. But in other cases they were retained and farmed out at so much the year by the wardens, pledges being expected for their safe custody. In some instances the sheep and cows belonging to the church or assigned to particular altars were numerous. Another form of live stock were hives of bees; offerings of this kind doubtless originated with a desire to provide pure wax for altar lights. Now and again the wardens sold honey. In addition to the parishes from whose accounts extracts are made, there are many particulars of sheep at Bardwell, Suffolk; Culworth, Northants; Stanford, Berks; Munden, Herts; and St. Michael, Bath. Also of cows at Worfield, Salop; and at Culworth, and Pulham St. Mary Magdalen, Norfolk; at the last of these there was a herd of 40. Pigs occur in the Morebath, Devon, accounts; and bees at Morebath and Culworth.

1407–8 (*Tavistock*). Letting of an ox xvj d., of . . . cows ij s. iiij d.
1411–2. Letting of cattle iiij s. viij d.; sale of wool ij s.; sale of four cows xlviij s. vj d.; sale of ten goats xij s. iiij d.

Bassingbourn, Cambs, was largely dependent for its church income on the farming of cows.

1478. M⁴ that Alis Rooge and William Rooge gaff and wyllyd a Cowe to kepe with their obyt yerly one daye in the yer the whiche Cowe the Chyrchwardens shuld be the betteres of the whiche John a Condall hath in his bandes and yerly keping the seid Obytt.

In 1515 the wardens received 3s. 1d. as rent for "ij mylchebestes." In the same year it was covenanted that one George Richardson should have—

> a cow of Mʳ Dalyrons obett for to pay thatt yere sche hath a cawyth iij s., and when sche hath non xx d., deliveryd at the annunciacion of our lady day, to pa by the halfe yer.

Among the receipts of 1519–20 were 3s. 1d. for "ij milche keyse," and three separate payments of 2s. for "one milche kowe." In 1524–5 there were four like payments of 2s. each, and two of 3s. 4d. each. In the same year the wardens bought a cow for 60s.

The wardens of Stoke Courcy, Somerset, made a profit out of a few parish cows, *temp.* Henry VII and VIII; 20d. was the usual fee for a year's hire of a cow.

> 1511 (*Pilton, Somerset*). Ric. Sergeant and Willyam Canard Wardens of the churche Key (Kine) a compte for iij yers.
> Friste for the hyre of vj key ij yer . . . . xij s.
> Item for the iij yer the hire of the key . . . vj s.
> Over all charges remaneth to the chirche stocke . . iiij s.
> The names of them that hath the key to hyr wt ther bonnd and plegge.
> Fyrste John Elyns j cow; Item William Canard of East Compton j cowe, plegge John Canard; Item Johan Knoll a cowe, plegge Johan Jennard; Item John Dunkerton a cowe, plegge Johan Barwn; Item Johan Brouse of Pultun a cowe, plegge Ric Sergeant; Wyllyam Knoll a cowe, plegge Wyllam Canard; Stephans Aylwarde for a cowe, plege Wylelm Aylwarde-at-Crosse; John Tannysende of West Compton a cowe, plege Edwarde Holdson; Rob. Stoke a cowe precid xiij s. iiij d.

In the 1543–4 accounts of Elmsett, Suffolk, there is a list of thirteen cows bestowed upon the parish, with the name of the donor and chief object of the gift, and also the name of the then farmer. They were all given to sustain lights "afore oʳ lady in the chauncell," "afore oʳ lady in the north syde of the churche," "in the Rode Lofte," "before Seynt Peter," or "to fynd the pascall and syngyng light." There is a list of nine parish cows under the year 1564.

>1511 (*St. Edmund, Sarum*). Of Master Chasey for the hire of xx shepe wiche John Ludlow did geve to the Mayntenyng of Seynt Sebastians light . . . . . vj s.
>1554 (*Worksop*). Rec. of John Roynes for xiij shepe and iij lambes . . . . xxvij s.

The Hants parish of Wootton had a considerable stock of sheep and cows. Twelve sheep were given to the church by ten donors in 1558. Among the receipts for 1600 were rents paid for four cows at 12d. each, and for twenty-seven sheep at 2½d. each. In 1623 it was agreed that they which had any of the church stock were henceforth to bring it to the churchwardens at any feast of All Saints, "or else give a pledge for the securitie of the Churche."

>1560 (*Weyhill, Hants*). The Stocke of the Church
>John North iiij shepe . . . . . xvj d.
>John Helliar for v shepe . . . . xij d.
>John Tarrant j shepe . . . . . . iiij d.
>John Knyght and John Tarrant a li. of wax p'annum Robt Manfeld hath in his landes of shepe viij the pryce of any shepe ij s. iiij d., or the shepe at the paryshe plesure and to pay for the viij shepe by the year iij s. iiij d.

The parish of Spelsbury, Oxon, held a large stock of sheep in the second quarter of the sixteenth century, termed in the church wardens' accounts *Oves Ecclesie*. They were hired out in lots of from 20 to 4 for periods varying from one to five years. A rental was paid of from 20d. to 16d. per sheep, but usually the former scale. Sureties were required for the due return of the sheep. The number of sheep hired in the first year of the accounts was 153. Afterwards they dwindled in numbers; they disappear from the accounts after 1556.

Funds for church expenses at Pittington, Durham, from 1584, were almost entirely raised from the profits of a flock of sheep, called "The Church Shepe," during the sixteenth century and the first quarter of the seventeenth century. These sheep were pastured gratis on the several farms, one sheep to be fed for every 4 rental. A special rate was only resorted to for some particular purpose on a few occasions. The accounts show year by year the receipts for sheep, lambs, and wool, and the disbursements and purchases of stock. But in 1674 the church flock, being in a decayed state, was sold for £6 3s. 2d.; it then consisted of six wethers, ten ewes, and five lambs. Thenceforth the system of regular rates was adopted.

Occasionally sheep were given or bequeathed to the wardens, and almost immediately sold. Thus at St. Columb Major two sheep were given by different donors, and were sold respectively for 3s. and 2s. 6d. In 1556 "one ew sheepe" was left by will to the church; it was sold for 4s.

> 1631 (*St. Mabyn, Cornwall*). For pitch tar and tallow for signe-
> ing ye Parish sheepe . . . . . 7s. 6d.

The keeping of a parish bull, even when there was no stock of parish kine, was by no means an exceptional incident, but was only part of the general semi-communistic principles upon which the unenclosed lands of England (*i.e.* by far the larger portion of the soil) were then, and for long afterwards, held. We have met with entries relative to the parish bull in old parish accounts of Allestree, Marston-on-Dove, and Tickenhall, and, in short, in all the old accounts of Derbyshire parishes that we have searched. At Eckington there was a parish boar.

> 1592 (*Repton*). It. given to Rycharde Prince for Recevynge the
> bull and looking to hym . . . . . j d.

At Bassingbourn, Cambs, the "comyn bull" was sold for 9s. in 1503-4, and for 12s. in 1515. A common bull was bought for 7s. in 1507, and another in 1500 for 10s. 9d. A "town bull" repeatedly occurs in the Culworth, Northants, accounts.

In 1458 the wardens of Tintinhull paid 3½d. for a beehive. Thomas Trychay, in 1529, "gave unto the store of Jesus and to the store of Saint Sidwell" a swarm of bees to maintain a taper before them in the church of Morebath.

> 1500 (*Worfield, Salop*). Pro duobus apiaribus (hives)   ij d.

In 1603 the parish of St. Columb Major owned "a but of bees with three swarmes with Mr. heugh Boscawen." In the following year Mr. Boscawen held four butts and had to give to the wardens an "inventory indented" to show that two butts were the parish property. In 1616 the parish sold honey to the extent of 12d. The wardens of Culworth and Fordwich also profited by the sale of honey from church hives.

In 1532 it was enacted (24 Hen. VIII, c. 10), in consequence of the "innumerable number" of rooks, crows, and choughs, that every parish, township, or hamlet was to provide itself with a net for their destruction, to maintain it for ten years, and to present it annually before the manor court steward. Twopence was to be paid for every 12 old crows, rooks, or choughs by the owner or occupier of the manor or lands.

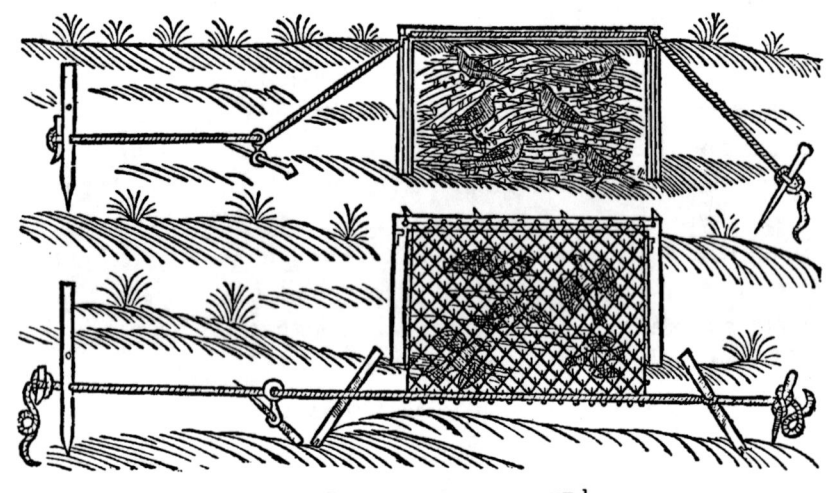

THE CROWE NET SET OR BENT [1]

In 1566 it was provided (8 Eliz. c. 15), in an Act for the preservation of grain, that the last-named Act as to rook nets be renewed. It was further provided that the churchwardens, with other six parishioners, should assess holders of land or tithe for the destruction of "Noyfull Fowles and Vermyn" to provide a fund to reward every person bringing "any Heades of old Crowes, Choughes, Pyes, or Rookes, for the heades of every three of them a penny, and for the Heades of everie syxe yong Crowes, etc., a penny, and for everie Syxe Egges of anye of them unbroken a penny,

[1] An exceedingly rare small 4to book, by L. M(ascall), was printed in 1590, termed *Sundrie Engines and Trappes*. It is full of woodcuts, from which this drawing of the parish Crow Net and the three following cuts of traps are taken.

and lykewise for everye twelve Stares (starlings) Heades a penny." Such heads and eggs were to be brought before the wardens and assessors at least once a month, and a time of account was to be made in writing as to what money had been paid for them, and also for "the Heades of suche other ravenyng Byrdes and Vermin. For everie Heade of Martyn Hawkes, Furskytte, Moldekytte, Busarde, Schagge, Carmerat, or Ryngtale (hen harrier), two pence; and for every two Egges of them one penny; for evry Iron (Heron) or Osprayes Head, fower pence; for the Heade of everie Woodwall (Green Woodpecker), Pye, Jaye, Raven or Kyte, one penny; for the Head of everie Byrde which is called the Kinges Fysshr, one penny; for the Head of everie Bulfynche or other Byrde that devowreth the blowth of Fruite, one penny; for the Heades of every Foxe or Gray, twelve pence; and for the Head of everie Fitchere, Polcatte, Wesell, Stote, Fayre bade or Wilde Catte, one penny; for the Heades of everie Otter or Hedgehogges, two pence; for the Heades of everie three Rattes or twelve Myse, one penny; for the Heades of everie Moldewarpe or Wante one halfpenny." The heads and eggs, after account had been taken of them, were "to be burned, consumed, or cut in sunder before Churchwardens and Taxours."

This Act was expressly renewed in 1572 (14 Eliz. c. 11), and again in 1598 (39 Eliz. c. 18).

In the Court Leet Records of Leominster for 1566 it is entered that—

> They (the jury) present the churchwardens of the towne to have incurred the penalty of the Statute in that case made and provided for not keeping of such netts as whereby crowes and such other vermine might be destroyed, which devoure and spoyle corne to the greate prejudice of many of the inhabitants within the Borough.

For a short time after the passing of the Elizabethan Act, it would appear that the statutable rate for the destruction of vermin was maintained. This was the case at St. Michael, Bishop Stortford, where Edward Waglley, "Collectore of all man' of veyrmane," received, between 12th April 1569 and the like date 1571, £2 12s. 7½d., in payment for the slaughter of 141 hedgehogs, 53 moles, 6 weasles, 1 polecat, 1476 mice, 80 rats, 202 crows' eggs,

128 pies' eggs, 154 heads of crows and jackdaws, 24 starlings, 5 hawks, and 5 kingfishers.

Five years earlier than the Elizabethan Act, the wardens of Woodbury, Devon, felt justified in charging a vermin destroyer in their accounts.

 1560–1. Paid to John Westcott and John Holwell for a fox nett bought this yere . . . . . iiij s. viij d.

There was evidently no intention in Elizabethan days of suffering the Act to become a dead letter. In 1575 the Shropshire parish of Worfield was "amased by the commysoners at bridge-north for not destroyinge foules and varmynt according to the Statute in that behalf xxx s. x d." As a consequence of this a general massacre took place in the following year of foxes, otters, badgers, polecats, hedgehogs, rats, and mice, as well as of magpies, rooks, crows, choughs, kites, bullfinches, and even of the innocent little titmice.

Rewards for the killing of urchins first appear in the accounts of St. Nicholas, Warwick, in the year 1570, when one John Seynte received 4d. "for kyllynge off serten urchyns," and a further penny "agayne for ye same doynge." In 1501, Henry Winfilde obtained 21 pence for "kyllinge off xxj orchins." The price had risen to twopence a head in 1585. Twelve urchins were paid for at twopence a head in 1589, "according to the statute." Twelve more urchins were slain in 1590, one of them by "Cawdelles wyffe." A few are mentioned almost each year down to 1618, when the numbers amounted to seventeen. In 1622 the number of those slaughtered had grown to thirty-two.

The entries as to the destruction of noxious fowls and vermin are frequent in the parish accounts of Minchinhampton, Gloucestershire; the victims included otters, badgers, foxes, and hedgehogs, also kites, jays, and pies.

 1575. For a crowe nett . . . . . ij s. iiij d.
  To John Boure at Gloucester for the forfuytinge of the statute of noysome fowles and vermyne lost in the tyme of John Hawkes and Thomas Kembridge . x s.
 1596. For a grayes head . . . . . xiij d.
 1634. For the destroying of noysum foule and varments 14s.

The accounts of Cratfield, Suffolk, about 1580, show that payments were made for the heads of buzzards, magpies, "cadowes" (jackdaws), "haupes" (bullfinches), and "hoddespyts" (probably woodpeckers, still locally called woodspites).

The wardens' accounts for 1585-6 enter six payments for "wilde cattes" at 6d. a head.

In 1619 the St. Columb Major accounts record payment to one John Bay for bringing in the heads of three "Auters." In the earlier years of the St. Columb accounts, which begin in 1585, the vermin entries are rare, but towards the end of the seventeenth century the cost sometimes ran up to £2 in the year. The vermin heads were brought into the church. In 1785 the parish "ordered that no more Fitchers Otters and Badgers Heads be paid for by the Church Wardens." In 1795, 3d. a dozen was offered for sparrows.

The amount of vermin destroyed in Cheddar parish, according to the accounts from 1612 to 1674, was simply prodigious. As to the birds, next in number to the sparrows, the payment for which was 1d. a dozen, came the "whoops" or bullfinches, the tariff price for which was 12d. the dozen heads. Choughs were valued at 6d. the dozen heads, and crows, rooks, jays, and "peimaggetes" or "meigetepeys" (magpies) at 12d. the dozen. Polecats and hedgehogs realised 2s. the dozen, whilst badgers and foxes fetched 12d. a head.

The parish accounts of St. Neots, Cornwall, are prolific in vermin entries throughout the seventeenth century. The ten following representative years give a fair idea of the nature and number of the vermin annually destroyed.

Year.	Fitches.	Foxes.	Wild Cats.	Badgers.	Kites.
1621	36	2	...	...	...
1640	28	4		3	
1658	33	9		6	...
1660	32	2		6	15
1670	37	9	...	...	6
1680	53	11	2	.	
1682	44	6	5		...
1687	35	9	22		18
1690	34		2		6
1700	56	...	5	...	...

Fitches, spelt also "fitchets" and "fitchews," was the usual name for polecats, but the term occasionally embraced stoats and weasels. An otter occurs once or twice, and now and again "vautors." Vautors appear to have been sea birds, but they were certainly not vultures, as has been somewhat wildly suggested. Rats to the number of 52 were paid for in 1677, and ten years later 28.

At the end of an inventory of goods in the church of Ragnall, Notts, occurs the following entry:—

If there is likwise a crow nett and a birdnet with the implements thereunto belonging in the hands of John Ashton 1620. These netts still remayneth in the hands of the sayd John Ashton, viz., anno 1621.

The parish accounts of Sidbury, Devon, hold the palm, so far as our experience goes, in the wholesale and varied destruction of fauna, not a few of which were as beautiful as they were harmless. The killing of "woopes," "oops," or bullfinches began in 1622; in 1667 a penny apiece was paid for 45 heads. Six greys or badgers were destroyed in 1622; they are of frequent subsequent occurrence, the reward varying from 6d. to 12d. In 1625 occurs one of the earliest references to sparrow slaughter:—

For the kyllinge of 8c sper' . . . . . . viij d.

Foxes became such a nuisance that in 1651 £2 was paid to a professional "fox catcher"; he was evidently a stranger from a distance, for one Richard Westcott was paid 1s. 2½d. "to show the fox-catcher about the parishe."

In 1667 four greys, two foxes, and seven jays were destroyed; but 1668 was a record year up to that date—the victims included four greys, eight foxes, five hedgehogs, forty-two jays, and fifty-seven "oops." In the following year the greys' heads numbered thirteen. In 1676 the "bag" of vermin was large and varied; it included a polecat, seven stoats, seven greys, a fox, twenty-one hedgehogs, forty-one jays, twenty-five "woops," seven "maggate pyes," sixteen rooks, and a sparrow hawk. The rooks were probably crows; the wardens also spent 7s. this year "for a Rooke net." In the following year two kites were among the victims, and the fashion having once been set in magpies, the wardens received eleven heads, though the reward was only a halfpenny each. In 1678 sixty-one beautiful magpies were slaughtered, and in this year the term rooks was dropped in favour of crows; the magpies' deaths rose to sixty-eight in 1679, and to seventy-five in 1682. The head of a "woodwall," or green woodpecker, obtained a penny. In 1686 the victims included nine kites.

The vermin payments for 1687 had increased so rapidly that the wardens gave up entering exact details in their accounts, and several times made entries such as this: "For diverse more for vermine 6s. 4½d." Foxes by this time had risen considerably in

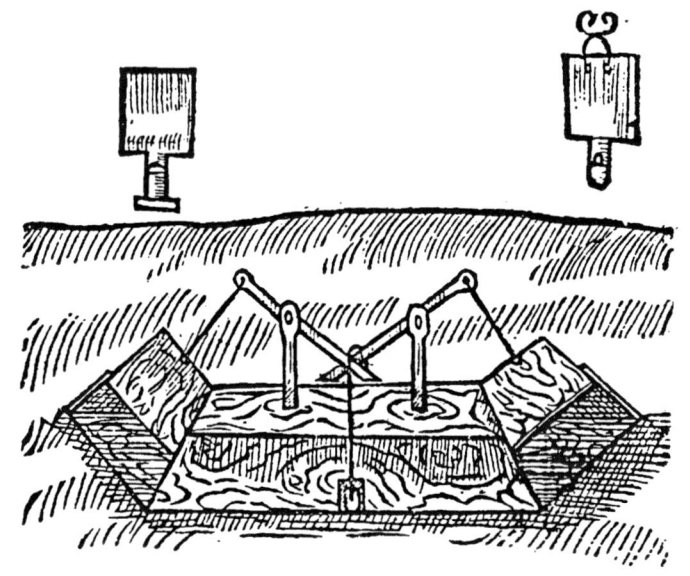

A HATCH TO TAKE POLECATS, AS ALSO OTHER VERMIN

value; 5s. was paid for an old fox and 2s. 6d. for a young one. The total vermin expenditure of this year was £2 11s. 3½d., or more than a tenth of the total disbursements, which in 1687 amounted to £21 15s. 6½d. In 1689 fifteen fitchers or polecats were killed; the term may sometimes perhaps be applied to a stoat or weasel, but not so in this case, as there are separate entries of these smaller animals; twelve fitchers occur in 1691. In 1703 twopence apiece was paid for sixty-one hedgehogs, and the same price for seventeen polecats. The last of these Sidbury accounts is that which was presented in 1724; the vermin enumerated are eight greys, three foxes, six polecats, ten stoats, fifteen hedgehogs, five sparrow hawks, thirteen jays, nine "hoops" or bullfinches, and absolutely fifty-five titmice at a farthing apiece!

There are many noteworthy vermin entries in seventeenth- and eighteenth-century accounts of Eastington, Gloucestershire.

1628. Layd out for crowes or devouring fowles		iiij d.
1663. Layd out to ye Sparrow Catcher		2 0
1697. For Hegogs and Ficbers		1 11
1699. For 18 hedghoggs and a fitche		3 4
1703. Pd for Hedghogs and other vermints		9 7
1714. P^d for Birds and Varments		1 7 2½
1722. P^d to Ed Stephens jun^r for seven Wood pickers		1 2
P^d my son for 3 Hedghoggs and 5 Hoops and 6 wood pickers		1 11
1724. Pd for wood peckers, hedgehoggs, hoops, Kites (9), joyes, fitchers, and foxes		1 2 7
1733. For all sorts of vermants		3 16 9

The payments for 1740 amounted to £3 2s. 10d., including 12s. "for sparrows and tomtits," and 9s. 10d. for "hickwalls." In 1744 the vermin charges rose to £4 19s. 10¼d. Hickwall or hackwall is a south-west provincialism for the smaller or blue tit.

At Pittington, co. Durham, in 1628—

> It was agreed upon by the gentlemen and twelve of this parish that whosaver shall take any fox, or pate or badger in this parish and bring the heade to the church shall have twelve pence paid by the churchwardens.

"Pate" is a north-country *alias* for a badger, and is still in occasional use.

The slaughter of ravens, foxes, and hedgehogs was excessive in Wirksworth, Derbyshire, and must have seriously interfered with the economy of nature. In 1688 sixteen foxes were killed. The wholesale destruction of ravens was grievous; in 1710 no fewer than 191 ravens were paid for, at 3d. a head. The following years were most fateful to hedgehogs: 64 in 1672, 62 in 1711, 103 in 1720, 123 in 1721, and 161 in 1725.

The Kendal accounts testify to much seventeenth-century destruction of vermin. In some years payment was made for as many as 20 fox heads and 18 badger heads. On 19th January 1679 the parish decided on the following scale of payments: " Fox head 12d.; brocke 6d.; otter 6d.; a clean mart 4d.; a foul mart 2d.; a wild catt 4d.; a raven 2d., if sane to flying. The said heads to be brused and caryed to the Kent side and thrown in to midle of the water."

There are other notable and frequent vermin entries in the accounts of Hartshorne, Derbyshire; Hartland, Devon; Camborne

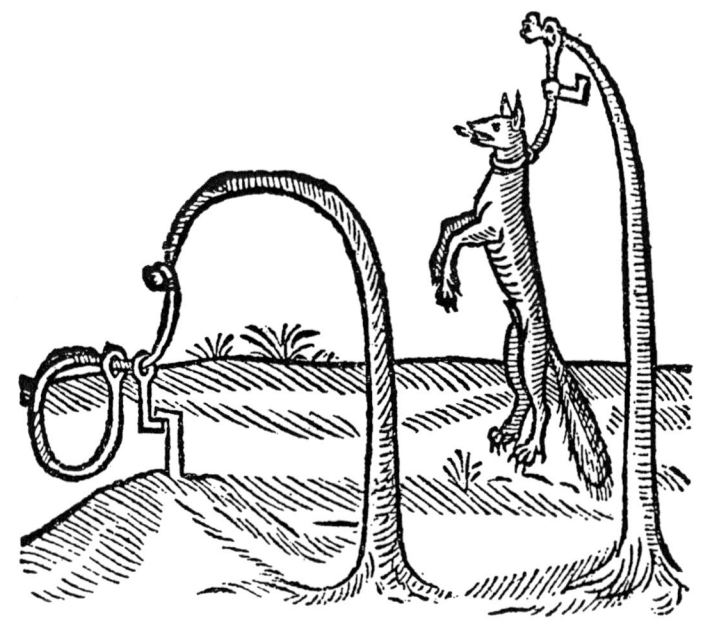

THE WHIPPE OR SPRINGE TRAPPE

and Liskeard, Cornwall, and Thruxton, Hants, for which space cannot be found.

The following are a further selection from vermin gleanings, needing no comments, from parish accounts up and down the country, arranged, so far as may be, chronologically:—

1566-7 (*Tavistock*). To William Gaye towards his charge of kyllyng of Foxes . . . . . . x s.
1573-4. To Willm Gaye for kyllyng of a Fox . xij d.
For Willm Gaye half yeres rent for takyng of Foxes ix s.
1627-8. For killinge of Fyve foxes . . . . . v s.

For killinge of seaven foaxes	vij s.
1567-8 (*S. Tawton, Devon*). For iij hopes heads	iij d.
For vj hopys and ij pyes	vj d.
1568. (*North Elmham*). For ij foxes heades accordinge to the statute	ij s.
For iiij polecattes and a wilde cattes hed	v d.
For a rooke net	ij s. viij d.
1569 (*Ludlow*). For xvij dosen of myce heades	xviij d.
For ix krowes heades	iij d.
For iiij young crowes beades unto Mr Smithes son of Crednyll	j d.
For iij crowes heades unto Mr Barnabes sone	j d.

THE MOULL TRAPPE

For vj chohes (choughs) beades	j d.
1572. Paid Mr Farrers man Coxshall for raittes heades, at the apoyntment of Mr Bayleff Mason	xij d.
1577. For a rattes head and a wontes (mole)	j d.
For xx wontes beades	x d.
1584 (*Burton Latimer*). For foure dosyn of mooles	xvj d.
1590. Paide to the molecatcher	vij s. vj d.
1601 (*Great Wigston, Leicestershire*). Twopenny levy a yerdland for catching moles	1 12 0
1620. Paid for 16 dozen of sparrows	1 4
1622. Paid to a man earnest to take 100 dozen sparrows	6
1608 (*St. Oswald, Durham*). To John Medcalf for three fox heads that he did kill within this parish	iij s.

1610. For two oulde foxheades . . . . . ij s.
For fower yong fox beades . . . . . xvj d.
[Also in various subsequent years.]
1636 (*Strood, Kent*). Paid to Thomas Coulter for Three Foxe heads . . . . 3 (
Paid to Henry Story for Two grayes beades 2 (
[Seven more fox heads and two badgers' heads this year.]
1657 (*Prestwich*). P^d to Robert Ward for killinge of 130 roackes, crowes, and pies 3 4
For ringteals (hen harriers) and kiets and one heron 1 6
Laid down for severall varments 15 9
1666 (*It imborne*). For 57 dozen of Sparrowes . . . 4s. 9d.
1674 (*St. Mabyn's, Cornwall*). To John Stevens for four Kites heads . . . . 8d.
1682. To Will Jory for two fitches head and one stotte 3d.
To John Philips for a wild cats head . . . 6d.
1709. For twelve polecats . . . . . . 2s.
1677 (*Ruardyn, Gloucestershire*). For 12 Fox's heads 12s.
1683 (*Methley, Yorks*). Given to Mr Savile boy for a fox head . . . .
Paid to Mr Savile man for two fox heads . . . 2 0
1684. To John Arnell for foure foumards heads . . . 1 0
Paid for two folmards heads 8
1686. For two fox heads 2 0
1689. Paid for an otters head 1 6
1684 (*Edenbridge*). For 4 Polcats Heads 8d., for 3 Hedgehoggs' heads 6d.
1730 (*Hawkshead, Lancashire*). For two foxes killing near Graithwaite 3s. 4d. per piece and 2 cubs in Claiffe 1s. 8d. per piece 10 0
1731. 4 Ravens killing 4d. p. piece 1 4
A fox killing 5 0
1732. For an old fox and one cubb 7 6
11 raven heads 3 8
1734. For one old fox and 3 cubbs 12 6
[Foxes and ravens continued to fetch similar prices for several later years.]

Occasional entries of payment for snakes appear in late eighteenth-century and early nineteenth-century accounts. Thus at Culworth, Northants, in 1715, 6s. 8d. was paid for a score of old snakes, and 6s. 6d. for 39 young snakes. In 1802, 10s. 6d. was paid for 143 young snakes.

Birds in Churches

Churchwardens were called upon from time to time, as they are at present, to deal with the nuisance of birds gaining entrance to churches. The following extracts will suffice to illustrate this trouble:—

1512	(*Wigtoft, Lincolnshire*). To Robert Haddenelle for stopping of Caddows (jackdaws) oute.	iiij d.
1555	(*Smarden, Kent*). Paid to the sexton for mendinge holes to kepe the culvers (pigeons) out of the churche	ij d.
1559	(*Worksop*). For makyng of the trellyeses to kepe out Crowes	ij s. vj d.
1566	(*St. Michael, Worcester*). To William the Tyler for ij dayes worke, stoppyng between the raughters of the churche to kepe furthe pygeons, etc.	xij d.
1588	(*Stanford, Berks*). For stoppinge out the pygeons.	iij d.
1587	(*Ludlow*). For stoppinge choughes out of the churche	iiij d.
1599	(*Morton, Derbyshire*). To John Lye for stoping the churche forth of the Caddowes (jackdaws) the 10th of May	...
1618	(*Sidbury, Devon*). For stopping out the Culvers (pigeons).	iij d.
1627	(*All Saints, Derby*). For powder and shott to kill pigeons in the Church	7½d.
1631	For stopping the pigeons out of Church	1 0.
1702	(*Hexham*). P^d for powder to banish the pidgeons	10d.
1711	(*Redenhall, Norfolk*). For worke and stuffe and nailes in stopping out ye owles at ye church.	3 6
1562-3	(*St. Martin, Leicester*). Payd for ij pound and a half of bird-lyme for to kyll the starlings abowt the churche	xx d.
1563-4.	P^d for gunpowder to beate ye starlings from ye churche	ij d.
1564-5.	Pade for iiij boltes for to shoute at starlins.	vj d.
	Payde for halfe a pound of gunpowder for to shout at starlins	ix d.
1625-6.	Pd for powther and shott to kill starlings in the Church	ij d.
1746.	(*Sapcote, Leicestershire*). For shooting sparrows in ye church and powder.	2 6
1759.	(*St. John, Chester*). Paid for bird lime to catch Owles in the Church	

The following entry in the wardens' accounts of Bradeston, Norfolk, probably refers to precautions against the entrance of birds:—

1544.	Paid for a hesppe of twynne for ye nette at ye church dore.	ij d. ob.

Rats in Churches

There is testimony in some of the earliest warden accounts of the mischief done by rats in churches. In 1457 the purchase of "rattes beyte" is mentioned in the accounts of St. Andrew Hubbard. Three "rat trappes for the chirche" were purchased by the wardens of St. Michael, Cornhill, at a cost of 6d. The following entries in the books of a third City church, St. Mary-at-Hill, tell of the definite mischief effected by rats, and of the means taken to destroy them:—

1501-2. For mendyng of the best Antyphones Cuveryng the whych the Rattes had hurte	xij d.
1523-4. For Milke and Rattisbane for the Rattes in the chirch	j d. ob.
1527-8. For an eln of fyne lynnyn cloth to amend the sepulture cloth wherat it was eiton with rattes	xij d.
1537-8. To the rat taker for laying of his bayts	iiij d.

The Dog-Whipper

In days long prior to a dog tax, dogs abounded in great numbers, and almost every cottager possessed one to aid in fetching his cow or a few sheep from the common. They were often in the habit of attending church with their masters, from the squire downwards. To regulate their behaviour and to remove the unseemly, almost every parish possessed a modestly paid official termed the dog-whipper. The absurd suggestion has been printed by several would-be folklorists, and repeated in a Herefordshire volume in 1912, that the custom of taking dogs to church was introduced by the Puritans to show their contempt for the sacraments, and for old-fashioned reverence. This is ridiculous, for entries as to dog-whippers occur in pre-Reformation wardens' accounts, and at the present time dogs attend mass in out-of-the-way chapels in Ireland; I have myself seen fine wolfhounds crouching behind the shepherds in churches of the French Pyrenees.

A dog-whip still hangs in the vestry of Baslow, Derbyshire; it has a stout lash, some three feet long, fastened to a short ash stick, with leather bound round the handle. See Cox's *Churches of Derbyshire*, ii. 61-2.

308 THE CHURCHWARDENS' ACCOUNTS

ROBERT SCARLETT, SEXTON OF PETERBOROUGH CATHEDRAL (OB. 1591), WITH DOG-WHIP

In the church of Clynnog Fanon, North Wales, there is a wonderful instrument for the removal of ill-behaved dogs. It is a long pair of iron "lazy keufs," with short spikes at the end for laying hold of the unhappy victim. There is another wooden pair at Llanynys, near Denbigh; when closed they are about 2 ft. 6 in. long, but when opened for use would extend to a distance of 6 or 7 feet. A third wooden pair used to be in the Herefordshire church of Clodock, but they have been removed to a Welsh museum.

The early sixteenth-century south door of St. Mullion, Cornwall, has at the base a diminutive latchet door 11 in. square, contrived to expedite the ejection of dogs without the necessity of opening the big door.

In later days it was customary to add the care of unruly young bipeds to the duties of the dog-whipper. The following are a selection from the very numerous references to this official which occur in old parish books:—

 1536 (*Culworth*). For
  whypps for
  dogges . ij d.

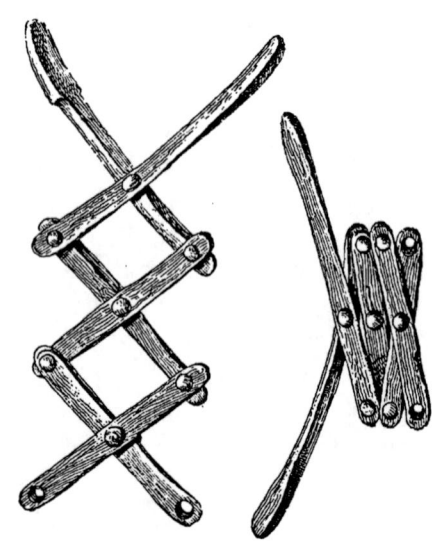

WOODEN DOG-TONGS, CLODOCK HEREFORDSHIRE

LIVE STOCK—VERMIN

1542 (*Ludlow*). For whippynge doges out of the church . . viij d.
1569. For ij belle for the whip to whip dogges out of church . iiij d.
1578 9. Payd Edward Humfries for his wage for keepinge doggs oute of the Chuche . . . . . . v s.

In the volume of churchwarden's accounts of St. Nicholas, Warwick, extending from 1547 to 1621, the dog-whipper is named almost every year. At first his annual salary was 6d., but after a time it increased to 12d. The various ways of describing his office are not a little amusing. In 1574 occurs the entry:—

"Payde to John Whetley for Rebukyng the dogges owt off the churche, xij d."

In 1581 other duties were assigned to this official:—

"Payde to John Whettley for whippynge dogges owt of the church and keepinge order amonge boys, xx d."

A little later these twofold duties received a further rise in salary, and the maximum of 2s. was reached. The following is the entry of 1596:—

"Paid to John Rose his wholl yeres waiges for Overseinge of the boyes, and to whipe the Doges forth of the church, ij s."

    1618 (*Staplegrove, Somerset*). To Richard Searll for whipping the dogges . . . . j s. iiij d.
    1663. For a Coard for Searll to whippe the dogs . . I d.
    1618 (*Bray, Berks*). Paid for a jerkin to Edward Johnson according to ancient custom for whipyng dogs out of the church vj s. iiij d.
    1631 (*Prestbury, Cheshire*). To a boy to beate dogs forth of the Church . . . . x d.
    1635 (*Hartshorne, Derby*). Geevin for a wip to wip dodges out of church . . . . ij d.
    Paid to Robert Cock for whiping the doges out of the church xij d.
    1647 (*Barnsley*). To Richard Hodgaris wife for whipping dogs . 2 0

One instance among very many of the manifold duties assigned to the dog-whipper in the eighteenth century may be cited:—

    1736 (*Prestwick, Manchester*). Resolved that 13s. a year be given to George Grimshaw and a new coat (not exceeding 20s.) every other year, for his trouble and pains in wakening sleepers in ye church whipping out dogs, keeping children quiet and orderly, and keeping ye pulpit and church walks clean.

CHAPTER XXI

OLLA PODRIDA

Incense—Juniper—Peter's Pence or Smoke Farthings—The Cap trade—Wine at weddings—Jewellery for brides—King's Evil—Sugar loaves—Plague—Fire appliances—Some odds and ends

THE entries as to the purchase of Incense are curiously few, considering its constant use, in pre-Reformation accounts. Mr. Atchley is probably right in saying that "in most places it was the business of the curate to provide incense; hence the churchwardens' accounts do not, as a rule, contain the notes of payment for it."[1] The All Saints, Bristol, accounts begin in 1407, and there is no incense entry until near the end of Henry VIII's reign. The following are all the incense entries for that parish :—

1533-4. Costes halowyng of the gret belle : payd for di a li of frankeinsens	jd. ob.
1539-40. Item frankeinsense	ij d.
1553-4. The Setting up Another Awter : pd for halfe a pounde of franceinnsense	j d.
1555-6. Payed for franckyn sense	iij d.
1557-8. Paid for frangencence . [Repeated three times].	ij d.
1559-60. Item for frangensence	iij d.

Mr. Atchley cites the comparatively few incense entries from printed accounts such as those of Ludlow, Weybridge, Morebath, Yatton, St. Mary Cambridge, and of several City churches. Those that I have noted in unprinted accounts confirm the statement that ceremonial incense entries seldom found their way into wardens' accounts. It is not, therefore, fair to argue that ceremonial incense ceased altogether in Edward VI or Elizabeth's reign because of lack of entries.

---
[1] *Incense in Divine Worship* (1903), pp. 359-60.

OLLA PODRIDA

Nevertheless it is but just to state that in the great majority of the numerous cases in which incense occurs in parish books from the accession of Elizabeth to the end of the eighteenth century, its use was obviously to perfume the building or to act as a disinfectant. The following are but a fourth of the instances collected :—

1562 (*St. Mary, Cambridge*). For frankincense to perfume the church	j d.
1579-80 (*St. Edmund, Sarum*). Coles and fronkinsence agains^{te} christmas	xiv d.
1588 (*St. Peter, Winchester*). For p'fume at Mrs Palmers buriall	iiij d.
1603. For the perfuminge the Churche the som of	2 0
1604 (*St. Ewen, Bristol*). For frankansence and holly for the Church	iij d.
1593-4 (*St. Thomas, Sarum*). Frankansence and sweete wood	12d.
1630-1. Frankinsense	2d.
1637 (*Redenhall, Norfolk*). For frankinsense for the church and sweete wood	vj d.
1639-40 (*St. Martin, Leicester*). P^{d} for sweete wood to burne in the church.	6d.

In three cases the use of frankincense has been noted in connection with the burial of paupers; it was probably placed on the body in infectious cases.

1541 (*St. Columb Major*). Paid George Collins for a shroude for ye pavers daughter and for an halfe pounde of Francke encence and for a penarde of threede, 8s. 5d.

An interesting entry occurs in 1595 of the non-ceremonial use of incense at St. Margaret, Westminster :—

Also pd for franckensence in the church in the time of visitation, iiij d.

This does not refer to any episcopal or archidiaconal visitation, but to an outbreak of plague.

During the period of the great Civil War, the church of St. Laurence, Reading, was repeatedly used as a temporary barrack by the soldiers of both parties. In 1664 a shilling was spent on frankincense to sweeten the church after one of these visits. The following entries in the next two years speak for themselves :—

1645. Pd to Val. Fallowe for mending seats in the church wch the souldiers broke downe	3 2

THE CHURCHWARDENS' ACCOUNTS

Pd to Dauid Browne for making clean the Church twice, and for pitch and frankincense	5 c
1646. Pd for 1ᵘ of frankincence and of pitch to perfume the church	8
Pd for 2ˡⁱ of pitch and 2li of frankincence used in the church	1 4
Pd to Dan. Browne for watching and making cleane the church when the soldiers were last here .	4 c
1665 (*Solihull, Warwickshire*). Payd for bread and wine and frankincense for the first Sacrament . . .	13s. 4d.
1741 (*St. Peter, Barnstaple*). Pd for Tobacco and Frankincense burnt in the Church.	2 6
1752. Pd for Frankincense, Senemon and Charcole	3 0

Sprigs of juniper, burnt on a brazier, were sometimes used in churches as an adjunct to, or in place of, frankincense for odorous or deodorising purposes.

1563 (*All Hallowes, Steyning*). In the time of the sickness: for gennefore for the Church	viij d.
1584 (*Cratfield, Suffolk*). Pd to William Clamp for a swete ode (hod) off Juneper	iiij d.
1589 (*Pittington, Durham*). To Bettres Dobson and her daughter for bringinge of two burthen of Jenepers to the church .	iij d.
1667 (*St. Nicholas, Durham*). For frankencence and juniper	6d.
1675. For juniper and frankincence to Robᵗ Healey upon the Lᵈ Bpps comeing into the church	
1680. For frenkincence, benjamin and juniper att the Bpp's preaching	2 6
[Benjamin, *i.e.* Benzoin, a drug much used as a perfume.]	
1677-8 (*St. Mary, Reading*). For oyle frankencence and juniper .	6s. 3d.

PETER'S PENCE

The nature and origin of Peter's Pence, known otherwise as Smoke farthings, Whitsun farthings, Pentecostals, etc., have been already set forth under St. Edmund, Sarum (pp. 73-4). St. Nicholas, Worcester, paid 5d. yearly to the Dean and Chapter as Whitsun farthings, but at St. Helen in the same city they were called Peter farthings. Milton Abbot, Devon, paid 5d. annually as Peter farthings. St. Neot, Cornwall, contributed 12d. a year to Exeter Cathedral down to 1642, usually under the title of Peter farthings. Smoke farthings is the term continually used in the

OLLA PODRIDA

accounts of St. Mary, Reading, from 1555 to 1642; the sum varied from 2s. 1d. to 2s. 3d. Smoke farthings occur in Yarnton, Oxford, accounts from 1611 to 1702.

1349 (*St. Michael, Bath*). Pro denariis beati Petri		vij d. ob.
1518 (*St. Giles, Reading*) For Petre pens to the official		iiij s. j d.
1574 „ To the Official for smoke ferthynges		iiij s. j d.
1544 „ To the official for petre pens alias smoke ferthynges		ij s. j d.
1547–8 (*St. Nicholas, Warwick*). Payd for whitson ferthynges to the Sumner		ij s.
1549–50 „ „ Payd to the bisshope of Wyssieters offyceres callyd Whytson Farthinges		ij s.
1557–8 (*Mere, Wilts*). For Smoke Ferthynges to Rome		xix d.
1575 (*Minchinhampton, Gloucester*). To the sumner for peterpense or smokye farthynges somtyme due to the Anthecrist of roome		x d.
1576. For Pentecost money, otherwyse peterpence, sometyme payed to Antechryst of Roome		xvj d.

In 1570 a sumptuary statute was passed for the supposed encouragement of home manufacture, whereby it was enacted that any male person over six years of age (except nobles, knights, gentlemen of 20 marks by year in land, or such as have "borne office of worship") who did not wear upon the Sundays and holy days a "cappe of wool, knit, thicked and dressed in England, and only dressed and finished by some of the trade of cappers, was to be fined 3s. 4d. for each day's transgression. This statute, like others of its class, speedily became a dead letter in most parts of England; and where it was put into operation the fines were much mitigated. There are various entries with respect to these caps in the Cratfield, Suffolk, accounts.

1578. Payde at Blybrough before the Comyssoners for caps		xj s.
1580. Payde to the baly for a default of wearing of cappes		ij s.
1582. Payed to the Baliffe for a mercyment for all the Townsmen for not wearing their Cappes according unto statute		ij s.
1585. To the Quenes Balye for not wearing of capps		ij s.
[Like entries for 1588, 1589, and 1592 show that the general fine on the township for not complying with this statute was reduced to 1s.]		
1588 (*Milton Abbot*). To John Cragge for the fyne of wearing of hats this year		xij d.

1598 (*Minchinhampton, Gloucester*). Payed for a forfett for not wearinge of Cappes . . . . . . iiij d.

1605 (*Tavistock*). Payd to Mr Thomas Mohun the Earll of Bedfords hundred Bayleif in burdewyke Court sett upon the p'ishners for that they offende the Statute in not wearing Capps on the Sondaie . . . iij s. iiij d.

A singular marriage custom was enjoined by the old Sarum Use. At the end of the Mass a bowl of wine was produced in which were soaked certain small cakes or wafers termed sops. The priest blessed the bowl or maser in these words :—

> Benedic Domine panem istum et hunc potum, et hoc vasculum, sicut benedixisti quinque panes in deserto, et sex hydrias in chanaan Galilee, sed sint sani et sobrii atque immaculate omnes gustantes ex iis.

The contents were then drunk by the bridegroom and bride.

An inventory of 1507 in the wardens' accounts of Pilton names

> A stonding maser to serve for brides at their weddyng.

A silver-gilt bridal cup of this nature was bequeathed to St. Laurence, Reading, in 1534. Prior to the visit of the marauding commissioners, the authorities astutely passed the following resolution to prevent its seizure :—

> St. Michael 25 Hen. VIII. At this day it is agreid that the Gilt Cupp of the gifte of Mrs. Hide always to remayne in the custodye of the Mayor, if the Mayor dwell in the p'sshe. And if the Mayor dwell out of the p'sshe then to remayne and be in the Custodye of hym that was last Mayor of the same p'sshe, to thuse declared in the will of the said Mrs. Hide.

An early Elizabethan entry adds :—

> The said Cuppe was given for the use to be carried before all brydds that were wedded in St. Lawrence Church. And now is turned to be occupied there at all tymes when nede is to occupie more than one commyon cuppe at one tyme, to use and occupye it y^n as a commyon cuppe.

This cup is also named in 1607, when it had reverted to its original custody :—

> A fayre cupp with a cover. Whosoever is mayor in this parishe keepeth him.

Various parish books testify to the fact that the use of the bridal cup in church by no means expired with the Reformation. Several entries, such as the following from Devonshire, have generally been misinterpreted to refer to celebration of the Eucharist at the wedding:—

1595 (*Talaton*). Paid for bread and wine for 3 weddings . 6d.
1601 Paid for bread and wine against a wedding 2d.

So firmly was the custom maintained that a Bristol church made special provision for the preparation.

1569 (*St. James, Bristol*). Payd for the little table to dress sops in wyne at any weddinge . . . . . ij s. vj d.

Shakespeare, in the *Taming of the Shrew* (iii, 2), alludes to the practice when Gremio relates how the bridegroom

". . . quaff'd off the muscadel,
And threw the sops all in the sexton's face;
Having no other reason
But that his beard grew thin and hungerly,
And seem'd to ask him sops as he was drinking."

In some churches it was the custom to provide special jewellery to be worn at the wedding. The most notable instance is that of the parish church of Henley, where a set of valuable jewels was presented in 1518, with the double object of decking maidens at the time of their marriage, and providing funds for maintaining lights before the Lady altar. If lent by the wardens outside the parish, a fee of 3s. 4d. was to be paid, if lent to the daughter of a burgess 20d., or to any other maiden within the town 2s. 4d. There are entries in the accounts of the loan of the jewels under the years 1529 and 1531. The set consisted of a fillet with 26 pearls, "a past with a stone set full of perlys," and also a coronal "with viij great stones and set full of perles." The "past," "paste," or "partlet" was the name of a collar or collaret, in this instance of silver gilt.

The wardens' accounts of Steyning, 1561, enter 6d. for the hire of "a Bryde paiste."

1540 (*St. Margaret, Westminster*). To Alice Lewis a goldsmiths wife for a serclett to marry maydens in . . iij li. x s.

1564 (*St. Margaret, Westminster*). One past for brydes set with perle and stone [Inventory].

The English custom of the royal touch for curing scrofula or the King's Evil can be traced back to the days of Edward the Confessor; it expired with the advent of George I, "who believed in little or nothing." Part of the ceremony consisted, according to the rubric, in the King "crossing the sore of the sick person with an angel noble; and the sick person to have the same angel hanged about his neck, and to wear it until he be full whole." Hence the ribband supplied by Minchinhampton. See *Parish Registers of England*, 179-183.

1634 (*Seal, Surrey*). To Will'm Giles for his charitie and travell to London with Widowe Hilles children to be cured of the King's evill, by a rate for that cause made by the parishe as appears under divers of their hands . ix s.

1663 (*Minchinhampton, Gloucester*). For one yeard of rebband to Jonathan Harris, his child that has the King's evill . 5d.
[Similar entries are continued up to 1736.]

In 1684, at St. Martin, Leicester, payment was made for his Majesty's declaration "for the times when his Majesty touches for healing."

1683-4 (*Mavesyn Ridware, Staffs*). For a boke for the Kings cure . 1s.

Sugar loaves were usual presents to dignitaries in the latter part of the sixteenth and seventeenth centuries. Dr. Wilmot, who was minister of All Saints, Derby, from 1632 to 1643, received such gifts from the parish on three occasions:—

1637. For a sugar loff to carry to Mr. Dr. . . . 1 1 6
1639. For a sugar loaf of 12^b 3 ounce given Dr Wilmott on New Years Day 1 0 0
1640. For 2 Sugar loavs 15^b 2 ounces for ye D^r . 1 2 6
1588 (*St. Christopher-le-Stocks*). For iiij sugar loffes wch was given to the Judges . . . . . iiij li. j s.
[Judgment had been given in favour of the parish in a lawsuit as to property in Fleet Street.]

In 1626, 1629, and 1634, sugar loaves were presented to the Bishop at Christmas by the parish of St. James, Bristol.

Much has been given in *The Parish Registers of England* (pp. 144-176) as to visitations of the plague; the subject is, however, dealt with after a different fashion in the wardens' accounts.

The parish of St. Martin's-in-the-Fields suffered much from the plague visitation of 1593; 40 bills were purchased on 10th August for 18d. for posting on the doors of the visited houses, and 4d. was spent on red wands which were carried by the searchers. On 22nd July "bearers and searchers" had been appointed, namely, two men and two women at a weekly wage. Collectors were appointed to gather from house to house to assist the visited; in the fourteen weeks beginning 19th September they collected £8 6s. 6d., and they also received "further benevolence of divers honorable and worshipfull men to the amount of £12 10s. 6d." It was also agreed by the vestry to employ Daniel Stocken of Westminster as dog-killer for the parish, allowing him 2d. for every killed dog; they were rightly considered "very apt cattell to carry the infection." Daniel had earned 3s. 4d. by 16th September. Further expenditure of a like character was incurred in 1603.

1573 (*St. Christopher-le-Stocks*). For red wandes and bylles for
    the plague . . . . vj d.
    For foure bookes set out by y[e] byshope for y[e] plague . viij d.
1628. P[d] for earthen Pannes, Charcolles, stare, pich, franconsence
    and Incense to burn in the streate according to my Lord
    Mayor his order . . . . . . 1s. 8d.
1592 (*St. Alphege, London Wall*). For redd wandes for the plage ij d.
    For two searchers for the plage . . . . viij d.
    For a booke of orders for the plage . . . . iij d.
1605. For settinge 5 red Crosses on the doores of vyseted houses . 1 8
    For red wands for serchers of vyseted houses to carry in
    their handes 2
1609. For settinge red crosses on houses infected . . . 1 4
1625. For setting up the Crosses on the visited houses   vj s. viij d.
1665. Distributed to the releefe of the poore infected that were
    shutt upp, and for the Coles which made the fires by
    order of the Lord Mair £52 12 7
1593-4 (*St. Martin, Leicester*). Paied for mendinge the beer whereon
    vysyted folkes were carried, and nayles to y[e] same . viij d.
1610-1. Given to Robert Humier in consideracon that he shoulde
    watche no more to the visited people nor could not have
    no worke . . . . iiij s.

THE CHURCHWARDENS' ACCOUNTS

1611–2. Payde to the Seckerston for burieyng of the poore visited people by Mr Maiors appoyntment . iijs. iiij d.

1626–7. Pd to the pariter for bringinge a letter from the Lord Bishop concerning the plagge . . . . vj d.

1602 (*St. Margaret, Westminster*). To two surgions to search a coarse suspected to be of the plague vj s. viij d.

1603. June 19th. To Robert Walls for killing of fore score dogs vj s. viij d.
[Walls was paid for killing 422 more dogs this summer at 1d. each.]
For the graves of 451 poor folke . . j li. xvij s. vij d.

1625. Rec. of the Lord Bishop of London, of money collected, for the relief of the poor visited of this city of Westminster . £300
For killing 14 dozen and ten dogs in time of visitacion . £1 9 8
For killing of 24 dozen of dogs 1 8 0

1626. For 272 loads of gravel for the churchyard . . 13 12 0
To the graves of 1447 poor people this year . 1 0 0

1631. For bills for visited houses 1 0

1639. To Bummer the beadle for watching a house all night in Gardiners Lane which was shut up and supposed to be visited 8

1642. Rec. out of the black chest at several tymes for the building of the new pest houses 200 0 0

1643. For relief of a child that died of the plague in the Still yard, and of a poore woman that was shutt up in her house there 10 0

1644. Disbursements for the poore visited with the plague this year 59 4 4
[In 1645, £81 1s. 5d. ; in 1646, £154 13s. 9d. ; in 1647, £165 10s. ; in 1648, £73 ; and in 1649, £1 16s.]

1603 (*St. Benedict, Gracechurch*). Pd for pitch and faggots yt were burnt in ye streete by my Lord Maiors command . £1 15 0

1627. Pd for putting forth of the perfumes in time of the sicknesse 10 0

1603 (*Melton Mowbray*). Payd to Walter Parker and Hickson for keepinge the townsfolke of Tythe and Asswell out of o^r market being suspected for the plague . vj d.

1625–6. Payde to Wydow Powlie for Vittelinge yonge Queniboroghe lodging in the feild being suspected of the plague for hys dyet j month and watching some nights of hym vij s. viij d.

1606 (*St. Mary, Cambridge*). For a double guilte boule, which was given to Mr. Wattes our minister for his extraordinary paines taking amoungst us in the parrishe at two severall tymes when the sickness was amongst us . . iiij li. v s. vj d.

Constables' accounts, of country districts, during the several outbreaks of Charles I's days bear witness to the fact of generous grants being made by one township to others of the same district during the time of visitations. Thus the parish of Stathern, Leicestershire, contributed seven several times in 1631-2 to the "visited people" of Loughborough sums varying from 3s. 4d. to 20s., and on three occasions in the same twelve months to the visited people of Plungar. From July to October in 1637, Stathern contributed monthly sums, varying from 12s. to 15s., to Melton Mowbray when in like sad plight.

> 1638 (*St. Giles, Northampton*). For pitch, tarre and roszen to perfume the church at the siknes time .
> 1666-7 (*Basingstoke*). Paid for three chafing dishes, resin, franckincense and tobacco sticks to burn in the church in the time of the Visitation . . . . . 1s. 6½d.

Appliances for the extinguishing of fires in towns and larger villages were almost invariably stored in the churches, usually under the tower. They chiefly consisted of leather buckets, ladders, and strong iron hooks attached to great poles. The hooks were used for the dragging down blazing timber houses to save the adjoining tenements. They were thrown over the ridge-beams, and there were generally iron rings at the ends of the poles and part way up to which horses were attached or companies of men. The poles varied from 20 to 30. ft in length. There is a fine pair in the church of Raunds, another pair at Stanwick and a single one at Harringworth, all in Northants. For the orders made as to buckets and hooks at Northampton, see *Borough Records*, ii. 240, 252, etc. The parish books of All Saints, Northampton, show that there were 190 buckets in the four churches of that town in 1628, and "one hundred and three-score and fyve buckets" in charge of the All Saints' churchwardens in 1629. A pair of fire-hooks are crossed over the west entrance to the parish church of Tunbridge, under the tower.

A 1598 inventory of St. Martin's-in-the-Fields names 23 leather buckets, the respective gifts of six parishioners, 5 ladders, and "ij greate fyer hoockes wth their Cheynes." In Michaelmas quarter, 1600, occurs the following entry:—

> Paide unto vj poore men for helping home with the hoockes and lathers from Durham house when the stable was a fier . xviij d.

The accounts of St. Bartholomew Exchange name two dozen

320 THE CHURCHWARDENS' ACCOUNTS

leather buckets, four ladders, and two great hooks yearly from 1597 to 1602, but in 1603 there were "iij greate poules with Iron hooks." In 1610 the hooks had increased to four. Shortly afterwards there were three dozen buckets and six ladders. There were also "six wooden scoopes." Their exact use is explained in an entry of 1624:—

> For six scoopes according to the Lord Mayors precept to cast water for daunger of scatte fyers, and for shooing them and binding them with plate . . . . . 12 (
>
> 1527 (*Wimborne*). For a fyre croke to help draw down the houses that are aventured with fyre. . . . . v d.
>
> 1583-4 (*St. Matthew, Friday Street*). Paid for 20 buckettes at ij s. iij d.   xlv s.
> Paid for payntinge them . . . . . ij s. v d.
>
> 1583 (*Ludlow*). Paied to a mason for hanginge up the new buckettes on the walle in the church . . . ij s. vj d.
>
> 1602 (*St. Botolph, Cambridge*). xij Leather Bucketts. Ye townes. One hooke of Iron with a handle of wood. Ye Townes.
>
> 1611 (*St. Benet Fink*). A fyer hook poiz 124 lbs sett upon a powle.
>
> 1618 (*St. Bartholomew Exchange*). For bringing home the hookes from the fyer in Cornhill . . . . 4d.
>
> 1632-3 (*St. Botolph, Aldersgate*). One Brasse Squirt to quench fire with in a case: thirtie two Leather Bucketts: two greate Ladders: two hooks.
>
> 1655 (*St. Christopher-le-Stocks*). Paid Porters for carrying the yron hooke when ye fire was in Threadneedle st
>
> 1661 (*St. Petrock, Exeter*). xlvj Lether Buccetts with the Parrish name on Them.
>
> 1677 (*Wellingborough*). Twelve new leather buckettes . 2 14 0
> Eight poles for Hookes 9 4
> Making the Hookes 13 0

The following are a bundle of odds and ends, which defy any kind of classification, arranged chronologically:—

> 1485-6 (*St. Andrew Hubbard*). For loppyng of the tree on the chircheyarde for caterpillars . . . . ij d.
>
> 1499-1500 (*St. Botolph, Aldersgate*). A tabyll for the Popys bull . vij d.
>
> 1546 (*St. Margaret, Westminster*). On Ascension even for bread ale beer and wyne for the prebendaries and quyer of the mynster after Mas was done . . . . xiiij d.
>
> 1583-4 (*Thatcham, Berks*). Payde for the ingoing to Burfield to the cunnyng woman for to make enquire for the comunione clothe and the ij outher clothes that were lost out of the church. . . . . xvj d.

FIRE-HOOKS IN RAUNDS CHURCH, NORTHANTS

1610 (*St. Margaret, Westminster*). To Goodwyfe Wells for salt to destroy the fleas in the churchwardens pew . vj d.
1611 ,, For five vines and one apricock tree and for planting of them before the vestry window . . .. x s.
For a pound of orris powder to put among the churche linon. x d.
1630 (*St. Benedict, Gracechurch*). Pd for paynting Queen Elizabeths tomb with ye frame of it . . . . 8 (

[This was a picture of the Queen lying on her tomb, which was common to several London churches.]

1641 (*St. Clement, Ipswich*). For wryghting faire of 700 names of them that took the protestation to deliver to Mr Bailies 3 12 0
1643 (*St. Margaret, Westminster*). For drawing out the names of all such persons as have taken the covenant and putting them in an alphabetical way: alsoe for the drawing up as well of all the names of such as had not taken the covenant, etc 3 11 4
1644. For a table with the Covenant to hang in the church 3 0
1643-4 (*St. Martin, Leicester*). Paid for a skin of Parchm^t to register their names that tooke the vow and covenant 0 0 6
Paid for engrossing the said vow and covenant 0 3 4
Paid for another sheete of parchment to enter their names that took the covenant 0 0 6
Paid for writing faire in two schedules ye names of all those that gave to the releife in Ireland . . . . 0 5 (

[The distinction between the Protestation and the Covenant is fully discussed in Cox's *Parish Registers*, pp. 198-200.]

1644 (*St. Margaret, Westminster*). Rec for 29 pound of fine brass at 4d. a pound, and 96 pound of coarse brass at 3d. a pound, taken off from sundrie toombe-stones in the church 1 13 6
1644 (*Loughborough*). Payd to John Wright and William Ragsbee for dressinge the Church after the Souldiers and for frankincense to sweeten it . . . . 2 ·
1645. Payd for dressing ye Church after ye Souldiers lay in yt 3 8
1646. Payd for helpe to dresse the Church and our charges when souldiers had lyen 2 nights and a day in it when ye scots mony was here 3 4
1645 (*St. Martin, Leicester*). The moneys received at the Communions on April 13th and May 11, being about 30s., were taken out of the of the poor man's box by the soldiers at the taking of Leicester.
1646 (*St. Martin, Leicester*). At a parish meeting it was put to the vote whether there should that day be the election of a minister in the room of Mr Grace; the ayes were 33 and

the noes 7. The choice fell upon Mʳ Thomas Palmer of the City of London.

1658 (*St. Margaret, Westminster*). To Richard May for informing of one that played at trap-ball on the Lords day . 18 0

1665–6 (*St. Mary, Leicester*). In beer and Tobacco from first to last 7 10

1671 (*St. Alphege, London Wall*). For Pipes and Tobaccoe in the Vestry 2 0

For a grosse of pipes at severall times . . . 2 0

1739. Ordered that there be no Smoaking nor Drinking for the future in the Vestry Room during the time business is doing on pain of forfieting one shilling, Assention Day excepted.

1783 (*Bramley, Yorks*). Dec. 8ᵗʰ, Expenses on bargaining with conjuror from Skipton to cure Matthew Hudson's daughter 1 0

1784. Feb 1ˢᵗ Astrological Doctor for Hudson's daughter 12 6

CHAPTER XXII

CONSTABLES' ACCOUNTS [1]

Office and Duty of Constable—Weights and Measures—Soldiers—Butts and Bows and Arrows—Parish Armour—Gunpowder—Saltpetre Men—Purveyance—Vagrants—Rogue Money—Gipsies—Beacons—Ducking Stool—Stocks and Whipping Posts—Constables Accounts of (1) Wimeswold, (2) Manchester, and (3) Combe

CONSTABLES' Accounts are often found, particularly in smaller parishes, blended with those of the churchwardens', or entered in the same books. Occasionally they are found set forth, with much valuable detail, in separate books, of which those of the Leicestershire parishes of Wimeswold and Stathern [2] are notable instances. Anything tending to throw light on the character and duties of an office which was founded fourteen centuries ago, and which, under the varying designation of Tythingman, Headborough, Provost, or Constable, was the very centre of our local self-government, is possessed of value, and throws a similar light on the secular history of the parish to that thrown on the religious history by Churchwardens' Accounts. The constabulary arrangements of our ancestors were based upon a very simple but sound view of human nature. That view is, as Toulmin Smith has remarked, that those most immediately concerned in the taking care of their own safety, and in the protection of their own property, are the most likely to take vigorous and efficient means to secure these ends. The constantly maintained policy of the old English system was to fix on all men the closest

[1] Everything connected with the office and duties of High Constables and Petty Constables will be found set forth at length or fully discussed in Dr. Cox's *Three Centuries of Derbyshire Annals*, 2 vols., 1890.

[2] A valuable annotated transcript of much of the Stathern Constable Accounts from 1630 to 1649 has appeared (as we go to press) in the *Archæological Journal*, vol. lxix. (1912), from the pen of Mr. Everard L. Guilford.

sense of their responsibility as citizens, and to impress upon them that those who would be well governed must take an active part in governing themselves.

For the right understanding of old constabulary records a few paragraphs dealing with the most important of their duties are necessary.

Watch and Ward were the terms used, from the earliest period of parochial law, to imply the general duties of the parish constable or constables. The number of men who were bound to keep night watch to arrest strangers, in each city, borough, and town or parish, is specified in the Statute of Winchester (13 Edward I). Every inhabitant was held responsible for the watch and ward—that is, for the due peace and safety of his neighbourhood—and inquests before sworn juries of freemen used to be periodically held in every place to see that the local arrangements were in working order. The present system of "Special Constables," by which every householder is called upon to act as a constable in certain emergencies, is a remnant of the old custom of watch and ward that used to be binding on all. Watching and warding was a serious tax upon the parish when kept strictly during troublous or tumultuous times. Certain inhabitants were generally nominated to discharge this duty during fair or week days.

All *Weights* and *Measures* used in the parish were under the constable's charge; they had to be stamped by a clerk of the market of the nearest town, and annually inspected by the same official. By the statute 11 Henry VII, cap. iv., only certain towns were allowed to keep imperial standards. Very few of the old standard weights and measures remain, owing doubtless to their frequent renewal consequent upon new statutes. Some good examples are preserved at Cambridge, Derby, Lancaster, and Northampton. An illustration is here given of an Elizabethan standard bushel from the last of these towns.

Ancient rights of *Purveyance*, or providing for the victualling and carriage of the sovereign and his household when in progress, came by degrees to assume the form of fixed charges levied throughout the county, whether royalty was in progress or not. The whole system was under the control of the central Board of Green Cloth in Elizabethan and Stuart days, and was a constant source of friction with both county and parish authorities. The authorised purveyors were supposed to pay "a reasonable price" for all they claimed by right of pre-emption, but in practice everything was exacted far below its market value, and in quantities infinitely beyond any possible requirements. The purveyors were usually open to a money composition. This odious system died out under the Commonwealth, and was never re-established.

Trained Soldiers and Mariners were relieved by parochial assessments, according to three acts of the latter part of Elizabeth's reign (35 Eliz. c. 4 ; 39 Eliz. c. 21 ; 43 Eliz. c. 3). By the first of these, the relief of maimed or sick-pressed soldiers or mariners was placed upon the rates, provided that no parish for this purpose

ELIZABETHAN STANDARD BUSHEL: NORTHAMPTON

was to be rated higher than 10d. a week or lower than 2d. a week. The rate to be collected by the churchwardens and petty constables. The pension had to be granted by the county treasurer ; it usually amounted to 12d. a week. The treasurer could grant a pass entitling them to relief in each parish through which they passed when travelling to their own county.

The main part of the *English Army* of old days was raised by means of the parishes, which were considered in all respects as the units of the State. Every parish, according to the Parliament Rolls of Edward II, was required to furnish one foot soldier, ready armed and equipped, for sixty days. When the forces required any sudden increase the additional numbers were usually procured by raising the quota supplied by the parishes ; thus, in 1449, proclamation was made "in every parishe" that every thirty men should furnish one horseman, the whole number so raised being computed at 60,000. Every parish was bound to keep ready for use a certain amount of armour, and a man or men, if necessity arose, properly trained to the use of this armour. This armour was not intended for merely local use, still less for show, but for practical service in the field, either at home or abroad, against the national enemies. At the conclusion of the inventory of armour in the parish accounts of Fulham, Middlesex, for the year 1583, is added in a later hand: "*N.B.* All sett owte into Flanders, anno 1585, by Rowland Fysher, except one harquobusse," etc.

According to the Statute of Winchester (1285), it was enjoined that "viewe of armour be made every yere two times, and in all hundredes and fraunchises two constables shal be chosen to make the view of armour, and the constables aforesaide shal present before Justices assigned such defautes as they doe see in the countrey about armour." This act was much elaborated by 4 & 5 Philip and Mary, cap. 2, which made many provisions as to parish armour, its custody, and its annual viewing.

The *Train Band* soldier, who was to a certain extent a volunteer, originated in the Armada days, when certain select men of the General Musters (pressed soldiers) were selected for training in bands both in the gun and long-bow. These trained bands assumed more definite form under James I.

The parish armour was almost invariably kept within the church, even in large town parishes such as St. Martin's-in-the-Fields, St. Margaret, Westminster, or the various churches of Colchester, Leicester, Bristol, or Taunton. In country parishes the room over the porch was often used as an armoury in Elizabethan and Stuart days, there being hardly any church valuables left requiring the guard of a church watch.

The following are brief explanations of the terms of constant occurrence in old constable accounts, in their inventories or entries as to parish or church armour.

The *musket* was a heavy gun, which could not be fired with any precision without the use of a forked support or rest. The *arquebuse* was a lighter form of hand gun with a curved stock. The *caliver* was the regulation firearm of Elizabethan days, so called from the calibre being according to standard; it had a wheel-lock, was 3 ft. 2 in. long, and usually had a magazine for bullets in the butt. The large *flasks* were for the powder, and the *touch-boxes* were diminutive flasks that held the priming powder. The *bandoleers* were small wooden or tin cases, covered with leather, each containing a single charge for the caliver, and fastened to a broad band of leather worn over the shoulder.

In addition to swords and daggers, certain soldiers of the sixteenth and seventeenth centuries carried *pikes*, weapons with very long shafts and a sharp head; or *bills*, a kind of concave battleaxe with long wooden handle; or *halberds*, which had shafts some 6 ft. long, surmounted by an axe-like instrument, balanced on the opposite side by a hook or pick.

The defensive armour of the old parish soldier consisted of a *morion*, an open helmet without beaver, or visor, or a *sallet*, a lighter form of helmet with a projection behind. Mere skullcaps of steel were also used. The *corslet*, usually of leather, was the only armour of pikemen or billmen. The *gorget* was plate armour for the defence of the throat. *Almayne-rivettes* was armour of German invention, made flexible by means of rivets. The *brigandine* was a corslet of leather upon which were sown a number of small plates of iron.

The Act of Parliament of 1466 directed that *Butts* should be made in every township at which the inhabitants were to shoot up and down on all Sundays and holy days under pain of a halfpenny fine for every omission. Every Englishman was to have a long bow of his own height, the price was fixed at 3s. 6d. for the best bow stave; this was confirmed in 1512, and again in 1542. References to butts are fairly frequent in parish accounts. The following entries occur in the parish books for 1538–9 of Cratfield, Suffolk:—

The Cost of Yᴇ Butts

Itm to Edmund Myllys for v dayes worke and for hys borde	. ij s. vj d.
Itm Thomas Smythes man for v dayes worke and hys borde	. ij s. j d.
Itm John Smythes man for one days worke and for hys borde	v d.
Itm John Sparham one dayes worke and for hys borde .	vj d.
Itm ye bryngyng downe of the tymber and for Thomas Smythes boyes worke	viij d.
	vj s. ij d.

There was further legislation with regard to butts in the days of Elizabeth and Charles I.

> 1568 (*North Elmham*). At the makinge of the buttes . . xij d.
> 1597, May 16th (*St. Margaret, Westminster*). For making of the butts in Tothil and for carting of a ditch about the butts . . . . 11s. 4d.
> 1603 (*Eltham, Kent*). Pd for felling three trees for the buts and cutting them out . . . . . . xij d.
> For carrying the same timber . . xij d.
> To Hamshere for 2 daies worck to mak the postes and pails for the buts, and set them up . ij s. iiij d.
> Pd to four men that digged turf and labord at the buts iiij s.
> For one hundreth and a half of nails . iij d.
> Pd in charges for their suppers for all them that wraght at the buts, which were three or four more than were hyred, becas we would end them in one day . iiij s.
> For the two bars for the buts, with the staples and ironwork thereunto . . . . . . ij s. ij d.
> 1621-6 (*Stockton, Norfolk*). For bread and beere when the butts were made 5
> To the Boweman for his fees 1
> [Expenditure on the butts as late as 1637.]
> 1628 (*Strood, Kent*). Pd for yᵉ Proclamacon that came from the Kinge for Bowes and Arrowes and going to the butts 1 0
> 1628 (*St. Mary, Reading*). To the repayrrng of the buttes 8 0

The wardens' accounts, where there were no separate constable accounts, occasionally mention *bows* and *arrows*. Yew bows were always considered the best, and various legislative acts endeavoured to prevent any exhaustion of the supply. Archery formed an important quota of the equipment of the general musters of 1558-9, and also of 1588. "A bowe of yew" could be purchased from "the Quenes Magistis Store" for 2s. 8d. and a sheaf of arrows (24) for 20d. The use of the long-bow in warfare lasted much longer in England than on the Continent; it played a considerable part in the lesser battles and skirmishes of the Commonwealth struggle. The parish constable of North Wingfield, Derbyshire, arrested a vagrant in 1633 for cutting boughs for bows from the churchyard yews.

> 1512 (*Shipdham, Norfolk*). Item for a bowe . . xxiij d.
> 1532 (*Cratfield, Suffolk*). Receyvd of Edmund Smyth for a scheff of arrows . . . . . . iij s.

CONSTABLES' ACCOUNTS

       Payd for heads for a scheff of arrows . . viij d.
1538 (*Cratfield*). For a bowe and arrowes . iij s. viij d.
1557-8 (*Ashburton, Devon*). For a sheff of arrows xx d.
1558-9. Rec. from loppng the yew tree . iij s. iiij d.
1559-60. To the Bowyer for makyng of bowes . . xij s.
1560-1. From Edmund Tayllr for 1 piece of le yew sold to him
   1558 (*St Michael, Worcester*). To John Oseland for a sheffe of
      arrowes . . . . ij s. vj d.
      To the same John for a bowe . . . iij s. iiij d.
   1598 (*Wigtoft, Lincolnshire*). Item ij bowes, whereof one fully
      furnyshed.

Some time before the Armada scare, namely, in 1569, commissioners were appointed to press the exercise of the bow, "which was then much decayed"; and for many years commissioners for this purpose moved about the country.

   1577 (*Cratfield*). Payde for the charges befor the Comyssiones
      for bowes . . . . ij s. vj d.
   1580. To the comyssioner for bowes and arrowes at Yaxford . ij s. iiij d.
   1581. Payed to Gregory Rown for agreying with the Comyssioner
      for the bowes when he was at Laxfield ij s. iiij d.

It was not long, however, after the appointment of the first Elizabethan bow commissioners that the superiority of weapons charged with gunpowder became generally admitted, and the harquebus or large form of pistol came into common use. The interesting Cratfield accounts make the first mention of gunpowder in 1577, when 8d. was spent on its purchase. In 1578 a Suffolk county meeting held at Stowmarket determined that "they should spend their time principally in the shot with the bullet." In 1585 the parish of Cratfield paid to the constables the great sum of £3 10s. "for powder and lynt" (match).

Henceforward, for fully a century, it became customary to place considerable stores of gunpowder, bullet, and match within the parish churches, ready for parochial use. In 1559, the fine church of St. Columb Major gave shelter to "twelve li of matchs and some gunpowder," and in 1591 to 56 lb. of gunpowder. In 1595 there was "a rate made for powlder" which brought in £3 15s. 5d. In 1596 a like rate brought in the large sum of £7 3s. 9d., and it is recorded that there was a store of 74 lb. of powder in barrel, besides 9 lb. of old powder. The churchwardens, here as elsewhere, occasionally traded in the parish store of powder. In 1595 Thomas Pollamaunter bought a pound of gunpowder for 18d., and Francis Benny a pound for 1s. In 1596 the parish actually sold £7 3s. 2d. worth, as well as some barrels and match, and even then had no less than 83 li. of powder left in store. In 1617 a barrel containing "five score pound weight" cost £4 10s. Eventually this church suffered severely from being used as a powder magazine. Through the conduct of some mischievous boys, in 1676, the grand chancel and fine chapels were greatly damaged by a powder explosion.

A score or two of cases could readily be cited of powder stored for many a long year in fine churches such as St. Martin's-in-the-Fields; St. Margaret, Westminster; Morpeth and Newcastle in the north; Mere, Wilts: Sidbury and Honiton, Devon; Minehead and Dunster, Somerset; Chelmsford, Essex; and Beccles and Worstead, East Anglia. The marvel is that more churches did not suffer.

> 1589 (*Mere, Wilts*). For a hundred pownd and a half of Gunpowder at xiiij d. ob. the pownd wth the barrell and the charge of fetching the gune powder .   vj li. iiij s.
> 1642 (*St. Margaret, Westminster*). For the carpenters worke of the floore over the stairs where the powder and bullets and match lyethe . . . . . . 1 15 (
> 1646 (*Basingstoke*). Paid for twice drawing and engrossing of the petition delivered to the Committee at Winchester for allowance towards the reparation of the church, being much torn by the blowing up of gunpowder lying in the church . . . . 3s. 4d.

The following are representative examples of parish armour and parish soldier extracts selected from upwards of fifty that we had copied :—

> 1546. (*Cratfield, Suffolk*). To John Newson for j harnes (set of armour) . . . . x s.
> To John Rowse for j sheve of arrows (24) . ij s. x d.
> To John Thurketyll for j dagger . . xiij d.
> To Thomas Smyth for j byll . . . . xij d.
> To William Crysp for a Sallet . . . ij s. iiij d.
> To Richard Baldry for a Sallet and a gorgett . iij d.
> 1569. For the corslet . . . . . . vj s. vj d.

1587.	For carrynge the Colyver to Beckles .	xvj d.
	For a head pese	v s.
	For a sworde .	vj s.
1588.	Payd to the constables for the cotes for the sowldyers	iij li. x s. viij d.
1596.	For powder for the Toune Mosket .	vj d.
1597.	Pd for the towne musket	21s. 6d.
1621.	For a hamper for the town armr	4s.
1625.	Paid to Mr. Stevun the armourer for triming of the two town Corslets and the new gorgetts .	£1 7 (
1628.	For powder and match for the 9 trained soldiers	15 (

Part of the church of St. Martin's-in-the-Fields served as a storehouse for the parish armour. One Abraham Leeds received 10s. a year in Elizabethan days "for kepeinge and lookinge unto the Armor." From 1550 onwards the references to armour in these accounts are incessant. In 1556, 3s. 9d. was paid for "fetherenge of thre sheaf of Arrowes." In 1569 "a newe presse for the armour" cost £3. There was an expenditure of 12d. in 1586 "for ye makinge cleane of ye shert of male." An inventory of 1598 records:—

IN THE ARMORY

Item iij Arming swordes. one horsemans sworde and ij backe swords. vj Calevers and a horsemans peece. iiij flaskes and touche boxes. iij Daggers. iiij white Corsettes and ij blacke Corslettes. iij Almayne Ryvettes. iiij morrions. iiij Sallettes. one buffe Jerkyn. one Coate of Mayle. ij blacke bills and vi Pykes.

1558	(*St. Margaret, Westminster*). To Law, fletcher, for fetheryng of iiij sheffe of arrowse and new triming of the heads	iiij s.
1562.	Ten pair of allmen rivettes, one harnis for a horseman, vj blak billes, vij shefs of arrowse, and vj daggers. For the new fethering of two sheaf of arrowes	ij s.
1567.	For mending and setting up the coate armour in Our Lady chapel	vj d.
1569.	P^d towards the harness that came from the Tower of London	v li.
1577.	For new stocking of five calyvers	xij s.
1579.	For scowering of the armor and shott against the muster in Totehel Fields	j li. vj s.
	For powder for the soldiers upon the mustering day	xij s. iiij d.
	P^d to the soiers, the ansyant (ensign) bearer and to him that played upon the drome .	j li. vij s. iiij d.
1574-5	(*Tavistock*). Delyvered to Mr. Constable for ij Costeletts bought at Plymnothe	iij li.

For one halberde	vj s. viij d.
For one flaske and touch box	. ij s. vj d.
Delyvered the Constable for settinge fourthe the sawdyers into Ireland and for armor at that tyme .	. vij li.
1594-5. For a Sword and a pyke	iiij s. iiij d.
For ij dayes service with the parish armor .	xvj d.
For makyng Cleane the armor and Carynge of the same to Plympton	. ij s. ij d.
1605-6. For keepynge Cleane of the Churche armour	. viij d.

In 1583, St. Columb Major, Cornwall, possessed 4 pairs of Corslettes, 6 long pikes, 3 Callyvers, 3 Flaskes and touche boxes, 7 swoordis, 3 daggers, 6 hangings for swoordes, 2 murryens.

In a later account were added "2 burgonettes (bayonets), 3 calyver mouldes, and some gunpowder."

1590. A Note of the armoure of *Repton* receaved into the handes of Rycharde Weatte, beyinge Constable.
Inprimis ij corsletts wth all that belongeth unto them.
It. ij platt' cotts (coats of plate armour).
It. ij swordes and iij daigers and ij gyrgells.
It. ij calevers wth flaxes and tuchboxe.
It. ij pyckes and ij halberds.
It. for the Tr'band Souldiar a cote and bowe and a shiffe of arowes and a quiver.

1601.	It. spent in gatheringe ye money for the meamed soldiers	. xviij d.
	It. payd to the meamed Souldiers for the whole year	iij s. iiij d.
	It. payd to Sir Homfry Ferrers, Knyght, at the Muster, ye 4 day of August	. xxx s.
	It. paid at same Muster in charges wth the Souldiers	iij s. vj d.
	It. paid for one letheringe for ye flaxe (flask)	vj d.
	It. for one dagger sheathe and a sworde scaber	xij d.
	It. payd for ye swordes	iij s.
	It. spent at Clockesmithes receavinge ye armore	iiij d.
	It. given to ye prest Souldiers	. xij s.
	It. pay^d for one Horse to carry ye armor, . .	. xiii. d.
	It. spent ledeinge ye armor to Darby . .	ij. d.
1597-8	(*Hartland, Devon*). Paid to George Husbande for iij bullet bagges for the iiij churche musquettes .	xij d.
	For lace to fasten the lyning of the morians belonginge to the churche corselettes	ij d.
	For mendinge the head of one of the churche pikes .	j d.
	For a hilt and handle and a scabart for a sworde and for mendinge a dagger of the church	ij s.

	Paid att Exon for a corslett furnished and iij musquettes furnished, haveinge one dagger and for a pike	vj li. xiij s.
1598-9.	Paid the x of November for the carriage of iij mens armor at Torrington, when the souldiers went into Ireland	xij d.
	Paid for the amendinge of one of the churche calivers, with a morian, flaske, a tochebox, and other furniture for the same	x s. vij d.
	Paid at Plymmouthe for two swordes for the pyoners	ij s. iij d.
	Paid for a black bill for the pyoners .	ij s. iij d.
1608	(*Wimeswold*). Payd for the swordes dressinge and for oyle for the harness	xxij d.
	Carryinge the Armour to fysson . . .	viij d.
1623	Payed to Rawlin for dressing the Armoure	iiij d.
	Payed for bandeleyres	ij s. iiij d.
1627.	Pd for a musket rest	10d.
	P^d for a sack to carry the armor in	1s.
	For carring of the Armor to Leicester . . .	2s.
1635.	For browninge two of the trained mens swordes	4d.
1637.	To the armor men for dressinge the Townes Armor for a yeare	4s.
1639.	For making a rest	5d.
	For mendinge a musket and for settinge the Irons upon 2^d rest	4d.
1640.	For a Picke mendinge, and for mendinge two Rests and a Gyrdle	20d.

It was agreed in 1622, by the parish of Pittington, Durham,

> That the comon Armes, being 3 muskets with the furniter belonging to them, and 3 costolets with the pikes and all the furneter belonginge to them shall be made complet and fully furnished att the charg of the whole parishe by generall sesment ... and that upon Easter Teueseday yearly in the fore noone the whole six common armors shalbe brought in and viewed by the Twelve of the parish, what case it is in, that it may be mantaned and kept as it ought to be.

1632	(*Cheddar*). For setting up a frame in the churche to hange the armor upon	xij s.
	For carryinge the armor to Bridgwater and Axbridge	vj s. vj d.
	For dressinge the armor	vj s. viij d.
1638.	John Bale hath agreed to keepe the armor of Chedder yearly at viij s. the year, vizt that is to keepe it cleane and other reparacions, as in former tyme it doth appeare hee hath done, that is with buckels, nailes, and leather.	

The searching for Saltpetre was a great source of trouble to constables in late Elizabethan and Stuart days. When the use of firearms became general towards the end of the sixteenth century, nitre was much needed for the manufacture of gunpowder. It was discovered that the top soil of farmyards, cattle stalls, stables, and other places exposed to the vapours of putrefying matter afforded, when mixed with ashes, a considerable supply of nitre. Hence these substances were claimed by the Crown, and granted to individuals or companies for the making of saltpetre. The rigour of these saltpetre men became most burdensome, as they insisted on the right of entering stables and even houses in search of material. Hence, to avoid such entrance, it became customary not only for individuals, but also for townships, to bribe or compound with the saltpetre men to escape their visits, and to be free from the privilege they claimed of using the parishioners' carts, without payment, for the conveyance of material to their works. A proclamation of 1627 by Charles I considerably increased the extent of this odious burden; but at last, in 1656, an Act of Parliament forbade any entry into houses or enclosed lands for this purpose without the leave of the owners.

 1596 (*Cratfield, Suffolk*). Layd out to the goodman Rous for the
  sault peter man . . . . . . xxxvj s.
 1602 (*Repton, Derby*). Spent with ye salt peter men   ij d.
 1601 (*Wimeswold, Leicester*). Pd for carryinge Ashes to Leicester
  to the sault peter worke . . . . vj s. viij d.

As to Purveyance, the wardens' accounts of Burton Latimer, Northants, for 1566, contain entries relative to that parish's share in the provisions for the Queen's household during her progress in June. Two men received 11d. "for dryvyng of ye Quenes cariege."

Queen Elizabeth visited Suffolk in 1572, 1573, 1577, 1578, and 1579, and in several subsequent years. The Cratfield accounts are eloquent as to the burden these visits imposed on her subjects.

 1572. Payed unto the Constables for the Quens gesse . xxvj s.
 1573. „ „ for a callfe for the Quene   iij s.
 1577. „ „ for the Quenes botter . xv s.
 1578. Payd to John Gylharde and John Smyth for bryngng forth
  the calves for the Quenes Majestyes house   x d.
  Payd for the losse of the calves to mak good the pryse   xvj s. iiij d.
  To John Melles for cairynge the Quenes botter . . vj d.

1586. To John Mells for a cafe to serve ye Quen . xiij s. iiij d.
1587. Laid out to Clark the purvar (purveyor) for the carriage of the Quenes chese and butter . . xvj d.

In 1585, Cratfield received from the royal purveyor 4s. 6d. for 4 capons, 5 pullets, and 6 hens, but these poultry had cost the parish 5s. 11d. in addition to carriage expenses.

1590. Pd to Willm Aldus for a calfe for the Quene . vj s. iiij d.
Pd to Willm Warne for a combe of wheate for the Quene . xj s.
Pd to chief constable for deliverye of same wheate . vj d.
Pd to Meeke for caring of the same wheate . xvj d.

The grievances in connection with the seizing of provisions for the royal household, and the inadequancy of the payment for the same, grew to such a pitch that the Queen was forced to permit the counties to arrange composition for the same. A scheme for Suffolk was drawn up at Stowmarket in September 1592. The high constable for each Hundred was ordered to present at sessions all who refused to pay. The Cratfield accounts for 1595 show that that parish was amerced at 30s. Before 1592 the loss sustained by Cratfield was frequently in excess of this commuted sum. Thus in one year the loss on two weighs of cheese and 1½ barrels of butter was 45s. 4d., which was the difference in the price given by the parish and that which was received from the purveyors. The purveyance composition varied greatly year by year; Cratfield's share ran up to £4 in 1597, but fell to £3 5s. in 1598.

Purveyance compositions were continued under James I, but after a lax fashion. In 1609, Cratfield paid as its share of the royal household provisions £3 16s., but had also to pay a further sum of 12s. 6d. as the county compoundes fell short by £135 "by reason of the great price of things."

1586 (*Mendlesham, Suffolk*). Item payd to the constables for that they layde oute more than the quenes price for on weight and three quarters of chese and six firkins of butter, and ther charges . . . . . . xxij s. vj d.
Item pay to them more for thre combe oates more than the quenes price . . . . x s.

The Leicestershire parish of Stathern, adjoining Belvoir Castle, has detailed constable accounts which bear testimony to the burdens of the visits of Charles I.

1633. Payed for the cart that went for the Kinges bysenes the
18th of May 6 8
It payed to Branston men for finding a part of a Drafte for
the Kings use Julie 22 . . . . . 1 4
It payed to Branston men finding a draughs to goe about the
Kings bysenes the 25 of Julie 10 4
It payed to Mr. Elson for his majestie provision 13th April . 1 0 0
It payed for poultree the same day 7 0
1634. It payed to foer men that went with the carrages about the
King busines . . . . 4 c
It payed for heay and straw and other the King provision . 12 0
It spent at that time at Belver . . . . . 1 c
It payed to Raph and William Walker when they went with
the cartt to Lessester about the Kings bisines august 9 . 5 0
It payed to Raph Baynes for carring capens to Lessester . 1 4
It payed for three capens and three pullites . 5 0
It payed to Mr Elson for cooles to make salt Peetr for the
Kinges servis the 1 of October 6 8
1636. It payed to Mr Elsten of Muston for otes hay straw carte
and carrages for his ma^{tie} Court at Belver August the 28 1 1 6
It payed for a aquittance for the same . . . 4
It spent when I was at lunson with the maire 2

There were few more constant drains on parish funds than the relief of licensed vagrants travelling with passes or passports, or other tramps in distress. The amount of traffic of this nature through parishes traversed by any main road can only be gathered from those few cases in which full constable accounts have been preserved. Here, for instance, are the particulars of the relief of this nature granted by the constable of Stathern in the single month of May 1630:—

Paid for a passe making ye jth of May . . . .
Geven to tow poore men ye vjth of May . . . .
Geven to one poore man ye vijth of May . . . .
Geven to a poore man that had a passe ye xvth of May 1
Pay^d for a passe making ye 18th of May . . . 2
Geven tow men and there wifes and one child ye 24th of May 6
Geven to one man and two children ye 25th of May 2
Geven to tow women and one child ye 26th of May
Geven to one man and a child that had pa yer 27th of May
Geven to one man and his wife and two children ye 29th of May
Geven to thre me ye 31th of May that had a passe . 2

Rog money or *Rogge money* is a fairly frequent entry in sixteenth-

and seventeenth-century constable or parish accounts in the north. It is thus defined in Houghton, Durham, accounts of 1658:—

> The Rogue money is a yearly payment by this Parish at Midsoumer, payable to the High Constable for prisoners in goale, correction, etc., and since the yeare 1623 the said payments hath bin eleven pound five shillings a yeare.

Early Elizabethan legislation (18 Eliz. c. 3) provided that in every shire there should be at least one *House of Correction* for rogues, vagabonds, and sturdy beggars. In the next reign the purpose of these houses, differing in several respects from regular gaols for convicted criminals, was more specifically defined; in addition to being places of detention of rogues and vagabonds, and all poor persons who would not employ themselves on appointed work, they were to provide temporary imprisonment for those who by incorrigible or dangerous habits set the parish constable at defiance.

DUCKING-STOOL FOR A SCOLD
(*From an old Chap book*)

Each parish also possessed its *stocks* and *whipping-post*, and the larger ones a *pillory*, a *ducking-stool* for scolds, and a *cage* or lock-up for immediate detention. The constable was responsible for the repair or reconstruction of all these implements of punishment.

1572 (*Kingston*). The making of the cucking stool	viij s.
Ironwork for the same	iij s.
Timber for the same	vij s. vj d.
Three brasses for the same and three wheels	iiij s. x d.

338 THE CHURCHWARDENS' ACCOUNTS

 1588-9 (*Berkhampstead*). For mendinge of the stockes .   vj d.
 1598 (*St. Michael, Cornhill*). For making of Irons to the pillory for a whipping place, for locks, paynting, and to the Carpenter in all . . . . . xiij s. ij d.
 1630 (*St. Alphege, London Wall*). For Irons for the Whippinge poste and a locke 2 0
 1631 It payd to Roger Lee for mending the stocks . 4d.
 1655 (*Cowden, Kent*). Yron for the stocks and whipping post, 23 cwt. 9 10
 Timber for the stocks and whipping post . 8 0

The constable was responsible for the usual *whipping* of men, women, and mere children for such crimes as begging without a licence. See *Parish Registers*, pp. 230-2. To find an executioner required a small outlay; and after the whipping, the vagrant had to receive a small sum, usually 2d., as an aid to proceeding to another parish.

 1598 (*St. Bartholomew Exchange*). For whipping of a poore man   vj d.
 For whipping one at the poste . . . . iiij d.
 1600. For whipping Elizabeth Justice . . . . iiij d.
 For her pasainge money . . . . . ij d.
 For her provision all night, being brought at vj of the Clocke at night . . . . . . vj d.
 1601. For the whippinge of Joan and Amys Brown and for ther pas to Norwich . . . . . . xij d.
 For whipping of Gillime Anderson the same day being a merchante daughter of newcastle, and for her pas   vj d.
 1602 (*Melton Mowbray*). Geven to Robert Moodee for wippin tow pore folkes . . . . . . ij d.
 And gave them when they were wipped . . . ij d.
 Geven to Tomlyn's boy for whippin a man and a woman ij d.
 And gave them when they went . . . . ij d.

At St. Columb Major the whipping was done by the same man who was the official vermin killer; in 1616 he was paid 7d. " for a precept for the Ayde and for whipping a beggar."

It is supposed that *Gipsies* did not come into England until about the year 1500. In 1530 their itinerancy was forbidden by statute, and they were expelled the realm. It was afterwards enacted by statutes 2 Philip and Mary, c. 4, and 5 Eliz. c. 20, that any gipsy remaining a month in the kingdom would be judged guilty of felony, without benefit of clergy. A further statute of 1562 adjudged anyone guilty of felony who consorted with

"Egyptians" for forty days. Under this last cruel Elizabethan statute five men were hung at Durham in 1596, and thirteen persons were executed under the same law at a single assize in the days of Charles I. This odious statute was not repealed until 1783. The gipsies, however, persisted in coming to England and were for the most part mercifully treated, in defiance of the laws, by the constables and parish authorities.

    1602 (*Repton, Derbyshire*). Given to Gipsies ye xxx daye of Januarye to avoyde ye towne . . . . xx d.
    1613 (*Melton Mowbray*). Gyven to the gippsis to ride the towne of them . . . . xij d.
    1632 (*Stathern*). Given to a great Companie of gipes 16 August . 1 4
    1638. Given to a companie of gepsies May the 2th . . . 1 0
    Given to a Companie of gepsies Sept the 15th 9

The Constable's Account Book of Helmdon, Northants, for the years 1653 to 1717, which is now in the Bodleian Library, contains among the entries of expenditures a number of references to money paid to bands of passing gipsies.

    Fol. 5v. (Between Sept. and Oct. 29, 1658.) Item giuen (un)to a Company of Gipsees that were brought with a passe from Wapenham, 4d.

    Fol. 26. Dec. 12, 1682, giuen to a Company of Geipsseys, 1 0.

    Fol. 27. April 10, 1683, giuen to a Company of Gippseys that had a passe, 1 0.

    July 24, giuen to a Company of Gipses, 1 0.

    Sept. 20, giuen to a Company of Gipeseses, 1 0.

        giuen to Jeningsis Boay to haue the Gipseses out of the towne, 1d.

    Fol. 37. Oct. 5, 1688, given a Company of Gipsyes 8 in Number who came with a Passe from Eaton in Kent to Passe into Cumberland. Witnesse Jo. Hawten, Sen., 6d.

    Fol. 38. Jan. 29, 1689. Giuen a Company of Gipsyes 12 in Number who Came with a Guide & to Pass into Essex, 6d.

    Fol. 41. March 14, 1689. Given to 14 Gipsyes who had a Pass, 6d.

    Fol. 42. May 27, 1689. Given a Company of Gipsyes nro. 15 who had a Pass to pass out of Kent into Cheshire, 1 2.

    Fol. 44. 1690. Given to a Company of Gipsyes 13 number who had a pass, 10d.

    Fol. 54. 1693-4. pd. to Nat. Crosse for 6 gipses laying their one Night ordered by Rich. Clarke, 1-06.

    Fol. 68. (Between Aug. 2 and 23, 1697.) giuen to 8 Gipsyes who had a Pass to goe to Robin Hoods Bay, 1 0.[1]

---

[1] These extracts kindly given me through Mr. R. A. S. Macfie, honorary secretary of the Gypsey Lore Society.

Another interesting duty pertaining to the office of constable in certain parishes was the building up, maintaining, and lighting of *Beacons*. Legislative enactments of Richard II, Henry IV, and Elizabeth provided for beacons to warn of dangers on various high lands, and more especially within sight of the coast. " Attached to the service of them, were some of the men called ' hoblers,' who are often named in old Acts among the men-at-arms. They were men lightly armed, who rode on a light nag or 'hobby,' and so could instantly and quickly carry intelligence if need were."

1566 (*Eltham, Kent*). Paid for watchinge the beacon on Shutters Hill	v s.
1570. Paid to Richard Bosi for the beacons	xxx s.
1574. Paid to John Bebley for making the beacon	iij s. iiij d.

In 1619 the wardens of Seal gave 2s. "to the constable tourdes billding the beakon."

It now remains to give a good general idea of the voluminous civil duties that used to fall to the lot of the parish constable by giving (1) an analysis of the seventeenth-century Wimeswold accounts, (2) a brief reference to the important printed Constable minutes of Manchester Manor, and finally (3) to the remarkable and more recent MS. documents of Combe, Oxon.

The Constable Accounts of Wimeswold, Leicestershire, from 1602 to 1669 (Brit. Mus. Add. 10,457) are contained in a MS. volume of 319 folios. Nicholls, the historian of the county, made some extracts from this highly interesting MS. in the second part of his third volume.

The following are the chief disbursements for 1608:—

To the payment of the seaventh fyfteene	iiij li.
To the mayned solldiers and hospitalls at Easter	iiij s. iiij d.
To the jeale att the same tyme	iij s. iiij d.
To the provysyon	xxxiij s.
To the provision of poultrye	vj s. viij d.
Spent when I went before the Clarke of the Markett wyth strikes, for our dinnour	xv d.
To one which had losses by fyre on saynt James day with passport	ij d.
Gyvyn to a poore woman which lay in the Church porch and to goe forth of the towne because she had a child which were borne in the toone for to take yt wyth her	vj d.

Seventeen tramps, with passports, were relieved this year by the Wimeswold constable; the relief varied from 1d. to 3d. a head. The total disbursements were £7 19s. 4d.

The levies made at Wimeswold in 1688 for the discharge of the usual constable's accounts were in the first instance raised at the rate of 1½d. a beast, and 6d. a score of sheep. The following are the first six entries of the levy of 17th April 1608, " for the payment of the Fyffteene."

Mr. Ballard, xiij score sheepe And xxiij bestes	ix s. x d.
Mr. Calton, iij score sheepe And ix bestes .	ij s. vij d.
Mr. Poulson, ix score and x sheepe And ij bestes	v s.
William Barrett, ix score sheepe And xx bestes	vij s.
Edward Blunt junior iij score and xv sheepe and vij bestes	ij s. viij d.
William Blunt senior iij score and xvij sheepe and xvij bestes	iiij s. ob.

There were no fewer than 92 cattle or sheep owners in the parish. The entries for this levy afford proof of general prosperity in connection with the unenclosed common system. Twenty-one householders possessed two cows, and nine owned a single "beste." The total of this levy amounted to £5 9s. 6d.

A second levy was made on 5th June of the same year for " A subply of soldiers, after xx[ti] Acres of Land iiij d. and Cottigers a 1d. a beaste." The total of this levy is missing. There were forty holders of land, varying from Mr. Ballard who held eleven score acres, down to " Thomas Wildman for beste and land ij d."

A third levy for general constable's expenses was collected on 5th August 1608, after a penny a beast; it produced 36s. 3d., showing that the kine numbered 435.

The following are among the items "layd forthe by Thomas Franke junior," constable for this year:—

Payd to the heigh Constable towardes bringe of gune powder for our majesties service the x day of Januarie	xiij s. iiij d.
Geven the xix day of januarie to a woman wch came forth of bedlam wyth passport	ij d.
Geven the same day to ij solldiers forth of Ireland with passporte	vj d.
Spent the first day of Februarie when we were before the Clarke of the Markett	ij s. ij d.
Paye for alowinge the wayghtes	iiij d.
Geven to a Bygg belly woman to goe forth of the towne	ij d.
Geven to a lame woman wh had but one legg	ij d.
Geven to a man and a woman with a child on horse backe which had losses by fyer wyth passport	iiij d.

Mendinge the stockes	ij d.
Provision for his majesties household	xxxj s.
The provision of poultrey	vj s. viij d.

The payments this year for maimed soldiers and hospitals were 4s. 4d. a quarter, and for the Fifteenth £4 2s. A considerable proportion of the passported tramps of 1608 were soldiers, one of whom was blind; some of the tramps came from the far north, one from Carlisle and another from Newcastle.

The following entries from these constable's accounts have been selected as showing the diversity of local and national subjects which they so abundantly illustrate during a critical period in England's history:—

1602.	Payd for carryinge Ashes to Leicester to the sault peter worke.	vj s. viij d.
1607.	Geven to a poore man and a woman which were punished accordinge to the statute	ij d.
1611.	Paide towardes the releiffe of the visited folke in Thrumaston	v s.
	Paid to the visited folkes in Leicester.	vj s.
	Paid to John Smyth and his wyef for three weeks when they were kepte in there house beinge suspected of the Plague	ix s.
1623.	Given to William Henson for catching of mooles	x s.
	Payed for a payre of stocks	v s. iiij d.
1627.	To a poore man with seaven children	iij d.
	For a criple with two children and for a horse to carye him to Burton	vij d.
1628.	For ye soulgers Coulors	4s.
	For a pound of gunpowder and 2 yards of match the second trayning	1s. 2d.
1630.	To two shouldgers wch ad beene commanders in ye lowe cuntreys	4d.
1632.	To a Seafaring man wh was taken by the Dunkerkes	3d.
1634.	For two Carts and Carriage for Carryinge the Kinges M^{ties} provision from Belvoire to Newarke	30s.
	Paid to Thomas Burton for wardinge and keepinge begars etc. forthe of the towne vij d. a weeke, for his whole years wages	30s. 4d.
1635.	Spent when I was before the Justices at Syston to presente the Recusantes and the punishinge of Roagues	2s. 6d.
	Spent when wee wente with the Poppitt Player before Mr. Roosley	1s.
	To the Postmayster to free the Towne of Post Horses for this yeare	

CONSTABLES' ACCOUNTS 343

To Foure men for wardinge on the Wake day		1s. 4d.
1636. For makinge a pass for a man which I sett in the Stockes which had 4 children with him		2d.
For makinge the Billes the last yeare and this yeare which the inhabitantes was severally taxed and assessed to pay towardes the makinge of his Maties Shippes		3s. 4d.
1637. Given to a great bellyed woman wch came from Hoton with a passe		6d.
Paid for a Carte and a Mydwyfe and two women to go with her to Wylloughby		1s. 4d.
1639. For two Loades and a half of Coales for the salt peter men		10s.
1640. Spent on myself and my horse goeinge two days to Leicester about the stayinge the Sessements of the Shipp Money		2s. 8d.
Paid to Mr. Browne the Salt Peter maker for freeing the towne for carryinge 2 lode of Ashes from Loughborro to Ashley		17s. 6d.
1643. To a blind minyster with a pass from Constable to Constable and for his charges for his super and his lodginge at Richard Leakes		6d.
1642. Given to James Dallenocke of Oukeham Relater for the King to see ther be nether Roogues Seminaries nor Jesuits inhabiting in our towne and y^t our buts and high wayes be in good repaire		1s.
Given to Richard Herbert of Christ Church in ye Ile of Man wch had great losse by fire by reason of ye pirats shooting wild fire into their Towne and had Certificate and manie Earls Lords and Knights hands at it		7s.

To Robert Leake for carieng the King's goods from Nottingan 1 0 0
To William Blunt for the like 10 0
1643. To John Hall for lodginge thre troophers . 3 9
[Several like entries.]
1644. For two hundered of Colles wch was burnte in the church when the troupers billited at o towne . 1 8
1647. Spent when the souldgers made their tickets at the Church 1 0
For the poore visited people of Loughborrow 14 0
A tax made the 20th of September for the Raysinge of money towardes the payment of Sr Thomas Fairefax armyes and for carryinge on the warr in Ireland by divers of the inhabitants of Wymeswoold (90 in all) 10 15 4
1649. Paid the souldiers to quarter themselves a weake Aprill 23^d 14 0
[Seven other like weekly entries.]
1651. To the Ringers when they Rong for ye Cottes (Scots) Route 2 0

1653. A Certificate from the Keepers of the liberties of England	3	0
1655. Paid for the Whipin post and the Ringes which are one it	1	8
1658. Given to two vagerand women that was stocked and whiped		4
1659. Given to fore soulgers which would have had horsses to ride after the Armie to Darbe	4	4
1660. Pd to fore men that wached the foolish man one night and for ale and bread and candles	1	2
1661. Warand for provition monie for the Kings househould		10
Given to a man that brought an order for bows and arrows	1	0
Pd to head Constable for proision monie for the Kings househould	1 10	1

STOCKS AND WHIPPING POST: UFFORD, SUFFOLK

1662. My charges going to Throggington to put in a bill of presentment of such as goe not to Church	1	4
Spent on the Kings Crownation Day with yᵉ Ringers	1	0
For Catching 4 dussen of Sparrows		6
1663. Spent at Gadsby when I went before the Justices with the auld souldgers baptists and quakers	6	0

The full and valuable Constable Accounts of the Manor of Manchester were transcribed and edited by Mr. J. P. Earwaker, in three volumes (1891-2); they extend from 1612 to 1776. The introduction supplies a good summary of the origin and duties of the office of constable. The following are among the entries relative to the Plague :—

1625. Oct. 19. Pd a Messenger which the Constables of Stafford sent to o^r Constable to Cartiefie against infectious goods in xij packes newlie come from London, and thus it were right they were put out of ye town . . . . 6d.

1631. July 24. Pd and given to 8 persons to cause them to retorne whence they came because they were Suspected to have been in some Infected place . . . . 20s.

1631. Oct. 27. For the releefe and watching of those at Cabbins £21 11 11
[Cabins or wooden huts were erected on Collyhurst Common for the isolation of those suffering from the plague.]

1645. Sept. 26. To Dr. Smith for pte of his wages for his service in ye tyme of visitacon £39

The diversity of subjects treated of in these volumes may be judged from the following list of headings:—

Aletasters, Alehouse Keepers, Ballad-singers, Beacons, Beadles, Bell (market), Branding, Cage, Candles for watch, Catchpole or Bailiff, Clerk of the Market, Coroners, Cuckstool, Cock-crowing, Drunkards, Fire Buckets and Engines, Fortune-tellers, Gibbet, Gipsies, Handcuffs, House of Correction, King's Evil, Lent, Leper, Market, Militia, Pillory, Plague, Players, Recusants, Rogues, Saltpeter-man, Scolds' Bridles, Searches (Privy), Soldiers, Stocks, Trained Bands, Whipping, and "Window Peepers."

The parish of Combe, near Woodstock, Oxfordshire, has Constable's accounts extending from 1788 to 1822. The mole-catcher was paid two guineas in 1791, and in the same year £1 16s. was paid for "crow-keeping in seedtime," a most unusual entry. The "stox" were repaired in 1792 at a charge of 18s. 4d. New stocks cost £3 4s. in 1805; they were repaired for 12s. in 1821. A pair of handcuffs was bought in 1802 for 5s. The chief annual charge was the levy under the head of Marshalsea (spelt with endless variants) money, chiefly for gaol expenses. It was paid twice a year and fluctuated considerably in amount; in 1788 it amounted to £6 7s. 9d.; in 1791, £4 14s. 9d.; in 1809, £4 10s.; in 1810, £8 15s.; and in 1813, £34 5s. At the head of each year's accounts is the entry as to the swearing-in of the constable and the tithingmen, his two assistants, at the Park Gate Court; this court was the Court Baron of the Duke of Marlborough, held at the Woodstock Park Gate, as Combe parish (with several other adjacent parishes) was a member of the Honour of Woodstock

Manor, formerly ancient demesne of the Crown. Other regular entries related to the preparing of the jury list and taking it to Oxford to be signed; and making the militia lists and attending at the balloting for the same. The constable's services for "keeping the peace at Combe feast" are usually entered at 1s. 6d., but he was occasionally able to discharge this duty at the lower fee of 1s. This feast is the annual fair held on the village green on the Monday and Tuesday after the 10th of August; the church is dedicated to St. Laurence. On two occasions the constable received 1s. for keeping the peace at the 5th of November "bonfire."

There is a highly remarkable entry in the last of these village constable records under date 28th September 1822:—

Paid Francis Norrays
John Slatter
Joseph Strickley
Wm. Motley } For guarding the Church Night and Day.
James Hone £1 4 0
Rich. Tallett
James Tallett
Timothy Slings

On the constable's accounts coming before the parish vestry, strong objections were raised to this charge. They considered it an "imposition as there were no orders issued from the churchwardens to the constable to guard the church, the churchwardens being present at the time, and the constable has declared repeatedly that Dr. Mavor as a magistrate had given him orders never to act on consecrated ground. Instead of the constable preserving the Peace, he came in the night with part of these men and most disgracefully violated the Peace."

This so-called "guarding of the church" was the culminating point of an unhappy parish scandal. The rectory of Combe was appropriated to the College of Lincoln in the fifteenth century, and the college was bound by statute to appoint a chaplain to serve the cure, instead of a duly instituted vicar in accordance with usual precedent. The chaplain was appointed by the Rector or Head of Lincoln College, and removable at will. Dr. Edward Tatham, who was Rector of Lincoln for forty years in the first half of last century, was a man of headstrong will and of a coarse, turbulent character. Sooner or later he seems to have violently quarrelled with every one with whom he came in contact. In 1817 he appointed Rev. Bartley Lee, M.A., to Combe chaplaincy, assuring him, as Mr. Lee stated, that it was a life appointment. For two years Mr. Lee lived quietly at the chaplain's house with his invalid wife, worked hard, and won the respect and affection of the parishioners. Then Dr. Tatham had some disagreement with the chaplain, and in November 1820 gave him peremptory notice to quit, and appointed another chaplain, who was to take duty on the Sunday following the letter. On Sunday, 3rd December, the new man, Mr. Rose, a fellow of the college, appeared in surplice in the church before the morning service, but found Mr. Lee (who had taken legal advice) already in the reading desk. Mr. Rose was ordered to leave by the churchwarden. The Rector then took action against Mr. Lee in the Court of Arches; the suit dragged on through the greater part of 1821, when it was dismissed with costs on the ground that the Court had no jurisdiction. Meanwhile the college withheld all payment of salary, and Mr. Lee had very small means. In the midst of the worry his wife died. But friends came to his support, and nothing would induce him to leave.

Dr. Tatham, furious at the chaplain's opposition, and having failed in his legal methods, determined to use force to carry out his purpose. Accordingly, in September 1822, he brought over to Combe, without warning, a locksmith, four Oxford constables, and two Lincoln undergraduates. The locksmith applied new locks to all the church doors, and handed the keys to the Rector, who intended to let himself into the church on the following Sunday and conduct the services. One of the constables was locked in the church on Saturday evening, with instructions to be ready to admit Dr. Tatham on the morrow and to assist to keep Mr. Lee out should he attempt to enter. This constable was supplied with provisions, but the night was cold, and he wrapped himself up in the altar cloth and some other church hangings—a fact that was brought up against Dr. Tatham at the subsequent trial. On Sunday morning, between ten and eleven, the Rector, carrying his surplice, appeared in the churchyard, and was startled to find the whole enclosure filled with a crowd of villagers, augmented by not a few from neighbouring parishes, forming a crowd of four or five hundred persons. Loud shouts were raised of "No Tatham! Lee for ever!" Tatham with his few partisans made for the south chancel door, but the crowd blocked his approach with threatening gestures, and he withdrew to the rectory, "in fear of his life," as he subsequently stated. Meanwhile Lee, ready vested and accompanied by his lawyer brother and by Lord Charles Churchill (brother of the Duke of Marlborough), approached the main doorway on the north side of the church. The door was soon wrenched from its hinges by the aid of crowbars, and fell with a crash into the church. The Oxford constable was found within ready to resist Mr. Lee's entrance, but he and his paid companions, who joined him, were flung out one by one from the church with their clothes torn to ribbons. Mr. Lee's friends completely filled the church, and the service proceeded. By the irony of events it was "a Sacrament Sunday."

This distressful event was the so-called Combe Riot. At the next Oxford assizes, Dr. Tatham indicted Mr. Lee, Lord Churchill, and twenty Combe labourers for riot with violence in Combe churchyard; three labourers were convicted and sentenced to short terms of imprisonment, the rest were acquitted. The chaplain's house was the freehold of the college, and the turbulent Rector, to the grief of nearly the whole parish, won the day by legally ejecting Mr. Lee from his residence. Tatham was burnt in effigy on the village green.

APPENDIX

CONSECRATION CROSSES

THERE are few subjects as to which more blunders have been made in the past (by myself included) than that of consecration crosses, and several misconceptions still survive.[1] The earliest English Pontifical, that of Egbert, Archbishop of York, 732–766, directs that at the dedication of a church, the bishop was to make crosses with his thumb dipped in chrism

ANOINTING A CONSECRATION CROSS
PONTIFICALUM ROMANUM VENITIIS, 1620

on the walls of his church. A Winchester Pontifical of the end of the tenth century directs the anointing of both the internal and external walls. Later Pontificals prescribe that the walls were to be anointed in twelve places within and twelve places without; it was also ordered that the places were to be marked beforehand by crosses, which were to be

---

[1] On this matter the earlier ecclesiological hand-books are all wrong. The two authoritative papers are those by the late Dr. Middleton (*Archæologia*, xlviii. 456) and by the Rev. E. S. Dewick (*Archæological Journal*, lxv., No. 257), but the former is wrong in the misapplication of the term.

placed within circles, and that brackets for candles were to be attached to each place. The best known instances of the survival of these crosses in an elaborate form is that of Salisbury Cathedral, where eight survive on the outside and a like number on the inside. The indents in this case were originally filled with metal crosses; about three inches below each cross is a small hole, to which the branch for the candle was attached, to be lit on the day of dedication. At Edington, Wilts, consecrated in 1361, eleven of the internal crosses remain, and eight on the outside; Uffington, Berks, consecrated in the thirteenth century, also has an almost perfect set of external crosses. In both these cases the indents were originally filled with metal. Two other notable instances occur at Ottery St. Mary, Devon, and at Liskeard, Cornwall. A great number of interior consecration crosses, simply painted on the walls, as at Tong, Cheltenham, and Worstead, have come to light during recent years. Mr. Dewick stated in 1908 that he had a list of one hundred and seventy English parish churches in which they had been noted. With a little industry, such a list might readily be extended to upwards of two hundred. During the present century several such crosses have, to our knowledge, been cleared away owing to ignorance and, in at least one case, to bigotry. Good examples may be readily noticed at Arundel, Sussex; Darenth, Kent; and Stansfield, Suffolk. In short, there are several instances extant, either interior or exterior, in almost every English county. In Cambridgeshire they occur at St. Botolph and Holy Trinity, Cambridge, Fen Ditton, Isleham, Lynton, and Winningham. In Norfolk they may be noted at the three Norwich churches of St. John Sepulchre, St. Saviour, and St. Peter Permentergate; also at Barningham Winter, Burcham Tofts, Blofield, Bodney, Carleton Rode, Horning, Ovington, Oxborough, North Repps, Shottisham All Saints, Thrigby, and Worstead. In Sussex external crosses, formed of black flints, may be noted at Boxgrove, Broadwater, Seaham, and Westham, and they are painted upon the inside walls at Amberley, Climping, Ford, Poling, Pevensey, Slindon, Trotton, and Warminghurst.

A few words are necessary as to the common habit of speaking of *consecration* crosses where they do not really exist. It is fairly common to find quite small crosses incised, with more or less care, on the jambs of doorways. Sometimes there are several in this position, the later ones probably careless imitations of the original. In certain cases such crosses have been incised with some care, as at Tideswell, Derbyshire, and Boston, Lincolnshire. Nevertheless, not one of these crosses has any right whatever to the word "consecration." Such a term is only to

APPENDIX

be used for crosses which were anointed with chrism by the bishop at the time of the church's dedication; this was never done on doorways, for the chrism was always applied at a sufficient height to avoid casual contact. Where these doorways crosses were made deliberately, it would be with the general idea of the power of the cross to keep off evil influences, just as it is expressed in the Roman Pontifical, when the officiant, on entering the church, makes the sign of the cross with the lower end of his crozier on the threshold, saying—

Ecce crucis signum fugiant phantasmata cuncta.

Again, the word consecration must not be applied to crosses painted or incised on church furniture, or in places impossible for anointing purposes, such as over a chancel arch, or in flints on an outer clerestory. At Cheltenham there is a cross on the piscina; at Lanreath, Cornwall, Bideford, Devon, and Windermere, Westmorland, there are incised crosses on the fonts; in each of these cases the word "consecration" is habitually but wrongfully applied.

ADDENDA

LIST OF WARDENS' ACCOUNTS

Date.	Place.	Printed References, etc.
Edw. III to Edw. IV	Bridgwater	Bishop Hobhouse's *Churchwardens' Accounts* (1893), 230-1
1509–1675	Rotherfield, Sussex	*Suss. Arch. Coll.*, vol. xli. 25-48
1515-1579	West Tarring, Sussex	*Suss. Arch. Coll.*, vol. xli. 68
1516-1603	Banwell, Somerset	Bishop Hobhouse's *Churchwardens' Accounts* (1890), 229-30
1527-1568	Lydd, Kent	Finn's *Records of Lydd* (1911), 329-427
1527	Great Dunmow, Essex	Scott's *Hist. of an Essex Parish* (1873)
1528	Great Witchingham, Norfolk	*Norfolk Archæology*, vol. xiii. 119-216
1524-1700	Burford, Oxon	Monk's *Hist. of Burford* (1891)
1547	Narborough, Norfolk	
Edw. VI	March, Cambs.	Rood entries interesting
1552-1628	Chelsea, Middlesex	Lyson's *Environs of London*, ii. 145-146
1560	Coventry, Holy Trinity	Sharp's *Holy Trinity* (1818)
1573-1636	Fulham, Middlesex	Lyson's *Environs of London*, ii. 394-6
1585-1709	Finedon, Northants	
1598-1762	Hastings, Sussex	*Suss. Arch. Coll.*, vol. xxiii. 85-118
1606	Deerhurst, Glouc.	
1644-1813	Preston, Lanc.	Smith's *Record of Par. Church* (1872)

INDEX TO WARDENS' ACCOUNTS
(ARRANGED UNDER COUNTIES)

BEDFORDSHIRE—
  Bolnhurst, 51
  Flitton, 48
BERKSHIRE—
  Bray, 48, 309
  Henley, 315
  Reading, St. Giles, 45, 313
    St. Laurence, 18-9, 91-3, 97, 109, 127, 131-2, 140, 142-4, 150, 152, 187-8, 213, 215, 217-8, 229-30, 242, 244, 247, 250-1, 262, 269-70, 282-4, 286-7, 311, 314
    St. Mary, 13, 46, 61, 94, 98-9, 104, 135, 157, 191, 197-8, 222, 232, 235, 242, 262, 286, 312, 313, 328
    Stanford, 46, 93, 219, 236, 288, 292, 306
    Thatcham, 46, 320
BUCKS—
  Marlow, 48, 280-1, 290
  Wing, 45, 285
CAMBRIDGESHIRE—
  Bassingbourn, 42, 108-9, 111, 130-1, 141-2, 145, 165, 179, 202, 226, 251, 262-3, 270-4, 289-90, 292-3, 295
  Boxford, 45, 247, 276
  Cambridge, Great St. Mary, 9, 44, 83-4, 105, 112, 114, 116, 118-9, 126, 132, 151-2, 167, 170, 179, 183-4, 192, 201, 221, 237, 246, 248, 250, 260, 310-1, 318
    Holy Trinity, 4, 44, 101, 103, 111, 126, 146, 164, 169-70, 202, 250, 260, 262
    St. Botolph, 48, 104, 135-6, 156, 180, 191, 320
  March, 353
CHESHIRE—
  Chester, St. John, 306
    St. Martin, 51
    St. Mary-on-the-Hill, 45, 244, 246, 256, 265
  Prestbury, 46, 118, 233, 243, 309
  Rostherne, 51
  Whitegate, 48
  Wilmslow, 46

CORNWALL—
  Bodmin, 81-3
  Camborne, 301
  Launceston, 39
  Liskeard, 51, 301
  St. Columb Major, 47, 235, 280, 295, 299, 311, 329-30, 322, 338
  St. Ives, 47, 205, 244, 280
  St. Mabyn, 49, 156, 295
  St. Neots, 48, 169, 299, 312
CUMBERLAND—
  Torpenhow, 51
  Waberthwaite, 51
DERBYSHIRE—
  Allestree, 295
  Ashborne, 204
  Derby, All Saints, 31-2, 105, 114, 116, 118, 134, 136, 163-4, 225-7, 235, 237, 244, 263, 306
    St. Mary-on-the-Bridge, 147-8
    St. Werburgh, 49
  Eckington, 295
  Hartshorne, 49, 173, 206, 234, 301, 309
  Hayfield, 102, 206, 243
  Marston-on-Dove, 48, 206, 295
  Morton, 48, 306
  North Wingfield, 328
  Repton, 12, 47, 121, 295, 332, 334, 339
  Tickenhall, 295
  Wirksworth, 50, 95, 118, 154-5, 158, 300
  Youlgrave, 48, 118-9, 157, 205
DEVON—
  Ashburton, 38-9, 93, 103, 180, 209, 217, 269, 329
  Barnstaple, 46, 232, 277, 312
  Chagford, 39
  Chudleigh, 46
  East Budleigh, 51
  Exeter, St. Petrock, 20, 122, 136-7, 229, 236, 242, 320
  Hartland, 156, 180, 301, 332
  Milton Abbot, 4, 48, 312-3
  Morebath, 12, 45, 125, 250, 292, 295, 310
  Otterton, 253
  Portsmouth, 46

355

356 THE CHURCHWARDENS' ACCOUNTS

DEVON (*continued*)—
  Sidbury, 5, 49, 90, 101, 136, 204, 264, 300-2, 306
  South Tawton, 45, 304
  Talaton, 315
  Tavistock, 17-8, 87-8, 106, 118, 128, 133, 135, 138, 204, 243, 277, 285, 292, 303, 314, 331
  Woodbury, 253, 298
DORSET—
  Langton-Long-Blandford, 50
  Wimborne, 38, 98, 103-4, 109-11, 118, 120, 127, 145, 147, 151, 195, 198-9, 215, 236, 251, 290, 320
DURHAM—
  Durham, St. Nicholas, 51, 312
  St. Oswald, 47, 102, 122, 158, 191, 216, 304
  Houghton-le-Spring, 48, 337
  Pittington, 13, 47, 100, 236, 245, 294, 300, 312, 333
ESSEX—
  Braintree, 274
  Chelmsford, 46, 277-9
  Great Dunmow, 353
  Saffron Walden, 20, 144, 214-5, 263
  Weybridge, 274
GLOUCESTERSHIRE—
  Bristol, All Saints, 18, 193, 202, 214-5, 310
    Christchurch, 45, 134, 218
    St. Ewen, 23, 128, 134, 139, 153, 166, 189, 245, 251, 256, 259, 311
    St. James, 47, 101, 210, 247, 315
    St. John Baptist, 35, 179, 218, 256, 266
    St. Mary-le-Port, 46, 246
    St. Mary Redcliffe, 34
    St. Michael, 47, 247
    St. Nicholas, 40
    St. Peter, 50, 224, 227, 242
    SS. Philip and James, 46, 204
    St. Thomas, 46
    St. Werburgh, 46, 104
  Clifton, St. Andrew, 43
  Deerhurst, 353
  Eastington, 45, 302
  Hampnett, 48
  Minchinhampton, 46, 236, 298, 313-4, 316
  Ruardon, 51
HAMPSHIRE—
  Basingstoke, 5, 49, 158, 172, 319, 330
  Bedhampton, 52
  Bourne, St. Mary, 49
  Bramley, 45
  Crondall, 45
  Ellingham, 46
  Ibsley, 51
  Lymington, 51, 235
  North Waltham, 48
  Ringwood, 48
  Sherfield-on-Loddon, 51

HAMPSHIRE (*continued*)—
  Silchester, 52
  Southampton, Holy Rood, 52
    St. Michael, 50
  Stoke Charity, 45
  Thruxton, 52, 301
  Upham, 50
  Weyhill, 294
  Winchester, St. John, 116, 118, 135
    St. Peter Chesil, 47, 311
    St. Swithin-on-Kingsgate, 51
  Wootton, 46, 281, 294
    St. Laurence, 48
  Yateley, 48
HERTFORDSHIRE—
  Berkhamstead, 47, 100, 233, 337
  Bishop Stortford, 297
  Hertford, St. Andrew, 145
  Knebworth, 48
  Munden, 292
HUNTINGDONSHIRE—
  Great Paxton, 48
  Huntingdon, All Saints, 253
KENT—
  Birchington, 49
  Canterbury, Holy Cross, 102, 225
    St. Dunstan, 90, 106, 109, 179, 213, 268
  Chiddingstone, 47
  Cobham, 50
  Cowden, 48, 338
  Deptford, 51, 264
  Dover, St. Mary, 45, 112, 167, 194, 215, 236, 261, 263
  Edenbridge, 136, 194
  Eltham, 46, 99, 328, 340
  Fordwich, 44, 296
  Greenwich, 50
  Hawkhurst, 45, 101, 152, 154, 264
  Hoo, All Saints, 46
  Hythe, 19
  Lydd, 353
  Rainham, 45
  Sandwich, St. Mary, 21, 80-1, 212
  Smarden, 147, 167, 203, 306
  Snowdon, 45
  Strood, 46, 116, 134, 153, 191, 218, 233, 328
  Woolwich, 52
LANCASHIRE—
  Ashton-under-Lyne, 50
  Bolton, 50
  Childwall, 48
  Flixton, 51
  Hawkshead, 52
  Middleton, 50
  Preston, 353
  Prestwick, 309
  Ribchester, 50
  St. Michael-on-Wyre, 51
  Wigan, 47

INDEX TO WARDENS' ACCOUNTS

LEICESTERSHIRE—
  Great Wigston, 118, 304
  Loughborough, 47, 321
  Leicester, St. Martin, 41, 94, 104-5, 120, 135-6, 152-3, 157-8, 173, 181-3, 191, 193, 214, 222, 224, 227, 231-3, 236, 245, 250, 263, 277, 286, 306, 311, 316-7, 321
    St. Mary-in-Castro, 42, 190, 193, 322
  Melton Mowbray, 12, 46, 97, 112, 318, 338-9
  Sapcote, 306
  Stathern, 319, 335-9
  Wimeswold, 333-5, 340-4
LINCOLNSHIRE—
  Kirton-in-Lindsey, 40
  Louth, 44, 128, 265
  Saxilby, 46
  Spalding, 212
  Sutterton, 39, 96, 126, 276
  Wigtoft, 147, 249, 306, 329
LONDON (including Westminster and Borough)—
  All Hallows the Great, 49
    the Less, 49
    Honey Lane, 49
    London Wall, 33
  All Hallows, Staining, 42
  St. Alphege, London Wall, 9, 45, 173, 179, 202, 217, 220, 223, 241, 252, 255, 265, 317, 322, 338
  St. Andrew Cheap, 258
    Holborn, 21-3, 81, 202, 217, 279
    Hubbard, 24, 139, 145, 166, 178, 193, 203, 209, 217, 240, 244, 255, 258, 307, 320
  St. Ann Aldersgate, 50
  St. Antholin, 47, 252
  St. Augustine, Farringdon Within, 48
  St. Bartholomew Exchange, 48, 104, 319-20, 338
    the Great, 49
  St. Benet Fink, 49, 320
    Gracechurch, 46, 221, 241, 318, 321
    Paul's Wharf, 48, 252
  St. Botolph Aldersgate, 32, 138-9, 145, 162-3, 210, 241, 244, 258, 320
    Aldgate, 46
    Billingsgate, 48
    Bishopsgate, 47
  St. Catherine Aldgate, 46
    Coleman, 49
  St. Christopher-le-Stocks, 47, 134-5, 142, 219, 317, 320
  St. Clement Eastcheap, 56
  St. Dionis Backchurch, 49
  St. Dunstan-in-the-East, 251
  St. Ethelburga Bishopsgate, 47
  St. George, Botolph Lane, 48
    Southwark, 49

LONDON (continued)—
  St. Helen Bishopsgate, 47, 200, 229
  St. James Clerkenwell, 47
  St. John Baptist Walbrook, 48
  St. John Zachary, 48
  St. Leonard Eastcheap, 51
  St. Magnus, 50
  St. Martin's-in-the-Fields, 8, 14, 100-1, 112, 136, 157, 172, 190, 212, 218-20, 236, 244, 257-8, 276, 317, 331
    Ludgate, 47, 140
    Ludgate Hill, 50
    Ongar, 34-5
    Outwich, 45, 258
  St. Margaret, New Fish Street, 47
    Pattens, 44, 190, 193, 240, 246, 251, 255
    Southwark, 22, 178, 201, 268
    Westminster, 27-8, 87, 90, 93, 100, 104-5, 111, 127, 134, 136, 139, 147, 155-6, 166-7, 172, 178, 180, 194, 209, 212, 216, 218-23, 234, 241, 242, 244-6, 251, 255, 257, 259, 262-3, 265, 285, 315-6, 318, 320-2, 330-1
  St. Mary Aldermanbury, 47
    -at-Hill, 5, 13, 19, 86-7, 93, 124, 129, 135, 156, 159, 161-2, 166, 176-8, 193, 199-200, 207-8, 212-3, 218, 239-40, 243, 245, 250, 254, 258, 259, 261-2, 307, 311
    Woodchurch, 46, 234-5
    Woolnoth, 45, 104, 118, 120, 202, 209, 236, 246, 252, 255, 277
  St. Mary Magdalene, Milk Street, 45
    Old Fish Street, 50
  St. Matthew, Friday Street, 46, 88, 156, 168, 190, 209, 241, 320
  St. Michael Cornhill, 24, 120, 127, 142, 147, 173, 178, 193, 203, 209, 218, 241, 251, 256, 258, 307, 338
    Wood Street, 49
  St. Nicholas, Cole Abbey, 209
  St. Olave Southwark, 46
  St. Pancras, Soper Lane, 46
  St. Peter Cheap, 20, 86-7, 94, 142, 147, 166, 179, 193, 200-1, 240, 246, 250-1, 254
  St. Saviour Southwark, 101
  St. Stephen Walbrook, 35-6, 133, 193, 201, 209, 255
  St. Swithin, London Wall, 48
MIDDLESEX—
  Chelsea, 353
  Fulham, 326, 353
  Hammersmith, 30
  Kensington, 51, 224
NORFOLK—
  Brockdish, 46
  Dunham Parva, 51
  East Dereham, 149

NORFOLK (*continued*)—
Forncett St. Peter, 51
Great Witchingham, 353
Harling, 268
Loddon, 46
Narborough, 353
North Elmham, 45, 86, 110, 139, 304, 328
Norwich, St. Benedict, 48
  St. Gregory, 47
  St. Laurence, 48
  St. Mary, 47
  St. Peter Mancroft, 47
  St. Stephen, 47
Pulham St. Mary, 46
  St. Mary Magdalene, 48, 292
Redenhall, 47, 99, 235, 306, 311
Shipdham, 45, 202, 289, 328
Snettisham, 36
Stockton, 152, 328
Swaffham, 23-4
Toft Monks, 48, 89
Yarmouth, 29, 276
NORTHAMPTON—
Aldwinkle St. Peter, 50
Ashby St. Legers, 51
Broughton, 51
Burton Latimer, 46, 304
Byfield, 49
Castle Ashby, 51
Colleyweston, 50
Collingtree, 50
Cottingham, 48
Culworth, 45, 286, 292, 295, 305, 308
East Haddon, 51
Finedon, 353
Glinton, 50
Great Harrowden, 51
  Haughton, 50
  Weldon, 49
Helmdon, 339
Kingsthorpe, 47
Lamport, 52
Lowick, 48, 89, 286
Marston Trussell, 48
Northampton, All Saints, 319
  St. Giles, 49, 114, 154, 232, 319
  St. Sepulchre, 49
Overstone, 51
Peterborough, St. John Baptist, 33-4, 106, 230
Piddington, 50
Stanford, 46, 93
Sudborough, 51
Thornby, 50
Thornhaugh, 50
Ufford, 50
Wecdon Bec, 49
Wellingborough, 5, 49, 320
Woodford Halse, 48
Yarwell, 51

NORTHUMBERLAND—
Hexham, 306
NOTTINGHAMSHIRE
Holme Pierrepoint, 46
Worksop, 45, 99, 111, 294, 306
OXFORDSHIRE—
Burford, 353
Enstone, 50
Oxford, St. Michael, 17
  St. Peter-in-the-East, 21
Spelsbury, 6, 45, 99, 164-5, 192, 294
Thame, 20-1, 178, 190, 230, 245, 250
Yarnton, 231, 263, 313
SHROPSHIRE—
Acton Round, 51
Alberbury, 50
Atcham, 52
Badger, 51
Barrington, 51
Barrow, 49
Bolas Magna, 52
Cheswardine, 45
Chetwynd, 50
Chirbury, 48
Church Pulverbatch, 50, 233
Clun, 51
Clunbury, 49
Clungunford, 51
Condover, 47
Cound, 49
Culmington, 52
Diddlebury, 51
Edgmond, 50
High Ercall, 51
Kenley, 48
Kinnerley, 50
Lilleshall, 48
Ludlow, 34, 81, 86-7, 104, 136, 146, 189, 202, 210, 230, 236, 244, 246, 250, 256, 304, 306, 309, 310, 320
Lydham, 51
Mainstone, 50
More, 50
Newport, 52
North Lydbury, 49
Oswestry, 47
Pitchford, 52
Prees, 51
Quatford, 51
Ryton, 48
Shawbury, 49
Shrewsbury, Abbey Church, 47
  St. Mary, 49
Stapleton, 51
Stockton, 48
Tong, 49
Uffington, 49, 234
Whitchurch, 49
Worfield, 12, 44, 127, 298

INDEX TO WARDENS' ACCOUNTS

SOMERSETSHIRE—
Banwell, 353
Bath, St. Michael, 15, 16, 79, 89, 106, 190, 268, 292, 313
Bridgwater, 353
Cheddar, 49, 299, 333
Croscombe, 36, 109, 112, 119, 146, 282, 290
Minehead, 218
Pilton, 4, 165, 179, 293, 314
Staplegrove, 47, 85, 101, 309
Stoke Courcy, 44, 251, 290, 293
Swainswick, 49
Tintinhull, 28, 94, 97, 118, 125, 159, 115-6, 230, 250, 289, 295
Yatton, 22, 93-4, 111, 112, 114, 116, 118-9, 124-5, 128, 138, 145, 151, 155, 165, 168, 175-6, 230, 233, 250, 288-9, 310
Yeovil, 26, 212, 262
STAFFORDSHIRE—
Leek, 102, 158
Mavesyn Ridware, 50, 316
SUFFOLK—
Bardwell, 45, 292
Beccles, 95, 235
Blythburgh, 35
Bungay, 43, 275
Cratfield, 41-2, 105, 201, 247, 289, 299, 312-3, 327-9, 335
Eastfield, 145
Elmsett, 45, 293
Exning, 86, 94, 236
Henley, 48
Huntingfield, 45
Ipswich, St. Clement, 48, 321
St. Mary-le-Tower, 49
St. Matthew, 47
St. Peter, 47, 54, 116, 119, 135, 154, 192, 263
St. Stephen, 49
Little Cornand, 47
Little Glenham, 253
Mellis, 49
Mendlesham, 45, 140
Walberswick, 23, 87, 127, 258, 265
Wenhaston, 50
Weybread, 48
SURREY
Bletchingley, 233
Elstead, 50
Hascombe, 267
Horley, 44, 192
Kingston-on-Thames, 42, 283-4, 337
Lambeth, 44, 234, 262
Mortlake, 47
Seal, 46, 101, 105, 114, 135-6, 205, 233, 290-1, 316
Weybridge, 310

SUSSEX—
Arlington, 26, 155
Bolney, 45, 97
Cowfold, 28, 150
Eastbourne, 50
Hastings, 353
Lindfield, 47
Mailsham, 245
Rotherfield, 353
Steyning, 7, 42, 312
West Tarring, 353
WARWICKSHIRE—
Coventry, Holy Trinity, 353
Solihull, 312
Southam, 48
Warwick, St. Mary, 170, 225, 235
St. Michael, 45
St. Nicholas, 112, 114, 116, 121, 153, 168, 172, 218, 290, 298, 309, 313
WESTMORELAND—
Kendal, 50, 245, 300
WILTSHIRE—
Chippenham, 233
Devizes, St. Mary, 112, 118, 121, 185, 203, 233, 236, 260
Mere, 5, 46, 97-8, 180, 203, 291, 313, 330
Salisbury, St. Edmund, 4, 29, 88, 90, 93, 96-7, 101, 103-4, 107, 110, 114-6, 118, 125, 128, 139, 154, 158, 166, 173, 192, 193, 208-9, 213, 222, 227, 232-4, 241, 246, 251, 254, 256, 294, 311
St. Martin, 47
St. Thomas, 4, 88, 100-4, 114, 118, 135-7, 154, 156, 173, 194, 210, 219, 222, 224, 232-4, 247, 253, 263, 286, 311
Steeple Ashton, 45, 269
WORCESTERSHIRE—
Badsey, 45
Bewdley, 47, 279
Tewkesbury, 280
Worcester, St. Helen, 45, 202, 246, 312
St. Mary, 152
St. Michael, 13, 101, 134-5, 217-8, 235, 246, 306, 329
St. Nicholas, 312
YORKSHIRE—
Barnsley, 49, 309, 322
Bramley, 322
Cundall, 194
Ecclesfield, 45
Hedon, St. Augustine, 16, 268
St. James, 16
St. Nicholas, 17, 145
Wakefield, 47
York, Holy Trinity, 46
St. John, 47

GENERAL INDEX

Ale. *See* Church-ale
Almayne-rivettes, 327
Altar cloths, stained, 132-3
    covers, 105
    rails, 104-5
Altars, 91-3
Antiphoners, 106-11
Apricot trees, 321
Archæologia, 44-7, 149, 186
Archers, 36
Armada, 219, 329
Armour, parish, 326-33
Army, English, 325-6
Arquebuse, 326
Ascension Day, 18, 240
Astrological doctor, 322
Atchley's *Incense in Divine Worship*, 310
Audit feasting, 9

Babington Conspiracy, 219
Badger skins, 130
Badgers, 297 *et seq.*
Baking, 20. *Also under* Church-ales
Baldrick, 211
Bandoleers, 327
Banners, 71-2, 263
Baslow, 307
Bastard (wine), 95
Bay, 242, 245
Beacons, 340
Beam-light, 162-3
Bede Roll, 62, 158-9
Beer stone, 80
Bells and bell-ringing, 211-27
    funeral, 56-8, 172-4
    small, 139, 205
Bibles, 116-8
Bier, 57-8, 170-4
Bills, 327
Birch, 238-40
Birds in churches, 306
Boar, common, 295
Bolingbroke, Mr., 247, 267
Bond's *Screens and Galleries*, 175
Bonfires, 28, 224
Bookbinding, 107-11
Book of Sports, 122
Books, 18-9, 106-22

Boulogne, peace of, 218
Bows and arrows, 327-9, 344
Boy-bishop, 40-1, 129
Boyle's *History of Hedon*, 16
Boy's *History of Sandwich*, 21
Bradshaw, Henry, 120
Brass pots, gifts of, 20, 37
Breviary or porthose, 108-11
Brewing, 201. *Also under* Church-ales
Bridal cup, 314-5
    jewellery, 315
Brigandine, 327
Bristol Past and Present, 18, 34-5, 44
Bucer, Martin, 126
Bull, common, 295
Bullfinches, 297 *et seq.*
Burial of criminals, 39
Burials in churches, 22, 24, 34, 169
Burke, Mr. A. M., 27
Burning of women, 33 *n.*
Butchers, 61, 251
Butts, 327-8
Buzzards, 297-305

Caen stone, 79, 80, 149
Cage, 337
Cakes, 71, 254-5
Calf's head, 71, 213
Caliver, 326
Canary, 95
Candles or tapers, 18, 27, 29, 39, 160-8
Candlesticks, 31, 40, 57-8, 138-42, 162, 241
Canopies for Blessed Sacrament, 101, 132
Cantell or cantle, 58-9
Cap trade, 313-4
Carols, 210
Caterpillars, 320
Cattle, 26, 29, 43, 292-5
Caxton's *Golden Legend*, 111
Celebrations, number of, 101-2
Censers and ships, 138-42
Chained books, 107, 119-21
Chair in quire, 73
Chalice, 138-42
Chapelwardens, 3

361

Charnel houses, 169-70
Choristers, 207-10
Choughs, 296-306
Chrismatories, 138-42, 151
Chrismatory cloths, 132, 151-2
Christening fees, 58
Christmastide, 245-7
Church-ale, 21, 22, 38-9, 41-2, 62-4, 287-91
  house, 20, 39, 287-8
  plate, 138-42
  rates, 2, 11-2, 75-8
Church Broughton, 206
Churching pew, 194
Churchwardens, office of, 1-14; solely ecclesiastical in origin, 1-2; post-Reformation civil duties, 2-3; their number, 4-5; all elected by parish, 5; fines for refusing office, 5-6; women wardens, 6-7; election and audit feasting, 7-9; time of audit, 10; election by vestry, 13-4; stipend of wardens, 16
Churchyard stalls, 61
Claverton stone, 79
Clerk's salary, 63, 73
Clocks, 19, 40, 73, 228-31
Clodock, 308
Clynnog, 308
Coffins, 57, 172-4
Combe, Constable Accounts, 345-8
  Riot, 346-8
Common Prayer, 112-4
Commons, House of, at Communion, 100
Communion Books, 112-4
"Conduct," 207-9
Confessionals, 193
Conjuror, 322
Consecration Crosses, 349-51
Constables' Accounts, 323-48
Cope, festival, 133
Cormorants, 297 *et seq.*
Corporation pews, 193
Corpse, passage of, 172
Corpus Christi, 40, 64, 239-41, 265-6
Corslet, 327
"Cotter," 211
Covenant, the, 321
Cowchers, 108-9
Cox's *Church Furniture*, 160, 175, 186, 233-5, 249
  Parish Registers, 172, 252, 316-7, 321, 338
  Three Centuries of Derbyshire Annals, 323
Creeping to the Cross, 259
"Croke," 37
Cromwell's funeral, 174
Crow net, 296, 298
Crows, 296-305

Cruets, 138-42
Cunning woman, 320

Dancing, 22, 36, 66, 255-6
Dewick, Rev. E. S., 123
Dials, 228-9
Directory, the, 114-5
Dog killers, 318-9
  whipper, the, 307-9
Dowsing, William, 89
Duck hunting, 227
Ducking-stool, 337
Duncan, Lord, 225
Durham, Bishop of, 216
Dyer's *Churchlore Gleanings*, 243, 253

Eagle brass, 142
Easter Sepulchre, 33, 60, 129
Election and audit feasting, 7-10
  of mayors in churches, 31
Elizabeth, Queen, 210, 215-6, 218-9
Epiphany, 247-8
Episcopal ringing, 216, 226
Erasmus' *Paraphrases*, 118-9
Eton College, 207
Eversden stone, 84-5

Fabric charges, 74-7
  of the church, 79-90
Fair of St. Bartholomew, 33
Fairs, 16, 61
Feasey's *Holy Week Ceremonial*, 254
Feasting at elections, 7-8, 10
Felton stone, 81
Fennel, 239-40
Fertur (fertor), 170
Fire, Holy, 55, 260-1
Fire buckets, 319-20
  hooks, 319-20
  scoops, 320
Fitchers (fitchets), etc., 298 *et seq.*
Fleas, 321
Flints, 85
Flodden Field, 217
Folkestone rag, 80
Font cloths, 153
  taper, 31, 54-5, 60, 161
  taps, 152-3
Fonts, 149-57
Forthfare or passing bell, 56-7
Foxes, 297 *et seq.*
Foxe's *Martyrs*, 119
Freewill offerings, 77, 79
Funeral gear, hire of, 26, 57-8, 173-4

Galleries, 90
Galpin's *English Musical Instruments*, 196, 206
Gang-week. See Rogationtide
Gardner's *History of Dunwich*, 23

GENERAL INDEX 363

Garlands, 239-41
Garments, gifts of, 37-8, 55-6
Garnishing of churches, 298 ff.
Gatherings at church door, 24
  in church, 17, 22, 25, 27, 28, 40, 42, 53-4
  in streets, 16, 24
Gazeley, 83
Genge, Abbot, 33
Gifts and bequests, 26, 28, 31, 37-8, 55-6, 147-8
Gilds, 31, 36-7, 39-41, 43, 59-60
Gillyflower, 239
Gipsies, 339
Glazing of windows, 87-9
Gloves, 135
Good Friday, 258-9
Gorget, 327
Goring, Lord, 216
Gorleston, 89
Gowns, 137
Gowrie Conspiracy, 220
Graduals, 108
Grasmere, 243
Grayles, 106-11
"Gudgeons," 212
Guilford, Mr. E. L., 323
Gunpowder, 329-30, 342

Hagglers, 36
Halberds, 327
Hallowing, 123-8
Hampton Court, 225
Harwich, 225
Havanah, 225
Hawks, 296-305
Hearse, 57, 170-2
Hedgehogs, 297 et seq.
Henry VIII, death of, 217
Herbs, 240-2
Hire of funeral gear, 26, 57-8, 173-4
Historical MSS. Commission, 19
Historical ringings, 217-25
Hobby-horse, 285-6
Hobhouse, Bishop, 11, 15, 21, 22, 286-7
Hocktide, 21, 64-5, 261-3
Hogmaney, 26
Hognell silver, 26
Holly (or holme), 241, 245-7
Holy Fire, 55, 260-1
  Loaf, 58-9, 96-8
Homilies, 116
Hoods, University, 135-6
Hope, John, 81
Hosier, John, 81
Hour-glasses, 232-3
House of Correction, 337
Houseling bread, 98
  cloths, 103-4, 132
  tokens, 100-1

Hughley stone, 81
Hugutio's *Vocabularium*, 107
Hunstanton Hall, 36

Image veils, 251
Images, 142-5
Incense, 31, 310-2
Indulgences, 19, 30-1
Ivry, battle of, 220
Ivy, 241, 245-7

Jack o' Clock, 73, 228-9
Jackdaws, 297 et seq.
Jays, 297-315
Jewellery, gifts of, 37-8, 55-6
Jewel's *Apology*, 119
Judas candles, 166, 177, 179
Juniper, 312

Kerry, Rev. C., *History of St. Laurence, Reading*, 19
Killiecrankie, 224
Kingfishers, 297 et seq.
Kingplay, 64, 284-5
King's Evil, 316
Kites, 297 et seq.

Lairstalls (laystalls), 34, 169
Laud, Archbishop, 288
Laurel, 242, 245
Lazy tongs, 308
Lee, Rev. Bartley, 347-8
Legenda, 19, 106-11
Lent, 249-53
Lenten Veil, 250
Libraries, 121
Licences for flesh in Lent, 251-2
Lights, 160-8
  wardens of, 4, 22, 59-60
Lincoln College, 345-6
Litany, 111-2
Live stock, 292-6
Llanynys, 308
Londinium Redivivium, 23, 45-7
Lotrier, Hugh, 81
Loughborough, 319
Luccombe, 206, 228

Magdala, castle of, 144
Magpies, 296-305
Maidens, 22, 37
Malmsey, 96
Manchester, Constable Accounts, 344-5
Manuals, 106-11
Marbeck's *Book of Common Prayer noted*, 206
Marlborough, Duke of, 224-5, 348
Marriage fees, 58
Mary, Queen of Scots, 219

364 THE CHURCHWARDENS' ACCOUNTS

Mascall, *Sundrie Engines and Trappes*, 296
Mattins, early, 213-4
Maundy Thursday, 31, 70-1
May games, 65-6, 284-5
Meynell, Mr. Godfrey, 31
Mice, 297 *et seq.*
Midsummer Day, 239-41
Midwife pew, 194
Missals, 106-11
Moldewarps (moles), 297 *et seq.*
Monstrance, 138
Morion, 327
Muscadel, 96
Muscadine, 96-7
Music, English Instruments of, 196
Musical instruments, 204-6
Musicians, 63
Muskets, 326

Nelson, Lord, 225

Obits, 21, 27, 35, 40
Organ books, 106
  makers, 197-204
Organists, 40, 198-204
Organs, 19, 195-204
Ornaments Rubric, 133-4
Orpin, 239
Otters, 297-305

Pall, 57-8, 170
Palm Sunday, 249, 253-8
Palms, 239, 254-8
Parwich, 249
Paschal Monday, 55, 99
  taper, 55, 60, 99, 161
Passes, 336, 343
Patens, 138-42
Penance, 252-3
Pentecostals. *See* Peter's Pence
Peter's Pence, 73-4, 312-3
Pews. *See* Seats
Pikes, 327
Pinkie, battle of, 217
Plague, 317-9, 342, 345
Plays and playing, 21, 22, 63-4, 267-86
Plough Monday, 42, 248-9
Plungar, 319
Pole, Cardinal, 218
Polecats, 297-305
Pollution of churchyard, 125
Pondicherry, 225
Pope, obit of, 23
Porch, chamber over, 23, 75, 86
Porthose or breviary, 106-11
Pricksong books, 109
Priests' chambers, 86
Printed books, 111
Processionals, 106-11

Processions, 38, 72
" Prophets " of Palm Sunday, 254-5
Protestation, the, 321
Psalter, 112-4
Pulpits, 155-8
Puritans, 307
Purveyance, 42, 324-5, 335-6
Pyrenees, 307
Pyx, 93-4, 138-42, 145

Quebec, 225

Rag stone, 80
Rates. *See* Church Rates
Rats, 297 *et seq.*
  in churches, 307
Raunds, 319
Raven's *Bells of England*, 211
Ravens, 297 *et seq.*
" Reconciliation " of church, 226
  of churchyard, 225
Reformation changes, 181-5
Reformed Service Books, 112-4
Ringers and ringing, 211-27
Robin Hood, 36, 280-4
Rochets, 136
Rock's *Hierurgia*, 160
Rodney, Admiral, 225
Rogationtide, 71-2, 263-5
Rogue money, 337
Rood-lights, 17, 60, 162, 166
  screens and roods, 17, 23, 83, 175-81
  Veil, 250-1
Rooks, 296-305
Rosemary, 240, 246-7
Roses, 239-41
Roundel, 165
Royal Arms, 41, 233-4
Rushes, 41, 243-5

Sack (wine), 96
Salisbury, Bishops of, 226
Sallet, 327
Saltpetre men, 333-4, 342-3
Salve Mass, 208
Scarlett, Robert, 308
Seats and Pews, 66-9, 186-94
Select Vestry, 12-4
Selworthy, 206
" Sentencial " or Great Sentence, 108
Serges, 161, 163-4
Shags, 296-305
Shingles, 85
Shriving pews, 193-211
Sidesmen, 3
Singing bread, 98, 139
Smith, Mr. Toulmin, 323
Smoke farthings. *See* Peter's Pence
Snakes, 305
Snuffers, 166

GENERAL INDEX

Sprat boats, 23
St. George, cult of, 142, 145–6
St. John's wort, 239
St. Mullion, 308
St. Osmund, 107
Staley's *Studies in Ceremonial*, 160
Stalls at church door, 24
  in churchyard, 26
Star of Epiphany, 247–8
Starlings, 297 *et seq.*
Stipend of wardens, 16
Stoats, 297 *et seq.*
Stocks, 337 *et seq.*
Stone-tiles, 85
Stourbridge fair, 165
Stowmarket, 329
Surplice, 134–6

Tabernacles, 142–3
Tallow candles, 18, 161, 167–8, 245–6
Tapers. *See* Candles
Tatham, Dr. Edward, 346–8
Tempests and bells, 212–3
Ten Commandments, 235–7
Tenebrae, 166, 256
Thorney Abbey, 85
Times of service, 26
Titmice, 297 *et seq.*
Tobacco, 322
  duty, 227
Tokens, houseling, 100–1
Torches, 39, 40, 160–1, 163
Tothill Fields, 174
Touch-boxes, 327
Tournay, 225
Train Bands, 326
Tregarthyn stone, 83
Trendal, 163, 167
Triplow, 83

Vallance, Aymer, 175
Vaux's *Church Folklore*, 243, 253

Veils, Lenten, 250–1
Vermin, 296–305
Vestment Controversy, 133–4
Vestments, 128–37
  hire of, 26, 61
Vestry, 10–4
Vigo, 225
Vines, 321

Wafer bread, 98–9
Wages of clerk, sexton, etc., 73
Waits, 63
Wakefield, 34 *n.*
Watch and Ward, 324
Waterloo, 226
Wax, 19, 26
Weasels, 297–305
Webbers, 36
Weights and Measures, 324
Whitewash, 34, 87–8
Whitsun farthings. *See* Peter's Pence
Whitsuntide, 265
  games, 285–6
Wild cat, 297 *et seq.*
Willow, 239, 256–7
Wilton, 216, 220
Winchelsea, Archbishop, 11
Winchester, Statute of, 326
Wine for Communion, 94–6
Wolsey, Cardinal, 150
Woman burnt, 33
Women wardens, 7
Woodruff, 239–40
Wood's *Scottish Pewter Ware*, 101
Woodwell (woodpecker), 297
Worcester, battle of, 174
Wright, Thomas, 34
Wyat's Rebellion, 218

Yew, 238–9, 254–5
York, Duke of, 34
Young men, 37

Printed by
MORRISON & GIBB LIMITED
Edinburgh

A SELECTION OF BOOKS PUBLISHED BY METHUEN AND CO. LTD., LONDON 36 ESSEX STREET W.C.

CONTENTS

	PAGE		PAGE
General Literature .	2	Little Quarto Shakespeare	19
Ancient Cities. .	12	Miniature Library .	19
Antiquary's Books.	12	New Library of Medicine	19
Arden Shakespeare	13	New Library of Music	19
Classics of Art .	13	Oxford Biographies	19
"Complete" Series	13	Three Plays . . .	20
Connoisseur's Library	14	States of Italy . .	20
Handbooks of English Church History	14	Westminster Commentaries	20
		"Young" Series .	20
Handbooks of Theology .	14	Shilling Library .	21
"Home Life" Series . .	14	Books for Travellers	21
Illustrated Pocket Library of Plain and Coloured Books	15	Some Books on Art. .	21
		Some Books on Italy	22
Leaders of Religion	15	Fiction . . .	23
Library of Devotion	16	Two-Shilling Novels	27
Little Books on Art	16	Books for Boys and Girls .	27
Little Galleries . . .	17	Shilling Novels . . .	28
Little Guides . . .	17	Novels of Alexandre Dumas	28
Little Library . . .	18	Sixpenny Books . .	29

JULY 1912

A SELECTION OF MESSRS. METHUEN'S PUBLICATIONS

In this Catalogue the order is according to authors. An asterisk denotes that the book is in the press.

Colonial Editions are published of all Messrs. METHUEN's Novels issued at a price above 2s. 6d., and similar editions are published of some works of General Literature. Colonial editions are only for circulation in the British Colonies and India.

All books marked net are not subject to discount, and cannot be bought at less than the published price. Books not marked net are subject to the discount which the bookseller allows.

Messrs. METHUEN's books are kept in stock by all good booksellers. If there is any difficulty in seeing copies, Messrs. Methuen will be very glad to have early information, and specimen copies of any books will be sent on receipt of the published price *plus* postage for net books, and of the published price for ordinary books.

This Catalogue contains only a selection of the more important books published by Messrs. Methuen. A complete and illustrated catalogue of their publications may be obtained on application.

Andrewes (Lancelot). PRECES PRIVATAE. Translated and edited, with Notes, by F. E. BRIGHTMAN. *Cr. 8vo.* 6s.

Aristotle. THE ETHICS. Edited, with an Introduction and Notes, by JOHN BURNET. *Demy 8vo.* 10s. 6d. net.

Atkinson (C. T.). A HISTORY OF GERMANY, 1715-1815. *Demy 8vo.* 12s. 6d. net.

Atkinson (T. D.). ENGLISH ARCHITECTURE. Illustrated. *Fcap. 8vo.* 3s. 6d. net.

A GLOSSARY OF TERMS USED IN ENGLISH ARCHITECTURE. Illustrated. *Second Edition. Fcap. 8vo.* 3s. 6d. net.

ENGLISH AND WELSH CATHEDRALS. Illustrated. *Demy 8vo.* 10s. 6d. net.

Bain (F. W.). A DIGIT OF THE MOON: A HINDOO LOVE STORY. *Ninth Edition. Fcap. 8vo.* 3s. 6d. net.

THE DESCENT OF THE SUN: A CYCLE OF BIRTH. *Fifth Edition. Fcap. 8vo.* 3s. 6d. net.

A HEIFER OF THE DAWN. *Seventh Edition. Fcap. 8vo.* 2s. 6d. net.

IN THE GREAT GOD'S HAIR. *Fifth Edition. Fcap. 8vo.* 2s. 6d. net.

A DRAUGHT OF THE BLUE. *Fourth Edition. Fcap. 8vo.* 2s. 6d. net.

AN ESSENCE OF THE DUSK. *Third Edition. Fcap. 8vo.* 2s. 6d. net.

AN INCARNATION OF THE SNOW. *Second Edition. Fcap. 8vo.* 3s. 6d. net.

A MINE OF FAULTS. *Second Edition. Fcap. 8vo.* 3s. 6d. net.

THE ASHES OF A GOD. *Fcap. 8vo.* 3s. 6d. net.

*BUBBLES OF THE FOAM. *Fcap 4to.* 5s. net. Also *Fcap. 8vo.* 3s. 6d. net.

Balfour (Graham). THE LIFE OF ROBERT LOUIS STEVENSON. Illustrated. *Fifth Edition in one Volume. Cr. 8vo.* Buckram, 6s. Also *Fcap. 8vo.* 1s. net.

Baring (Hon. Maurice). A YEAR IN RUSSIA. *Second Edition. Demy 8vo.* 10s. 6d. net.

LANDMARKS IN RUSSIAN LITERATURE. *Second Edition. Crown 8vo.* 6s. net.

RUSSIAN ESSAYS AND STORIES. *Second Edition. Crown 8vo.* 5s. net.

THE RUSSIAN PEOPLE. *Demy 8vo.* 15s. net.

Baring-Gould (S.). THE LIFE OF NAPOLEON BONAPARTE. Illustrated. *Second Edition. Royal 8vo.* 10s. 6d. net.

General Literature

THE TRAGEDY OF THE CÆSARS: A History of the Emperors of the Julian and Claudian Houses. Illustrated. *Seventh Edition. Royal 8vo. 10s. 6d. net.*
THE VICAR OF MORWENSTOW. With a Portrait. *Third Edition. Cr. 8vo. 3s. 6d.*
Also Fcap. 8vo. 1s. net.
OLD COUNTRY LIFE. Illustrated. *Fifth Edition. Large Cr. 8vo. 6s.*
A BOOK OF CORNWALL. Illustrated. *Third Edition. Cr. 8vo. 6s.*
A BOOK OF DARTMOOR. Illustrated. *Second Edition. Cr. 8vo. 6s.*
A BOOK OF DEVON. Illustrated. *Third Edition. Cr. 8vo. 6s.*

Baring-Gould (S.) and **Sheppard (H. Fleetwood).** A GARLAND OF COUNTRY SONG. English Folk Songs with their Traditional Melodies. *Demy 4to. 6s.*
SONGS OF THE WEST: Folk Songs of Devon and Cornwall. Collected from the Mouths of the People. New and Revised Edition, under the musical editorship of Cecil J. Sharp. *Large Imperial 8vo. 5s. net.*

Barker (E.). THE POLITICAL THOUGHT OF PLATO AND ARISTOTLE. *Demy 8vo. 10s. 6d. net.*

Bastable (C. F.). THE COMMERCE OF NATIONS. *Fifth Edition. Cr. 8vo. 2s. 6d.*

Beckford (Peter). THOUGHTS ON HUNTING. Edited by J. Otho Paget. Illustrated. *Third Edition. Demy 8vo. 6s.*

Belloc (H.). PARIS. Illustrated. *Second Edition, Revised. Cr. 8vo. 6s.*
HILLS AND THE SEA. *Fourth Edition. Fcap. 8vo. 5s.*
ON NOTHING AND KINDRED SUBJECTS. *Third Edition. Fcap. 8vo. 5s.*
ON EVERYTHING. *Third Edition. Fcap. 8vo. 5s.*
ON SOMETHING. *Second Edition. Fcap. 8vo. 5s.*
FIRST AND LAST. *Second Edition. Fcap. 8vo. 5s.*
MARIE ANTOINETTE. Illustrated. *Third Edition. Demy 8vo. 15s. net.*
THE PYRENEES. Illustrated. *Second Edition. Demy 8vo. 7s. 6d. net.*

Bennett (W. H.). A PRIMER OF THE BIBLE. *Fifth Edition. Cr. 8vo. 2s. 6d.*

Bennett (W. H.) and **Adeney (W. F.).** A BIBLICAL INTRODUCTION. With a concise Bibliography. *Sixth Edition. Cr. 8vo. 7s. 6d. Also in Two Volumes. Cr. 8vo. Each 3s. 6d. net.*

Benson (Archbishop). GOD'S BOARD. Communion Addresses. *Second Edition. Fcap. 8vo. 3s. 6d. net.*

Bicknell (Ethel E.). PARIS AND HER TREASURES. Illustrated. *Fcap. 8vo. Round corners. 5s. net.*

Blake (William). ILLUSTRATIONS OF THE BOOK OF JOB. With a General Introduction by Laurence Binyon. Illustrated. *Quarto. 21s. net.*

Bloemfontein (Bishop of). ARA CŒLI: An Essay in Mystical Theology. *Fifth Edition. Cr. 8vo. 3s. 6d. net.*
FAITH AND EXPERIENCE. *Second Edition. Cr. 8vo. 3s. 6d. net.*

Bowden (E. M.). THE IMITATION OF BUDDHA: Quotations from Buddhist Literature for each Day in the Year. *Sixth Edition. Cr. 16mo. 2s. 6d.*

Brabant (F. G.). RAMBLES IN SUSSEX. Illustrated. *Cr. 8vo. 6s.*

Bradley (A. G.). ROUND ABOUT WILTSHIRE. Illustrated. *Second Edition. Cr. 8vo. 6s.*
THE ROMANCE OF NORTHUMBERLAND. Illustrated. *Second Edition. Demy 8vo. 7s. 6d. net.*

Braid (James). ADVANCED GOLF. Illustrated. *Seventh Edition. Demy 8vo. 10s. 6d. net.*

Brodrick (Mary) and **Morton (A. Anderson).** A CONCISE DICTIONARY OF EGYPTIAN ARCHÆOLOGY. A Handbook for Students and Travellers. Illustrated. *Cr. 8vo. 3s. 6d.*

Browning (Robert). PARACELSUS. Edited with an Introduction, Notes, and Bibliography by Margaret L. Lee and Katharine B. Locock. *Fcap. 8vo. 3s. 6d. net.*

Buckton (A. M.). EAGER HEART: A Christmas Mystery-Play. *Tenth Edition. Cr. 8vo. 1s. net.*

Bull (Paul). GOD AND OUR SOLDIERS. *Second Edition. Cr. 8vo. 6s.*

Burns (Robert). THE POEMS AND SONGS. Edited by Andrew Lang and W. A. Craigie. With Portrait. *Third Edition. Wide Demy 8vo. 6s.*

Calman (W. T.). THE LIFE OF CRUSTACEA. Illustrated. *Cr. 8vo. 6s.*

Carlyle (Thomas). THE FRENCH REVOLUTION. Edited by C. R. L. Fletcher. *Three Volumes. Cr. 8vo. 18s.*
THE LETTERS AND SPEECHES OF OLIVER CROMWELL. With an Introduction by C. H. Firth, and Notes and Appendices by S. C. Lomas. *Three Volumes. Demy 8vo. 18s. net.*

Methuen and Company Limited

Celano (Brother Thomas of). THE LIVES OF S. FRANCIS OF ASSISI. Translated by A. G. FERRERS HOWELL. With a Frontispiece. *Cr. 8vo.* 5s. net.

Chambers (Mrs. Lambert). LAWN TENNIS FOR LADIES. Illustrated. *Cr. 8vo.* 2s. 6d. net.

*****Chesser, (Elizabeth Sloan).** PERFECT HEALTH FOR WOMEN AND CHILDREN. *Cr. 8vo.* 3s. 6d. net.

Chesterfield (Lord). THE LETTERS OF THE EARL OF CHESTERFIELD TO HIS SON. Edited, with an Introduction by C. STRACHEY, and Notes by A. CALTHROP. *Two Volumes. Cr. 8vo.* 12s.

Chesterton (G.K.). CHARLES DICKENS. With two Portraits in Photogravure. *Seventh Edition. Cr. 8vo.* 6s.
ALL THINGS CONSIDERED. *Sixth Edition. Fcap. 8vo.* 5s.
TREMENDOUS TRIFLES. *Fourth Edition. Fcap. 8vo.* 5s.
ALARMS AND DISCURSIONS. *Second Edition. Fcap. 8vo.* 5s.
THE BALLAD OF THE WHITE HORSE. *Third Edition. Fcap. 8vo.* 5s.
*TYPES OF MEN. *Fcap. 8vo.* 5s.

Clausen (George). SIX LECTURES ON PAINTING. Illustrated. *Third Edition. Large Post 8vo.* 3s. 6d. net.
AIMS AND IDEALS IN ART. Eight Lectures delivered to the Students of the Royal Academy of Arts. Illustrated. *Second Edition. Large Post 8vo.* 5s. net.

Clutton-Brock (A.) SHELLEY: THE MAN AND THE POET. Illustrated. *Demy 8vo.* 7s. 6d. net.

Cobb (W.F.). THE BOOK OF PSALMS. With an Introduction and Notes. *Demy 8vo.* 10s. 6d. net.

Conrad (Joseph). THE MIRROR OF THE SEA: Memories and Impressions. *Third Edition. Cr. 8vo.* 6s.

Coolidge (W. A. B.). THE ALPS: IN NATURE AND HISTORY. Illustrated. *Demy 8vo.* 7s. 6d. net.

*****Correvon (H.).** ALPINE FLORA. Translated and enlarged by E. W. CLAYFORTH. Illustrated. *Square Demy 8vo.* 16s. net.

Coulton (G. G.). CHAUCER AND HIS ENGLAND. Illustrated. *Second Edition. Demy 8vo.* 10s. 6d. net.

Cowper (William). THE POEMS. Edited with an Introduction and Notes by J. C. BAILEY. Illustrated. *Demy 8vo.* 10s. 6d. net.

Cox (J. C.). RAMBLES IN SURREY. *Second Edition. Cr. 8vo.* 6s.

Crowley (Ralph H.). THE HYGIENE OF SCHOOL LIFE. Illustrated. *Cr. 8vo.* 3s. 6d. net.

Davis (H. W. C.). ENGLAND UNDER THE NORMANS AND ANGEVINS: 1066-1272. *Third Edition. Demy 8vo.* 10s. 6d. net.

Dawbarn (Charles). FRANCE AND THE FRENCH. Illustrated. *Demy 8vo.* 10s. 6d. net.

Dearmer (Mabel). A CHILD'S LIFE OF CHRIST. Illustrated. *Large Cr. 8vo.* 6s.

Deffand (Madame du). LETTRES DE MADAME DU DEFFAND À HORACE WALPOLE. Edited, with Introduction, Notes, and Index, by Mrs. PAGET TOYNBEE. *In Three Volumes. Demy 8vo.* £3 3s. net.

Dickinson (G. L.). THE GREEK VIEW OF LIFE. *Seventh Edition. Crown 8vo.* 2s. 6d. net.

Ditchfield (P. H.). THE PARISH CLERK. Illustrated. *Third Edition. Demy 8vo.* 7s. 6d. net.
THE OLD-TIME PARSON. Illustrated. *Second Edition. Demy 8vo.* 7s. 6d. net.
*THE OLD ENGLISH COUNTRY SQUIRE. Illustrated. *Demy 8vo.* 10s. 6d. net.

Ditchfield (P. H.) and Roe (Fred). VANISHING ENGLAND. The Book by P. H. Ditchfield. Illustrated by FRED ROE. *Second Edition. Wide Demy 8vo.* 15s. net.

Douglas (Hugh A.). VENICE ON FOOT. With the Itinerary of the Grand Canal. Illustrated. *Second Edition. Round corners. Fcap. 8vo.* 5s. net.
VENICE AND HER TREASURES. Illustrated. *Round corners. Fcap. 8vo.* 5s. net.

Dowden (J.). FURTHER STUDIES IN THE PRAYER BOOK. *Cr. 8vo.* 6s.

Driver (S. R.). SERMONS ON SUBJECTS CONNECTED WITH THE OLD TESTAMENT. *Cr. 8vo.* 6s.

Dumas (Alexandre). THE CRIMES OF THE BORGIAS AND OTHERS. With an Introduction by R. S. GARNETT. Illustrated. *Second Edition. Cr. 8vo.* 6s.
THE CRIMES OF URBAIN GRANDIER AND OTHERS. Illustrated. *Cr. 8vo.* 6s.
THE CRIMES OF THE MARQUISE DE BRINVILLIERS AND OTHERS. Illustrated *Cr. 8vo.* 6s.
THE CRIMES OF ALI PACHA AND OTHERS. Illustrated. *Cr. 8vo.* 6s.

General Literature

MY MEMOIRS. Translated by E. M Waller. With an Introduction by Andrew Lang. With Frontispieces in Photogravure. In six Volumes. *Cr. 8vo. 6s. each volume*
Vol. I. 1802-1821. Vol. IV. 1830-1831.
Vol II. 1822-1825. Vol. V. 1831-1832.
Vol III. 1826-1830. Vol. VI. 1832-1833.
MY PETS. Newly translated by A. R. Allinson. Illustrated. *Cr. 8vo. 6s.*

Duncan (F. M.). OUR INSECT FRIENDS AND FOES. Illustrated. *Cr. 8vo. 6s.*

Dunn-Pattison (R. P.). NAPOLEON'S MARSHALS. Illustrated. *Demy 8vo. Second Edition. 12s 6d net.*
THE BLACK PRINCE. Illustrated. *Second Edition. Demy 8vo. 7s. 6d. net.*

Durham (The Earl of). THE REPORT ON CANADA. With an Introductory Note. *Demy 8vo. 4s. 6d. net.*

Dutt (W. A.). THE NORFOLK BROADS. Illustrated. *Second Edition. Cr. 8vo. 6s.*

Egerton (H. E.). A SHORT HISTORY OF BRITISH COLONIAL POLICY. *Third Edition. Demy 8vo. 7s. 6d. net.*

Evans (Herbert A.). CASTLES OF ENGLAND AND WALES. Illustrated. *Demy 8vo. 12s. 6d. net.*

Exeter (Bishop of). REGNUM DEI. (The Bampton Lectures of 1901.) *A Cheaper Edition. Demy 8vo. 7s. 6d. net.*

Ewald (Carl). MY LITTLE BOY. Translated by Alexander Teixeira de Mattos. Illustrated. *Fcap. 8vo. 5s.*

Fairbrother (W. H.). THE PHILOSOPHY OF T. H. GREEN. *Second Edition. Cr. 8vo. 3s. 6d.*

*ffoulkes (Charles). THE ARMOURER AND HIS CRAFT. Illustrated. *Royal 4to. £2 2s. net.*

Firth (C. H.). CROMWELL'S ARMY: A History of the English Soldier during the Civil Wars, the Commonwealth, and the Protectorate. Illustrated. *Second Edition. Cr. 8vo. 6s.*

Fisher (H. A. L.). THE REPUBLICAN TRADITION IN EUROPE. *Cr. 8vo. 6s. net.*

FitzGerald (Edward). THE RUBA'IYAT OF OMAR KHAYYÁM. Printed from the Fifth and last Edition. With a Commentary by H. M. Batson, and a Biographical Introduction by E. D. Ross. *Cr. 8vo. 6s.*

Flux (A. W.). ECONOMIC PRINCIPLES. *Demy 8vo. 7s. 6d. net.*

Fraser (J. F.). ROUND THE WORLD ON A WHEEL. Illustrated. *Fifth Edition. Cr. 8vo. 6s.*

Galton (Sir Francis). MEMORIES OF MY LIFE. Illustrated. *Third Edition. Demy 8vo. 10s. 6d. net.*

Gibbins (H. de B.). INDUSTRY IN ENGLAND: HISTORICAL OUTLINES. With Maps and Plans. *Seventh Edition, Revised. Demy 8vo. 10s 6d.*
THE INDUSTRIAL HISTORY OF ENGLAND. With 5 Maps and a Plan. *Eighteenth and Revised Edition. Cr. 8vo. 3s.*
ENGLISH SOCIAL REFORMERS. *Second Edition. Cr. 8vo. 2s. 6d.*

Gibbon (Edward). THE MEMOIRS OF THE LIFE OF EDWARD GIBBON. Edited by G. Birkbeck Hill. *Cr. 8vo. 6s.*
THE DECLINE AND FALL OF THE ROMAN EMPIRE. Edited, with Notes, Appendices, and Maps, by J. B. Bury, Illustrated. *In Seven Volumes. Demy 8vo. Each 10s. 6d. net. Also in Seven Volumes. Cr. 8vo. 6s. each.*

Glover (T. R.). THE CONFLICT OF RELIGIONS IN THE EARLY ROMAN EMPIRE. *Fourth Edition. Demy 8vo. 7s. 6d. net.*

Godley (A. D.). LYRA FRIVOLA. *Fourth Edition. Fcap. 8vo. 2s. 6d.*
VERSES TO ORDER. *Second Edition. Fcap. 8vo. 2s. 6d.*
SECOND STRINGS. *Fcap. 8vo. 2s. 6d.*

Gostling (Frances M.). THE BRETONS AT HOME. Illustrated. *Third Edition. Cr. 8vo. 6s.*
AUVERGNE AND ITS PEOPLE. Illustrated. *Demy 8vo. 10s. 6d. net.*

*Gray (Arthur). CAMBRIDGE AND ITS STORY. Illustrated. *Demy 8vo. 7s. 6d. net.*

Grahame (Kenneth). THE WIND IN THE WILLOWS. Illustrated. *Sixth Edition. Cr. 8vo. 6s.*

Granger (Frank). HISTORICAL SOCIOLOGY: a Text-Book of Politics. *Cr. 8vo. 3s. 6d. net.*

Grew (Edwin Sharpe). THE GROWTH OF A PLANET. Illustrated. *Cr. 8vo. 6s.*

Griffin (W. Hall) and Minchin (H. C.). THE LIFE OF ROBERT BROWNING. Illustrated. *Second Edition. Demy 8vo. 12s. 6d. net.*

Hale (J. R.). FAMOUS SEA FIGHTS: from Salamis to Tsu-shima. Illustrated. *Cr. 8vo. 6s. net.*

*Hall (H. R.). THE ANCIENT HISTORY OF THE NEAR EAST FROM THE EARLIEST PERIOD TO THE PERSIAN INVASION OF GREECE. Illustrated. *Demy 8vo. 15s. net.*

Hannay (D.). A SHORT HISTORY OF THE ROYAL NAVY. Vol. I., 1217-1688. Vol. II., 1689-1815. *Demy 8vo. Each 7s. 6d. net.*

Harper (Charles G.). THE AUTOCAR ROAD-BOOK. With Maps. *In Four Volumes. Cr. 8vo. Each 7s. 6d. net.*
Vol. I.—SOUTH OF THE THAMES.
Vol. II.—NORTH AND SOUTH WALES AND WEST MIDLANDS.
Vol. III.—EAST ANGLIA AND EAST MIDLANDS.
*Vol. IV.—THE NORTH OF ENGLAND AND SOUTH OF SCOTLAND.

Harris (Frank). THE WOMEN OF SHAKESPEARE. *Demy 8vo. 7s. 6d. net.*

Hassall (Arthur). THE LIFE OF NAPOLEON. Illustrated. *Demy 8vo. 7s. 6d. net.*

Headley (F. W.). DARWINISM AND MODERN SOCIALISM. *Second Edition. Cr. 8vo. 5s. net.*

Henderson (M. Sturge). GEORGE MEREDITH: NOVELIST, POET, REFORMER. With a Portrait. *Second Edition. Cr. 8vo. 6s.*

Henley (W. E.). ENGLISH LYRICS: CHAUCER TO POE. *Second Edition. Cr. 8vo. 2s. 6d. net.*

Hill (George Francis). ONE HUNDRED MASTERPIECES OF SCULPTURE. Illustrated. *Demy 8vo. 10s. 6d. net.*

Hind (C. Lewis). DAYS IN CORNWALL. Illustrated. *Third Edition. Cr. 8vo. 6s.*

Hobhouse (L. T.). THE THEORY OF KNOWLEDGE. *Demy 8vo. 10s. 6d. net.*

Hobson (J. A.). INTERNATIONAL TRADE: AN APPLICATION OF ECONOMIC THEORY. *Cr. 8vo. 2s. 6d. net.*
PROBLEMS OF POVERTY: AN INQUIRY INTO THE INDUSTRIAL CONDITION OF THE POOR. *Seventh Edition. Cr. 8vo. 2s. 6d.*
THE PROBLEM OF THE UNEMPLOYED : AN ENQUIRY AND AN ECONOMI - POLICY. *Fifth Edition. Cr. 8vo. 2s. 6d.*

Hodgson (Mrs. W.). HOW TO IDENTIFY OLD CHINESE PORCELAIN. Illustrated. *Third Edition. Post 8vo. 6s.*

Holdich (Sir T. H.). THE INDIAN BORDERLAND, 1880-1900. Illustrated. *Second Edition. Demy 8vo. 10s. 6d. net.*

Holdsworth (W. S.). A HISTORY OF ENGLISH LAW. *In Four Volumes. Vols. I., II., III. Demy 8vo. Each 10s. 6d. net.*

Holland (Clive). TYROL AND ITS PEOPLE. Illustrated. *Demy 8vo. 10s. 6d. net.*
THE BELGIANS AT HOME. Illustrated. *Demy 8vo. 10s. 6d. net.*

Horsburgh (E. L. S.). LORENZO THE MAGNIFICENT : AND FLORENCE IN HER GOLDEN AGE. Illustrated. *Second Edition. Demy 8vo. 15s. net.*
WATERLOO: A NARRATIVE AND A CRITICISM. With Plans. *Second Edition. Cr. 8vo. 5s.*
THE LIFE OF SAVONAROLA. Illustrated. *Cr. 8vo. 5s. net.*

Hosie (Alexander). MANCHURIA. Illustrated. *Second Edition. Demy 8vo. 7s. 6d. net.*

Hudson (W. H.). A SHEPHERD'S LIFE: IMPRESSIONS OF THE SOUTH WILTSHIRE DOWNS. Illustrated. *Third Edition. Demy 8vo. 7s. 6d. net.*

Humphreys (John H.). PROPORTIONAL REPRESENTATION. *Cr. 8vo. 5s. net.*

Hutchinson (Horace G.). THE NEW FOREST. Illustrated. *Fourth Edition. Cr. 8vo. 6s.*

Hutton (Edward). THE CITIES OF SPAIN. Illustrated. *Fourth Edition. Cr. 8vo. 6s.*
THE CITIES OF UMBRIA. Illustrated. *Fourth Edition. Cr. 8vo. 6s.*
*THE CITIES OF LOMBARDY. Illustrated. *Cr. 8vo. 6s.*
FLORENCE AND NORTHERN TUSCANY WITH GENOA. Illustrated. *Second Edition. Cr. 8vo. 6s.*
SIENA AND SOUTHERN TUSCANY. Illustrated. *Second Edition. Cr. 8vo. 6s.*
VENICE AND VENETIA. Illustrated. *Cr. 8vo. 6s.*
ROME. Illustrated. *Third Edition. Cr. 8vo. 6s.*
COUNTRY WALKS ABOUT FLORENCE. Illustrated. *Second Edition. Fcap. 8vo. 5s. net.*
IN UNKNOWN TUSCANY. With Notes by WILLIAM HEYWOOD. Illustrated. *Second Edition. Demy 8vo. 7s. 6d. net.*
A BOOK OF THE WYE. Illustrated. *Demy 8vo. 7s. 6d. net.*

Ibsen (Henrik). BRAND. A Dramatic Poem, Translated by WILLIAM WILSON. *Fourth Edition. Cr. 8vo. 3s. 6d.*

Inge (W. R.). CHRISTIAN MYSTICISM. (The Bampton Lectures of 1899.) *Second and Cheaper Edition. Cr. 8vo. 5s. net.*

General Literature

Innes (A. D.). A HISTORY OF THE BRITISH IN INDIA. With Maps and Plans. *Cr. 8vo.* 6s.
ENGLAND UNDER THE TUDORS. With Maps. *Third Edition. Demy 8vo.* 10s. 6d. *net.*

Innes (Mary). SCHOOLS OF PAINTING. Illustrated. *Second Edition. Cr. 8vo.* 5s. *net.*

Jenks (E.). AN OUTLINE OF ENGLISH LOCAL GOVERNMENT. *Second Edition.* Revised by R. C. K. Ensor, *Cr. 8vo.* 2s. 6d. *net.*
A SHORT HISTORY OF ENGLISH LAW: FROM THE EARLIEST TIMES TO THE END OF THE YEAR 1911. *Demy 8vo.* 10s. 6d. *net.*

Jerningham (Charles Edward). THE MAXIMS OF MARMADUKE. *Second Edition. Cr. 8vo.* 5s.

Johnston (Sir H. H.). BRITISH CENTRAL AFRICA. Illustrated. *Third Edition. Cr. 4to.* 18s. *net.*
THE NEGRO IN THE NEW WORLD. Illustrated. *Demy 8vo.* 21s. *net.*

Julian (Lady) of Norwich. REVELATIONS OF DIVINE LOVE. Edited by Grace Warrack. *Fourth Edition. Cr. 8vo.* 3s. 6d.

Keats (John). THE POEMS. Edited with Introduction and Notes by E. de Sélincourt. With a Frontispiece in Photogravure. *Third Edition. Demy 8vo.* 7s. 6d. *net.*

Keble (John). THE CHRISTIAN YEAR. With an Introduction and Notes by W. Lock. Illustrated. *Third Edition. Fcap. 8vo.* 3s. 6d.

Kempis (Thomas à). THE IMITATION OF CHRIST. From the Latin, with an Introduction by Dean Farrar. Illustrated. *Third Edition. Fcap. 8vo.* 3s. 6d.

Kingston (Edward). A GUIDE TO THE BRITISH PICTURES IN THE NATIONAL GALLERY. Illustrated. *Fcap. 8vo.* 3s. 6d. *net.*

Kipling (Rudyard). BARRACK-ROOM BALLADS. 108th *Thousand. Thirty-first Edition. Cr. 8vo.* 6s. Also *Fcap. 8vo, Leather.* 5s. *net.*
HE SEVEN SEAS. 89th *Thousand. Nineteenth Edition. Cr. 8vo.* 6s. Also *Fcap. 8vo, Leather.* 5s. *net.*
THE FIVE NATIONS. 72nd *Thousand. Eighth Edition. Cr. 8vo.* 6s. Also *Fcap. 8vo, Leather.* 5s. *net.*
DEPARTMENTAL DITTIES. *Twentieth Edition. Cr. 8vo.* 6s. Also *Fcap. 8vo, Leather.* 5s. *net.*

Lamb (Charles and Mary). THE COMPLETE WORKS. Edited with an Introduction and Notes by E. V. Lucas. *A New and Revised Edition in Six Volumes. With Frontispiece. Fcap 8vo.* 5s. *each.*
The volumes are:—
I. Miscellaneous Prose. II. Elia and the Last Essays of Elia. III. Books for Children. IV. Plays and Poems. V. and VI. Letters.

Lankester (Sir Ray). SCIENCE FROM AN EASY CHAIR. Illustrated. *Fifth Edition. Cr. 8vo.* 6s.

Le Braz (Anatole). THE LAND OF PARDONS. Translated by Frances M. Gostling. Illustrated. *Third Edition. Cr. 8vo.* 6s.

Lock (Walter). ST. PAUL, THE MASTER-BUILDER. *Third Edition. Cr. 8vo.* 3s. 6d.
THE BIBLE AND CHRISTIAN LIFE. *Cr. 8vo.* 6s.

Lodge (Sir Oliver). THE SUBSTANCE OF FAITH, ALLIED WITH SCIENCE: A Catechism for Parents and Teachers. *Eleventh Edition. Cr. 8vo.* 2s. *net.*
MAN AND THE UNIVERSE: A Study of the Influence of the Advance in Scientific Knowledge upon our Understanding of Christianity. *Ninth Edition. Demy 8vo.* 5s. *net.* Also *Fcap. 8vo.* 1s. *net.*
THE SURVIVAL OF MAN. A Study in Unrecognised Human Faculty. *Fifth Edition. Wide Crown 8vo.* 5s. *net.*
REASON AND BELIEF. *Fifth Edition. Cr. 8vo.* 3s. 6d. *net*
*MODERN PROBLEMS. *Cr. 8vo.* 5s. *net.*

Lorimer (George Horace). LETTERS FROM A SELF-MADE MERCHANT TO HIS SON. Illustrated. *Twenty-second Edition. Cr. 8vo.* 3s. 6d. Also *Fcap. 8vo.* 1s. *net.*
OLD GORGON GRAHAM. Illustrated. *Second Edition. Cr. 8vo.* 6s.

Lucas (E. V.). THE LIFE OF CHARLES LAMB. Illustrated. *Fifth Edition. Demy 8vo.* 7s. 6d. *net.*
A WANDERER IN HOLLAND. Illustrated. *Thirteenth Edition. Cr. 8vo.* 6s.
A WANDERER IN LONDON. Illustrated. *Twelfth Edition. Cr. 8vo.* 6s.
A WANDERER IN PARIS. Illustrated. *Ninth Edition. Cr. 8vo.* 6s. Also *Fcap. 8vo.* 5
*A WANDERER IN FLORENCE. Illustrated. *Cr. 8vo.* 6s.
THE OPEN ROAD: A Little Book for Wayfarers. *Eighteenth Edition. Fcap. 8vo.* 5s.; *India Paper,* 7s. 6d.
*Also *Illustrated in colour. Cr. 4to* 15s. *net.*

THE FRIENDLY TOWN: A Little Book for the Urbane. *Sixth Edition. Fcap. 8vo.* 5s.; *India Paper*, 7s. 6d.
FIRESIDE AND SUNSHINE. *Sixth Edition. Fcap. 8vo.* 5s.
CHARACTER AND COMEDY. *Sixth Edition. Fcap. 8vo.* 5s.
THE GENTLEST ART. A Choice of Letters by Entertaining Hands. *Seventh Edition. Fcap 8vo.* 5s.
THE SECOND POST. *Third Edition. Fcap. 8vo.* 5s.
HER INFINITE VARIETY: A FEMININE PORTRAIT GALLERY. *Sixth Edition. Fcap. 8vo.* 5s.
GOOD COMPANY: A RALLY OF MEN. *Second Edition. Fcap. 8vo.* 5s.
ONE DAY AND ANOTHER. *Fifth Edition. Fcap. 8vo.* 5s.
OLD LAMPS FOR NEW. *Fourth Edition. Fcap. 8vo.* 5s.
LISTENER'S LURE: AN OBLIQUE NARRATION. *Ninth Edition. Fcap. 8vo.* 5s.
OVER BEMERTON'S: AN EASY-GOING CHRONICLE. *Ninth Edition. Fcap. 8vo.* 5s.
MR. INGLESIDE. *Ninth Edition. Fcap. 8vo.* 5s.
See also Lamb (Charles).

Lydekker (R. and Others). REPTILES, AMPHIBIA, FISHES, AND LOWER CHORDATA. Edited by J. C. CUNNINGHAM. Illustrated. *Demy 8vo.* 10s. 6d. net.

Lydekker (R.). THE OX AND ITS KINDRED. Illustrated. *Cr. 8vo.* 6s.

Macaulay (Lord). CRITICAL AND HISTORICAL ESSAYS. Edited by F. C. MONTAGUE. *Three Volumes. Cr. 8vo.* 18s.

McCabe (Joseph). THE DECAY OF THE CHURCH OF ROME. *Third Edition. Demy 8vo.* 7s. 6d. net.
THE EMPRESSES OF ROME. Illustrated. *Demy 8vo.* 12s. 6d. net.

MacCarthy (Desmond) and Russell (Agatha). LADY JOHN RUSSELL: A MEMOIR. Illustrated. *Fourth Edition. Demy 8vo.* 10s. 6d. net.

McCullagh (Francis). THE FALL OF ABD-UL-HAMID. Illustrated. *Demy 8vo.* 10s. 6d. net.

McDougall (William). AN INTRODUCTION TO SOCIAL PSYCHOLOGY. *Fourth Edition. Cr. 8vo.* 5s. net.
BODY AND MIND: A HISTORY AND A DEFENCE OF ANIMISM. *Demy 8vo.* 10s. 6d. net.

'Mdlle. Mori' (Author of). ST. CATHERINE OF SIENA AND HER TIMES. Illustrated. *Second Edition. Demy 8vo.* 7s. 6d. net.

Maeterlinck (Maurice). THE BLUE BIRD: A FAIRY PLAY IN SIX ACTS. Translated by ALEXANDER TEIXEIRA DE MATTOS. *Fcap. 8vo. Deckle Edges.* 3s. 6d. net. Also *Fcap. 8vo. Cloth*, 1s. net. An Edition, illustrated in colour by F. CAYLEY ROBINSON, is also published. *Cr. 4to. Gilt top.* 21s. net. Of the above book Twenty-nine Editions in all have been issued.
MARY MAGDALENE: A PLAY IN THREE ACTS. Translated by ALEXANDER TEIXEIRA DE MATTOS. *Third Edition. Fcap. 8vo. Deckle Edges.* 3s. 6d. net. Also *Fcap. 8vo.* 1s. net.
DEATH. Translated by ALEXANDER TEIXEIRA DE MATTOS. *Fourth Edition. Fcap. 8vo.* 3s. 6d. net.

Mahaffy (J. P.). A HISTORY OF EGYPT UNDER THE PTOLEMAIC DYNASTY. Illustrated. *Cr. 8vo.* 6s.

Maitland (F. W.). ROMAN CANON LAW IN THE CHURCH OF ENGLAND. *Royal 8vo.* 7s. 6d.

Marett (R. R.). THE THRESHOLD OF RELIGION. *Cr. 8vo.* 3s. 6d. net.

Marriott (Charles). A SPANISH HOLIDAY. Illustrated. *Demy 8vo.* 7s. 6d. net.
THE ROMANCE OF THE RHINE. Illustrated. *Demy 8vo.* 10s. 6d. net.

Marriott (J. A. R.). THE LIFE AND TIMES OF LUCIUS CARY, VISCOUNT FALKLAND. Illustrated. *Second Edition. Demy 8vo.* 7s. 6d. net.

Masefield (John). SEA LIFE IN NELSON'S TIME. Illustrated. *Cr. 8vo.* 3s. 6d. net.
A SAILOR'S GARLAND. Selected and Edited. *Second Edition. Cr. 8vo.* 3s. 6d. net.

Masterman (C. F. G.). TENNYSON AS A RELIGIOUS TEACHER. *Second Edition. Cr. 8vo.* 6s.
THE CONDITION OF ENGLAND. *Fourth Edition. Cr. 8vo.* 6s. Also *Fcap. 8vo.* 1s. net.

*Mayne (Ethel Colburn). BYRON. Illustrated. *In two volumes. Demy 8vo.* 21s. net.

Medley (D. J.). ORIGINAL ILLUSTRATIONS OF ENGLISH CONSTITUTIONAL HISTORY. *Cr. 8vo.* 7s. 6d. net.

Methuen (A. M. S.). ENGLAND'S RUIN: DISCUSSED IN FOURTEEN LETTERS TO A PROTECTIONIST. *Ninth Edition. Cr. 8vo.* 3d. net.

Miles (Eustace). LIFE AFTER LIFE: OR, THE THEORY OF REINCARNATION. *Cr. 8vo.* 2s. 6d. net.
THE POWER OF CONCENTRATION: HOW TO ACQUIRE IT. *Fourth Edition. Cr. 8vo.* 3s. 6d. net.

General Literature

Millais (J. G.). THE LIFE AND LETTERS OF SIR JOHN EVERETT MILLAIS. Illustrated. *New Edition. Demy 8vo.* 7s. 6d. net.

Milne (J. G.). A HISTORY OF EGYPT UNDER ROMAN RULE. Illustrated. *Cr. 8vo.* 6s.

Moffat (Mary M.). QUEEN LOUISA OF PRUSSIA. Illustrated. *Fourth Edition. Cr. 8vo.* 6s.
MARIA THERESA. Illustrated. *Demy 8vo.* 10s. 6d. net.

Money (L. G. Chiozza). RICHES AND POVERTY, 1910. *Tenth and Revised Edition. Demy 8vo.* 5s. net.
MONEY'S FISCAL DICTIONARY, 1910. *Second Edition. Demy 8vo.* 5s. net.
INSURANCE VERSUS POVERTY. *Cr. 8vo.* 5s. net.
THINGS THAT MATTER: Papers on Subjects which are, or ought to be, under Discussion. *Demy 8vo.* 5s. net.

Montague (C. E.). DRAMATIC VALUES. *Second Edition. Fcap. 8vo.* 5s.

Moorhouse (E. Hallam). NELSON'S LADY HAMILTON. Illustrated. *Third Edition. Demy 8vo.* 7s. 6d. net.

*****Morgan (C. Lloyd).** INSTINCT AND EXPERIENCE. *Cr. 8vo.* 5s. net.

*****Nevill (Lady Dorothy).** MY OWN TIMES. Edited by her son. *Demy 8vo.* 15s. net.

Norway (A. H.). NAPLES: Past and Present. Illustrated. *Fourth Edition. Cr. 8vo.* 6s.

*****O'Donnell (Elliott).** WEREWOLVES. *Cr. 8vo.* 5s. net.

Oman (C. W. C.), A HISTORY OF THE ART OF WAR IN THE MIDDLE AGES. Illustrated. *Demy 8vo.* 10s. 6d. net.
ENGLAND BEFORE THE NORMAN CONQUEST. With Maps. *Second Edition. Demy 8vo.* 10s. 6d. net.

Oxford (M. N.), A HANDBOOK OF NURSING. *Sixth Edition, Revised. Cr. 8vo.* 3s. 6d. net.

Pakes (W. C. C.). THE SCIENCE OF HYGIENE. Illustrated. *Second and Cheaper Edition.* Revised by A. T. Nankivell. *Cr. 8vo.* 5s. net.

Parker (Eric). THE BOOK OF THE ZOO. Illustrated. *Second Edition. Cr. 8vo.* 6s.

Pears (Sir Edwin). TURKEY AND ITS PEOPLE. *Second Edition. Demy 8vo.* 12s. 6d. net.

Petrie (W. M. Flinders). A HISTORY OF EGYPT. Illustrated. *In Six Volumes. Cr. 8vo.* 6s. each.
Vol. I. From the Ist to the XVIth Dynasty. *Seventh Edition.*
Vol. II. The XVIIth and XVIIIth Dynasties. *Fourth Edition.*
Vol. III. XIXth to XXXth Dynasties.
Vol. IV. Egypt under the Ptolemaic Dynasty. J. P. Mahaffy.
Vol. V. Egypt under Roman Rule. J. G. Milne.
Vol. VI. Egypt in the Middle Ages. Stanley Lane-Poole.
RELIGION AND CONSCIENCE IN ANCIENT EGYPT. Illustrated. *Cr. 8vo.* 2s. 6d.
SYRIA AND EGYPT, FROM THE TELL EL AMARNA LETTERS. *Cr. 8vo.* 2s. 6d.
EGYPTIAN TALES. Translated from the Papyri. First Series, ivth to xiith Dynasty. Illustrated. *Second Edition. Cr. 8vo.* 3s. 6d.
EGYPTIAN TALES. Translated from the Papyri. Second Series, xviiith to xixth Dynasty. Illustrated. *Cr. 8vo.* 3s. 6d.
EGYPTIAN DECORATIVE ART. Illustrated. *Cr. 8vo.* 3s. 6d.

Phelps (Ruth S.). SKIES ITALIAN: A Little Breviary for Travellers in Italy. *Fcap. 8vo. Leather.* 5s. net.

Pollard (Alfred W.). SHAKESPEARE FOLIOS AND QUARTOS. A Study in the Bibliography of Shakespeare's Plays, 1594-1685. Illustrated. *Folio.* 21s. net.

Porter (G. R.). THE PROGRESS OF THE NATION. A New Edition. Edited by F. W. Hirst. *Demy 8vo.* 21s. net.

Power (J. O'Connor). THE MAKING OF AN ORATOR. *Cr. 8vo.* 6s.

Price (Eleanor C.). CARDINAL DE RICHELIEU. Illustrated. *Second Edition. Demy 8vo.* 10s. 6d. net.

Price (L. L.), A SHORT HISTORY OF POLITICAL ECONOMY IN ENGLAND FROM ADAM SMITH TO ARNOLD TOYNBEE. *Seventh Edition. Cr. 8vo.* 2s. 6d.

Pycraft (W. P.). A HISTORY OF BIRDS. Illustrated. *Demy 8vo.* 10s. 6d. net.

Rawlings (Gertrude B.). COINS AND HOW TO KNOW THEM. Illustrated. *Third Edition. Cr. 8vo.* 6s.

Regan (C. Tate). THE FRESHWATER FISHES OF THE BRITISH ISLES. Illustrated. *Cr. 8vo.* 6s.

Reid (Archdall). THE LAWS OF HEREDITY. *Second Edition. Demy 8vo.* 21s. net.

METHUEN AND COMPANY LIMITED

Robertson (C. Grant). SELECT STATUTES, CASES, AND DOCUMENTS, 1660-1894. *Demy 8vo.* 10s. 6d. net.
ENGLAND UNDER THE HANOVERIANS. Illustrated. *Second Edition. Demy 8vo.* 10s. 6d. net.

Roe (Fred). OLD OAK FURNITURE. Illustrated. *Second Edition. Demy 8vo.* 10s. 6d. net.

*Ryan (P. F. W.). STUART LIFE AND MANNERS: A SOCIAL HISTORY. Illustrated. *Demy 8vo.* 10s. 6d. net.

St. Francis of Assisi. THE LITTLE FLOWERS OF THE GLORIOUS MESSER, AND OF HIS FRIARS. Done into English, with Notes by WILLIAM HEYWOOD. Illustrated. *Demy 8vo.* 5s. net.

'Saki' (H. H. Munro). REGINALD. *Third Edition. Fcap. 8vo.* 2s. 6d. net.
REGINALD IN RUSSIA. *Fcap. 8vo.* 2s. 6d. net.

Sandeman (G. A. C.). METTERNICH. Illustrated. *Demy 8vo.* 10s. 6d. net.

Schidrowitz (Philip). RUBBER. Illustrated. *Demy 8vo.* 10s. 6d. net.

Selous (Edmund). TOMMY SMITH'S ANIMALS. Illustrated. *Eleventh Edition. Fcap. 8vo.* 2s. 6d.
TOMMY SMITH'S OTHER ANIMALS. Illustrated. *Fifth Edition. Fcap. 8vo.* 2s. 6d.
JACK'S INSECTS. Illustrated. *Cr. 8vo.* 6s.

Shakespeare (William).
THE FOUR FOLIOS, 1623; 1632; 1664; 1685. Each £4 4s. *net*, or a complete set, £12 12s. *net*.
THE POEMS OF WILLIAM SHAKESPEARE. With an Introduction and Notes by GEORGE WYNDHAM. *Demy 8vo.* Buckram. 10s. 6d.

Shelley (Percy Bysshe). THE POEMS OF PERCY BYSSHE SHELLEY. With an Introduction by A. CLUTTON-BROCK and notes by C. D. LOCOCK. *Two Volumes. Demy 8vo.* 21s. net.

Sladen (Douglas). SICILY: The New Winter Resort. Illustrated. *Second Edition. Cr. 8vo.* 5s. net.

Smith (Adam). THE WEALTH OF NATIONS. Edited by EDWIN CANNAN. *Two Volumes. Demy 8vo.* 21s. net.

Smith (G. Herbert). GEM-STONES AND THEIR DISTINCTIVE CHARACTERS. Illustrated. *Cr. 8vo.* 6s. net.

Snell (F. J). A BOOK OF EXMOOR. Illustrated. *Cr. 8vo.* 6s.
THE CUSTOMS OF OLD ENGLAND. Illustrated. *Cr. 8vo.* 6s.

'Stancliffe.' GOLF DO'S AND DONT'S *Fourth Edition. Fcap. 8vo.* 1s. net.

Stevenson (R. L.). THE LETTERS OF ROBERT LOUIS STEVENSON. Edited by Sir SIDNEY COLVIN. *A New and Enlarged Edition in four volumes. Third Edition. Fcap. 8vo.* Each 5s. Leather, each 5s. net.

Stevenson (M. L). FROM SARANAC TO THE MARQUESAS AND BEYOND Being Letters written by Mrs. M. I. STEVENSON during 1887-88. Illustrated. *Cr. 8vo* 6s. net.
LETTERS FROM SAMOA, 1891-95. Edited and arranged by M. C. BALFOUR. Illustrated. *Second Edition. Cr. 8vo.* 6s. net.

Storr (Vernon F.). DEVELOPMENT AND DIVINE PURPOSE. *Cr. 8vo.* 5s. net.

Streatfeild (R. A.). MODERN MUSIC AND MUSICIANS. Illustrated. *Second Edition. Demy 8vo.* 7s. 6d. net.

Swanton (E. W.). FUNGI AND HOW TO KNOW THEM. Illustrated. *Cr. 8vo.* 6s. net.

Symes (J E.). THE FRENCH REVOLUTION. *Second Edition. Cr. 8vo.* 2s. 6d

Tabor (Margaret E.). THE SAINTS IN ART. Illustrated. *Fcap. 8vo.* 3s. 6d. net

Taylor (A. E). ELEMENTS OF METAPHYSICS. *Second Edition. Demy 8vo.* 10s 6d. net.

Taylor (Mrs. Basil) (Harriet Osgood). JAPANESE GARDENS. Illustrated *Cr. 4to.* 21s. net.

Thibaudeau (A. C.). BONAPARTE AND THE CONSULATE. Translated and Edited by G. K. FORTESCUE. Illustrated. *Demy 8vo.* 10s. 6d. net.

Thomas (Edward). MAURICE MAETERLINCK. Illustrated. *Second Edition. Cr. 8vo.* 5s. net.

Thompson (Francis). SELECTED POEMS OF FRANCIS THOMPSON. With a Biographical Note by WILFRID MEYNELL. With a Portrait in Photogravure. *Seventh Edition. Fcap. 8vo.* 5s. net.

Tileston (Mary W.). DAILY STRENGTH FOR DAILY NEEDS. *Nineteenth Edition. Medium 16mo.* 2s. 6d net. Lambskin 3s. 6d. net. Also an edition in superior binding, 6s.
THE STRONGHOLD OF HOPE. *Medium 16mo.* 2s. 6d. net.

Toynbee (Paget). DANTE ALIGHIERI HIS LIFE AND WORKS. With 16 Illustrations. *Fourth and Enlarged Edition. Cr. 8vo.* 5s. net.

General Literature

Trevelyan (G. M.). ENGLAND UNDER THE STUARTS. With Maps and Plans. *Fifth Edition. Demy 8vo.* 10s. 6d. net.

Triggs (H. Inigo). TOWN PLANNING: PAST, PRESENT, AND POSSIBLE. Illustrated. *Second Edition. Wide Royal 8vo.* 15s. net.

*Turner (Sir Alfred E.). SIXTY YEARS OF A SOLDIER'S LIFE. *Demy 8vo.* 12s. 6d. net.

Underhill (Evelyn). MYSTICISM. A Study in the Nature and Development of Man's Spiritual Consciousness. *Fourth Edition. Demy 8vo.* 15s. net.

*Underwood (F. M.). UNITED ITALY. *Demy 8vo.* 10s. 6d. net.

Urwick (E. J.). A PHILOSOPHY OF SOCIAL PROGRESS. *Cr. 8vo.* 6s.

Vaughan (Herbert M.). THE NAPLES RIVIERA. Illustrated. *Second Edition. Cr. 8vo.* 6s.
FLORENCE AND HER TREASURES. Illustrated. *Fcap. 8vo. Round corners.* 5s. net.

Vernon (Hon. W. Warren). READINGS ON THE INFERNO OF DANTE. With an Introduction by the REV. DR. MOORE. *Two Volumes. Second Edition. Cr. 8vo.* 15s. net.
READINGS ON THE PURGATORIO OF DANTE. With an Introduction by the late DEAN CHURCH. *Two Volumes. Third Edition. Cr. 8vo.* 15s. net.
READINGS ON THE PARADISO OF DANTE. With an Introduction by the BISHOP OF RIPON. *Two Volumes. Second Edition. Cr. 8vo.* 15s. net.

Wade (G. W.), and Wade (J. H.). RAMBLES IN SOMERSET. Illustrated. *Cr 8vo.* 6s.

Waddell (L. A.). LHASA AND ITS MYSTERIES. With a Record of the Expedition of 1903-1904. Illustrated. *Third and Cheaper Edition. Medium 8vo.* 7s. 6d. net.

Wagner (Richard). RICHARD WAGNER'S MUSIC DRAMAS: Interpretations, embodying Wagner's own explanations. By ALICE LEIGHTON CLEATHER and BASIL CRUMP. *Fcap. 8vo.* 2s. 6d. each.
THE RING OF THE NIBELUNG.
 Fifth Edition.
PARSIFAL, LOHENGRIN, AND THE HOLY GRAIL.
TRISTAN AND ISOLDE.
TANNHÄUSER AND THE MASTERSINGERS OF NUREMBERG.

Waterhouse (Elizabeth). WITH THE SIMPLE-HEARTED: Little Homilies to Women in Country Places. *Third Edition. Small Pott 8vo.* 2s. net.
THE HOUSE BY THE CHERRY TREE. A Second Series of Little Homilies to Women in Country Places. *Small Pott 8vo.* 2s. net.
COMPANIONS OF THE WAY. Being Selections for Morning and Evening Reading. Chosen and arranged by ELIZABETH WATERHOUSE. *Large Cr. 8vo.* 5s. net.
THOUGHTS OF A TERTIARY. *Small Pott 8vo.* 1s. net.

Waters (W. G.). ITALIAN SCULPTORS AND SMITHS. Illustrated. *Cr. 8vo.* 7s. 6d. net.

Watt (Francis). EDINBURGH AND THE LOTHIANS. Illustrated. *Second Edition. Cr. 8vo.* 10s. 6d. net.

*Wedmore (Sir Frederick). MEMORIES. *Demy 8vo.* 7s. 6d. net.

Weigall (Arthur E. P.). A GUIDE TO THE ANTIQUITIES OF UPPER EGYPT: From Abydos to the Sudan Frontier. Illustrated. *Cr. 8vo.* 7s. 6d. net.

Welch (Catharine). THE LITTLE DAUPHIN. Illustrated. *Cr. 8vo.* 6s.

Wells (J.). OXFORD AND OXFORD LIFE. *Third Edition. Cr. 8vo.* 3s. 6d.
A SHORT HISTORY OF ROME. *Eleventh Edition.* With 3 Maps. *Cr. 8vo.* 3s. 6d.

Wilde (Oscar). THE WORKS OF OSCAR WILDE. *In Twelve Volumes. Fcap. 8vo.* 5s. net each volume.
I. LORD ARTHUR SAVILE'S CRIME AND THE PORTRAIT OF MR. W. H. II. THE DUCHESS OF PADUA. III. POEMS. IV. LADY WINDERMERE'S FAN. V. A WOMAN OF NO IMPORTANCE. VI. AN IDEAL HUSBAND. VII. THE IMPORTANCE OF BEING EARNEST. VIII. A HOUSE OF POMEGRANATES. IX. INTENTIONS. X. DE PROFUNDIS AND PRISON LETTERS. XI. ESSAYS. XII. SALOMÉ, A FLORENTINE TRAGEDY, and LA SAINTE COURTISANE.

Williams (H. Noel). THE WOMEN BONAPARTES. The Mother and three Sisters of Napoleon. Illustrated. *Two Volumes. Demy 8vo.* 24s. net.
A ROSE OF SAVOY: MARIE ADÉLAÏDE OF SAVOY, DUCHESSE DE BOURGOGNE, MOTHER OF LOUIS XV. Illustrated. *Second Edition. Demy 8vo.* 15s. net.
THE FASCINATING DUC DE RICHELIEU: LOUIS FRANÇOIS ARMAND DU PLESSIS (1696-1788). Illustrated. *Demy 8vo.* 15s. net.
A PRINCESS OF ADVENTURE: MARIE CAROLINE, DUCHESSE DE BERRY (1798-1870). Illustrated. *Demy 8vo.* 15s. net.

Wood (Sir Evelyn). FROM MIDSHIPMAN TO FIELD-MARSHAL. Illustrated. *Fifth Edition. Demy 8vo. 7s. 6d. net. Also Fcap. 8vo. 1s. net.*

THE REVOLT IN HINDUSTAN (1857-59). Illustrated. *Second Edition. Cr. 8vo. 6s.*

Wood (W. Birkbeck), and Edmonds (Col. J. E.). A HISTORY OF THE CIVIL WAR IN THE UNITED STATES (1861-5). With an Introduction by SPENSER WILKINSON. With 24 Maps and Plans. *Third Edition. Demy 8vo. 12s. 6d. net.*

Wordsworth (W.). THE POEMS. With an Introduction and Notes by NOWELL C. SMITH. *In Three Volumes. Demy 8vo. 15s. net.*

Yeats (W. B.). A BOOK OF IRISH VERSE. *Third Edition. Cr. 8vo. 3s. 6d.*

PART II.—A SELECTION OF SERIES.

Ancient Cities.

General Editor, B. C. A. WINDLE.

Cr. 8vo. 4s. 6d. net each volume.

With Illustrations by E. H. NEW, and other Artists.

BRISTOL. Alfred Harvey.
CANTERBURY. J. C. Cox.
CHESTER. B. C. A. Windle.
DUBLIN. S. A. O. Fitzpatrick.

EDINBURGH. M. G. Williamson.
LINCOLN. E. Mansel Sympson.
SHREWSBURY. T. Auden.
WELLS and GLASTONBURY. T. S. Holmes.

The Antiquary's Books.

General Editor, J. CHARLES COX

Demy 8vo. 7s. 6d. net each volume.

With Numerous Illustrations.

ARCHÆOLOGY AND FALSE ANTIQUITIES. R. Munro.
BELLS OF ENGLAND, THE. Canon J. J. Raven. *Second Edition.*
BRASSES OF ENGLAND, THE. Herbert W. Macklin. *Second Edition.*
CELTIC ART IN PAGAN AND CHRISTIAN TIMES. J. Romilly Allen. *Second Edition.*
CASTLES AND WALLED TOWNS OF ENGLAND, THE. A. Harvey.
DOMESDAY INQUEST, THE. Adolphus Ballard.
ENGLISH CHURCH FURNITURE. J. C. Cox and A. Harvey. *Second Edition.*
ENGLISH COSTUME. From Prehistoric Times to the End of the Eighteenth Century. George Clinch.
ENGLISH MONASTIC LIFE. Abbot Gasquet. *Fourth Edition.*
ENGLISH SEALS. J. Harvey Bloom.
FOLK-LORE AS AN HISTORICAL SCIENCE. Sir G. L. Gomme.
GILDS AND COMPANIES OF LONDON, THE. George Unwin.

MANOR AND MANORIAL RECORDS, THE Nathaniel J. Hone. *Second Edition.*
MEDIÆVAL HOSPITALS OF ENGLAND, THE. Rotha Mary Clay.
OLD ENGLISH INSTRUMENTS OF MUSIC. F. W. Galpin. *Second Edition.*
OLD ENGLISH LIBRARIES. James Hutt.
OLD SERVICE BOOKS OF THE ENGLISH CHURCH. Christopher Wordsworth, and Henry Littlehales. *Second Edition.*
PARISH LIFE IN MEDIÆVAL ENGLAND. Abbot Gasquet. *Third Edition.*
PARISH REGISTERS OF ENGLAND, THE. J. C. Cox.
REMAINS OF THE PREHISTORIC AGE IN ENGLAND. B. C. A. Windle. *Second Edition.*
ROMAN ERA IN BRITAIN, THE. J. Ward.
ROMANO-BRITISH BUILDINGS AND EARTHWORKS. J. Ward.
ROYAL FORESTS OF ENGLAND, THE. J. C. Cox.
SHRINES OF BRITISH SAINTS. J. C. Wall.

GENERAL LITERATURE

The Arden Shakespeare.

Demy 8vo. 2s. 6d. net each volume.

An edition of Shakespeare in single Plays; each edited with a full Introduction, Textual Notes, and a Commentary at the foot of the page.

ALL'S WELL THAT ENDS WELL.
ANTONY AND CLEOPATRA.
CYMBELINE.
COMEDY OF ERRORS, THE.
HAMLET. *Third Edition.*
JULIUS CAESAR.
*KING HENRY IV. PT. I.
KING HENRY V.
KING HENRY VI. PT. I.
KING HENRY VI. PT. II.
KING HENRY VI. PT. III.
KING LEAR.
*KING RICHARD II.
KING RICHARD III.
LIFE AND DEATH OF KING JOHN, THE.
LOVE'S LABOUR'S LOST.
MACBETH.
MEASURE FOR MEASURE.
MERCHANT OF VENICE, THE.
MERRY WIVES OF WINDSOR, THE.
MIDSUMMER NIGHT'S DREAM, A.
OTHELLO.
PERICLES.
ROMEO AND JULIET.
TAMING OF THE SHREW, THE.
TEMPEST, THE.
TIMON OF ATHENS.
TITUS ANDRONICUS.
TROILUS AND CRESSIDA.
TWO GENTLEMEN OF VERONA, THE.
TWELFTH NIGHT.
VENUS AND ADONIS.
*WINTER'S TALE, THE.

Classics of Art.

Edited by DR. J. H. W. LAING.

With numerous Illustrations. Wide Royal 8vo.

THE ART OF THE GREEKS. H. B. Walters. 12s. 6d. net.
THE ART OF THE ROMANS. H. B. Walters. 15s. net.
CHARDIN. H. E. A. Furst. 12s. 6d. net.
DONATELLO. Maud Cruttwell. 15s. net.
FLORENTINE SCULPTORS OF THE RENAISSANCE. Wilhelm Bode. Translated by Jessie Haynes. 12s. 6d. net.
GEORGE ROMNEY. Arthur B. Chamberlain. 12s. 6d. net.
GHIRLANDAIO. Gerald S. Davies. *Second Edition.* 10s. 6d.
MICHELANGELO. Gerald S. Davies. 12s. 6d. net.
RUBENS. Edward Dillon. 25s. net.
RAPHAEL. A. P. Oppé. 12s. 6d. net.
REMBRANDT'S ETCHINGS. A. M. Hind.
*SIR THOMAS LAWRENCE. Sir Walter Armstrong. 21s. net.
TITIAN. Charles Ricketts. 15s. net.
TINTORETTO. Evelyn March Phillipps. 15s. net.
TURNER'S SKETCHES AND DRAWINGS. A. J. Finberg. 12s. 6d. net. *Second Edition.*
VELAZQUEZ. A. de Beruete. 10s. 6d. net.

The "Complete" Series.

Fully Illustrated. Demy 8vo.

THE COMPLETE BILLIARD PLAYER. Charles Roberts. 10s. 6d. net.
THE COMPLETE COOK. Lilian Whitling. 7s. 6d. net.
THE COMPLETE CRICKETER. Albert E. Knight. 7s. 6d. net. *Second Edition.*
THE COMPLETE FOXHUNTER. Charles Richardson. 12s. 6d. net. *Second Edition.*
THE COMPLETE GOLFER. Harry Vardon. 10s. 6d. net. *Twelfth Edition.*
THE COMPLETE HOCKEY-PLAYER. Eustace E. White. 5s. net. *Second Edition.*
THE COMPLETE LAWN TENNIS PLAYER. A. Wallis Myers. 10s. 6d. net. *Third Edition, Revised.*
THE COMPLETE MOTORIST. Filson Young. 12s. 6d. net. *New Edition (Seventh).*
THE COMPLETE MOUNTAINEER. G. D. Abraham. 15s. net. *Second Edition.*
THE COMPLETE OARSMAN. R. C. Lehmann. 10s. 6d. net.
THE COMPLETE PHOTOGRAPHER. R. Child Bayley. 10s. 6d. net. *Fourth Edition.*
THE COMPLETE RUGBY FOOTBALLER, ON THE NEW ZEALAND SYSTEM. D. Gallaher and W. J. Stead. 10s. 6d. net. *Second Edition.*
THE COMPLETE SHOT. G. T. Teasdale-Buckell. 12s. 6d. net. *Third Edition.*
THE COMPLETE SWIMMER. F. Sachs. 7s. 6d. net.
*THE COMPLETE YACHTSMAN. B. Heckstall-Smith and E. du Boulay. 15s. net.

METHUEN AND COMPANY LIMITED

The Connoisseur's Library.

With numerous Illustrations. Wide Royal 8vo. 25s. net each volume.

ENGLISH FURNITURE. F. S. Robinson.
ENGLISH COLOURED BOOKS. Martin Hardie.
ETCHINGS. Sir F. Wedmore. *Second Edition.*
EUROPEAN ENAMELS. Henry H. Cunynghame.
GLASS. Edward Dillon.
GOLDSMITHS' AND SILVERSMITHS' WORK. Nelson Dawson. *Second Edition.*
ILLUMINATED MANUSCRIPTS. J. A. Herbert. *Second Edition.*

IVORIES. Alfred Maskell.
JEWELLERY. H. Clifford Smith. *Second Edition.*
MEZZOTINTS. Cyril Davenport.
MINIATURES. Dudley Heath.
PORCELAIN. Edward Dillon.
*FINE BOOKS. A. W. Pollard.
SEALS. Walter de Gray Birch.
WOOD SCULPTURE. Alfred Maskell. *Second Edition.*

Handbooks of English Church History.

Edited by J. H. BURN. *Crown 8vo. 2s. 6d. net each volume.*

THE FOUNDATIONS OF THE ENGLISH CHURCH. J. H. Maude.
THE SAXON CHURCH AND THE NORMAN CONQUEST. C. T. Cruttwell.
THE MEDIÆVAL CHURCH AND THE PAPACY. A. C. Jennings.

THE REFORMATION PERIOD. Henry Gee.
THE STRUGGLE WITH PURITANISM. Bruce Blaxland.
THE CHURCH OF ENGLAND IN THE EIGHTEENTH CENTURY. Alfred Plummer.

Handbooks of Theology.

THE DOCTRINE OF THE INCARNATION. R. L. Ottley. *Fifth Edition, Revised.* Demy 8vo. 12s. 6d.
A HISTORY OF EARLY CHRISTIAN DOCTRINE. J. F. Bethune-Baker. *Demy 8vo.* 10s. 6d.
AN INTRODUCTION TO THE HISTORY OF RELIGION. F. B. Jevons. *Fifth Edition.* Demy 8vo. 10s. 6d.

AN INTRODUCTION TO THE HISTORY OF THE CREEDS. A. E. Burn. *Demy 8vo.* 10s. 6d.
THE PHILOSOPHY OF RELIGION IN ENGLAND AND AMERICA. Alfred Caldecott. *Demy 8vo.* 10s. 6d.
THE XXXIX ARTICLES OF THE CHURCH OF ENGLAND. Edited by E. C. S. Gibson, *Seventh Edition. Demy 8vo.* 12s. 6d.

The "Home Life" Series.

Illustrated. Demy 8vo. 6s. to 10s. 6d. net.

HOME LIFE IN AMERICA. Katherine G. Busbey. *Second Edition.*
HOME LIFE IN FRANCE. Miss Betham-Edwards. *Fifth Edition.*
HOME LIFE IN GERMANY. Mrs. A. Sidgwick. *Second Edition.*
HOME LIFE IN HOLLAND. D. S. Meldrum. *Second Edition.*

HOME LIFE IN ITALY. Lina Duff Gordon. *Second Edition.*
HOME LIFE IN NORWAY. H. K. Daniels.
HOME LIFE IN RUSSIA. Dr. A. S. Rappoport.
HOME LIFE IN SPAIN. S. L. Bensusan. *Second Edition.*

General Literature

The Illustrated Pocket Library of Plain and Coloured Books.
Fcap. 8vo. 3s. 6d. net each volume.

WITH COLOURED ILLUSTRATIONS.

OLD COLOURED BOOKS. George Paston. 2s. net.

THE LIFE AND DEATH OF JOHN MYTTON, ESQ. Nimrod. *Fifth Edition.*

THE LIFE OF A SPORTSMAN. Nimrod.

HANDLEY CROSS. R. S. Surtees. *Fourth Edition.*

MR. SPONGE'S SPORTING TOUR. R. S. Surtees. *Second Edition.*

JORROCKS'S JAUNTS AND JOLLITIES. R. S. Surtees. *Third Edition.*

ASK MAMMA. R. S. Surtees.

THE ANALYSIS OF THE HUNTING FIELD. R. S. Surtees.

THE TOUR OF DR. SYNTAX IN SEARCH OF THE PICTURESQUE. William Combe.

THE TOUR OF DR. SYNTAX IN SEARCH OF CONSOLATION. William Combe.

THE THIRD TOUR OF DR. SYNTAX IN SEARCH OF A WIFE. William Combe.

THE HISTORY OF JOHNNY QUAE GENUS. The Author of 'The Three Tours.'

THE ENGLISH DANCE OF DEATH, from the Designs of T. Rowlandson, with Metrical Illustrations by the Author of 'Doctor Syntax.' *Two Volumes.*

THE DANCE OF LIFE: A Poem. The Author of 'Dr. Syntax.'

LIFE IN LONDON. Pierce Egan.

REAL LIFE IN LONDON. An Amateur (Pierce Egan). *Two Volumes.*

THE LIFE OF AN ACTOR. Pierce Egan.

THE VICAR OF WAKEFIELD. Oliver Goldsmith.

THE MILITARY ADVENTURES OF JOHNNY NEWCOME. An Officer.

THE NATIONAL SPORTS OF GREAT BRITAIN. With Descriptions and 50 Coloured Plates by Henry Alken.

THE ADVENTURES OF A POST CAPTAIN. A Naval Officer.

GAMONIA. Lawrence Rawstorne.

AN ACADEMY FOR GROWN HORSEMEN. Geoffrey Gambado.

REAL LIFE IN IRELAND. A Real Paddy.

THE ADVENTURES OF JOHNNY NEWCOME IN THE NAVY. Alfred Burton.

THE OLD ENGLISH SQUIRE. John Careless.

THE ENGLISH SPY. Bernard Blackmantle. *Two Volumes. 7s. net.*

WITH PLAIN ILLUSTRATIONS.

THE GRAVE: A Poem. Robert Blair.

ILLUSTRATIONS OF THE BOOK OF JOB. Invented and engraved by William Blake.

WINDSOR CASTLE. W. Harrison Ainsworth.

THE TOWER OF LONDON. W. Harrison Ainsworth.

FRANK FAIRLEGH. F. E. Smedley.

THE COMPLEAT ANGLER. Izaak Walton and Charles Cotton.

THE PICKWICK PAPERS. Charles Dickens.

Leaders of Religion.
Edited by H. C. BEECHING. *With Portraits.*
Crown 8vo. 2s. net each volume.

CARDINAL NEWMAN. R. H. Hutton.

JOHN WESLEY. J. H. Overton.

BISHOP WILBERFORCE. G. W. Daniell.

CARDINAL MANNING. A. W. Hutton.

CHARLES SIMEON. H. C. G. Moule.

JOHN KNOX. F. MacCunn. *Second Edition.*

JOHN HOWE. R. F. Horton.

THOMAS KEN. F. A. Clarke.

GEORGE FOX, THE QUAKER. T. Hodgkin. *Third Edition.*

JOHN KEBLE. Walter Lock.

THOMAS CHALMERS. Mrs. Oliphant. *Second Edition.*

LANCELOT ANDREWES. R. L. Ottley. *Second Edition.*

AUGUSTINE OF CANTERBURY. E. L. Cutts.

WILLIAM LAUD. W. H. Hutton. *Third Ed.*

JOHN DONNE. Augustus Jessop.

THOMAS CRANMER. A. J. Mason.

LATIMER. R. M. Carlyle and A. J. Carlyle.

BISHOP BUTLER. W. A. Spooner.

METHUEN AND COMPANY LIMITED

The Library of Devotion.
With Introductions and (where necessary) Notes.
Small Pott 8vo, cloth, 2s. ; leather, 2s. 6d. net each volume.

The Confessions of St. Augustine. *Seventh Edition.*
The Imitation of Christ. *Sixth Edition.*
The Christian Year. *Fifth Edition.*
Lyra Innocentium. *Third Edition.*
The Temple. *Second Edition.*
A Book of Devotions. *Second Edition.*
A Serious Call to a Devout and Holy Life. *Fourth Edition.*
A Guide to Eternity.
The Inner Way. *Second Edition.*
On the Love of God
The Psalms of David.
Lyra Apostolica.
The Song of Songs.
The Thoughts of Pascal. *Second Edition.*
A Manual of Consolation from the Saints and Fathers.
Devotions from the Apocrypha.
The Spiritual Combat.
The Devotions of St. Anselm.
Bishop Wilson's Sacra Privata.
Grace Abounding to the Chief of Sinners.
Lyra Sacra: A Book of Sacred Verse. *Second Edition.*
A Day Book from the Saints and Fathers.
A Little Book of Heavenly Wisdom. A Selection from the English Mystics.
Light, Life, and Love. A Selection from the German Mystics.
An Introduction to the Devout Life.
The Little Flowers of the Glorious Messer St. Francis and of his Friars.
Death and Immortality.
The Spiritual Guide. *Second Edition.*
Devotions for Every Day in the Week and the Great Festivals.
Preces Privatae.
Horae Mysticae: A Day Book from the Writings of Mystics of Many Nations.

Little Books on Art.
With many Illustrations. Demy 16mo. 2s. 6d. net each volume.
Each volume consists of about 200 pages, and contains from 30 to 40 Illustrations including a Frontispiece in Photogravure.

Albrecht Dürer. L. J. Allen.
Arts of Japan, The. E. Dillon. *Third Edition.*
Bookplates. E. Almack.
Botticelli. Mary L. Bonnor.
Burne-Jones. F. de Lisle.
Cellini. R. H. H. Cust.
Christian Symbolism. Mrs. H. Jenner.
Christ in Art. Mrs. H. Jenner.
Claude. E. Dillon.
Constable. H. W. Tompkins. *Second Edition.*
Corot. A. Pollard and E. Birnstingl.
Enamels. Mrs. N. Dawson. *Second Edition.*
Frederic Leighton. A. Corkran.
George Romney. G. Paston.
Greek Art. H. B. Walters. *Fourth Edition.*
Greuze and Boucher. E. F. Pollard.
Holbein. Mrs. G. Fortescue.
Illuminated Manuscripts. J. W. Bradley.
Jewellery. C. Davenport.
John Hoppner. H. P. K. Skipton.
Sir Joshua Reynolds. J. Sime. *Second Edition.*
Millet. N. Peacock.
Miniatures. C. Davenport.
Our Lady in Art. Mrs. H. Jenner.
Raphael. A. R. Dryhurst.
Rembrandt. Mrs. E. A. Sharp.
*Rodin. Muriel Ciolkowska.
Turner. F. Tyrrell-Gill.
Vandyck. M. G. Smallwood.
Velazquez. W. Wilberforce and A. R. Gilbert.
Watts. R. E. D. Sketchley. *Second Edition.*

General Literature

The Little Galleries.

Demy 16mo. 2s. 6d. net each volume.

Each volume contains 20 plates in Photogravure, together with a short outline of the life and work of the master to whom the book is devoted.

A LITTLE GALLERY OF REYNOLDS.
A LITTLE GALLERY OF ROMNEY.
A LITTLE GALLERY OF HOPPNER.

A LITTLE GALLERY OF MILLAIS.
A LITTLE GALLERY OF ENGLISH POETS.

The Little Guides.

With many Illustrations by E. H. NEW and other artists and from photographs.

Small Pott 8vo, cloth, 2s. 6d. net; leather, 3s. 6d. net, each volume.

The main features of these Guides are (1) a handy and charming form; (2) illustrations from photographs and by well-known artists; (3) good plans and maps; (4) an adequate but compact presentation of everything that is interesting in the natural features, history, archæology, and architecture of the town or district treated.

CAMBRIDGE AND ITS COLLEGES. A. H. Thompson. *Third Edition, Revised.*
CHANNEL ISLANDS, THE. E. E. Bicknell.
ENGLISH LAKES, THE. F. G. Brabant.
ISLE OF WIGHT, THE. G. Clinch.
LONDON. G. Clinch.
MALVERN COUNTRY, THE. B. C. A. Windle.
NORTH WALES. A. T. Story.
OXFORD AND ITS COLLEGES. J. Wells. *Ninth Edition.*
SHAKESPEARE'S COUNTRY. B. C. A. Windle. *Fourth Edition.*
ST. PAUL'S CATHEDRAL. G. Clinch.
WESTMINSTER ABBEY. G. E. Troutbeck. *Second Edition.*

BERKSHIRE. F. G. Brabant.
BUCKINGHAMSHIRE. E. S. Roscoe.
CHESHIRE. W. M. Gallichan.
CORNWALL. A. L. Salmon.
DERBYSHIRE. J. C. Cox.
DEVON. S. Baring-Gould. *Second Edition.*
DORSET. F. R. Heath. *Second Edition.*
ESSEX. J. C. Cox.
HAMPSHIRE. J. C. Cox.
HERTFORDSHIRE. H. W. Tompkins.
KENT. G. Clinch.
KERRY. C. P. Crane.

LEICESTERSHIRE AND RUTLAND. A. Harvey and V. B. Crowther-Beynon.
MIDDLESEX. J. B. Firth.
MONMOUTHSHIRE. G. W. Wade and J. H. Wade.
NORFOLK. W. A. Dutt. *Second Edition, Revised.*
NORTHAMPTONSHIRE. W. Dry. *Second Ed.*
NORTHUMBERLAND. J. E. Morris.
NOTTINGHAMSHIRE. L. Guilford.
OXFORDSHIRE. F. G. Brabant.
SHROPSHIRE. J. E. Auden.
SOMERSET. G. W. and J. H. Wade. *Second Edition.*
STAFFORDSHIRE. C. Masefield.
SUFFOLK. W. A. Dutt.
SURREY. J. C. Cox.
SUSSEX. F. G. Brabant. *Third Edition.*
WILTSHIRE. F. R. Heath.
YORKSHIRE, THE EAST RIDING. J. E. Morris.
YORKSHIRE, THE NORTH RIDING. J. E. Morris.
YORKSHIRE, THE WEST RIDING. J. E. Morris. *Cloth, 3s. 6d. net; leather 4s. 6d. net.*

BRITTANY. S. Baring-Gould.
NORMANDY. C. Scudamore.
ROME. C. G. Ellaby.
SICILY. F. H. Jackson.

The Little Library.

With Introductions, Notes, and Photogravure Frontispieces.

Small Pott 8vo. Each Volume, cloth, 1s. 6d. net.

Anon. A LITTLE BOOK OF ENGLISH LYRICS. *Second Edition.*

Austen (Jane). PRIDE AND PREJUDICE. *Two Volumes.*
NORTHANGER ABBEY.

Bacon (Francis). THE ESSAYS OF LORD BACON.

Barham (R. H.). THE INGOLDSBY LEGENDS. *Two Volumes.*

Barnett (Annie). A LITTLE BOOK OF ENGLISH PROSE.

Beckford (William). THE HISTORY OF THE CALIPH VATHEK.

Blake (William). SELECTIONS FROM THE WORKS OF WILLIAM BLAKE.

Borrow (George). LAVENGRO. *Two Volumes.*
THE ROMANY RYE.

Browning (Robert). SELECTIONS FROM THE EARLY POEMS OF ROBERT BROWNING.

Canning (George). SELECTIONS FROM THE ANTI-JACOBIN : with some later Poems by GEORGE CANNING.

Cowley (Abraham). THE ESSAYS OF ABRAHAM COWLEY.

Crabbe (George). SELECTIONS FROM THE POEMS OF GEORGE CRABBE.

Craik (Mrs.). JOHN HALIFAX, GENTLEMAN. *Two Volumes.*

Crashaw (Richard). THE ENGLISH POEMS OF RICHARD CRASHAW.

Dante Alighieri. THE INFERNO OF DANTE. Translated by H. F. CARY.
THE PURGATORIO OF DANTE. Translated by H. F. CARY.
THE PARADISO OF DANTE. Translated by H. F. CARY

Darley (George). SELECTIONS FROM THE POEMS OF GEORGE DARLEY.

Deane (A. C.). A LITTLE BOOK OF LIGHT VERSE.

Dickens (Charles). CHRISTMAS BOOKS. *Two Volumes.*

Ferrier (Susan). MARRIAGE. *Two Volumes.*
THE INHERITANCE. *Two Volumes.*

Gaskell (Mrs.). CRANFORD. *Second Ed.*

Hawthorne (Nathaniel). THE SCARLET LETTER.

Henderson (T. F.). A LITTLE BOOK OF SCOTTISH VERSE.

Kinglake (A. W.). EOTHEN. *Second Edition.*

Lamb (Charles). ELIA, AND THE LAST ESSAYS OF ELIA.

Locker (F.). LONDON LYRICS.

Marvell (Andrew). THE POEMS OF ANDREW MARVELL.

Milton (John). THE MINOR POEMS OF JOHN MILTON.

Moir (D. M.). MANSIE WAUCH.

Nichols (Bowyer). A LITTLE BOOK OF ENGLISH SONNETS.

Smith (Horace and James). REJECTED ADDRESSES.

Sterne (Laurence). A SENTIMENTAL JOURNEY.

Tennyson (Alfred, Lord). THE EARLY POEMS OF ALFRED, LORD TENNYSON.
IN MEMORIAM.
THE PRINCESS.
MAUD.

Thackeray (W. M.). VANITY FAIR. *Three Volumes.*
PENDENNIS. *Three Volumes.*
HENRY ESMOND.
CHRISTMAS BOOKS.

Vaughan (Henry). THE POEMS OF HENRY VAUGHAN.

Waterhouse (Elizabeth). A LITTLE BOOK OF LIFE AND DEATH. *Thirteenth Edition.*

Wordsworth (W.). SELECTIONS FROM THE POEMS OF WILLIAM WORDSWORTH.

Wordsworth (W.) and Coleridge (S. T.). LYRICAL BALLADS. *Second Edition.*

The Little Quarto Shakespeare.
Edited by W. J. CRAIG. With Introductions and Notes.
Pott 16mo. In 40 Volumes. Leather, price 1s. net each volume.
Mahogany Revolving Book Case. 10s. net.

Miniature Library.
Demy 32mo. Leather, 1s. net each volume.

EUPHRANOR: A Dialogue on Youth. Edward FitzGerald.

THE LIFE OF EDWARD, LORD HERBERT OF CHERBURY. Written by himself.

POLONIUS: or Wise Saws and Modern Instances. Edward FitzGerald.

THE RUBÁIYÁT OF OMAR KHAYYÁM. Edward FitzGerald. *Fourth Edition.*

The New Library of Medicine.
Edited by C. W. SALEEBY. *Demy 8vo.*

CARE OF THE BODY, THE. F. Cavanagh. *Second Edition.* 7s. 6d. net.

CHILDREN OF THE NATION, THE. The Right Hon. Sir John Gorst. *Second Edition.* 7s. 6d. net.

CONTROL OF A SCOURGE; or, How Cancer is Curable, The. Chas. P. Childe. 7s. 6d. net.

DISEASES OF OCCUPATION. Sir Thomas Oliver. 10s. 6d. net. *Second Edition.*

DRINK PROBLEM, in its Medico-Sociological Aspects, The. Edited by T. N. Kelynack. 7s. 6d. net.

DRUGS AND THE DRUG HABIT. H. Sainsbury.

FUNCTIONAL NERVE DISEASES. A. T. Schofield. 7s. 6d. net.

HYGIENE OF MIND, THE. T. S. Clouston. *Fifth Edition.* 7s. 6d. net.

INFANT MORTALITY. Sir George Newman. 7s. 6d. net.

PREVENTION OF TUBERCULOSIS (CONSUMPTION), THE. Arthur Newsholme. 10s. 6d. net. *Second Edition.*

AIR AND HEALTH. Ronald C. Macfie. 7s. 6d net. *Second Edition.*

The New Library of Music.
Edited by ERNEST NEWMAN. *Illustrated. Demy 8vo.* 7s. 6d. net.

BRAHMS. J. A. Fuller-Maitland. *Second Edition.*

HANDEL. R. A. Streatfeild. *Second Edition.*

HUGO WOLF. Ernest Newman.

Oxford Biographies.
Illustrated. Fcap. 8vo. Each volume, cloth, 2s. 6d. net; leather, 3s. 6d. net.

DANTE ALIGHIERI. Paget Toynbee. *Third Edition.*

GIROLAMO SAVONAROLA. E. L. S. Horsburgh. *Fourth Edition.*

JOHN HOWARD. E. C. S. Gibson.

ALFRED TENNYSON. A. C. Benson. *Second Edition.*

SIR WALTER RALEIGH. I. A. Taylor.

ERASMUS. E. F. H. Capey.

THE YOUNG PRETENDER. C. S. Terry.

ROBERT BURNS. T. F. Henderson.

CHATHAM. A. S. McDowall.

FRANCIS OF ASSISI. Anna M. Stoddart.

CANNING. W. Alison Phillips.

BEACONSFIELD. Walter Sichel.

JOHANN WOLFGANG GOETHE. H. G. Atkins.

FRANÇOIS DE FÉNELON. Viscount St. Cyres.

Three Plays.

Fcap. 8vo. 2s. net.

THE HONEYMOON. A Comedy in Three Acts. Arnold Bennett. *Second Edition.*

KISMET. Edward Knoblauch.

MILESTONES. Arnold Bennett and Edward Knoblauch. *Second Edition.*

The States of Italy.

Edited by E ARMSTRONG and R. LANGTON DOUGLAS.

Illustrated. Demy 8vo.

A HISTORY OF MILAN UNDER THE SFORZA. Cecilia M. Ady. 10s. 6d. net.

A HISTORY OF PERUGIA. W. Heywood. 12s. 6d. net.

A HISTORY OF VERONA. A. M. Allen. 12s. 6d. net.

The Westminster Commentaries.

General Editor, WALTER LOCK.

Demy 8vo.

THE ACTS OF THE APOSTLES. Edited by R. B. Rackham. *Sixth Edition.* 10s. 6d.

THE FIRST EPISTLE OF PAUL THE APOSTLE TO THE CORINTHIANS. Edited by H. L. Goudge. *Third Edition.* 6s.

THE BOOK OF EXODUS Edited by A. H. M'Neile. With a Map and 3 Plans. 10s. 6d.

THE BOOK OF EZEKIEL. Edited by H. A. Redpath. 10s. 6d.

THE BOOK OF GENESIS. Edited with Introduction and Notes by S. R. Driver. *Eighth Edition.* 10s. 6d.

THE BOOK OF THE PROPHET ISAIAH. Edited by G. W. Wade. 10s. 6d.

ADDITIONS AND CORRECTIONS IN THE SEVENTH AND EIGHTH EDITIONS OF THE BOOK OF GENESIS. S. R. Driver. 1s.

THE BOOK OF JOB. Edited by E. C. S. Gibson. *Second Edition.* 6s.

THE EPISTLE OF ST. JAMES. Edited with Introduction and Notes by R. J. Knowling. *Second Edition.* 6s.

The "Young" Series.

Illustrated. Crown 8vo.

THE YOUNG BOTANIST. W. P. Westell and C. S. Cooper. 3s. 6d. net.

THE YOUNG CARPENTER. Cyril Hall. 5s.

THE YOUNG ELECTRICIAN. Hammond Hall. 5s.

THE YOUNG ENGINEER. Hammond Hall. *Third Edition.* 5s.

THE YOUNG NATURALIST. W. P. Westell. *Second Edition.* 6s.

THE YOUNG ORNITHOLOGIST. W. P. Westell. 5s.

General Literature

Methuen's Shilling Library

Fcap. 8vo. 1s. net.

CONDITION OF ENGLAND, THE. G. F. G. Masterman.
DE PROFUNDIS. Oscar Wilde.
FROM MIDSHIPMAN TO FIELD-MARSHAL. Sir Evelyn Wood, F.M., V.C.
*IDEAL HUSBAND, AN. Oscar Wilde.
*JIMMY GLOVER, HIS BOOK. James M. Glover.
*JOHN BOYES, KING OF THE WA-KIKUYU. John Boyes.
LADY WINDERMERE'S FAN. Oscar Wilde.
LETTERS FROM A SELF-MADE MERCHANT TO HIS SON. George Horace Lorimer.
LIFE OF JOHN RUSKIN, THE. W. G. Collingwood.
LIFE OF ROBERT LOUIS STEVENSON, THE. Graham Balfour.
*LIFE OF TENNYSON, THE. A. C. Benson.
*LITTLE OF EVERYTHING, A. E. V. Lucas.
LORD ARTHUR SAVILE'S CRIME. Oscar Wilde.
LORE OF THE HONEY-BEE, THE. Tickner Edwardes.
MAN AND THE UNIVERSE. Sir Oliver Lodge.
MARY MAGDALENE. Maurice Maeterlinck.
SELECTED POEMS. Oscar Wilde.
SEVASTOPOL, AND OTHER STORIES. Leo Tolstoy.
THE BLUE BIRD. Maurice Maeterlinck.
UNDER FIVE REIGNS. Lady Dorothy Nevill.
*VAILIMA LETTERS. Robert Louis Stevenson.
*VICAR OF MORWENSTOW, THE. S. Baring-Gould.

Books for Travellers.

Crown 8vo. 6s. each.

Each volume contains a number of Illustrations in Colour.

*A WANDERER IN FLORENCE. E. V. Lucas.
A WANDERER IN PARIS. E. V. Lucas.
A WANDERER IN HOLLAND. E. V. Lucas.
A WANDERER IN LONDON. E. V. Lucas.
THE NORFOLK BROADS. W. A. Dutt.
THE NEW FOREST. Horace G. Hutchinson.
NAPLES. Arthur H. Norway.
THE CITIES OF UMBRIA. Edward Hutton.
THE CITIES OF SPAIN. Edward Hutton.
*THE CITIES OF LOMBARDY. Edward Hutton.
FLORENCE AND NORTHERN TUSCANY, WITH GENOA. Edward Hutton.
SIENA AND SOUTHERN TUSCANY. Edward Hutton.
ROME. Edward Hutton.
VENICE AND VENETIA. Edward Hutton.
THE BRETONS AT HOME. F. M. Gostling.
THE LAND OF PARDONS (Brittany). Anatole Le Braz.
A BOOK OF THE RHINE. S. Baring-Gould.
THE NAPLES RIVIERA. H. M. Vaughan.
DAYS IN CORNWALL. C. Lewis Hind.
THROUGH EAST ANGLIA IN A MOTOR CAR. J. E. Vincent.
THE SKIRTS OF THE GREAT CITY. Mrs. A. G. Bell.
ROUND ABOUT WILTSHIRE. A. G. Bradley.
SCOTLAND OF TO-DAY. T. F. Henderson and Francis Watt.
NORWAY AND ITS FJORDS. M. A. Wyllie.

Some Books on Art.

ART AND LIFE. T. Sturge Moore. Illustrated. *Cr. 8vo. 5s. net.*

AIMS AND IDEALS IN ART. George Clausen. Illustrated. *Second Edition. Large Post 8vo. 5s. net.*

SIX LECTURES ON PAINTING. George Clausen. Illustrated. *Third Edition. Large Post 8vo. 3s. 6d. net.*

FRANCESCO GUARDI, 1712-1793. G. A. Simonson. Illustrated. *Imperial 4to. £2 2s. net.*

ILLUSTRATIONS OF THE BOOK OF JOB. William Blake. *Quarto. £1 1s. net.*

JOHN LUCAS, PORTRAIT PAINTER, 1828-1874. Arthur Lucas. Illustrated. *Imperial 4to. £3 3s. net.*

ONE HUNDRED MASTERPIECES OF PAINTING. With an Introduction by R. C. Witt. Illustrated. *Second Edition. Demy 8vo. 10s. 6d. net.*

A GUIDE TO THE BRITISH PICTURES IN THE NATIONAL GALLERY. Edward Kingston. Illustrated. *Fcap. 8vo. 3s. 6d. net.*

METHUEN AND COMPANY LIMITED

SOME BOOKS ON ART—*continued*.

ONE HUNDRED MASTERPIECES OF SCULPTURE. With an Introduction by G. F. Hill. Illustrated. *Demy 8vo.* 10s. 6d. *net*.
ROMNEY FOLIO. With an Essay by A. B. Chamberlain. *Imperial Folio.* £15 15s. *net*.
THE SAINTS IN ART. Margaret E. Tabor. Illustrated. *Fcap. 8vo.* 3s. 6d. *net*.
SCHOOLS OF PAINTING. Mary Innes. Illustrated. *Cr. 8vo.* 5s. *net*.

THE POST IMPRESSIONISTS. C. Lewis Hind. Illustrated. *Royal 8vo.* 7s. 6d. *net*.
CELTIC ART IN PAGAN AND CHRISTIAN TIMES. J. R. Allen. Illustrated. *Second Edition*. *Demy 8vo.* 7s. 6d. *net*.
"CLASSICS OF ART." See page 13.
"THE CONNOISSEUR'S LIBRARY." See page 14
"LITTLE BOOKS ON ART." See page 16.
"THE LITTLE GALLERIES." See page 17.

Some Books on Italy.

A HISTORY OF MILAN UNDER THE SFORZA. Cecilia M. Ady. Illustrated. *Demy 8vo.* 10s. 6d. *net*.
A HISTORY OF VERONA. A. M. Allen. Illustrated. *Demy 8vo.* 12s. 6d. *net*.
A HISTORY OF PERUGIA. William Heywood. Illustrated. *Demy 8vo.* 12s. 6d. *net*.
THE LAKES OF NORTHERN ITALY. Richard Bagot. Illustrated. *Fcap 8vo.* 5s. *net*.
WOMAN IN ITALY. W. Boulting. Illustrated. *Demy 8vo.* 10s. 6d. *net*.
OLD ETRURIA AND MODERN TUSCANY. Mary L. Cameron. Illustrated. *Second Edition*. *Cr. 8vo.* 6s. *net*.
FLORENCE AND THE CITIES OF NORTHERN TUSCANY, WITH GENOA. Edward Hutton. Illustrated. *Second Edition*. *Cr. 8vo.* 6s.
SIENA AND SOUTHERN TUSCANY. Edward Hutton. Illustrated. *Second Edition*. *Cr. 8vo.* 6s.
IN UNKNOWN TUSCANY. Edward Hutton. Illustrated. *Second Edition*. *Demy 8vo.* 7s. 6d. *net*.
VENICE AND VENETIA. Edward Hutton. Illustrated. *Cr. 8vo.* 6s.
VENICE ON FOOT. H. A Douglas. Illustrated. *Fcap. 8vo.* 5s. *net*.
VENICE AND HER TREASURES. H. A. Douglas. Illustrated. *Fcap. 8vo.* 5s. *net*.
*THE DOGES OF VENICE. Mrs. Aubrey Richardson. Illustrated. *Demy 8vo.* 10s. 6d. *net*.
FLORENCE: Her History and Art to the Fall of the Republic. F. A. Hyett. *Demy 8vo.* 7s. 6d. *net*.
FLORENCE AND HER TREASURES. H. M. Vaughan. Illustrated. *Fcap. 8vo.* 5s. *net*.
COUNTRY WALKS ABOUT FLORENCE. Edward Hutton. Illustrated. *Fcap. 8vo.* 5s. *net*.
NAPLES: Past and Present. A. H. Norway. Illustrated. *Third Edition*. *Cr. 8vo.* 6s.
THE NAPLES RIVIERA. H. M. Vaughan. Illustrated. *Second Edition*. *Cr. 8vo.* 6s.
SICILY: The New Winter Resort. Douglas Sladen. Illustrated. *Second Edition*. *Cr. 8vo.* 5s. *net*.

SICILY. F. H. Jackson. Illustrated. *Small Pott 8vo.* Cloth, 2s. 6d. *net*, leather, 3s. 6d. *net*.
ROME. Edward Hutton. Illustrated. *Second Edition*. *Cr. 8vo.* 6s.
A ROMAN PILGRIMAGE. R. E. Roberts Illustrated. *Demy 8vo.* 10s. 6d. *net*.
ROME. C. G. Ellaby. Illustrated. *Small Pott 8vo.* Cloth, 2s. 6d. *net*; leather, 3s. 6d. *net*.
THE CITIES OF UMBRIA. Edward Hutton. Illustrated. *Fourth Edition*. *Cr. 8vo.* 6s.
*THE CITIES OF LOMBARDY. Edward Hutton. Illustrated. *Cr. 8vo.* 6s.
THE LIVES OF S. FRANCIS OF ASSISI. Brother Thomas of Celano. *Cr. 8vo.* 5s. *net*.
LORENZO THE MAGNIFICENT. E. L. S. Horsburgh. Illustrated. *Second Edition*. *Demy 8vo.* 15s. *net*.
GIROLAMO SAVONAROLA. E. L. S. Horsburgh. Illustrated. *Cr. 8vo.* 5s. *net*.
ST. CATHERINE OF SIENA AND HER TIMES By the Author of "Mdlle Mori." Illustrated *Second Edition*. *Demy 8vo.* 7s. 6d. *net*.
DANTE AND HIS ITALY. Lonsdale Ragg. Illustrated. *Demy 8vo.* 12s. 6d. *net*.
DANTE ALIGHIERI: His Life and Works Paget Toynbee. Illustrated. *Cr. 8vo.* 5s. *net*.
THE MEDICI POPES. H. M. Vaughan. Illustrated. *Demy 8vo.* 15s. *net*.
SHELLEY AND HIS FRIENDS IN ITALY. Helen R. Angeli. Illustrated. *Demy 8vo.* 10s. 6d. *net*.
HOME LIFE IN ITALY. Lina Duff Gordon. Illustrated. *Second Edition*. *Demy 8vo.* 10s. 6d. *net*.
SKIES ITALIAN: A Little Breviary for Travellers in Italy. Ruth S. Phelps. *Fcap. 8vo.* 5s. *net*.
*A WANDERER IN FLORENCE. E. V. Lucas Illustrated. *Cr. 8vo.* 6s.
*UNITED ITALY. F. M. Underwood. *Demy 8vo.* 10s. 6d. *net*.

PART III.—A SELECTION OF WORKS OF FICTION

Albanesi (E. Maria). SUSANNAH AND ONE OTHER. *Fourth Edition. Cr. 8vo. 6s.*
LOVE AND LOUISA. *Second Edition. Cr. 8vo. 6s.*
THE BROWN EYES OF MARY. *Third Edition. Cr. 8vo. 6s.*
I KNOW A MAIDEN. *Third Edition. Cr. 8vo. 6s.*
THE INVINCIBLE AMELIA: OR, THE POLITE ADVENTURESS. *Third Edition. Cr. 8vo. 3s. 6d.*
THE GLAD HEART. *Fifth Edition. Cr. 8vo. 6s.*
*OLIVIA MARY. *Cr. 8vo. 6s.*

Bagot (Richard). A ROMAN MYSTERY. *Third Edition. Cr. 8vo. 6s.*
THE PASSPORT. *Fourth Edition. Cr. 8vo. 6s.*
ANTHONY CUTHBERT. *Fourth Edition. Cr. 8vo. 6s.*
LOVE'S PROXY. *Cr. 8vo. 6s.*
DONNA DIANA. *Second Edition. Cr. 8vo. 6s.*
CASTING OF NETS. *Twelfth Edition. Cr. 8vo. 6s.*
THE HOUSE OF SERRAVALLE. *Third Edition Cr. 8vo. 6s.*

Bailey (H. C.). STORM AND TREASURE. *Third Edition. Cr. 8vo. 6s.*
THE LONELY QUEEN. *Third Edition. Cr. 8vo. 6s.*

Baring-Gould (S.). IN THE ROAR OF THE SEA. *Eighth Edition. Cr. 8vo. 6s.*
MARGERY OF QUETHER. *Second Edition. Cr. 8vo. 6s.*
THE QUEEN OF LOVE. *Fifth Edition. Cr. 8vo. 6s.*
JACQUETTA. *Third Edition. Cr. 8vo. 6s.*
KITTY ALONE. *Fifth Edition. Cr. 8vo. 6s.*
NOÉMI. Illustrated. *Fourth Edition. Cr. 8vo. 6s.*
THE BROOM-SQUIRE. Illustrated. *Fifth Edition. Cr. 8vo. 6s.*
DARTMOOR IDYLLS. *Cr. 8vo. 6s.*
GUAVAS THE TINNER. Illustrated. *Second Edition. Cr. 8vo. 6s.*
BLADYS OF THE STEWPONEY. Illustrated. *Second Edition. Cr. 8vo. 6s.*
PABO THE PRIEST. *Cr. 8vo. 6s.*
WINEFRED. Illustrated. *Second Edition. Cr. 8vo. 6s.*
ROYAL GEORGIE. Illustrated. *Cr. 8vo. 6s.*
CHRIS OF ALL SORTS. *Cr. 8vo. 6s.*
IN DEWISLAND. *Second Edition. Cr. 8vo. 6s.*
MRS. CURGENVEN OF CURGENVEN. *Fifth Edition. Cr. 8vo. 6s.*

Barr (Robert). IN THE MIDST OF ALARMS. *Third Edition. Cr. 8vo. 6s.*
THE COUNTESS TEKLA. *Fifth Edition. Cr. 8vo. 6s.*
THE MUTABLE MANY. *Third Edition. Cr. 8vo. 6s.*

Begbie (Harold). THE CURIOUS AND DIVERTING ADVENTURES OF SIR JOHN SPARROW, BART.; OR, THE PROGRESS OF AN OPEN MIND. *Second Edition. Cr. 8vo. 6s.*

Belloc (H.). EMMANUEL BURDEN, MERCHANT. Illustrated. *Second Edition. Cr. 8vo. 6s.*
A CHANGE IN THE CABINET. *Third Edition. Cr. 8vo. 6s.*

Belloc-Lowndes (Mrs.). THE CHINK IN THE ARMOUR. *Fourth Edition. Cr. 8vo. 6s.*
*MARY PECHELL. *Cr. 8vo. 6s.*

Bennett (Arnold). CLAYHANGER. *Tenth Edition. Cr. 8vo. 6s.*
THE CARD. *Sixth Edition. Cr. 8vo. 6s.*
HILDA LESSWAYS. *Seventh Edition. Cr. 8vo. 6s.*
*BURIED ALIVE. *A New Edition. Cr. 8vo. 6s.*
A MAN FROM THE NORTH. *A New Edition. Cr. 8vo. 6s.*
THE MATADOR OF THE FIVE TOWNS. *Second Edition. Cr. 8vo. 6s.*

Benson (E. F.). DODO: A DETAIL OF THE DAY. *Sixteenth Edition. Cr. 8vo. 6s.*

Birmingham (George A.). SPANISH GOLD. *Sixth Edition. Cr. 8vo. 6s.*
THE SEARCH PARTY. *Fifth Edition. Cr. 8vo. 6s.*
LALAGE'S LOVERS. *Third Edition. Cr. 8vo. 6s.*

Bowen (Marjorie). I WILL MAINTAIN. *Seventh Edition. Cr. 8vo. 6s.*
DEFENDER OF THE FAITH. *Fifth Edition. Cr. 8vo. 6s.*
*A KNIGHT OF SPAIN. *Cr. 8vo. 6s.*
THE QUEST OF GLORY. *Third Edition. Cr. 8vo. 6s.*
GOD AND THE KING. *Fourth Edition. Cr. 8vo. 6s.*

Clifford (Mrs. W. K.). THE GETTING WELL OF DOROTHY. Illustrated. *Second Edition. Cr. 8vo. 3s. 6d.*

Conrad (Joseph). THE SECRET AGENT: A Simple Tale. *Fourth Ed. Cr. 8vo. 6s.*
A SET OF SIX. *Fourth Edition. Cr. 8vo. 6s.*
UNDER WESTERN EYES. *Second Ed. Cr. 8vo. 6s.*

Conyers (Dorothea.). THE LONELY MAN. *Cr. 8vo.* 6s.

Corelli (Marie). A ROMANCE OF TWO WORLDS. *Thirty-first Ed. Cr. 8vo.* 6s.
VENDETTA; OR, THE STORY OF ONE FORGOTTEN. *Twenty-ninth Edition. Cr. 8vo.* 6s.
THELMA: A NORWEGIAN PRINCESS. *Forty-second Edition. Cr. 8vo.* 6s.
ARDATH: THE STORY OF A DEAD SELF. *Twentieth Edition. Cr. 8vo.* 6s.
THE SOUL OF LILITH. *Seventeenth Edition. Cr. 8vo.* 6s.
WORMWOOD: A DRAMA OF PARIS. *Eighteenth Edition. Cr. 8vo.* 6s.
BARABBAS: A DREAM OF THE WORLD'S TRAGEDY. *Forty-sixth Edition. Cr. 8vo.* 6s.
THE SORROWS OF SATAN. *Fifty-seventh Edition. Cr. 8vo.* 6s.
THE MASTER-CHRISTIAN. *Thirteenth Edition.* 179th Thousand. *Cr. 8vo.* 6s.
TEMPORAL POWER: A STUDY IN SUPREMACY. *Second Edition.* 150th Thousand. *Cr. 8vo.* 6s.
GOD'S GOOD MAN: A SIMPLE LOVE STORY. *Fifteenth Edition.* 154th Thousand. *Cr. 8vo.* 6s.
HOLY ORDERS: THE TRAGEDY OF A QUIET LIFE. *Second Edition.* 120th Thousand. *Crown 8vo.* 6s.
THE MIGHTY ATOM. *Twenty-ninth Edition. Cr. 8vo.* 6s.
BOY: a Sketch. *Twelfth Edition. Cr. 8vo.* 6s.
CAMEOS. *Fourteenth Edition. Cr. 8vo.* 6s.
THE LIFE EVERLASTING. *Fifth Ed. Cr. 8vo.* 6s.

Crockett (S. R.). LOCHINVAR. Illustrated. *Third Edition. Cr. 8vo.* 6s.
THE STANDARD BEARER. *Second Edition. Cr. 8vo.* 6s.

Croker (B. M.). THE OLD CANTONMENT. *Second Edition. Cr. 8vo.* 6s.
JOHANNA. *Second Edition. Cr. 8vo.* 6s.
THE HAPPY VALLEY. *Fourth Edition. Cr. 8vo.* 6s.
A NINE DAYS' WONDER. *Fourth Edition. Cr. 8vo.* 6s.
PEGGY OF THE BARTONS. *Seventh Edition. Cr. 8vo.* 6s.
ANGEL. *Fifth Edition. Cr. 8vo.* 6s.
KATHERINE THE ARROGANT. *Sixth Edition. Cr. 8vo.* 6s.
BABES IN THE WOOD. *Fourth Edition. Cr. 8vo.* 6s.

Danby (Frank.). JOSEPH IN JEOPARDY. *Third Edition. Cr. 8vo.* 6s.

Doyle (Sir A. Conan). ROUND THE RED LAMP. *Twelfth Edition. Cr. 8vo.* 6s.

Fenn (G. Manville). SYD BELTON: THE BOY WHO WOULD NOT GO TO SEA. Illustrated. *Second Ed. Cr. 8vo.* 3s. 6d.

Findlater (J. H.). THE GREEN GRAVES OF BALGOWRIE. *Fifth Edition. Cr. 8vo.* 6s.
THE LADDER TO THE STARS. *Second Edition. Cr. 8vo.* 6s.

Findlater (Mary). A NARROW WAY. *Third Edition. Cr. 8vo.* 6s.
OVER THE HILLS. *Second Edition. Cr. 8vo.* 6s.
THE ROSE OF JOY. *Third Edition. Cr. 8vo.* 6s.
A BLIND BIRD'S NEST. Illustrated. *Second Edition. Cr. 8vo.* 6s.

Fry (B. and C. B.). A MOTHER'S SON *Fifth Edition. Cr. 8vo.* 6s.

Harraden (Beatrice). IN VARYING MOODS. *Fourteenth Edition. Cr. 8vo.* 6s.
HILDA STRAFFORD and THE REMITTANCE MAN. *Twelfth Ed. Cr. 8vo.* 6s.
INTERPLAY. *Fifth Edition. Cr. 8vo.* 6s.

Hichens (Robert). THE PROPHET OF BERKELEY SQUARE. *Second Edition. Cr. 8vo.* 6s.
TONGUES OF CONSCIENCE. *Third Edition. Cr. 8vo.* 6s.
THE WOMAN WITH THE FAN. *Eighth Edition. Cr. 8vo.* 6s.
BYEWAYS. *Cr. 8vo.* 6s.
THE GARDEN OF ALLAH. *Twenty-first Edition. Cr. 8vo.* 6s.
THE BLACK SPANIEL. *Cr. 8vo.* 6s.
THE CALL OF THE BLOOD. *Seventh Edition. Cr. 8vo.* 6s.
BARBARY SHEEP. *Second Edition. Cr. 8vo.* 3s. 6d.
THE DWELLER ON THE THRESHOLD. *Cr. 8vo.* 6s.

Hope (Anthony). THE GOD IN THE CAR. *Eleventh Edition. Cr. 8vo.* 6s.
A CHANGE OF AIR. *Sixth Edition. Cr. 8vo.* 6s.
A MAN OF MARK. *Seventh Ed. Cr. 8vo.* 6s.
THE CHRONICLES OF COUNT ANTONIO. *Sixth Edition. Cr. 8vo.* 6s.
PHROSO. Illustrated. *Eighth Edition. Cr. 8vo.* 6s.
SIMON DALE. Illustrated. *Eighth Edition. Cr. 8vo.* 6s.
THE KING'S MIRROR. *Fifth Edition. Cr. 8vo.* 6s.
QUISANTÉ. *Fourth Edition. Cr. 8vo.* 6s.
THE DOLLY DIALOGUES. *Cr. 8vo.* 6s.
TALES OF TWO PEOPLE. *Third Edition. Cr. 8vo.* 6s.
THE GREAT MISS DRIVER. *Fourth Edition. Cr. 8vo.* 6s.
MRS. MAXON PROTESTS. *Third Edition. Cr. 8vo.* 6s.

Hutten (Baroness von). THE HALO. *Fifth Edition. Cr. 8vo.* 6s.

FICTION

'Inner Shrine' (Author of the). THE WILD OLIVE. *Third Edition. Cr. 8vo.* 6s.

Jacobs (W. W.). MANY CARGOES. *Thirty-second Edition. Cr. 8vo.* 3s. 6d. *Also Illustrated in colour. Demy 8vo.* 7s. 6d. net.
SEA URCHINS. *Sixteenth Edition. Cr. 8vo.* 3s. 6d.
A MASTER OF CRAFT. Illustrated. *Ninth Edition. Cr. 8vo.* 3s. 6d.
LIGHT FREIGHTS. Illustrated. *Eighth Edition. Cr. 8vo.* 3s. 6d.
THE SKIPPER'S WOOING. *Eleventh Edition. Cr. 8vo.* 3s. 6d.
AT SUNWICH PORT. Illustrated. *Tenth Edition. Cr. 8vo.* 3s. 6d.
DIALSTONE LANE. Illustrated. *Eighth Edition. Cr. 8vo.* 3s. 6d.
ODD CRAFT. Illustrated. *Fifth Edition. Cr. 8vo.* 3s. 6d.
THE LADY OF THE BARGE. Illustrated. *Ninth Edition. Cr. 8vo.* 3s. 6d.
SALTHAVEN. Illustrated. *Third Edition. Cr. 8vo.* 3s. 6d.
SAILORS' KNOTS. Illustrated. *Fifth Edition. Cr. 8vo.* 3s. 6d.
SHORT CRUISES. *Third Edition. Cr. 8vo.* 3s. 6d.

James (Henry). THE GOLDEN BOWL. *Third Edition. Cr. 8vo.* 6s

Le Queux (William). THE HUNCHBACK OF WESTMINSTER. *Third Edition. Cr. 8vo.* 6s.
THE CLOSED BOOK. *Third Edition. Cr. 8vo.* 6s.
THE VALLEY OF THE SHADOW. Illustrated. *Third Edition. Cr. 8vo.* 6s.
BEHIND THE THRONE. *Third Edition. Cr. 8vo.* 6s.

London (Jack). WHITE FANG. *Eighth Edition. Cr. 8vo.* 6s.

Lucas (E. V.). LISTENER'S LURE: AN OBLIQUE NARRATION. *Eighth Edition. Fcap. 8vo.* 5s.
OVER BEMERTON'S: AN EASY-GOING CHRONICLE. *Ninth Edition. Fcap 8vo.* 5s.
MR. INGLESIDE. *Eighth Edition. Fcap. 8vo.* 5s.
LONDON LAVENDER. *Cr. 8vo.* 6s.

Lyall (Edna). DERRICK VAUGHAN, NOVELIST. *44th Thousand. Cr. 8vo.* 3s. 6d.

Macnaughtan (S.). THE FORTUNE OF CHRISTINA M'NAB. *Fifth Edition. Cr. 8vo.* 6s.
PETER AND JANE. *Fourth Edition. Cr. 8vo.* 6s.

Malet (Lucas). A COUNSEL OF PERFECTION. *Second Edition. Cr. 8vo.* 6s.

THE WAGES OF SIN. *Sixteenth Edition. Cr. 8vo.* 6s.
THE CARISSIMA. *Fifth Ed. Cr. 8vo.* 6s.
THE GATELESS BARRIER. *Fifth Edition. Cr. 8vo.* 6s.

Maxwell (W. B.). THE RAGGED MESSENGER. *Third Edition. Cr. 8vo.* 6s.
THE GUARDED FLAME. *Seventh Edition. Cr. 8vo.* 6s.
ODD LENGTHS. *Second Ed. Cr. 8vo.* 6s.
HILL RISE. *Fourth Edition. Cr. 8vo.* 6s.
THE COUNTESS OF MAYBURY: BETWEEN YOU AND I. *Fourth Edition. Cr. 8vo.* 6s.
THE REST CURE. *Fourth Edition. Cr. 8vo.* 6s.

Milne (A. A.). THE DAY'S PLAY. *Third Edition. Cr. 8vo.* 6s.
*THE HOLIDAY ROUND. *Cr. 8vo.* 6s.

Montague (C. E.). A HIND LET LOOSE. *Third Edition. Cr. 8vo.* 6s.

Morrison (Arthur). TALES OF MEAN STREETS. *Seventh Edition. Cr. 8vo.* 6s.
A CHILD OF THE JAGO. *Sixth Edition. Cr. 8vo.* 6s.
THE HOLE IN THE WALL. *Fourth Edition. Cr. 8vo.* 6s.
DIVERS VANITIES. *Cr. 8vo.* 6s.

Ollivant (Alfred). OWD BOB, THE GREY DOG OF KENMUIR. With a Frontispiece. *Eleventh Ed. Cr. 8vo.* 6s.
THE TAMING OF JOHN BLUNT. *Second Edition. Cr. 8vo.* 6s.
*THE ROYAL ROAD. *Cr. 8vo.* 6s.

Onions (Oliver). GOOD BOY SELDOM: A ROMANCE OF ADVERTISEMENT. *Second Edition. Cr. 8vo.* 6s.

Oppenheim (E. Phillips). MASTER OF MEN. *Fifth Edition. Cr. 8vo.* 6s.
THE MISSING DELORA. Illustrated. *Fourth Edition. Cr. 8vo.* 6s.

Orczy (Baroness). FIRE IN STUBBLE. *Fifth Edition. Cr. 8vo.* 6s.

Oxenham (John). A WEAVER OF WEBS. Illustrated. *Fifth Ed. Cr. 8vo.* 6s.
PROFIT AND LOSS. *Fourth Edition. Cr. 8vo.* 6s.
THE LONG ROAD. *Fourth Edition. Cr. 8vo.* 6s.
THE SONG OF HYACINTH, AND OTHER STORIES. *Second Edition. Cr. 8vo.* 6s.
MY LADY OF SHADOWS. *Fourth Edition. Cr. 8vo.* 6s.
LAURISTONS. *Fourth Edition. Cr. 8vo.* 6s.
THE COIL OF CARNE. *Sixth Edition. Cr 8vo.* 6s.
*THE QUEST OF THE GOLDEN ROSE. *Cr. 8vo.* 6s.

Parker (Gilbert). PIERRE AND HIS PEOPLE. *Seventh Edition. Cr. 8vo. 6s.*
MRS. FALCHION. *Fifth Edition. Cr. 8vo. 6s.*
THE TRANSLATION OF A SAVAGE. *Fourth Edition. Cr. 8vo. 6s.*
THE TRAIL OF THE SWORD. Illustrated. *Tenth Edition. Cr. 8vo. 6s.*
WHEN VALMOND CAME TO PONTIAC: The Story of a Lost Napoleon. *Seventh Edition. Cr. 8vo. 6s.*
AN ADVENTURER OF THE NORTH. The Last Adventures of 'Pretty Pierre.' *Fifth Edition. Cr. 8vo. 6s.*
THE BATTLE OF THE STRONG: a Romance of Two Kingdoms. Illustrated. *Seventh Edition. Cr. 8vo. 6s.*
THE POMP OF THE LAVILETTES. *Third Edition. Cr. 8vo. 3s. 6d.*
NORTHERN LIGHTS. *Fourth Edition. Cr. 8vo. 6s.*

Pasture (Mrs. Henry de la). THE TYRANT. *Fourth Edition. Cr. 8vo. 6s.*

Pemberton (Max). THE FOOTSTEPS OF A THRONE. Illustrated. *Fourth Edition. Cr. 8vo. 6s.*
I CROWN THEE KING. Illustrated. *Cr. 8vo. 6s.*
LOVE THE HARVESTER: A Story of the Shires. Illustrated. *Third Edition. Cr. 8vo. 3s. 6d.*
THE MYSTERY OF THE GREEN HEART. *Third Edition. Cr. 8vo. 6s.*

Perrin (Alice). THE CHARM. *Fifth Edition. Cr. 8vo. 6s.*
*THE ANGLO-INDIANS. *Cr. 8vo. 6s.*

Phillpotts (Eden). LYING PROPHETS. *Third Edition. Cr. 8vo. 6s.*
CHILDREN OF THE MIST. *Sixth Edition. Cr. 8vo. 6s.*
THE HUMAN BOY. With a Frontispiece. *Seventh Edition. Cr. 8vo. 6s.*
SONS OF THE MORNING. *Second Edition. Cr. 8vo. 6s.*
THE RIVER. *Fourth Edition. Cr. 8vo. 6s.*
THE AMERICAN PRISONER. *Fourth Edition. Cr. 8vo. 6s.*
KNOCK AT A VENTURE. *Third Edition. Cr. 8vo. 6s.*
THE PORTREEVE. *Fourth Edition. Cr. 8vo. 6s.*
THE POACHER'S WIFE. *Second Edition. Cr. 8vo. 6s.*
THE STRIKING HOURS. *Second Edition. Cr. 8vo. 6s.*
DEMETER'S DAUGHTER. *Third Edition. Cr. 8vo. 6s.*

Pickthall (Marmaduke). SAÏD THE FISHERMAN. *Eighth Edition. Cr. 8vo. 6s.*

'Q' (A. T. Quiller Couch). THE WHITE WOLF. *Second Edition. Cr. 8vo. 6s.*

THE MAYOR OF TROY. *Fourth Edition. Cr. 8vo. 6s.*
MERRY-GARDEN and other Stories. *Cr. 8vo. 6s.*
MAJOR VIGOUREUX. *Third Edition. Cr. 8vo. 6s.*

Ridge (W. Pett). ERB. *Second Edition. Cr. 8vo. 6s.*
A SON OF THE STATE. *Third Edition. Cr. 8vo. 3s. 6d.*
A BREAKER OF LAWS. *Cr. 8vo. 3s. 6d.*
MRS. GALER'S BUSINESS. Illustrated. *Second Edition. Cr. 8vo. 6s.*
THE WICKHAMSES. *Fourth Edition. Cr. 8vo. 6s.*
NAME OF GARLAND. *Third Edition. Cr. 8vo. 6s.*
SPLENDID BROTHER. *Fourth Edition. Cr. 8vo. 6s.*
NINE TO SIX-THIRTY. *Third Edition. Cr. 8vo. 6s.*
THANKS TO SANDERSON. *Second Edition. Cr. 8vo. 6s.*
*DEVOTED SPARKES. *Cr. 8vo. 6s.*

Russell (W. Clark). MASTER ROCKAFELLAR'S VOYAGE. Illustrated. *Fourth Edition. Cr. 8vo. 3s. 6d.*

Sidgwick (Mrs. Alfred). THE KINSMAN. Illustrated. *Third Edition. Cr. 8vo. 6s.*
THE LANTERN-BEARERS. *Third Edition. Cr. 8vo. 6s.*
ANTHEA'S GUEST. *Fifth Edition. Cr. 8vo. 6s.*
*LAMORNA. *Cr. 8vo. 6s.*

Somerville (E. Œ.) and Ross (Martin). DAN RUSSEL THE FOX. Illustrated. *Fourth Edition. Cr. 8vo. 6s.*

Thurston (E. Temple). MIRAGE. *Fourth Edition. Cr. 8vo. 6s.*

Watson (H. B. Marriott). THE HIGH TOBY. *Third Edition. Cr. 8vo. 6s.*
THE PRIVATEERS. Illustrated. *Second Edition. Cr. 8vo. 6s.*
ALISE OF ASTRA. *Third Edition. Cr. 8vo. 6s.*
THE BIG FISH. *Second Edition. Cr. 8vo. 6s.*

Webling (Peggy). THE STORY OF VIRGINIA PERFECT. *Third Edition. Cr. 8vo. 6s.*
THE SPIRIT OF MIRTH. *Fifth Edition Cr. 8vo. 6s.*
FELIX CHRISTIE. *Second Edition. Cr. 8vo. 6s.*

Weyman (Stanley). UNDER THE RED ROBE. Illustrated. *Twenty-third Edition. Cr. 8vo. 6s.*

Whitby (Beatrice). ROSAMUND. *Second Edition. Cr. 8vo. 6s.*

FICTION

Williamson (C. N. and A. M.). THE LIGHTNING CONDUCTOR. The Strange Adventures of a Motor Car. Illustrated. *Seventeenth Edition. Cr. 8vo. 6s.* Also *Cr. 8vo. 1s. net.*

THE PRINCESS PASSES: A Romance of a Motor. Illustrated. *Ninth Edition. Cr. 8vo. 6s.*

LADY BETTY ACROSS THE WATER. *Eleventh Edition. Cr. 8vo. 6s.*

SCARLET RUNNER. Illustrated. *Third Edition. Cr. 8vo. 6s.*

SET IN SILVER. Illustrated. *Fourth Edition. Cr. 8vo. 6s.*

LORD LOVELAND DISCOVERS AMERICA. *Second Edition. Cr. 8vo. 6s.*

THE GOLDEN SILENCE. *Sixth Edition. Cr. 8vo. 6s.*

THE GUESTS OF HERCULES. *Third Edition. Cr. 8vo. 6s.*

*THE HEATHER MOON. *Cr. 8vo. 6s.*

Wyllarde (Dolf). THE PATHWAY OF THE PIONEER (Nous Autres). *Sixth Edition. Cr. 8vo. 6s.*

THE UNOFFICIAL HONEYMOON *Seventh Edition. Cr. 8vo. 6s.*

THE CAREER OF BEAUTY DARLING. *Cr. 8vo. 6s.*

Methuen's Two-Shilling Novels.

Crown 8vo. 2s. net.

*BOTOR CHAPERON, THE. C. N. and A. M. Williamson.

*CALL OF THE BLOOD, THE. Robert Hichens.

CAR OF DESTINY AND ITS ERRAND IN SPAIN, THE. C. N. and A. M. Williamson.

CLEMENTINA. A. E. W. Mason.

COLONEL ENDERBY'S WIFE. Lucas Malet.

FELIX. Robert Hichens.

GATE OF THE DESERT, THE. John Oxenham.

MY FRIEND THE CHAUFFEUR. C. N. and A. M. Williamson.

PRINCESS VIRGINIA, THE. C. N. and A. M. Williamson.

SEATS OF THE MIGHTY, THE. Sir Gilbert Parker.

SERVANT OF THE PUBLIC, A. Anthony Hope.

*SET IN SILVER. C. N. and A. M. Williamson.

SEVERINS, THE. Mrs. Alfred Sidgwick.

SIR RICHARD CALMADY. Lucas Malet.

*VIVIEN. W. B. Maxwell.

Books for Boys and Girls.

Illustrated. Crown 8vo. 3s. 6d.

CROSS AND DAGGER. The Crusade of the Children, 1212. W. Scott Durrant.

GETTING WELL OF DOROTHY, THE. Mrs. W. K. Clifford.

GIRL OF THE PEOPLE, A. L. T. Meade.

HEPSY GIPSY. L. T. Meade. 2s. 6d.

HONOURABLE MISS, THE. L. T. Meade.

MASTER ROCKAFELLAR'S VOYAGE. W. Clark Russell.

ONLY A GUARD-ROOM DOG. Edith E. Cuthell.

RED GRANGE, THE. Mrs. Molesworth.

SYD BELTON: The Boy who would not go to Sea. G. Manville Fenn.

THERE WAS ONCE A PRINCE. Mrs. M. E. Mann.

Methuen's Shilling Novels.

*Anna of the Five Towns. Arnold Bennett.
Barbary Sheep. Robert Hichens.
Charm, The. Alice Perrin.
*Demon, The. C. N. and A. M. Williamson.
Guarded Flame, The. W. B. Maxwell.
Jane. Marie Corelli.
Lady Betty Across the Water. C. N. & A. M. Williamson.
*Long Road, The. John Oxenham.
Mighty Atom, The. Marie Corelli.
Mirage. E. Temple Thurston.
Missing Delora, The. E. Phillips Oppenheim.
Round the Red Lamp. Sir A. Conan Doyle
*Secret Woman, The. Eden Phillpotts.
*Severins, The. Mrs. Alfred Sidgwick.
Spanish Gold. G. A. Birmingham.
Tales of Mean Streets. Arthur Morrison
The Halo. The Baroness von Hutten.
*Tyrant, The. Mrs. Henry de la Pasture.
Under the Red Robe. Stanley J. Weyman.
Virginia Perfect. Peggy Webling
Woman with the Fan, The. Robert Hichens.

The Novels of Alexandre Dumas.

Medium 8vo. Price 6d. Double Volumes, 1s.

Acté.
Adventures of Captain Pamphile, The.
Amaury.
Bird of Fate, The.
Black Tulip, The.
Black: the Story of a Dog.
Castle of Eppstein, The.
Catherine Blum.
Cécile.
Châtelet, The.
Chevalier D'Harmental, The. (Double volume.)
Chicot the Jester.
Chicot Redivivus.
Comte de Montgommery, The.
Conscience.
Convict's Son, The.
Corsican Brothers, The; and Otho the Archer.
Crop-Eared Jacquot.
Dom Gorenflot.
Duc d'Anjou, The.
Fatal Combat, The.
Fencing Master, The.
Fernande.
Gabriel Lambert
Georges.
Great Massacre, The.
Henri de Navarre.
Hélène de Chaverny.
Horoscope, The.
Leone-Leona.
Louise de la Vallière. (Double volume.)
Man in the Iron Mask, The. (Double volume.)
Maître Adam.
Mouth of Hell, The.
Nanon. (Double volume.)
Olympia.
Pauline; Pascal Bruno; and Bontekoe.
Père la Ruine.
Porte Saint-Antoine, The.
Prince of Thieves, The.
Reminiscences of Antony, The.
St. Quentin.
Robin Hood.
Samuel Gelb.
Snowball and the Sultanetta, The.
Sylvandire.
Taking of Calais, The.
Tales of the Supernatural.
Tales of Strange Adventure.
Tales of Terror.
Three Musketeers, The. (Double volume.)
Tourney of the Rue St. Antoine.
Tragedy of Nantes, The.
Twenty Years After. (Double volume.)
Wild-Duck Shooter, The.
Wolf-Leader, The

FICTION

Methuen's Sixpenny Books.
Medium 8vo.

Albanesi (E. Maria). LOVE AND LOUISA.
I KNOW A MAIDEN.
THE BLUNDER OF AN INNOCENT.
PETER A PARASITE.
*THE INVINCIBLE AMELIA.

Anstey (F.). A BAYARD OF BENGAL.

Austen (J.). PRIDE AND PREJUDICE.

Bagot (Richard). A ROMAN MYSTERY.
CASTING OF NETS.
DONNA DIANA.

Balfour (Andrew). BY STROKE OF SWORD.

Baring-Gould (S.). FURZE BLOOM.
CHEAP JACK ZITA.
KITTY ALONE.
URITH.
THE BROOM SQUIRE.
IN THE ROAR OF THE SEA.
NOÉMI.
A BOOK OF FAIRY TALES. Illustrated.
LITTLE TU'PENNY.
WINEFRED.
THE FROBISHERS.
THE QUEEN OF LOVE.
ARMINELL.
BLADYS OF THE STEWPONEY.
CHRIS OF ALL SORTS.

Barr (Robert). JENNIE BAXTER.
IN THE MIDST OF ALARMS.
THE COUNTESS TEKLA.
THE MUTABLE MANY.

Benson (E. F.). DODO.
THE VINTAGE.

Brontë (Charlotte). SHIRLEY.

Brownell (C. L.). THE HEART OF JAPAN.

Burton (J. Bloundelle). ACROSS THE SALT SEAS.

Caffyn (Mrs.). ANNE MAULEVERER.

Capes (Bernard). THE GREAT SKENE MYSTERY.

Clifford (Mrs. W. K.). A FLASH OF SUMMER.
MRS. KEITH'S CRIME.

Corbett (Julian). A BUSINESS IN GREAT WATERS.

Croker (Mrs. B. M.). ANGEL.
A STATE SECRET.
PEGGY OF THE BARTONS.
JOHANNA.

Dante (Alighieri). THE DIVINE COMEDY (Cary).

Doyle (Sir A. Conan). ROUND THE RED LAMP.

Duncan (Sara Jeannette). THOSE DELIGHTFUL AMERICANS.

Eliot (George). THE MILL ON THE FLOSS.

Findlater (Jane H.). THE GREEN GRAVES OF BALGOWRIE.

Gallon (Tom). RICKERBY'S FOLLY.

Gaskell (Mrs.). CRANFORD.
MARY BARTON.
NORTH AND SOUTH.

Gerard (Dorothea). HOLY MATRIMONY.
THE CONQUEST OF LONDON.
MADE OF MONEY.

Gissing (G.). THE TOWN TRAVELLER.
THE CROWN OF LIFE.

Glanville (Ernest). THE INCA'S TREASURE.
THE KLOOF BRIDE.

Gleig (Charles). BUNTER'S CRUISE.

Grimm (The Brothers). GRIMM'S FAIRY TALES.

Hope (Anthony). A MAN OF MARK.
A CHANGE OF AIR.
THE CHRONICLES OF COUNT ANTONIO.
PHROSO.
THE DOLLY DIALOGUES.

Hornung (E. W.). DEAD MEN TELL NO TALES.

Hyne (C. J C.). PRINCE RUPERT THE BUCCANEER.

Ingraham (J. H.). THE THRONE OF DAVID.

Le Queux (W.). THE HUNCHBACK OF WESTMINSTER.
THE CROOKED WAY.
THE VALLEY OF THE SHADOW.

Levett-Yeats (S. K.). THE TRAITOR'S WAY.
ORRAIN.

Linton (E. Lynn). THE TRUE HISTORY OF JOSHUA DAVIDSON.

Lyall (Edna). DERRICK VAUGHAN.

Malet (Lucas). THE CARISSIMA.
A COUNSEL OF PERFECTION.

Mann (Mrs. M. E.). MRS. PETER HOWARD.
A LOST ESTATE.
THE CEDAR STAR.
THE PATTEN EXPERIMENT.
A WINTER'S TALE.

Marchmont (A. W.). MISER HOADLEY'S SECRET.
A MOMENT'S ERROR.

Marryat (Captain). PETER SIMPLE.
JACOB FAITHFUL.

March (Richard). A METAMORPHOSIS.
THE TWICKENHAM PEERAGE.
THE GODDESS.
THE JOSS.

Mason (A. E. W.). CLEMENTINA.

Mathers (Helen). HONEY.
GRIFF OF GRIFFITHSCOURT.
SAM'S SWEETHEART.
THE FERRYMAN.

Meade (Mrs. L. T.). DRIFT.

Miller (Esther). LIVING LIES.

Mitford (Bertram). THE SIGN OF THE SPIDER.

Montrésor (F. F.). THE ALIEN.

Morrison (Arthur). THE HOLE IN THE WALL.

Nesbit (E.). THE RED HOUSE.

Norris (W. E.). HIS GRACE.
GILES INGILBY.
THE CREDIT OF THE COUNTY.
LORD LEONARD THE LUCKLESS.
MATTHEW AUSTEN.
CLARISSA FURIOSA.

Oliphant (Mrs.). THE LADY'S WALK.
SIR ROBERT'S FORTUNE.

THE PRODIGALS.
THE TWO MARYS.

Oppenheim (E. P.). MASTER OF MEN.

Parker (Sir Gilbert). THE POMP OF THE LAVILETTES.
WHEN VALMOND CAME TO PONTIAC.
THE TRAIL OF THE SWORD.

Pemberton (Max). THE FOOTSTEPS OF A THRONE.
I CROWN THEE KING.

Phillpotts (Eden). THE HUMAN BOY.
CHILDREN OF THE MIST.
THE POACHER'S WIFE.
THE RIVER.

'Q' (A. T. Quiller Couch). THE WHITE WOLF.

Ridge (W. Pett). A SON OF THE STATE.
LOST PROPERTY.
GEORGE and THE GENERAL.
A BREAKER OF LAWS.
ERB.

Russell (W. Clark). ABANDONED.
A MARRIAGE AT SEA.
MY DANISH SWEETHEART.
HIS ISLAND PRINCESS.

Sergeant (Adeline). THE MASTER OF BEECHWOOD.
BALBARA'S MONEY.
THE YELLOW DIAMOND.
THE LOVE THAT OVERCAME.

Sidgwick (Mrs. Alfred). THE KINSMAN.

Surtees (R. S.). HANDLEY CROSS.
MR. SPONGE'S SPORTING TOUR.
ASK MAMMA.

Walford (Mrs. L. B.). MR. SMITH.
COUSINS.
THE BABY'S GRANDMOTHER.
TROUBLESOME DAUGHTERS.

Wallace (General Lew). BEN-HUR.
THE FAIR GOD.

Watson (H. B. Marriott). THE ADVENTURERS.
CAPTAIN FORTUNE.

Weekes (A. B.). PRISONERS OF WAR.

Wells (H. G.). THE SEA LADY.

Whitby (Beatrice). THE RESULT OF AN ACCIDENT.

White (Percy). A PASSIONATE PILGRIM.

Williamson (Mrs. C. N.). PAPA.

PRINTED BY
UNWIN BROTHERS, LIMITED,
LONDON AND WOKING.

UNIVERSITY OF CALIFORNIA LIBRARY
Los Angeles

This book is DUE on the last date stamped below.

MAR 31 1960

REC'D LD-URL
LD-URL FEB 20 1967

RECHARGE OR RENEW WITH NEW
REC'D LD-URL REGISTRATION OR LIBRARY
CARD ONLY
SEP 26 1972 NEW CARD VERIFIED ☐

REC'D LD-URL
APR 01 1987

Form L9–40m-7,'56(C790s4)444

CPSIA information can be obtained at www.ICGtesting.com
Printed in the USA
LVOW10s1512210915

455063LV00002B/448/P

9 781331 877066